The Future of Education

Transformative Methods and Cutting-Edge Tools for Enhancing Learning and Achieving Academic Excellence

Freddie Dancer

ISBN: 978-1-77961-096-6
Imprint: Telephasic Workshop

Contents

Introduction

Importance of Transformative Education

Defining Transformative Education

Transformative education is an approach to learning that goes beyond acquiring knowledge and skills. It aims to create profound and lasting changes in students' attitudes, beliefs, and behaviors, empowering them to become active participants in their own learning and agents of change in their communities. This type of education is rooted in the belief that education has the power to transform individuals, societies, and the world.

At its core, transformative education involves a shift from a traditional, teacher-centered model to a student-centered approach. It recognizes that students are not passive recipients of information but active participants in the learning process. The emphasis is on engaging students in critical thinking, reflection, and self-discovery, rather than simply transmitting information to them.

In transformative education, the goal is not just to impart knowledge but to foster the development of a wide range of competencies, including problem-solving, communication, collaboration, creativity, and adaptability. It seeks to empower students to think critically, challenge assumptions, and take ownership of their learning.

This approach also recognizes the importance of addressing social and emotional aspects of learning. It promotes the development of emotional intelligence, empathy, and compassion, as well as the cultivation of values such as social responsibility, equity, and justice. Transformative education aims to prepare students not only for academic success but also for responsible citizenship and active engagement in their communities.

The key principles that underpin transformative education include:

1. Engagement: Transformative education promotes active engagement and

participation in the learning process. It encourages students to ask questions, explore ideas, and apply their learning to real-world contexts.

2. Relevance: Transformative education connects learning to students' lives and experiences. It emphasizes the application of knowledge and skills to authentic problems and challenges, making the learning meaningful and relevant.

3. Critical Thinking: Transformative education fosters critical thinking skills, enabling students to analyze information, evaluate evidence, and think independently. It encourages them to question assumptions, challenge biases, and consider multiple perspectives.

4. Reflection: Transformative education values reflection as a key process for deepening learning and promoting personal growth. It encourages students to reflect on their experiences, identify their strengths and areas for improvement, and make connections between their learning and their values and goals.

5. Empowerment: Transformative education aims to empower students to take control of their own learning. It fosters a sense of agency and self-efficacy, enabling students to set goals, make decisions, and take responsibility for their own learning.

By focusing on these principles, transformative education aims to create learning experiences that inspire students, challenge their assumptions, and enable them to develop the knowledge, skills, and attitudes needed to thrive in an ever-changing world.

Transformative education is not without its challenges. Implementing this approach requires a shift in pedagogical practices, a reconfiguration of curriculum and assessment methods, and the integration of technology and other innovative tools. It also requires ongoing professional development for teachers to equip them with the skills and mindset necessary to facilitate transformative learning experiences.

Despite these challenges, the benefits of transformative education are significant. Research has shown that students who experience transformative education develop a deeper understanding of content, demonstrate higher-order thinking skills, and are more motivated and engaged in their learning. They also develop a sense of agency, empathy, and social responsibility, which are crucial in today's interconnected and rapidly changing world.

In conclusion, transformative education is a powerful approach to learning that seeks to go beyond the transmission of knowledge and skills. It aims to foster profound and lasting changes in students, empowering them to become active learners and agents of positive change in the world. By emphasizing student-centered learning, critical thinking, reflection, and empowerment, transformative education prepares students for success in an increasingly complex and interconnected world.

Regular education focuses on imparting knowledge and skills to students, but transformative education goes beyond that. It aims to bring about profound personal and social change in learners. This section will explore the benefits of transformative education and how it has the potential to revolutionize the way we learn and interact with the world.

1. Empowerment: Transformative education empowers individuals to take ownership of their learning journey and become active participants in society. By engaging in critical reflection and self-awareness, learners gain the necessary tools to challenge existing systems, think critically, and make informed decisions. This empowerment leads to a sense of agency and the ability to effect positive change in their communities.

2. Holistic Development: Rather than focusing solely on academic achievements and knowledge acquisition, transformative education takes a holistic approach to student development. It nurtures the intellectual, emotional, social, and ethical dimensions of individuals, enabling them to become well-rounded individuals who are better equipped to navigate the complexities of the modern world.

3. Deep Learning: Transformative education encourages deep learning, where students are actively engaged in constructing knowledge rather than passively receiving information. By applying knowledge to real-life situations, students develop a deeper understanding of concepts, enhance problem-solving abilities, and foster critical thinking skills. This deep learning leads to greater retention of knowledge and better application of what has been learned.

4. Creativity and Innovation: Transformative education nurtures creativity and innovation by fostering a safe and supportive learning environment. It encourages students to think outside the box, challenge conventional wisdom, and explore new ideas and perspectives. By promoting creativity and innovation, transformative education equips students with the necessary skills to tackle complex problems and adapt to rapidly changing environments.

5. Social Justice and Equity: Transformative education places a strong emphasis on social justice and equity. It recognizes the importance of creating inclusive learning environments that address issues of discrimination, inequality, and social injustices. Through transformative education, students develop a deep awareness of social issues and acquire the knowledge and skills to become advocates for a more just and equitable society.

6. Global Citizenship: Transformative education prepares students to become responsible global citizens. It promotes global awareness, cultural sensitivity, and an understanding of global challenges and interconnectedness. By encouraging students to engage in cross-cultural dialogue, collaborative problem-solving, and

international cooperation, transformative education cultivates a sense of global citizenship, empathy, and respect for diverse perspectives.

7. Personal Growth and Well-being: Transformative education values the holistic development and well-being of individuals. It supports the social-emotional growth of students, fostering self-confidence, resilience, and positive mental health. By addressing the social and emotional needs of students, transformative education creates a conducive learning environment in which students can thrive academically and personally.

8. Lifelong Learning: Transformative education instills a love for learning and a desire to continue learning throughout one's life. It equips students with essential lifelong learning skills such as critical thinking, problem-solving, adaptability, and self-directed learning. By fostering a growth mindset and the ability to embrace change, transformative education prepares individuals to navigate a rapidly evolving world and continuously acquire new knowledge and skills.

In conclusion, transformative education offers numerous benefits that go beyond traditional education. It empowers individuals, promotes holistic development, fosters deep learning, encourages creativity and innovation, addresses social justice and equity, cultivates global citizenship, supports personal growth and well-being, and instills a love for lifelong learning. By embracing transformative education, we can create a brighter future where individuals are equipped with the knowledge, skills, and values to shape a more just, sustainable, and inclusive world.

The role of technology in transformative education

In today's rapidly evolving world, technology plays a crucial role in transforming the landscape of education. It has the potential to revolutionize the way students learn and teachers teach, making education more engaging, personalized, and accessible. In this section, we will explore the various ways technology can enhance and facilitate transformative education.

Enhancing engagement and motivation

Technology has the power to captivate students' attention and make learning more interactive and immersive. It provides an array of multimedia resources such as videos, simulations, and interactive games that can engage students in ways that traditional textbooks cannot. For example, virtual reality (VR) can transport students to different environments or historical periods, enabling them to experience and explore concepts firsthand. This immersive experience can boost motivation, curiosity, and retention of knowledge.

Additionally, technology offers opportunities for personalized learning experiences, allowing students to learn at their own pace and in their preferred style. Adaptive learning software, for instance, can tailor content and activities based on students' individual needs, strengths, and weaknesses. This personalized approach fosters a sense of ownership and empowerment, leading to increased engagement and motivation.

Facilitating collaboration and communication

Technology has revolutionized the way students interact and collaborate with one another, breaking down geographical barriers and enabling global connections. Through various web-based tools and platforms, students can engage in meaningful discussions, share ideas, and collaborate on projects with peers from different regions and cultures. This not only broadens their perspectives but also enhances their critical thinking, communication, and teamwork skills.

Social media platforms, specifically designed for educational purposes, can facilitate collaborative learning and knowledge sharing. Students can participate in virtual communities or online forums to ask questions, seek feedback, and benefit from the collective wisdom of their peers. Such collaborative interactions foster a sense of community and help students develop important 21st-century skills needed for success in a rapidly changing world.

Enabling access to resources and information

One of the most significant advantages of technology in transformative education is the access it provides to a vast amount of resources and information. The internet has revolutionized the way we acquire knowledge, making information readily available at our fingertips. Students can access a wide range of research articles, books, educational videos, and online courses, greatly expanding their learning opportunities.

Furthermore, technology can bridge the digital divide and provide equal educational opportunities for students from diverse backgrounds. Online learning platforms and open educational resources enable learners from remote areas or underprivileged communities to access high-quality education. This inclusivity and democratization of education ensure that no student is left behind and everyone has the opportunity to achieve academic excellence.

Promoting critical thinking and problem-solving skills

Technology can serve as a powerful tool for promoting critical thinking, problem-solving, and creativity among students. Educational software and apps often incorporate interactive exercises and puzzles that require students to think critically, analyze information, and apply knowledge to solve complex problems. These activities not only enhance cognitive abilities but also foster a growth mindset, encouraging students to persist in the face of challenges and develop resilience.

Additionally, technology can provide real-world context and authenticity to learning experiences. Simulations, virtual laboratories, and online experiments allow students to explore scientific phenomena, conduct experiments, and observe the outcomes in a risk-free environment. This hands-on approach to learning enhances problem-solving skills, encourages experimentation, and prepares students for future careers that require innovation and adaptability.

Addressing challenges and ethical considerations

While technology brings numerous benefits to transformative education, it is essential to address the challenges and ethical considerations associated with its use. Teachers and policymakers need to be mindful of issues such as data privacy, security, and digital citizenship. There is a responsibility to ensure that the use of technology in education is done in an ethically responsible manner, respecting student privacy and safeguarding their personal information.

Moreover, the digital divide remains a significant challenge. Despite the increasing accessibility of technology, there are still regions and communities with limited infrastructure and connectivity. Efforts should be made to bridge this gap and ensure equitable access to technology-enhanced education for all students.

In conclusion, technology is a powerful catalyst for transformative education. It enhances engagement, facilitates collaboration, provides access to resources, promotes critical thinking, and prepares students for the challenges of the future. However, it is essential to employ technology thoughtfully, addressing ethical considerations and ensuring that it is used in ways that foster inclusive and equitable education for all. By harnessing the potential of technology, we can create a future of education that empowers learners and prepares them to thrive in a rapidly changing world.

Challenges in implementing transformative education

Transformative education holds great potential for revolutionizing the learning experience and preparing students for the challenges of the future. However, its implementation is not without its challenges. In this section, we will explore some of the key challenges that educators may face when trying to implement transformative education in their classrooms.

Resistance to change

One of the primary challenges in implementing transformative education is resistance to change. Many educators and stakeholders may be hesitant to adopt new teaching methods and technologies due to fear of the unknown, lack of understanding, or concerns about the effectiveness of these approaches. Resistance to change can create barriers and slow down the process of implementing transformative education.

To address this challenge, it is important to provide clear communication and support for educators. Professional development programs can help teachers overcome their fears and develop the necessary skills to implement transformative methods. Administrators and educational leaders should also provide ongoing support, encourage collaboration among teachers, and create a culture of innovation and experimentation within the school community.

Lack of resources

Another significant challenge is the lack of resources, both financial and technological, that are necessary to implement transformative education. Many schools may struggle to secure funding for the purchase of new technologies, updating infrastructure, or providing professional development opportunities for teachers.

To overcome this challenge, schools can explore alternative sources of funding such as grants, partnerships with local businesses or universities, or crowdfunding campaigns. Additionally, schools can prioritize their spending to allocate resources towards educational technologies and provide ongoing support for teachers to effectively integrate these tools into their teaching practices.

Inequitable access to technology

Transformative education relies heavily on the use of technology tools and resources. However, inequitable access to technology can create challenges in implementing transformative practices. Students from disadvantaged communities may not have the same access to technology at home or within the school, which can further widen the digital divide and hinder their learning opportunities.

Schools can address this challenge by providing equitable access to technology within the school environment. This may include establishing technology centers or providing loaner devices for students to use at home. Additionally, schools can partner with community organizations or government agencies to extend internet access to underserved communities and ensure that students have adequate resources for learning.

Teacher training and professional development

Implementing transformative education requires teachers to develop new skills and competencies to effectively integrate technology and innovative teaching methods into their classrooms. However, many educators may lack the necessary training and professional development opportunities to acquire these skills.

To address this challenge, schools should prioritize ongoing professional development programs for teachers. These programs should focus on building digital literacy skills, promoting pedagogical innovation, and providing support for teachers to navigate the complexities of transformative education. Collaborative and peer-led professional learning communities can also be an effective way for teachers to share best practices, receive feedback, and continuously improve their teaching methods.

Assessment and accountability

Traditional assessment methods may not align with the goals and principles of transformative education. Standardized testing and high-stakes assessments often emphasize rote memorization and regurgitation of information, which can hinder the development of critical thinking, creativity, and problem-solving skills.

To address this challenge, educators should explore alternative assessment approaches that align with the transformative goals of education. This may include portfolio assessments, project-based assessments, or performance-based assessments that focus on real-world application of knowledge and skills. Additionally, educators should work towards creating a culture of assessment for learning, where assessment is seen as a tool for growth and improvement rather than a measure of success or failure.

Societal and cultural norms

The implementation of transformative education can also be influenced by societal and cultural norms. Some communities may have traditional views of education that prioritize memorization, conformity, and uniformity, which may conflict with the principles of transformative education.

To address this challenge, it is important to engage and involve all stakeholders, including parents, community members, and policymakers, in the conversation about the benefits and importance of transformative education. Building awareness and understanding of the changing needs of the 21st century and the value of innovation and creativity in education can help overcome these societal and cultural barriers.

In conclusion, while transformative education offers numerous benefits and opportunities, implementing it in practice can be challenging. Resistance to change, lack of resources, inequitable access to technology, teacher training and professional development, assessment and accountability, and societal and cultural norms are just a few of the challenges that educators may face. By addressing these challenges head-on and implementing strategies to overcome them, educators can gradually transform their classrooms and create positive learning environments for students.

The Future of Education and the Need for Transformative Methods

As we navigate the ever-changing landscape of education, it becomes increasingly clear that traditional teaching methods are no longer sufficient to prepare students for the challenges of the future. The world is evolving at an unprecedented pace, with advancements in technology, globalization, and societal shifts reshaping the way we live and work. In order to equip our students with the skills they need to thrive in this rapidly changing world, we must embrace transformative methods in education.

Transformative education can be defined as an approach that goes beyond content delivery and rote memorization. It aims to empower students to become critical thinkers, problem solvers, and lifelong learners. By focusing on developing skills such as creativity, collaboration, critical thinking, and adaptability, transformative education prepares students to face the uncertainties of the future.

One of the key drivers of the need for transformative methods in education is the rapid advancement of technology. Technology is revolutionizing every aspect of our lives, and education is no exception. In order to stay relevant, education must adapt and leverage the power of technology to enhance the learning experience. From virtual reality and artificial intelligence to gamification and mobile learning, cutting-edge tools have the potential to engage students in new and exciting ways, making learning more interactive, personalized, and immersive.

However, implementing transformative education is not without its challenges. Resistance to change, lack of resources, and limited teacher training are some of the obstacles that schools and educators face. It is crucial to address these challenges and provide the necessary support and professional development opportunities for teachers to effectively implement transformative methods in their classrooms.

The future of education will require a paradigm shift in the role of teachers. In transformative classrooms, teachers will no longer be seen as mere disseminators of knowledge, but as facilitators of learning. They will embrace new roles such as mentors, guides, and coaches, focusing on fostering creativity, critical thinking skills, and fostering a growth mindset in students.

Additionally, promoting inclusivity and diversity will be of utmost importance in the future of education. As societies become increasingly diverse, classrooms should reflect this diversity and provide an inclusive learning environment where every student feels valued and supported. This involves creating culturally responsive instruction, incorporating diverse perspectives in the curriculum, and addressing biases and discrimination in educational technology.

Moreover, ethical considerations play a crucial role in transformative education. As we integrate technology into classrooms, we must be mindful of issues such as data privacy, security, and the responsible use of artificial intelligence. It is important to establish ethical guidelines and educate both students and educators about digital citizenship, ensuring that technology is used in an ethical and responsible manner.

In conclusion, the future of education rests upon transformative methods and cutting-edge tools that can enhance learning and help students achieve academic excellence. By embracing these methods, we can prepare students to thrive in a rapidly changing world, where critical thinking, adaptability, and creativity are paramount. This shift requires a reimagining of the role of teachers, a focus on inclusivity and diversity, and a commitment to ethical considerations. Only by embracing this transformative approach can we ensure that our education system remains relevant, empowering, and impactful for generations to come.

Overview of Cutting-edge Tools

Introduction to Educational Technologies

In today's rapidly evolving digital era, educational technologies have become an integral part of the education landscape. These technologies have the potential to enhance teaching and learning experiences, engage students in meaningful ways, and open up new possibilities for personalized and interactive education. In this section, we will explore the various types of educational technologies and their applications in the classroom.

The Evolution of Educational Technologies

Educational technologies have come a long way since the early days of computers in the classroom. Advancements in technology have drastically transformed the educational landscape, making learning more interactive, accessible, and engaging. From the introduction of personal computers and the internet to the rise of mobile devices and cloud computing, the possibilities for integrating technology into education have exponentially grown.

Types of Educational Technologies

Educational technologies encompass a wide range of tools and applications that can enhance teaching and learning experiences. In this section, we will introduce some of the key types of educational technologies that are commonly used in classrooms today.

Learning Management Systems (LMS) Learning Management Systems, or LMS, are online platforms that facilitate the delivery and management of educational resources, assignments, assessments, and communication between teachers and students. LMS provide a centralized digital space where teachers can organize course materials, interact with students, and track their progress. Popular LMS include Moodle, Canvas, and Blackboard.

Educational Apps Educational apps are software applications designed specifically to support learning and skill development. These apps can be used on mobile devices, such as smartphones and tablets, and cover a wide range of subjects and learning objectives. From interactive language learning apps to math practice games, these apps provide students with opportunities for independent learning and practice.

Virtual Reality (VR) and Augmented Reality (AR) Virtual Reality (VR) and Augmented Reality (AR) technologies provide immersive experiences that can revolutionize the way students learn. VR creates a simulated environment that allows students to interact with virtual objects and explore concepts in a hands-on manner. AR overlays digital content onto the real world, enhancing the learning experience by adding contextual information and interactive elements.

Artificial Intelligence (AI) Artificial Intelligence (AI) is an emerging field that has the potential to transform education. AI technologies can analyze large amounts of data, adapt to individual learners, and provide personalized recommendations. AI-powered educational tools can provide intelligent tutoring, automated grading and assessment, and adaptive learning experiences tailored to each student's needs.

Gamification Gamification refers to the integration of game elements, such as competition, rewards, and challenges, into educational experiences. By incorporating game-like features, educators can increase student engagement and motivation. Gamification can be applied to various subjects and learning objectives, from math quizzes to language learning games.

Online Collaboration Tools Online collaboration tools enable students to work together and communicate effectively, regardless of their physical location. These tools allow for real-time collaboration on projects, document sharing, and instant messaging. From Google Docs for collaborative writing to video conferencing platforms for virtual group discussions, these tools promote teamwork and foster a sense of community among students.

Adaptive Learning Technologies Adaptive learning technologies employ advanced algorithms to dynamically personalize the learning experience for each student. These technologies assess students' strengths and weaknesses and provide targeted content and resources based on their individual needs. Adaptive learning platforms can monitor student progress, identify areas where they are struggling, and deliver personalized feedback and interventions.

Data Analytics and Learning Analytics Data analytics and learning analytics involve the collection and analysis of student data to gain insights into their learning processes. Learning analytics can help educators understand how students engage with educational materials and identify areas where additional support may be needed. By analyzing data on student performance, behavior, and engagement, educators can make informed instructional decisions and design targeted interventions.

Benefits of Educational Technologies

The integration of educational technologies offers numerous benefits that can significantly enhance teaching and learning experiences:

- Improved engagement and motivation: Educational technologies provide interactive and immersive learning experiences that can capture students' interest and motivation. By incorporating game elements, virtual reality, and personalized learning experiences, educational technologies can create a more engaging and enjoyable learning environment.

- Personalized learning: Educational technologies can adapt to individual students' needs, providing personalized content, feedback, and support. This tailored approach allows students to learn at their own pace and focus on areas where they need more assistance, leading to improved learning outcomes.

- Access to a wealth of resources: With educational technologies, students and teachers have access to a vast amount of online resources, including textbooks, articles, videos, and interactive simulations. This accessibility allows for self-directed learning and exploration beyond traditional classroom boundaries.

- Collaborative learning opportunities: Educational technologies enable students to collaborate with their peers, whether in the same physical space or across different locations. Online collaboration tools facilitate group projects, discussions, and knowledge sharing, fostering teamwork and communication skills.

- Real-time feedback and assessment: Through educational technologies, teachers can provide immediate feedback on students' progress, enabling them to monitor their understanding and address misconceptions promptly. Automated assessment tools can also save teachers time by grading assignments and providing detailed feedback.

- Enhanced teaching and instructional strategies: Educational technologies provide educators with new tools and resources to enhance their teaching practices. From virtual simulations to data analytics, teachers can leverage these technologies to create more interactive and effective instructional strategies.

While the benefits of educational technologies are substantial, their implementation also presents challenges that educators need to consider. In the next section, we will explore the challenges and considerations involved in integrating educational technologies into the classroom.

Virtual Reality in Education

Virtual reality (VR) is a technology that has gained significant attention in recent years for its potential to revolutionize education. With VR, students can be transported to virtual worlds that provide immersive and interactive learning experiences. This section will explore the concept of virtual reality in education, its benefits, and how it can be effectively incorporated to enhance teaching and learning.

Understanding Virtual Reality

Virtual reality refers to a computer-simulated environment that can simulate real or imaginary experiences. It typically involves the use of a head-mounted display (HMD) and hand controllers to create a fully immersive experience for the user. The user feels as if they are physically present in the virtual world and can interact with objects and environments.

In the context of education, virtual reality can provide students with a simulated environment that allows them to explore concepts, practice skills, and engage in realistic scenarios. It offers a unique opportunity to bridge the gap between theory and practice by providing hands-on experiences that might otherwise be difficult, dangerous, or costly to replicate in the real world.

Benefits of Virtual Reality in Education

Virtual reality offers several key benefits for education:

1. Enhanced Visualization: VR can provide visualizations of complex concepts that are difficult to grasp through traditional teaching methods. For example, students studying astronomy can explore the solar system in a virtual environment, allowing them to better understand the scale and relationships between celestial objects.

2. Immersive Experiences: VR can create immersive learning environments that actively engage students in the learning process. This level of immersion

boosts motivation, curiosity, and retention of information. Students can explore historical events, visit foreign countries, or even travel back in time to better understand different eras.

3. Experiential Learning: Virtual reality allows students to actively participate and learn by doing. For example, medical students can practice surgical procedures in a realistic virtual operating room, enabling them to gain hands-on experience and develop crucial skills before working with real patients.

4. Personalized Learning: VR can adapt to each student's needs, allowing for personalized learning experiences. Students can progress at their own pace, receive immediate feedback, and revisit challenging concepts until they are mastered. This individualized approach can enhance learning outcomes and cater to diverse learning styles.

5. Collaboration and Communication: VR can facilitate collaborative learning experiences by enabling students and teachers to interact with each other within the virtual environment. Students can work together on virtual projects, solve problems collectively, and communicate with experts or peers from different locations.

Integration of Virtual Reality in Education

To effectively integrate virtual reality in education, thoughtful planning and consideration of curricular goals are necessary. Here are some strategies for integrating VR into the classroom:

1. Identify Learning Objectives: Determine the specific learning objectives that VR can enhance or support. VR should be used purposefully to achieve desired outcomes and align with the curriculum.

2. Select Appropriate VR Content: Choose VR applications or experiences that align with the learning objectives and provide meaningful learning opportunities. Consider the quality of the content, its accuracy, and its suitability for the target audience.

3. Provide Guidance and Support: Ensure that students receive proper guidance and support while using VR. Familiarize them with the technology, set clear expectations, and provide instructions on how to navigate the virtual environment effectively.

4. Create Reflection and Discussion Opportunities: Encourage students to reflect on their VR experiences and engage in discussions about what they learned. This helps deepen their understanding, promotes critical thinking, and encourages the application of knowledge gained.

5. Evaluate and Assess Learning Outcomes: Assess the effectiveness of VR in achieving the desired learning outcomes. Use appropriate evaluation methods,

such as quizzes, projects, or observations, to assess students' knowledge and skills acquired through VR experiences.

Challenges and Considerations

While virtual reality holds immense potential, there are several challenges and considerations that need to be acknowledged:

1. Cost and Accessibility: VR equipment and software can be expensive, limiting access for some schools or individuals. Considerations should be made to ensure equitable access to VR experiences or alternative solutions explored.
2. Technical Limitations: VR technology is still evolving, and there can be technical limitations such as limited field of view, motion sickness, or hardware constraints. These limitations need to be recognized and addressed for a seamless VR experience.
3. Ethical Considerations: Privacy, safety, and ethical implications should be carefully considered when implementing VR. Protecting students' personal data and ensuring their emotional well-being are paramount.
4. Content Curation: It is essential to curate and review VR content for accuracy, relevance, and quality. Only reliable and age-appropriate content should be selected to ensure a valuable learning experience.

Real-World Examples

Here are a few examples of how virtual reality is being used in education:

1. Science Education: VR is used to simulate scientific experiments, allowing students to observe phenomena that are otherwise difficult to replicate in a traditional lab setting.
2. Historical Simulations: Students can immerse themselves in historical events, such as the American Revolution or World War II, to gain a deeper understanding of the period and its impact.
3. Language Learning: VR provides immersive environments where students can practice language skills and interact with native speakers, fostering language acquisition and cultural understanding.
4. Medical Training: Virtual reality is used to simulate medical procedures, enabling students to develop skills and experience realistic scenarios without risking patient safety.

Resources for Virtual Reality in Education

Here are some resources to explore virtual reality in education further:

- Google Expeditions: Offers a library of virtual field trips and educational experiences for various subjects. - Nearpod VR: Provides interactive VR lessons and experiences for classrooms. - Labster: Offers VR lab simulations for biology, chemistry, and other science subjects. - Engage: A platform for creating and sharing VR educational experiences in various subjects. - CoSpaces Edu: Allows students to create their own VR experiences and projects.

Conclusion

Virtual reality has the potential to transform education by providing immersive and engaging learning experiences. It offers unique opportunities for visualization, experiential learning, and personalized instruction. However, careful consideration of curriculum alignment, content selection, and ethical considerations is necessary for successful integration. With the right approach, virtual reality can empower students, enhance learning outcomes, and prepare them for the challenges of the future.

Artificial Intelligence in Education

Artificial intelligence (AI) is revolutionizing various aspects of our lives, and education is no exception. In recent years, AI has gained significant attention and has the potential to transform the way we teach and learn. AI in education refers to the use of intelligent machines or systems that can simulate human intelligence and perform tasks that typically require human intelligence, such as understanding natural language, recognizing patterns, and making decisions.

1.2.3.1 Benefits of AI in Education

The integration of AI in education offers several potential benefits:

- Personalized Learning: AI can analyze vast amounts of data on individual students' learning patterns and preferences to provide personalized recommendations. This customization ensures that students receive tailored instruction and support, maximizing their learning outcomes.

- Intelligent Tutoring: AI-powered virtual tutors can interact with students in a conversational manner, providing guidance, answering questions, and assessing their understanding. These intelligent systems can adapt the educational content and pace to meet the needs of individual students.

- Automated Grading: Evaluating large volumes of student work can be time-consuming for teachers. AI algorithms can be employed to automate grading processes, providing quicker and more consistent feedback to students.

- Enhancing Accessibility: AI can assist students with disabilities by providing real-time transcription, captioning, or sign language interpretation in educational settings. This technology helps create more inclusive and accessible learning environments.

- Data Analytics for Improvement: AI can analyze educational data gathered from various sources, such as student performance, engagement, and feedback, to generate insights and inform instructional decisions. Teachers and administrators can use these analytics to identify areas for improvement and enhance the effectiveness of teaching practices.

- Supporting Teachers: AI can help reduce the administrative workload for teachers by automating tasks such as lesson planning, content curation, and classroom management. This allows teachers to focus more on individual instruction and fostering positive student-teacher relationships.

1.2.3.2 Challenges and Considerations

While AI holds great promise for education, it also poses certain challenges and ethical considerations:

- Data Privacy and Security: The use of AI in education involves collecting and analyzing sensitive student data. It is crucial to ensure data privacy and implement robust security measures to protect students' personal information from unauthorized access or misuse.

- Bias and Fairness: AI systems can inadvertently perpetuate bias or discrimination if the training data used to develop them contains inherent biases. It is essential to address these biases and develop AI algorithms that are fair and unbiased, promoting equal opportunities for all learners.

- Ethical Decision-making: AI systems that make autonomous decisions, such as personalized learning recommendations or grading, raise questions about accountability, transparency, and the ethics of delegating decisions to machines. It is important to establish ethical guidelines and ensure that AI systems operate in line with societal values and standards.

- Digital Skills Gap: The successful integration of AI in education requires both educators and students to possess the necessary digital literacy and computational thinking skills. Closing the digital skills gap is crucial to ensure that everyone can effectively participate in and benefit from AI-powered educational environments.

1.2.3.3 Future Directions of AI in Education

The future of AI in education looks promising, with several areas showing great potential:

- Natural Language Processing: Further advancements in natural language processing can enhance AI-based chatbots and virtual tutors, making them even more conversational and capable of understanding and responding to complex student inquiries.
- Adaptive Learning Systems: Building more sophisticated adaptive learning systems that utilize AI to analyze individual student data and adjust learning content and strategies in real-time will enable more personalized and effective instruction.
- Intelligent Feedback and Assessment: AI can provide intelligent feedback to students, not only on their answers but also on their problem-solving approaches. AI algorithms can analyze students' thinking processes to provide personalized feedback that promotes critical thinking and metacognitive skills.
- Augmented Reality (AR) and Virtual Reality (VR): Integrating AI with AR and VR technologies can create immersive learning experiences in virtual environments, enabling students to explore and interact with complex concepts and scenarios.
- Lifelong Learning and Skill Development: AI can play a significant role in supporting lifelong learning and upskilling by providing personalized learning pathways and targeted recommendations for continuous education and professional development.

In conclusion, AI has the potential to revolutionize education by providing personalized learning experiences, intelligent tutoring, automated grading, and valuable data analytics. However, careful consideration of ethical concerns, data privacy, and bridging the digital skills gap is necessary to ensure equitable and responsible use of AI in education. The future of AI in education holds immense possibilities for enhancing teaching and learning processes and improving educational outcomes for all.

Gamification in Education

Gamification is a powerful educational approach that has gained significant attention in recent years. It involves incorporating game elements and mechanics into the learning experience to increase engagement, motivation, and overall learning outcomes. By applying game design principles, educators can transform traditional classroom activities into interactive and enjoyable experiences for students. In this section, we will explore the concept of gamification in education, its benefits, strategies for implementation, and future directions in this field.

Understanding Gamification

Gamification in education refers to the integration of game elements, such as competition, rewards, achievements, and challenges, into the learning process. It aims to make learning more engaging, interactive, and enjoyable for students. By leveraging the inherent motivational aspects of games, educators can create a dynamic learning environment that promotes active participation and deepens students' understanding of the subject matter.

Benefits of Gamification

Gamification in education offers several benefits for both students and teachers. Some of the key advantages include:

1. Increased Motivation: Gamification provides intrinsic motivation by tapping into students' desire for achievement, recognition, and mastery. By incorporating game elements, students become more motivated to actively participate in learning activities.

2. Enhanced Engagement: Games are inherently engaging, and gamification brings this engagement into the classroom. It creates an immersive and interactive learning experience that captures students' attention and encourages active involvement in the learning process.

3. Improved Retention: Gamified learning experiences often require students to apply their knowledge in realistic or challenging situations, promoting better retention of learned concepts. The use of repetition and immediate feedback in games also reinforces learning.

4. Personalized Learning: Gamification allows for customization and adaptability to individual students' needs and preferences. With a variety of game elements, educators can create personalized learning paths and experiences tailored to each student's learning style.

5. Collaborative Learning: Gamification can foster collaboration and teamwork among students. By incorporating multiplayer elements or team challenges, students can work together, share knowledge, and develop important social and communication skills.

Strategies for Implementing Gamification

Implementing gamification in education requires careful planning and consideration. Here are some strategies to effectively integrate gamification into the classroom:

1. Set Clear Learning Objectives: Clearly define the learning goals and outcomes to align game elements with educational objectives. This ensures that gamification supports the desired learning outcomes.

2. Choose Appropriate Game Elements: Select game elements that align with the subject matter and learning objectives. This could include points, badges, leaderboards, levels, quests, or challenges.

3. Provide Immediate Feedback: Timely and constructive feedback is essential in gamified learning. Incorporate feedback mechanisms that provide students with information on their progress, achievements, and areas for improvement.

4. Encourage Healthy Competition: Competition can foster motivation and engagement when used in a healthy and supportive way. Design multiplayer games or leaderboards that encourage friendly competition and cooperation among students.

5. Balance Challenge and Reward: Strike a balance between challenging tasks and rewards to maintain students' motivation. Gradually increase the difficulty level of activities and offer appropriate rewards for accomplishments.

6. Monitor Progress and Assess Learning: Utilize technology tools and learning management systems to track students' progress, assess their learning, and provide individualized support.

Examples of Gamification in Education

Here are a few examples of how gamification can be applied in different educational contexts:

1. Language Learning: Gamify language learning by incorporating vocabulary challenges, interactive quizzes, and virtual language exchanges with native speakers.

2. Science and Math: Create virtual labs or simulations that allow students to conduct experiments or solve complex math problems in a game-like environment.

3. History and Social Studies: Design role-playing games where students assume historical personas and make decisions that shape historical events.

4. Programming and Coding: Use game-based platforms that teach coding principles through interactive challenges and puzzles.

Future Directions of Gamification

The field of gamification in education is continuously evolving, with exciting future directions. Some emerging trends and possibilities include:

1. Immersive Technologies: Virtual reality (VR) and augmented reality (AR) have the potential to revolutionize gamification in education. These technologies can provide immersive and interactive learning experiences that enhance student engagement and understanding.

2. Adaptive Gamification: With advancements in artificial intelligence and learning analytics, gamification can become more adaptive and personalized. By tracking and analyzing student performance, games can dynamically adjust the difficulty level and content to meet individual needs.

3. Gamification for Soft Skills: Gamified approaches are increasingly being used to teach and assess important skills such as communication, problem-solving, and critical thinking. Gamification can provide a safe and engaging environment for students to develop and practice these skills.

4. Gamification for Professional Development: Gamified approaches can be extended to teacher professional development. By incorporating game elements into training programs, educators can enhance their skills and knowledge in a fun and interactive way.

5. Gamification in Online Learning: As online and remote learning becomes more prevalent, gamification can play a crucial role in keeping students engaged and motivated in virtual environments. Gamified elements can be integrated into online courses, discussion forums, and collaborative activities.

In conclusion, gamification in education offers a powerful approach to engage and motivate students, enhance learning outcomes, and create an immersive and enjoyable learning experience. By leveraging game elements and mechanics, educators can transform traditional classrooms into dynamic and interactive spaces. With ongoing advancements in technology, the future of gamification in education holds great potential for further innovation and impact.

Mobile Learning and Personalized Education

Mobile devices, such as smartphones and tablets, have become increasingly popular and have had a significant impact on various aspects of our lives, including education. Mobile learning, also known as m-learning, refers to the use of mobile devices and technologies to facilitate learning and provide educational content to students. In this section, we will explore the concept of mobile learning and its relationship to personalized education.

Understanding Mobile Learning

Mobile learning leverages the ubiquity of mobile devices to enable anytime, anywhere learning. It allows students to access educational resources, engage in collaborative activities, and interact with learning materials on their mobile devices. Mobile learning can take various forms, including mobile applications, online courses, e-books, videos, podcasts, and educational games.

The rise of mobile learning is driven by several factors. First, mobile devices offer convenience and flexibility, allowing students to learn at their own pace and on their own schedule. Second, mobile learning promotes personalized and individualized learning experiences. Students can access content that caters to their specific needs and learning preferences. Third, mobile devices are versatile and can offer rich multimedia content, interactive features, and real-time feedback, enhancing student engagement and motivation.

Benefits of Mobile Learning

Mobile learning offers several benefits that contribute to enhancing the learning experience and improving academic achievement. Some of these benefits include:

1. Increased Access to Education: Mobile learning provides opportunities for individuals who may have limited access to formal education. It allows learners in remote areas, those with physical disabilities, or those with other personal constraints to access educational resources and participate in learning activities.

2. Personalized Learning: Mobile learning supports personalized education by providing students with tailored content that matches their interests, learning styles, and abilities. Adaptive learning technologies, coupled with mobile devices, can track students' progress, identify their strengths and weaknesses, and adjust the learning experience accordingly.

3. Active and Engaged Learning: Mobile devices enable interactive and multimedia-rich learning experiences, encouraging students to actively engage with the content. This active learning approach fosters higher levels of understanding, critical thinking, and problem-solving skills.

4. Collaborative Learning: Mobile learning facilitates collaborative activities and social interaction among students. Through mobile applications and online

platforms, students can connect with peers, share ideas, work on group projects, and engage in peer learning, irrespective of geographical boundaries.

5. Seamless Integration of Formal and Informal Learning: Mobile devices blur the line between formal and informal learning. Students can continue their learning beyond the classroom by accessing educational resources, online communities, and informal learning opportunities through their mobile devices.

Implementing Mobile Learning

To effectively implement mobile learning, educators and institutions need to consider several factors:

1. Infrastructure and Technical Considerations: Ensuring reliable internet connectivity and addressing any technical limitations or compatibility issues related to mobile devices and educational applications is crucial. Institutions must invest in robust Wi-Fi networks and provide sufficient support to students to troubleshoot technical problems.

2. Digital Content Development: Developing high-quality digital content that suits the mobile learning environment is essential. Content should be interactive, engaging, and optimized for mobile devices. Educators should also ensure that the content aligns with the learning objectives and promotes active and personalized learning experiences.

3. Teacher Training and Professional Development: Teachers play a crucial role in implementing mobile learning effectively. They need to be trained on how to integrate mobile devices into their teaching practices, leverage mobile applications, and create meaningful learning experiences. Professional development opportunities should be provided to keep educators updated with the latest trends and best practices in mobile learning.

4. Privacy and Security Considerations: Given the sensitive nature of educational data, it is crucial to address privacy and security concerns related to mobile learning. Institutions need to have robust security measures in place, ensuring data protection, safeguarding student information, and complying with relevant regulations and policies.

Case Studies and Best Practices

Mobile learning has been successfully implemented in various educational settings, leading to improved student outcomes. Here are a few examples of case studies and best practices in mobile learning:

1. Flipped Classroom Approach: In a flipped classroom model, students learn new concepts through pre-recorded video lectures on their mobile devices before attending class. Class time is then utilized for discussion, collaborative activities, and problem-solving. This approach promotes personalized learning and active engagement.

2. Mobile Apps for Language Learning: Language learning apps, such as Duolingo and Babbel, have gained popularity due to their mobile-first approach. These apps offer interactive lessons, gamification elements, and personalized feedback, allowing learners to practice their language skills at their own pace.

3. Virtual Reality Field Trips: Mobile virtual reality (VR) applications allow students to embark on virtual field trips to historical sites, natural wonders, or even outer space. These immersive experiences enhance student engagement, deepen understanding, and bring the curriculum to life.

Future Directions of Mobile Learning

The future of mobile learning holds great potential for further innovation and transformation. Some of the future directions include:

1. Augmented Reality (AR) Integration: AR technology can overlay digital information onto the real-world environment, creating interactive learning experiences. With the integration of AR into mobile devices, students can explore concepts, visualize complex phenomena, and interact with virtual objects in their physical environment.

2. Artificial Intelligence (AI) Personalization: AI-powered mobile applications can adapt to students' individual needs and provide personalized recommendations, adaptive assessments, and intelligent tutoring. AI algorithms can analyze data collected from student interactions and provide targeted feedback and learning pathways.

3. Mobile Learning Analytics: Analyzing the data generated by mobile learning activities can provide valuable insights into student engagement, progress, and learning outcomes. Mobile learning analytics can enable educators to identify patterns, personalize instruction, and make data-informed decisions to enhance teaching and learning.

In conclusion, mobile learning offers opportunities for personalized and flexible education, enabling students to access educational content anytime and anywhere. By leveraging the potential of mobile devices and technologies, educators can create engaging and meaningful learning experiences that cater to individual student needs and enhance academic achievement. The future of mobile learning holds promise for continued innovation and integration with emerging technologies, further enhancing the transformative potential of education.

Social Media and Collaborative Learning

In today's digital age, social media has become an integral part of our daily lives, transforming the way we connect, communicate, and learn. Social media platforms such as Facebook, Twitter, Instagram, and YouTube have revolutionized the way we share information, collaborate, and engage with others. This section explores the role of social media in fostering collaborative learning, discussing its benefits, challenges, and future directions.

Benefits of Social Media in Collaborative Learning

Social media provides numerous benefits in the context of collaborative learning. Here are some of the key advantages:

- **Facilitating communication and collaboration:** Social media platforms enable students and educators to connect and collaborate beyond the constraints of physical classrooms. Through shared spaces, discussions, and messaging features, students can actively engage with their peers, exchange ideas, receive feedback, and work on group projects.

- **Promoting active learning:** Social media platforms offer a wide range of multimedia tools including videos, images, and interactive content. These resources can enhance the learning experience by making it more engaging, interactive, and personalized. Students can actively participate in discussions, share their thoughts, and learn from each other's perspectives.

- **Enhancing critical thinking and digital literacy skills:** Engaging with social media requires students to critically evaluate and analyze information. By navigating through various sources, students can develop their digital literacy skills, distinguish between credible and unreliable sources, and think critically about the content they consume and share.

- **Increasing access to diverse perspectives:** Social media provides a platform for students from different cultural backgrounds, geographical locations, and educational institutions to connect and share their knowledge and experiences. This exposure to diverse perspectives fosters a global mindset, promotes cultural understanding, and encourages empathy and collaboration.

- **Encouraging active participation and student agency:** Social media empowers students to take ownership of their learning as they actively contribute to discussions, create content, and share their work with a wider audience. This active participation fosters a sense of agency, motivation, and self-directed learning.

Challenges in Implementing Social Media for Collaborative Learning

While social media offers numerous benefits, there are also challenges that need to be addressed for its effective implementation in the context of collaborative learning. Some key challenges include:

- **Privacy and safety concerns:** Social media platforms raise concerns about students' privacy, as they involve sharing personal information and engaging in online interactions. Educators must ensure a safe and secure learning environment, establishing guidelines for responsible social media usage and addressing cyberbullying or harassment incidents.

- **Digital divide and accessibility:** Not all students have equal access to technology and the internet, creating a digital divide. Educators must be mindful of this disparity and explore strategies to bridge the gap, such as providing internet access or utilizing offline alternatives for collaborative learning activities.

- **Information overload and credibility:** The vast amount of information available on social media can be overwhelming for students. Educators should guide students in developing information literacy skills to effectively evaluate sources, verify information, and discern misinformation or fake news.

- **Maintaining focus and academic integrity:** Social media platforms can serve as distractions, potentially diverting students' attention away from learning tasks. Educators should establish clear expectations, provide guidelines, and facilitate structured activities to ensure that social media is used for educational purposes and does not compromise academic integrity.

- **Digital well-being and time management:** Excessive use of social media can negatively impact students' well-being, leading to issues such as addiction, anxiety, and poor time management. Educators should promote healthy habits, encourage digital detoxes, and provide guidance on balancing online and offline activities.

Future Directions of Social Media in Collaborative Learning

The future of social media in collaborative learning is promising, with several trends and developments shaping its potential. Here are some future directions:

- **Integration of artificial intelligence:** AI-powered features, such as automated feedback, personalized recommendations, and intelligent data analytics, can enhance the collaborative learning experience on social media platforms. AI algorithms can facilitate adaptive learning, identify knowledge gaps, and provide tailored learning experiences for students.
- **Augmented and virtual reality integration:** Social media platforms may incorporate augmented reality (AR) and virtual reality (VR) technologies to create immersive and interactive learning experiences. These technologies can transport students to virtual environments, enabling them to explore concepts, engage in simulations, and collaborate with others in a virtual setting.
- **Emphasis on digital citizenship and online ethics:** With the growing use of social media, there is an increased need to promote digital citizenship and ethical online behavior. Future directions may involve integrating digital citizenship education into the curriculum, training students on responsible social media use, and addressing ethical considerations associated with data privacy and algorithmic bias.
- **Integration with learning management systems:** Integration between social media platforms and learning management systems (LMS) can enable seamless integration of collaborative learning activities into coursework. This integration can streamline communication, assignment submission, grading, and tracking student progress, providing a comprehensive learning experience.
- **Exploration of emerging social media platforms:** As new social media platforms continue to emerge, educators can explore their potential for collaborative learning. Platforms such as TikTok or Clubhouse offer unique features that can engage students in creative ways and facilitate collaborative learning experiences in diverse formats.

In conclusion, social media can play a transformative role in collaborative learning, fostering communication, active engagement, and the development of critical thinking skills. However, educators must address the challenges of privacy, accessibility, information credibility, focus, and well-being to effectively harness the potential of social media. Looking ahead, the integration of AI, AR/VR, digital citizenship education, integration with LMS, and exploration of emerging platforms will shape the future of social media in collaborative learning.

Data Analytics and Learning Analytics

Data analytics and learning analytics play a crucial role in modern education. These approaches leverage data to gain insights into student learning and enhance the overall educational experience. By analyzing large amounts of data, educators can make data-driven decisions and implement personalized and adaptive learning strategies. In this section, we will explore the principles and applications of data analytics and learning analytics in education.

Principles of Data Analytics

Data analytics involves the process of collecting, analyzing, and interpreting data to gain meaningful insights and inform decision-making. In the context of education, data analytics focuses on using educational data to understand student performance, identify patterns, and optimize instructional strategies. The following are key principles of data analytics in education:

1. Data Collection: Data collection involves gathering relevant information from various educational sources, such as student assessments, learning management systems, online platforms, and classroom observations. It is essential to ensure that the data collected is accurate, reliable, and representative of the learning process.

2. Data Analysis: Data analysis involves exploring, cleaning, and transforming the collected data to identify patterns, trends, and relationships. This process often utilizes statistical techniques to uncover insights and make data-driven decisions. Data analysis can be quantitative, involving numerical data, or qualitative, involving text and narrative data.

3. Data Visualization: Data visualization is the process of presenting data in a graphical or visual format to facilitate understanding and interpretation. Visualizing educational data can help educators identify patterns, outliers, and trends more effectively. It enables stakeholders to make informed decisions based on clear, concise, and visually appealing representations of data.

4. Data Interpretation: Data interpretation involves deriving meaningful insights and actionable recommendations from the analyzed data. It requires understanding the context, considering different perspectives, and drawing

conclusions based on evidence. The interpretation of data should be guided by the research question or educational objective at hand.

5. Continuous Improvement: Data analytics in education is an iterative process. It involves continuously collecting, analyzing, and interpreting data to improve teaching and learning practices. By using feedback from data analysis, educators can make evidence-based adjustments to their instructional strategies, interventions, and curriculum.

Applications of Data Analytics in Education

Data analytics has diverse applications in education, supporting decision-making at various levels, from individual student support to systemic improvements. The following are some key applications of data analytics in education:

1. Identifying At-Risk Students: By analyzing student data, such as grades, attendance records, and behavior indicators, educators can identify students who may be at risk of falling behind academically or disengaging from the learning process. This allows for early intervention strategies to address their needs and improve their chances of success.

2. Personalization and Adaptive Learning: Data analytics enables educators to personalize the learning experience for individual students. By analyzing student performance and preferences, educators can tailor instructional materials, learning activities, and assessments to match each student's unique needs and learning style. Adaptive learning systems use data analytics to dynamically adjust the content and pacing of instruction based on a student's progress and performance.

3. Curriculum Design and Alignment: Data analytics can inform curriculum design by identifying areas of strength and weakness in the current curriculum. By analyzing student performance data, educators can align curriculum objectives, instructional materials, and assessments to ensure that students are achieving the desired learning outcomes.

4. Program Evaluation and Improvement: Data analytics can assess the effectiveness of educational programs, interventions, and policies. By analyzing data on student outcomes, educators and policymakers can identify successful practices and areas for improvement. This facilitates evidence-based decision-making in education and helps allocate resources more efficiently.

5. Predictive Analytics: Predictive analytics uses historical data to forecast student outcomes, such as graduation rates or subject performance. By analyzing patterns and trends, educators can identify factors contributing to success or failure and take proactive measures to support struggling students.

6. Learning Analytics: Learning analytics focuses on understanding and improving the learning process itself. By analyzing data generated by educational technologies, such as learning management systems, online platforms, and digital assessments, educators can gain insights into how students learn, their engagement levels, and their learning strategies. This information can be used to optimize instructional design and enhance pedagogical approaches.

Challenges and Limitations of Data Analytics in Education

While data analytics has immense potential to transform education, there are several challenges and limitations that need to be addressed. These include:

1. Data Quality and Privacy: Data accuracy, completeness, and representativeness are critical for reliable analysis. Maintaining data privacy and security is also essential to protect sensitive student information. Educators must adhere to ethical guidelines and ensure that data is collected and used responsibly.

2. Data Integration and Interoperability: Educational data is often scattered across various systems and platforms, making it challenging to integrate and analyze effectively. Establishing data interoperability standards and implementing robust data management practices are necessary to overcome these challenges.

3. Ethical and Bias Considerations: Analysis of educational data should be conducted with ethical considerations in mind. Educators must be cautious of potential biases in data collection and analysis that may perpetuate inequalities or discrimination. It is crucial to address these biases and ensure fairness and equity in the educational system.

4. Teacher Training and Support: Educators need training and support to effectively utilize data analytics tools and techniques. Professional development programs should provide opportunities for teachers to enhance their data literacy skills and apply data-driven decision-making in their classrooms.

5. Technical Infrastructure and Resources: Implementing data analytics in education requires robust technical infrastructure and resources. Educational institutions need to invest in technology, software, and data storage capabilities to support data analytics efforts effectively.

6. Human Factors: Data analytics should complement the expertise and experience of educators rather than replace them. It is crucial to strike a balance between data-driven decision-making and professional judgment. Educators should be empowered to interpret and act upon data insights while considering the unique needs and context of their students.

Real-World Example: Using Learning Analytics for Intervention

Imagine a high school implementing learning analytics to support academic interventions. The school collects data on student attendance, grades, and engagement through an online learning management system. Using learning analytics, the school identifies a group of students with consistently low attendance and declining grades in mathematics.

The learning analytics platform generates visualizations and reports that highlight specific students' performance and identify patterns of disengagement. The data reveals that a significant number of these students struggle with the concepts introduced in the early stages of the math curriculum.

Based on these insights, the school implements targeted interventions to address these students' needs. The math teachers collaborate with support staff to design additional resources, personalized tutoring sessions, and interactive activities specifically focused on the challenging concepts. The school then monitors the students' progress using ongoing data collection and analysis to determine the effectiveness of the interventions.

Through this data-driven approach, the school can intervene early, provide personalized support, and help students overcome their difficulties in mathematics. This example demonstrates how learning analytics can empower educators to identify at-risk students, tailor interventions, and improve academic outcomes.

Conclusion

Data analytics and learning analytics offer powerful tools for transforming education. By harnessing the potential of educational data, educators can gain insights into student learning, optimize instructional practices, and promote personalized and adaptive learning experiences. However, it is crucial to address challenges related to data quality, privacy, bias, and educator training. By doing so, we can leverage data analytics to create more equitable, inclusive, and effective education systems.

Augmented Reality in Education

Augmented Reality (AR) is an innovative technology that blends the real world with digital elements, creating a unique and interactive learning experience. In education, AR has the potential to revolutionize the way students engage with content by providing immersive and contextual learning opportunities. This section will explore the principles and applications of AR in education, highlighting its benefits, challenges, and future directions.

Principles of Augmented Reality

AR is based on the principle of overlaying digital information onto the real world, enhancing the user's perception and interaction with their environment. It achieves this by utilizing computer vision techniques, marker-based and markerless tracking systems, and the integration of real-time data. By using a device such as a smartphone, tablet, or AR headset, users can view and interact with the digital content superimposed onto the physical world.

Benefits of Augmented Reality in Education

The integration of AR into education offers numerous benefits for both teachers and students. Firstly, AR provides a highly engaging and interactive learning experience, as it allows students to visualize complex concepts and ideas in a three-dimensional and dynamic manner. This visual and interactive approach enhances understanding and retention of information.

Secondly, AR can overcome the limitations of traditional teaching methods by providing personalized and immersive learning experiences. Students can explore virtual objects, conduct virtual experiments, and engage in simulations that would otherwise be impossible or impractical in a traditional classroom setting. This hands-on approach fosters creativity, critical thinking, and problem-solving skills.

Furthermore, AR promotes active learning and student engagement by giving learners the opportunity to actively participate in the learning process. Students can explore and manipulate virtual objects, collaborate with peers, and solve real-world problems, thereby enhancing their learning motivation and autonomy.

AR also promotes inclusivity in education by providing alternative modes of representation and interaction. Students with diverse learning styles or disabilities can benefit from AR's multimodal and customizable learning experiences. Additionally, AR can bridge language and cultural barriers by providing real-time translations or contextual explanations, making education accessible to a wider range of students.

Challenges and Considerations

While AR holds immense potential, there are several challenges that need to be addressed for its effective implementation in education. One of the main challenges is the cost and accessibility of AR devices and software. Schools and institutions need to invest in the necessary hardware and software infrastructure to ensure equitable access to AR experiences for all students.

Another challenge is the development of high-quality and curriculum-aligned AR content. Educators need access to a wide range of educational AR applications, simulations, and resources that align with their learning objectives and standards. Collaborative efforts between educators, developers, and researchers are essential to ensure the availability of high-quality AR content.

Additionally, privacy and ethical considerations should be taken into account when using AR in the classroom. Student data privacy and permissions must be respected, and proper guidelines and policies should be in place to protect student information and ensure responsible use of AR technologies.

Examples and Applications

AR can be applied across various subject areas in education. In science, students can explore virtual anatomy models, conduct virtual chemistry experiments, or visualize astronomical phenomena. In history, AR can bring historical events to life by overlaying digital artifacts and interactive narratives onto real-world locations. In languages, students can practice vocabulary and pronunciation through AR-enhanced language learning apps. The possibilities are vast, limited only by the creativity and imagination of educators.

One example of AR in education is the "Elements 4D" app, which enables students to explore the properties and interactions of chemical elements by manipulating physical cubes that trigger digital animations and information. Another example is "WWF Free Rivers," an AR app that allows students to understand the impact of river systems on ecosystems by creating virtual rivers in their physical environment.

Future Directions

The future of AR in education holds immense potential. As technology advances and becomes more accessible, AR experiences will become even more immersive, realistic, and seamlessly integrated into the learning process.

One exciting direction is the integration of AR with other emerging technologies, such as artificial intelligence and virtual reality. This fusion can create a truly transformative learning experience, where AR not only provides information but also adapts to individual learning needs and preferences.

Another future direction is the widespread adoption of AR in remote and online learning contexts. AR can bridge the physical separation between teachers and students, providing remote learners with interactive and engaging experiences that mimic the benefits of face-to-face instruction.

In conclusion, augmented reality has the power to redefine education by creating immersive, interactive, and personalized learning experiences. By leveraging the principles of AR, educators can engage students in deep learning, foster creativity and critical thinking, and promote inclusivity in the classroom. As technology continues to evolve, the future of AR in education is bright, promising a revolution in teaching and learning.

Robotics and Education

In recent years, robotics has emerged as a powerful tool for enhancing education and providing students with hands-on learning experiences. This section explores the integration of robotics in education, discussing its benefits, challenges, and future directions.

Benefits of Robotics in Education

Integrating robotics into education offers numerous benefits to students. Firstly, it promotes engagement and motivation by providing students with interactive and stimulating learning environments. Robotics allows students to actively participate in problem-solving activities, where they can apply their knowledge in real-world contexts. This hands-on approach encourages critical thinking, creativity, and collaboration among students.

Secondly, robotics helps develop technical and computational skills. By working with robots, students learn how to program, design, and control their creations. These practical skills are highly valuable in today's technology-driven world, where automation and robotics are becoming increasingly prevalent.

Furthermore, robotics fosters interdisciplinary learning. Students are exposed to concepts from various subjects such as science, technology, engineering, and mathematics (STEM). They learn to apply knowledge from these subjects to solve complex problems, promoting a holistic understanding of the interconnectedness of these disciplines.

Robotics also cultivates important soft skills such as teamwork, communication, and problem-solving. Students often work in groups to design and build robots, requiring effective collaboration and communication. Additionally, when facing challenges during the robot-building process, students develop problem-solving skills by analyzing and troubleshooting issues.

Challenges in Implementing Robotics in Education

While robotics presents numerous benefits, its implementation in education also faces challenges. One primary challenge is the cost of robotics equipment and resources. High-quality robots can be expensive, making it difficult for schools with limited budgets to invest in such technology. However, with advancements in technology and increased availability of affordable robotics kits, this challenge is gradually being addressed.

Another challenge is the need for specialized training and support for teachers. Integrating robotics into the curriculum requires educators to have the necessary technical knowledge and skills to effectively utilize robotics tools. Professional development programs and resources play a crucial role in empowering teachers with the skills needed to integrate robotics into their teaching practices.

Moreover, integrating robotics into the curriculum requires careful planning and alignment with academic standards. Educators need to design appropriate lesson plans and activities that seamlessly incorporate robotics while addressing specific learning objectives. This requires collaboration between teachers, curriculum developers, and robotics experts to ensure the integration is smooth and effective.

Finally, robotics may introduce ethical considerations. While robotics offers immense potential, ethical issues such as privacy, security, and the impact of automation on employment need to be addressed. Educators and policymakers must navigate these ethical dilemmas and ensure the responsible use of robotics technology in educational settings.

Future Directions of Robotics in Education

The future of robotics in education holds exciting possibilities. As advancements in technology continue, robotics will become more accessible and affordable, allowing a wider range of schools and students to benefit from its integration.

One promising area is the use of artificial intelligence (AI) in robotics education. AI-powered robots can analyze student data and provide personalized feedback, creating adaptive learning environments tailored to each student's needs. This individualized approach enhances the learning experience and promotes student engagement and achievement.

Furthermore, the integration of robotics with other emerging technologies such as virtual reality (VR) and augmented reality (AR) offers new opportunities for immersive learning experiences. Students can interact with virtual robots, explore robotic simulations, and gain practical skills in a safe and controlled virtual environment.

Robotics also holds potential in bridging the gap between physical and virtual learning spaces. With the rise of online and blended learning, robots can serve as physical avatars, allowing remote students to interact and participate in physical classrooms.

In conclusion, robotics has transformative potential in education by promoting engagement, fostering technical and computational skills, and nurturing interdisciplinary and soft skills. Despite challenges such as cost and teacher training, the future of robotics in education looks promising with the integration of AI, VR, and AR. By embracing robotics and preparing students for a technology-driven future, we can provide them with the skills and knowledge they need to succeed in the 21st century.

Blockchain Technology in Education

Blockchain technology has gained significant attention in recent years, primarily known for its association with cryptocurrencies like Bitcoin. However, blockchain technology has abundant potential beyond cryptocurrencies and has started to make its way into various domains, including education. In this section, we will explore the concept of blockchain technology and its applications in the field of education.

Understanding Blockchain Technology

Blockchain is a decentralized and distributed ledger that records transactions or data across multiple computers or nodes. It is characterized by its transparency, security, and immutability, making it an ideal technology for managing digital assets and information.

At its core, a blockchain is a chain of blocks, where each block contains a collection of transactions or data. These blocks are linked together using cryptographic hashes, creating a sequential chain. Each block contains a unique identifier, called a hash, which is generated based on the content of the block and the hash of the previous block. This linkage between blocks ensures that any modification in one block would require changes in all subsequent blocks, making the blockchain highly secure and tamper-proof.

Applications of Blockchain Technology in Education

Blockchain technology has the potential to revolutionize various aspects of education, from credentialing and certification to improving administrative processes. Here are some key applications of blockchain technology in education:

Secure Credentials and Certificates: One of the significant challenges in education is the verification of credentials and certificates. Blockchain provides a secure and decentralized platform for issuing, sharing, and verifying educational credentials. The use of blockchain technology ensures the authenticity of certificates, reducing the risk of fraud or misrepresentation. Employers and educational institutions can easily verify the legitimacy of an individual's educational achievements through a blockchain-based platform.

Student Records and Transcripts: Managing student records and transcripts is a critical aspect of education systems. Traditional paper-based records are often prone to errors, loss, or manipulation. With blockchain, student records can be securely stored and accessed, ensuring their integrity and privacy. Blockchain-based student records allow for seamless sharing between different institutions while maintaining confidentiality and data security.

Micro-Credentials and Badges: In addition to formal degrees and certificates, blockchain technology enables the creation and recognition of micro-credentials and digital badges. Micro-credentials represent smaller units of achievement or competencies, allowing individuals to showcase their specific skills and knowledge. Blockchain-based badges and micro-credentials can be easily shared and verified, facilitating lifelong learning and professional development.

Secure Digital Rights Management: Blockchain technology can play a significant role in protecting intellectual property rights in the education sector. With blockchain, content creators, such as researchers or authors, can securely publish and manage their work, ensuring proper attribution and ownership. This decentralized approach to digital rights management reduces the dependence on intermediaries and enhances the transparency and fairness of content distribution.

Smart Contracts and Payments: Blockchain technology enables the use of smart contracts, which are self-executing contracts with predefined conditions. Smart contracts can automate various administrative processes in education, including tuition payments, financial aid disbursement, and contract management. By leveraging blockchain and smart contracts, educational institutions can streamline their operations, reduce administrative costs, and enhance transparency.

Challenges and Considerations

While blockchain technology holds immense potential for transforming education, several challenges and considerations need to be addressed:

Scalability and Performance: Blockchain networks, especially public ones like Bitcoin and Ethereum, can face scalability and performance issues when dealing with a large volume of transactions. To ensure widespread adoption of blockchain technology in education, scalability solutions and optimization techniques need to be developed.

Data Privacy and Security: While blockchain technology provides inherent security and immutability, ensuring data privacy is crucial, especially in educational settings. Blockchain systems should implement robust encryption and permission mechanisms to protect sensitive student data and comply with privacy regulations like GDPR (General Data Protection Regulation).

Standardization and Interoperability: To fully realize the potential of blockchain in education, interoperability standards should be established to enable seamless integration with existing educational systems and platforms. Standardization efforts and collaborations among educational institutions, governments, and technology providers are necessary for widespread adoption.

Digital Divide and Accessibility: The digital divide, which refers to the gap in access to technology and digital resources, can pose challenges in implementing blockchain technology in education. Efforts should be made to ensure equitable access and inclusion, making blockchain-based solutions accessible to all learners.

Case Studies and Best Practices

Several initiatives and projects have already explored the application of blockchain technology in education. Here are a few notable examples:

Holberton School: The Holberton School, a San Francisco-based coding school, has implemented blockchain technology to issue and verify academic certificates. Employers can easily verify the authenticity of a candidate's credentials using a blockchain-based platform.

MIT Media Lab: The MIT Media Lab has developed the "Blockcerts" open standard for issuing and verifying blockchain-based credentials. Blockcerts allows individuals to have complete ownership and control over their digital certificates, enabling seamless sharing and verification.

Learning Machine: Learning Machine, a software company, has partnered with governments and educational institutions to create and manage blockchain-based digital transcripts. Their solution ensures the interoperability and validity of educational credentials across different institutions and regions.

Future Directions

As blockchain technology continues to mature, its applications in education are likely to expand. Here are some potential future directions of blockchain technology in education:

Immutable Learning Records: Blockchain-based learning records could create lifelong learning portfolios for individuals, capturing their achievements, skills, and competencies. These immutable records can provide a comprehensive view of an individual's learning journey and enhance employability.

Decentralized Learning Networks: Blockchain can enable the creation of decentralized learning networks, where learners can connect directly with content creators, educators, and employers. These networks can facilitate personalized and learner-centric educational experiences.

Credential and Skills Marketplace: Blockchain-based platforms could emerge as marketplaces for credentials and skills, connecting learners directly with employers or organizations seeking specific skills. These platforms can foster a more efficient and transparent job market, focused on skills and competencies rather than traditional qualifications.

Blockchain for Learning Analytics: Blockchain technology can enhance the collection and analysis of learning data, enabling more accurate learning analytics. The immutability and transparency of blockchain can provide a reliable source of data for personalized learning recommendations and educational research.

In conclusion, blockchain technology has the potential to transform various aspects of education, from credentialing and record management to revolutionizing administrative processes. While challenges and considerations exist, ongoing research and innovation will pave the way for realizing the full potential of blockchain technology in education. By leveraging blockchain, we can create a more secure, transparent, and learner-centric education system.

The Role of Teachers in Transformative Education

Shifting role of teachers in the digital age

The digital age has brought about significant changes in various aspects of our lives, including education. As technology continues to advance, the role of teachers is also evolving to adapt to the new demands and opportunities presented by the digital age. In this section, we will explore the shifting role of teachers in the digital age and examine how they can leverage technology to enhance their teaching practices and support student learning.

Understanding the changing landscape

The traditional role of teachers has often been centered around delivering content and guiding students through the learning process. However, with the proliferation of digital technologies, information is readily accessible to students from various sources. This has shifted the focus of teaching from being the primary source of knowledge to becoming a facilitator of learning.

In the digital age, teachers are expected to go beyond simply imparting information and instead, foster critical thinking, problem-solving, and collaboration skills among their students. They need to create rich and meaningful learning experiences that engage students in active learning and help them connect concepts to real-world applications.

Embracing technology as an instructional tool

Technology has become an integral part of the modern classroom, and teachers must embrace its use to enhance their instructional practices. They need to familiarize themselves with various educational technologies, such as learning management systems, collaborative tools, and multimedia resources, to deliver engaging and interactive lessons.

By incorporating digital tools into their teaching, teachers can create personalized learning experiences that cater to the diverse needs and interests of their students. They can utilize online platforms to distribute resources, provide timely feedback, and facilitate discussions both inside and outside the classroom. Technology also enables teachers to differentiate instruction, track student progress, and address individual learning gaps more effectively.

Facilitating student-centered learning

In the digital age, the focus of education has shifted towards student-centered learning. Teachers are now encouraged to adopt pedagogical approaches that empower students to take ownership of their learning journey. This requires them to create inclusive and collaborative learning environments where students are actively involved in knowledge construction.

Teachers can leverage technology to facilitate student-centered learning by incorporating interactive multimedia resources, online simulations, and virtual learning environments. These tools can provide students with opportunities for exploration, experimentation, and self-directed learning. Teachers should also encourage students to create their own digital content, collaborate with peers, and engage in authentic real-world tasks to develop deeper understanding and critical thinking skills.

Supporting digital literacy and digital citizenship

In the digital age, teachers play a crucial role in fostering digital literacy and promoting responsible digital citizenship among their students. They need to educate students on how to critically evaluate online information, navigate digital platforms safely, and respect and protect their digital identities.

Teachers can integrate digital literacy skills into their curriculum by guiding students through the process of conducting online research, identifying reliable sources of information, and distinguishing between credible and unreliable online content. They should also address issues related to online privacy, cyberbullying, and ethical use of technology.

Collaborating with technology specialists

As technology continues to advance rapidly, teachers may find it challenging to keep pace with the latest tools and trends. To support their professional development and ensure effective integration of technology in their teaching practices, collaboration with technology specialists is crucial.

Teachers can collaborate with technology specialists within their school or district to gain insights into emerging technologies, effective pedagogical strategies, and troubleshooting technical issues. Technology specialists can provide guidance, training, and ongoing support to teachers, enabling them to make the most of available technology resources and create impactful learning experiences for their students.

Promoting lifelong learning

In the digital age, learning is an ongoing process for both teachers and students. Teachers must adopt a growth mindset and be open to continuous professional development to stay abreast of the latest trends and developments in educational technology.

Teachers can engage in various professional learning opportunities, such as attending conferences, participating in online courses, and joining professional learning communities. They can also connect with other educators through social media platforms and online forums to share ideas, resources, and best practices.

By embracing lifelong learning, teachers can adapt to the evolving needs of their students and harness the power of technology to create transformative learning experiences in the digital age.

Key Takeaways

- The role of teachers in the digital age is shifting from being the primary source of knowledge to that of a facilitator of learning.
- Teachers should embrace technology as an instructional tool to enhance their teaching practices and support student learning.
- Student-centered learning should be prioritized, with teachers creating inclusive and collaborative environments that empower students to take ownership of their learning.
- Teachers should support digital literacy and promote responsible digital citizenship among their students.

- Collaboration with technology specialists is essential to support teachers' professional development and ensure effective integration of technology in the classroom.
- Lifelong learning is crucial for teachers to stay updated with the latest trends and innovations in educational technology.

Discussion Questions

1. How has technology changed the role of teachers in the digital age?
2. In what ways can teachers leverage technology to enhance student learning experiences?
3. What challenges might teachers face in adopting technology in their teaching practices, and how can they overcome them?
4. How can teachers promote digital literacy and responsible digital citizenship among their students?
5. What are some strategies that teachers can employ to stay updated with the latest trends and innovations in educational technology?

Teacher Professional Development for Transformative Education

Teacher professional development plays a crucial role in implementing transformative education in the digital age. This section will explore the importance of professional development, various models and approaches to enhance teacher skills and knowledge, and the future of teacher professional development.

Importance of Professional Development

Professional development is essential for teachers to stay updated with the latest educational trends, research, and techniques. It ensures that teachers are equipped with the necessary skills and knowledge to effectively implement transformative education in their classrooms.

Transformative education requires teachers to adopt new pedagogical strategies, incorporate technology into their teaching practices, and create inclusive and culturally responsive learning environments. Professional development provides opportunities for teachers to learn and develop these skills, enabling them to create meaningful and engaging learning experiences for their students.

Research has shown that effective professional development leads to improved teaching practices, increased student achievement, and overall school improvement. It empowers teachers, enhances their confidence, and supports their continuous growth as educational professionals.

Models and Approaches to Professional Development

There are various models and approaches to teacher professional development that can be effective in promoting transformative education. Here are some key models and approaches:

1. **Collaborative Learning Communities:** This model focuses on creating communities of practice where teachers come together to share ideas, collaborate, and learn from each other. It encourages peer support, reflection, and the exchange of best practices. Collaborative learning communities can take the form of professional learning communities (PLCs), grade-level or subject-area teams, or online communities.
2. **Job-Embedded Professional Development:** This approach emphasizes integrating professional development into teachers' daily work. It involves providing support and coaching within the context of teachers' classrooms. Job-embedded professional development can include lesson study, co-teaching, and instructional coaching.
3. **Online and Virtual Professional Development:** With the advancement of technology, online and virtual professional development has gained popularity. This approach provides flexibility and accessibility for teachers to engage in professional development activities at their own pace and convenience. Online platforms, webinars, virtual conferences, and online courses offer opportunities for teachers to expand their knowledge and skills.
4. **Micro-credentials and Digital Badges:** Micro-credentials and digital badges are a form of competency-based professional development. Teachers can earn micro-credentials by demonstrating mastery of specific skills or knowledge areas. These credentials can be showcased as digital badges, providing evidence of professional growth and achievement.
5. **Traditional Workshops and Conferences:** Despite the growth of online professional development, traditional workshops and conferences continue to be valuable avenues for teachers to learn and network. They offer opportunities for attending presentations, participating in hands-on workshops, engaging in discussions, and networking with other educators.
6. **Action Research and Reflective Practice:** Action research involves teachers conducting research in their own classrooms to improve their teaching practices. It

promotes reflective practice, inquiry, and continuous improvement. Teachers can collaborate with colleagues, collect data, analyze and reflect on their findings, and make informed decisions to enhance their teaching practices.

Building Effective Professional Development Programs

To ensure the success of professional development programs for transformative education, several key principles should be considered:

1. **Needs Assessment:** Professional development should be based on a thorough needs assessment, taking into account the specific needs and goals of teachers and the school community. This assessment should involve input from teachers, administrators, and other stakeholders to ensure that the professional development aligns with the vision and context of the school.
2. **Sustained and Ongoing Support:** Professional development should not be a one-time event but rather a continuous and sustained effort. Teachers need ongoing support, feedback, and opportunities for collaboration to implement new strategies effectively. Follow-up sessions, coaching, and mentoring can help teachers integrate their learning into their practice.
3. **Active Learning and Collaboration:** Professional development should be designed to actively engage teachers in the learning process. It should include hands-on activities, collaboration, and opportunities for reflection. Teachers should be encouraged to share their experiences, ask questions, and learn from each other.
4. **Alignment with School Goals:** Professional development should align with the overall goals and vision of the school or district. It should focus on addressing specific challenges and needs identified by the school community. When professional development is aligned with the broader goals of the school, it is more likely to have a lasting impact.
5. **Integration of Technology:** Professional development programs should model the use of technology in transformative education. Teachers should have opportunities to explore and gain hands-on experience with educational technologies that can enhance their teaching and student learning.

Challenges in Professional Development for Transformative Education

Implementing effective professional development for transformative education comes with its challenges. Some common challenges include:

1. **Time Constraints:** Teachers often face time constraints due to their busy schedules and workload. Finding dedicated time for professional development can

be challenging. Finding innovative ways to provide professional development without adding to teachers' workload is crucial.

2. **Resistance to Change:** Implementing transformative education requires a mindset shift and changes in teaching practices. Some teachers may resist these changes due to fear, lack of confidence, or a reluctance to leave their comfort zones. Supporting teachers in overcoming these barriers is essential.

3. **Access to Resources and Support:** Providing equitable access to resources and support is vital for effective professional development. Teachers in underserved communities or rural areas may face challenges in accessing high-quality professional development opportunities. Ensuring that all teachers have equal access to resources and support is crucial for promoting transformative education.

4. **Cost and Funding:** Professional development programs can be costly, especially when considering the costs of trainers, materials, and technology. Securing funding and resources to support professional development can be a challenge, particularly for schools or districts with limited budgets.

The Future of Teacher Professional Development

The future of teacher professional development is likely to be shaped by technological advancements, changing educational paradigms, and the evolving needs of students and teachers. Here are some trends and considerations for the future:

1. **Personalized Professional Development:** The future of professional development is likely to be more personalized, allowing teachers to choose learning paths based on their individual needs and interests. Adaptive learning technologies and personalized approaches will enable teachers to engage in targeted and relevant professional development.

2. **Data-Driven Professional Development:** The use of data and learning analytics will play a significant role in informing and improving professional development. Analyzing data on teacher performance, student outcomes, and learning needs can help identify areas of growth and tailor professional development programs accordingly.

3. **Virtual and Augmented Reality:** Virtual and augmented reality technologies have the potential to revolutionize professional development by providing immersive and interactive learning experiences for teachers. Virtual simulations can allow teachers to practice new skills, experiment with new pedagogies, and receive feedback in a safe and realistic environment.

4. **Collaboration and Global Connections:** Technology enables teachers to connect and collaborate with educators from around the world. Online platforms

and social media can facilitate the sharing of ideas, resources, and best practices. Collaborative projects and virtual exchanges can provide opportunities for teachers to broaden their perspectives and engage in global professional development.

5. **Continued Emphasis on Equity and Inclusion:** The future of professional development must prioritize equity and inclusion. Efforts should be made to ensure that professional development opportunities are accessible to all teachers, including those in remote areas or underserved communities. Culturally responsive and inclusive approaches should be embedded in professional development programs.

In conclusion, teacher professional development is essential for implementing transformative education. It should be designed to address the specific needs and goals of teachers and the school community. Providing sustained support, active learning experiences, and integration of technology are essential elements of effective professional development. Overcoming challenges and addressing future trends will shape the future of professional development, enabling teachers to create transformative learning environments for their students.

Building Strong Teacher-Student Relationships in Transformative Classrooms

In transformative classrooms, building strong teacher-student relationships is crucial for creating an environment that fosters learning and growth. These relationships go beyond traditional teacher-student dynamics and focus on empowering students to take an active role in their education. This section explores the importance of strong teacher-student relationships in transformative classrooms and provides strategies for cultivating such relationships.

The Importance of Teacher-Student Relationships

Strong teacher-student relationships have a profound impact on student engagement, motivation, and academic success. When students feel connected and supported by their teachers, they are more likely to actively participate in class, take risks in their learning, and persevere through challenges. Additionally, positive teacher-student relationships contribute to students' social-emotional development, well-being, and overall satisfaction with school.

In transformative classrooms, where the goal is to empower students and promote their agency, teacher-student relationships become even more critical. These relationships serve as a foundation for trust, collaboration, and open communication. They create a sense of belonging and a safe space for students to express their thoughts, ideas, and concerns. Moreover, strong teacher-student relationships allow teachers to better understand individual students' strengths, needs, and interests, enabling them to provide personalized support and guidance.

Strategies for Building Strong Teacher-Student Relationships

Building strong teacher-student relationships requires intentional effort and a genuine commitment from teachers. The following strategies can help cultivate these relationships in transformative classrooms:

1. **Get to know your students individually:** Take the time to learn about each student's background, interests, and learning styles. This understanding will help you tailor your teaching approach and create personalized learning experiences. Engage in informal conversations, use interest inventories, and conduct student conferences to connect with students on a deeper level.

2. **Show care and empathy:** Demonstrate genuine care and concern for your students' well-being. Acknowledge their emotions, validate their experiences, and create a supportive classroom culture. Be approachable, actively listen, and provide guidance when needed. Empathy is crucial in building trust and establishing strong connections with students.

3. **Foster positive and respectful communication:** Cultivate an environment where open and respectful communication is encouraged. Create opportunities for students to voice their opinions, ask questions, and engage in meaningful discussions. Respond to student inquiries promptly and thoughtfully. Use positive language and provide constructive feedback that encourages growth and improvement.

4. **Create collaborative learning experiences:** Foster collaborative learning opportunities that promote teamwork and cooperation among students. Encourage peer-to-peer interactions, group work, and problem-solving activities. Collaborative learning experiences help build strong relationships among students, as well as between students and teachers.

5. **Provide support and guidance:** Offer support and timely guidance to students based on their individual needs. Be proactive in identifying and addressing any challenges or barriers to learning. Provide resources, interventions,

and additional assistance when necessary. By offering support, teachers demonstrate their commitment to their students' success.

6. Celebrate student achievements: Recognize and celebrate the achievements, both academic and personal, of your students. Whether it's a small milestone or a significant accomplishment, acknowledge their efforts and progress. Celebrations can take various forms, such as verbal praise, certificates, or classroom-wide acknowledgments. These gestures reinforce the positive teacher-student relationship and motivate students to continue their growth.

7. Engage in reflective practice: Engage in reflective practice to continually evaluate and refine your teaching approaches. Reflect on the effectiveness of your interactions with students, identify areas for improvement, and seek feedback from students themselves. Reflective practice promotes self-awareness and helps teachers strengthen their relationships with students.

Real-World Example: Building Trust through Shared Experiences

To illustrate the impact of strong teacher-student relationships, let's consider a real-world example of building trust and connection through shared experiences. In a high school science class, the teacher wanted to create an environment that encouraged student curiosity and inquiry. The teacher recognized the importance of building relationships with each student and decided to start the semester with a group project.

The project involved students working in small groups to design and carry out their own scientific experiments. The teacher provided guidance and resources but gave students the freedom to explore their interests and develop their hypotheses. Throughout the project, the teacher engaged in one-on-one conversations with each student, providing personalized feedback and encouragement.

As students collaborated with their peers and the teacher, trust began to flourish. The teacher listened attentively to students' ideas, challenged their thinking, and supported their decision-making process. Students felt valued and heard, which motivated them to take ownership of their learning and push their boundaries. By the end of the project, students not only developed a deeper understanding of scientific concepts but also formed strong connections with their teacher and peers.

Additional Resources

For further exploration of building strong teacher-student relationships in transformative classrooms, the following resources are highly recommended:

- Book: "The Power of Relationships in Transformative Education" by Jane M. Braun
- Research Article: "Teacher-Student Relationships Matter: Exploring Impact on Student Engagement and Achievement" by Karen L. Mapp et al.
- Website: Edutopia - "Building Relationships with Students" (edutopia.org)
- Podcast: Cult of Pedagogy with Jennifer Gonzalez - "The Power of Human Connections" (cultofpedagogy.com)

Remember, strong teacher-student relationships are the cornerstone of transformative classrooms. By investing in these relationships, teachers can create an empowering learning environment that nurtures students' growth, curiosity, and academic success.

Fostering Creativity and Critical Thinking Skills in Students

Fostering creativity and critical thinking skills is essential in today's rapidly changing world. As the future of education moves towards transformative methods and cutting-edge tools, it becomes increasingly important for educators to empower students with the ability to think critically, solve complex problems, and think creatively.

Definition and Importance

Creativity can be defined as the ability to generate original and valuable ideas or solutions. Critical thinking, on the other hand, involves analyzing, evaluating, and synthesizing information to make informed decisions and solve problems effectively. Both of these skills are crucial for students to thrive in their personal lives, careers, and as active citizens in a global society.

Fostering creativity and critical thinking skills in students is important for several reasons:

1. Problem-solving: Creativity and critical thinking enable students to approach problems from different angles, come up with innovative solutions, and make informed decisions.

2. Adaptability: In a rapidly changing world, students need to be adaptable and flexible. Creativity and critical thinking skills help them to navigate new challenges and adapt to different situations.

3. Innovation: By nurturing creativity, students can become innovators who can bring about positive change in their communities and society as a whole.

4. Empowerment: Creativity and critical thinking empower students to take ownership of their learning, explore their passions, and develop their unique strengths and talents.

5. Lifelong learning: These skills lay the foundation for lifelong learning, enabling students to continue growing intellectually, professionally, and personally throughout their lives.

Strategies for Fostering Creativity and Critical Thinking Skills

To foster creativity and critical thinking skills in students, educators can implement various strategies and techniques:

1. Encourage questioning: Encourage students to ask questions, explore multiple perspectives, and challenge assumptions. By creating a safe and supportive learning environment, students will feel comfortable thinking critically and expressing their ideas.

2. Provide open-ended tasks and projects: Assign open-ended tasks that require creativity and critical thinking. These tasks should allow students to generate multiple solutions, consider different viewpoints, and engage in problem-solving.

3. Promote divergent thinking: Divergent thinking refers to the ability to generate multiple ideas and solutions. Encourage students to think divergently by using brainstorming sessions, mind mapping, and other creative thinking techniques.

4. Foster collaboration and teamwork: Collaborative activities provide opportunities for students to engage in critical discussions, share perspectives, and work together to solve problems. Encourage collaboration through group projects, debates, and presentations.

5. Emphasize reflection: Reflection plays a crucial role in developing critical thinking skills. Encourage students to reflect on their learning experiences, evaluate their thinking processes, and identify areas for improvement.

6. Incorporate real-world examples: Connect classroom learning to real-world examples and problems. By anchoring learning in context, students can see the relevance of their education and apply critical thinking skills to real-life situations.

7. Provide opportunities for creative expression: Allow students to express their creativity through various mediums, such as art, writing, music, or design. Provide platforms for showcasing their work and foster an appreciation for diverse forms of expression.

8. Embrace technology and digital tools: Integrate technology tools that promote creativity and critical thinking, such as multimedia presentations, digital storytelling, coding platforms, and simulation software. These tools can enhance student engagement and provide opportunities for interdisciplinary learning.

9. Encourage risk-taking and resilience: Foster a growth mindset in students by encouraging risk-taking and embracing mistakes as opportunities for learning and growth. Help students develop resilience, perseverance, and the ability to overcome challenges.

10. Cultivate curiosity and a love for learning: Nurture students' natural curiosity and encourage a lifelong love for learning. Provide opportunities for independent exploration, self-directed projects, and intellectual curiosity.

Example: Fostering Creativity and Critical Thinking Skills in Science Education

In science education, fostering creativity and critical thinking skills is crucial for future scientists and innovators. Consider the example of a biology class focusing on ecological conservation. Instead of a traditional lecture-based approach, the class could engage in a project-based learning experience.

The students could be tasked with designing a sustainable ecosystem using their knowledge of ecological principles. They would need to consider factors such as interdependence, energy flow, and biodiversity. Throughout the project, they would be required to think critically, analyze information, make informed decisions, and creatively design an ecosystem that promotes sustainability and conservation.

This project would allow students to apply their creativity in designing an ecosystem and develop critical thinking skills by considering the potential challenges and trade-offs involved. They would need to research and analyze different strategies, evaluate the ecological impact of their design, and adjust their plans based on feedback and new information.

By engaging in this hands-on, inquiry-based project, students would not only deepen their understanding of ecological concepts but also develop the creativity and critical thinking skills necessary for future environmental scientists and conservationists.

Resources for Fostering Creativity and Critical Thinking

Here are some resources that can help educators foster creativity and critical thinking skills in their students:

1. Creativity in the Classroom: Schools of Curious Delight by Alane Starko 2. Unleashing Creativity and Innovation: Nine Lessons from Nature for Enterprise Growth and Career Success by Jim Dewald 3. Developing Critical Thinking Skills: A Handbook for Teachers in Primary and Secondary Schools by Stephen Bowkett 4. Teaching for Critical Thinking: Tools and Techniques to Help Students Question Their Assumptions by Stephen D. Brookfield 5. The Art of Critical Pedagogy: Possibilities for Moving from Theory to Practice in Urban Schools by Jeffrey M. Duncan-Andrade and Ernest Morrell

In addition to these books, educators can explore online platforms, such as the Global Digital Citizen Foundation, the Buck Institute for Education, and the National Science Teachers Association, which provide a wealth of resources, lesson plans, and professional development opportunities to support creativity and critical thinking in education.

Conclusion

Fostering creativity and critical thinking skills is essential in preparing students for the future. By providing opportunities for creative expression, encouraging questioning and reflection, and integrating real-world examples, educators can empower students to become critical thinkers, problem solvers, and innovators. By nurturing their creativity and critical thinking skills, we can help them thrive in an ever-changing world and contribute to positive societal change. Strengthening these skills in students not only benefits their academic success but also prepares them to become active and engaged citizens who can navigate the complexities of the world around them.

Cultivating a growth mindset in students

In order to ensure the success of students in the future of education, it is crucial to cultivate a growth mindset in them. A growth mindset is the belief that one's abilities and intelligence can be developed through effort, dedication, and resilience. This contrasts with a fixed mindset, which believes that abilities are fixed and cannot be changed.

1. Background:

The concept of growth mindset was first introduced by psychologist Carol Dweck. According to Dweck, individuals with a growth mindset are more likely to embrace challenges, persist in the face of obstacles, and view failures as opportunities for learning. On the other hand, individuals with a fixed mindset tend to avoid challenges, give up easily, and see failures as proof of their limitations.

2. Principles of cultivating a growth mindset:

2.1 Emphasize effort over outcome: To cultivate a growth mindset, it is important to shift the focus from grades and performance to the process of learning and the effort put into it. By recognizing and praising students' efforts, rather than merely their achievements, they learn to see the value in perseverance and hard work.

2.2 Provide opportunities for reflection and self-assessment: Encourage students to reflect on their learning journey and assess their progress. This enables them to recognize areas where they have made improvements and identify areas where they can still grow. Self-assessment also helps in setting realistic goals and creating a sense of ownership over the learning process.

2.3 Promote a positive and supportive learning environment: Create a classroom culture that celebrates effort, encourages risk-taking, and supports collaboration. Provide opportunities for students to support and uplift one another, fostering an environment where mistakes are seen as opportunities for growth rather than sources of embarrassment.

2.4 Teach the neuroscience of learning: Help students understand that the brain is adaptable and can grow through effort and practice. By explaining the concept of neuroplasticity and how the brain forms new connections when learning new information or skills, students can develop a more positive outlook on their own abilities.

3. Strategies for cultivating a growth mindset:

3.1 Encourage the use of "yet": Encourage students to adopt a growth mindset language by using the word "yet" in their statements. For example, instead of saying "I can't solve this problem," they can say "I can't solve this problem yet." This simple shift in language reinforces the belief that success is achievable with effort and persistence.

3.2 Teach metacognitive strategies: Metacognitive strategies, such as goal setting, planning, self-monitoring, and reflection, help students become aware of their own thinking processes and regulate their learning. By teaching these strategies, students develop a greater understanding of their own strengths and weaknesses, and can take steps to improve their learning outcomes.

3.3 Provide constructive feedback: Feedback plays a critical role in cultivating a growth mindset. It should focus on specific aspects of the student's work or performance, highlight successes, and provide guidance for improvement. By framing feedback as an opportunity for growth, students are more likely to view it as valuable input rather than as a judgement of their abilities.

3.4 Teach resilience and embrace failures: Help students understand that setbacks and failures are a natural part of the learning process. Teach them to see failures as opportunities to learn, grow, and try again. Provide support and guidance in developing resilience, teaching them to bounce back from challenges and develop problem-solving skills.

4. Real-world example:

Let's take the example of a student who struggles with math. Instead of viewing their difficulty as a fixed limitation, cultivate a growth mindset by providing targeted support, encouraging a positive attitude, and emphasizing the importance of effort and perseverance. Use specific strategies, such as breaking down complex problems into smaller steps, promoting collaborative learning, and providing opportunities for practice and feedback. Through this process, the student can develop confidence in their ability to improve and approach math problems with a growth mindset.

5. Resources for cultivating a growth mindset:

- "Mindset: The New Psychology of Success" by Carol S. Dweck: This book provides further insights into the concept of growth mindset and practical strategies for fostering it in students. - Khan Academy: This online platform offers a variety of resources and interactive lessons that promote growth mindset and emphasize the importance of effort in learning. - ClassDojo: This classroom management tool includes a growth mindset curriculum with videos, activities, and discussion points to help teachers cultivate a growth mindset in their students.

In conclusion, cultivating a growth mindset in students is crucial for their success in the future of education. By emphasizing effort, promoting reflection, creating a supportive environment, and teaching resilience, teachers can help students develop the belief that they can continually grow and improve. This mindset not only enhances academic performance but also equips students with the skills and mindset needed to navigate an ever-changing world.

Promoting Inclusivity and Diversity in the Classroom

Inclusive education refers to an approach that aims to ensure that all students, regardless of their background or ability, have equitable access to quality education and are actively involved in the learning process. It recognizes that every student is unique and has different strengths, challenges, and learning styles. Inclusive classrooms foster a sense of belonging, where diversity is celebrated and every student feels valued and supported.

1. Importance of Inclusivity and Diversity in Education Promoting inclusivity and diversity in the classroom is crucial for several reasons:

1.1 Enhancing Learning Outcomes: Inclusive classrooms provide opportunities for students to learn from and with each other, bringing varied perspectives and experiences to the learning environment. This diversity enriches discussions, critical thinking, and problem-solving, enhancing the overall learning outcomes for all students.

1.2 Fostering Empathy and Understanding: Inclusive classrooms expose students to diverse backgrounds, cultures, and perspectives, fostering empathy, understanding, and respect for others. This helps students develop social and emotional skills, such as empathy, cooperation, and tolerance, which are essential for their personal growth and future success in a diverse society.

1.3 Creating Safe and Supportive Environments: Inclusive classrooms create safe and supportive environments where every student feels accepted, valued, and supported. This enhances their self-esteem and motivation to learn, leading to improved academic performance and overall well-being.

1.4 Addressing Inequality and Discrimination: Inclusive education is a powerful tool to address inequality and discrimination. It promotes equal opportunities for all students, irrespective of their background, ethnicity, gender, socio-economic status, or disabilities. By challenging stereotypes and promoting social justice, inclusive classrooms contribute to building a more equitable society.

2. Strategies for Promoting Inclusivity and Diversity

2.1 Culturally Responsive Teaching: Culturally responsive teaching is an effective approach to promote inclusivity and diversity in the classroom. It involves incorporating students' cultural backgrounds, experiences, and values into the curriculum and teaching practices. This can be done by using culturally relevant materials, providing examples and perspectives from diverse cultures, and creating inclusive learning activities that reflect students' identities and interests.

2.2 Differentiated Instruction: Differentiated instruction acknowledges that students learn at different paces and have different learning needs. It involves adapting teaching methods, materials, and assessments to accommodate these differences, ensuring that all students can actively engage in the learning process regardless of their abilities or challenges. This approach promotes inclusivity by catering to individual differences and creating a supportive learning environment.

2.3 Collaboration and Cooperative Learning: Collaboration and cooperative learning activities promote inclusivity and diversity by encouraging students to work together and learn from one another. These activities foster peer interaction, cooperation, and the sharing of knowledge and perspectives. They can be structured in a way that ensures equal participation and values the contributions of every student, promoting a sense of belonging and equity in the classroom.

2.4 Sensitivity to Learning Styles: Students have different learning styles, such as auditory, visual, or kinesthetic. Inclusive classrooms accommodate these differences by providing a variety of instructional strategies and resources that cater to different learning styles. This allows students to engage with the content in ways that are most effective for them, promoting their active participation and success in the learning process.

2.5 Universal Design for Learning (UDL): Universal Design for Learning is an inclusive instructional framework that aims to provide multiple means of representation, expression, and engagement to meet the diverse needs of all students. It involves incorporating various teaching methods, technologies, and assessment options that allow students to access and demonstrate their learning in ways that are most comfortable and effective for them.

3. Challenges and Considerations

Promoting inclusivity and diversity in the classroom may face certain challenges that educators need to be aware of and address:

3.1 Implicit Bias: Educators should be mindful of their own biases and stereotypes that may inadvertently impact their interactions with students. Implicit bias training and self-reflection are essential for creating a non-discriminatory and inclusive classroom environment.

3.2 Language and Communication: Inclusive classrooms may have students with different language backgrounds or those who are English language learners. Teachers should provide appropriate support and resources to ensure effective communication and equal participation for all students.

3.3 Resource Allocation: Classrooms with diverse and inclusive environments may require additional resources, such as assistive technologies, learning materials, or support personnel, to accommodate students' diverse learning needs. School systems should ensure equitable allocation of resources to support inclusive education.

3.4 Collaboration with Families and Communities: Inclusive education can be strengthened by collaborating with families and communities. This collaboration ensures that cultural, linguistic, and other community-specific aspects are respected and incorporated into the classroom environment and teaching practices.

4. Case Study: Promoting Inclusivity and Diversity in a Science Classroom

In a science classroom, promoting inclusivity and diversity can be achieved by adopting the following strategies:

4.1 Incorporating Relevant Examples: Introduce scientific concepts using examples that are relevant to students' cultures or communities. This makes the content more relatable and ensures all students feel represented in the learning material.

4.2 Group Projects: Assign group projects that bring together students with diverse backgrounds and interests. These projects encourage collaboration, teamwork, and shared learning experiences where each student's input is valued and respected.

4.3 Using Multi-modal Materials: Provide science learning materials (such as videos, illustrations, and hands-on experiments) that cater to different learning styles and abilities. This ensures that all students can engage with the content in ways that suit their strengths and preferences.

4.4 Building an Inclusive Classroom Culture: Foster a classroom culture that values inclusivity, diversity, and respect. Encourage open discussions where students can share their perspectives, ask questions, and challenge ideas in a supportive and respectful environment.

4.5 Celebrating Diversity: Organize activities or events that celebrate the diversity of cultures, traditions, and languages represented in the classroom. This can include inviting guest speakers from different backgrounds or arranging field trips to culturally significant locations.

5. Resources for Promoting Inclusivity and Diversity

- Teaching Tolerance: Provides resources, professional development, and classroom materials to help educators promote inclusivity and diversity. Website: `https://www.tolerance.org/`

- Edutopia: Offers articles, videos, and practical strategies for implementing inclusive practices in the classroom. Website: `https://www.edutopia.org/article/creating-inclusive-classrooms`

- National Center on Universal Design for Learning: Provides information, research, and practical resources on implementing Universal Design for Learning in classrooms. Website: `https://www.udlcenter.org/`

- Multicultural Pavilions: Offers resources and lesson plans for promoting cultural diversity and understanding in the classroom. Website: `http://www.edchange.org/multicultural/`

- Equity Alliance: Provides resources and tools to support educators in addressing equity and promoting inclusive practices in education. Website: `https://www.equityallianceatasu.org/`

In conclusion, promoting inclusivity and diversity in the classroom is essential for creating equitable learning environments where all students can thrive. By implementing strategies such as culturally responsive teaching, differentiated instruction, collaboration, and sensitivity to learning styles, educators can foster inclusivity, celebrate diversity, and ensure that every student feels valued and supported in their educational journey.

Ethical Considerations in Transformative Education

Ethical considerations play a crucial role in transformative education. As we implement cutting-edge tools and transformative methods in the classroom, it is essential to ensure that we are upholding ethical principles and promoting responsible use of technology. In this section, we will explore some of the key ethical considerations that educators should keep in mind when transforming education.

Privacy and Data Protection

One of the most important ethical considerations in transformative education is ensuring the privacy and protection of student data. With the integration of technology in the classroom, a significant amount of personal information is being collected and stored. It is crucial for educators to understand and comply with data protection laws, and to ensure that student data is not misused or accessed by unauthorized individuals.

Educators must be transparent with students and their families about the types of data that are being collected, how it will be used, and the steps taken to protect it. It is also essential to obtain informed consent from students and their parents/guardians before collecting any personally identifiable information.

Additionally, educators should carefully evaluate the technology tools they use in the classroom to ensure that they have appropriate data privacy policies in place. They should also regularly review and update their privacy practices to stay current with changing laws and regulations.

Equity and Access

Transformative education aims to provide equal opportunities for all students, regardless of their socio-economic background, race, gender, or abilities. Therefore, it is important to consider equity and access when implementing transformative methods and tools.

Educators should be mindful of the digital divide that exists in many communities, where not all students have access to the same technology and resources. They should strive to minimize this divide by providing equal access to technology and ensuring that all students have the opportunity to benefit from transformative educational experiences.

Furthermore, educators should be aware of potential biases in the technology tools they use. Algorithms and artificial intelligence systems can unintentionally perpetuate biases and discrimination. It is crucial to critically evaluate these tools to ensure they do not reinforce stereotypes or discriminate against certain groups of students.

Digital Citizenship and Responsible Use of Technology

In transformative education, it is essential to promote digital citizenship and responsible use of technology. Educators should teach students about ethical behavior online, including topics such as cyberbullying, plagiarism, and intellectual property rights. Students should understand the impact of their digital footprint and the potential consequences of their actions.

Teachers must also model responsible use of technology and guide students in making ethical decisions when using digital resources. This can be achieved through discussions, workshops, and incorporating digital citizenship lessons into the curriculum.

Informed Consent and Autonomy

When implementing transformative methods and tools, educators should ensure that students have the right to make informed decisions about their participation. Informed consent is crucial when using innovative technologies that may collect sensitive data or require students to engage in online activities.

Students should have the autonomy to participate or opt-out of activities that they are uncomfortable with or that may compromise their privacy. Educators should provide clear information about the purpose, benefits, and potential risks of participating in transformative experiences and seek consent from students and their parents/guardians.

Social and Emotional Well-being

Transformative education should prioritize the social and emotional well-being of students. Educators should be mindful of the potential impacts that technology and transformative methods may have on students' mental health and emotional well-being.

For example, excessive screen time or the use of immersive technologies could have negative effects on students' sleep patterns, attention spans, and overall well-being. It is important to strike a balance and prioritize the holistic development of students.

Educators should also be attentive to signs of technology addiction or social isolation among students. They should promote healthy and meaningful interactions both online and offline, fostering empathy, and promoting student well-being.

Ethics of AI and Algorithmic Decision-making

As artificial intelligence (AI) becomes more prevalent in education, educators must carefully consider the ethical implications of AI and algorithmic decision-making. AI systems can perpetuate biases, limit opportunities, and reinforce existing inequalities.

Educators should critically evaluate AI tools and algorithms to ensure that they are fair, unbiased, and transparent. They should also teach students about the limitations of AI and the importance of human judgment and ethical decision-making.

Furthermore, educators should advocate for ethical AI policies and participate in discussions around the development and implementation of AI systems in education. They should advocate for the responsible use of AI, ensuring that it serves the best interests of students and promotes equity, diversity, and inclusivity.

Professional Conduct and Integrity

In transformative education, educators must uphold professional conduct and integrity. This includes adhering to ethical standards, maintaining confidentiality, and avoiding conflicts of interest.

Educators should be transparent about their roles and responsibilities, avoiding any actions that may compromise their professional integrity. They should also be vigilant in identifying and addressing ethical dilemmas that may arise in the context of transformative education.

Additionally, educators should continue to engage in professional development opportunities focused on ethical considerations in transformative education. This will enable them to stay informed about emerging ethical issues in educational technology and ensure their practices align with ethical principles.

In conclusion, ethical considerations are paramount in transformative education. Educators must prioritize privacy and data protection, promote equity and access, foster responsible use of technology, obtain informed consent, prioritize students' social and emotional well-being, address the ethical implications of AI, and uphold professional integrity. By staying mindful of these ethical principles, educators can create transformative learning environments that are inclusive, equitable, and beneficial for all students.

Overcoming Resistance to Change Among Teachers

Teachers play a crucial role in implementing transformative education in the classroom. However, embracing new methods and technologies can be met with resistance and challenges. In this section, we will explore strategies for overcoming resistance to change among teachers and promoting a culture of innovation and continuous improvement.

Understanding the Nature of Resistance

Resistance to change is a natural human reaction and can stem from various factors. Some common reasons for resistance among teachers include fear of the unknown, lack of confidence in using new tools, concerns about increased workload, and skepticism about the effectiveness of new methods. It is important to acknowledge and understand these concerns in order to address them effectively.

Communicating the Vision

One of the key strategies to overcome resistance is effective communication of the vision and benefits of transformative education. Teachers need to understand why the change is necessary and how it aligns with their goals as educators. Highlighting the positive impact on student learning outcomes, creativity, engagement, and critical thinking can be persuasive. Sharing success stories and case studies from other schools or educators who have successfully embraced change can also provide inspiration and motivation.

Providing Adequate Support and Training

Teachers may resist change if they feel ill-equipped to implement new methods or use technological tools. Providing ongoing support and training is crucial to empower teachers and build their confidence. Professional development workshops, webinars, and hands-on training sessions can be organized to familiarize teachers with the concepts, tools, and techniques related to transformative education. Encouraging teachers to collaborate and learn from each other can also help to alleviate concerns and promote a sense of community.

Creating a Safe and Supportive Environment

Creating a safe and supportive environment is essential for overcoming resistance. Teachers need to feel that they have permission to take risks, make mistakes, and learn from them. School leaders and administrators should encourage an open and non-judgmental culture where teachers can freely share their thoughts, concerns, and ideas. Celebrating small victories and recognizing the efforts of teachers who embrace change can boost morale and encourage others to do the same.

Providing Time for Implementation

Implementing transformative methods and using cutting-edge tools may require additional time and effort from teachers. It is important to acknowledge and address these concerns by providing sufficient time for planning, preparation, and implementation. Schools can consider allocating dedicated time during professional development days or setting aside regular periods for teachers to collaborate, experiment, and reflect on their practice. Reducing non-essential administrative tasks can also alleviate the workload and allow teachers to focus on implementing transformative education effectively.

Monitoring and Evaluation

Monitoring and evaluation play a crucial role in addressing resistance to change. Regularly assessing the impact of transformative methods and tools can provide valuable feedback to teachers and help identify areas of improvement. Collecting data on student outcomes, engagement levels, and teacher satisfaction can help to measure the effectiveness of the changes and address any concerns or challenges that arise. Sharing this data with teachers and involving them in the evaluation process can foster a sense of ownership and encourage continuous improvement.

Building a Community of Practice

Building a community of practice is an effective strategy to overcome resistance and promote collaboration among teachers. Encouraging informal discussions, sharing of ideas, and expertise can help teachers learn from each other and address their concerns collectively. Establishing mentorship programs, peer coaching, or action research groups can provide additional support and guidance to teachers as they navigate the challenges of implementing transformative education.

Rewarding and Recognizing Efforts

Rewarding and recognizing teachers' efforts and achievements in embracing change is crucial to sustaining their motivation and commitment. Schools can consider various strategies such as acknowledging innovative practices through a recognition program, creating opportunities for teachers to present their work at conferences or workshops, or providing incentives such as additional professional development opportunities or leadership roles. Celebrating teachers' successes publicly can inspire others and create a culture where innovation is valued and encouraged.

By addressing the concerns of teachers, providing support and training, creating a safe and supportive environment, and fostering collaboration and recognition, schools can overcome resistance to change and create a culture of continuous improvement and transformation. Embracing transformative education requires a collective effort from all stakeholders, and by working together, we can create learning environments that prepare students for the future.

Collaborative Teaching and Co-Teaching Models

Collaborative teaching and co-teaching models are approaches to instruction that involve two or more teachers working together in the classroom. These models are based on the belief that by combining their expertise and sharing responsibilities, teachers can create more inclusive and effective learning environments for their students. This section explores the benefits, strategies, and challenges of collaborative teaching and co-teaching models, as well as the future directions of these approaches in education.

Benefits of Collaborative Teaching and Co-Teaching

Collaborative teaching and co-teaching models offer several benefits for both teachers and students. These models promote:

1. Enhanced Differentiation: With multiple teachers in the classroom, students receive more individualized attention and support. Teachers can address diverse learning needs, styles, and abilities more effectively, ensuring that all students have access to high-quality instruction.

2. Increased Student Engagement: Collaborative teaching encourages active participation from students as they have the opportunity to interact with multiple teachers. This dynamic environment promotes dialogue and discussion, stimulating critical thinking and fostering a deeper understanding of the content.

3. Improved Classroom Management: By sharing responsibilities, teachers can better manage classroom dynamics, behavior, and instructional time. They can

monitor student progress, provide timely feedback, and address any challenges that arise more effectively.

4. Professional Growth: Collaborative teaching provides an opportunity for teachers to learn from one another, share best practices, and develop new instructional strategies. It encourages reflective practice and professional dialogue, contributing to ongoing teacher development.

5. Enhanced Creativity: Collaborative teaching fosters a culture of innovation and creativity. Teachers can brainstorm ideas, design engaging lessons, and integrate diverse perspectives and teaching styles, resulting in a more vibrant and dynamic learning experience for the students.

Strategies for Collaborative Teaching and Co-Teaching

Effective implementation of collaborative teaching and co-teaching models requires careful planning and coordination. Here are some strategies to consider:

1. Clear Roles and Responsibilities: Clearly define the roles and responsibilities of each teacher involved in the collaboration. Establish common expectations and protocols to ensure smooth coordination and effective use of instructional time.

2. Shared Planning and Preparation: Collaborate on lesson planning and curriculum development to align objectives, instructional strategies, and assessments. Teachers can leverage their expertise to create engaging and cohesive learning experiences.

3. Communication and Reflection: Maintain open lines of communication between the collaborating teachers through regular meetings, shared documents, and digital platforms. Reflect on instructional practices, adjust strategies based on student needs, and celebrate successes together.

4. Coordinated Instruction: Coordinate instruction by dividing content delivery, grouping students for small-group instruction or collaborative activities, or alternating teaching responsibilities throughout a lesson or unit. Ensure a seamless flow of instruction and engagement for all students.

5. Differentiated Instruction: Utilize the diverse expertise of the collaborating teachers to meet the needs of all learners. Apply various instructional strategies, scaffold learning, and provide targeted support for struggling students while challenging advanced learners.

6. Co-Assessment and Feedback: Collaborate on the assessment of student learning and provide feedback to students. Use formative and summative assessment data to guide instructional decisions and promote continuous improvement.

7. Building Relationships: Foster a positive and supportive classroom environment by promoting strong relationships among collaborating teachers and between teachers and students. Encourage a sense of community, respect, and inclusivity.

Challenges and Considerations

While collaborative teaching and co-teaching models offer numerous benefits, they also present some challenges. It is important to address these challenges proactively to ensure successful implementation:

1. Time and Scheduling: Collaborating teachers need time for planning, coordination, and reflection. Finding common planning time within busy schedules can be challenging. Schools should prioritize dedicated collaboration time and provide necessary resources to facilitate effective co-teaching.
2. Communication and Collaboration: Effective communication and collaboration require a shared vision, open dialogue, and mutual respect among teachers. Investing in professional development to enhance collaboration skills is crucial.
3. Power Dynamics: Collaborating teachers should establish equal partnership and shared decision-making to prevent power imbalances. Openly discuss expectations, roles, and responsibilities to ensure a balanced collaborative environment.
4. Classroom Management: Co-teaching can complicate classroom management. Collaborating teachers need to establish consistent behavior management strategies, routines, and procedures to maintain a positive and productive classroom environment.
5. Resistance to Change: Some teachers may resist collaborative teaching models due to a fear of losing autonomy or unfamiliarity with this approach. Providing professional development, coaching, and creating a supportive culture of collaboration can help overcome resistance to change.

Examples and Case Studies

Example 1 - Co-Teaching in Inclusion Classrooms: In an inclusion classroom, a special education teacher and a general education teacher collaborate to support students with diverse learning needs. They use a co-teaching model where both teachers share equal responsibility for instruction, provide differentiated support, and adjust instructional strategies to meet individual student needs.

Example 2 - Collaboration in Project-Based Learning: In a high school science class, the science teacher and the arts teacher collaborate to provide an interdisciplinary project-based learning experience. Students work on a project that combines scientific concepts with artistic expression, encouraging creativity, critical thinking, and collaboration among students.

Resources for Collaborative Teaching and Co-Teaching

1. "Co-Teaching That Works: Structures and Strategies for Maximizing Student Learning" by Anne M. Beninghof 2. "Collaboration and Co-Teaching: Strategies for English Learners" by Andrea Honigsfeld and Maria Dove 3. "Differentiated Instructional Strategies: One Size Doesn't Fit All" by Gayle H. Gregory and Carolyn M. Chapman

Conclusion

Collaborative teaching and co-teaching models provide powerful opportunities to create inclusive, engaging, and effective learning environments. By combining the expertise and resources of multiple teachers, these models can enhance differentiation, student engagement, classroom management, and professional growth. Implementing collaboration strategies, addressing challenges, and promoting effective communication are essential for successful collaborative teaching experiences. As educators continue to explore innovative teaching practices, collaborative teaching and co-teaching models are likely to play a significant role in shaping the future of education.

The Future of Teaching: AI-Assisted Instruction

In recent years, advancements in artificial intelligence (AI) have revolutionized various sectors, including education. AI has the potential to transform teaching and learning, making education more personalized, adaptive, and efficient. AI-assisted instruction is a promising approach that combines the power of technology and machine learning algorithms to enhance the teaching and learning experience. In this section, we will explore the future of teaching with AI-assisted instruction, its benefits, challenges, and potential applications.

Understanding AI-Assisted Instruction

AI-assisted instruction refers to the use of AI technologies to support and enhance the instructional process. It involves the integration of intelligent tutoring systems, chatbots, and other AI tools into the teaching and learning environment. These AI systems can provide personalized guidance, feedback, and support to students, helping them navigate through complex concepts and improve their learning outcomes. Moreover, AI-assisted instruction can assist teachers in various tasks such as lesson planning, assessment, and data analysis, enabling them to focus more on individual student needs and instructional design.

Benefits of AI-Assisted Instruction

The integration of AI in teaching offers several benefits:

1. Personalized Learning: AI algorithms can analyze vast amounts of student data and provide personalized learning pathways tailored to individual student needs. This helps students learn at their own pace, receive targeted feedback, and address their specific learning gaps.

2. Adaptive and Interactive Learning: AI tools can adapt to students' learning patterns and adjust the instructional content and pace accordingly. Additionally, AI systems can provide interactive and engaging learning experiences through the use of virtual simulations, gamification, and multimedia resources.

3. Enhanced Student Engagement: AI systems can provide real-time feedback and support, fostering active student engagement. Chatbots and virtual assistants, for example, can engage students in interactive conversations and answer their questions, promoting deeper understanding and critical thinking.

4. Efficient Classroom Management: AI tools can automate administrative tasks, such as grading assignments and generating reports, saving teachers significant time and effort. This allows teachers to focus more on instructional activities and individual student needs.

5. Data-Driven Insights: By analyzing student data, AI systems can provide valuable insights into student learning patterns, strengths, and weaknesses. This data can inform instructional decision-making, enabling teachers to design targeted interventions and instructional strategies.

Challenges of AI-Assisted Instruction

While AI-assisted instruction offers promising benefits, there are several challenges that need to be addressed:

1. Ethical Considerations: The collection and use of student data raise ethical concerns regarding data privacy, security, and algorithm biases. It is essential to establish clear policies and guidelines to ensure the responsible and ethical use of AI technologies in education.

2. Teacher Training and Support: Teachers need professional development opportunities to familiarize themselves with AI tools and understand their pedagogical implications. Training programs should equip teachers with the necessary skills to effectively integrate AI into their instructional practices.

3. Equity and Access: The widespread implementation of AI-assisted instruction should ensure equitable access to technology and digital resources for all students. Addressing the digital divide and ensuring equal opportunities for learning is critical in realizing the benefits of AI in education.

4. Overreliance on Technology: AI-assisted instruction should not replace human teachers but rather complement their expertise. It is crucial to strike a balance between AI-supported instruction and the human aspects of teaching, such as building relationships, empathy, and emotional support.

Applications of AI-Assisted Instruction

AI-assisted instruction can be applied in various ways across different educational settings and subject areas:

1. Intelligent Tutoring Systems: These AI systems provide personalized instruction based on individual student needs, tracking their progress and adapting the material accordingly. They can provide immediate feedback, clarify misconceptions, and suggest additional resources.

2. Chatbots and Virtual Assistants: AI-powered chatbots and virtual assistants can engage students in natural language conversations, answering their questions, and providing guidance. They can assist students in problem-solving, offer explanations, and even engage in interactive dialogues.

3. Automated Grading and Feedback: AI algorithms can analyze student work, such as essays and quizzes, and provide automated grading and feedback. This frees up teachers' time, allowing them to focus on higher-level instructional tasks.

4. Personalized Learning Platforms: AI can power adaptive learning platforms that tailor the learning experience to each student's needs. These platforms can provide customized content, adaptive assessments, and personalized recommendations for further study.

5. Data Analytics for Instructional Design: AI technologies can analyze student data and provide insights for instructional design. This includes identifying common misconceptions, determining the effectiveness of instructional materials, and designing targeted interventions for specific student needs.

Overall, AI-assisted instruction holds great potential in transforming the future of teaching. By leveraging the power of AI technologies, educators can create more personalized, adaptive, and engaging learning experiences for their students. However, it is important to address the ethical considerations, provide adequate support for teachers, and ensure equitable access to technology to fully harness the benefits of AI in education.

Transformative Pedagogies

Project-Based Learning

Defining project-based learning

Project-based learning (PBL) is an instructional approach that emphasizes active and authentic learning experiences through the completion of real-world projects. In PBL, students actively engage in investigating complex problems, designing and implementing solutions, and presenting their findings to a real audience. PBL is rooted in constructivist theories of learning, which emphasize the importance of learners constructing their own knowledge and meaning through hands-on experiences.

At its core, PBL involves the following key elements:

1. **Real-world relevance:** Project-based learning focuses on solving authentic, meaningful problems that have real-world applications. Projects should reflect the challenges and complexities of the real world, allowing students to connect their learning to their everyday lives and future careers.

2. **Inquiry and investigation:** PBL encourages students to ask meaningful questions, explore topics of interest, and conduct in-depth research to find answers. The process of inquiry and investigation helps students develop critical thinking, problem-solving, and information literacy skills.

3. **Collaboration:** Collaboration is an essential component of PBL. Students work in teams to complete projects, allowing them to develop communication, teamwork, and interpersonal skills. Collaboration also fosters a sense of collective responsibility and ownership of the project.

4. **Authentic assessment:** In PBL, assessment is focused on evaluating students' knowledge, skills, and abilities demonstrated through the completion of projects. Authentic assessment methods, such as presentations, portfolios, and performance tasks, are used to measure students' mastery of content and their ability to apply it

in real-world contexts.

5. **Teacher facilitation:** In PBL, the role of the teacher is transformed from being a traditional lecturer to that of a facilitator or guide. Teachers provide structure, resources, and support to help students navigate the project, monitor their progress, and provide feedback. The role of the teacher is to scaffold students' learning and foster their independence and self-directedness.

6. **Reflection and metacognition:** Reflection is a crucial aspect of PBL as it enables students to think critically about their learning experiences, evaluate their progress, and identify areas for improvement. Metacognitive skills, such as goal-setting, self-assessment, and self-reflection, are developed through the process of PBL.

PBL offers numerous benefits to students. It enhances their engagement and motivation by making learning relevant and meaningful. It develops their critical thinking, problem-solving, and creativity skills, as they have to think critically and apply their knowledge to real-world situations. PBL also promotes collaboration, communication, and leadership skills, which are essential for success in the 21st-century workforce.

To illustrate the concept of PBL, let's consider an example in the field of environmental science. Imagine a project where students are tasked with designing a sustainable solution to address a local pollution problem. They would first conduct research on the causes and impacts of pollution, explore various mitigation strategies, and gather data on pollution levels in the community. Based on their findings, they would then propose and implement a plan to reduce pollution, such as organizing a community cleanup event or designing a recycling program. Finally, they would assess the effectiveness of their solution and present their findings to local stakeholders.

Through this example, students engage in authentic, hands-on learning experiences, develop a deep understanding of the environmental issues, collaborate with their peers, and apply their knowledge and skills to solve a real-world problem. They also develop a sense of agency and become more environmentally conscious citizens.

In conclusion, project-based learning is a powerful instructional approach that promotes active learning, critical thinking, collaboration, and real-world problem-solving. By engaging in meaningful projects, students develop the knowledge, skills, and attitudes necessary for success in the 21st century. PBL provides an opportunity for students to become active participants in their own learning and prepares them to tackle the challenges of the future.

Benefits of Project-Based Learning

Project-based learning (PBL) offers a variety of benefits for both students and educators. By engaging students in authentic and hands-on projects, PBL allows for a more active and meaningful learning experience. In this section, we will explore some of the key benefits of project-based learning.

Enhanced Understanding and Retention of Concepts

One of the main advantages of PBL is its ability to deepen students' understanding and retention of concepts. Instead of passively receiving information, students actively apply their knowledge and skills to solve real-world problems. This promotes a deeper level of understanding, as they see the relevance and practicality of what they are learning. Research shows that when students are actively engaged in a project, they are more likely to remember and internalize the information they encounter.

Developing Critical Thinking and Problem-Solving Skills

PBL encourages the development of critical thinking and problem-solving skills, which are essential for success in the 21st century. By working on complex projects, students are challenged to analyze information, evaluate different perspectives, and generate creative solutions. They learn to identify problems, collaborate with their peers, and develop effective strategies to address the challenges they encounter. These skills are highly transferable and can be applied to various real-life situations.

Promoting Collaboration and Communication

In project-based learning, students often work in teams to accomplish their project goals. This collaborative environment fosters effective communication and teamwork skills. Students learn to express their ideas, listen to others' viewpoints, and negotiate and compromise to reach a common goal. They also develop interpersonal skills such as leadership, conflict resolution, and delegation. These skills are crucial in today's interconnected and globalized world.

Increasing Engagement and Motivation

Project-based learning has been shown to increase student engagement and motivation. When students are given the opportunity to work on projects that align with their interests and passions, they become more invested in their learning. PBL allows for a more personalized and student-centered approach, which can tap into students' intrinsic motivation. Additionally, the tangible outcomes of projects, such as presentations, products, or exhibitions, provide a sense of accomplishment and pride, further enhancing motivation.

Building 21st Century Skills

The integration of technology and other resources in project-based learning helps students develop essential 21st century skills. Through the use of digital tools, students learn to navigate through information, evaluate its credibility, and effectively communicate their findings. They also gain experience in using different software applications and online platforms, improving their digital literacy. These skills are highly valued in today's workplace and prepare students for future career opportunities.

Cultivating Creativity and Innovation

PBL nurtures students' creativity and encourages them to think innovatively. By working on open-ended projects, students are given the freedom to explore, experiment, and come up with unique solutions. They are encouraged to think outside the box, take risks, and learn from failure. This cultivates an entrepreneurial mindset and fosters a culture of innovation, which is essential in an ever-changing and evolving world.

Real-World Connectio

PBL provides students with the opportunity to make real-world connections. By working on authentic and meaningful projects, students can see the relevance and application of what they are learning in the classroom. They can explore issues and topics that are relevant to their lives, communities, or society as a whole. This not only makes learning more meaningful but also helps students develop a sense of agency and social responsibility.

In conclusion, project-based learning offers a range of benefits for students and educators alike. It enhances understanding and retention of concepts, develops critical thinking and problem-solving skills, promotes collaboration and communication, increases engagement and motivation, builds 21st century skills, cultivates creativity and innovation, and establishes real-world connections. By incorporating project-based learning into the classroom, educators can create a transformative learning experience that prepares students for success in the future.

Designing Effective Project-Based Learning Experiences

Project-based learning (PBL) is an innovative and engaging instructional approach that shifts the focus from traditional teacher-centered classrooms to student-centered, hands-on learning experiences. In project-based learning, students actively explore real-world problems and challenges, work collaboratively, and create meaningful and authentic products or solutions.

Designing effective project-based learning experiences involves careful planning and consideration of several key elements. In this section, we will explore these elements and provide guidelines for designing and implementing impactful project-based learning experiences.

1. Define Clear Learning Objectives

Before starting any project-based learning experience, it is crucial to define clear learning objectives that align with curriculum standards and desired learning outcomes. These objectives should be specific, measurable, achievable, relevant, and time-bound (SMART). Clear objectives provide a roadmap for both teachers and students and ensure that the project is purposeful and meaningful.

2. Select a Real-World Problem or Challenge

Choose a problem or challenge that is relevant and meaningful to students' lives and connects to real-world contexts. Authenticity is a key aspect of project-based learning, as it increases student engagement and motivation. The problem should be open-ended, allowing for multiple perspectives and possible solutions. Consider current issues, community needs, or interdisciplinary topics that can spark students' curiosity and drive their learning.

3. Plan the Project Timeline and Milestones

A well-structured project timeline is essential for managing the project effectively. Clearly define the starting and ending dates of the project, as well as intermediate milestones or checkpoints. This allows for monitoring progress, providing feedback, and ensuring that the project stays on track. Remember to allocate time for research, planning, design, implementation, and reflection.

4. Scaffold Learning with Strategic Questions

To guide students' inquiry and critical thinking, develop a set of strategic questions that scaffold the learning process. These questions should encourage students to explore the problem, generate ideas, analyze information, make connections, and evaluate their solutions. The questions should promote higher-order thinking skills and stimulate students' curiosity and creativity.

5. Support Collaboration and Communication

Project-based learning often involves collaboration and teamwork. Create opportunities for students to work in teams, assign roles, and encourage effective communication and collaboration skills. Use digital tools and platforms for online collaboration, sharing resources, and providing timely feedback. Emphasize the importance of active listening, respectful communication, and compromise in a team setting.

6. Provide Resources and Materials

Ensure that students have access to a variety of resources and materials to support their learning and research. These may include textbooks, articles, websites, multimedia content, experts in the field, and hands-on materials. Foster a culture of inquiry by encouraging students to seek out and evaluate information from diverse sources.

7. Integrate Technology

Technology plays a crucial role in project-based learning, enabling students to leverage digital tools and resources, conduct online research, create multimedia presentations, and collaborate with peers. Integrate technology into the project design to enhance student learning and engagement. Consider using tools such as online collaboration platforms, multimedia software, data analysis tools, and virtual simulations.

8. Provide Ongoing Feedback and Assessment

Continuous feedback and assessment are essential components of project-based learning. Provide formative feedback throughout the project to guide students' progress and support their learning. Consider using rubrics, checklists, or peer assessments to assess the quality of their work and provide constructive feedback. Encourage self-reflection and self-assessment to promote metacognitive skills.

9. Foster Reflection and Evaluation

At the end of the project, provide opportunities for students to reflect on their learning experience and evaluate their work. Encourage them to critically evaluate their solutions, reflect on the processes and challenges faced, and identify areas for improvement. Reflective practices enhance metacognition and enable students to transfer their learning to future projects or real-life situations.

10. Celebrate and Share Student Work

Finally, celebrate and showcase students' final products or solutions. Provide opportunities for students to present their work to peers, teachers, parents, or the wider community. This allows students to develop public speaking skills, build confidence, and receive recognition for their achievements. Additionally, sharing student work inspires and motivates others, creating a culture of collaboration and excellence.

Overall, effective project-based learning experiences require thoughtful planning, clear objectives, authentic problems, scaffolding, collaboration, and technology integration. By implementing these guidelines, educators can design engaging and transformative learning experiences that promote critical thinking, collaboration, and the development of essential 21st-century skills in students.

Assessing Student Learning in Project-Based Learning

Assessing student learning in project-based learning (PBL) is crucial for both teachers and students to gauge the effectiveness of the learning process and to ensure that students are meeting the intended learning outcomes. Traditional assessment methods, such as tests and quizzes, may not capture the full range of skills and knowledge that students develop through PBL. Therefore, alternative assessment strategies need to be implemented to align with the nature of PBL and provide a comprehensive evaluation of student learning.

Authentic Assessment

One of the key principles of assessing student learning in PBL is the use of authentic assessment. Authentic assessment refers to the evaluation of student performance on real-world tasks that have relevance and meaning outside the classroom. In the context of PBL, authentic assessment methods allow students to apply their knowledge and skills to solve authentic problems, similar to those they may encounter in the real world.

Examples of authentic assessment in PBL include:

- **Presentations and Exhibitions:** Students can showcase their project outcomes to an audience, such as classmates, teachers, or even professionals in the field. This allows students to demonstrate their understanding and communicate their ideas effectively.

- **Portfolios:** Students can create portfolios to document their work throughout the project. Portfolios can include artifacts, reflections, and evidence of the learning process. They provide a holistic view of student progress, allowing for a deeper understanding of individual growth and achievements.

- **Performance Assessments:** Students can participate in performances or simulations that require them to demonstrate specific skills relevant to the project. For example, in a project on environmental sustainability, students could design and implement a recycling program and measure its impact.

Authentic assessment emphasizes the application of knowledge and skills in real-world contexts, promoting deeper learning and critical thinking.

Rubrics

To ensure consistency and fairness in the assessment process, rubrics are commonly used in PBL. A rubric is a scoring tool that provides criteria or a set of guidelines for evaluating student work. Rubrics help both teachers and students understand the expectations for each component of the project and the quality of work at different levels.

When designing a rubric for PBL, it is important to align the criteria with the learning objectives and project goals. The criteria should reflect the skills and knowledge that students are expected to acquire through the project. Rubrics can include multiple dimensions, such as content knowledge, problem-solving skills, collaboration, communication, and creativity.

For example, a rubric for a project on renewable energy could include criteria such as research and understanding of renewable energy sources, design and implementation of a renewable energy system, analysis of data collected, and presentation skills.

Rubrics provide transparency in the assessment process, enabling students to understand their strengths and areas for improvement. They also help teachers provide targeted feedback that supports student learning and growth.

Self and Peer Assessment

In PBL, self and peer assessment play a vital role in enhancing student learning and promoting metacognitive skills. Self-assessment allows students to reflect on their progress, identify their strengths and weaknesses, and set goals for improvement. Peer assessment provides an opportunity for students to give and receive feedback, promoting collaboration and a deeper understanding of the project's content and processes.

When implementing self and peer assessment in PBL, clear guidelines and criteria should be provided to students. This ensures that students are assessing the project based on the intended learning outcomes and project goals. Peer assessment can be conducted through structured protocols, where students evaluate each other's work using a rubric or specific guidelines.

Self and peer assessment help students develop a deeper understanding of their own learning process and contribute to a more holistic view of their abilities. It also encourages students to take ownership of their learning and promotes a growth mindset.

Reflection and Metacognition

Reflection and metacognition are critical components of assessing student learning in PBL. Reflection allows students to think deeply about their learning experience, the challenges they encountered, and the strategies they used to overcome those challenges. Metacognition, or thinking about one's own thinking, helps students develop an awareness of their learning strategies and preferences.

Teachers can incorporate reflection and metacognition as part of the assessment process by including prompts for students to reflect on the project, their contributions, and their learning outcomes. This can be done through written reflections, group discussions, or even video reflections. Students can share their insights and lessons learned, as well as identify areas for improvement and future goals.

Reflection and metacognition enhance students' ability to analyze their own learning, make connections between different experiences and concepts, and transfer knowledge to new situations. It also provides valuable information for teachers to understand students' learning processes and tailor instruction to meet individual needs.

Conclusion

Assessing student learning in project-based learning requires a shift from traditional assessment methods to more authentic and comprehensive approaches. Authentic assessment, the use of rubrics, self and peer assessment, and reflection and metacognition all contribute to a more holistic view of student learning in the context of PBL. These assessment strategies promote deeper understanding, critical thinking, collaboration, and metacognitive skills. By aligning assessments with the goals and nature of PBL, teachers can provide valuable feedback and support student growth and achievement.

Overcoming Challenges in Implementing Project-Based Learning

Project-based learning (PBL) is a student-centered instructional approach that involves students working on real-world projects to develop deeper understanding and critical-thinking skills. While PBL offers numerous benefits, such as fostering creativity, collaboration, and problem-solving abilities, it also presents several challenges that educators and schools need to address to ensure successful implementation. In this section, we will explore some of these challenges and discuss strategies to overcome them.

1. **Time Management:** One of the biggest challenges in implementing PBL is managing the time required to complete projects. PBL often involves a longer timeframe compared to traditional instructional methods, as students need sufficient time to engage in project planning, research, and reflection. To overcome this challenge, teachers can:

- Set clear project timelines and milestones to keep students on track. - Break larger projects into smaller tasks with deadlines to ensure progress. - Incorporate time management strategies and tools into the project framework. - Provide guidance and support in prioritizing tasks and managing time effectively.

2. **Assessment of Learning:** Assessing student learning in PBL can be complex, as it goes beyond traditional assessments such as exams and quizzes. Teachers need to develop appropriate assessment methods that align with the project objectives and emphasize the process of learning along with the final product. To address this challenge, teachers can:

- Establish clear and measurable learning outcomes for each project. - Design rubrics or scoring guides that align with the project goals and criteria. - Provide ongoing formative feedback to guide student learning and improvement. - Incorporate innovative assessment methods, such as self and peer evaluations. -

Use a combination of individual and group assessments to capture diverse contributions.

3. **Managing Group Dynamics:** Collaborative group work is a fundamental aspect of PBL, but it can present challenges related to group dynamics, such as conflicts, unequal participation, and varying levels of motivation. To address this challenge, teachers can:

- Teach students effective communication and teamwork skills. - Establish clear roles and responsibilities for each group member. - Monitor group interactions and intervene when necessary to address conflicts. - Encourage reflection and provide guidance on conflict resolution strategies. - Provide scaffolding and support, especially for students with weaker collaboration skills.

4. **Addressing Diverse Learning Needs:** PBL should be inclusive and cater to the diverse learning needs of students. This can be challenging when students have different abilities, interests, and learning styles. To address this challenge, teachers can:

- Differentiate instruction by providing multiple entry points and pathways. - Offer a range of project options that allow students to choose based on interest. - Provide necessary supports and resources to accommodate diverse learning needs. - Foster a culture of respect and inclusion, where all voices are valued and heard. - Collaborate with special education teachers or specialists to support students with disabilities.

5. **Engaging Parental Support:** Involving parents in the PBL process can enhance student motivation and success. However, securing parental support and engagement can be a challenge, particularly if parents are not familiar with the PBL approach or have concerns about its effectiveness. To address this challenge, teachers can:

- Communicate the goals and benefits of PBL to parents through newsletters or informational sessions. - Provide resources and examples of successful PBL projects. - Engage parents in the project by seeking their expertise or input. - Encourage parents to attend project showcases or presentations to see student work firsthand. - Address any concerns or misconceptions through open and ongoing communication.

By recognizing and addressing these challenges, educators can create a supportive and conducive environment for implementing project-based learning. Overcoming these hurdles not only ensures successful implementation of PBL but also maximizes its potential to enhance student learning and engagement. Remember, the journey of PBL implementation may present obstacles, but with creative problem-solving and a growth mindset, these challenges can be overcome, leading to transformative educational experiences for students.

Case Studies and Best Practices in Project-Based Learning

Project-based learning (PBL) is an effective pedagogical approach that promotes active learning and the application of knowledge and skills to real-world situations. In this section, we will explore case studies and best practices in project-based learning, highlighting successful implementations and providing practical insights for educators.

Case Study 1: Sustainable Energy Project

In this case study, students in a high school science class were tasked with designing and implementing a sustainable energy project. They were divided into teams and given the challenge to create a renewable energy system for their school.

During the project, students conducted research on various renewable energy sources such as solar, wind, and hydroelectric power. They learned about the technical aspects of each energy source, as well as the environmental and economic considerations.

To gain hands-on experience, students built small models of renewable energy systems and tested their efficiency. They also visited a local solar farm and interviewed industry professionals to gather insights and advice.

Throughout the project, students collaborated with their teammates, communicating their ideas and dividing tasks effectively. They also developed skills in critical thinking, problem-solving, and data analysis as they evaluated the feasibility of their energy system designs.

The project culminated in a presentation where students showcased their energy systems and explained their design choices. They also outlined the potential benefits of their systems, such as reducing the school's carbon footprint and saving on energy costs.

This case study highlights the importance of integrating real-world challenges into project-based learning. By working on a sustainable energy project, students not only deepened their understanding of scientific concepts but also developed skills in collaboration, research, and communication.

Best Practices

Based on successful project-based learning implementations, here are some best practices for educators:

1. Clear objectives: Clearly define the learning objectives of the project and communicate them to students. This helps students understand the purpose of the project and stay focused on the desired outcomes.

2. Authentic context: Incorporate real-world problems or challenges that reflect the relevance of the subject matter. This motivates students and helps them see the practical applications of their learning.

3. Student autonomy: Give students freedom and autonomy in designing and managing their projects. This allows them to take ownership of their learning and fosters creativity and critical thinking.

4. Scaffolded support: Provide scaffolds and guidance to support students throughout the project. This can include checklists, rubrics, and structured milestones to help students stay on track and make progress.

5. Collaboration and reflection: Encourage collaboration among students, both within their teams and with external stakeholders. Regular reflection on the project process and outcomes promotes metacognition and learning from experience.

6. Assessment for learning: Design formative assessments that align with the project's objectives and provide opportunities for feedback and reflection. This helps students monitor their progress and make improvements.

7. Showcase and celebration: Provide opportunities for students to showcase their projects to a broader audience, such as parents, community members, or industry professionals. Celebrating their achievements boosts confidence and reinforces the value of their work.

By implementing these best practices, educators can create engaging and meaningful project-based learning experiences that foster deep learning and transferable skills.

Resources

Here are some resources that can support educators in implementing project-based learning:

1. Project-Based Learning Handbook: This comprehensive guide by the Buck Institute for Education provides practical tips, strategies, and examples of project-based learning across different subject areas.

2. Edutopia: This educational website features a wide range of articles, videos, and case studies on project-based learning. It offers insights from experienced educators and showcases best practices.

3. National Geographic Education: National Geographic offers a collection of project-based learning resources focused on environmental science, geography, and social studies. These resources provide ideas and guidelines for implementing engaging projects.

4. PBLWorks: Formerly known as the Buck Institute for Education, PBLWorks offers professional development and resources for educators interested

in project-based learning. Their website includes project ideas, rubrics, and research-based strategies.

5. Virtual Project-Based Learning: In virtual or blended learning environments, platforms like ePals and Virtual PBL provide opportunities for global collaboration and project-based learning experiences.

These resources can help educators deepen their understanding of project-based learning principles and provide practical guidance for implementation.

Conclusion

In conclusion, project-based learning offers a transformative approach to education by engaging students in real-world challenges and promoting the application of knowledge and skills. The case studies and best practices highlighted in this section provide insights and resources for educators to enhance their project-based learning initiatives. By implementing effective strategies and supporting students through authentic and meaningful projects, educators can create impactful learning experiences that prepare students for future success.

Incorporating technology into project-based learning

In project-based learning (PBL), students engage in inquiry and problem-solving activities to gain knowledge and skills through real-world projects. Technology can play a crucial role in enhancing project-based learning experiences by providing tools and resources that facilitate collaboration, research, and creativity. Integrating technology into project-based learning can enable students to develop 21st-century skills, such as critical thinking, communication, and problem-solving, while engaging in authentic, hands-on learning experiences.

Benefits of incorporating technology

Incorporating technology into project-based learning offers numerous benefits for students. First, technology provides access to a vast amount of information and resources that can support students' research and exploration. Through the internet, students can access multimedia content, online databases, and virtual libraries to gather relevant information for their projects.

Second, technology enables collaboration and communication among students and with external experts. Online platforms, such as video conferencing tools and project management software, allow students to work together, share ideas, and receive feedback from their peers and experts in the field. Collaborative technologies also foster teamwork and help students develop interpersonal skills.

Third, technology allows for the creation of multimedia presentations and demonstrations. Students can use digital tools, such as video editing software, graphic design applications, and presentation platforms, to produce high-quality deliverables that showcase their learning outcomes effectively. These multimedia elements can enhance students' communication skills and creativity.

Finally, technology supports the documentation and reflection process in project-based learning. Digital portfolios, blogs, or online journals can be used to capture students' progress, reflections, and self-assessments throughout the project. This documentation not only helps students track their learning but also allows for the assessment and evaluation of their work.

Integrating technology tools into project-based learning

When integrating technology tools into project-based learning, it is essential to select tools that align with the project's goals, students' needs, and the availability of resources. Here are some examples of technology tools that can enhance different aspects of project-based learning:

- **Collaboration tools:** Tools like Google Docs, Microsoft Teams, or project management platforms enable students to work together on shared documents, communicate in real-time, and track project progress. These tools facilitate effective collaboration and promote teamwork skills.
- **Research tools:** Online databases, search engines, and digital libraries such as JSTOR or Google Scholar provide students with access to scholarly resources and research materials. Teachers can also introduce students to citation management tools like Zotero or Mendeley to teach them how to properly cite their sources.
- **Presentation tools:** Presentation software like PowerPoint or Prezi allows students to create visually appealing and interactive presentations. Students can incorporate multimedia elements, such as images, videos, or infographics, to enhance the impact of their presentations.
- **Digital storytelling tools:** Tools like Adobe Spark or Storybird enable students to create digital stories, incorporating text, images, and narration. Digital storytelling fosters creativity and enables students to express their ideas in a compelling and engaging manner.
- **Simulation and modeling tools:** Simulations and modeling tools, such as PhET or Scratch, allow students to explore complex concepts and scenarios

in a virtual environment. These tools promote critical thinking and problem-solving skills by providing students with opportunities for experimentation and analysis.

- **Data visualization tools:** Tools like Tableau or Google Data Studio can help students visualize and analyze data collected during their projects. By creating visual representations of data, students can gain insights and draw conclusions from their findings effectively.

Considerations for successful implementation

While incorporating technology into project-based learning offers numerous benefits, it is essential to consider some factors for successful implementation:

- **Access to technology:** Ensure that all students have equal access to technology tools and resources. Addressing the digital divide through initiatives like providing laptops or tablets, internet connectivity, or utilizing school computer labs can ensure equitable opportunities for all students.

- **Digital literacy skills:** Provide necessary support and training to students to ensure they have the digital literacy skills required to effectively use technology tools. Offer guidance on using specific software or platforms, promoting responsible digital citizenship, and addressing issues like online safety and privacy.

- **Teacher professional development:** Support teachers in gaining the necessary skills and knowledge to integrate technology into project-based learning effectively. Offer professional development opportunities, workshops, or mentorship programs to help teachers explore and master technology tools that align with their teaching practices.

- **Alignment with curriculum standards:** Ensure that the selected technology tools align with curriculum standards and learning objectives. Technology should not be used for the sake of using technology but should enhance and extend the learning experience.

- **Continuous assessment and feedback:** Incorporate formative and summative assessments to gauge students' understanding and progress throughout the project. Use technology tools for providing timely feedback, tracking student performance, and reflecting on their learning journey.

Incorporating technology into project-based learning allows students to engage in meaningful and authentic learning experiences. By leveraging appropriate technology tools, teachers can enhance collaboration, research, communication, and creativity within project-based learning environments. By carefully selecting and integrating technology, educators can create transformative learning experiences that prepare students for the future.

Collaborative Project-Based Learning

Collaborative project-based learning is an approach that combines teamwork and hands-on projects to enhance student learning and engagement. It involves students working together in groups to investigate and solve real-world problems, applying their knowledge and skills to create meaningful outcomes. This section will explore the principles and benefits of collaborative project-based learning, provide strategies for successful implementation, and discuss its future directions.

Principles of Collaborative Project-Based Learning

Collaborative project-based learning is guided by a set of principles that drive its effectiveness and success. These principles include:

1. Active Learning: Collaborative project-based learning promotes active learning, where students actively participate in the learning process rather than passively receiving information. Students engage in hands-on tasks that require critical thinking, problem-solving, and decision-making skills.
2. Authentic Context: Projects in collaborative project-based learning are designed to reflect real-world scenarios or problems. This authentic context provides students with opportunities to apply their knowledge and skills in a meaningful and relevant way.
3. Student Autonomy: Collaborative project-based learning fosters student autonomy and ownership of the learning process. Students have the freedom to make decisions, set goals, and take responsibility for their learning outcomes.
4. Social Interaction: Collaboration is a key component of collaborative project-based learning. Students work together in groups, helping and supporting each other, sharing ideas, and engaging in collective problem-solving.
5. Reflection and Feedback: Reflection and feedback are integral parts of collaborative project-based learning. Students are encouraged to reflect on their learning experiences, assess their progress, and provide feedback to their peers. This process enhances metacognitive skills and promotes continuous improvement.

Benefits of Collaborative Project-Based Learning

Collaborative project-based learning offers numerous benefits for students, educators, and the learning environment. Some of the key benefits include:

1. Enhanced Learning Outcomes: Collaborative project-based learning promotes deep learning, as students actively engage in complex tasks that require higher-order thinking skills. It helps students develop a deeper understanding of the subject matter as they apply their knowledge in real-world contexts.

2. Improved Communication and Collaboration Skills: Working collaboratively on projects develops students' communication and collaboration skills. They learn to express their ideas, actively listen to others, negotiate, and work effectively in a team. These skills are essential for success in the modern workforce.

3. Increased Motivation and Engagement: Collaborative project-based learning increases student motivation and engagement. The authentic and meaningful nature of projects, along with the opportunity to work with peers, fosters a sense of ownership and purpose in the learning process.

4. Development of 21st-Century Skills: Collaborative project-based learning aligns with the development of 21st-century skills, such as critical thinking, problem-solving, creativity, and collaboration. These skills are highly valued in today's rapidly changing society and workplace.

5. Cultivation of Social and Emotional Skills: Collaborative project-based learning provides a platform for students to develop social and emotional skills, such as empathy, teamwork, and self-regulation. Students learn to navigate diverse perspectives, resolve conflicts, and develop a sense of empathy towards others.

Strategies for Successful Implementation

Implementing collaborative project-based learning effectively requires careful planning and implementation strategies. Here are some strategies to ensure successful implementation:

1. Clearly Define Learning Goals and Outcomes: Begin by defining clear learning objectives and outcomes for the project. This helps students understand the purpose of the project and what they are expected to learn.

2. Form Heterogeneous Groups: Form groups that consist of students with diverse abilities, interests, and backgrounds. Heterogeneous groups encourage collaboration and allow students to learn from each other's strengths.

3. Provide Structured Guidelines: Provide students with structured guidelines and project frameworks to ensure they stay on track and meet the project requirements. This helps maintain focus and clarity throughout the project.

4. Facilitate Student Reflection and Self-Assessment: Incorporate regular opportunities for students to reflect on their learning experiences and assess their progress. This reflection helps students deepen their understanding and promotes metacognitive skills.

5. Foster Effective Communication and Collaboration: Encourage open communication and collaboration within the groups. Provide opportunities for students to practice effective communication skills, such as active listening, providing constructive feedback, and resolving conflicts.

6. Scaffold the Project: Break down the project into smaller manageable tasks and provide necessary support and resources to ensure students can successfully complete the project. Scaffold the learning process by gradually releasing responsibility to the students.

7. Emphasize Process and Product: Place equal emphasis on both the process and product of the project. Encourage students to focus on the learning experience and the skills developed along the way, rather than solely on the final product.

8. Provide Timely Feedback: Provide timely and constructive feedback to guide students' progress and help them improve. Feedback can come from both the teacher and peers, fostering a culture of continuous improvement.

Example: Designing a Sustainable Energy Solution

To illustrate collaborative project-based learning, let's consider an example of designing a sustainable energy solution. In this project, students work in groups to develop a proposal for a renewable energy project in their community. The project could involve designing a solar panel installation, wind turbine farm, or a hydroelectric power system.

Throughout the project, students will:

1. Research renewable energy sources and assess the feasibility of different options. 2. Identify the energy needs of their community and analyze the environmental impact. 3. Calculate the costs and benefits of the proposed energy solution. 4. Develop a detailed plan, including the design, implementation, and maintenance of the renewable energy system. 5. Create a persuasive presentation to pitch their proposal to the local community.

Students will collaborate within their groups to divide tasks, gather information, analyze data, and design the renewable energy solution. They will engage in discussions, share ideas, and collectively make decisions. This collaborative approach ensures that diverse perspectives are considered, leading to a more comprehensive and innovative solution.

Throughout the project, the teacher plays the role of facilitator, providing guidance, resources, and feedback. The emphasis is on student-led learning, where students take ownership of their learning and develop valuable 21st-century skills.

Resources for Collaborative Project-Based Learning

Here are some resources that can support the implementation of collaborative project-based learning:

1. Project-Based Learning Institute: The Buck Institute for Education provides resources, professional development, and project examples for educators interested in implementing project-based learning.
2. Collaboration Tools: There are a variety of online collaboration tools available, such as Google Docs, Microsoft Teams, and Slack, that facilitate communication and collaboration among students.
3. Project Examples: Explore project examples and case studies to gather ideas and inspiration for designing collaborative projects. Websites like the New Tech Network and Edutopia offer a wealth of project-based learning resources.
4. Professional Development Opportunities: Take advantage of professional development opportunities focused on project-based learning. Attend workshops, webinars, or conferences to enhance your understanding of the approach and learn from experienced practitioners.

Challenges and Considerations

Implementing collaborative project-based learning may come with certain challenges and considerations. Some of these include:

1. Group Dynamics: Group work can sometimes be challenging, with issues such as unequal contributions, conflicts, and a lack of accountability. Effective group management strategies and clear expectations can address these challenges.
2. Time Management: Collaborative projects may require a significant amount of time, both in and outside of class. Proper planning and scheduling can help ensure that project timelines are realistic and manageable.
3. Assessment: Assessing individual learning and contributions in collaborative projects can be challenging. Design clear assessment criteria and provide opportunities for both individual and group evaluations.
4. Teacher Support and Training: Teachers may need support and training to effectively implement collaborative project-based learning. Professional development opportunities and mentorship can help teachers gain the necessary skills and knowledge.

5. Resource Availability: Availability of resources, both physical and technological, can impact the feasibility of collaborative projects. Ensure that students have access to necessary materials and technology to support their project work.

Addressing these challenges and considerations through careful planning, teacher support, and ongoing reflection can contribute to the successful implementation of collaborative project-based learning.

Future Directions

As education continues to evolve, collaborative project-based learning will play an increasingly significant role. The future of collaborative project-based learning will see advancements in technology integration, increased emphasis on global collaboration, and deeper connections with the real world. Here are some future directions to consider:

1. Virtual Collaboration: With the rise of technology, collaborative project-based learning can transcend physical boundaries. Virtual collaboration tools and platforms will provide opportunities for students to work on projects with peers from different cultural backgrounds and geographical locations.

2. Integration of AI and Machine Learning: Artificial intelligence (AI) and machine learning can enhance collaborative project-based learning by providing personalized support, automating certain tasks, and analyzing large amounts of data to offer insights into student progress and project outcomes.

3. Community Engagement: Collaborative project-based learning will increasingly focus on engaging with the community and addressing local issues. Students will collaborate with community members, experts, and organizations to design solutions for real-world problems.

4. Sustainable Development Goals: Collaborative project-based learning will align with the United Nations' Sustainable Development Goals (SDGs). Students will identify global challenges related to the SDGs and work collaboratively to devise innovative solutions.

5. Entrepreneurship and Innovation: Collaborative project-based learning will foster an entrepreneurial mindset, encouraging students to think creatively and become innovators. Students will explore opportunities to turn their project ideas into tangible products or services.

Collaborative project-based learning has the potential to transform education by equipping students with the skills needed for success in the 21st century. By providing students with opportunities to work collaboratively, engage in authentic projects, and apply their knowledge in real-world contexts, we can create a learning environment that prepares students for the challenges and opportunities of the future.

Project-Based Learning in Different Subject Areas

Project-based learning is a highly effective educational approach that allows students to engage in real-world, hands-on projects that are relevant to their learning objectives. This approach encourages students to actively explore and apply their knowledge and skills in authentic contexts, leading to deeper understanding and meaningful learning experiences. Project-based learning can be implemented in various subject areas, including but not limited to:

Science

In science education, project-based learning provides students with opportunities to investigate and explore scientific phenomena in a practical and meaningful way. For example, students can design and conduct experiments to explore the effects of different variables on plant growth or study the impact of pollution on local ecosystems. Through these projects, students develop critical thinking skills, enhance their understanding of scientific principles, and learn to analyze and interpret data.

Example: Students can design a project to investigate the water quality of a local river. They can collect water samples, test for various parameters such as pH, dissolved oxygen, and turbidity, and analyze the results to assess the health of the river ecosystem. This project not only allows students to apply their knowledge of water chemistry but also raises awareness about environmental issues and the importance of water conservation.

Mathematics

In mathematics education, project-based learning helps students connect mathematical concepts to real-life situations, making the subject more meaningful and applicable. Projects can involve solving real-world problems, analyzing data, or designing mathematical models. Through these projects, students develop essential mathematical skills such as problem-solving, critical thinking, and logical reasoning.

Example: Students can engage in a project to design a budget for a hypothetical event, such as a school fair or a community fundraiser. They need to analyze costs, create a budget, predict attendance, and determine ticket prices to ensure that the event is profitable. This project requires students to apply various mathematical concepts such as arithmetic, percentages, and algebraic equations in a practical context, enhancing their financial literacy and math skills.

Social Studies

In social studies education, project-based learning allows students to explore historical events, analyze societal issues, and develop a deeper understanding of different cultures and perspectives. Projects can involve researching, creating presentations, conducting interviews, or organizing community-based initiatives. Through these projects, students develop critical thinking skills, research skills, and cross-cultural understanding.

Example: Students can work on a project to research and present on a significant historical event or person. They can create multimedia presentations, conduct interviews with community members who have personal connections to the event, and analyze primary and secondary sources to gain a comprehensive understanding of the historical context. This project enhances students' research skills, presentation skills, and historical empathy.

Language Arts

In language arts education, project-based learning provides students with opportunities to develop and apply their language skills in authentic and meaningful ways. Projects can involve writing and publishing stories, creating multimedia presentations, or organizing literary events. Through these projects, students improve their communication skills, critical thinking skills, and creativity.

Example: Students can engage in a project to write and publish their own books. They can develop their stories, create illustrations, and design the layout of their books. This project allows students to apply their language skills in a creative and meaningful way, fostering their love for reading and writing.

Conclusion

Project-based learning is a versatile and effective approach that can be implemented in various subject areas. By engaging in hands-on projects that are relevant to their learning objectives, students can develop essential skills and knowledge while experiencing the joy of learning. Whether it's in science, mathematics, social studies, or language arts, project-based learning provides students with the opportunity to explore, create, and apply their learning in real-world contexts.

Future directions of project-based learning

Project-based learning (PBL) has emerged as a powerful educational approach that promotes student engagement, critical thinking, collaboration, and problem-solving skills. As we look ahead to the future of education, there are several exciting directions and possibilities for the further development and implementation of PBL. In this section, we explore some of these future directions and their potential impact on transformative education.

Integrating emerging technologies

One key area where PBL can evolve is through the integration of emerging technologies. As technology continues to advance, there are new opportunities to enhance the PBL experience and expand its possibilities. For example, the use of virtual reality (VR) and augmented reality (AR) can transport students to virtual environments that simulate real-world scenarios, allowing for immersive and interactive project experiences. By incorporating VR and AR into PBL, students can gain practical skills and knowledge in a safe and controlled environment.

Furthermore, artificial intelligence (AI) can play a significant role in supporting PBL. AI-powered tools can assist students in the research, data analysis, and problem-solving stages of their projects, providing personalized feedback and guidance. These tools can also help teachers in managing and assessing PBL assignments more effectively.

Global collaboration

In an increasingly interconnected world, PBL can transcend geographical boundaries and facilitate global collaboration among students. Through technology platforms and virtual exchange programs, students from different parts of the world can collaborate on projects, share ideas, and learn from diverse perspectives. This global collaboration not only exposes students to different cultures and ways of thinking but also helps them develop skills for effective communication, teamwork, and understanding of global issues.

Educators can design PBL experiences that foster cross-cultural understanding and empathy, leveraging technology and online platforms to connect their students with peers from different countries. By incorporating global collaboration into PBL, students can develop a global mindset and become better prepared for the challenges of an interconnected world.

Authentic and real-world connections

To make PBL more relevant and meaningful, educators can strengthen the connection between projects and real-world contexts. By incorporating authentic assessments and real-world challenges into PBL, students can see the direct application and impact of their learning. This approach not only enhances student motivation but also fosters a deeper understanding of how knowledge and skills are used in practical situations.

Furthermore, partnerships with local organizations, businesses, and community members can provide students with authentic learning opportunities and guidance throughout their PBL projects. This collaboration with external stakeholders can offer students insights into real-world problems, professional expertise, and opportunities for mentorship.

Interdisciplinary projects

As the world becomes more interconnected and complex, the boundaries between disciplines are becoming increasingly blurred. In the future, PBL can move beyond subject-specific projects and embrace interdisciplinary approaches. By integrating knowledge and skills from multiple disciplines, students can explore complex problems that require a holistic understanding and innovative solutions.

Interdisciplinary PBL projects can help students develop critical thinking skills, creativity, and the ability to make connections across different fields. Educators can design projects that tackle real-world issues, such as sustainability, climate change, global health, or social justice, which often require interdisciplinary perspectives.

Assessment and continuous improvement

In the future, PBL assessment approaches can evolve to focus more on the process of learning rather than just the final product. Formative assessments, including self-reflection, peer feedback, and regular check-ins, can be integrated throughout the project to provide ongoing feedback and support student growth. These assessment strategies can help students develop metacognitive skills, self-regulation, and the ability to continuously improve their work.

Additionally, technology-enhanced assessment tools and learning analytics can provide educators with insights into student progress and facilitate data-driven decision-making. By leveraging data and analytics, teachers can better understand student needs, adapt instructional strategies, and identify areas for improvement in PBL implementation.

Professional development for teachers

As PBL continues to evolve, there is a need for ongoing professional development opportunities for teachers. Educators need the knowledge, skills, and support to design and implement effective PBL experiences that align with the evolving demands of the future. Professional development programs should provide teachers with the necessary pedagogical strategies, technological skills, and collaboration opportunities to enhance their PBL practices.

Collaborative professional learning communities can play a crucial role in supporting teachers in their implementation of PBL. By sharing best practices, exchanging ideas, and providing support, teachers can continually learn and refine their PBL approaches. Online and virtual professional development opportunities can also enable teachers to access resources, training, and mentorship from experts in the field.

Conclusion

As education moves forward, project-based learning has the potential to continue evolving and shaping the future of transformative education. By integrating emerging technologies, fostering global collaboration, creating authentic connections to the real world, embracing interdisciplinary approaches, rethinking assessment, and providing ongoing professional development for teachers, PBL can become even more effective in preparing students for the challenges and opportunities of the future. By embracing these future directions, educators can ensure that PBL remains a valuable and transformative approach to learning.

Flipped Classroom

Understanding the flipped classroom model

In the traditional classroom model, students receive instruction during class time and then complete assignments and practice outside of class. However, in the flipped classroom model, this sequence is reversed. Students are first exposed to new content outside of class, typically through pre-recorded video lectures or online resources. Class time is then dedicated to activities, discussions, and problem-solving, where students can apply and deepen their understanding of the concepts.

The flipped classroom model is based on the principle of active learning, where students have more opportunities to engage with the material and work collaboratively with their peers. This approach shifts the role of the teacher from a lecturer to a facilitator of learning, allowing students to take ownership of their learning process.

Benefits of the flipped classroom model

The flipped classroom model offers several benefits for both students and teachers. Here are some key advantages:

1. **Flexible learning:** The flipped classroom gives students the flexibility to learn at their own pace, accessing the instructional materials when and where they choose. Students can review the content as many times as needed to grasp the concepts.
2. **Active engagement:** With the traditional model, students often passively receive information during lectures. In the flipped classroom, students actively engage with the content by watching videos, reading materials, and completing interactive exercises outside of class. This active engagement enhances their understanding and retention of the material.
3. **Classroom interaction:** By moving lectures outside of class, valuable class time is freed up for interactive discussions, collaborative activities, and problem-solving. This allows students to delve deeper into the material, ask questions, and receive immediate feedback from both their peers and the teacher.
4. **Individualized support:** In the traditional classroom, it can be challenging for teachers to provide personalized attention to each student. In the flipped classroom, the teacher has more time to work closely with individual students, providing targeted support and addressing specific learning needs.
5. **Critical thinking and problem-solving:** The flipped classroom promotes higher-order thinking skills, as students have the opportunity to apply their knowledge to real-world problems and engage in meaningful discussions. This prepares them to think critically and solve complex problems beyond the classroom.

Implementation of the flipped classroom model

Implementing the flipped classroom model effectively requires careful planning and consideration. Here are some key steps to consider:

1. **Content selection:** Choose or develop high-quality instructional materials that students can access outside of class. These materials should be engaging, concise, and aligned with the learning objectives.
2. **Communication and expectations:** Clearly communicate to students the expectations and guidelines for the flipped classroom model. Explain how they

should access the content, what they should do to prepare for class, and how class time will be structured.

3. **Active learning activities:** Design activities for class time that actively engage students with the material. This could include group discussions, problem-solving exercises, simulations, debates, or hands-on experiments. These activities should align with the learning objectives and provide opportunities for application and critical thinking.

4. **Feedback and assessment:** Provide opportunities for ongoing feedback and assessment during class time. This can include formative assessments, peer feedback, and teacher-guided discussions. It is important to assess students' understanding and address any misconceptions or gaps in knowledge.

5. **Reflection and iteration:** Regularly reflect on the effectiveness of the flipped classroom model and make adjustments as needed. Seek feedback from students and use their input to improve the learning experience.

Challenges and considerations

While the flipped classroom model has many benefits, it is important to be aware of the challenges and considerations in its implementation:

1. **Access to resources:** Flipping the classroom requires access to technology and reliable internet connection for students to access the instructional materials outside of class. It is crucial to ensure equitable access to resources for all students.

2. **Self-regulated learning:** The flipped classroom places greater responsibility on students to independently engage with the content outside of class. Some students may struggle with managing their time and staying motivated. Teachers need to provide guidance and support to help students develop effective self-regulated learning skills.

3. **Teacher preparation:** The role of the teacher shifts from being the primary source of information to a facilitator of learning. Teachers need to be prepared to design and facilitate meaningful activities, provide individualized support, and assess student progress effectively.

4. **Technology challenges:** Technical issues with online resources or lack of familiarity with technology can create barriers to implementing the flipped classroom model. Adequate training and support should be provided to both teachers and students.

5. **Resistance to change:** Implementing a new teaching approach may encounter resistance from both students and teachers who are accustomed to the traditional classroom model. Clear communication and ongoing support can help address concerns and build confidence in the flipped classroom approach.

In conclusion, the flipped classroom model offers a transformative approach to teaching and learning. By shifting the traditional lecture-based instruction to outside of class, students engage with the content actively and have more opportunities for collaboration and problem-solving during class time. However, successful implementation requires careful planning, flexible resources, and ongoing support for both students and teachers. The flipped classroom can enhance student engagement, deepen understanding, and promote critical thinking skills, preparing students for success in the digital age.

Benefits of the Flipped Classroom Approach

The flipped classroom approach is a pedagogical model that has gained significant attention in recent years. It involves reversing the traditional sequence of teaching, where students first learn new content in class and then apply it through homework assignments. Instead, in the flipped classroom, students are exposed to new content outside of class, often through pre-recorded lectures or online resources, and then use class time for active learning activities, such as discussions, group work, and problem-solving.

The benefits of the flipped classroom approach are numerous and have been supported by research and testimonials from educators and students alike. In this section, we will explore the key benefits of adopting the flipped classroom model.

Enhanced Engagement and Active Learning

One of the primary benefits of the flipped classroom approach is the increase in student engagement and active learning. By shifting the lecture portion of the learning to outside of class, students come to class with a solid foundation of knowledge and can engage in more meaningful activities during class time. This active learning approach allows students to apply their knowledge, ask questions, and participate in discussions and group activities. It creates a dynamic and interactive learning environment that promotes deeper engagement and a higher level of participation from students.

Personalized and Self-paced Learning

The flipped classroom model allows for personalized and self-paced learning. Students can access the pre-recorded lectures or online resources at their own convenience and review the content as many times as needed to grasp the concepts. This flexibility enables students to learn at their own pace and accommodate different learning styles and preferences. Students who grasp the material quickly can move ahead, while those who need additional time can review the content until they feel confident. This individualized approach promotes a deeper understanding of the material and allows students to take ownership of their learning.

Opportunity for Differentiated Instruction

The flipped classroom approach provides an opportunity for differentiated instruction. Teachers can use class time to provide targeted support and guidance to students based on their individual needs. Since the traditional lecture is moved outside of class, teachers can spend more time working one-on-one or in small groups with students who require additional help or challenge. This targeted instruction helps to meet the diverse needs of students, promote academic growth, and ensure that all students are progressing at an appropriate pace.

Improved Classroom Management

By shifting the delivery of lecture content outside of class, teachers have more time and flexibility to focus on classroom management during actual class time. They can devote their attention to facilitating discussions, monitoring group activities, and providing immediate feedback to students. This increased focus on classroom management enhances the overall learning environment and allows for a more efficient use of instructional time.

Promotion of Higher-order Thinking Skills

The flipped classroom approach promotes the development of higher-order thinking skills, such as critical thinking, problem-solving, and analytical skills. With the traditional lecture moved outside of class, students have more opportunities to engage in active learning activities that require them to apply their knowledge and think critically. Class discussions, group work, and problem-solving activities encourage students to analyze information, evaluate different perspectives, and synthesize their understanding. These higher-order thinking skills are vital for success in the modern workforce and in higher education.

Increased Student-Teacher Interaction

The flipped classroom approach fosters increased student-teacher interaction. With the lecture portion moved outside of class, teachers have more time to interact individually with students and provide personalized feedback. This close interaction allows teachers to assess student understanding, address misconceptions, and provide immediate support. Students also have more opportunities to seek clarifications, ask questions, and engage in meaningful discussions with their teacher. This personalized interaction strengthens the student-teacher relationship and promotes a positive and supportive learning environment.

Development of Digital Literacy Skills

In the flipped classroom model, students engage with online resources, pre-recorded lectures, and various digital tools. This exposure to digital resources and technology develops essential digital literacy skills. Students learn how to navigate online platforms, access information, evaluate online sources for credibility and reliability, and collaborate online. These skills are increasingly necessary in the digital age and prepare students for future education and careers.

Increased Student Autonomy and Responsibility

The flipped classroom approach encourages student autonomy and responsibility in their learning. Students take the initiative to access the pre-recorded lectures or online resources, plan their study time, and pace their learning. They become active participants in their education and develop skills such as time management, organization, and self-discipline. This increased autonomy and responsibility prepare students for higher education and the workplace, where self-directed learning is highly valued.

Cost and Resource Efficiency

The flipped classroom approach can contribute to cost and resource efficiency. By eliminating the need for extensive in-class lectures, teachers can make more efficient use of class time and reduce the need for additional resources, such as textbooks. Additionally, the use of online resources and pre-recorded lectures can minimize printing and paper usage, reducing the overall environmental impact. The flipped classroom model allows for a more sustainable approach to education while maximizing the use of available resources.

In conclusion, the flipped classroom approach offers numerous benefits that enhance the learning experience for students. It promotes engagement, active learning, personalized instruction, and the development of critical thinking skills. It also increases student-teacher interaction, fosters autonomy and responsibility, and prepares students for success in the digital age. With its many advantages, the flipped classroom approach is transforming education and shaping the future of teaching and learning.

It is important to note that while the flipped classroom approach has significant benefits, it may not be suitable for all subjects or learning objectives. Educators should consider the specific needs of their students and the content they teach when deciding whether to implement the flipped classroom model. Additionally, proper planning, support, and training for both teachers and students are essential for successful implementation and realization of the benefits of the flipped classroom approach.

Flipped Classroom Design and Implementation Strategies

The flipped classroom model is a form of instructional delivery where the traditional classroom instruction and homework components are reversed. Students engage in self-paced learning outside the classroom, typically through video lectures or online modules, while in-class time is dedicated to hands-on activities, problem-solving, and discussions facilitated by the teacher. This section will discuss the design and implementation strategies for the flipped classroom model.

Designing Flipped Classroom Lessons

Designing effective flipped classroom lessons requires careful planning to ensure that students engage with the content before coming to class. Here are some key considerations:

label=• **Identify learning objectives:** Clearly define the learning objectives for each lesson. What knowledge or skills should students acquire by the end of the lesson?

lbbel=• **Break the content into manageable chunks:** Divide the content into smaller sections or topics that can be easily understood in a self-paced manner. This helps students absorb the information more effectively.

lcbel=• **Create engaging and concise video lectures:** Develop video lectures or online modules that are concise, engaging, and aligned with the learning objectives. Use multimedia elements, such as graphics and animations, to enhance understanding.

ldbel=• **Provide guided notes or study guides:** Accompany the video lectures or online modules with guided notes or study guides that help students focus on key concepts and take structured notes.

lebel=• **Include formative assessments:** Integrate formative assessments, such as quiz questions or short quizzes, into the video lectures or online modules. This helps students check their understanding and identify areas that need further clarification.

Implementing Flipped Classroom Lessons

Implementing flipped classroom lessons effectively involves creating a supportive and engaging learning environment both inside and outside the classroom. Consider the following strategies:

label=• **Communicate expectations:** Clearly communicate the expectations and guidelines for engaging with the pre-class materials. Students should understand the importance of completing the assigned tasks before coming to class.

lbbel=• **Provide resources and support:** Ensure that students have access to the necessary resources, such as a reliable internet connection and devices to watch video lectures or access online modules. Offer technical support if needed.

lcbel=• **Encourage active learning in class:** Design in-class activities that promote active learning, collaboration, and critical thinking. This can include problem-solving exercises, group discussions, simulations, experiments, or case studies related to the pre-class materials.

ldbel=• **Individualize instruction:** Use in-class time to provide individualized support and feedback to students. Identify areas where students may be struggling and offer additional explanations or resources as needed.

lebel=• **Promote student engagement:** Use various instructional strategies to keep students engaged during in-class activities, such as interactive technologies, hands-on experiments, group projects, or role-playing scenarios. Encourage peer-to-peer interaction and collaboration.

lfbel=• **Assess student learning:** Assess student understanding and progress through formative and summative assessments. Use a mix of traditional methods, such as quizzes or exams, as well as alternative assessment strategies, such as projects, presentations, or portfolios.

Challenges and Solutions

Implementing the flipped classroom model may come with certain challenges. Here are some common challenges and possible solutions:

label=• **Student accountability:** Some students may struggle with self-paced learning outside the classroom. To address this, establish an accountability system, such as quizzes or assignments that must be completed before the in-class session.

lbbel=• **Access to technology:** Not all students may have access to the required technology at home. Provide alternative options for accessing the pre-class materials, such as making them available for offline viewing or providing printed materials.

lcbel=• **Time management:** Students may face difficulties managing their time effectively to complete the pre-class materials. Provide clear deadlines and prioritize key concepts or materials to help students focus on the most important content.

ldbel=• **Resistance to change:** Both teachers and students may initially resist the flipped classroom model due to its departure from traditional teaching methods. Offer professional development opportunities for teachers to understand the benefits and address concerns. Communicate the benefits of flipped learning to students to increase their motivation and engagement.

Real-World Example

To exemplify the implementation of the flipped classroom model, consider a high school mathematics class. The teacher designs a lesson on solving quadratic equations using the flipped classroom approach. Here is how the lesson is structured:

1. Before the class session:

    - Students watch a video lecture on the basics of quadratic equations and how to solve them.
    - They complete guided notes while watching the video.
    - Students attempt formative assessment questions embedded in the video.

2. In the class session:
    - The teacher starts with a brief review of the key concepts covered in the video lecture.
    - Students work in pairs or small groups to solve a set of quadratic equation problems.
    - The teacher circulates the classroom, offering guidance and clarification as necessary.
    - Students present their solutions to the class, promoting peer-to-peer learning and critical thinking.
    - The teacher concludes the session by summarizing the key concepts and addressing any remaining questions.

This approach allows students to engage with the content at their own pace, actively participate in problem-solving activities during the class session, and receive immediate feedback and support from the teacher. It promotes deeper understanding and application of the mathematical concepts.

Additional Resources

For further exploration of the flipped classroom model, refer to the following resources:

- *Flip Your Classroom: Reach Every Student in Every Class Every Day* by Jonathan Bergmann and Aaron Sams
- *Flipped Learning: Gateway to Student Engagement* by Jon Bergmann, Aaron Sams, and Taki R. Moore
- *The Flipped Learning Revolution: How to Overcome Barriers, Engage Students, and Increase Class Time* by Jonathan Bergmann and Aaron Sams

Additionally, websites such as the Flipped Learning Network (flippedlearning.org) and the Khan Academy (khanacademy.org) provide valuable resources, case studies, and best practices for implementing the flipped classroom model.

In conclusion, the flipped classroom model offers a learner-centered approach to instruction, allowing students to take responsibility for their own learning and engage actively in class. By carefully designing and implementing flipped classroom lessons, educators can create a dynamic and interactive learning environment that enhances student understanding and promotes higher-order thinking skills.

Assessing Student Learning in the Flipped Classroom

Assessing student learning is a critical component of the flipped classroom model. In a traditional classroom, assessment often takes the form of quizzes or exams administered after the teacher has delivered the content. However, in a flipped classroom, where students learn the content outside of the classroom, assessment needs to be carefully designed to align with the unique characteristics and goals of this approach.

Goals of Assessment in the Flipped Classroom

Assessment in the flipped classroom serves several purposes. First and foremost, it allows teachers to gauge the students' understanding of the content they have learned independently. This helps identify areas of strength and weakness and allows the teacher to provide targeted support and feedback. Additionally, assessment helps students consolidate their learning, reinforce key concepts, and develop metacognitive skills.

Furthermore, assessment in the flipped classroom can also serve as a formative tool to inform instructional decisions. By gathering data on student learning, teachers can identify misconceptions or gaps in understanding and adjust their teaching strategies accordingly. This ongoing feedback loop ensures that instruction is responsive to the needs of the students.

Designing Effective Assessments

When designing assessments for the flipped classroom, it is important to consider a variety of factors. The assessments should be aligned with the learning objectives and should measure the desired knowledge, skills, and competencies. Here are some key considerations:

1. **Authenticity:** Assessments should be authentic and reflect real-world applications of the content. This allows students to see the relevance of what they have learned and helps them transfer knowledge to different contexts. For example, instead of traditional multiple-choice questions, consider designing open-ended tasks or projects that require problem-solving and critical thinking skills.

2. **Active Learning:** Assessments should encourage active learning and student engagement. Rather than passive recall of information, assessments should require students to apply, analyze, synthesize, and evaluate knowledge. This can be done through hands-on activities, group projects, presentations, or debates.

3. **Differentiation:** Provide opportunities for students to demonstrate their understanding in different ways. Some students may excel at written assessments,

while others may prefer creating videos, giving oral presentations, or designing visual representations. Giving students choice and flexibility in how they demonstrate their learning promotes ownership and engagement in the assessment process.

4. **Timeliness:** Assessments should be timely to provide immediate feedback and allow for timely interventions if needed. Consider using frequent low-stakes assessments, such as weekly quizzes or brief online discussions, to monitor student progress. This formative assessment approach helps students stay on track and allows the teacher to address misconceptions in a timely manner.

Overcoming Challenges in Flipped Classroom Assessment

Assessing student learning in the flipped classroom comes with its own set of challenges. Here are some common challenges and strategies to overcome them:

1. **Limited In-Class Time:** One of the primary challenges is the limited amount of in-class time available for assessments. To maximize the use of class time, consider using technology-based assessments that allow for quick and efficient data collection. This could include online quizzes, interactive activities, or real-time response systems.

2. **Ensuring Accountability:** With students learning independently outside of class, it can be challenging to ensure that each student is actively engaging with the content. To address this, consider incorporating pre-class assignments or activities that serve as evidence of student preparation. Additionally, provide opportunities for peer assessment or reflection to hold students accountable for their learning.

3. **Addressing Equity and Access:** It is important to ensure that assessment tools and resources are accessible to all students, regardless of their background or learning needs. Provide alternative formats for assessments (e.g., audio recordings, printed materials) and offer support to students who may face technological or connectivity challenges. Consider using inclusive assessment practices that value diverse forms of expression and representation.

Case Studies and Best Practices

Here are a few examples of how assessment can be conducted in a flipped classroom:

1. **Peer Feedback and Self-Assessment:** In a flipped classroom, students can engage in peer feedback and self-assessment activities to reflect on their learning. This can be done through structured protocols, rubrics, or online tools that facilitate anonymous peer feedback. Encouraging students to assess their own understanding and progress promotes metacognition and autonomy.

2. **Project-Based Assessments:** Instead of traditional exams, consider implementing project-based assessments that require students to apply their knowledge to real-world problems. This could involve designing a solution, conducting a research study, or creating a multimedia presentation. These types of assessments allow for collaboration, creativity, and critical thinking.

3. **Real-Time Formative Assessments:** Use technology tools, such as online quizzes or polling apps, to conduct real-time formative assessments during class. These tools provide immediate feedback to both students and teachers, allowing for on-the-spot clarification or redirection. It also promotes active engagement and participation.

Resources for Flipped Classroom Assessment

Here are some resources that can help you design effective assessments for the flipped classroom:

- **Flipped Learning Network:** The Flipped Learning Network (flippedlearning.org) provides resources, case studies, and best practices for implementing the flipped classroom model, including assessment strategies.

- **National Education Association:** The National Education Association (nea.org) offers articles, guides, and professional development resources related to assessment practices in the flipped classroom.

- **Khan Academy:** Khan Academy (khanacademy.org) provides a wide range of online resources and assessment tools that align with various subject areas and can be used in the flipped classroom.

- **Assessment Design Toolkit:** The Assessment Design Toolkit by the Christensen Institute provides a step-by-step process for designing assessments that align with the goals of the flipped classroom model.

- **Online Learning Consortium:** The Online Learning Consortium (onlinelearningconsortium.org) offers webinars, workshops, and research articles on assessment in online and blended learning environments, which can be applicable to the flipped classroom.

In conclusion, assessing student learning in the flipped classroom requires careful consideration of the unique characteristics and goals of this instructional approach. Designing effective assessments that align with learning objectives, promote active engagement, and provide timely feedback is crucial for student success. By implementing a variety of assessment methods and leveraging technology tools, teachers can gather valuable data to inform instruction and support the learning needs of their students.

Overcoming challenges in implementing the flipped classroom

Implementing the flipped classroom approach comes with its own set of challenges. In this section, we will discuss some of these challenges and explore strategies to overcome them.

1. **Resistance to Change:** One of the biggest challenges in implementing the flipped classroom is the resistance to change from both teachers and students. Teachers may be hesitant to abandon the traditional lecture-style teaching they are accustomed to, while students may struggle with the increased responsibility for their own learning.

To overcome this challenge, it is important to provide professional development and training opportunities for teachers to familiarize themselves with the flipped classroom model. This can include workshops, webinars, and ongoing support to address any concerns or doubts. Additionally, it is crucial to communicate the benefits of the flipped classroom to both teachers and students, emphasizing the shift towards a more student-centered and interactive learning experience.

2. **Lack of Technological Infrastructure:** Another challenge is the lack of access to reliable technology and internet connectivity, especially in resource-constrained environments. The success of the flipped classroom relies heavily on students having access to the necessary devices and reliable internet connection to access online learning materials.

To address this challenge, educators can explore alternative methods for delivering content, such as providing offline resources or using low-tech options like DVDs or USB drives. It is also important to collaborate with school administrators and IT personnel to ensure that the necessary infrastructure is in place to support flipped classroom implementation.

3. **Student Engagement and Accountability:** In a flipped classroom, students are expected to take a more active role in their learning, which can be a challenge for some students who are used to a more passive learning environment. It can be difficult to ensure that all students come prepared to class, having watched the video lectures or completed the pre-class assignments.

To address this challenge, teachers can implement strategies to promote student accountability, such as tracking completion of pre-class assignments and incorporating formative assessments at the beginning of each class to gauge students' understanding. Providing timely feedback and support to students who may be struggling can also help improve engagement and motivation.

4. **Time Management:** The flipped classroom model requires careful planning and time management both for teachers and students. Teachers need to allocate time for creating and curating high-quality video lectures, while students need to allocate time outside of class to watch the lectures and complete pre-class assignments.

To overcome this challenge, teachers can provide clear guidelines and expectations regarding the time commitment required for the flipped classroom. They can also offer support to students in managing their time effectively, such as providing study schedules or helping them set goals and prioritize tasks.

5. **Assessment and Evaluation:** Assessing student learning in a flipped classroom can be different from traditional methods, as students may have already gained initial exposure to the content outside of class. This requires teachers to design assessments that go beyond simple recall and focus on higher-order thinking skills and application of knowledge.

To address this challenge, teachers can incorporate more project-based assessments, problem-solving tasks, and collaborative activities that require students to apply their knowledge in meaningful ways. Providing timely and constructive feedback is also important to guide students' learning and help them improve.

In conclusion, while the flipped classroom has the potential to enhance student engagement and learning outcomes, it is important to acknowledge and address the challenges that may arise during implementation. By addressing resistance to change, ensuring access to technology, promoting student engagement and accountability, managing time effectively, and designing appropriate assessments, educators can create a successful flipped classroom environment that maximizes the potential of this transformative teaching approach.

Case studies and best practices in the flipped classroom

In this section, we will explore some case studies and best practices in implementing the flipped classroom model. The flipped classroom approach has gained popularity due to its potential to enhance student engagement, improve understanding of complex concepts, and promote active learning. By flipping the traditional classroom model, students are able to engage with new content before attending class, allowing for more interactive and collaborative activities during face-to-face instructional time.

Case Study 1: Mathematics Flipped Classroom

In a high school mathematics class, the teacher implemented the flipped classroom model to improve student understanding and problem-solving skills. Before each class, the teacher assigned video lessons covering the new topics, which students were required to watch at home. The videos were created by the teacher and made available on the school's learning management system.

During class time, students participated in collaborative activities such as group problem-solving, discussions, and hands-on exercises. The teacher provided guidance and support as students worked through challenging problems. In addition to in-class activities, the teacher also created online quizzes and interactive assignments to assess students' understanding of the material.

The results of this case study showed significant improvements in student engagement and achievement. Students reported feeling more confident in their problem-solving abilities and appreciated the opportunity to work together in a supportive environment. The flipped classroom model allowed for personalized instruction and targeted interventions, ensuring that students received individualized support when needed.

Best Practice 1: Creating Engaging Video Lessons

One key aspect of the flipped classroom model is the creation of engaging and effective video lessons. When designing video content, consider the following best practices:

- Keep the videos short and focused: Break down complex topics into digestible chunks of information. Aim for videos that are no longer than 10-15 minutes to maintain student attention and facilitate comprehension.

- Use a conversational tone: Speak directly to the students as if you are having a conversation with them. This helps create a more personal and engaging learning experience.

- Incorporate visuals and multimedia: Use graphics, diagrams, animations, and real-world examples to aid understanding and make the content more visually appealing.

- Encourage student interaction: Include questions or prompts throughout the video to encourage students to pause and reflect on the material or respond to discussion prompts.

- Provide guided practice opportunities: Offer opportunities for students to apply what they have learned in the video by including example problems or interactive activities.

By following these best practices, teachers can create video lessons that not only effectively deliver content but also enhance student engagement and understanding.

Best Practice 2: Facilitating Active Learning

One of the primary goals of the flipped classroom model is to promote active learning during class time. Here are some best practices for facilitating active learning in a flipped classroom:

- Use collaborative learning strategies: Assign students to work in small groups or pairs to solve problems, engage in discussions, or complete projects. This fosters peer-to-peer interaction and encourages active participation.

- Incorporate hands-on activities: Provide opportunities for students to engage in hands-on experiments, simulations, or real-world applications of the concepts learned through the video lessons. This helps students make meaningful connections and deepen their understanding.

- Offer immediate feedback: Provide timely feedback to students during in-class activities to address misconceptions, reinforce correct understanding, and guide further learning. This feedback can be given by the teacher or through peer review.

- Promote reflection and metacognition: Encourage students to reflect on their learning process, identify areas of strength and improvement, and set goals for future learning. This helps develop self-regulated learning skills and promotes deeper understanding.

- Foster a supportive and inclusive classroom environment: Create a classroom culture where students feel comfortable asking questions, sharing their thoughts, and supporting each other's learning. Promote inclusivity and celebrate diverse perspectives.

By applying these best practices, teachers can create a dynamic and interactive learning environment that maximizes the benefits of the flipped classroom model.

Case Study 2: Science Flipped Classroom

In a middle school science class, the teacher implemented the flipped classroom model to enhance students' understanding of scientific concepts and promote scientific inquiry. The teacher assigned pre-class readings and video lessons that introduced new content and provided background information for in-class activities.

During class time, students engaged in various hands-on experiments, laboratory investigations, and group discussions. The teacher acted as a facilitator, guiding students through the scientific inquiry process and encouraging critical thinking and problem-solving skills. Students used online resources and interactive simulations to further explore scientific concepts and apply their knowledge.

The results of this case study showed increased student motivation, improved understanding of scientific concepts, and higher levels of engagement during in-class activities. Students developed a deeper appreciation for the scientific process and gained valuable research and analytical skills.

Best Practice 3: Assessing Learning in the Flipped Classroom

Assessment is a crucial component of the flipped classroom model. Here are some best practices for assessing student learning in a flipped classroom:

- Use formative assessment strategies: Regularly check student understanding through quizzes, online activities, or in-class discussions. This allows for immediate feedback and helps identify areas where additional support or clarification is needed.

- Incorporate both individual and group assessments: Assess individual students' grasp of the content through quizzes or short assignments. Additionally, include group projects or presentations to assess collaborative skills, communication, and critical thinking.

- Provide opportunities for self-assessment and reflection: Encourage students to reflect on their learning progress and evaluate their own understanding through self-assessment activities. This helps develop metacognitive skills and promotes a sense of ownership over learning.

- Use a variety of assessment methods: Consider using a mix of traditional assessments (e.g., written tests) and more authentic assessments (e.g., performance tasks, portfolios) to provide a comprehensive view of student learning and skills development.

- Leverage technology for assessment: Take advantage of online tools and platforms that allow for automated grading, immediate feedback, and data analysis. This can save time for both teachers and students and provide valuable insights into student progress.

By incorporating these best practices into the assessment process, teachers can effectively measure and monitor student learning in the flipped classroom.

In conclusion, case studies and best practices demonstrate the benefits of the flipped classroom model in promoting student engagement, critical thinking skills, and content understanding. By designing engaging video lessons, facilitating active learning, and implementing effective assessment strategies, teachers can create transformative learning experiences for their students. The flipped classroom model offers endless possibilities for enhancing education and preparing students for success in the digital age.

Incorporating Technology in the Flipped Classroom Model

The flipped classroom model has gained significant popularity in recent years due to its ability to enhance student engagement and promote active learning. In this section, we will explore how technology can be effectively incorporated into the flipped classroom model to optimize student learning outcomes and foster a more personalized and interactive learning environment.

Benefits of Technology in the Flipped Classroom

Before delving into the specific ways technology can be integrated into the flipped classroom, let us briefly discuss the benefits it brings to this educational approach. Technology provides several advantages that complement the flipped classroom model:

1. **Access to Resources:** Technology allows students to access a wide range of digital resources, such as online videos, interactive simulations, e-books, and educational websites. These resources can support self-paced learning, enabling students to revisit content and reinforce their understanding.

2. **Flexibility in Learning:** With technology, students can learn at their own pace and in their preferred learning style. They can review and revisit materials as needed, catering to individual needs and promoting a more personalized learning experience.

3. **Engagement and Interactivity:** Technology offers various tools and applications that make learning more engaging and interactive. Students can participate in online discussions, collaborate on projects, and engage in virtual experiments or simulations, resulting in higher levels of active participation and deeper understanding of the subject matter.

4. **Immediate Feedback:** Technology allows for instant feedback, which is crucial for effective learning. Teachers can use online quizzes, interactive assessments, and automated grading systems to provide timely feedback to students, allowing them to gauge their progress and identify areas for improvement.

5. **Data Analytics:** By leveraging learning analytics tools, teachers can gain insights into student performance, progress, and participation. Analyzing data generated from student interactions with technology can help identify learning gaps, implement targeted interventions, and customize instruction to meet individual needs.

Flipped Classroom Technology Tools

To incorporate technology effectively in the flipped classroom, educators can choose from a wide array of tools and technologies. Let's explore some key tools that can enhance the learning experience in a flipped classroom setting:

1. **Video Creation and Sharing Tools:** Video is a fundamental component of the flipped classroom model. Teachers can create instructional videos using tools like *Screencast-O-Matic* or *Camtasia*, which allow educators to record their screens, add annotations, and incorporate voiceovers. These videos can then be shared with students through platforms like YouTube, where they can access the content at their convenience.

2. **Learning Management Systems (LMS):** An LMS serves as a central hub for managing and delivering online content. Platforms like *Moodle, Canvas,* or *Google Classroom* allow teachers to organize resources, post assignments, facilitate discussions, and track student progress. LMSs also provide a means for communication and collaboration, enabling students to engage with course materials and interact with their peers.

3. **Collaboration Tools:** Technology enables collaboration and teamwork even outside the physical classroom. Tools such as *Google Docs, Microsoft Teams,* or *Trello* provide platforms for students to collaborate on projects, share

documents, and offer real-time feedback to their peers. Such tools foster active learning, enhance communication skills, and promote a sense of community among students.

4. **Interactive Simulations and Virtual Labs:** Technology offers a wide range of interactive simulations and virtual labs that provide practical learning experiences. Tools such as *PhET Simulations, Labster,* or *ChemCollective,* provide virtual environments where students can conduct experiments, explore scientific concepts, and apply their knowledge in a risk-free setting. These resources enhance student engagement and offer hands-on experiences that may be otherwise inaccessible.

5. **Online Assessment Tools:** Technology facilitates the creation and administration of quizzes, tests, and assessments. Platforms like *Kahoot, Quizlet,* or *EdPuzzle* provide engaging and interactive assessment features, including gamified quizzes, multimedia-based questions, and immediate feedback. These tools help teachers assess student learning and provide valuable insights into student progress.

Implementation Strategies for Incorporating Technology

To ensure the effective integration of technology in the flipped classroom model, educators can consider the following strategies:

1. **Align Technology with Learning Objectives:** When selecting technology tools, it is essential to align them with the learning objectives of the flipped classroom. The chosen tools should support the intended learning outcomes and enrich the instructional content.

2. **Provide Clear Instructions and Support:** As students engage with technology outside the classroom, it is crucial to provide clear instructions on how to access and navigate these tools. Additionally, offering technical support and troubleshooting guidelines ensures students can effectively utilize the technology without unnecessary hurdles.

3. **Promote Digital Citizenship and Online Etiquette:** With the increased use of technology, educators must emphasize the importance of responsible digital citizenship and appropriate online behavior. Discussions around internet safety, privacy, and ethical considerations should be integrated into the curriculum to prepare students for safe and responsible online interactions.

4. **Continuous Professional Development:** Teachers need ongoing professional development to stay abreast of emerging technologies and best practices. Providing relevant training and support equips teachers with the necessary skills to effectively incorporate technology and adapt their instructional practices to meet the evolving needs of students.

5. **Evaluate Technological Tools:** After implementing technology in the flipped classroom, it is essential to evaluate its effectiveness in enhancing student learning outcomes. Collecting feedback from students, conducting formative assessments, and analyzing learning analytics can help identify strengths and weaknesses in the technology integration.

Challenges and Considerations

While technology offers immense potential in the flipped classroom, there are certain challenges and considerations that educators should be aware of:

1. **Access and Equity:** Not all students may have equal access to technology resources outside the classroom. It is crucial to address the digital divide and ensure that all students have equitable access to the necessary devices and internet connectivity.

2. **Training and Support:** Teachers may require training and support to effectively integrate technology tools into their instructional practices. Professional development opportunities should be provided to enhance teachers' technological literacy and pedagogical knowledge.

3. **Technical Issues:** Regardless of careful planning, technological issues may arise during the implementation of the flipped classroom model. Having contingency plans in place and providing technical support can help mitigate disruptions and ensure the smooth functioning of the learning environment.

4. **Data Privacy and Security:** When incorporating technology, it is essential to prioritize student data privacy and security. Careful selection of tools, compliance with data protection regulations, and thoughtful use of personal information are paramount in maintaining a safe and secure learning environment.

Case Study: Flipped Classroom with Technology Integration

Let's consider a case study of a high school biology teacher, Ms. Johnson, who successfully implements technology in her flipped classroom.

Ms. Johnson creates instructional videos using screencasting tools to explain complex biological processes and concepts. She uploads these videos to an online platform, accessible to her students at any time. In addition, she uses an LMS to provide supplementary resources, facilitate discussions, and assign online quizzes.

To encourage collaboration, Ms. Johnson incorporates online group projects using collaborative tools like Google Docs. Students use these tools to collaborate, co-create documents, and exchange feedback. Additionally, she utilizes virtual labs and simulations to provide hands-on experiences that enhance student engagement and deep understanding.

Ms. Johnson regularly analyzes student engagement and performance data provided by the learning analytics tools integrated into her LMS. This data helps her identify struggling students, customize interventions, and differentiate instruction to meet individual needs.

By incorporating technology tools strategically, Ms. Johnson creates an engaging and interactive learning environment that fosters active learning, student collaboration, and personalized instruction.

Conclusion

Incorporating technology in the flipped classroom model offers significant benefits and opportunities to enhance student learning outcomes. The use of video creation tools, learning management systems, collaboration tools, virtual labs, and online assessments can optimize the flipped classroom experience for both teachers and students. However, it is crucial to address challenges related to access, training, technical issues, and data privacy to ensure equitable and effective technology integration. By employing thoughtful implementation strategies and considering the unique needs of students, educators can leverage technology to create transformative learning experiences in the flipped classroom.

Blended Learning and the Flipped Classroom

Blended learning is an innovative approach to education that combines traditional face-to-face instruction with online elements. It aims to create a flexible and personalized learning experience by leveraging the advantages of both online and offline learning environments. In blended learning, students have the opportunity to engage with educational materials and activities through online platforms, while also benefiting from in-person interactions with their peers and teachers.

The flipped classroom model is a specific form of blended learning that has gained popularity in recent years. In a flipped classroom, the traditional notion of homework and classroom activities is reversed. Students are introduced to new concepts and learning materials through online resources, such as videos, podcasts, or interactive modules, before coming to class. Class time is then devoted to discussions, collaborative activities, and problem-solving exercises, allowing students to apply and deepen their understanding of the content.

The combination of blended learning and the flipped classroom offers several advantages for both students and teachers. Firstly, it allows for greater flexibility in learning, as students can access educational materials at their own pace and review them as needed. This personalized approach to learning helps to cater to the individual needs and learning styles of each student.

Furthermore, blended learning and the flipped classroom promote active engagement and participation. By providing students with online resources to learn the foundational concepts at home, class time can be dedicated to interactive and hands-on activities. This active learning approach fosters critical thinking, collaboration, and problem-solving skills among students. It also allows teachers to serve as facilitators and mentors, guiding students through their learning journey and providing individualized support.

Implementing blended learning and the flipped classroom requires thoughtful planning and integration of technology into the curriculum. Teachers need to curate and create high-quality online resources that align with the learning objectives and student needs. They also need to design meaningful and engaging in-class activities that build upon the pre-class online learning. Additionally, teachers must establish clear expectations and guidelines for student participation and ensure access to necessary technology tools and resources.

One challenge in implementing blended learning and the flipped classroom is addressing the digital divide. Not all students have equal access to technology and internet connectivity outside of the classroom. To mitigate this issue, schools can explore ways to provide students with the necessary devices and internet access or provide alternative offline resources for those who do not have access to technology.

Another challenge is ensuring that students engage with the online resources and come to class prepared. Teachers can address this by integrating formative assessments and interactive elements into the online materials, encouraging students to actively participate and track their progress. Setting clear expectations and providing structured guidance can also incentivize students to complete the pre-class activities.

Blended learning and the flipped classroom have been successfully implemented in various subject areas, from mathematics and science to language arts and social sciences. The flexibility of this approach allows teachers to tailor the learning experience to the specific needs of each discipline.

To illustrate the concept of blended learning and the flipped classroom, let's consider an example from a high school physics class. The teacher records short video lectures covering the fundamental principles of physics and uploads them to an online platform accessible to students. Before coming to class, students watch the videos and take quizzes to assess their understanding. In the classroom, the teacher facilitates hands-on experiments and group discussions, where students apply their knowledge to solve real-world physics problems. This interactive and collaborative approach enhances students' comprehension and retention of the subject matter.

In summary, blended learning and the flipped classroom offer a transformative approach to education by combining online and in-person learning experiences. They promote active engagement, personalized learning, and the development of critical thinking skills. While challenges exist, with careful planning and thoughtful integration of technology, these methods have the potential to enhance student learning outcomes and create a more dynamic and interactive classroom environment. By embracing these innovative approaches, educators can prepare students for the demands of the future and equip them with the skills necessary for academic excellence and lifelong learning.

Flipped Classroom in Different Subject Areas

In recent years, the flipped classroom model has gained popularity as an innovative approach to teaching and learning across various subject areas. In a flipped classroom, traditional classroom activities such as lectures are moved outside of the class, typically through pre-recorded videos or online resources, while in-class time is dedicated to collaborative and interactive activities. This instructional method has shown great potential in promoting active learning, student engagement, and critical thinking skills. Let's explore how the flipped classroom can be implemented in different subject areas.

Mathematics

The flipped classroom model can be particularly effective in teaching mathematics. Instead of spending valuable class time lecturing, teachers can provide students with pre-recorded video lessons covering the foundational concepts and problem-solving techniques. Students can access these videos at their own pace, allowing them to review the material or pause and rewind as needed.

During class time, teachers can facilitate discussions and engage students in problem-solving activities. This allows students to apply what they have learned in a collaborative and supportive environment. In addition, teachers can provide one-on-one assistance to students who may be struggling with specific concepts or skills. The flipped classroom approach in mathematics helps students develop a deep understanding of mathematical concepts through active participation and problem-solving.

Science

The flipped classroom model is also well-suited for teaching science subjects. In science education, hands-on experiments and inquiry-based learning are essential for developing critical thinking and problem-solving skills. By flipping the classroom, teachers can assign pre-lab readings or videos to students before they come to class. This enables students to familiarize themselves with the scientific concepts and procedures, making the lab activities more meaningful and engaging.

During class time, teachers can provide guidance and facilitate discussions related to the lab experiments. Students can work collaboratively in groups to design and conduct experiments, analyze data, and draw conclusions. The flipped classroom approach in science encourages students to actively participate in the scientific process, fostering a deeper understanding of scientific principles and nurturing their curiosity and scientific thinking skills.

Language Arts

In language arts, the flipped classroom model can enhance students' reading comprehension, writing, and critical analysis skills. Teachers can assign pre-reading activities, such as reading passages or literary texts, to students before class. This allows students to familiarize themselves with the content and develop their own initial interpretations and questions.

During class time, teachers can facilitate discussions and guide students in analyzing the text in-depth. Students can engage in interactive activities, such as group discussions, debates, or collaborative writing exercises, to deepen their understanding of the text and strengthen their communication skills. The flipped classroom approach in language arts encourages students to actively engage with the material and develop their interpretation and critical thinking skills, fostering a love for literature and effective communication.

Social Studies

The flipped classroom model can be applied to social studies to foster a deeper understanding of historical events, cultural phenomena, and social issues. Teachers can assign pre-class readings or videos that provide background information and context for the topics to be discussed in class. This allows students to acquire the necessary knowledge and develop their own questions and perspectives.

During class time, teachers can facilitate debates, simulations, or group activities that encourage critical thinking and analysis of historical events or social issues. Students can explore multiple perspectives, engage in discussions, and collaboratively work on projects that deepen their understanding of the subject matter. The flipped classroom approach in social studies empowers students to become active and informed citizens by developing their research, analytical, and critical thinking skills.

Physical Education

The flipped classroom model can even be applied in physical education (PE) classes to enhance students' understanding of fitness concepts and promote healthy living. Teachers can assign pre-class videos or articles that cover topics such as nutrition, exercise techniques, or specific sports skills. This allows students to gain knowledge about personal health and fitness outside of the PE class.

During class time, teachers can focus on engaging students in physical activities, sports, or fitness challenges. By providing a foundation of knowledge beforehand, students can participate more actively and make informed choices about their physical activities. The flipped classroom approach in physical education helps students develop a lifelong commitment to physical fitness by providing a balance between theoretical knowledge and practical application.

In conclusion, the flipped classroom model has proven to be a versatile and effective instructional approach in various subject areas. By leveraging technology and providing students with pre-class materials, teachers can create engaging and interactive learning experiences inside the classroom. Whether it's mathematics, science, language arts, social studies, or physical education, the flipped classroom approach promotes active learning, critical thinking, and collaboration, preparing students for success in different disciplines.

Future directions of the flipped classroom

The flipped classroom model has gained significant popularity in recent years, offering a more student-centered approach to learning. As technology continues to advance and pedagogical strategies evolve, the future of the flipped classroom holds great potential for further enhancement and innovation. In this section, we will explore some of the future directions that the flipped classroom could take.

1. Integration of Augmented Reality (AR) and Virtual Reality (VR)

One exciting direction for the flipped classroom is the integration of Augmented Reality (AR) and Virtual Reality (VR) technologies. These immersive technologies can provide students with an enriched learning experience by enabling them to explore virtual worlds, manipulate digital objects, and engage in realistic simulations.

For example, in a science class, students can use AR to visualize complex concepts, such as the human anatomy, by overlaying virtual 3D models onto real-world objects. Similarly, VR can transport students to historical events, allowing them to experience significant moments firsthand. By incorporating AR and VR into the flipped classroom, students can engage with content in a more interactive and experiential way.

2. Adaptive Learning and Personalized Instruction

Another future direction for the flipped classroom lies in the integration of adaptive learning technologies. Adaptive learning systems use data and analytics to tailor instruction and learning resources to meet individual students' needs and preferences. By analyzing students' performance and progress data, these systems can provide personalized recommendations for further study and offer targeted remediation when necessary.

In a flipped classroom setting, adaptive learning platforms can be used to deliver pre-recorded video lectures and interactive activities that are specifically designed to address each student's unique learning gaps and challenges. This individualized approach to instruction can maximize students' learning outcomes and help them achieve mastery of the subject matter.

3. Gamification and Game-Based Learning

Gamification and game-based learning are emerging trends in education, and they hold great potential for the future of the flipped classroom. By incorporating game elements and mechanics into the learning process, educators can increase student engagement and motivation.

In a flipped classroom, gamification can be applied to various aspects of the learning experience. For example, teachers can design interactive quizzes, quests, or challenges that students can complete to earn badges or unlock rewards. These gamified elements can promote friendly competition, foster collaboration, and encourage students to take an active role in their learning.

Additionally, game-based learning environments can provide students with opportunities to apply their knowledge and skills in simulated real-world scenarios. For instance, in a business class, students can participate in a virtual business simulation, making strategic decisions and experiencing the consequences of their actions. This hands-on approach can enhance critical thinking, problem-solving, and decision-making skills.

4. Mobile Learning and Microlearning

As the use of mobile devices continues to rise, mobile learning (m-learning) is becoming an integral part of education. The future of the flipped classroom may involve leveraging mobile devices such as smartphones and tablets to deliver content and engage students outside the classroom.

With mobile learning, students can access bite-sized learning modules or microlearning resources that are tailored to their specific learning objectives. These resources can include short videos, interactive quizzes, infographics, or podcasts. By providing flexible and on-the-go learning opportunities, mobile learning can support self-directed learning and enable students to learn at their own pace.

Furthermore, mobile devices can facilitate seamless communication and collaboration among students and between students and teachers. Through mobile apps or online platforms, students can engage in discussions, share ideas, and collaborate on projects, regardless of their physical location.

5. Artificial Intelligence (AI) and Learning Analytics

Artificial Intelligence (AI) and learning analytics have the potential to revolutionize the flipped classroom by providing valuable insights about students' learning patterns, preferences, and progress. AI algorithms can analyze large amounts of data generated by students' online interactions, assignments, and assessments to provide customized recommendations and interventions.

For instance, AI-powered chatbots can assist students in finding resources, answering questions, and providing real-time feedback. These chatbots can be programmed to adapt to students' individual needs and learning styles, providing instant support and guidance.

Furthermore, learning analytics can enable educators to use data-driven decision-making to improve the effectiveness of their instructional strategies. By analyzing students' learning data, educators can identify areas of improvement, adjust their teaching approaches, and provide timely interventions for struggling students.

Conclusion

The future of the flipped classroom is filled with exciting possibilities. The integration of immersive technologies like AR and VR, the adoption of adaptive learning and personalized instruction, the incorporation of gamification and game-based learning, the utilization of mobile learning and microlearning, as well as the integration of AI and learning analytics, can greatly enhance the effectiveness of the flipped classroom model.

By embracing these future directions, educators can create engaging and dynamic learning environments that foster critical thinking, collaboration, and self-directed learning. The flipped classroom, combined with emerging technologies and innovative pedagogies, can truly transform education and prepare students to thrive in an ever-evolving digital world.

Inquiry-Based Learning

Defining inquiry-based learning

Inquiry-based learning is an educational approach that places the learner at the center of the learning process. It is a student-centered and active learning approach that fosters curiosity, critical thinking, and problem-solving skills. In this section, we will explore the key characteristics and principles of inquiry-based learning, its benefits, and how it can be effectively implemented in the classroom.

Key Characteristics of Inquiry-Based Learning

Inquiry-based learning is characterized by the following key principles:

- **Questioning and curiosity:** Inquiry-based learning begins with posing questions and stimulating curiosity in students. Students are encouraged to ask their own questions, investigate problems, and explore topics of interest.
- **Active engagement:** In inquiry-based learning, students actively engage in the learning process. They investigate, analyze, interpret, and evaluate information to construct their own understanding. This active engagement promotes deeper learning and a sense of ownership.
- **Problem-solving and critical thinking:** Inquiry-based learning focuses on developing problem-solving and critical thinking skills. Students learn to analyze and evaluate information, make informed decisions, and draw conclusions based on evidence.

- **Collaboration and communication:** Collaboration and communication are essential in inquiry-based learning. Students work together, share ideas, and engage in meaningful discussions. They learn to listen to others' perspectives, negotiate, and communicate their findings effectively.
- **Reflection and metacognition:** Inquiry-based learning encourages students to reflect on their learning process, evaluate their understanding, and make connections to real-world contexts. Metacognition, or thinking about one's learning, is promoted to enhance self-awareness and self-regulation.

Benefits of Inquiry-Based Learning

Inquiry-based learning offers numerous benefits for students. It promotes deep understanding, critical thinking, and problem-solving skills. By actively engaging in the learning process, students develop a sense of ownership and responsibility for their learning. Some other key benefits of inquiry-based learning include:

- **Improved knowledge retention:** Inquiry-based learning promotes a deeper level of understanding and knowledge retention compared to traditional rote learning methods. When students actively explore and discover information, they are more likely to remember and apply it in different contexts.
- **Enhanced critical thinking skills:** Inquiry-based learning allows students to practice critical thinking skills such as analyzing information, evaluating evidence, and making informed decisions. These skills are invaluable for future academic and real-world challenges.
- **Increased motivation and engagement:** By focusing on students' interests and questions, inquiry-based learning enhances motivation and engagement. Students are more eager to learn when they have a personal connection to the topic and can actively participate in the learning process.
- **Developing lifelong learning skills:** Inquiry-based learning equips students with essential lifelong learning skills. They learn how to ask meaningful questions, seek information, evaluate sources, and solve complex problems independently. These skills are transferable to various domains beyond the classroom.
- **Preparation for the future workforce:** In today's rapidly changing world, the ability to adapt, think critically, and solve problems is highly valued in the workforce. Inquiry-based learning prepares students to thrive in a dynamic and uncertain future by developing these essential skills.

Implementing Inquiry-Based Learning

Implementing inquiry-based learning requires careful planning and design. Here are some key considerations for effective implementation:

- **Designing open-ended questions:** Start by posing open-ended questions that encourage exploration and critical thinking. These questions should be thought-provoking and allow for multiple possible answers and approaches.
- **Providing supportive resources:** Offer a variety of resources, such as books, articles, videos, and websites, to guide students' investigation. These resources should be accessible and age-appropriate, enabling students to gather information and develop a solid foundation.
- **Facilitating student inquiry:** The role of the teacher in inquiry-based learning is that of a facilitator or guide. Teachers should encourage student inquiry, provide guidance when needed, and scaffold the learning process. It is essential to strike a balance between providing support and allowing students to explore independently.
- **Creating opportunities for reflection:** Build in regular opportunities for students to reflect on their learning. Encourage them to think critically about their findings, evaluate their understanding, and make connections to real-world applications. Reflection helps solidify learning and enhances metacognitive skills.
- **Promoting collaboration:** Foster a collaborative learning environment where students can work together, share ideas, and learn from one another. Collaborative projects and discussions allow for different perspectives and promote a deeper understanding of the subject matter.
- **Assessing learning outcomes:** Assess student learning based on the process, skills, and knowledge acquired. Traditional summative assessments may not capture the full scope of inquiry-based learning. Consider using alternative assessment methods, such as portfolios, presentations, and self-assessments, to evaluate students' progress.

Example of Inquiry-Based Learning

To illustrate the concept of inquiry-based learning, let's consider an example in the field of environmental science. The teacher poses the guiding question, "How can we reduce plastic waste in our school?" Students are encouraged to explore the topic, gather information, and propose possible solutions.

In the initial stage, students might brainstorm ideas, conduct research on the environmental impact of plastic waste, and analyze data on the amount of waste generated in the school. They could then reach out to local organizations or experts for further insights and possible partnerships.

During the investigation phase, students might explore various approaches, such as organizing recycling programs, implementing a composting system, or advocating for alternatives to single-use plastics. They collaborate in teams, critically analyze the effectiveness and feasibility of their proposals, and modify their plans accordingly.

In the final stage, students present their findings and proposed solutions to the school community, seeking feedback, and support. Through this inquiry-based learning experience, students not only acquire knowledge about plastic waste but also develop critical thinking, problem-solving, and communication skills.

Resources for Inquiry-Based Learning

Here are some resources that can support the implementation of inquiry-based learning in the classroom:

1. **Project-Based Learning:** Project-Based Learning (PBL) is a related instructional approach that aligns well with inquiry-based learning. The Buck Institute for Education (`https://www.bie.org/`) offers a wealth of resources, project ideas, and professional development opportunities for implementing PBL effectively.

2. **National Geographic Education:** National Geographic Education (`https://www.nationalgeographic.org/education/`) provides a wide range of lesson plans, activities, and multimedia resources that can support inquiry-based learning across various subjects, particularly in the areas of science, geography, and social studies.

3. **Smithsonian Learning Lab:** The Smithsonian Learning Lab (`https://learning.si.edu/`) offers a vast collection of digital resources from the Smithsonian Institution, including curated collections, lesson plans, and interactive tools that can spark inquiry and promote interdisciplinary learning.

4. **Teaching Channel:** Teaching Channel (`https://www.teachingchannel.com/`) is an online platform that

features a wealth of videos, articles, and resources on a wide range of teaching practices, including inquiry-based learning. Educators can find inspiration, lesson ideas, and classroom examples from expert teachers on the platform.

Conclusion

Inquiry-based learning is a powerful educational approach that promotes active engagement, critical thinking, and problem-solving skills. By fostering curiosity, collaborative learning, and reflection, inquiry-based learning prepares students for lifelong learning and equips them with essential skills for the future. Through careful planning, facilitation, and assessment, teachers can effectively implement inquiry-based learning in their classrooms and create a transformative learning experience for their students.

Benefits of Inquiry-Based Learning

Inquiry-based learning is a student-centered approach to education that focuses on promoting curiosity, critical thinking, and problem-solving skills. This approach encourages students to actively engage in the learning process by asking questions, investigating real-world problems, and constructing their own knowledge. Here are some of the key benefits of inquiry-based learning:

1. Enhanced Critical Thinking Skills: Inquiry-based learning promotes higher-order thinking skills such as analysis, synthesis, and evaluation. By actively exploring and investigating topics, students develop the ability to think critically, make connections, and evaluate evidence. This enables them to develop a deeper understanding of concepts and apply their knowledge in new and complex situations.

2. Improved Problem-Solving Abilities: In inquiry-based learning, students are presented with real-world problems or scenarios that require them to use their knowledge and skills to find solutions. Through this process, students develop problem-solving abilities, including identifying and defining problems, generating and evaluating possible solutions, and implementing effective strategies. These problem-solving skills are transferable and can be applied in various contexts beyond the classroom.

3. Increased Engagement and Motivation: Inquiry-based learning places the learner at the center of the educational experience, making it more personally relevant and meaningful. Students are actively involved in the learning process, which increases their engagement and motivation. By pursuing their own

questions and interests, students feel a sense of ownership and responsibility for their learning, leading to greater motivation to acquire knowledge and skills.

4. Deeper Understanding and Retention of Knowledge: In inquiry-based learning, students construct their own understanding of concepts by actively exploring and investigating. This hands-on approach allows for a deeper understanding of the subject matter, as students connect new information to existing knowledge and experiences. Research has shown that inquiry-based learning promotes long-term retention of knowledge, as students are more likely to remember what they have discovered and explored on their own.

5. Development of Research and Information Literacy Skills: In inquiry-based learning, students learn how to effectively search for and evaluate information from various sources. They develop research and information literacy skills by identifying relevant sources, analyzing the credibility and reliability of information, and synthesizing their findings. These skills are essential in the digital age, where the abundance of information requires students to be critical consumers and producers of knowledge.

6. Collaboration and Communication Skills: Inquiry-based learning often involves collaborative work and communication among students. Through working in groups, students learn how to effectively collaborate, communicate, and share ideas. This enhances their interpersonal skills, teamwork abilities, and the capacity to express their thoughts and opinions articulately. These skills are essential for success in the 21st-century workplace and in building positive relationships with others.

7. Fostering a Lifelong Love for Learning: By engaging in inquiry-based learning, students develop a passion for learning that extends beyond the classroom. They become lifelong learners who are curious, self-directed, and motivated to seek knowledge and solutions. Inquiry-based learning encourages students to ask questions, explore new ideas, and pursue their own interests, fostering a love for learning that goes far beyond the completion of specific academic tasks.

Overall, inquiry-based learning empowers students to take ownership of their learning, develop critical and analytical thinking skills, and prepare them for success in an ever-changing world. It promotes active engagement, deep understanding, and lifelong learning habits, making it a valuable approach in contemporary education.

Designing Effective Inquiry-Based Learning Experiences

Inquiry-based learning is an instructional approach that promotes active engagement and critical thinking skills by allowing students to explore and investigate complex problems or questions. In this section, we will discuss the key principles and strategies for designing effective inquiry-based learning experiences.

Principles of Inquiry-Based Learning

Designing inquiry-based learning experiences requires a deep understanding of the principles that underpin this approach. These principles include:

1. Authenticity: Inquiry-based learning should involve real-world problems and tasks that are relevant and meaningful to students. This promotes a sense of authenticity and helps students see the value of their learning.
2. Student autonomy: Inquiry-based learning empowers students to take ownership of their learning by allowing them to define their own questions, make decisions, and take responsibility for their work.
3. Collaboration: Inquiry-based learning encourages collaboration and teamwork, as students often work together to gather information, analyze data, and solve problems. Collaborative learning not only enhances students' social and emotional skills but also fosters a deeper understanding of the subject matter.
4. Reflection: Inquiry-based learning includes opportunities for students to reflect on their learning experiences and think critically about their methods, findings, and conclusions. Reflection promotes metacognition and helps students develop a deeper understanding of the learning process.

Designing the Inquiry-Based Learning Process

To design effective inquiry-based learning experiences, educators should consider the following steps:

1. Engage students: Begin by presenting a compelling question or real-world problem that captures students' interest and sets the context for inquiry. This can be achieved through thought-provoking scenarios, multimedia resources, or relevant case studies.
2. Establish learning goals: Clearly define the learning goals and objectives of the inquiry. This helps guide students' investigations and ensures they stay focused on the desired outcomes.
3. Scaffold learning: Provide students with the necessary background knowledge, skills, and resources to start their inquiry. This can include mini-lessons, demonstrations, readings, or access to relevant experts or online platforms.
4. Encourage exploration and data gathering: Allow students to explore the topic independently or in small groups. This may involve conducting experiments,

gathering data from different sources, or conducting surveys or interviews. Encourage students to document their findings and observations.

5. Support data analysis and interpretation: Guide students in analyzing and interpreting the data they have collected. This may involve using various analytical tools, creating visual representations (such as graphs or charts), or conducting statistical analysis.

6. Foster critical thinking and problem-solving: Help students develop critical thinking skills by encouraging them to analyze the evidence, evaluate different perspectives, and construct well-reasoned arguments or solutions. Provide opportunities for peer discussions, debates, or presentations to further develop these skills.

7. Facilitate reflection and synthesis: Provide time for students to reflect on their learning experience and synthesize their findings. Encourage them to connect their new knowledge to what they already know and consider the implications or applications of their findings.

8. Showcase and celebrate student work: Create opportunities for students to showcase and share their inquiry projects with others. This can be done through presentations, exhibitions, or online platforms. Celebrating student work not only recognizes their achievements but also motivates and inspires other students.

Challenges and Solutions

While inquiry-based learning can be highly effective, it is not without its challenges. Some common challenges include:

1. Time management: Inquiry-based learning requires more time than traditional instructional methods. However, careful planning, prioritizing learning objectives, and providing structured guidance can help manage time effectively.

2. Assessing learning: Assessing student learning in inquiry-based activities can be challenging due to the open-ended nature of the process. To address this, educators can develop rubrics or criteria that align with the learning goals and encourage students to self-assess and reflect on their progress.

3. Student engagement: Maintaining student engagement throughout the inquiry process can be a challenge. To address this, educators can provide ongoing support and guidance, offer choice and autonomy, and incorporate technology tools or simulations to enhance engagement.

4. Access to resources: In some cases, students may face barriers to accessing necessary resources or materials for their inquiry. Educators can address this challenge by providing alternative resources, leveraging online platforms or virtual simulations, or facilitating collaboration among students to share resources.

Example

Let's consider an example of an inquiry-based learning experience in a science classroom. The learning goal is for students to understand the impact of environmental pollution on a specific ecosystem. Here is the step-by-step process:

1. Engage students: Begin by showing students images and videos of polluted ecosystems and ask them to think about the possible consequences of pollution.
2. Establish learning goals: Clearly define the learning goals, such as understanding the effects of pollution on biodiversity, water quality, and ecosystem stability.
3. Scaffold learning: Provide students with background information on the ecosystem and the concept of pollution. This can be done through a mini-lesson, readings, or watching educational videos.
4. Encourage exploration and data gathering: In small groups, students select a specific ecosystem to investigate. They collect data by conducting field observations, analyzing water and soil samples, and conducting interviews with local experts.
5. Support data analysis and interpretation: Students analyze their data and identify patterns or relationships between pollution levels and ecosystem health. They use graphs, charts, or other visual representations to present their findings.
6. Foster critical thinking and problem-solving: Students critically evaluate the impact of pollution on the ecosystem and propose potential solutions or mitigation strategies. They consider different perspectives and evaluate the effectiveness of different approaches.
7. Facilitate reflection and synthesis: Students reflect on their learning experience and consider the broader implications of their findings. They synthesize their knowledge by creating presentations or reports that highlight their research process, findings, and recommendations.
8. Showcase and celebrate student work: Students present their projects to the class or a wider audience, such as parents or community members, through a poster session or a virtual exhibition. This allows them to share their knowledge and inspire others to take action.

By following this inquiry-based learning process, students are actively engaged in their learning, developing critical thinking skills, and gaining a deeper understanding of the impact of pollution on ecosystems.

Resources for Inquiry-Based Learning

Here are some resources that can support the design and implementation of inquiry-based learning experiences:

1. National Science Teaching Association (NSTA): NSTA provides a wide range of resources, including lesson plans, articles, and publications, to support inquiry-based teaching in science.

2. Buck Institute for Education: The Buck Institute offers resources and professional development for designing and implementing project-based learning experiences, which often include elements of inquiry-based learning.

3. The Inquiry Project: Developed by TERC, The Inquiry Project provides curriculum materials and professional development resources to support K-5 teachers in implementing inquiry-based science education.

4. Smithsonian Science Education Center: The Smithsonian Science Education Center offers a variety of free resources and programs that integrate inquiry-based approaches into science education.

5. TeachThought: TeachThought is an educational website that offers articles, blog posts, and resources on inquiry-based learning and other innovative teaching approaches.

Remember that these resources should be tailored to the specific needs and context of your students and subject area.

Exercises

1. Choose a topic of interest and design an inquiry-based learning experience for your students. Describe the steps you would take, the learning goals you would set, and the resources you would use.

2. Identify a current global issue, such as climate change or biodiversity loss, and design an inquiry-based learning experience that addresses this issue. Outline the steps, learning goals, and assessments you would use.

3. Reflect on your own teaching practice and think about how you could incorporate more inquiry-based learning experiences. Identify one subject or topic in your curriculum where inquiry-based learning would be particularly effective and develop a plan to implement it.

4. Explore online platforms or resources that support inquiry-based learning. Choose one resource that aligns with your subject area and evaluate its suitability for your classroom. Write a brief reflection on how you could integrate it into your teaching.

Key Takeaways

- Inquiry-based learning promotes active engagement and critical thinking skills by allowing students to explore and investigate problems or questions. - Designing effective inquiry-based learning experiences requires an understanding of the principles of authenticity, student autonomy, collaboration, and reflection. - The inquiry-based learning process involves steps such as engaging students, establishing learning goals, scaffolding learning, encouraging exploration and data gathering, supporting data analysis and interpretation, fostering critical thinking, facilitating reflection and synthesis, and showcasing student work. - Challenges in inquiry-based learning include time management, assessing learning, student engagement, and access to resources. These challenges can be addressed through careful planning, providing support and guidance, offering choice and autonomy, and leveraging technology tools. - Resources such as professional organizations, curriculum materials, and online platforms can support the design and implementation of inquiry-based learning experiences. - Exercises provide an opportunity for educators to apply the concepts and principles discussed and reflect on their own teaching practice.

Assessing Student Learning in Inquiry-Based Learning

Assessing student learning is a critical component of any educational approach, and inquiry-based learning is no exception. In inquiry-based learning, the emphasis is on students actively engaging in exploration, investigation, and problem-solving. Therefore, assessment should align with the principles and goals of this approach, focusing on evaluating students' abilities to generate questions, conduct research, analyze data, and present their findings.

To effectively assess student learning in inquiry-based learning, educators can employ a variety of assessment methods. Here, we will explore some key strategies and tools that can be utilized:

1. Rubrics: Rubrics are an excellent tool for assessing inquiry-based learning. They provide clear criteria and expectations for students' work, enabling them to understand what is expected and allowing educators to provide objective feedback. Rubrics can be used to assess various aspects of inquiry-based learning, such as the quality of research questions, the depth of investigation, the analysis of data, and the clarity of presentations or reports.

For example, a rubric for assessing research questions may include criteria such as the clarity and specificity of the question, the relevance to the topic, and the feasibility of investigation. Each criterion can be assigned a score or level of achievement, allowing for a comprehensive assessment of student performance.

2. Reflections and Learning Journals: In inquiry-based learning, students are encouraged to reflect on their learning process and document their thoughts and

insights in learning journals. These reflections can provide valuable insights into students' understanding, problem-solving strategies, and growth over time.

Educators can assess these reflections by looking for evidence of critical thinking, metacognitive awareness, and connections to the learning objectives. For example, students may analyze the effectiveness of their research methods, reflect on challenges they encountered, or discuss new insights gained. By reading and responding to these reflections, educators can gain a deeper understanding of each student's learning journey and provide personalized feedback.

3. Presentations and Demonstrations: In inquiry-based learning, students often present their findings or demonstrate their understanding through presentations, exhibitions, or interactive demonstrations. These assessments allow students to showcase their knowledge, communication skills, and ability to articulate complex concepts.

To assess presentations effectively, educators can use criteria such as organization of content, clarity of explanations, use of visual aids, and engagement with the audience. Additionally, peer assessments and feedback can be incorporated to promote collaborative learning and peer evaluation skills.

4. Authentic Assessments and Real-World Applications: Inquiry-based learning focuses on the application of knowledge and skills to real-world scenarios. Therefore, assessments should also reflect these authentic contexts. For example, students could be tasked with solving a real-world problem, conducting fieldwork or experiments, or developing innovative solutions to existing challenges.

Authentic assessments can take various forms, such as designing prototypes, writing reports, developing multimedia presentations, or participating in community-based projects. These assessments provide students with opportunities to apply their learning in meaningful ways and demonstrate their abilities in real-world settings.

5. Peer Assessment and Collaboration: Peer assessment plays a vital role in inquiry-based learning. Engaging students in the evaluation of their peers' work not only promotes a deeper understanding of the subject matter but also cultivates critical thinking and constructive feedback skills.

Peer assessment can be structured using rubrics or checklists, where students evaluate their peers' work based on specific criteria. To ensure fairness and reliability, clear guidelines and training on assessment processes can be provided to students. Peer feedback can be used to enhance the learning experience and encourage collaborative learning, as students gain insights from different perspectives and learn from one another.

In conclusion, assessing student learning in inquiry-based learning requires a multifaceted approach that aligns with the principles of the approach itself.

Through the use of rubrics, reflections, presentations, authentic assessments, and peer collaboration, educators can effectively evaluate students' abilities to engage in inquiry, think critically, and apply their learning to real-world contexts. By implementing these assessment strategies, educators can provide valuable feedback to students, foster their growth, and ensure that inquiry-based learning is impactful and meaningful.

Overcoming Challenges in Implementing Inquiry-Based Learning

Inquiry-based learning is an approach that promotes active and student-centered learning, allowing students to develop critical thinking, problem-solving, and research skills. However, implementing inquiry-based learning in the classroom can be challenging. In this section, we will explore and discuss some of the common challenges teachers may face and provide strategies to overcome them.

Lack of Teacher Guidance

One of the biggest challenges in implementing inquiry-based learning is the shift from a teacher-centered approach to a student-centered approach. Teachers may feel uncertain about how to facilitate inquiry-based learning without being the primary source of information and guidance. To overcome this challenge, educators can:

- Provide clear instructions and expectations for students during the inquiry process.
- Offer scaffolding and support to help students develop research and problem-solving skills.
- Guide students in formulating research questions and identifying credible sources of information.
- Use questioning techniques to stimulate critical thinking and guide students' inquiry.
- Monitor student progress and provide timely feedback to ensure they stay on track.

By providing structure and support, teachers can gradually shift the responsibility to students while still maintaining their role as facilitators.

Limited Time and Resources

Another common challenge in implementing inquiry-based learning is the limited time and resources available in the classroom. Teachers may worry about covering the curriculum and meeting academic standards. To address this challenge, educators can:

- Identify key concepts or topics that lend themselves well to inquiry-based learning and focus on those.
- Integrate inquiry-based activities into existing lessons to save time.
- Use technology to access a wide range of resources and make research more efficient.
- Collaborate with other teachers to share resources and expertise, allowing for more diverse and engaging inquiry experiences.
- Leverage community resources and partnerships to provide students with real-world connections and experiences.

By being strategic and creative with time and resources, teachers can successfully implement inquiry-based learning without sacrificing curriculum coverage.

Student Resistance and Lack of Engagement

Engaging students and getting them excited about inquiry-based learning can be a challenge, especially if they are accustomed to more traditional methods. To overcome this challenge, educators can:

- Clearly communicate the purpose and benefits of inquiry-based learning to students.
- Design inquiry activities that tap into students' interests and real-world problems.
- Incorporate hands-on experiments, field trips, and guest speakers to make the learning experience more engaging.
- Provide opportunities for students to collaborate and work in groups, fostering peer support and motivation.

- Offer choice and autonomy in the inquiry process, allowing students to pursue topics they are passionate about.
- Celebrate and showcase students' inquiry projects to promote a sense of pride and accomplishment.

By making inquiry-based learning relevant, engaging, and student-centered, teachers can overcome student resistance and foster a positive learning environment.

Assessment Challenges

Assessing student learning in inquiry-based activities can be challenging due to the open-ended nature of the process. To address this challenge, educators can:

- Clearly define the learning objectives and criteria for successful inquiry.
- Develop rubrics or scoring guides that align with the learning objectives and provide clear expectations.
- Use a variety of assessment methods, such as presentations, portfolios, and discussions, to capture the multifaceted nature of inquiry.
- Provide ongoing feedback and formative assessment throughout the inquiry process to guide student learning.
- Encourage self-reflection and metacognition, asking students to reflect on their learning and growth during the inquiry process.

By implementing thoughtful and meaningful assessment strategies, teachers can effectively evaluate and recognize students' learning in inquiry-based activities.

Integration with Existing Curriculum

Integrating inquiry-based learning into an already established curriculum can be challenging, especially if there is a heavy emphasis on knowledge transmission and memorization of facts. To address this challenge, educators can:

- Identify opportunities within the existing curriculum where inquiry-based learning can be integrated, such as research projects or problem-solving activities.

- Align inquiry-based activities with academic standards to ensure they address the required content and skills.
- Collaborate with colleagues to create cross-curricular connections and develop inquiry-based units that span multiple subjects.
- Advocate for the importance of inquiry-based learning and its alignment with educational goals and outcomes.

By aligning inquiry-based learning with existing curriculum goals and making a case for its value, teachers can successfully integrate it into their teaching practice.

In conclusion, while implementing inquiry-based learning in the classroom may present challenges, with careful planning, guidance, and support, teachers can overcome these obstacles. By providing structure, using available time and resources effectively, engaging students, addressing assessment concerns, and integrating inquiry-based learning with the existing curriculum, educators can create rich and meaningful learning experiences for their students.

Case studies and best practices in inquiry-based learning

Inquiry-based learning is an instructional approach that promotes active engagement, critical thinking, and problem-solving skills among students. By encouraging students to ask questions, explore topics of interest, and seek answers through investigations, inquiry-based learning fosters a deep understanding of concepts and promotes independent learning. In this section, we will explore some case studies and best practices that demonstrate the effectiveness of inquiry-based learning.

Case Study 1: Science Inquiry in Elementary School

In a 4th-grade science class, the teacher implemented an inquiry-based learning approach to teach the concept of the water cycle. The students were divided into small groups and given the task of investigating the process of evaporation. They were provided with materials such as water, containers, thermometers, and heat sources to conduct their experiments.

The students started by formulating their own research questions, such as "How does temperature affect the rate of evaporation?" and "Does the surface area of the water affect the rate of evaporation?" They designed experiments, collected data, and analyzed their findings. Throughout the process, the teacher acted as a facilitator, guiding the students to develop scientific skills and promoting collaboration among group members.

At the end of the unit, the students presented their findings to the class and discussed the implications of their research. This case study demonstrates how inquiry-based learning can enhance scientific inquiry skills, critical thinking, and collaboration among elementary school students.

Case Study 2: History Inquiry in High School

In a 10th-grade history class, the teacher employed an inquiry-based learning approach to teach about the causes and consequences of World War II. Instead of delivering lectures, the teacher posed open-ended questions to the students, such as "What were the underlying factors that led to the outbreak of World War II?" and "What were the long-term effects of the war on global politics?"

The students were tasked with conducting research, analyzing primary and secondary sources, and presenting their findings through various mediums such as essays, presentations, and debates. They were encouraged to explore different perspectives and critically evaluate historical events.

To facilitate the inquiry process, the teacher provided guidance on research methods, source reliability, and historiography. The students engaged in group discussions, debates, and peer feedback sessions. This case study highlights how inquiry-based learning can promote historical thinking, research skills, and the ability to analyze and interpret historical events.

Best Practices in Inquiry-Based Learning

Based on the case studies and research in inquiry-based learning, here are some best practices to effectively implement this approach:

- Begin with an engaging and thought-provoking question that stimulates curiosity and inquiry. This sets the stage for students to explore the topic further.

- Provide opportunities for hands-on experiences, experiments, and investigations. These activities allow students to actively engage in the learning process and make meaningful connections.

- Foster a safe and supportive learning environment where students feel comfortable asking questions, taking risks, and sharing their ideas. Encourage collaboration, respect for diverse perspectives, and open-mindedness.

- Scaffold the inquiry process by providing guidance and support as needed. Offer resources, research tools, and help students develop critical thinking and problem-solving skills.

- Incorporate technology and digital resources to enhance the inquiry process. Utilize online databases, virtual simulations, and multimedia tools to facilitate research and presentation of findings.

- Emphasize the importance of reflection and metacognition. Encourage students to think about their thinking, evaluate their progress, and make connections between their discoveries and real-world applications.

- Assess student learning through a variety of formative and summative methods. Focus on assessing disciplinary knowledge, critical thinking skills, effective communication, and collaboration.

- Encourage students to become self-directed learners by setting individual or group inquiry-based projects. Provide autonomy and choices, allowing students to pursue their interests within the given framework.

By following these best practices, educators can create a rich and engaging learning environment that fosters curiosity, critical thinking, and a deeper understanding of the subject matter through inquiry-based learning.

Exercises

1. Choose a topic from your subject area and design an inquiry-based learning activity for students at the middle-school level. Clearly outline the research question, materials, and investigation procedures involved.

2. Reflect on your own teaching practices and identify one area where you could incorporate inquiry-based learning strategies. Explain how you would implement these strategies and the potential benefits for your students.

3. Explore an online database or digital resource that can support inquiry-based learning in your subject area. Share the resource with your colleagues and explain how it can enhance student engagement and learning.

4. Form a group with your colleagues and collaborate on designing an interdisciplinary inquiry-based learning project. Consider how different subject areas can be integrated to provide a holistic learning experience for students.

5. Conduct a literature review on the effectiveness of inquiry-based learning in your subject area. Summarize the key findings and propose areas for future research.

Additional Resources

1. Bell, S. (2010). Project-based learning for the 21st century: Skills for the future. The Clearing House, 83(2), 39-43.

2. Kolodner, J. L., Camp, P. J., Crismond, D., Fasse, B., Gray, J., Holbrook, J., & Ryan, M. (2003). Problem-based learning meets case-based reasoning in the middle-school science classroom: Putting Learning by DesignTM into practice. Journal of the Learning Sciences, 12(4), 495-547.

3. National Research Council. (2012). Education for Life and Work: Developing Transferable Knowledge and Skills in the 21st Century. National Academies Press.

4. Sinatra, G. M., Kienhues, D., & Reyna, V. F. (Eds.). (2012). The Cambridge Handbook of the Learning Sciences. Cambridge University Press.

5. Wiggins, G. P., & McTighe, J. (2005). Understanding by Design. ASCD.

These resources provide further insights into inquiry-based learning and offer practical strategies for implementation in different subject areas.

Incorporating Technology in Inquiry-Based Learning

Inquiry-based learning is an approach to education that focuses on fostering students' curiosity, critical thinking, and problem-solving skills. It encourages students to ask questions, investigate topics of interest, and explore possible solutions through research and experimentation. By incorporating technology into inquiry-based learning, educators can enhance students' learning experiences and provide them with new tools and resources to support their investigations.

Benefits of Technology in Inquiry-Based Learning

The integration of technology in inquiry-based learning offers several benefits to both students and educators. Here are some key advantages:

1. Access to Information: Technology provides students with instant access to a vast amount of information and resources. Online databases, digital libraries, and educational websites offer a wealth of information that students can explore to deepen their understanding of the topics they are investigating.

2. Authentic Research Opportunities: Technology enables students to engage in authentic research experiences. They can conduct online surveys, interviews, or experiments, collect and analyze data using digital tools, and collaborate with experts or professionals in the field through virtual platforms.

3. Multimedia Presentations: Technology allows students to present their findings in engaging and creative ways. They can create multimedia presentations,

videos, or animations to communicate their ideas effectively. This helps develop their communication and digital literacy skills.

4. Collaboration and Communication: Technology tools facilitate collaboration and communication among students. Online platforms, such as discussion forums or collaborative document editors, enable students to share ideas, exchange feedback, and work together on projects, regardless of their physical location.

5. Real-World Connections: Technology can help students make connections between their inquiries and real-world contexts. Virtual simulations, interactive models, or augmented reality applications can provide students with immersive experiences that bridge the gap between theory and practice.

Examples of Technology Integration

Here are a few examples of how technology can be integrated into inquiry-based learning:

1. Virtual Labs: Instead of traditional science labs, virtual labs can provide students with interactive simulations and experiments. They can manipulate variables, gather data, and observe outcomes in a safe and cost-effective environment.

2. Online Research Tools: Students can use online research tools, such as databases, search engines, or academic journals, to find reliable and up-to-date information on their chosen topics. Educators can guide them in selecting appropriate sources and evaluating the credibility of online information.

3. Collaborative Digital Platforms: Educators can incorporate collaborative digital platforms, like Google Docs or Microsoft Teams, to facilitate group work and peer feedback. Students can work together on shared documents, provide comments and suggestions, and collaborate in real-time.

4. Data Visualization Tools: Students can use data visualization tools, such as graphs, charts, or infographics, to analyze and present their findings visually. These tools can help them identify patterns, trends, or relationships in the data they collect during their inquiries.

5. Online Communication Platforms: Educators can implement online communication platforms, such as discussion boards or video conferencing tools, to facilitate student engagement and interaction. Students can engage in online discussions, share their progress, seek advice, and receive support from their peers or educators.

Challenges and Considerations

While incorporating technology in inquiry-based learning offers numerous benefits, there are also challenges and considerations that educators need to address:

1. Digital Divide: Access to technology and the internet may vary among students, leading to inequalities in their learning experiences. Educators should ensure equitable access to technology resources and support students who may have limited or no access outside the classroom.

2. Digital Literacy: Students need to develop digital literacy skills to effectively navigate and evaluate online resources. Educators should provide guidance on how to critically evaluate information, cite sources, and use technology ethically.

3. Information Overload: The vast amount of information available online can be overwhelming for students. Educators should guide students in conducting focused searches, selecting relevant information, and distinguishing reliable sources from misinformation.

4. Technological Downtime and Technical Issues: Technology can sometimes be unreliable, leading to downtime or technical issues. Educators should have contingency plans in place and be prepared to switch to alternative teaching strategies or resources if necessary.

Best Practices and Strategies

To effectively incorporate technology in inquiry-based learning, educators can consider the following best practices and strategies:

1. Purposeful Integration: Select technology tools and resources that align with the learning goals and objectives of the inquiry. Ensure that technology enhances and supports the inquiry process, rather than being used for the sake of using technology.

2. Scaffolded Learning: Provide guidance and support to students as they navigate and use technology tools. Gradually release responsibility to students, allowing them to become more independent in their technological skills and decision-making.

3. Digital Citizenship Education: Integrate digital citizenship education into the inquiry process. Teach students about responsible and ethical technology use, including topics such as online safety, privacy, copyright, and respectful online communication.

4. Ongoing Assessment: Continuously assess students' technological skills, as well as their inquiry process and outcomes. Provide timely feedback and offer

opportunities for students to reflect on their use of technology and make improvements.

5. Professional Development: Support educators in developing their own technological skills and pedagogical strategies for integrating technology in inquiry-based learning. Offer professional development opportunities, collaborative learning communities, and resources to help educators stay updated with the latest technologies and teaching practices.

Conclusion

Incorporating technology in inquiry-based learning can enrich students' learning experiences, enhance their critical thinking skills, and provide them with authentic opportunities for research and exploration. By leveraging technology tools and resources effectively, educators can empower students to become lifelong learners, capable of navigating the digital world and addressing real-world problems through inquiry and discovery.

Collaborative inquiry-based learning

Collaborative inquiry-based learning is a powerful educational approach that promotes active engagement, critical thinking, and problem-solving skills in students. This section will explore the principles, benefits, challenges, and strategies for implementing collaborative inquiry-based learning in the classroom.

Principles of Collaborative Inquiry-Based Learning

Collaborative inquiry-based learning is rooted in constructivist theories of learning, which emphasize the active construction of knowledge through social interaction and meaningful experiences. The principles of collaborative inquiry-based learning include:

1. Active engagement: Students actively participate in the learning process through questioning, investigating, and exploring ideas together with their peers.

2. Shared responsibility: Students take joint responsibility for their own learning and the learning of their peers, fostering a sense of ownership and accountability.

3. Social interaction: Collaboration and communication among students are essential for sharing ideas, perspectives, and insights, leading to deeper understanding and knowledge construction.

4. Inquiry-driven approach: Students engage in authentic and open-ended inquiries to explore complex problems, generate hypotheses, and seek evidence to support their ideas.

5. Reflection and metacognition: Students reflect on their learning processes, self-assess their understanding, and identify areas for further investigation and improvement.

Benefits of Collaborative Inquiry-Based Learning

Collaborative inquiry-based learning offers numerous benefits for students, including:

1. Enhanced critical thinking skills: By engaging in collaborative problem-solving activities, students learn to analyze information, evaluate evidence, and develop reasoned arguments.

2. Improved communication and teamwork: Collaborative learning fosters effective communication and teamwork skills, promoting respectful dialogue, active listening, and the ability to work collaboratively towards a common goal.

3. Deeper understanding: Through discussions and interactions with peers, students gain multiple perspectives, which leads to a deeper understanding of the subject matter.

4. Increased motivation and engagement: Collaboration fosters an inclusive and supportive learning environment, creating a sense of belonging and intrinsic motivation among students.

5. Preparation for real-world challenges: Collaborative inquiry-based learning equips students with the skills and mindset necessary to navigate complex challenges and work collaboratively in professional and personal contexts.

Challenges of Collaborative Inquiry-Based Learning

Implementing collaborative inquiry-based learning may present some challenges, which teachers must address to ensure successful implementation. These challenges include:

1. Managing group dynamics: Group work can sometimes face issues related to unequal participation, conflicts, or dominant personalities. Teachers need to facilitate the process by setting clear expectations, providing guidance, and creating strategies to ensure equal participation and respectful collaboration.

2. Assessing individual contributions: Assessing individual learning and contributions within a collaborative setting can be challenging. Teachers should

design assessments that measure both individual growth and the group's collective outcome, using a combination of individual and group assessments.

3. Time management: Collaborative inquiry-based learning requires adequate time for discussions, investigations, and reflection. Teachers must plan their lessons effectively to ensure sufficient time for deep engagement and reflection.

4. Different learning styles and abilities: Students have diverse learning styles and abilities. Teachers should design collaborative activities that accommodate different learning preferences and provide necessary support to ensure equitable participation and learning outcomes.

Strategies for Implementing Collaborative Inquiry-Based Learning

To successfully implement collaborative inquiry-based learning, teachers can employ the following strategies:

1. Establish clear expectations: Clearly communicate the goals, procedures, and expected outcomes for collaborative inquiry-based learning activities. This helps students understand their role and responsibilities within the group.

2. Scaffold the process: Provide students with structure and support to guide their collaborative inquiry process. This may include providing guiding questions, providing resources, or modeling effective collaboration strategies.

3. Foster a supportive learning environment: Create a safe and inclusive learning environment where students feel comfortable sharing their ideas, taking risks, and learning from each other. Encourage mutual respect, active listening, and constructive feedback.

4. Monitor and facilitate group dynamics: Observe the group interactions and provide guidance and support as needed to ensure equal participation, respectful communication, and effective collaboration.

5. Integrate technology tools: Utilize technology tools such as online collaborative platforms, discussion forums, or shared documents to facilitate communication, information sharing, and collaboration among students.

6. Provide formative feedback: Regularly provide feedback on students' collaborative processes, contributions, and group outcomes. This feedback helps students reflect on their learning and improve their collaborative skills.

7. Reflect on the learning process: Encourage students to reflect on their collaborative experiences, identify what worked well, and suggest improvements for future collaborations. Reflection promotes metacognition and deepens understanding of the inquiry process.

Example: Collaborative Inquiry-Based Learning in Science Education

In a high school science classroom, collaborative inquiry-based learning can be implemented to investigate a complex scientific concept, such as climate change. Students form small groups and engage in inquiry-driven investigations to explore the causes, impacts, and potential solutions to climate change.

The teacher introduces the topic and provides relevant resources, such as articles, videos, and data sets, to support students' exploration. Each group conducts investigations, collects data, and analyzes findings collaboratively. They use their collective knowledge to create presentations or reports that communicate their understanding and propose actions to mitigate climate change.

Throughout the process, the teacher facilitates group discussions, provides guidance on data analysis and interpretation, and encourages critical thinking and reflection. The teacher also assesses students' individual understanding through individual reflections, quizzes, or presentations.

This collaborative inquiry-based learning experience allows students to develop scientific inquiry skills, deepen their understanding of climate change, and work collaboratively towards meaningful solutions. It also promotes critical thinking, communication, and teamwork skills essential for scientific inquiry and real-world problem-solving.

Resources for Collaborative Inquiry-Based Learning

Teachers can utilize various resources to support the implementation of collaborative inquiry-based learning in the classroom. Some recommended resources include:

1. Project-Based Learning Checklists: Checklists or rubrics that outline the key components of collaborative inquiry-based learning projects can help students stay focused and meet the desired learning outcomes.

2. Online Collaboration Tools: Platforms like Google Docs, Microsoft Teams, or Padlet enable students to collaborate online, share ideas, and co-create content in real-time.

3. Collaboration Support Materials: Printable resources, such as role cards, discussion prompts, or graphic organizers, can assist students in effective collaboration and inquiry.

4. Professional Development Opportunities: Workshops, webinars, or online courses on collaborative inquiry-based learning offer teachers the chance to enhance their instructional practices and gain new insights and strategies.

5. Research Articles and Books: Reading research articles and books on collaborative learning and inquiry-based instruction can deepen teachers'

understanding of the theoretical underpinnings and practical applications of this approach.

Overall, collaborative inquiry-based learning is a powerful approach that enhances critical thinking skills, promotes collaboration, and cultivates a deep understanding of subject matter. By implementing effective strategies and addressing potential challenges, teachers can create engaging and transformative educational experiences for their students.

Inquiry-based Learning in Different Subject Areas

Inquiry-based learning is a teaching and learning approach that emphasizes the importance of student inquiry, investigation, and discovery. It involves posing questions, conducting investigations, and seeking answers to develop knowledge and understanding. While inquiry-based learning is applicable to all subject areas, its implementation may vary depending on the specific discipline. In this section, we will explore how inquiry-based learning can be incorporated in different subject areas, highlighting its benefits, challenges, and strategies for effective implementation.

Science

Inquiry-based learning is particularly well-suited for science education as it aligns with the nature of scientific inquiry. In a science classroom, students can engage in hands-on experiments, data collection, and analysis to investigate scientific phenomena. They can formulate research questions, design experiments, and draw conclusions based on evidence and observations.

For example, in a biology class, students can explore the effects of different environmental factors on the growth of plants. They can design experiments to test variables such as light intensity, temperature, or soil composition, and analyze the data to identify patterns and relationships. Through this process, students not only develop a deeper understanding of concepts but also enhance their critical thinking and problem-solving skills.

One of the challenges in implementing inquiry-based learning in science is the availability of resources and laboratory equipment. However, teachers can overcome this challenge by integrating virtual simulations or using alternative materials that are readily accessible. Additionally, providing guidance and scaffolding during the inquiry process can support students in developing inquiry skills and scientific reasoning.

Mathematics

Inquiry-based learning can also be applied to mathematics education, promoting a deeper understanding of mathematical concepts and problem-solving skills. In a mathematics classroom, students can engage in investigations and explore patterns, relationships, and real-world applications of mathematical principles.

For instance, in a geometry class, students can investigate the properties of different shapes and their relationships. They can explore the concept of symmetry through hands-on activities, such as creating symmetrical patterns using reflective materials or designing tessellations. By engaging in these inquiries, students develop spatial reasoning, logical thinking, and mathematical communication skills.

One challenge of inquiry-based learning in mathematics is the balance between student exploration and the coverage of curriculum content. Teachers need to carefully design inquiry activities that align with the learning objectives and provide support to ensure students are making progress towards mastery of mathematical concepts.

Social Studies

Inquiry-based learning is highly applicable to social studies, as it encourages students to critically examine historical events, societal issues, and diverse perspectives. In a social studies classroom, students can engage in research, analyze primary and secondary sources, and construct arguments based on evidence.

For example, in a history class, students can investigate a particular time period or an event to understand its causes, consequences, and broader historical context. They can analyze primary sources such as letters, photographs, or speeches, and draw connections between different events to form a comprehensive understanding. Through these inquiries, students develop historical thinking skills, such as analyzing sources, constructing narratives, and interpreting multiple perspectives.

However, implementing inquiry-based learning in social studies may require addressing sensitive or controversial topics. Teachers must create a safe and inclusive learning environment where students feel comfortable discussing different viewpoints and engaging in respectful dialogue.

Language Arts

Inquiry-based learning can also be integrated into language arts instruction to foster critical thinking, communication, and creativity. In a language arts classroom, students can engage in inquiry to explore literary themes, analyze texts, and develop their writing skills.

For instance, in an English literature class, students can engage in an inquiry project where they investigate a specific theme or motif across different texts. They can analyze the use of symbolism, character development, or narrative techniques in different works of literature and present their findings through oral presentations, written essays, or creative projects. Through this process, students develop close reading skills, literary analysis, and effective communication.

One challenge in implementing inquiry-based learning in language arts is providing guidance and scaffolding to support students in their research and analysis. Teachers can provide models, frameworks, and clear evaluation criteria to help students navigate the inquiry process and develop their independent thinking and critical analysis skills.

In summary, inquiry-based learning can be effectively implemented across various subject areas. Whether it is in science, mathematics, social studies, or language arts, inquiry-based learning promotes deeper understanding, critical thinking, and problem-solving skills. However, teachers must carefully plan and scaffold the inquiry process to ensure students are engaged, supported, and making meaningful connections between their inquiries and the subject matter.

Future directions of inquiry-based learning

Inquiry-based learning has gained significant momentum in education due to its ability to foster critical thinking, problem-solving skills, and a deep understanding of concepts. As education continues to evolve, it is important to explore the future directions of inquiry-based learning and how it can be enhanced to meet the emerging needs of students and society. This section will discuss some key trends and advancements that can shape the future of inquiry-based learning.

Trend 1: Integration of technology

Technology has become an integral part of education, and its integration in inquiry-based learning holds great potential. In the future, we can expect to see more sophisticated tools and platforms that support inquiry-based learning experiences. For example, virtual and augmented reality technologies can immerse students in realistic and interactive learning environments, allowing them to explore scientific phenomena, historical events, or complex concepts in a hands-on manner. These technologies can provide students with unique opportunities to develop investigative skills and gain a deep understanding of the subject matter.

Moreover, artificial intelligence (AI) can play a pivotal role in inquiry-based learning by providing personalized guidance and feedback to students. AI-powered virtual assistants can help students formulate research questions, suggest relevant resources, and facilitate the data analysis process. This integration of technology can not only enhance the efficiency and effectiveness of inquiry-based learning but also make it more accessible and inclusive for diverse learners.

Trend 2: Authentic and real-world connections

Inquiry-based learning has always emphasized the connection between classroom learning and real-world applications. As we look to the future, there will be an increased emphasis on authentic learning experiences that allow students to address real-world problems and challenges. This can involve partnerships with local businesses, community organizations, and government agencies to provide students with meaningful opportunities to apply their knowledge and skills.

For instance, students may engage in community-based research projects, where they work collaboratively with experts and community members to address environmental issues, social justice concerns, or technological innovations. By engaging in authentic inquiry, students develop a sense of agency and purpose, as they understand the value and impact of their learning beyond the classroom.

Trend 3: Interdisciplinary and cross-curricular approaches

As the boundaries between disciplines continue to blur, future inquiry-based learning will increasingly adopt interdisciplinary and cross-curricular approaches. This means that students will have opportunities to explore connections between different subject areas, fostering a holistic understanding of complex problems and phenomena.

For example, a science inquiry project may involve elements of mathematics, language arts, and social sciences, allowing students to make connections across multiple disciplines. This interdisciplinary approach can enhance students' critical thinking skills, as they learn to analyze problems from different perspectives and integrate diverse knowledge and skills.

Trend 4: Global and cultural perspectives

Inquiry-based learning can also play a crucial role in preparing students for a globally connected world. The future of inquiry-based learning will highlight the importance of global and cultural perspectives, where students engage in investigations that explore different cultural, social, and environmental contexts.

Through global collaborations and virtual exchanges, students can investigate global issues, compare and contrast cultural practices, and develop empathy and intercultural competencies. This global perspective fosters a sense of interconnectedness and prepares students to be active and responsible global citizens.

Trend 5: Assessment for learning

Traditional assessment methods may not be well-aligned with the principles of inquiry-based learning, where the focus is on the process rather than just the end product. In the future, there will be a shift towards assessment approaches that align with the overarching goals of inquiry-based learning.

Assessment for learning, also known as formative assessment, will take center stage in evaluating students' progress and providing timely feedback. This can involve the use of technology-enhanced assessment tools, such as online quizzes, simulations, and multimedia presentations, to capture the multifaceted nature of students' inquiry processes and outcomes. By providing continuous feedback and opportunities for reflection, assessment for learning can support students' metacognitive development and improve their inquiry skills.

Conclusion

The future of inquiry-based learning looks promising, with the integration of technology, emphasis on authentic and real-world connections, adoption of interdisciplinary approaches, focus on global and cultural perspectives, and the transformation of assessment practices. These trends will not only enhance the effectiveness of inquiry-based learning but also ensure its relevance and impact in preparing students for the challenges of the future. As educators, it is crucial to embrace these future directions and continually innovate our instructional practices to provide students with meaningful and engaging inquiry-based learning experiences.

Problem-Based Learning

Defining Problem-Based Learning

Problem-based learning (PBL) is an instructional approach that centers on addressing real-world problems and challenges. In PBL, students actively engage in investigating and solving complex, authentic problems, thereby developing their critical thinking, problem-solving, and collaboration skills. This section will provide a comprehensive definition of PBL, highlight its key features, and explain the principles that guide its implementation.

Key Features of Problem-Based Learning

Problem-based learning incorporates several key features that distinguish it from traditional instructional approaches. These features include:

1. Real-world problems: PBL tasks are designed to reflect real-world issues or challenges that students might encounter in their future professions. These problems are often interdisciplinary in nature, requiring students to draw from multiple subject areas to develop solutions.

2. Student-centered inquiry: In PBL, students take ownership of their learning by actively exploring the problem, asking questions, and seeking relevant information. They are encouraged to identify knowledge gaps and develop strategies to acquire the necessary knowledge and skills to address the problem.

3. Collaborative learning: PBL emphasizes collaboration and teamwork. Students work in small groups to analyze the problem, propose solutions, and present their findings. This collaboration enhances their communication, negotiation, and interpersonal skills.

4. Authentic assessment: Instead of relying solely on traditional tests and exams, PBL uses authentic assessments to evaluate students' knowledge and skills. These assessments may include presentations, reports, portfolios, and performance-based tasks that demonstrate their ability to apply their knowledge to real-world problems.

Principles of Problem-Based Learning

There are several principles that guide the implementation of problem-based learning:

1. Learning through solving problems: PBL places problem-solving at the center of the learning experience. By actively engaging with real-world problems, students develop a deep understanding of the subject matter and acquire critical thinking and problem-solving skills.

2. Student autonomy and responsibility: PBL promotes student autonomy and responsibility for their learning. Students are encouraged to set their own learning goals, determine the strategies they will use to solve the problem, and reflect on their learning process.

3. Facilitator role of the teacher: In PBL, the teacher acts as a facilitator rather than a provider of knowledge. The teacher guides and supports students throughout

the learning process, helping them develop essential skills such as problem-solving, critical thinking, and self-direction.

4. Integration of disciplines: PBL encourages the integration of knowledge from different subject areas. By addressing interdisciplinary problems, students gain a holistic understanding of complex issues and develop the ability to draw connections between different fields of study.

5. Reflection and metacognition: PBL emphasizes reflection and metacognition, enabling students to think about their thinking and learning process. Through reflection, students gain insights into their strengths and weaknesses, allowing them to make informed decisions for future learning.

Example and Application

To better understand the application of PBL, let's consider an example in the field of environmental science. Suppose a group of high school students is tasked with addressing the issue of plastic pollution in their local community. They must analyze the problem, identify its root causes, and propose sustainable solutions.

In this PBL scenario, students will engage in research, data collection, and analysis to understand the impact of plastic pollution on the environment and human health. They may conduct field investigations, interview local community members, and collaborate with experts in the field. Through this process, students will develop a deep understanding of the complex nature of the problem and explore a range of innovative solutions.

As part of their assessment, students might prepare a comprehensive report detailing their findings and proposed solutions. They could also present their recommendations to a panel of experts, community members, and policymakers, showcasing their ability to communicate and defend their ideas effectively.

This example demonstrates how problem-based learning allows students to tackle real-world problems, apply their knowledge and skills, collaborate with others, and develop a deeper understanding of the subject matter.

Advantages and Considerations

Problem-based learning offers various advantages for students and educators. Some of the key advantages include:

1. Development of critical thinking skills: PBL cultivates students' ability to analyze complex problems, think critically, and develop creative solutions. These skills are highly valuable in both academic and professional settings.

2. Authentic and engaging learning experiences: By working on real-world problems, students find relevance and meaning in their learning. This enhances their motivation and engagement, leading to deeper and more meaningful learning outcomes.

3. Collaboration and teamwork skills: PBL promotes collaboration and teamwork, enabling students to develop effective communication and interpersonal skills. These skills are essential for success in the workplace and in life.

4. Transfer of knowledge and skills: PBL encourages the application of knowledge and skills to real-world contexts, facilitating the transfer of learning to new situations. Students develop a deeper understanding of the subject matter and the ability to apply their knowledge to solve complex problems.

However, there are also some considerations to keep in mind when implementing PBL:

1. Time and resource constraints: PBL requires sufficient time for students to engage in problem-solving and collaboration. Educators need to carefully plan and allocate time to ensure that all learning objectives are met within the available timeframe.

2. Assessment challenges: Assessing student learning in PBL can be complex due to the multifaceted nature of the problems and the diverse range of solutions. Educators need to design authentic assessment methods that align with the learning objectives and provide meaningful feedback to students.

3. Facilitator training: Educators facilitating PBL need appropriate training and support to effectively guide students through the learning process. They must be skilled in asking probing questions, facilitating group discussions, and providing constructive feedback.

Overall, problem-based learning offers a powerful approach to education that prepares students for the complexities of the real world. By engaging in authentic problem-solving experiences, students develop essential skills and knowledge that go beyond memorization and rote learning. They become active learners who can tackle complex challenges with confidence and creativity.

Exercises

1. Identify a real-world problem related to your field of study or interest. Develop a plan on how you would incorporate problem-based learning to address this problem. Consider the learning objectives, resources needed, and assessment methods.

2. Reflect on a challenging problem you have encountered in your life and describe how you approached finding a solution. Analyze your problem-solving

process using the principles of problem-based learning. Identify areas where you could have applied PBL principles more effectively.

3. In a group setting, select a current global issue such as climate change or poverty. Apply the principles of problem-based learning to analyze the issue, propose solutions, and create an action plan for raising awareness or implementing change. Present your findings to the class.

4. Interview a professional in your field of study or interest and ask them how they have applied problem-based learning in their career. Explore the benefits and challenges they have encountered and the impact it has had on their problem-solving skills.

5. Design a problem-based learning activity for elementary school students to introduce them to the concept of recycling. Consider the age of the students, available resources, and how you would assess their learning outcomes.

Note: Remember that the key to effective problem-based learning is to choose authentic, relevant, and challenging problems that stimulate students' curiosity and engage them in critical thinking and problem-solving.

Benefits of Problem-Based Learning

Problem-based learning (PBL) is an approach to education that emphasizes solving real-world problems as a core method of learning. It is a student-centered, inquiry-based pedagogy that fosters critical thinking, problem-solving skills, collaboration, and self-directed learning. In this section, we will explore the various benefits of problem-based learning and why it is an effective method for enhancing learning outcomes and academic excellence.

Promotes Active Learning

One of the significant advantages of problem-based learning is that it promotes active learning. Unlike traditional lecture-style teaching, where students passively receive information, PBL engages students in actively seeking solutions to real problems. This active participation in problem-solving enhances students' understanding and retention of the subject matter. Through hands-on activities, students become active participants in their learning process, leading to a deeper comprehension of the concepts and ideas being taught.

Develops Critical Thinking Skills

Problem-solving lies at the core of problem-based learning. By engaging in real-world problems, students are required to think critically, analyze information, and develop logical reasoning. PBL encourages students to generate hypotheses, gather and evaluate data, and make informed decisions. These critical thinking skills are vital in preparing students for the complex challenges of the modern world and equipping them with the necessary skills to solve problems in various contexts.

Enhances Collaborative Skills

Another benefit of problem-based learning is that it enhances collaborative skills. PBL often involves group work, where students work together to solve a problem. In these collaborative settings, students learn to communicate effectively, share ideas, negotiate and resolve conflicts, and work towards a common goal. Collaborative learning fosters the development of teamwork and interpersonal skills, which are crucial in the professional world. Additionally, students learn from each other's perspectives and diverse backgrounds, broadening their understanding of the problem and increasing their cultural competence.

Improves Problem-Solving Abilities

Problem-solving is a critical skill required in various aspects of life. PBL enhances students' problem-solving abilities by providing opportunities to apply their knowledge to real-world challenges. Through repeated practice, students develop a systematic approach to problem-solving, identify patterns, and find innovative solutions. By engaging with problems that do not have a straightforward answer, students become comfortable with ambiguity and learn to think creatively. These problem-solving skills are transferable to different domains and prepare students for lifelong learning.

Motivates and Engages Students

PBL often presents students with authentic problems that are meaningful and relevant to their lives. This approach creates intrinsic motivation and engages students in their learning. By connecting academic concepts to real-world applications, students see the value and purpose of their education. This motivation drives students to actively participate, take ownership of their learning, and persist in solving complex problems. The dynamic and interactive nature of problem-based learning also keeps students engaged, preventing boredom and fostering a positive learning experience.

Prepares Students for the Future

In an increasingly complex and interconnected world, problem-based learning helps students develop essential skills for the future. By focusing on problem-solving, critical thinking, collaboration, and self-directed learning, PBL prepares students with the skills needed to tackle real-world challenges. These skills are highly valued by employers and in various professions, as they enable individuals to adapt, innovate, and continuously learn throughout their careers. Problem-based learning equips students with a growth mindset, resilience, and the ability to navigate through uncertainty, making them future-ready.

Example: Designing Sustainable Energy Solutions

To illustrate the benefits of problem-based learning, let's consider an example in the context of sustainable energy. Suppose a group of students is tasked with designing an innovative and sustainable energy solution to address the growing energy demands of a local community. The students would need to apply their knowledge of renewable energy sources, environmental impact, and engineering principles to develop a viable solution. Through collaboration, critical thinking, and hands-on research, the students would enhance their understanding of sustainable energy while fostering skills in problem-solving, communication, and project management.

By tackling a real-world problem, students gain a deeper appreciation for the complexities and challenges involved in sustainable energy solutions. They develop a sense of ownership and responsibility towards finding innovative solutions and comprehend the importance of sustainable practices in addressing global energy needs. This example demonstrates how problem-based learning not only improves academic performance but also instills a sense of purpose and empowers students to make a positive impact on the world.

In conclusion, problem-based learning offers numerous benefits to students. It promotes active learning, develops critical thinking and collaboration skills, improves problem-solving abilities, motivates and engages students, and prepares them for the future. By incorporating real-world problems into the curriculum, educators can create transformative learning experiences that foster academic excellence and equip students with the skills necessary to thrive in the modern world.

Designing effective problem-based learning experiences

Problem-based learning (PBL) is a student-centered instructional approach that focuses on real-world problems and engages students in critical thinking, problem-solving, collaboration, and communication skills. In PBL, students actively explore meaningful problems and construct their knowledge through inquiry and discovery.

Principles of PBL

To design effective problem-based learning experiences, it is essential to understand the key principles of PBL. These principles serve as the foundation for creating engaging and authentic learning opportunities for students. The following principles are essential in designing PBL experiences:

1. **Authenticity:** Problems should be authentic, relevant, and relatable to real-world situations. They should challenge students to apply knowledge and skills in meaningful ways.

2. **Open-endedness:** Problems should be open-ended, allowing for multiple perspectives and potential solutions. This encourages students to think critically, analyze information, and develop creative solutions.

3. **Student-driven inquiry:** Students should take an active role in driving their learning. They should ask questions, conduct research, gather and analyze information, and seek solutions independently or collaboratively.

4. **Interdisciplinary connections:** Problems should allow for connections across different subject areas. This fosters the integration of knowledge and skills from various disciplines, providing a holistic learning experience.

5. **Collaboration and teamwork:** PBL promotes collaboration and teamwork among students. Students work together, share ideas, and contribute to the problem-solving process. This cultivates communication and interpersonal skills.

6. **Reflection and metacognition:** Students reflect on their learning experiences, evaluate their progress, and assess their problem-solving strategies. Metacognitive skills such as self-regulation and self-reflection are developed through the process of PBL.

7. **Scaffolding and support:** Students are provided with appropriate support and scaffolding throughout the PBL process. Teachers offer guidance, resources, and feedback to facilitate student learning.

Steps in designing a PBL experience

Designing an effective problem-based learning experience involves a systematic approach that ensures the integration of the principles mentioned above. The following steps can guide the design process:

Step 1: Identify the problem: Start by identifying a problem or scenario that is relevant to the learning objectives and connects with real-life experiences. The problem should be challenging, engaging, and align with the students' prior knowledge and skills.

Step 2: Develop the problem statement: Craft a clear and concise problem statement that outlines the task or challenge students need to address. The problem statement should be open-ended, allowing for multiple possible solutions and encouraging critical thinking.

Step 3: Define learning outcomes: Identify the specific learning outcomes or objectives that students should achieve through the PBL experience. These objectives should align with the curriculum and encompass both content knowledge and skills development.

Step 4: Plan and structure the learning process: Determine how students will approach the problem and outline the stages or phases of the PBL process. This may include conducting research, analyzing data, proposing solutions, and evaluating outcomes. Design activities and resources that support each stage of the process.

Step 5: Facilitate and guide student learning: As the facilitator, provide guidance and support to students throughout the PBL experience. Encourage students to ask questions, seek resources, and collaborate with peers. Offer feedback and prompt reflection to deepen their understanding and metacognitive skills.

Step 6: Assess student learning: Develop assessment strategies that align with the learning outcomes. Use a combination of formative and summative assessments to evaluate students' knowledge, skills, and ability to apply their learning to solve the problem.

Examples of PBL experiences

To illustrate how PBL experiences can be designed, consider the following examples:

Example 1: Sustainable Energy Solutions

Problem Statement: Design a sustainable energy solution for a community that relies heavily on fossil fuels.

Learning Outcomes: 1. Analyze the environmental impact of fossil fuels. 2. Research and apply knowledge of renewable energy sources. 3. Collaborate to develop a proposal for a sustainable energy solution. 4. Evaluate the feasibility and effectiveness of the proposed solution.

Learning Process: 1. Research and discuss the environmental consequences of fossil fuels. 2. Investigate renewable energy sources such as solar, wind, and hydroelectric power. 3. Collaboratively design a sustainable energy plan for the community, considering factors like cost, efficiency, and community impact. 4. Present the proposal and justify the chosen solution. 5. Evaluate the strengths, weaknesses, and potential improvements of the proposed solution.

Assessment: 1. Formative assessments: Research notes, group discussions, and peer feedback on the proposal development process. 2. Summative assessments: Presentation of the sustainable energy plan and a written evaluation of the proposed solution.

Example 2: Addressing Water Scarcity

Problem Statement: Develop an innovative solution to address water scarcity in a region facing drought.

Learning Outcomes: 1. Investigate the causes and impacts of water scarcity. 2. Apply knowledge of water conservation strategies and techniques. 3. Analyze the social, economic, and environmental aspects of potential water solutions. 4. Design a sustainable water management plan for the region.

Learning Process: 1. Research and discuss the causes and consequences of water scarcity. 2. Explore water conservation methods, such as rainwater harvesting and water recycling. 3. Collaboratively analyze the feasibility and potential impacts of different water management strategies (e.g., desalination, water distribution systems, water-efficient agriculture). 4. Design and present a comprehensive water management plan, considering factors like cost, environmental impact, and community engagement.

Assessment: 1. Formative assessments: Individual reflections on research findings, group discussions on potential solutions, and peer feedback on the plan development process. 2. Summative assessments: Presentation of the water management plan and a written evaluation of the proposed solution.

Challenges and considerations in PBL

While problem-based learning offers numerous benefits, there are also challenges to consider in its design and implementation. Some key challenges include:

1. **Time management:** PBL can be time-consuming, requiring careful planning and coordination to ensure that students have sufficient time to engage in the problem-solving process.

2. **Facilitator role:** The role of the facilitator is crucial in PBL. Teachers need to strike a balance between providing guidance and allowing students to take ownership of their learning. Facilitation skills, including effective questioning and feedback techniques, are essential.

3. **Group dynamics:** Collaborative work in PBL may face challenges related to group dynamics. Some students may dominate discussions, while others may be passive. Facilitators must create a supportive and inclusive environment that encourages equal participation and respectful communication.

4. **Assessment strategies:** Assessing student understanding and performance in PBL can be complex. Teachers must develop appropriate assessment strategies that align with the learning outcomes and provide a comprehensive view of student competencies.

5. **Resource availability:** PBL often requires access to resources beyond the classroom. Teachers need to ensure that students have access to relevant information, technology tools, and community resources to support their inquiry and problem-solving process.

Despite these challenges, the benefits of PBL in fostering deep learning, critical thinking skills, and engagement make it a powerful instructional approach worth implementing.

Resources and tools for designing PBL experiences

Designing effective PBL experiences can be facilitated by utilizing various resources and tools. Here are some recommended resources:

- **Buck Institute for Education** (www.bie.org): Provides resources, project examples, and professional development for PBL implementation.

- **PBLWorks** (www.pblworks.org): Offers a wide range of PBL resources, including project ideas, planning tools, and online courses for educators.

- **Google Suite for Education** (edu.google.com): Provides collaborative tools like Google Docs, Sheets, and Slides for students to work together on PBL projects.

- **Design Thinking Toolkit for Educators** by IDEO.org: Offers a human-centered design approach that can be incorporated into PBL experiences.

These resources can provide valuable guidance, examples, and strategies for designing and implementing effective problem-based learning experiences.

Conclusion

Designing effective problem-based learning experiences requires careful consideration of the principles, steps, and challenges involved in this instructional approach. By providing authentic and engaging problems, integrating interdisciplinary connections, fostering collaboration and reflection, and aligning assessment strategies, educators can create transformative learning experiences that promote deep understanding, critical thinking, and real-world application of knowledge and skills. Embracing the principles and techniques of PBL can help prepare students for the challenges and complexities of the future.

Assessing Student Learning in Problem-Based Learning

Assessment is a crucial aspect of problem-based learning (PBL) in order to determine the effectiveness of the learning experience and ensure that students are achieving the desired learning outcomes. In this section, we will explore various methods and strategies for assessing student learning in PBL.

Traditional Assessment Methods

While PBL focuses on active, student-centered learning, traditional assessment methods such as quizzes and tests still have a role to play in evaluating student understanding. These methods can be used to assess foundational knowledge and skills that are essential for engaging in PBL activities.

However, it is important to note that traditional assessments alone may not capture the full range of student learning in PBL. They may overlook students' abilities to critically analyze complex problems, collaborate with others, and apply knowledge to real-world situations. Therefore, it is necessary to supplement traditional assessments with other strategies to obtain a comprehensive understanding of student learning in PBL.

Authentic Assessments

One of the key benefits of PBL is its emphasis on real-world relevance. Therefore, authentic assessments that mirror the types of tasks and challenges encountered in professional settings are well-suited to evaluate student learning in PBL. These assessments can take various forms, such as:

- **Projects:** Students can be assessed based on their ability to develop and present a solution to a real-world problem. The project could involve conducting research, gathering data, analyzing information, and presenting their findings to an authentic audience.
- **Portfolios:** Students can compile a portfolio of their work throughout the PBL process, showcasing their problem-solving skills, critical thinking abilities, and collaborative efforts. Portfolios can include artifacts such as written reflections, research reports, and multimedia presentations.
- **Simulations:** Simulations provide an opportunity for students to apply their knowledge and skills in a realistic and controlled environment. By engaging in simulated scenarios, students can demonstrate their ability to think critically, make decisions, and solve problems within a context that mirrors real-world challenges.

Authentic assessments not only evaluate students' knowledge and skills but also promote deeper learning and engagement. They provide students with opportunities to demonstrate their ability to transfer knowledge to real-world contexts and develop skills that are relevant for future professional endeavors.

Peer and Self-Assessment

In addition to traditional and authentic assessments, peer and self-assessment can be valuable tools for evaluating student learning in PBL. These strategies encourage students to reflect on their own learning processes and provide constructive feedback to their peers.

Peer assessment involves students evaluating the work of their classmates, while self-assessment requires students to critically reflect on their own strengths, weaknesses, and learning progress. Both methods can support metacognitive skills and encourage students to take ownership of their learning.

When implementing peer and self-assessment in PBL, it is important to provide clear guidelines and criteria for evaluation. This ensures that assessments are fair, consistent, and focused on the desired learning outcomes. It is also important to provide opportunities for students to give and receive feedback, as this promotes a culture of collaboration and continuous improvement.

Rubrics and Criteria-Based Assessment

To ensure consistency and fairness in assessing student learning in PBL, rubrics and criteria-based assessment can be utilized. Rubrics provide a clear framework for evaluating student performance by outlining the specific criteria and levels of achievement.

When designing rubrics for PBL, it is important to align them with the learning objectives and the specific skills and knowledge that students are expected to develop through the problem-solving process. Rubrics should include both content-related criteria, such as accuracy and depth of knowledge, as well as process-related criteria, such as collaboration and critical thinking.

By using rubrics and criteria-based assessment, educators can provide students with clear expectations and feedback, facilitating their self-assessment and helping them identify areas for improvement. Rubrics also assist educators in ensuring consistency and fairness in grading across multiple assessors.

Assessment Strategies for Group Work

Collaboration and teamwork are integral components of PBL. Therefore, it is essential to assess not only individual student performance but also the effectiveness of group work and collaboration in achieving the learning outcomes.

To assess group work in PBL, a combination of individual and group assessments can be employed. Individual assessments allow educators to evaluate each student's contributions and understanding, while group assessments provide insights into the overall effectiveness of the collaborative process.

Some assessment strategies for group work in PBL include:

- **Group presentations:** Groups can be required to present their findings, solutions, or recommendations to the class or an external audience. The presentation can be followed by a question-and-answer session to assess individual understanding.

- **Peer evaluations:** Group members can evaluate each other's contributions, highlighting strengths, areas for improvement, and fairness of workload distribution. Peer evaluations can provide valuable insights into individual accountability and collaboration skills.

- **Group reflections:** Groups can engage in reflective discussions or submit written reflections on the group dynamics, challenges faced, and lessons learned. This allows students to critically evaluate their own and their group's performance.

By incorporating these assessment strategies, educators can ensure that individual students' contributions are evaluated, and the effectiveness of collaboration and teamwork is assessed.

Emphasizing Feedback and Reflection

In PBL, feedback and reflection are fundamental to the learning process. Providing timely and constructive feedback is essential for guiding students' progress and helping them improve their problem-solving skills.

Educators should provide feedback on both the content of students' work and the process they employed to arrive at their solutions. This feedback promotes metacognitive awareness and enhances students' ability to assess their own work.

Additionally, incorporating opportunities for structured reflection allows students to analyze their learning experiences, identify strengths and weaknesses, and set goals for future learning. Reflection activities can take various forms, such as group discussions, journaling, or online reflections.

By emphasizing feedback and reflection, educators can support students in developing a growth mindset, fostering continuous learning, and further enhancing their problem-solving abilities.

Conclusion

Assessing student learning in problem-based learning goes beyond traditional assessment methods and requires a comprehensive approach that evaluates students' knowledge, skills, and abilities to solve real-world problems. Authentic assessments, peer and self-assessment, rubrics, and assessment strategies for group work are essential components of assessing student learning in PBL. Additionally, feedback and reflection play a crucial role in supporting continuous improvement and the development of metacognitive skills. By employing these assessment strategies, educators can effectively evaluate the effectiveness of PBL and promote meaningful and transformative learning experiences for students.

Overcoming challenges in implementing problem-based learning

Implementing problem-based learning (PBL) can present several challenges for educators. However, with careful planning and effective strategies, these challenges can be overcome to create a successful PBL experience for students. In this section, we will explore some common challenges in implementing PBL and discuss strategies to address them.

Challenge 1: Resistance from Students

One of the primary challenges in implementing PBL is student resistance. Many students are accustomed to traditional lecture-based instruction, and PBL requires a shift in their role as active participants in the learning process. To overcome this challenge, it is crucial to help students understand the benefits of PBL and create a supportive learning environment. Here are some strategies:

1. **Clear communication:** Clearly communicate the goals, expectations, and rationale for using PBL. Explain how PBL can enhance critical thinking, problem-solving, and collaboration skills.

2. **Provide examples:** Share success stories and examples of previous PBL projects to showcase the value and relevance of this approach. Highlight how PBL can prepare students for real-world challenges.

3. **Gradual implementation:** Start with smaller, well-structured PBL activities to ease students into the process. This allows them to become familiar with the problem-solving and collaboration skills required.

4. **Supportive learning environment:** Foster a supportive and inclusive classroom environment where students feel comfortable taking risks, sharing ideas, and making mistakes. Encourage peer collaboration and provide adequate scaffolding throughout the PBL process.

Challenge 2: Designing Authentic and Engaging Problems

Designing authentic and engaging problems for PBL is essential to capture students' interest and motivation. However, it can be challenging to create problems that are relevant, meaningful, and aligned with the curriculum. Here are some strategies to address this challenge:

1. **Real-world connections:** Ensure that the problems presented to students have real-world connections and are aligned with their interests and experiences. Use examples and scenarios that students can relate to and find meaningful.

2. **Interdisciplinary approach:** Incorporate interdisciplinary elements when designing problems. This helps students see the relevance of the problem across multiple subject areas and fosters a holistic understanding of the topic.

3. **Authentic assessment:** Integrate authentic assessments into the PBL process to motivate students and provide a sense of purpose. Instead of traditional exams, consider using presentations, portfolios, or group discussions to evaluate student learning.

4. **Student voice and choice:** Involve students in the problem design process by giving them the opportunity to provide input or suggest problems related to their interests. This enhances engagement and ownership in the learning process.

Challenge 3: Facilitating Effective Group Work

PBL often requires students to work in groups to solve complex problems collaboratively. However, group dynamics and collaboration can present challenges. To address this, educators can implement the following strategies:

1. **Group formation:** Carefully consider the composition of student groups. Strive for a diverse mix of strengths, backgrounds, and perspectives to foster effective collaboration. Provide clear guidelines on group roles and responsibilities.

2. **Group norms and expectations:** Establish clear expectations for group work, including communication protocols, decision-making processes, and conflict resolution strategies. Promote open and respectful communication within groups.

3. **Facilitator role:** Act as a facilitator and guide during group work. Offer support, ask probing questions, and encourage active participation from all group members. Monitor group progress and intervene when necessary.

4. **Individual accountability:** Ensure that each student has a designated role and responsibility within the group. Set milestones and deadlines for individual contributions to hold students accountable for their work.

5. **Reflection and feedback:** Provide opportunities for students to reflect on their group work experience. Encourage self-assessment and peer feedback to foster continuous improvement and enhance collaboration skills.

Challenge 4: Time Management

Implementing PBL requires careful time management to ensure that all aspects of the project are covered within the allocated timeframe. Here are some strategies to address this challenge:

1. **Project timeline:** Develop a clear project timeline with specific milestones and deadlines. Share this timeline with students to help them plan and manage their time effectively.

2. **Chunking activities:** Break the project into smaller, manageable tasks or activities. Provide guidelines and templates to scaffold students' progress and assist them in organizing their work.

3. **Flexible scheduling:** Allow for flexibility in scheduling to accommodate individual or group needs. Offer opportunities for students to adjust their timelines if necessary, while ensuring that overall project goals are met.

4. **Monitoring progress:** Regularly monitor student progress and provide constructive feedback. Use formative assessments to assess student understanding and identify any gaps or misconceptions.

Challenge 5: Assessment and Evaluation

Assessing and evaluating student learning in PBL can be challenging due to the dynamic and multidimensional nature of the process. Here are some strategies to address this challenge:

1. **Criteria-based assessment:** Design clear assessment criteria and rubrics that align with the project objectives. Communicate these criteria to students at the outset of the project to set expectations and guide their work.

2. **Multiple assessment methods:** Implement a variety of assessment methods to capture different aspects of student learning, including individual and group assessments, formative and summative assessments, and self and peer evaluations.

3. **Feedback and reflection:** Provide timely and constructive feedback to students throughout the project. Encourage students to reflect on their work, identify areas for improvement, and set goals for future learning.

4. **Continuous evaluation:** Emphasize the process of learning rather than just the final product. Encourage students to document their progress, challenges encountered, and strategies employed throughout the PBL experience.

By addressing these common challenges, educators can create a supportive and engaging environment for implementing problem-based learning. By overcoming these obstacles, students can develop critical thinking, problem-solving, collaboration, and self-directed learning skills that will serve them well in their future endeavors. PBL not only enhances academic achievement but also prepares students to tackle real-world challenges with confidence and competence.

Case Studies and Best Practices in Problem-Based Learning

Problem-based learning (PBL) is an innovative pedagogical approach that engages students in active learning by presenting them with real-world problems to solve. By focusing on real-world problems, PBL aims to develop students' critical thinking, problem-solving, collaboration, and communication skills. In this section, we will explore case studies and best practices that illustrate the effectiveness of PBL in different educational settings and subject areas.

Case Study 1: Applying PBL in Science Education

In a high school science classroom, the teacher implemented PBL to teach a unit on environmental sustainability. The students were divided into small groups and given the task of designing a renewable energy solution for their community. Throughout the project, students engaged in research, conducted experiments, and collaborated with experts in the field. They presented their solutions to a panel of community leaders.

This case study demonstrates how PBL can foster interdisciplinary learning, as students were required to apply knowledge from various scientific disciplines to address a real-world issue. It also highlights the importance of collaboration and inquiry-based learning in PBL, as students worked together to find innovative solutions to the problem.

Best Practice 1: Designing Authentic Problems

One of the key elements of successful PBL is the use of authentic, complex problems that reflect real-world challenges. When designing problems for PBL, educators should consider the following principles:

- Relevance: The problem should be meaningful and relatable to students' lives and future careers.
- Complexity: The problem should require students to critically analyze, synthesize information, and think creatively.
- Open-endedness: The problem should have multiple possible solutions and allow for different approaches and perspectives.
- Connection to curriculum: The problem should align with the learning goals and objectives of the curriculum.

By designing authentic problems, educators can create engaging learning experiences that promote deep understanding and skill development.

Case Study 2: PBL in Mathematics Education

In a middle school mathematics classroom, the teacher introduced a PBL unit on financial literacy. The students were tasked with creating a budget and financial plan for a virtual business. They had to consider costs, revenue, profit, and potential risks. Throughout the project, students used mathematical concepts and skills to make informed decisions and solve real-world problems related to finance.

This case study demonstrates how PBL can enhance students' mathematical understanding and its application in practical situations. It also highlights the ability of PBL to promote critical thinking, problem-solving, and financial literacy skills.

Best Practice 2: Facilitating Student Reflection

Reflection is a crucial element of the PBL process. It allows students to analyze their thinking, reflect on their learning experiences, and make connections between theory and practice. Educators can facilitate reflection by:

- Providing structured reflection prompts or journals for students to record their thoughts and observations.
- Incorporating class discussions or presentations where students can share their insights and lessons learned.
- Encouraging students to identify the skills and knowledge they have developed through the PBL experience.
- Guiding students to self-assess their strengths, weaknesses, and areas for improvement.

By incorporating reflection into the PBL process, educators can help students develop metacognitive skills and deepen their understanding of the topics they are studying.

Case Study 3: PBL in Social Studies Education

In a high school social studies classroom, students engaged in PBL to explore the causes and consequences of global migration. The teacher divided the class into small groups and assigned each group a specific region or country to study. Students conducted research, interviewed immigrants, and analyzed historical data to understand the complexities of migration. They collaboratively created multimedia presentations to raise awareness about migration issues.

This case study highlights how PBL can foster empathy, cultural understanding, and global awareness among students. It also demonstrates the power of collaboration and communication skills in PBL, as students worked together to engage with real-world issues and present their findings to an authentic audience.

Best Practice 3: Providing Ongoing Support and Feedback

In a PBL environment, it is essential for educators to provide ongoing support and feedback to students. This support can come in the form of:

- Regular check-ins: The teacher can schedule individual or group meetings to provide guidance, answer questions, and ensure students are on track.
- Formative assessment: Educators can design checkpoints and rubrics to assess students' progress throughout the PBL process and provide timely feedback for improvement.

- Scaffolded resources: Teachers can provide resources, such as reference materials, examples, or models, to support students' problem-solving and critical thinking skills.
- Peer collaboration: Encouraging peer feedback and collaboration allows students to learn from each other and develop interpersonal skills.

By providing ongoing support and feedback, educators can help students navigate challenges, stay motivated, and achieve their learning goals in the PBL process.

In conclusion, case studies and best practices demonstrate the effectiveness of problem-based learning in various educational contexts. By incorporating authentic problems, facilitating reflection, and providing ongoing support, educators can create engaging and impactful learning experiences that promote critical thinking, collaboration, and real-world problem-solving skills. As PBL continues to evolve, educators should embrace its potential to transform education and prepare students for the challenges and opportunities of the future.

If you have any specific questions or need assistance with a particular aspect of incorporating technology in problem-based learning, I would be happy to help.

Collaborative problem-based learning

In this section, we will explore the concept of collaborative problem-based learning (CPBL) and its significance in transformative education. CPBL is a student-centered approach that integrates problem-solving and collaboration skills to enhance learning outcomes. It involves students working together in small groups to solve real-world problems, fostering critical thinking, communication, and teamwork skills. CPBL promotes active engagement, deep understanding, and knowledge transfer.

Principles of Collaborative Problem-Based Learning

CPBL is built on several key principles:

1. **Authentic problems:** Students engage with real-world problems that are relevant and meaningful. These problems are often open-ended, complex, and require higher-order thinking.
2. **Collaboration:** Through teamwork, students learn to communicate effectively, share ideas, and leverage diverse perspectives. Collaboration fosters mutual responsibility, social skills, and the ability to work in interdisciplinary groups.

3. **Problem-solving process:** CPBL emphasizes a structured problem-solving process, which typically involves problem identification, analysis, research, solution generation, implementation, and reflection.

4. **Facilitator role:** The role of the teacher shifts from being a traditional instructor to that of a facilitator. The facilitator supports and guides students' learning process, encourages critical thinking, and monitors group dynamics.

5. **Reflection:** Regular reflection is a crucial component of CPBL. It encourages students to evaluate their problem-solving strategies, reflect on their learning process, and make connections to prior knowledge and real-life experiences.

Implementing Collaborative Problem-Based Learning

To implement CPBL effectively, educators should consider the following guidelines:

1. **Selecting appropriate problems:** Choose problems that are relevant to the students' lives and align with the learning objectives. Ensure that the problems are authentic, open-ended, and challenging enough to stimulate critical thinking.

2. **Creating collaborative groups:** Form groups of 3-6 students to encourage collaboration and ensure diverse perspectives. Consider students' strengths and weaknesses, as well as their cultural and social backgrounds, when forming groups.

3. **Providing clear guidelines:** Clearly outline the expectations, roles, and responsibilities of each group member. Set guidelines for communication, decision-making, and conflict resolution to ensure effective collaboration.

4. **Facilitating the learning process:** Act as a facilitator rather than a lecturer. Guide students through the problem-solving process, ask open-ended questions, provide scaffolding when necessary, and facilitate discussions and knowledge sharing.

5. **Promoting reflection:** Incorporate regular reflection activities to help students make connections between their problem-solving process, acquired knowledge, and real-life applications. This can be done through written reflections, group discussions, or presentations.

6. **Assessing learning outcomes:** Develop appropriate assessment strategies that align with the CPBL approach. Assess both individual and group performance, problem-solving skills, collaboration, and the ability to apply knowledge in real-world contexts.

Benefits of Collaborative Problem-Based Learning

CPBL offers numerous benefits for students, including:

1. **Deep understanding:** CPBL promotes a deeper understanding of concepts and fosters the application of knowledge in real-world scenarios. It enhances critical thinking skills and problem-solving abilities.

2. **Collaboration skills:** Students develop effective communication, teamwork, and interpersonal skills through collaboration. They learn to value diverse perspectives, appreciate different viewpoints, and work towards a collective solution.

3. **Higher-order thinking:** CPBL encourages students to think critically, analyze problems from multiple angles, and generate innovative solutions. It promotes creativity, analytical reasoning, and the ability to think on their feet.

4. **Transferable skills:** The skills gained through CPBL, such as critical thinking, collaboration, and problem-solving, are transferable to various domains of life and future careers. Students become lifelong learners and adaptable problem solvers.

Case Study: CPBL in a Science Classroom

Imagine a high school science classroom where students are learning about environmental conservation. The teacher poses a problem to the class: "How can we reduce plastic waste in our school?" Students form small groups and begin their CPBL journey.

In the problem-solving process, students identify the sources of plastic waste, research eco-friendly alternatives, and design a recycling program for their school. They collaborate by dividing tasks, discussing ideas, and pooling resources. They present their solutions to the class, encouraging feedback and reflection.

Throughout the CPBL experience, students develop a deep understanding of environmental issues, critical thinking skills, and teamwork abilities. They analyze the impact of their solutions, reflect on the challenges faced, and propose improvements for future projects. This collaborative and problem-based approach fosters a sense of ownership and empowers students to become active contributors to their community.

Resources for Collaborative Problem-Based Learning

To facilitate the implementation of CPBL, educators can utilize various resources, such as:

1. Online platforms: Platforms like Google Workspace, Microsoft Teams, or Schoology provide tools for communication, collaboration, and sharing resources among students.

2. Project-based learning resources: Explore project-based learning websites and databases that offer a wide range of authentic problems and project ideas suitable for CPBL.

3. Professional development programs: Attend workshops or online courses that focus on CPBL strategies, facilitation techniques, and assessment methods. These programs can support teachers in effectively implementing CPBL in their classrooms.

4. Collaborative tools: Utilize digital tools like Padlet, Trello, or Slack to facilitate group collaboration, task management, and effective communication among students.

5. Educational apps: Incorporate educational apps that promote collaboration and problem-solving skills. Apps like Tinkercad, CoSpaces, or Scratch enable students to create and share solutions collaboratively.

Caveats and Challenges

While CPBL offers numerous benefits, it also presents some challenges that educators should be aware of:

1. **Group dynamics:** Group work may result in varying levels of engagement, conflicts, or imbalances among group members. Teachers should monitor and support group dynamics to ensure equal participation.

2. **Time management:** CPBL projects may require careful time management to meet deadlines and ensure students have enough time for reflection and the problem-solving process.

3. **Teacher facilitation skills:** Facilitating CPBL requires teachers to adopt a facilitator role and guide students' learning process effectively. Professional development and ongoing reflection can help teachers develop the necessary facilitation skills.

4. **Assessment complexity:** Assessing individual and group performance in CPBL can be challenging. Teachers need to design assessment strategies that accurately measure both collaborative skills and content knowledge.

Conclusion

Collaborative problem-based learning (CPBL) is a transformative educational approach that fosters critical thinking, collaboration, and problem-solving skills. By engaging students in authentic, real-world problems and promoting collaboration, CPBL enhances learning outcomes and prepares students for the challenges of the future. Educators play a crucial role as facilitators, guiding students through the problem-solving process and encouraging reflection. Through CPBL, students become active agents of their learning, developing important skills that go beyond the classroom.

Problem-based learning in different subject areas

Problem-based learning (PBL) is a teaching methodology that emphasizes student-centered learning and encourages critical thinking and problem-solving skills. It involves students actively engaging in real-world problems and collaboratively finding solutions. PBL has gained popularity across various subject areas due to its effectiveness in enhancing students' understanding and application of knowledge. In this section, we will explore how PBL can be implemented in different subject areas to promote deep learning and prepare students for real-life challenges.

Mathematics

PBL in mathematics provides students with opportunities to apply mathematical concepts and techniques to solve authentic problems. For example, students can be presented with a real-life scenario where they need to design a budgeting plan for a family or analyze data to make informed decisions. By exploring such problems, students not only develop a deeper understanding of mathematical concepts but also enhance their analytical and critical thinking skills.

One example of a PBL task in mathematics could be related to financial literacy. Students could be given a budget and asked to solve problems involving budgeting, saving, and investing. They can work in groups to create financial plans, analyze the impact of different financial decisions, and present their findings to the class. This task not only reinforces mathematical skills but also fosters financial literacy and responsible decision-making.

Science

PBL is particularly beneficial in science education as it allows students to engage in authentic scientific inquiry, just like real scientists. Students can explore scientific phenomena, conduct experiments, and analyze data to develop scientific explanations. For instance, a PBL task in biology could involve students investigating the impact of environmental factors on plant growth. They can design experiments, collect data, and draw conclusions based on their findings.

PBL in science also provides an opportunity for interdisciplinary learning. Students can integrate concepts from different scientific disciplines to solve complex problems. For example, they can explore the effects of pollution on an ecosystem by analyzing data from chemistry, biology, and environmental science. This interdisciplinary approach enhances students' understanding of the interconnectedness of scientific concepts and prepares them for real-world scientific challenges.

Social Sciences

In the social sciences, PBL enables students to delve into complex social issues and develop a deeper understanding of societal challenges. For example, in history, students can engage in a PBL task where they analyze primary sources and artifacts to develop historical narratives. They can work collaboratively to investigate the causes and consequences of historical events and present their findings to the class.

PBL can also be effective in subjects like geography, economics, and sociology. Students can explore real-world problems such as urbanization, poverty, or globalization and analyze the underlying social, economic, and political factors. By engaging in PBL, students develop a deeper appreciation for social issues and become more engaged citizens.

Language Arts

PBL in language arts encourages students to actively apply their language and communication skills in authentic and meaningful contexts. Students can engage in PBL tasks such as creating a podcast, writing a persuasive essay, or producing a short film. These tasks require students to research, analyze information, and effectively communicate their ideas to an audience.

For example, students can be tasked with addressing a social issue through a persuasive speech or documentary. They can conduct research, gather evidence, and craft arguments to support their position. This PBL task not only enhances students' language skills but also fosters critical thinking, public speaking, and media literacy.

Arts and Creativity

PBL can also be incorporated into arts education to promote creativity, innovation, and problem-solving skills. In subjects like visual arts, music, or drama, students can engage in project-based tasks that allow them to express their creativity while addressing real-world problems. For example, students can create artistic installations that raise awareness about environmental conservation or compose music that reflects social justice issues.

PBL encourages students to think outside the box, explore different perspectives, and take risks in their artistic expressions. It fosters collaboration and provides opportunities for students to showcase their artistic talents and make a positive impact on their communities.

In conclusion, problem-based learning (PBL) can be effectively implemented in various subject areas to enhance students' understanding, critical thinking, and problem-solving skills. By engaging in real-world problems, students can develop a deeper appreciation for the subject matter and apply their knowledge in meaningful ways. PBL promotes collaboration, interdisciplinary learning, and prepares students for the challenges they will encounter in their future careers.

Future directions of problem-based learning

Problem-based learning (PBL) has gained popularity in recent years as an effective instructional approach that focuses on student-centered learning. By engaging students in real-world problems, PBL promotes critical thinking, problem-solving, collaboration, and communication skills. As we look to the future, there are several exciting directions and opportunities for further development and enhancement of PBL.

Integration of emerging technologies

One promising direction for the future of PBL is the integration of emerging technologies. Technology can provide tools and resources that enhance the problem-solving process and create more engaging and immersive learning experiences. For example, virtual reality (VR) can be used to simulate complex scenarios and enable students to explore and interact with problem situations in a controlled and realistic environment. Augmented reality (AR) can overlay digital information onto the physical world, allowing students to interact with virtual objects and collect data for problem-solving.

Additionally, artificial intelligence (AI) and machine learning can be incorporated into PBL to provide intelligent feedback, personalize learning paths, and assist students in finding relevant resources and solutions. AI-powered chatbots can serve as virtual mentors, guiding students through the problem-solving process and providing support and guidance.

Interdisciplinary and real-world connections

Another future direction of PBL is the emphasis on interdisciplinary learning and making real-world connections. Many of the problems students will encounter in their future careers do not fit neatly into subject-specific categories. Therefore, incorporating multiple disciplines in PBL can help students develop a holistic understanding of complex real-world problems and foster the ability to approach challenges from different perspectives.

Furthermore, connecting PBL to real-world issues and contexts can increase student motivation and engagement. By addressing authentic problems that have relevance beyond the classroom, students can see the practical applications of their learning and understand the impact their solutions can have on the world. This approach also promotes the development of skills such as empathy, ethical reasoning, and global citizenship.

Integration of data-driven decision making

The future of PBL can also benefit from the integration of data-driven decision making. With the increasing availability of educational data and learning analytics, PBL can be enhanced by using data to inform the design and implementation of problems, as well as to assess student progress and performance. By analyzing data on student interactions, collaboration, and problem-solving strategies, educators can gain valuable insights into students' learning processes and provide targeted feedback and support.

Furthermore, the integration of data and analytics allows for adaptive and personalized PBL experiences. By tailoring the level of challenge and support based on individual student needs and preferences, educators can create a more effective and engaging learning environment.

Promotion of lifelong learning skills

In the fast-paced, ever-changing world we live in, the ability to learn and adapt is becoming increasingly important. Therefore, a future direction of PBL is the explicit promotion of lifelong learning skills. PBL can be used not only to teach subject-specific knowledge but also to develop essential skills such as critical thinking, problem-solving, creativity, collaboration, and communication.

Moreover, fostering a growth mindset, which emphasizes the belief that intelligence and abilities can be developed through hard work and perseverance, is crucial for lifelong learning. PBL provides opportunities for students to face challenges, learn from failures, and develop resilience and a thirst for continuous improvement.

Collaborative problem-solving beyond the classroom

Finally, the future of PBL can extend beyond the boundaries of the classroom to engage students in collaborative problem-solving on a larger scale. The advent of technology and the interconnectedness of the world allow for global collaboration and the tackling of complex, global challenges.

By leveraging digital platforms and tools, students can connect with peers from diverse backgrounds and cultures, bringing together different perspectives and expertise to solve problems collaboratively. This approach not only enhances problem-solving abilities but also promotes cross-cultural understanding, empathy, and global citizenship.

In conclusion, the future of problem-based learning is full of exciting possibilities. Integration of emerging technologies, interdisciplinary and real-world connections, data-driven decision making, promotion of lifelong learning skills, and collaborative problem-solving beyond the classroom are all promising directions for the advancement and evolution of PBL. By embracing these future directions, educators can create transformative learning experiences that prepare students for success in an ever-changing world.

Experiential Learning

Defining Experiential Learning

Experiential learning is an educational approach that emphasizes the importance of learning through personal experience and reflection. It is based on the idea that individuals learn best when they actively participate in an experience, analyze it, and then apply their newfound knowledge and skills. This approach is rooted in the principles of constructivism and pragmatism, which highlight the importance of active engagement and the relevance of knowledge in real-world contexts.

In experiential learning, the focus is not only on acquiring knowledge and facts but also on applying that knowledge in practical situations. The goal is to develop a deeper understanding of concepts and skills by actively engaging with them, rather than simply passively receiving information. Experiences can range from hands-on activities, field trips, simulations, internships, community service projects, and other forms of real-world engagement.

Experiential learning is often characterized by the following key principles:

1. Active Engagement: Learners actively participate in experiences, taking on new roles and responsibilities, and applying their knowledge and skills in practical

situations. This active participation fosters a deeper level of understanding and promotes the development of critical thinking and problem-solving skills.

2. Reflection: After engaging in an experience, learners are encouraged to reflect on their actions, observations, and outcomes. Reflection involves analyzing the experience, identifying what was learned, and making connections to theoretical concepts or previous knowledge. This reflection is a crucial component of experiential learning, as it helps to consolidate learning and encourage metacognitive thinking.

3. Application and Transfer: Experiential learning emphasizes the application of knowledge and skills gained through experiences to new and unfamiliar contexts. Learners are encouraged to transfer their learning from one situation to another, demonstrating the ability to adapt and apply their knowledge in practical ways.

4. Collaboration and Feedback: Collaboration with others is often a central aspect of experiential learning. Learners engage in group work, discussions, and feedback sessions to enhance their understanding and learn from the perspectives of others. Collaboration fosters teamwork, communication skills, and the ability to consider multiple viewpoints.

5. Authenticity: Experiences in experiential learning should strive to be authentic and closely aligned with real-world situations. This authenticity enhances the relevance of the learning and enables learners to develop skills and knowledge that are directly applicable to their future careers or personal lives.

Experiential learning has many benefits for learners. It helps to promote a deeper understanding of concepts by providing opportunities for active engagement and application. It also enhances motivation and engagement, as learners are actively involved in the learning process and see the direct relevance of their learning. Experiential learning also supports the development of critical thinking, problem-solving, and decision-making skills, which are essential for success in the 21st century.

However, implementing experiential learning in educational settings can present challenges. It requires careful planning and organization to ensure that experiences are meaningful and aligned with learning objectives. It also requires effective facilitation and guidance from educators to support reflection and transfer of learning. Additionally, providing experiential learning opportunities for all students, including those with disabilities or diverse backgrounds, may require extra considerations and adaptations.

Incorporating technology into experiential learning can also enhance the learning experience. Virtual reality simulations, online collaborative platforms, and interactive multimedia resources can provide immersive and engaging experiences that may not be possible in traditional settings. However, it is important to strike a balance between the use of technology and the authentic, real-world nature of experiential learning.

Overall, experiential learning offers a powerful and effective approach to education that promotes active engagement, deep learning, and the development of practical skills. By providing opportunities for learners to actively participate, reflect, and apply their knowledge, experiential learning prepares them for success in the complex and dynamic environments of the future.

Benefits of Experiential Learning

Experiential learning is a powerful educational approach that involves learning through experiences, reflection, and application. It emphasizes the importance of actively engaging learners in hands-on activities that allow them to explore real-life situations and apply their knowledge in practical contexts. This section will explore the numerous benefits of experiential learning for students.

Enhances Engagement and Motivation

One of the key benefits of experiential learning is that it actively involves students in the learning process, making it highly engaging and motivating. By immersing themselves in real-world experiences and activities, students become active participants rather than passive recipients of knowledge. This active engagement helps to capture students' interest and curiosity, leading to better retention of information and a deeper understanding of concepts.

Promotes Critical Thinking and Problem-Solving Skills

Experiential learning provides students with opportunities to analyze and solve real-life problems, fostering the development of critical thinking and problem-solving skills. Through hands-on activities and real-world challenges, students are encouraged to examine issues from different perspectives, evaluate evidence, and make informed decisions. This helps them to develop their analytical and problem-solving abilities, which are essential skills for success in both academic and professional settings.

Encourages Collaboration and Communication

Experiential learning often involves collaborative activities, where students work together in teams to achieve common goals. This promotes the development of effective communication and teamwork skills, as students learn to share ideas, listen to others, communicate their thoughts clearly, and negotiate conflicts. Collaboration in experiential learning also exposes students to diverse perspectives and encourages inclusive practices, fostering a sense of empathy and understanding.

Increases Retention and Application of Knowledge

Research has shown that experiential learning has a lasting impact on students' retention and application of knowledge. When students engage in hands-on experiences and actively participate in their own learning, they are more likely to remember and apply what they have learned. The practical application of knowledge in real-world contexts helps students to see the relevance and practicality of the concepts they are learning, making the learning experience more meaningful and memorable.

Develops Emotional and Social Skills

Experiential learning not only focuses on academic knowledge but also emphasizes the development of emotional and social skills. Through experiential activities, students learn to manage their emotions, adapt to new environments, and be resilient in the face of challenges. They also have opportunities to interact with peers and mentors, enhancing their social skills, empathy, and ability to work effectively in diverse groups. These emotional and social skills are vital for students' personal growth and success in their future careers.

Prepares Students for the Real World

Experiential learning provides students with a taste of real-world experiences, preparing them for the challenges and demands they will face in their future careers. By engaging in authentic tasks and activities, students develop skills and competencies that are highly valued in the workplace, such as problem-solving, critical thinking, communication, collaboration, and adaptability. Experiential learning also allows students to explore different careers and gain insight into their own interests and strengths, helping them make informed decisions about their future.

Promotes Self-Reflection and Metacognitive Skills

Experiential learning encourages self-reflection, metacognition, and the development of self-awareness. By engaging in reflective practices, students are able to think critically about their experiences, examine their learning process, and identify areas for improvement. Through such self-reflection, students become actively involved in monitoring and evaluating their own learning, leading to greater self-regulation and self-directed learning skills.

In conclusion, experiential learning offers numerous benefits for students, including increased engagement and motivation, the promotion of critical thinking and problem-solving skills, the development of collaboration and communication abilities, improved retention and application of knowledge, the cultivation of emotional and social skills, preparation for the real world, and the fostering of self-reflection and metacognitive skills. By integrating experiential learning approaches into education, we can provide students with a holistic and impactful learning experience that prepares them for success in their personal and professional lives.

Designing effective experiential learning experiences

Experiential learning is a powerful pedagogical approach that promotes active engagement, critical thinking, and the application of knowledge in real-world contexts. It involves providing students with hands-on experiences and opportunities to reflect on their learning, gaining a deeper understanding of concepts and developing essential skills for success in their future careers. In this section, we will explore the key principles and strategies for designing effective experiential learning experiences.

Key Principles of Experiential Learning

Effective experiential learning experiences are guided by a set of key principles that help ensure meaningful and impactful learning outcomes. These principles include:

1. Active Engagement: Students should be actively involved in the learning process through hands-on activities and real-world problem-solving tasks. This promotes a sense of ownership and enhances motivation and interest in the subject matter.

2. Reflection: The opportunity for reflection is essential in experiential learning. Reflection prompts students to think critically about their experiences, analyze their actions, and link them to theoretical concepts, resulting in deeper learning and the ability to transfer knowledge to new situations.

3. Authenticity: Experiences should closely resemble real-world scenarios to provide students with genuine opportunities to apply their knowledge and skills. Authentic experiences foster a sense of relevance and help students understand the practical applications of what they are learning.

4. Collaboration: Experiential learning often involves collaborative activities that encourage teamwork, communication, and the sharing of ideas. Collaborative learning enhances social and interpersonal skills while offering diverse perspectives and fostering a sense of community.

5. Continuous Feedback: Timely and constructive feedback plays a crucial role in experiential learning. Feedback helps students understand their strengths and areas for improvement, enabling them to refine their skills and deepen their understanding.

6. Goal Orientation: Experiential learning experiences should have clear learning goals and objectives. These goals guide students' actions, motivate their efforts, and provide a sense of direction and purpose throughout the learning process.

Strategies for Designing Experiential Learning Experiences

Designing effective experiential learning experiences requires careful planning and consideration of various factors. Here are some strategies to help educators create impactful experiential learning opportunities for their students:

1. Identify Learning Objectives: Begin by identifying specific learning objectives that align with the content and skills you want students to develop. Consider what knowledge, skills, and attitudes students should acquire through the experience.

2. Design Real-World Scenarios: Create real-world scenarios that closely resemble situations students may encounter in their future careers or everyday lives. These scenarios should present authentic problems or challenges that require students to apply their knowledge and skills.

3. Integrate Theory and Practice: Ensure that students have a solid foundation of theoretical knowledge before engaging in experiential learning activities. Integrate theoretical concepts into the hands-on experiences, providing opportunities for students to see the relevance and practical applications of what they have learned.

4. Provide Structured Guidance: While experiential learning encourages hands-on exploration, it is important to provide students with structured guidance and scaffolding. Offer clear instructions, models, and resources to support their learning and help them navigate through the experience.

5. Incorporate Reflection Activities: Integrate reflection activities into the experiential learning process. Provide time and space for students to think critically about their experiences, ask questions, and make connections between theory and practice. Encourage journaling, group discussions, or guided reflection prompts to deepen their learning.

6. Foster Collaboration: Incorporate group activities or projects that foster collaboration and teamwork. Assign roles and responsibilities to encourage active participation and ensure that every student contributes to the collective learning experience.

7. Include Feedback Mechanisms: Provide regular feedback to students throughout the experiential learning process. Offer both formative and summative feedback to help students understand their progress, strengths, and areas for improvement.

8. Celebrate Successes: Recognize and celebrate student achievements and successes during and after the experiential learning experience. This fosters a positive learning environment and motivates students to continue engaging in hands-on learning opportunities.

Example: Designing an Experiential Learning Activity in Biology

Let's consider designing an experiential learning activity in a biology class focused on studying ecosystem dynamics. The learning objective is for students to understand the interconnectedness of organisms in an ecosystem and the impact of human activities on ecological balance.

1. Identify Learning Objectives: The objective is for students to analyze the impact of a specific human activity on an ecosystem and propose mitigation strategies.

2. Design Real-World Scenarios: Students could explore a local park or natural area to observe firsthand the ecosystem they will study. They can collect data on population dynamics, biodiversity, and environmental factors affected by human activities.

3. Integrate Theory and Practice: Before the field trip, students learn about ecological concepts such as food chains, energy transfer, and human impacts on ecosystems. During the trip, they apply this knowledge to analyze the specific ecosystem they are studying.

4. Provide Structured Guidance: Students receive instructions on data collection methods, use of equipment, and recording observations. They have access to field guides, data sheets, and sampling protocols to ensure accurate and systematic data collection.

5. Incorporate Reflection Activities: After the field trip, students engage in guided reflection activities. They analyze their data, identify trends, and discuss the potential impact of human activities on the ecosystem they studied.

6. Foster Collaboration: Students work in small groups to collect and analyze data. They collaborate to synthesize their findings and propose mitigation strategies. Group discussions encourage sharing ideas, debating perspectives, and collaboratively problem-solving.

7. Include Feedback Mechanisms: The educator provides formative feedback during group discussions and provides written feedback on the quality of students' data analysis and proposed solutions.

8. Celebrate Successes: Students present their findings and mitigation strategies to the class, fostering a sense of achievement and recognition for their efforts. This presentation can be followed by a class discussion on the importance of ecosystem conservation.

Utilizing these strategies, educators can create experiential learning activities that enhance student understanding, engagement, and application of knowledge in real-world contexts. By integrating theory and practice, fostering collaborative learning, and incorporating reflection activities, experiential learning offers students a transformative and enriching educational experience.

Assessing Student Learning in Experiential Learning

Assessing student learning in experiential learning is a crucial aspect of ensuring the effectiveness of this pedagogical approach. Since experiential learning focuses on active engagement and hands-on experiences, traditional assessment methods may not always be the most appropriate or accurate measure of student learning outcomes. In this section, we will explore various assessment strategies and tools that can be used to assess student learning in experiential learning settings.

Authentic Assessment

Authentic assessment is a natural fit for experiential learning as it aligns with the philosophy of providing real-world and meaningful learning experiences. Unlike traditional assessments that rely on memorization and regurgitation of information, authentic assessment focuses on evaluating students' ability to apply knowledge and skills in authentic, real-life situations. This type of assessment is often performance-based and requires students to demonstrate their understanding through practical tasks or projects.

In experiential learning, authentic assessment can take the form of case studies, simulations, role-playing exercises, or project-based assignments. For example, in a science class, students might be tasked with conducting a research project or designing and conducting experiments to test hypotheses. These types of assessments provide students with the opportunity to develop critical thinking, problem-solving, and decision-making skills while also demonstrating their understanding of the subject matter.

When designing authentic assessments for experiential learning, it is important to clearly define the assessment criteria and provide clear guidelines and rubrics to guide students' performance. Rubrics can help ensure consistency and objectivity in the assessment process, allowing students to understand the expectations and criteria for success. It is also important to provide timely and constructive feedback to students, highlighting their strengths and areas for improvement.

Reflection and Self-Assessment

Reflection is an integral part of the experiential learning process, and it can also serve as a valuable form of assessment. By asking students to reflect on their experiences and learning outcomes, educators can gain insights into students' understanding, insights, and personal growth. Reflective assessments can take the form of journal entries, reflective essays, or group discussions.

In addition to external assessments, self-assessment can be a powerful tool for students to gauge their own learning and growth. By encouraging students to self-assess their performance, educators promote metacognition and self-awareness, enabling students to take ownership of their learning process. Self-assessment can be facilitated through checklists, rating scales, or learner portfolios. It is important to provide students with clear guidelines and examples to help them accurately assess their own work.

To enhance the effectiveness of reflection and self-assessment in experiential learning, educators can incorporate structured prompts or guiding questions. These prompts can help students critically analyze their experiences, consider alternative perspectives, and identify areas for improvement. Providing students with opportunities for peer feedback and discussion can further enrich the reflective process and promote collaborative learning.

Performance Assessments

Performance assessments assess students' ability to perform specific tasks or skills in a real-world context. In experiential learning, performance assessments emphasize the application of knowledge and skills rather than the mere recall of information. Performance assessments can take various forms, such as presentations, debates, demonstrations, or exhibitions.

For example, in a history class, students might be asked to create a museum exhibit on a specific historical event, showcasing their knowledge and understanding through visual displays, written explanations, and interactive components. This type of performance assessment allows students to demonstrate their understanding of historical concepts while also developing their creativity, presentation skills, and ability to communicate effectively.

When designing performance assessments, it is essential to align the tasks with the learning objectives and provide clear evaluation criteria. Rubrics can be used to assess students' performance holistically, considering various dimensions such as content knowledge, critical thinking skills, communication skills, and creativity. It is also important to provide students with opportunities for self-reflection and self-assessment to promote metacognitive skills and foster a growth mindset.

Portfolios

Portfolios provide a comprehensive and multifaceted approach to assessing student learning in experiential learning. A portfolio is a collection of student work that demonstrates their progress, achievements, and learning outcomes over a period of time. In experiential learning, portfolios can showcase a range of artifacts, such as project reports, reflections, multimedia presentations, research papers, or artistic creations.

Portfolios can serve as a formative assessment tool, allowing students to document their learning journey and showcase their growth and development. They also provide a platform for students to reflect on their experiences, set goals, and plan their future learning. Additionally, portfolios can be used as a summative assessment tool, allowing educators to evaluate students' overall performance and mastery of learning outcomes.

When implementing portfolios in experiential learning, it is important to establish clear guidelines and criteria for portfolio creation and assessment. Educators can provide templates or frameworks to guide students in organizing and structuring their portfolio. It is also essential to provide ongoing feedback and support to students throughout the portfolio development process to ensure the quality and depth of reflection.

Integrated Assessments

Integrated assessments involve the integration of various assessment methods and tools to provide a comprehensive and holistic view of student learning in experiential learning. These assessments consider multiple dimensions of learning, including knowledge acquisition, critical thinking, problem-solving, creativity, communication, and collaboration.

For example, in a science class, an integrated assessment might involve a combination of a hands-on laboratory experiment, a written reflection on the experiment, a group presentation on the findings, and a self-assessment of the collaborative process. This integrated assessment approach allows educators to evaluate students' performance across multiple domains and provides a more complete picture of their learning outcomes.

When implementing integrated assessments, it is important to ensure alignment between the assessment methods and the learning objectives. It is also crucial to provide students with clear expectations and guidelines for each component of the assessment and to establish criteria for evaluating the integration of different components. Integrated assessments should promote meaningful learning experiences and provide students with opportunities to apply their knowledge and skills in authentic contexts.

Conclusion

Assessing student learning in experiential learning is essential for evaluating the effectiveness of this pedagogical approach. Authentic assessment methods, such as performance assessments, portfolios, and integrated assessments, focus on real-world application and provide a comprehensive view of students' learning outcomes. Reflection and self-assessment promote metacognition and self-awareness, enabling students to take ownership of their learning. By employing a variety of assessment strategies and tools, educators can ensure that experiential learning leads to meaningful and impactful learning experiences for students. In the next section, we will explore the role of problem-based learning in transformative education.

Overcoming Challenges in Implementing Experiential Learning

Experiential learning is a powerful pedagogical approach that engages students in active, hands-on experiences to deepen their understanding and enhance their skills. However, implementing experiential learning can come with its own set of challenges. In this section, we will explore some of the common obstacles faced by educators and provide strategies to overcome them.

Lack of Resources

One of the main challenges in implementing experiential learning is the lack of resources. Experiential learning often requires materials, equipment, and resources that may not be readily available in educational settings. This can limit the scope and effectiveness of experiential learning activities.

To overcome this challenge, educators can explore alternative resources and low-cost options. They can collaborate with local community organizations, museums, or businesses that may be willing to provide resources or collaborate on projects. Additionally, educators can leverage technology to create virtual simulations or utilize online resources to supplement hands-on experiences. By thinking creatively and being resourceful, educators can overcome the challenge of limited resources and provide meaningful experiential learning opportunities for their students.

Time Constraints

Another challenge in implementing experiential learning is the constraint of time. Traditional classroom settings often have a tightly packed curriculum, leaving little room for extended experiential learning activities. Educators may feel pressured to complete the prescribed syllabus, leaving limited time for hands-on experiences.

To address this challenge, educators can integrate experiential learning into existing curriculum units. They can identify key concepts or skills that can be reinforced through hands-on activities and align them with learning objectives. By purposefully selecting experiential learning opportunities that complement the curriculum, educators can ensure that both content knowledge and practical skills are covered within the available time frame.

Additionally, educators can leverage technology to streamline and optimize experiential learning activities. For example, using online platforms or tools can help facilitate virtual collaborations, save time on administrative tasks, and allow for asynchronous learning. By maximizing the available time and optimizing the use of technology, educators can overcome the time constraints associated with experiential learning.

Assessment and Evaluation

Assessing and evaluating the learning outcomes of experiential learning can be challenging. Traditional assessment methods, such as tests and exams, may not effectively capture the skills and knowledge acquired through hands-on experiences. This can make it difficult to demonstrate the effectiveness of experiential learning to stakeholders.

To address this challenge, educators can employ a variety of assessment strategies that align with the nature of experiential learning. For example, portfolios, reflective journals, or multimedia presentations can be used to document and showcase the learning process and outcomes. Peer and self-assessment can also be valuable tools in assessing collaboration, problem-solving, and critical thinking skills developed through experiential learning. Additionally, educators can leverage technology to implement real-time feedback and assessment mechanisms, such as online quizzes or digital simulations.

It is important for educators to clearly communicate the assessment criteria and expectations to students at the beginning of experiential learning activities. This will help students understand the purpose of the assessment and enable them to actively engage in self-reflection and self-assessment.

Safety Concerns

Safety concerns can be a significant challenge when implementing experiential learning, especially when working with potentially hazardous materials or equipment. Ensuring the well-being of students is a top priority, and educators must take appropriate measures to create a safe learning environment.

To address safety concerns, educators should conduct a thorough risk assessment before implementing any experiential learning activities. They should identify and mitigate potential risks by using safety equipment, establishing clear guidelines and protocols, and providing proper training to students. Educators should also closely supervise students during hands-on activities to ensure their safety and respond promptly to any emergencies or accidents.

In addition, educators can collaborate with experts or professionals in the field to ensure that safety guidelines and best practices are followed. This can provide students with valuable insights into real-world safety protocols and enhance their understanding of responsible and ethical practices.

Lack of Support and Awareness

Implementing experiential learning may face resistance or lack of support from various stakeholders, including administrators, parents, or colleagues. Some may be skeptical about the effectiveness or feasibility of experiential learning, while others may have concerns about its alignment with standardized tests or traditional educational models.

To address this challenge, educators can actively engage in professional development opportunities to build their knowledge and skills in experiential learning. They can seek out research and evidence that demonstrate the benefits and positive outcomes of experiential learning approaches. By becoming advocates for experiential learning, educators can share their experiences, success stories, and research findings with colleagues, administrators, parents, and the wider community.

It is essential to involve stakeholders in the planning and implementation of experiential learning initiatives to garner support and understanding. Educators can organize workshops, presentations, or open houses to showcase the value and impact of experiential learning on student engagement, motivation, and learning outcomes.

Conclusion

While implementing experiential learning may present challenges, educators can overcome these obstacles by leveraging available resources, integrating experiential learning into existing curriculum, employing appropriate assessment and evaluation strategies, ensuring safety, and building support and awareness. By embracing experiential learning and actively addressing the challenges, educators can create transformative learning experiences that empower students and enhance their academic and personal growth.

Case studies and best practices in experiential learning

Experiential learning is an approach to education that emphasizes learning through real-world experiences, hands-on activities, and reflection. It allows students to actively engage with concepts and apply their knowledge in practical situations. In this section, we will explore some case studies and best practices that demonstrate the effectiveness of experiential learning in both traditional and non-traditional educational settings.

Case Study 1: Outdoor Environmental Education

One of the most well-known examples of experiential learning is outdoor environmental education, where students learn about ecology, sustainability, and conservation through hands-on activities in natural settings. For instance, a group of middle school students may go on a week-long camping trip to study a local ecosystem.

During the camping trip, students actively participate in activities such as identifying plant and animal species, collecting and analyzing water samples, and mapping the ecosystem. By immersing themselves in the environment, students gain a deep understanding of the interconnectedness of living organisms and the impact of human activities on the ecosystem.

After the camping trip, students engage in reflection activities, such as journaling or group discussions, to process their experiences and connect them to larger concepts. This reflection component helps to solidify learning and develop critical thinking skills.

Best Practice 1: Service-Learning Projects

Service-learning projects are an effective way to engage students in experiential learning while making a positive impact in their communities. In a service-learning project, students collaborate with local organizations or community members to address real-world challenges.

For example, a high school physics class might partner with a local homeless shelter to design and build solar-powered devices for off-grid lighting. Through this project, students not only learn about solar energy and circuitry but also develop problem-solving and teamwork skills.

To ensure the success of service-learning projects, it is important to provide clear objectives, establish authentic partnerships, and guide students in reflecting on their experiences. The integration of community service with academic learning creates a meaningful and impactful educational experience.

Case Study 2: Simulations and Role-Playing

Simulations and role-playing activities are effective tools for experiential learning, especially in subjects such as history, social studies, and business. These activities allow students to step into the shoes of historical or fictional characters and make decisions based on their perspectives.

For example, in a history class studying the American Revolution, students may participate in a simulation where they take on the roles of key figures such as George Washington or King George III. They engage in debates, negotiations, and decision-making processes similar to those that occurred during the revolution.

Through simulations, students gain a deeper understanding of historical events and the complex factors that influenced them. They also develop empathy, critical thinking, and communication skills as they navigate the challenges and conflicts inherent in the scenarios.

Best Practice 2: Internships and Work-Based Learning

Internships and work-based learning experiences provide students with the opportunity to apply their classroom knowledge in real-world work settings. These experiences are especially valuable in vocational subjects such as healthcare, engineering, or culinary arts.

For instance, a college nursing program may require students to complete a clinical internship at a local hospital. During the internship, students work alongside healthcare professionals, providing direct patient care and applying their theoretical knowledge in a practical setting. This hands-on experience helps students develop clinical skills, professional competencies, and a deeper understanding of the healthcare industry.

To ensure the success of internships and work-based learning experiences, it is important to establish partnerships with industry professionals, provide adequate supervision and support, and encourage reflection and debriefing sessions to enhance the learning process.

Conclusion

Experiential learning, as exemplified by case studies and best practices in various educational settings, offers numerous benefits for students. It promotes active engagement, critical thinking, problem-solving skills, and deeper understanding of concepts. By connecting theoretical knowledge to real-world applications, experiential learning prepares students for success in their future careers and fosters a lifelong love for learning.

As educators, it is important to integrate experiential learning strategies into our teaching practices, considering the unique needs and interests of our students. By providing opportunities for hands-on experiences, reflection, and real-world connections, we can create transformative learning environments that inspire and empower students.

Incorporating technology in experiential learning

Experiential learning is an educational approach that emphasizes learning through direct hands-on experiences. It involves activities such as experiments, simulations, field trips, and other immersive experiences that engage learners in real-world situations. By actively participating in these experiences, students gain a deeper understanding of concepts and develop important skills, such as critical thinking, problem-solving, and collaboration.

Incorporating technology into experiential learning can enhance and extend these experiences, providing learners with new opportunities to explore, investigate, and analyze concepts and phenomena. Technology can also facilitate the collection and analysis of data, enabling learners to make evidence-based conclusions and decisions. In this section, we will explore different ways technology can be integrated into experiential learning activities.

Virtual and augmented reality

Virtual and augmented reality (VR/AR) technologies offer immersive and interactive experiences that can simulate real-world environments or enhance the existing environment with virtual elements. These technologies can be used to create virtual laboratories, simulated scenarios, or interactive field trips, allowing students to explore and interact with scientific phenomena, historical events, or cultural sites.

For example, in a biology class, students can use VR headsets to explore the human body in three dimensions, navigate through different organs, and observe how they function. In a history class, AR technology can overlay virtual artifacts and historical information onto physical museum exhibits, allowing students to engage with the past in a more interactive and tangible way.

Sensor-based data collection

Technology can enable students to collect real-time data through various sensors and tools. For instance, in a physics experiment, students can use motion sensors to measure velocity and acceleration, or light sensors to investigate the behavior of light. These sensors can provide precise measurements and instantly display data on computer screens or smartphones.

By using data collection tools, students can compare and analyze data sets, make predictions, and draw conclusions. This allows them to engage in the scientific process more effectively and develop critical thinking skills. Additionally, technology enables students to collect a larger amount of data, facilitating more accurate analysis and deeper understanding of the concepts being explored.

Simulations and modeling

Simulation software and computer models allow students to explore complex systems or processes that may be difficult to observe or manipulate directly. For example, in a chemistry class, students can use molecular simulation software to visualize and understand the behavior of atoms and molecules. In a business class, students can use financial modeling software to simulate different scenarios and evaluate potential outcomes.

These simulations provide learners with opportunities to experiment, test hypotheses, and observe the consequences of their actions or decisions in a controlled and safe environment. By interacting with these virtual models, students can develop a deeper understanding of the underlying principles and apply their knowledge to real-world situations.

Online collaboration and communication

Technology facilitates collaboration and communication among students, allowing them to work together on experiential learning activities, regardless of physical location. Online platforms, such as video conferencing tools and collaborative workspaces, make it possible for students to engage in group projects, discussions, and problem-solving activities.

For example, in a geography class, students from different schools or countries can collaborate on a virtual mapping project, sharing data and insights to create a comprehensive and accurate map. In a science class, students can remotely access and control scientific equipment, enabling them to conduct experiments collaboratively from different locations.

Digital documentation and reflection

Technology enables students to document their experiential learning activities, reflect on their experiences, and showcase their work in digital formats. This can include creating digital portfolios, blogs, videos, or multimedia presentations that capture their learning journey and highlight their achievements.

By engaging in the process of documenting and reflecting on their experiences, students develop metacognitive skills and become more aware of their learning progress and growth. Digital documentation also allows students to receive feedback from peers and teachers, providing them with opportunities for self-assessment and improvement.

Ethical considerations and challenges

While incorporating technology in experiential learning offers numerous benefits, it is important to consider ethical considerations and address potential challenges. These include ensuring students' data privacy and security, promoting digital citizenship and responsible use of technology, and addressing potential biases or limitations of the technologies being used.

It is crucial to provide proper guidance and support to students to help them navigate these ethical considerations and develop responsible technology practices. Teachers should also stay updated on the latest technologies and research, and continually evaluate and adapt their use of technology in experiential learning activities to foster positive and meaningful learning experiences.

In conclusion, incorporating technology in experiential learning can enhance students' engagement, deepen their understanding, and develop important skills. By leveraging virtual and augmented reality, sensor-based data collection, simulations and modeling, online collaboration, and digital documentation, educators can create rich and immersive experiential learning experiences. However, it is essential to address ethical considerations and guide students in using technology responsibly to maximize the benefits of technology-enhanced experiential learning.

Collaborative Experiential Learning

Collaborative experiential learning is an approach to education that combines hands-on experiences with group collaboration to enhance student learning. It emphasizes active participation, problem-solving, and critical thinking skills through real-world activities. In this section, we will explore the principles, benefits, and strategies of collaborative experiential learning and discuss how technology can enhance this approach.

Principles of Collaborative Experiential Learning

Collaborative experiential learning is grounded in several key principles that guide its implementation:

- **Authenticity:** Experiences should be authentic and relevant to real-world contexts to promote meaningful learning. This can include simulations, fieldwork, or projects that mirror professional or community settings.
- **Active engagement:** Students should actively engage in the learning process by participating in hands-on activities and problem-solving tasks. This promotes deeper understanding and retention of knowledge.
- **Collaboration:** Students work together in groups or teams to solve problems, share ideas, and learn from each other. Collaboration fosters communication skills, teamwork, and the ability to consider diverse perspectives.
- **Reflection:** Students reflect on their experiences, analyzing what they have learned and how it connects to their prior knowledge and future goals. Reflection promotes metacognition and helps students make connections between theory and practice.
- **Feedback:** Continuous feedback from peers and instructors is crucial in collaborative experiential learning. It helps students improve their skills, identify areas for growth, and develop a growth mindset.
- **Assessment:** Assessment focuses on both individual and group achievements. It should be aligned with the learning objectives and emphasize the process as well as the product of the collaborative experiential learning experience.

Benefits of Collaborative Experiential Learning

Collaborative experiential learning offers numerous benefits for students, including:

- **Active and engaged learning:** Students are actively involved in their learning process, which enhances their motivation, curiosity, and interest in the subject matter.
- **Enhanced problem-solving skills:** By working collaboratively, students learn to approach problems from different perspectives, leading to more effective and creative problem-solving skills.
- **Improved communication and teamwork:** Collaborative experiences require effective communication, collaboration, and teamwork. Students develop interpersonal skills essential for their personal and professional lives.
- **Transferable skills:** Collaborative experiential learning helps students develop transferable skills such as leadership, critical thinking, decision-making, and adaptability that are valuable in various contexts.
- **Deeper understanding:** Experiential learning allows students to apply theoretical knowledge in real-world situations, resulting in a deeper understanding of concepts and their practical applications.
- **Social and emotional growth:** Through collaboration and reflection, students develop social and emotional skills, such as empathy, self-awareness, and resilience.

Strategies for Collaborative Experiential Learning

Implementing collaborative experiential learning involves thoughtful planning and the use of effective strategies. Here are some strategies to consider:

- **Establishing clear learning objectives:** Clearly define the learning goals and outcomes to guide the collaborative experiential learning activities. This ensures that the experiences align with the desired outcomes.
- **Group formation:** Form diverse groups to maximize the exchange of ideas and perspectives. Consider a mix of skills, backgrounds, and learning styles to enhance collaboration.

- **Structured tasks:** Provide clear instructions and guidelines for the tasks to be completed. Structure the activities in a way that encourages equal participation and accountability within the group.

- **Facilitating communication and collaboration:** Use strategies and tools that promote effective communication and collaboration among group members. This can include group discussions, online forums, project management tools, and video conferencing platforms.

- **Reflection activities:** Incorporate regular reflection activities to encourage students to analyze their experiences, share insights, and connect their learnings to broader concepts.

- **Formative feedback:** Offer timely and constructive feedback to guide students' progress and promote continuous improvement. Encourage both peer feedback and feedback from the instructor.

- **Assessment methods:** Design assessment methods that align with the collaborative nature of the learning experiences. Consider assessing both individual contributions and group achievements.

Technology-Enhanced Collaborative Experiential Learning

Technology can play a crucial role in enhancing collaborative experiential learning experiences. Here are examples of how technology can be integrated into this approach:

- **Collaboration tools:** Online platforms and tools enable students to collaborate remotely, share resources, and work on group projects together. Examples include shared document editors, project management software, and virtual whiteboards.

- **Virtual simulations:** Virtual simulations provide opportunities for students to immerse themselves in realistic scenarios without physical constraints. They can replicate complex real-world situations and provide a safe environment for exploration and problem-solving.

- **Digital portfolios:** Students can showcase their collaborative experiential learning experiences through digital portfolios. This allows them to reflect on their growth, share their work with others, and showcase their skills to potential employers or educational institutions.

- **Virtual reality (VR) and augmented reality (AR):** VR and AR technologies can provide immersive experiences that allow students to interact with virtual environments. They can simulate real-world scenarios, enabling students to practice skills and gain practical experience.

- **Online communication and discussion platforms:** Online platforms, such as discussion forums or social media groups, facilitate communication and collaboration among students. They provide opportunities for asynchronous discussions and exchange of ideas beyond the classroom.

Case Study: Collaborative Experiential Learning in Environmental Science

Let's consider a case study where collaborative experiential learning is applied in an environmental science course. The learning objective is for students to understand the impact of human activities on the local ecosystem and develop sustainable solutions. Here's an overview of how this could be implemented:

- **Designing the experience:** Students are divided into groups and assigned different local ecosystems to study. Each group conducts fieldwork to collect data on the ecosystem, including biodiversity, water quality, and human activities that may affect it.

- **Collaborative analysis:** Back in the classroom, groups collaborate to analyze and interpret their findings. They share their data, compare results, and identify patterns or trends.

- **Developing sustainable solutions:** Each group formulates sustainable solutions to address the identified issues. They research innovative approaches, such as eco-friendly practices, conservation strategies, or community engagement initiatives.

- **Sharing findings:** Groups prepare presentations to share their findings and proposed solutions with the class. They receive formative feedback from classmates and the instructor, promoting further refinement of their ideas.

- **Reflection and assessment:** Students reflect on their collaborative experiences, comparing their individual contributions to the group's achievements. They consider the challenges faced, the skills developed, and the personal growth achieved through the project. Assessment is based on both individual reflections and group presentations.

This case study demonstrates how collaborative experiential learning can enable students to apply their knowledge, collaborate with peers, and develop an understanding of the real-world implications of their studies.

Exercises

1. Choose a subject area of interest to you and design a collaborative experiential learning activity for that context. Outline the learning objectives, tasks, desired outcomes, and assessment strategies.

2. Reflect on a past collaborative learning experience you have had. What were the strengths and weaknesses of the experience? How did it impact your learning?

3. Research a technology tool or platform that can enhance collaborative experiential learning. Describe how it can be integrated into a specific learning activity.

4. Explore different assessment methods that can effectively capture individual and group achievements in collaborative experiential learning. Discuss the benefits and challenges of each method.

Conclusion

Collaborative experiential learning offers a powerful approach to education, combining hands-on experiences with group collaboration. It engages students in authentic learning activities, develops essential skills, and fosters deeper understanding. By incorporating technology, educators can enhance and expand the possibilities of collaborative experiential learning, creating innovative and impactful learning experiences for students.

Experiential Learning in Different Subject Areas

Experiential learning is a pedagogical approach that emphasizes the importance of hands-on experiences in the learning process. It involves actively engaging students in real-world tasks and situations, allowing them to apply their knowledge and skills in practical contexts. This section explores how experiential learning can be implemented in different subject areas, providing examples and strategies to enhance the learning experience.

Science

Science is a subject that naturally lends itself to experiential learning. By incorporating hands-on experiments, students can develop a deeper understanding of scientific concepts and principles. For example, in biology, students can engage in fieldwork to study ecosystems and biodiversity. They can collect samples, analyze data, and make observations to learn about the interrelationships between organisms and their environment.

In chemistry, students can conduct laboratory experiments to understand chemical reactions and explore the properties of different substances. By actively participating in experiments, students can observe firsthand how the variables affect the outcomes and deepen their understanding of chemical principles.

In physics, students can engage in activities that involve building and testing physical models to explore concepts such as motion, forces, and energy. By designing and conducting experiments, students can apply theoretical concepts and develop a better grasp of the underlying principles.

Experiential learning in science can also involve real-world applications. For instance, students can work on engineering projects to solve practical problems, such as designing and building a simple machine or creating a sustainable energy solution. These experiences allow students to see the direct application of scientific principles and develop critical thinking and problem-solving skills.

Mathematics

Mathematics often presents a challenge for students due to its abstract nature. Experiential learning can help students bridge the gap between theoretical concepts and their practical application. By engaging in hands-on activities, students can develop a deeper understanding of mathematical principles and improve their problem-solving skills.

In geometry, students can work with manipulatives and visual models to explore geometric concepts such as shapes, angles, and symmetry. Manipulatives like pattern blocks or tangrams can help students develop spatial reasoning and understand geometrical relationships.

In statistics, students can analyze real-world data to draw conclusions and make predictions. They can collect and analyze data from surveys or experiments and use statistical tools to interpret the results. This allows students to see the relevance of statistics in everyday life and develop data literacy skills.

In algebra, students can solve real-world problems using mathematical equations and formulas. They can apply algebraic concepts to scenarios like budgeting, investing, or solving engineering problems. By working on practical applications of algebra, students can see the value and relevance of mathematical concepts in their lives.

Social Sciences

Experiential learning can also be applied to the social sciences, allowing students to engage with complex social issues and develop a deeper understanding of human behavior and society.

In history, students can participate in simulations or role-plays to experience historical events and understand the perspectives of different individuals or groups. These interactive experiences enable students to critically analyze historical events and develop empathy and a broader understanding of historical context.

In geography, students can engage in fieldwork to study and analyze physical and human landscapes. They can conduct surveys, gather data, and create maps to understand the relationship between people and their environment. By actively exploring and investigating different geographical features, students can develop a deep understanding of geographic concepts.

In psychology, students can conduct experiments or case studies to explore different aspects of human behavior and cognition. They can design experiments to test hypotheses and collect data to analyze psychological processes. Experiential learning in psychology allows students to critically analyze human behavior and develop research skills.

Arts and Humanities

Experiential learning can also be incorporated into arts and humanities subjects, allowing students to develop creativity and critical thinking skills while engaging with various art forms and cultural expressions.

In visual arts, students can engage in hands-on artistic processes, such as painting, sculpture, or photography, to express their ideas and emotions. Through experiential learning, students can explore different art techniques, experiment with materials, and develop their artistic skills while expressing their own unique perspectives.

In literature and language arts, students can participate in interactive storytelling or performative activities to bring literary works to life. They can engage in drama, role-plays, or creative writing exercises to deepen their understanding of literary elements and explore different narrative techniques.

In music, students can actively participate in playing instruments, singing, or composing their own music. By experiencing music firsthand, students can develop a deeper appreciation for musical elements, such as melody, rhythm, and harmony, and enhance their understanding of music theory.

Experiential learning in arts and humanities subjects allows students to develop their creativity, express their emotions, and critically engage with various art forms. It also fosters cultural appreciation and understanding by exposing students to diverse artistic and cultural expressions.

Physical Education

Experiential learning can also be integrated into physical education to enhance students' physical skills, promote teamwork, and develop a lifelong commitment to health and fitness.

In sports, students can actively participate in various games and activities to improve their physical abilities and learn important skills like teamwork, communication, and sportsmanship. By engaging in practical sports experiences, students can develop a deeper understanding of game strategies, rules, and tactics.

In fitness and wellness, students can engage in hands-on activities that promote physical well-being, such as creating personal fitness plans, tracking progress, and learning about nutrition. Experiential learning in physical education allows students to apply theoretical knowledge about health and fitness to real-world contexts, empowering them to make informed lifestyle choices.

Overall, experiential learning offers endless possibilities for engaging students in different subject areas. By providing hands-on experiences and real-world applications, educators can foster deep learning, critical thinking, and a lifelong love for learning in students across diverse disciplines.

Future Directions of Experiential Learning

As we move into the future, experiential learning continues to play a vital role in education, offering students unique opportunities for active engagement and practical skill development. Building upon the current practices and principles of experiential learning, several future directions emerge that have the potential to further enhance the effectiveness and impact of this approach. In this section, we will explore some of these potential future directions and their implications.

Integration of Virtual and Augmented Reality

One exciting avenue for future development in experiential learning is the integration of virtual reality (VR) and augmented reality (AR) technologies. VR immerses students in realistic simulated environments, allowing them to experience situations that would be otherwise impractical or impossible. AR, on the other hand, overlays digital information onto the real world, providing students with additional context and resources. By incorporating these technologies into experiential learning, students can engage in hands-on experiences that transcend traditional boundaries. For example, medical students can practice complex surgical procedures in a safe and controlled virtual environment, or history students can visit ancient civilizations through interactive AR tours. The integration of VR and AR technologies holds great promise for expanding the possibilities of experiential learning and enriching the educational experience for students.

Application of Artificial Intelligence

Artificial intelligence (AI) has the potential to revolutionize experiential learning by providing intelligent support and personalized feedback to students. AI algorithms can analyze student performance data in real-time, identify areas of improvement, and offer tailored advice. For instance, in a science experiment, AI-powered virtual assistants can guide students through the process, providing instant feedback and suggesting alternative approaches. Additionally, AI can create adaptive simulations that adjust the difficulty level based on the individual student's abilities, ensuring an optimal learning experience for each learner. By leveraging the power of AI, experiential learning can become more personalized, efficient, and effective.

Integration of Authentic Assessment Practices

Authentic assessment practices, such as performance-based evaluations and real-world application of knowledge and skills, are becoming increasingly valued in education. In the future, experiential learning will continue to align closely with authentic assessment, enabling students to showcase their abilities in practical contexts. By integrating authentic assessment practices into experiential learning, educators can provide students with opportunities to demonstrate their skills and knowledge in real-world scenarios. For example, rather than taking a traditional written exam, students might design and execute a community service project to apply their learning in a meaningful way. This alignment between experiential learning and authentic assessment not only enhances student engagement and motivation but also better prepares them for future careers and life beyond the classroom.

Collaborative Experiential Learning

Collaboration is a critical skill in today's interconnected world, and it will continue to be important in the future. As such, future directions of experiential learning will emphasize collaborative experiences that foster teamwork, communication, and problem-solving skills. In these collaborative experiential learning environments, students will work together to tackle complex challenges, combining their diverse perspectives, knowledge, and expertise. For instance, students from different disciplines could collaborate on a multidisciplinary project that addresses real-world problems. Through collaborative experiential learning, students can develop crucial interpersonal skills and learn how to work effectively as part of a team, which are essential for success in the workplace and society.

Integration of Environmental Sustainability

Environmental sustainability is a pressing global concern, and its integration into education is becoming increasingly important. In the future, experiential learning will place a greater emphasis on environmental sustainability by incorporating projects and activities that promote ecological awareness and responsibility. Students may engage in experiential learning opportunities that involve sustainable practices, such as designing and implementing renewable energy solutions or participating in ecological restoration projects. By integrating environmental sustainability into experiential learning, students not only develop an understanding of environmental issues but also learn how to apply sustainable principles to their own lives and future careers.

In summary, the future directions of experiential learning hold tremendous potential for enhancing student engagement, skill development, and real-world application of knowledge. The integration of virtual and augmented reality, the application of artificial intelligence, the alignment with authentic assessment practices, the emphasis on collaborative learning, and the integration of environmental sustainability are just a few examples of the exciting possibilities ahead. By embracing these future directions, educators can create transformative learning experiences that prepare students for success in the complex and rapidly changing world.

Technology-Enhanced Assessment

Formative Assessment

Understanding Formative Assessment

Formative assessment plays a crucial role in the educational process by providing immediate feedback to both teachers and students. It is a process of gathering and using evidence to continuously adjust and improve learning. Unlike summative assessment, which is used to evaluate student learning at the end of a unit or course, formative assessment focuses on monitoring progress and adjusting instruction in real-time.

Importance of Formative Assessment

Formative assessment serves multiple purposes in the education system. Firstly, it helps teachers identify students' strengths and weaknesses, allowing them to tailor instruction to meet individual needs. By understanding how well students understand and are progressing towards desired learning goals, teachers can modify their teaching strategies and provide additional support or challenges as necessary.

Furthermore, formative assessment empowers students to take ownership of their learning. By receiving timely feedback on their performance, students can reflect on their understanding, identify areas of improvement, and set goals for future learning. This reflective process fosters metacognition and self-regulation, promoting deeper learning and long-term retention of knowledge.

In addition to its impact on instruction and student learning, formative assessment also informs educational decision-making at the systemic level. Aggregated data from formative assessments can be analyzed to identify trends and patterns, allowing policymakers to make informed choices about curriculum development and resource allocation.

Principles of Formative Assessment

To effectively implement formative assessment, educators should adhere to the following principles:

1. Clarity of learning goals: Clear, specific, and measurable learning goals need to be established so that both teachers and students understand what success looks like. These goals provide a framework for assessment practices and help guide instruction.

2. Continuous and ongoing feedback: Feedback should be provided to students in real-time, highlighting their progress towards the learning goals and identifying areas for improvement. It should be constructive, specific, and actionable, focusing on both strengths and weaknesses. Feedback should be timely to enable students to make immediate adjustments to their learning strategies.

3. Learner involvement: Students should actively participate in the formative assessment process. They should be encouraged to engage in self-assessment, peer assessment, and reflection on their own learning. This involvement promotes a deeper understanding of their progress and fosters a sense of ownership and responsibility for their learning.

4. Use of multiple assessment strategies: Formative assessment is not limited to tests and quizzes. It encompasses a variety of assessment strategies, including observation, questioning, student work analysis, portfolios, and digital tools. By employing a range of assessment methods, teachers gain a more comprehensive picture of students' understanding and skills.

5. Adjustments to instruction: Formative assessment data should inform instructional decisions. Teachers should use the information gathered from assessments to adjust their teaching strategies, provide targeted interventions, and differentiate instruction to meet the diverse needs of their students. Instructional adjustments should be aimed at closing the gap between the current and desired levels of student understanding.

Examples of Formative Assessment Practices

Formative assessment can take many forms, depending on the subject area, grade level, and teaching context. Here are a few examples of effective formative assessment practices:

1. **Exit Tickets:** At the end of a lesson, students are given a prompt or a question related to the learning goals of the day. They have a few minutes to respond individually, and their responses provide valuable insights into their level of understanding.

2. **One-Minute Papers:** Students are asked to summarize their learning or pose a question about the topic of study in a brief, one-minute written response. This activity encourages reflection and helps teachers gauge student comprehension and misconceptions.

3. **Peer Feedback and Self-Assessment:** Students engage in constructive feedback by providing comments on each other's work or using rubrics to assess their own progress. This process not only supports peer learning but also helps students develop critical thinking and analytical skills.

4. **Think-Pair-Share:** Students are given a question or problem to consider individually, then discuss their thoughts with a partner, and finally share their ideas with the whole class. This strategy promotes active engagement and gives students the opportunity to refine their thinking through discussion.

5. **Concept Maps:** Students create visual representations of their understanding, connecting key concepts and relationships. Concept maps allow teachers to identify areas of misconception or incomplete understanding while providing students with a holistic view of their own learning.

Challenges and Solutions

Implementing effective formative assessment practices can be challenging. Some common challenges include:

- **Time constraints:** Teachers often feel pressured to cover a large curriculum within a specified timeframe, leaving limited time for formative assessment. To address this, educators can embed formative assessment practices seamlessly into their instruction, making it an integral part of the teaching and learning process.

- **Limited resources and access to technology:** In some educational contexts, there may be limited resources or access to technology tools for formative assessment. Teachers can adapt low-tech strategies, such as whiteboard responses, exit tickets, or peer feedback, to gather real-time information about student understanding.

- **Over-reliance on traditional assessment methods:** Teachers and students may be more accustomed to traditional assessment methods, such as quizzes and exams, which are often summative in nature. Educators can provide professional development and support for teachers to build their capacity in using a wider range of formative assessment techniques.

- **Lack of student buy-in:** Students may not fully understand the purpose and benefits of formative assessment, leading to resistance or disengagement. Educators should communicate the value of formative assessment, involve students in setting learning goals, and provide ongoing feedback that helps students see the connection between assessment and improvement.

Conclusion

Formative assessment is a powerful tool for enhancing student learning, supporting teacher decision-making, and shaping educational policies and practices. By understanding its principles, implementing effective strategies, and overcoming the associated challenges, educators can create an environment that fosters continuous improvement and empowers students to reach their full potential. Through formative assessment, we can transform education into a dynamic and personalized experience that caters to the diverse needs of learners.

Benefits of formative assessment

Formative assessment, also known as assessment for learning, plays a crucial role in enhancing the learning process and improving student outcomes. This section explores the various benefits of formative assessment and its impact on students, teachers, and the overall educational system.

Empowers students in their learning journey

One of the primary benefits of formative assessment is that it empowers students to take ownership of their learning. By providing regular feedback and opportunities for self-reflection, formative assessment helps students understand their strengths and areas for improvement. This fosters a growth mindset and encourages students to set goals and take concrete steps to achieve them.

For example, a mathematics teacher may use formative assessment in the form of quizzes or problem-solving tasks. Based on the feedback received, students can identify their weaknesses and work on improving their understanding of specific concepts. This iterative process allows students to monitor their progress and make necessary adjustments to their learning strategies.

Enhances learning and retention of knowledge

Formative assessment provides ongoing feedback, giving students a clear understanding of their current level of understanding. This feedback helps students to identify gaps in their knowledge and make corrections in real-time. By addressing misconceptions and focusing on areas that need improvement, formative assessment promotes deeper learning, leading to better retention of knowledge.

Research has shown that when students engage in self-assessment and reflective activities, it improves their understanding and long-term retention of the subject matter. By actively participating in the assessment process, students become more aware of their learning journey and are better able to connect new information with their existing knowledge.

Supports differentiated instruction

Formative assessment allows teachers to gather valuable data about each student's progress and understanding. This information can be used to tailor instruction to meet the diverse needs of students. By identifying areas of strength and weakness, teachers can provide targeted support and adjust instructional strategies accordingly.

For example, in a language arts class, a teacher may use formative assessment techniques such as exit tickets, class discussions, or quick-writes to gauge students' understanding of a particular concept. Based on the data collected, the teacher can differentiate instruction by providing additional resources or modifying instructional activities to meet the specific needs of individual students.

Promotes active engagement and metacognition

Formative assessment engages students actively in the learning process, encouraging them to think critically and reflect on their own learning. Through self-assessment and peer assessment activities, students become more self-aware and develop metacognitive skills. Metacognition refers to the ability to understand one's own thinking processes and regulate one's own learning.

When students are actively engaged in assessing their own understanding, they become aware of their learning strengths and weaknesses. This awareness helps them to generate strategies to further enhance their learning. Additionally, through peer assessment activities, students learn to give and receive feedback, which further deepens their understanding and promotes collaborative learning.

Informs instructional decisions and improves teaching practices

Formative assessment not only benefits students but also provides valuable information for teachers to make informed instructional decisions. By collecting and analyzing data from formative assessments, teachers can identify areas where students are struggling and adapt their teaching methods accordingly.

For instance, if a teacher notices that a significant number of students are struggling with a particular concept, they can modify their instructional approach, re-teach the material, or provide additional examples to clarify any misconceptions. This ongoing feedback loop allows teachers to continuously refine their teaching practices and ensure that all students are effectively learning.

Reduces achievement gaps and promotes equity

Formative assessment has the potential to reduce achievement gaps among students from different backgrounds. By providing continuous feedback and support, formative assessment helps identify and address learning gaps early on, preventing potential learning disparities from widening.

In a diverse classroom, formative assessment provides teachers with insights into individual student needs and allows for targeted interventions. By tailoring instruction to meet the specific needs of students, teachers can create an equitable learning environment and promote success for all learners.

Encourages self-regulated learning

Formative assessment plays a crucial role in developing students' self-regulated learning skills. Self-regulated learners have the ability to set goals, monitor their own progress, and take proactive steps to achieve them. Through formative assessment, students learn to reflect on their learning process, identify strategies that work best for them, and make adjustments accordingly.

By engaging in self-assessment, students become more autonomous learners, taking responsibility for their own learning journey. This skill is essential not only in the classroom but also in real-world contexts, where individuals must take charge of their own professional growth and development.

Overall, formative assessment offers numerous benefits that contribute to the holistic growth and development of students. By empowering students, enhancing learning and retention, supporting differentiated instruction, promoting active engagement and metacognition, informing instructional decisions, reducing achievement gaps, and encouraging self-regulated learning, formative assessment plays a vital role in achieving academic excellence and fostering lifelong learning.

Formative assessment strategies and tools

Formative assessment is an essential component of the learning process, providing valuable feedback to both teachers and students. It involves ongoing, real-time assessment of student learning to identify strengths and areas that need improvement. In this section, we will explore various formative assessment strategies and tools that can enhance the learning experience.

Classroom Observations

One effective strategy for formative assessment is classroom observations. The teacher can observe students during class activities, discussions, and group work to gauge their understanding and engagement. This can be done through informal observations, checklists, or structured observation protocols.

For example, in a science class, the teacher may observe students conducting an experiment and note their ability to follow procedures, ask questions, and make predictions. This observation provides valuable insights into students' conceptual understanding and their application of scientific skills.

Questioning Techniques

Asking thoughtful and purposeful questions is another powerful formative assessment strategy. Teachers can use a variety of questioning techniques to promote critical thinking and assess students' understanding.

One technique is the use of open-ended questions. These questions require students to provide detailed responses and demonstrate their understanding of a concept. For instance, in a history class, a teacher may ask students to explain the causes and consequences of a historical event, allowing them to showcase their knowledge and analytical skills.

Another technique is the use of probing questions. These questions are used to delve deeper into students' responses and push them to think more critically. By asking follow-up questions, teachers can assess students' ability to reason, justify their answers, and think beyond surface-level understanding.

Formative Assessment Tools

Technology has revolutionized the way we conduct formative assessments. There are numerous digital tools available that can help teachers gather real-time data, provide instant feedback, and track students' progress. Here are some popular formative assessment tools:

1. Kahoot: Kahoot is an interactive quiz platform that allows teachers to create engaging quizzes, polls, and surveys. It provides instant feedback and generates detailed reports to identify areas of improvement.

2. Socrative: Socrative is a versatile formative assessment tool that offers various question types, including multiple-choice, true/false, and short answer. Teachers can create quizzes, exit tickets, and quick assessments to gauge student understanding.

3. Nearpod: Nearpod is a collaborative platform that enables teachers to create interactive lessons and assessments. Teachers can embed quizzes, polls, and open-ended questions into their presentations and receive immediate feedback from students.

4. Padlet: Padlet is a virtual bulletin board that allows teachers and students to post notes, images, and other multimedia content. Teachers can create formative assessments by asking students to contribute their responses and ideas.

5. Google Forms: Google Forms is a versatile tool that enables teachers to create surveys, quizzes, and self-assessments. It provides real-time data and automatic grading features, making it easy to track student progress.

These tools not only facilitate formative assessment but also make the process more engaging and interactive for students.

Peer and Self-assessment

In addition to teacher-led assessments, peer and self-assessment strategies can be valuable formative assessment tools. Peer assessment involves students providing feedback to their peers, while self-assessment requires students to reflect on their own learning and progress.

Peer assessment encourages students to develop critical evaluation skills and learn from each other. For example, in a language class, students can exchange written assignments and provide constructive feedback based on predetermined criteria. This process allows students to actively engage in the assessment process, develop a deeper understanding of the subject, and improve their own work.

Self-assessment, on the other hand, empowers students to take ownership of their learning. They can reflect on their strengths, weaknesses, and areas for improvement. This can be done through journals, reflection exercises, or self-assessment rubrics. By engaging in self-assessment, students become more self-aware and develop metacognitive skills, fostering their ability to identify and regulate their own learning needs.

Using Data for Differentiation

Formative assessment data can provide invaluable information for differentiating instruction. By analyzing students' strengths and weaknesses, teachers can tailor their instruction to meet individual needs and promote academic growth.

For instance, if the data shows that a group of students is struggling with a particular concept, the teacher can provide additional instruction, resources, or targeted interventions to support their learning. On the other hand, if some students have already mastered a concept, they can be provided with more challenging tasks or enrichment opportunities.

Teachers can also use formative assessment data to group students based on their learning needs. By creating flexible groups, teachers can provide targeted instruction and support to specific groups of students, maximizing their learning potential.

Caveats and Challenges

While formative assessment has numerous benefits, there are some caveats and challenges to consider. First, teachers need to ensure that formative assessments are aligned with learning goals and objectives. The assessments should focus on capturing evidence of student understanding and progress towards the desired outcomes.

Another challenge is providing timely and meaningful feedback. With large class sizes, it can be challenging for teachers to provide individualized feedback to each student. Technology can help automate the feedback process and provide instant feedback to students, saving teachers time and enabling them to provide personalized guidance.

Furthermore, it is essential to create a safe and supportive classroom environment for formative assessment. Students should feel comfortable taking risks, making mistakes, and seeking feedback. Creating a positive classroom culture that values growth and learning can enhance the effectiveness of formative assessment strategies.

Conclusion

Formative assessment strategies and tools are essential for promoting student learning and improving instructional practices. Classroom observations, questioning techniques, and digital tools can provide valuable insights into student understanding. Peer and self-assessment encourage active student engagement, while data analysis enables teachers to differentiate instruction effectively. By harnessing the power of formative assessment, teachers can create more engaging and personalized learning experiences for their students.

Technology-Enhanced Formative Assessment

Formative assessment plays a crucial role in the learning process by providing ongoing feedback to students and teachers. It helps to identify students' strengths and weaknesses, informs instruction, and promotes deeper understanding of the subject matter. With the advancements in educational technology, formative assessment has become more effective and efficient. In this section, we will explore various technology-enhanced tools and strategies for formative assessment.

Benefits of Technology-Enhanced Formative Assessment

Technology-enhanced formative assessment offers several advantages over traditional methods. Here are some key benefits:

1. **Instant feedback:** Technology allows students to receive real-time feedback on their performance. This immediate feedback helps students understand their mistakes and make corrections promptly, leading to faster learning.

2. **Engagement:** Technology-based assessments can be interactive, engaging, and visually appealing. They can include multimedia elements such as videos, simulations, and interactive graphs, making the assessment experience more enjoyable and motivating for students.

3. **Personalization:** Technology enables personalized assessments tailored to each student's needs and learning pace. Adaptive assessment tools can dynamically

adjust the difficulty level of questions based on students' responses, ensuring appropriate challenges for every learner.

4. **Data-driven insights:** Technology allows educators to collect and analyze large amounts of data to gain insights into student learning patterns, misconceptions, and progress. This data can inform instructional decisions and interventions for individual students or the whole class.

5. **Efficiency:** Technology streamlines the assessment process by automating tasks such as scoring and data analysis, saving valuable time for teachers. It also enables the administration of assessments across multiple platforms and devices, making it easier to reach a large number of students efficiently.

Technology-Enhanced Formative Assessment Strategies

Now let's explore some of the technology-enhanced strategies and tools that can be used for formative assessment:

1. **Online Quizzes and Surveys:** Online platforms and learning management systems provide features to create and administer quizzes and surveys. These tools allow for automatic scoring, immediate feedback, and the option to track students' progress over time.

2. **Interactive Simulations:** Simulations allow students to explore and manipulate virtual environments, facilitating hands-on learning. Educators can embed questions within simulations to assess students' understanding and critical thinking skills.

3. **Clicker Systems:** Clicker systems, or student response systems, allow students to respond to multiple-choice questions using handheld devices. Results can be instantly displayed, providing feedback to both students and teachers.

4. **Digital Whiteboarding:** Digital whiteboarding tools enable collaborative problem-solving activities. Students can work together to solve problems, and teachers can provide instant feedback on their work.

5. **Peer Assessment Tools:** Technology can facilitate peer assessment by providing digital platforms for students to review and provide feedback on their peers' work. These tools can also include rubrics and guidelines to ensure fair and consistent assessment.

Implementing Technology-Enhanced Formative Assessment

To effectively implement technology-enhanced formative assessment, educators need to consider the following:

1. **Purpose and Learning Objectives:** Clearly define the purpose of the assessment and align it with the learning objectives. Determine what specific knowledge or skills you want to assess and choose appropriate technology tools accordingly.

2. **Accessibility and Compatibility:** Ensure that the technology tools and platforms used for assessment are accessible to all students. Consider students with disabilities, limited access to technology, or language barriers to ensure equity.

3. **Training and Support:** Provide training and support to both students and teachers on how to effectively use the technology tools for formative assessment. This includes guidance on navigating the tools, interpreting feedback, and implementing changes based on the assessment results.

4. **Data Privacy and Security:** Be mindful of data privacy and security when using technology tools for assessments. Choose tools that comply with relevant privacy regulations and ensure that student data is protected.

Case Studies and Best Practices

Let's explore a couple of case studies that highlight effective implementation of technology-enhanced formative assessment:

Case Study 1: Kahoot!: Kahoot! is a popular game-based learning platform that allows teachers to create quizzes, surveys, and discussions. Students participate by using their devices to answer multiple-choice questions, and results are instantly displayed. Kahoot! encourages active engagement, competition, and peer learning.

Case Study 2: Adaptive Learning Platforms: Adaptive learning platforms like Khan Academy and Smart Sparrow use intelligent algorithms to tailor assessments based on individual student performance. These platforms provide personalized feedback and adaptive instruction, helping students focus on their specific learning needs.

Conclusion

Technology-enhanced formative assessment offers numerous benefits and opportunities for enhancing student learning. By leveraging the power of technology, educators can provide timely and personalized feedback, engage students in interactive assessments, and gain valuable insights into student progress. To successfully implement technology-enhanced formative assessment, educators must carefully choose appropriate tools, provide training and support, and ensure data privacy and security. By embracing these strategies and practices, educators can optimize the formative assessment process and ultimately improve student outcomes.

Overcoming challenges in implementing formative assessment

Formative assessment is an essential tool for supporting student learning and providing timely feedback. However, implementing formative assessment strategies in the classroom can be challenging. In this section, we will explore some of the common challenges faced by educators and discuss strategies to overcome them.

Lack of clarity in learning goals

One of the main challenges in implementing formative assessment is the lack of clarity in learning goals. Teachers need to clearly define what they expect students to know and be able to do at the end of a lesson or unit. Without clear learning goals, it becomes difficult to design formative assessment activities that effectively measure student progress. To overcome this challenge, teachers should:

- Clearly articulate learning goals and objectives to students at the beginning of each lesson or unit.
- Use rubrics or checklists to provide explicit criteria for success.
- Align formative assessment activities with the learning goals to ensure they provide meaningful feedback.

Limited time and resources

Time constraints and limited resources are common challenges faced by teachers. It can be challenging to implement formative assessment strategies when there are competing demands and a lack of time for in-depth analysis of student work. To address this challenge, teachers can:

- Incorporate quick and easy formative assessment strategies, such as exit tickets or thumbs-up/thumbs-down responses, that can be easily incorporated into regular classroom activities.
- Leverage technology tools and resources to streamline the formative assessment process, such as online quizzes or digital rubrics.
- Collaborate with colleagues to share the workload and exchange ideas on effective formative assessment practices.

Resistance to change

Resistance to change is a common challenge when implementing any educational innovation, including formative assessment. Some teachers may be hesitant to try new strategies or may feel overwhelmed by the additional workload. To overcome resistance to change, it is important to:

- Provide professional development and training opportunities for teachers to learn about the benefits and best practices of formative assessment.
- Offer ongoing support and mentorship to teachers as they implement formative assessment strategies.
- Highlight success stories and share examples of how formative assessment has positively impacted student learning.
- Foster a collaborative and supportive school culture that encourages experimentation and continuous improvement.

Limited student engagement

Engaging students in the formative assessment process can be a challenge. Students may not see the value in providing feedback or may not fully understand how their actions and choices impact their learning. To increase student engagement in formative assessment, teachers can:

- Communicate the purpose and benefits of formative assessment to students, emphasizing how it can help them improve their learning.
- Design formative assessment activities that are interactive and meaningful, such as peer feedback or self-reflection exercises.
- Provide specific and timely feedback to students, highlighting their strengths and areas for improvement.
- Involve students in setting learning goals and tracking their own progress.

Insufficient use of data

Formative assessment generates a wealth of data that can inform instructional decisions. However, teachers may struggle to effectively analyze and use this data to guide their teaching. To address this challenge, teachers can:

- Use data analysis tools or software to efficiently analyze and interpret formative assessment data.
- Collaborate with colleagues to discuss and interpret data, share insights, and identify trends or patterns.
- Use data to inform instructional decisions, such as adjusting teaching strategies or providing targeted interventions for struggling students.
- Provide opportunities for students to reflect on their own data and set goals for improvement.

In conclusion, implementing formative assessment strategies in the classroom comes with its own set of challenges. By addressing these challenges head-on and adopting effective strategies, educators can overcome obstacles and create meaningful formative assessment experiences that positively impact student learning and growth.

Case studies and best practices in formative assessment

Formative assessment is an essential component of the teaching-learning process, providing valuable feedback to both teachers and students to measure progress and guide instructional decisions. In this section, we will explore some case studies and best practices in formative assessment that highlight its effectiveness in different educational contexts. These examples will demonstrate the diverse ways in which formative assessment can be implemented to enhance student learning and achievement.

Case Study 1: Using Digital Tools for Real-Time Feedback

In Mrs. Johnson's fifth-grade math class, students use digital tools to solve math problems, which allows for instant feedback on their responses. For instance, the class utilizes an online math platform that provides immediate corrections and explanations for incorrect answers. The platform enables Mrs. Johnson to monitor individual student progress and identify common misconceptions or areas of weakness in real-time. With this information, she can address specific needs and adapt her instruction accordingly. Furthermore, students can track their own progress and identify areas where they need additional practice. This digital formative assessment approach not only enhances student engagement but also promotes self-regulated learning.

Best Practice 1: Questioning Techniques and Think-Pair-Share

One effective formative assessment strategy involves the use of questioning techniques, such as think-pair-share. In this approach, teachers pose a thought-provoking question or scenario to students, giving them time to think individually about their response. Next, students pair up with a peer to discuss their thoughts, share their reasoning, and possibly revise their initial answers. Finally, the teacher initiates a whole-class discussion, allowing students to share their revised answers and engage in collaborative sense-making. This process not only assesses students' understanding but also promotes metacognitive skills, critical thinking, and peer learning.

Case Study 2: Student Self-Assessment and Reflection

In Mr. Lee's high school English literature class, students are actively involved in their own formative assessment process. After a writing assignment, students self-assess their work using a rubric provided by the teacher. They evaluate their writing based on specified criteria, such as clarity, organization, and use of evidence. Additionally, students are encouraged to reflect on their writing process, identifying strengths and areas for improvement. Mr. Lee then provides feedback and engages in one-on-one conferences with each student to discuss their self-assessment and reflection. This approach not only empowers students to take ownership of their learning but also fosters metacognitive skills and promotes goal setting.

Best Practice 2: Exit Tickets and Quick Checks

Exit tickets and quick checks are simple and effective formative assessment strategies that provide teachers with valuable insights into student understanding. At the end of a lesson or class period, teachers can distribute exit tickets to gauge student comprehension. These tickets typically consist of a brief question or prompt related to the key concepts or skills covered in the lesson. Students respond individually and submit their answers before leaving the class. The teacher can then quickly review the responses to identify common misconceptions or areas that need further instruction. This formative assessment technique helps prioritize instructional decisions, tailoring future lessons to address identified gaps.

Case Study 3: Peer Feedback and Peer Assessment

In Ms. Rodriguez's middle school science class, students engage in peer feedback and peer assessment activities to promote deeper learning. For example, during a group project on the water cycle, students provide feedback on their peers' work using a structured rubric. They evaluate the clarity of the explanations, the accuracy of the diagrams, and the overall organization of the project. This formative assessment approach encourages students to critically evaluate their peers' work and provide constructive feedback. It not only helps students refine their own understanding but also promotes collaboration and communication skills.

Best Practice 3: Ongoing Observations and Anecdotal Notes

An effective formative assessment practice involves ongoing observations and anecdotal notes. Teachers actively monitor students during instructional activities, taking note of their participation, engagement, and levels of understanding. These observations can help teachers identify students who are struggling or excelling, allowing for timely interventions or additional challenges. Anecdotal notes complement quantitative data with qualitative information about students' progress, strengths, and areas for improvement. By continuously gathering anecdotal evidence, teachers can make informed instructional decisions and provide targeted feedback to support student learning.

These case studies and best practices illustrate the multifaceted nature of formative assessment and its versatility across grade levels and subject areas. By implementing these strategies, educators can create a more inclusive and student-centered learning environment while promoting continuous growth and academic excellence. Remember, the key to effective formative assessment lies in purposeful planning, ongoing reflection, and meaningful feedback to support student progress.

Adaptive learning and formative assessment

In the field of education, adaptive learning refers to a teaching approach that uses technology and data to personalize the learning experience for each individual student. It is a dynamic and responsive method that tailors instruction to meet the unique needs and abilities of students. Adaptive learning systems use a combination of assessment, data analysis, and feedback to adjust the pace, content, and delivery of instruction. This section will explore the concept of adaptive learning in relation to formative assessment, which is a key component of the learning process.

Understanding adaptive learning

Adaptive learning leverages technology to create personalized learning paths for students. It starts with an initial assessment to gauge the student's knowledge and skills in a particular area. Based on the results, the adaptive learning platform generates a customized learning plan that takes into account the student's strengths, weaknesses, and individual learning style. The learning plan may include a variety of instructional materials, such as videos, simulations, interactive modules, and practice exercises.

The adaptive learning system continuously monitors the student's progress and performance. It collects data on the student's responses, time taken to complete tasks, and level of mastery. Through machine learning algorithms, the system analyzes this data to make informed decisions about the next steps in the learning process. It adapts the content, pace, and level of difficulty to ensure optimal learning for the student.

Benefits of adaptive learning

Adaptive learning offers several benefits for both students and teachers. First and foremost, it allows for personalized instruction. By tailoring the learning experience to the individual needs of each student, adaptive learning increases engagement and motivation. Students can learn at their own pace, which helps to build confidence and a sense of ownership over their learning journey.

Furthermore, adaptive learning promotes mastery-based learning. The system identifies areas of weakness and provides additional practice and support until the student demonstrates mastery. As a result, students are able to achieve a deeper understanding of the content and develop higher-order thinking skills.

Additionally, adaptive learning provides real-time feedback to students. It offers immediate guidance and corrective feedback, enabling students to identify and address misconceptions or errors as they occur. This timely feedback promotes self-reflection and enhances metacognitive skills.

For teachers, adaptive learning systems offer valuable insights into student performance. They provide detailed analytics and progress reports, allowing teachers to track individual and class-level progress. This data-driven approach enables teachers to make informed instructional decisions and provide targeted support to students who need it the most.

Integrating formative assessment into adaptive learning

Formative assessment is an essential component of adaptive learning. It is a process of gathering feedback and monitoring student progress during the learning process. Formative assessment provides information that guides instruction and helps identify areas for improvement.

In the context of adaptive learning, formative assessment is used to collect data on student performance and understanding. The adaptive learning system incorporates formative assessment tasks, such as quizzes or interactive exercises, at regular intervals. These tasks allow students to demonstrate their knowledge and skills in a specific area and provide the system with valuable data.

The adaptive learning system analyzes the results of the formative assessments to make informed decisions about the next steps in the learning process. It identifies areas of weakness or misconceptions and generates targeted instructional materials to address these gaps. The system may provide additional practice exercises, offer explanatory videos, or suggest alternative learning resources based on the student's performance.

Formative assessment in adaptive learning goes beyond traditional quizzes or tests. It can include a variety of interactive activities, such as simulations, problem-solving tasks, or collaborative projects. These activities provide a more comprehensive picture of the student's skills and understanding.

Challenges and considerations

While adaptive learning and formative assessment offer great potential for enhancing student learning, there are challenges and considerations to be mindful of.

One challenge is ensuring the validity and reliability of the assessment data. It is important to align the formative assessment tasks with the intended learning outcomes and ensure that they effectively measure the desired knowledge and skills. Continuous validation and refinement of the assessment tasks are necessary to maintain the integrity of the adaptive learning system.

Ethical considerations also come into play in the context of adaptive learning and formative assessment. It is crucial to handle student data with care and respect privacy rights. Adequate measures should be taken to protect student information and ensure data security.

Another consideration is the need for professional development for teachers. Adopting adaptive learning and implementing formative assessment practices require teachers to develop new skills and pedagogical strategies. Ongoing support and training are essential to enable teachers to effectively integrate adaptive learning into their instructional practices.

Case studies and best practices

Several educational institutions have successfully implemented adaptive learning and formative assessment practices. For example, at Arizona State University, adaptive learning has been integrated into large-enrollment math courses. Through the use of adaptive technology, students receive personalized instruction that targets their specific needs and allows for self-paced learning. This approach has led to improved student outcomes and decreased withdrawal rates.

Another best practice is the use of data analytics to inform instructional decisions. The Summit Learning program, developed by Summit Public Schools, uses personalized learning plans and ongoing formative assessments to tailor instruction to students' needs. The platform collects data on student performance and provides insights to teachers, enabling them to adjust instruction and provide targeted support.

Conclusion

Adaptive learning and formative assessment are powerful tools for enhancing the learning experience. By personalizing instruction and providing real-time feedback, these approaches support students' individual needs and promote deeper learning. Integrating formative assessment into adaptive learning allows for continuous monitoring of student progress and ensures that instruction is tailored to address students' specific needs. However, it is important to address challenges such as validity, ethics, and teacher professional development to ensure the successful implementation of adaptive learning and formative assessment. By leveraging technology and data, educators can create transformative learning environments that empower students to achieve academic excellence.

Peer and self-assessment in formative assessment

Formative assessment is a crucial component of the learning process as it provides feedback to both students and teachers on the progress and understanding of the subject matter. Traditional formative assessment methods involve teachers evaluating student work and providing feedback. However, peer and self-assessment can be valuable additions to formative assessment practices. Peer assessment involves students evaluating the work of their peers, while self-assessment involves students reflecting on their own work. Both approaches have been shown to have numerous benefits for student learning and development.

Benefits of peer assessment

Peer assessment has several advantages in the formative assessment process. Firstly, it promotes active learning as students take responsibility for their own learning and engage with the work of others. By assessing their peers' work, students reinforce their understanding of the subject matter and develop a deeper knowledge of the topic. Peer assessment also encourages critical thinking skills and the ability to provide constructive feedback. By evaluating their peers' work, students are required to think critically about the strengths and weaknesses of the work, leading to a deeper understanding of the material. Additionally, peer assessment promotes self-regulation and autonomy as students are empowered to assess and improve their own work based on feedback from their peers. This process enhances student metacognition and self-reflection skills.

Implementing peer assessment

Implementing peer assessment in the classroom requires careful planning and clear guidelines. Here are some steps to consider:

1. Clear expectations: Provide students with clear guidelines and criteria for assessing their peers' work. This ensures consistency and fairness in the assessment process.

2. Training: Before engaging in peer assessment, students should be trained on how to provide constructive feedback and how to use the assessment criteria. This can be done through modeling, examples, and practice sessions.

3. Peer feedback workshops: Plan structured workshops where students can exchange their work and provide feedback to their peers. This helps them develop their assessment skills and learn from each other.

4. Anonymous assessments: To avoid bias and promote fairness, consider implementing anonymous assessments where students assess the work of their peers without knowing the identity of the author. This encourages objective and unbiased evaluations.

5. Reflection and discussion: After completing the peer assessment process, provide opportunities for students to reflect on the feedback they received and discuss their findings with their peers. This promotes deeper understanding and encourages students to take ownership of their learning.

Benefits of self-assessment

Self-assessment is an essential aspect of formative assessment as it enables students to become actively involved in their learning process. By evaluating their own work, students become more self-aware of their strengths and weaknesses. They develop a greater understanding of the learning objectives and can set goals accordingly. Self-assessment also nurtures a sense of responsibility and ownership in students as they take charge of their own learning and strive for improvement.

Implementing self-assessment

To incorporate self-assessment effectively, here are some strategies to consider:

1. Clear criteria: Provide students with explicit criteria and standards for self-assessment. This helps them understand what is expected and enables them to assess their work accurately.
2. Reflection and goal-setting: Encourage students to reflect on their work and identify areas for improvement. Have them set specific and achievable goals based on their self-assessment.
3. Checklists and rubrics: Provide checklists or rubrics to guide students in assessing their work. These tools can help students focus on specific aspects of their work and encourage self-reflection.
4. Peer discussions: Engage students in discussions with their peers to gain different perspectives on their work. This can enhance self-assessment by facilitating deeper reflection and the identification of areas for improvement.
5. Teacher feedback: Provide timely and constructive feedback to students on their self-assessment. This helps them validate their judgments and provides guidance for further improvement.

Challenges and considerations

While peer and self-assessment offer valuable benefits, there are challenges and considerations to keep in mind:

1. Training and support: Students need guidance on how to assess their peers' work effectively and how to self-assess accurately. Providing training and ongoing support is crucial for successful implementation.
2. Consistency and fairness: Ensuring consistency and fairness in peer assessments can be challenging. Clear guidelines and assessment criteria can help mitigate this issue.

3. External validation: It is important to validate peer and self-assessment by comparing them with teacher assessments. This helps maintain accuracy and reliability.

4. Confidence and cultural factors: Students may lack confidence in their ability to assess their peers' work or may hesitate to provide constructive feedback. Cultural factors can also influence the assessment process, requiring sensitivity and inclusivity.

Despite these challenges, incorporating peer and self-assessment into formative assessment practices enhances student engagement, critical thinking skills, and self-regulation. It empowers students to take an active role in their learning and promotes a deeper understanding of the subject matter. Through careful planning, training, and support, educators can effectively implement peer and self-assessment methods in their classrooms to improve student learning outcomes.

Formative assessment in different subject areas

Formative assessment is a crucial component of the learning process in any subject area. It provides valuable feedback to both students and teachers, allowing for the identification of strengths and areas in need of improvement. In this section, we will explore how formative assessment can be applied in different subject areas, highlighting specific strategies and examples.

Mathematics

Formative assessment in mathematics plays a vital role in helping students develop conceptual understanding and problem-solving skills. Here are some effective strategies for assessing student learning in mathematics:

1. **Diagnostic questioning:** Ask open-ended questions that encourage students to explain their thought processes and reasoning in solving mathematical problems. This helps identify any misconceptions or gaps in understanding.

Example: Suppose a student is struggling with multiplying fractions. A diagnostic question could be: "Explain why multiplying two fractions results in a product that is smaller than the original fractions."

2. **Mathematical tasks:** Assign challenging and real-world mathematical tasks that require students to apply their knowledge and skills in different problem-solving scenarios. This can help gauge their ability to transfer learning to new situations.

Example: Provide a problem-solving task where students need to calculate the dimensions of a pyramid given the volume and height.

3. **Mathematical discourse:** Encourage classroom discussions and peer-to-peer interactions that focus on mathematical reasoning and justification. This allows students to articulate their mathematical thinking and engage in collaborative learning.

Example: Organize a group activity where students work together to solve a complex mathematical problem and explain their reasoning to their peers.

4. **Mathematical journals:** Ask students to maintain mathematical journals where they can reflect on their learning, document problem-solving strategies, and explain the steps taken to arrive at a solution. This provides insight into their thinking processes and allows for ongoing feedback.

Example: Students can keep a journal entry after solving a challenging word problem, describing the approach used and any difficulties encountered.

By implementing these formative assessment strategies in mathematics, teachers can identify areas of improvement, tailor instruction to meet individual student needs, and help students develop a deep understanding of mathematical concepts.

Science

Formative assessment is an essential tool in science education, as it helps students develop critical thinking skills, scientific inquiry abilities, and content knowledge. Here are some effective formative assessment strategies for assessing student learning in science:

1. **Concept maps:** Ask students to create concept maps that illustrate their understanding of the connections between scientific concepts. This visual representation of their knowledge helps identify any misunderstandings or gaps.

Example: Have students create a concept map to demonstrate their understanding of the water cycle, including key terms and their relationships to each other.

2. **Lab reports:** Assess students' understanding of scientific inquiry by evaluating their lab reports. Pay attention to their experimental design, data analysis, and conclusions drawn from the results. This allows for feedback on their scientific thinking and communication skills.

Example: Provide a lab activity where students investigate the effect of light intensity on the rate of photosynthesis in plants. Evaluate their lab reports for accurate data collection and interpretation.

3. **Scientific models:** Ask students to create models that represent scientific phenomena or concepts. This helps assess their understanding of the underlying principles and their ability to communicate scientific ideas.

Example: Have students create a model of the solar system, considering the relative sizes, distances, and motions of the planets.

4. **Classroom discussions:** Engage students in scientific discourse through classroom discussions. Encourage them to explain their reasoning, critique the ideas of others, and support their arguments with evidence.

Example: Initiate a discussion on climate change, where students present evidence supporting or refuting the claim that human activities contribute to global warming.

By incorporating these formative assessment strategies in science classrooms, teachers can gain valuable insight into student learning, provide timely feedback, and guide students towards a deeper understanding of scientific concepts.

Language Arts

Formative assessment in language arts focuses on developing students' reading, writing, speaking, and listening skills. It enables teachers to identify areas of improvement and provide targeted support. Here are some formative assessment strategies for assessing student learning in language arts:

1. **Reading conferences:** Conduct one-on-one reading conferences with students to assess their reading comprehension, fluency, and vocabulary acquisition. Use prompts and questions to encourage student reflection and discussion.

Example: During a reading conference, ask students to summarize what they have read, make predictions, or make connections between the text and their own experiences.

2. **Writing portfolios:** Have students maintain writing portfolios where they collect their written work and reflections. Regularly review their writing samples to assess their progress, provide feedback, and guide them in developing their writing skills.

Example: Ask students to include a variety of writing genres in their portfolios, such as narrative, persuasive, and informative essays.

3. **Listening and speaking tasks:** Design listening and speaking tasks that require students to demonstrate their understanding and ability to communicate effectively. These tasks can include presentations, debates, and small group discussions.

Example: Organize a debate on a controversial topic, such as the use of technology in education, where students must present arguments backed by evidence.

4. **Performance-based assessments:** Assign performance-based assessments that allow students to demonstrate their language arts skills in real-world contexts. This can include creating multimedia presentations, participating in literary performances, or producing podcasts.

Example: Have students create a multimedia presentation on a favorite book, incorporating elements such as visuals, audio recordings, and written reflections.

By utilizing these formative assessment strategies in language arts, teachers can gain insights into students' literacy development and provide targeted instruction to support their growth as readers, writers, speakers, and listeners.

These subject-specific examples provide a starting point for implementing formative assessment in various disciplines. However, it is essential to tailor these strategies to the specific needs and goals of your classroom and students. By using formative assessment effectively, educators can create a student-centered learning environment that promotes growth and academic success.

Future directions of formative assessment

Formative assessment plays a crucial role in the educational process, providing continuous feedback to students and teachers to gauge student understanding, identify knowledge gaps, and inform instructional decisions. As education continues to evolve in response to technological advancements and changing learning needs, the future of formative assessment is poised to embrace innovative approaches and tools that enhance its effectiveness and efficiency. In this section, we will explore some exciting future directions of formative assessment.

Adaptive formative assessment

One promising direction for formative assessment is the integration of adaptive technology. Adaptive formative assessment leverages artificial intelligence and machine learning algorithms to tailor assessment experiences to individual student needs. Through the use of adaptive algorithms, assessments can dynamically adjust the difficulty and content based on student responses. This personalized approach allows students to receive targeted feedback and support, leading to more efficient and effective learning.

For example, a digital learning platform could adaptively generate questions based on the student's performance and previous responses, challenging them at an appropriate level and providing immediate feedback. This adaptive formative assessment not only enhances student engagement but also optimizes learning outcomes by addressing each student's specific learning needs.

Multimodal formative assessment

Another exciting direction for formative assessment is the incorporation of multimodal assessment methods. Traditional formative assessments often focus on written or multiple-choice questions, limiting the range of skills and abilities that can be assessed. However, by embracing multimodal assessment, we can capture a broader spectrum of student learning and provide more comprehensive feedback.

Multimodal formative assessment may include elements such as oral presentations, multimedia projects, demonstrations, and performances. By evaluating student work across multiple modes, educators can gain a deeper understanding of students' knowledge, skills, and competencies. This approach also encourages students to express their understanding using various forms of media, promoting creativity, critical thinking, and communication skills.

Real-time analytics

The future of formative assessment also lies in the integration of real-time analytics. With the increasing availability of educational technologies and learning management systems, educators can leverage data analytics to gain valuable insights into student progress and performance. Real-time analytics enable teachers to monitor students' engagement, identify misconceptions, and adapt instructional strategies accordingly.

For instance, an online platform can generate visual dashboards that display key indicators of student learning in real-time, such as completion rates, mastery levels, and time spent on specific tasks. These analytics can inform timely intervention and targeted feedback, enabling educators to provide immediate support to struggling students and challenge high-achieving students further.

Gamified formative assessment

Gamification, the integration of game elements and mechanics in non-game contexts, holds immense potential in transforming formative assessment. By incorporating game elements such as point systems, leaderboards, badges, and quests, educators can create engaging assessment experiences that motivate students to actively participate in the learning process and strive for improvement.

For example, a teacher could design a virtual learning environment where students earn points or badges for completing formative assessments or demonstrating progress in specific learning goals. These gamified elements provide immediate feedback, foster a sense of accomplishment, and create a supportive and competitive learning environment. By aligning assessments with gamified elements, educators can increase student engagement and intrinsic motivation for learning.

Socio-emotional formative assessment

As the importance of socio-emotional learning is recognized in education, integrating socio-emotional formative assessment is likely to be a future direction. Socio-emotional formative assessment aims to assess and develop students' social and emotional competencies, such as self-awareness, self-management, social awareness, relationship skills, and responsible decision-making.

Educators can use a variety of assessment methods, including self-assessments, peer assessments, and teacher observations, to gather data on students' socio-emotional development. This data can inform targeted interventions and support the growth of these critical skills. By promoting socio-emotional formative assessment, educators can create nurturing and inclusive learning environments that foster students' holistic development.

Ethical considerations

As the future of formative assessment unfolds, it is crucial to consider the ethical implications of these new approaches. Educators and policymakers must ensure that formative assessment practices prioritize student well-being, privacy, and data security. Additionally, attention should be given to address potential biases in adaptive algorithms and the impact of gamified assessments on student motivation and equity.

To navigate these ethical considerations, interdisciplinary collaboration among educators, psychologists, technologists, researchers, and policymakers is necessary. Together, they can develop guidelines, policies, and frameworks that promote the responsible and ethical use of formative assessment technologies.

Conclusion

The future of formative assessment holds great promise in enhancing learning experiences and improving student outcomes. Through the integration of adaptive technology, multimodal assessment methods, real-time analytics, gamification, and socio-emotional assessment, we can transform formative assessment into a dynamic and personalized process that supports individual student needs and promotes holistic development. However, as we embrace these future directions, it is essential to remain vigilant about the ethical considerations and ensure that the benefits of formative assessment are accessible to all learners. By embracing these advancements and addressing their ethical implications, we can shape a future of formative assessment that empowers educators and learners alike.

Summative Assessment

Understanding Summative Assessment

Summative assessment is an important aspect of education that aims to evaluate students' learning outcomes and provide an overall judgment of their academic performance. Unlike formative assessment, which is ongoing and focuses on providing feedback for learning, summative assessment is conducted at the end of a unit, course, or academic period to determine the extent to which students have mastered the content and achieved the intended learning outcomes. In this section, we will delve into the key aspects of summative assessment, its benefits, strategies, and challenges.

Purpose of Summative Assessment

The primary purpose of summative assessment is to measure and evaluate students' knowledge, skills, and abilities acquired over a specific period. It aims to provide a comprehensive measure of student achievement and determine the extent to which they have met the learning objectives. Summative assessment plays a crucial role in making high-stakes decisions, such as grading students, promotion to the next level, or certification of competency.

Characteristics of Summative Assessment

Summative assessment typically has certain characteristics that distinguish it from formative assessment:

- **Endpoint assessment:** Summative assessment is conducted at the end of a learning period or a specific unit of study.
- **Judgment-oriented:** It focuses on evaluating the overall performance and determining the level of achievement of students.
- **Standardized:** Summative assessments often follow predefined criteria or rubrics to ensure consistency and fairness in evaluating student work.
- **Graded:** Scores or grades are assigned to students based on their performance in summative assessments.

- **External feedback:** Summative assessment provides feedback to students regarding their overall performance and helps them identify areas for improvement.

Types of Summative Assessment

There are various types of summative assessment methods that educators can employ to evaluate student learning:

- **Examinations:** Traditional exams, such as multiple-choice tests, short answer questions, and essay-style exams, are commonly used as summative assessments to measure students' knowledge and understanding of a subject.

- **Projects:** Students may be required to complete a research project, design a solution to a problem, or create a product that demonstrates their mastery of content and skills.

- **Portfolios:** Portfolios consist of a collection of students' work over a period of time, showcasing their progress and achievements in different areas.

- **Presentations:** Students may be assessed on their ability to deliver an oral presentation on a specific topic, demonstrating their knowledge and communication skills.

- **Performance assessments:** In certain disciplines like music, dance, or physical education, performance assessments evaluate students' practical skills and abilities.

- **Standardized tests:** External standardized tests, such as SAT, ACT, or state assessments, are often used for summative assessment purposes to compare students' performance at a national or international level.

Benefits of Summative Assessment

Summative assessment offers several benefits to students, educators, and educational institutions:

- **Determining achievement:** Summative assessment provides a comprehensive measure of students' achievement and their ability to meet the learning objectives.

- **Feedback for improvement:** Students receive feedback on their overall performance, enabling them to identify their strengths and weaknesses and make necessary improvements.
- **Curriculum evaluation:** Summative assessment results help evaluate the effectiveness of the curriculum and instructional strategies used in a course or program.
- **Accountability:** Summative assessments provide accountability for both students and educators, as they demonstrate the extent to which learning outcomes have been met.
- **External recognition:** Summative assessment results can be used as proof of competency or qualification, recognized by external entities such as employers or higher education institutions.

Strategies for Summative Assessment

To ensure the effectiveness and validity of summative assessment, educators can employ various strategies:

1. **Clearly defined learning objectives:** The learning objectives for the assessment should be well-defined, aligned with the curriculum, and communicated to students in advance.
2. **Rubrics and grading criteria:** Clear criteria and rubrics should be established to provide transparency and consistency in grading. This helps both students and educators understand the expectations for each level of achievement.
3. **Authentic tasks:** Design tasks that mirror real-world challenges and allow students to apply their knowledge and skills in context. This enhances the relevance and authenticity of the assessment.
4. **Multiple measures:** Use a combination of assessment methods to capture a more comprehensive view of students' learning, considering their diverse strengths and talents.
5. **Timely feedback:** Provide timely feedback to students, highlighting their strengths and areas for improvement. This helps students to reflect on their performance and take necessary actions for growth.

Challenges in Implementing Summative Assessment

Implementing summative assessment can present several challenges:

- **Overemphasis on grades:** The focus on grades can put excessive pressure on students and overshadow the importance of learning for the sake of learning.
- **Limited scope:** Summative assessment might not capture all aspects of a student's abilities or provide a holistic view of their learning outcomes.
- **Standardized assessment bias:** Standardized summative assessments may be biased towards certain cultural, socioeconomic, or linguistic groups, leading to inequitable outcomes.
- **Assessment overload:** Conducting too many summative assessments can lead to assessment fatigue and take away valuable learning time.

Future Directions of Summative Assessment

As education continues to evolve, so does the approach to summative assessment. Here are a few future directions that hold promise:

- **Authentic digital assessments:** With advancements in technology, the future will see the development of more authentic digital assessments that simulate real-world scenarios and require higher-order thinking skills.
- **Competency-based assessments:** There is a growing shift towards competency-based education, where assessments focus on measuring specific skills and abilities rather than traditional subject-based knowledge.
- **Online proctoring and security:** The future of summative assessment may involve the use of advanced online proctoring systems to ensure security and integrity during remote exams.
- **Adaptive assessments:** Adaptive assessments tailor the difficulty and content based on students' responses, providing a personalized and efficient evaluation of their abilities.

In conclusion, summative assessment serves as a vital tool in evaluating students' overall performance and determining their level of achievement. By understanding the purpose, characteristics, strategies, and challenges associated with summative assessment, educators can make informed decisions and design effective assessments that support meaningful learning outcomes. As education continues to evolve, the future of summative assessment holds exciting possibilities for more personalized, authentic, and inclusive assessment practices.

Benefits of Summative Assessment

Summative assessment plays a crucial role in the educational process by evaluating students' overall learning and achievement. It is typically conducted at the end of a learning unit, course, or academic term to determine the extent to which students have met the learning objectives and standards. This section will discuss the various benefits of summative assessment in education.

Measuring Learning Outcomes

One of the key benefits of summative assessment is its ability to measure students' learning outcomes. By using a standardized evaluation method, such as exams, projects, or presentations, educators can effectively assess the knowledge, skills, and competencies that students have acquired throughout the learning process. It provides a comprehensive view of students' achievements, allowing educators to gauge their level of understanding and mastery of the subject matter.

Providing Feedback for Improvement

Summative assessment also serves as a valuable tool for providing feedback to students. While formative assessment focuses on the ongoing process of learning and provides immediate feedback for improvement, summative assessment provides students with a comprehensive overview of their performance. This feedback can help students identify their strengths and weaknesses, enabling them to make targeted improvements in their learning strategies and study habits.

Recognizing Achievement and Progress

In addition to evaluating learning outcomes, summative assessment helps recognize students' achievements and progress. It provides a measure of success and accomplishment, giving students a sense of accomplishment and boosting their confidence. The act of being formally assessed and receiving a grade or a certificate serves as recognition for their hard work and dedication.

Informing Instructional Decisions

Summative assessment results not only benefit students but also inform instructional decisions for educators. By analyzing the assessment data, educators can identify areas of strength and areas that need improvement in their teaching methods and curriculum design. This information helps guide instructional planning and enables educators to make informed decisions about adjusting their teaching strategies and interventions to better support student learning.

Evaluating Program Effectiveness

Furthermore, summative assessment is critical for evaluating the effectiveness of educational programs and curriculum. It provides valuable insights into the overall performance of students and allows educators and policymakers to determine the efficiency of instructional practices, teaching resources, and curriculum implementation. This information can guide program improvement efforts, ensuring that educational initiatives are aligned with desired learning outcomes.

Preparing for Higher Education and Employment

Summative assessment also plays a vital role in preparing students for higher education and the workforce. By evaluating students' knowledge and skills against established standards, it helps ensure that they are adequately prepared for the challenges and expectations of higher education institutions or employment opportunities. It provides an objective measure of their readiness to pursue further education or enter the professional world.

Promoting Accountability and Quality Assurance

Lastly, summative assessment promotes accountability and quality assurance in the educational system. By providing a standardized evaluation method, it ensures that all students are held to the same standards and are assessed fairly and consistently. Summative assessment results also contribute to quality assurance initiatives by providing evidence of the effectiveness and quality of educational institutions and programs.

In conclusion, summative assessment offers several benefits in the educational context. It measures learning outcomes, provides feedback for improvement, recognizes achievement and progress, informs instructional decisions, evaluates program effectiveness, prepares students for higher education and employment, and promotes accountability and quality assurance. By utilizing summative assessment methods effectively, educators can gain valuable insights into students' learning and make informed decisions to enhance educational outcomes.

Summative Assessment Strategies and Tools

Summative assessment is a method of evaluating student learning at the end of a unit, course, or program. It focuses on measuring the overall achievement of students and determining their level of mastery of the learning objectives. In this section, we will explore various strategies and tools that can be used for summative assessment in educational settings.

Traditional Methods

1. **Exams and Tests:** Written exams and tests are commonly used for summative assessment. They can be designed in various formats, including multiple choice, short answer, essay, or problem-solving questions. These assessments provide a snapshot of students' knowledge and understanding of the material covered.
2. **Performance Assessments:** Performance assessments require students to demonstrate their skills or competencies in real-world contexts. Examples include presentations, portfolios, exhibitions, and practical assessments. These assessments provide a holistic view of students' abilities beyond just knowledge recall.
3. **Projects and Assignments:** Project-based assessments involve the completion of an extended project or assignment that showcases students' understanding, critical thinking, research, and problem-solving skills. These assessments can be individual or group-based and allow for creativity and application of knowledge.
4. **Oral Examinations:** Oral examinations involve a one-on-one conversation between the student and the examiner. This assessment method allows for in-depth exploration of the student's understanding, reasoning, and communication skills. It is particularly useful for assessing language proficiency, public speaking, or subject-specific discussions.

Technology-Enhanced Methods

1. **Online Quizzes and Assessments:** Online platforms and learning management systems provide tools for creating and administering quizzes and assessments. These tools often include features such as automated grading, immediate feedback, and question randomization. They allow for efficient administration and analysis of assessment results.

2. **Simulations and Virtual Assessments:** Simulations and virtual environments can be used to assess students' skills and decision-making abilities in realistic scenarios. For example, medical students can simulate patient consultations, and engineering students can engage in virtual experiments. These assessments provide an interactive and immersive experience for students.

3. **E-Portfolios:** E-portfolios are digital collections of student work that demonstrate their progress, achievements, and reflections over time. They allow students to showcase a range of artifacts, such as essays, projects, videos, and presentations. E-portfolios provide a comprehensive view of students' growth and development.

4. **Peer and Self-Assessment Tools:** Technology can facilitate the process of peer and self-assessment by providing structured frameworks and rubrics. Online tools enable students to evaluate their own work or provide feedback to their peers. This promotes self-reflection, metacognition, and the development of critical evaluation skills.

Considerations and Best Practices

When implementing summative assessment strategies and tools, it is essential to consider the following best practices:

1. **Alignment with Learning Objectives:** All summative assessments should align with the intended learning outcomes of the course or program. The assessment should accurately measure what students are expected to know and be able to do.

2. **Validity and Reliability:** It is crucial to ensure that the summative assessments are valid and reliable. Validity refers to the extent to which the assessment measures what it intends to measure, while reliability refers to the consistency of the assessment results.

3. **Clear Rubrics and Grading Criteria:** Providing clear rubrics and grading criteria helps maintain consistency and fairness in evaluating student work. Rubrics outline the expectations and criteria for performance at different levels, making the grading process transparent and understandable for students.

4. **Timely and Constructive Feedback:** Providing timely and constructive feedback is essential for students to understand their performance and areas for improvement. Feedback should be specific, actionable, and focused on helping students grow and develop.

5. **Ethical Considerations:** When using technology-enhanced assessment methods, it is important to consider ethical considerations such as data privacy, security, and equitable access to technology. Protecting student privacy and ensuring fairness in assessment are crucial.

6. **Balance of Assessment Methods:** A variety of assessment methods should be used to provide a well-rounded picture of students' learning. Combining traditional and technology-enhanced methods can encourage different types of skills and accommodate diverse learning styles.

In summary, summative assessment serves as a valuable tool to evaluate student learning and determine the level of achievement of learning objectives. Effective summative assessment strategies and tools should align with the learning objectives, be valid and reliable, provide clear grading criteria and timely feedback, and consider ethical considerations. By incorporating a mix of traditional and technology-enhanced methods, educators can gather comprehensive evidence of student achievement and promote continuous improvement.

Technology-enhanced Summative Assessment

Assessment plays a vital role in education, providing teachers with valuable insights into students' learning progress and helping to measure the effectiveness of educational programs. Summative assessment, in particular, focuses on evaluating students' understanding and knowledge acquisition at the end of a learning period. In this section, we will explore how technology can enhance the process of summative assessment, making it more efficient, valid, and reliable.

Benefits of Technology-enhanced Summative Assessment

Integrating technology into summative assessment brings several benefits to both educators and students. Firstly, technology allows for the efficient administration of assessments, reducing the time and effort required for tasks such as grading and data analysis. Automated grading systems, for example, can quickly process multiple-choice or fill-in-the-blank questions, providing instant feedback to students.

Secondly, technology-enhanced assessments provide more flexibility in the types of questions and tasks that can be included. Multimedia elements such as videos, images, and interactive simulations can be incorporated to assess students' abilities to analyze, synthesize, and evaluate information. This approach enhances the authenticity of the assessment by creating real-world scenarios, engaging students in more meaningful ways.

Furthermore, technology enables the use of adaptive assessments, which adjust the difficulty level of questions based on a student's previous responses. Adaptive assessments can provide a more accurate measure of a student's knowledge and understanding by tailoring the questions to their individual capabilities. This personalized approach ensures that students are appropriately challenged and prevents them from feeling overwhelmed or bored.

Lastly, technology allows for efficient and secure storage of assessment data, making it readily available for analysis and reporting. Digital platforms and learning management systems can provide comprehensive reports on individual and group performance, enabling educators to identify areas of strength and weakness in their teaching and curriculum. This data-driven approach enables informed decision-making and targeted interventions to improve learning outcomes.

Designing Technology-enhanced Summative Assessments

Designing effective technology-enhanced summative assessments requires careful consideration of various factors. Here are some key principles to consider:

1. **Alignment with learning objectives:** The assessments should align closely with the learning objectives and content covered in the instruction. This ensures that the assessment measures what students were intended to learn and provides a meaningful evaluation of their knowledge and skills.

2. **Authenticity:** The assessment tasks should mirror real-life situations or problems relevant to the subject area. This encourages students to apply their knowledge and skills in practical contexts, enhancing the authenticity and relevance of the assessment.

3. **Validity and reliability:** Validity refers to the extent to which an assessment accurately measures what it is intended to measure, while reliability refers to the consistency and dependability of assessment results. It is crucial to ensure that technology-enhanced assessments are valid and reliable by following established assessment principles and procedures.

4. **Clear instructions and expectations:** Clear instructions should be provided to students regarding the assessment tasks and expectations. This helps to minimize confusion and ensure that students understand what is required of them.

5. **Accessibility and inclusivity:** Technology-enhanced assessments should be accessible to all students, regardless of their varying abilities or characteristics. Designing assessments that accommodate diverse learners, such as providing alternative formats or assistive technologies, promotes equity and inclusion.

6. **Engagement and interactivity:** Leveraging the capabilities of technology, assessments should be designed to engage and interact with students. Incorporating interactive elements, multimedia, and gamification techniques can enhance student motivation and involvement in the assessment process.

Challenges and Considerations

While technology-enhanced summative assessment offers many advantages, there are also challenges and considerations that educators must address:

1. **Technical infrastructure:** Adequate technical infrastructure, including reliable internet connectivity and access to devices, is essential for implementing technology-enhanced assessments. Without proper infrastructure, students may face difficulties in completing assessments or accessing the necessary resources.

2. **Data privacy and security:** Protecting student data privacy and ensuring the security of assessment platforms and systems are critical considerations. Educators must follow ethical guidelines and adhere to relevant data protection laws when using technology to collect and store student assessment data.

3. **Equity and accessibility:** Providing equal opportunities for all students to access and participate in technology-enhanced assessments is crucial. Educators should consider the potential barriers that students may face, such as language proficiency, socioeconomic status, or disabilities, and provide appropriate accommodations to promote inclusivity.

4. **Teacher training and support:** Educators need adequate training and support to effectively design, administer, and interpret technology-enhanced summative assessments. Ongoing professional development opportunities can help educators stay updated on emerging assessment technologies and best practices.

5. **Validity and fairness:** It is essential to ensure that technology-enhanced assessments are valid and fair measures of student learning. Careful consideration should be given to the selection of appropriate assessment methods, alignment with learning outcomes, and the prevention of bias or discrimination in assessment design and scoring.

Case Studies

Let's explore two case studies that demonstrate the effective use of technology-enhanced summative assessment:

Case Study 1: Online Exam Proctoring

In this case study, an educational institution implemented online proctoring software to monitor remote exams securely. The software utilized facial recognition technology and machine learning algorithms to detect potential cheating behaviors, such as using external resources during the exam. This technology enhanced the reliability and integrity of summative assessments, ensuring that students' achievements were accurately measured.

Case Study 2: Digital Portfolios

In this case study, students in a fine arts program created digital portfolios to showcase their artistic skills and growth over time. The portfolios included multimedia elements such as images, videos, and written reflections. This technology-enhanced summative assessment allowed students to demonstrate their creativity, critical thinking, and artistic abilities in a more comprehensive and engaging manner.

Resources and Tools

Educators can leverage a range of resources and tools to implement technology-enhanced summative assessments effectively. Here are some examples:

1. **Assessment platforms:** Platforms such as Google Forms, Moodle, or Learning Management Systems (LMS) provide features for creating and administering technology-enhanced assessments. These platforms offer a variety of question types, automated grading, and data analysis functionalities.

2. **Multimedia creation tools:** Tools like Adobe Spark, Canva, or Piktochart can be used to create visually appealing and interactive multimedia elements, enhancing the authenticity and engagement of assessments.

3. **Online collaboration tools:** Tools such as Google Docs, Microsoft Teams, or Padlet enable collaborative assessment activities, allowing students to work together on projects, share their work, and provide feedback to each other.

4. **Digital portfolio platforms:** Platforms like Seesaw, Pathbrite, or Google Sites support the creation and sharing of digital portfolios, enabling students to document and showcase their learning progress and achievements.

5. **Simulation and virtual lab software:** Simulators and virtual lab software, such as ChemCollective, PhET Interactive Simulations, or Labster, allow students to perform virtual experiments and simulations, providing opportunities for authentic assessment in science and other STEM subjects.

Exercises

1. Consider a high school history class. Design a technology-enhanced summative assessment that assesses students' understanding of a specific historical event. Describe the assessment format, question types, and multimedia elements you would include to make it engaging and authentic.

2. Research an adaptive assessment tool or software and explain how it can be used in a mathematics class to provide personalized summative assessment. Discuss the benefits and potential challenges of implementing such a tool.

3. Reflecting on the challenges and considerations discussed earlier, propose strategies to address the digital divide and ensure equitable access to technology-enhanced summative assessments for students from diverse backgrounds.

Conclusion

Technology-enhanced summative assessment offers numerous benefits, from efficient administration and flexibility in question types to personalization and data-driven insights. By carefully considering design principles, addressing challenges, and leveraging available resources, educators can create meaningful and effective summative assessments that enhance the learning experience and foster student success.

Overcoming Challenges in Implementing Summative Assessment

Summative assessment plays a crucial role in determining students' overall learning outcomes and achievements. It is used to measure the extent to which students have met the learning goals and objectives set by the curriculum. However, implementing summative assessment can present various challenges for educators. In this section, we will discuss some common challenges and explore strategies to overcome them.

Challenge 1: Aligning Assessment with Curriculum and Standards

One of the major challenges in implementing summative assessment is ensuring alignment with the curriculum and standards. Assessment tasks need to accurately reflect the content, skills, and knowledge outlined in the curriculum. Misalignment can lead to inaccurate assessment results and a misunderstanding of students' true abilities.

To overcome this challenge, educators can:

- Clearly define the learning objectives and desired outcomes of the curriculum.
- Develop assessment tasks that directly align with these objectives and outcomes.
- Continuously review and update assessment tasks to ensure alignment with evolving curriculum standards.

For example, in a mathematics class, if the curriculum emphasizes problem-solving skills, summative assessment tasks can be designed to evaluate students' ability to apply mathematical concepts in real-life scenarios.

Challenge 2: Designing Valid and Reliable Assessment Tools

Designing valid and reliable assessment tools is another challenge in summative assessment. Validity ensures that the assessment measures what it intends to measure, while reliability ensures consistent and accurate results.

To address this challenge, educators should:

- Clearly define the learning outcomes and knowledge/skill areas to be assessed.
- Develop clear assessment criteria or rubrics to ensure consistent evaluation.
- Pilot test the assessment tools with a small group of students to identify any issues or ambiguities.
- Regularly review and refine the assessment tools to improve validity and reliability.

For instance, if assessing students' writing skills, educators can design rubrics that clearly define the criteria for content, organization, language, and mechanics. This helps ensure consistency and objectivity in grading.

Challenge 3: Managing Time Constraints

Time constraints often pose challenges in administering and grading summative assessments. Educators may find it difficult to allocate sufficient time for students to complete the assessments, especially when covering a large curriculum.

To overcome time constraints, educators can:

- Establish realistic timelines for completing the assessments, considering the complexity of the tasks and students' abilities.
- Incorporate time-management skills as part of classroom instruction, teaching students how to effectively manage their time during assessments.
- Use technology tools to automate certain aspects of assessment administration and grading, which can save time and ensure efficiency.

For example, educators can use online assessment platforms that provide automated grading and immediate feedback, alleviating the need for manual grading.

Challenge 4: Addressing Student Anxiety and Stress

Summative assessments can create anxiety and stress among students, which may impact their performance. High-stakes exams or the fear of failure can hinder students' ability to demonstrate their true knowledge and skills.

To address student anxiety and stress, educators can:

- Foster a positive and supportive classroom environment, where mistakes are seen as learning opportunities and assessment is viewed as a tool for growth.
- Provide students with clear guidelines and expectations for the assessment, reducing uncertainty and anxiety.
- Incorporate formative assessment practices throughout the learning process, allowing students to receive feedback and learn from their mistakes before the summative assessment.
- Teach students stress-management techniques, such as deep breathing or mindfulness exercises, to help them relax during assessments.

Educators can also consider alternative assessment methods, such as performance-based assessments or portfolios, which can help alleviate stress and provide a more comprehensive view of students' abilities.

Challenge 5: Ensuring Fairness and Equity in Assessment

Ensuring fairness and equity in summative assessment is a critical challenge for educators. Students from diverse backgrounds may face different barriers or challenges that affect their performance. It is important to create a level playing field and provide equal opportunities for all students.

To address this challenge, educators should:

- Provide clear instructions and guidelines for assessment tasks, so that all students have a clear understanding of expectations.
- Consider cultural and linguistic diversity when designing assessment tasks to avoid bias and unfair disadvantage.
- Provide accommodations or modifications for students with special needs or disabilities, ensuring they can fully access and participate in the assessments.
- Regularly review the assessment process for potential biases or inequities, and make necessary adjustments to promote fairness.

Educators can also provide additional support and resources to students who may require extra assistance, ensuring that everyone has an equal opportunity to succeed.

Example: Addressing Equity in Mathematics Assessment

In a mathematics class, educators may encounter challenges related to equity in summative assessment. Students from different socio-economic backgrounds may have varying access to resources and support, which can influence their performance in assessments.

To address this challenge, educators can:

- Provide extra resources and support to students who may require additional assistance.
- Incorporate real-life and culturally diverse examples in assessment tasks to make them relatable and inclusive.
- Offer multiple ways for students to demonstrate their understanding, such as through oral presentations or visual representations, to accommodate different learning styles and abilities.

By addressing equity in summative assessment, educators can ensure that all students have an equal opportunity to succeed and demonstrate their mathematical knowledge and skills.

In conclusion, implementing summative assessment can present several challenges for educators. However, by actively addressing issues related to alignment, validity and reliability, time constraints, student anxiety, fairness, and equity, educators can overcome these challenges and create a more effective and inclusive summative assessment process. This ultimately leads to a better understanding of students' achievements and promotes their overall academic growth.

Case studies and best practices in summative assessment

In this section, we will explore case studies and best practices in summative assessment. Summative assessment plays a crucial role in measuring students' learning outcomes and determining their level of achievement at the end of a learning period. It provides a comprehensive evaluation of students' knowledge, skills, and competencies in a specific subject area.

1. Case Study: Standardized Tests in Mathematics

One common example of summative assessment in education is standardized tests. Let's consider a case study of summative assessment in mathematics using a standardized test.

Background: A school district decides to administer a standardized math test to evaluate students' understanding of key concepts and skills covered in the curriculum.

Principles: The purpose of this summative assessment is to determine students' proficiency levels and compare their performance with state or national standards. The standardized test provides objective and reliable data for evaluating the effectiveness of the math curriculum and identifying areas where improvement is needed.

Process: The standardized math test is administered to all students in the district, with a predetermined set of questions assessing various math topics and skills. The test is timed, allowing students to demonstrate their ability to solve problems within a given timeframe. The test is designed to cover a range of difficulty levels to gauge students' depth of understanding.

Analysis: Once the test is completed by all students, the results are analyzed to identify patterns and trends. The district compares students' performance with established benchmarks, such as grade-level expectations or national standards. This analysis provides valuable insights into the effectiveness of the math curriculum and helps identify areas for improvement.

Interventions: Based on the analysis of the test results, the school district may identify specific areas where students are struggling and provide targeted interventions. For example, if a significant number of students demonstrate a lack of understanding in a particular math concept, additional instructional support or resources may be allocated to address these gaps.

Benefits: Standardized tests provide a standardized measure of student achievement, allowing for comparisons across different schools, districts, or even countries. The results help educators, policymakers, and parents make informed decisions regarding curriculum development, instructional strategies, and resource allocation.

Challenges: Standardized tests have faced criticism for their emphasis on rote memorization and recall rather than deep understanding and critical thinking skills. It is crucial for educators to strike a balance between the need for standardized measures of assessment and the importance of fostering higher-order thinking skills in students.

2. Best Practices in Summative Assessment: Authentic Performance Tasks

In addition to standardized tests, incorporating authentic performance tasks in summative assessment can provide a more comprehensive and meaningful evaluation of students' learning. Authentic performance tasks are real-world or problem-based assessments that require students to apply their knowledge and skills in contextually rich situations.

Benefits: Authentic performance tasks allow students to demonstrate their ability to transfer learning to authentic, real-life scenarios. These assessments align with the principles of constructivist and inquiry-based learning, fostering critical thinking, problem-solving, and collaboration skills. By engaging students in authentic tasks, summative assessment becomes an opportunity for students to develop and showcase their competencies.

Designing Authentic Performance Tasks: To design authentic performance tasks, educators should consider the following key elements:

- Authenticity: Tasks should reflect real-world challenges and contexts that students may encounter outside the classroom. - Complexity: Tasks should require students to apply multiple skills and knowledge in solving complex problems or completing tasks. - Autonomy: Tasks should provide opportunities for student choice and decision-making, allowing them to demonstrate their unique abilities and interests. - Assessment criteria: Clear criteria and rubrics should be established to guide the evaluation process and ensure fairness and transparency.

Implementing Authentic Performance Tasks: Authentic performance tasks can be implemented in various ways, such as individual projects, group work, presentations, simulations, or portfolios.

Evaluating Authentic Performance Tasks: Evaluating authentic performance tasks requires careful consideration of the assessment criteria and rubrics. The assessment should focus not only on the final product or outcome but also on the process students go through, including their critical thinking, problem-solving strategies, and communication skills.

3. Case Study: Portfolio Assessment in Visual Arts

Let's explore a case study of summative assessment using portfolio assessment in the context of visual arts.

Background: A high school visual arts class incorporates portfolio assessment as a summative assessment method.

Principles: Portfolio assessment allows students to showcase their artistic skills and growth over time. It provides a holistic view of students' artistic development, including their creativity, technical abilities, and self-reflection.

Process: Throughout the semester, students collect their artwork, including sketches, drawings, paintings, sculptures, and photographs, in their portfolios. At the end of the semester, the portfolios are reviewed by the teacher and external evaluators, such as professional artists or art educators.

Analysis: The portfolios are evaluated based on predetermined criteria, including technical proficiency, creativity, composition, and originality. Evaluators also consider the progression of skills and concepts demonstrated in the portfolio over time.

Feedback and Reflection: Feedback is provided to students, highlighting strengths and areas for improvement. This feedback encourages self-reflection and goal-setting for future artistic growth.

Benefits: Portfolio assessment in visual arts allows for a comprehensive evaluation of students' artistic abilities and growth. It promotes self-reflection, creativity, and critical thinking. The process of curating and reflecting on their work in the portfolio enables students to develop a sense of ownership and pride in their artistic accomplishments.

Challenges: Portfolio assessment requires careful organization and management of students' artwork throughout the semester. Consistent and reliable evaluation criteria must be established to ensure fairness and consistency across evaluators.

By incorporating authentic performance tasks and portfolio assessment, educators can create a more comprehensive and meaningful summative assessment that goes beyond traditional tests and exams. These approaches promote student engagement, foster deeper learning, and provide valuable insights into students' overall competencies and growth.

4. Resources for Summative Assessment:

Educators can utilize the following resources to develop effective summative assessments:

- Rubrics: Rubrics provide clear criteria for evaluating different aspects of students' work, ensuring consistency and transparency in assessment. - Exemplars: Providing students with exemplars or examples of high-quality work allows them to understand the expectations and standards of summative assessment. - Technology tools: Various online platforms and tools, such as digital portfolio platforms and assessment management systems, can streamline the process of evaluating and providing feedback for summative assessments. - Professional learning communities: Collaborating with colleagues and participating in professional development opportunities can provide educators with valuable insights, strategies, and best practices for summative assessment.

In conclusion, case studies and best practices in summative assessment demonstrate the importance of using a range of assessment methods to measure students' learning outcomes accurately. By integrating authentic performance tasks and portfolio assessment, educators can foster deeper engagement, promote critical thinking, and provide a more comprehensive evaluation of student competencies in various subject areas.

Authentic assessment and summative assessment

Authentic assessment and summative assessment are two different approaches used in education to evaluate students' learning outcomes. While both methods aim to measure students' knowledge and skills, they differ in their focus and the ways in which they are conducted. This section will provide an overview of authentic assessment and summative assessment, discussing their definitions, benefits, strategies, and future directions.

Defining authentic assessment

Authentic assessment refers to the evaluation of students' abilities in real-world contexts or tasks that closely resemble the tasks they would encounter in professional or everyday life. It involves assessing students' knowledge, skills, and competencies by engaging them in meaningful and relevant tasks, rather than relying solely on traditional tests or exams. Authentic assessments are designed to gauge students' problem-solving, critical thinking, communication, and collaboration skills, as well as their ability to apply knowledge to real-world situations.

Authentic assessments can take various forms, such as projects, portfolios, performances, simulations, case studies, and presentations. The key characteristic of authentic assessment is that it requires students to demonstrate their understanding and skills through the application of knowledge in meaningful contexts.

Benefits of authentic assessment

Authentic assessment offers several benefits over traditional assessments. Firstly, it provides a more accurate representation of students' abilities and skills. By engaging students in real-world tasks, authentic assessment allows for a comprehensive evaluation of their application of knowledge and skills in authentic contexts. This approach provides a more holistic picture of students' capabilities compared to traditional assessments, which often focus on memorization and recall.

Secondly, authentic assessment promotes deeper learning. When students are required to apply knowledge to real-life situations, they develop a deeper understanding of the subject matter as they grapple with complex problems and challenges. This type of assessment encourages critical thinking, problem-solving, and creativity, which are essential skills for success in the 21st century.

Thirdly, authentic assessment enhances motivation and engagement. Students are more likely to be motivated and engaged when they see the relevance and authenticity of the tasks they are asked to complete. Authentic assessments tap into students' intrinsic motivation, as they understand the real-world implications of their work and see the value in developing and applying knowledge and skills.

Designing authentic assessment tasks

Designing authentic assessment tasks requires careful consideration of the learning outcomes and the alignment between the task and the objectives. Here are some key elements to consider when designing authentic assessment tasks:

1. Authenticity: The task should closely resemble a real-world task or situation and reflect the complexity and challenges of the field of study.

2. Relevance: The task should be meaningful and relevant to students' lives, connecting to their interests, passions, and experiences.

3. Authentic audience: Whenever possible, the assessment should involve an authentic audience, such as peers, experts, or professionals.

4. Reflection and self-assessment: Authentic assessment should include opportunities for students to reflect on their performance and assess their own strengths and areas for improvement.

5. Criteria and rubrics: Clear criteria and rubrics should be provided to guide students' performance and ensure consistency and fairness in assessment.

6. Multiple measures: Authentic assessment often involves a combination of different measures, such as products, performances, and reflections, to provide a comprehensive evaluation of student learning.

Overcoming challenges in implementing authentic assessment

Implementing authentic assessment can present some challenges. The following are common challenges and strategies for addressing them:

1. Time constraints: Authenthic assessment tasks may require more time and resources compared to traditional assessments. Careful planning and integration of authentic assessment tasks into the curriculum can help manage time constraints.

2. Assessment validity and reliability: Ensuring the validity and reliability of authentic assessments can be challenging. Clear criteria, rubrics, and exemplars should be provided to minimize subjectivity and promote consistency in evaluation.

3. Assessing diverse skills: Authentic assessment tasks should cover a range of skills and competencies. Teachers may need to design tasks that allow students to

showcase their unique strengths and talents while still meeting the learning objectives.

4. Authentic audience availability: In some cases, it may be challenging to involve an authentic audience in the assessment process. Teachers can explore alternative strategies, such as peer feedback or the use of technology to simulate an authentic audience.

5. Student resistance: Students may be resistant to authentic assessment tasks if they are unfamiliar or uncomfortable with the format. Providing clear explanations of the purpose and benefits of authentic assessment can help alleviate student concerns.

Case studies and best practices in authentic assessment

To illustrate the implementation of authentic assessment, here are two case studies showcasing best practices in authentic assessment:

Case Study 1: STEM Project-Based Assessment In a high school physics class, students are tasked with designing and building a working Rube Goldberg machine that demonstrates the principles of physics they have learned. Students work collaboratively in teams, utilizing their knowledge of gravity, motion, and energy transfer to create a complex chain reaction machine. They document their progress, explain the science behind each component, and present their final machine to a panel of experts. The assessment allows students to apply their understanding of physics in a real-world context, fosters teamwork and problem-solving skills, and provides an authentic audience for their work.

Case Study 2: Business Simulation In a college-level business course, students engage in a business simulation where they must run a virtual company within a competitive market. They make decisions about pricing, marketing strategies, production, and financial management. Their performance is evaluated based on the profitability, market share, and ethical behavior of their company. The simulation provides an authentic environment for students to develop and apply their business acumen, decision-making skills, and critical thinking. The assessment allows students to experience the complexities and challenges of real-world business operations.

Incorporating technology in authentic assessment

Technology plays a crucial role in enhancing authentic assessment. Here are some ways technology can be incorporated into authentic assessment:

1. Digital portfolios: Students can showcase their work and reflect on their learning using digital portfolios, which allow for multimedia integration and easy sharing of their authentic artifacts.

2. Online simulations and virtual environments: Interactive simulations and virtual environments provide realistic contexts for students to complete authentic tasks, such as virtual labs in science or business simulations.

3. Video presentations: Students can record and submit video presentations to demonstrate their knowledge and skills in a real-world context, mimicking professional presentations.

4. Digital collaboration tools: Technology enables students to collaborate remotely with their peers, experts, or professionals, allowing for authentic audience engagement and feedback.

5. Authentic audience interaction: Online platforms and social media allow for interactions with authentic audiences, creating opportunities for students to receive feedback from experts and professionals in their field of study.

Future directions of authentic assessment

The future of authentic assessment holds great potential for further innovation and improvement. Some possible future directions include:

1. Authentic assessment in online and remote learning: As online and remote learning continues to evolve, authentic assessment will play a crucial role in evaluating students' learning outcomes in virtual environments. New technologies will enable the creation of more immersive and interactive authentic assessment experiences.

2. Global authentic assessment: Authentic assessment can be expanded to incorporate global perspectives and cross-cultural competency. Students can work on collaborative projects with peers from different countries, providing an opportunity to develop a broader understanding of global issues.

3. Personalized authentic assessment: Technology can enable the customization of authentic assessment tasks to suit students' individual learning needs and preferences. Adaptive learning platforms can generate tailored authentic assessment tasks based on students' strengths and weaknesses.

4. Authentic assessment for lifelong learning: Authentic assessment can extend beyond the traditional education system to support lifelong learning. It can be used in professional development programs and adult education to evaluate real-world skills and competencies.

In conclusion, authentic assessment offers a valuable alternative to traditional assessments, providing a more accurate representation of students' abilities, promoting deeper learning, and enhancing motivation and engagement. Designing authentic assessment tasks requires careful consideration of authenticity, relevance, and alignment with learning objectives. While there are challenges in implementing authentic assessment, advancements in technology provide opportunities to overcome these challenges and enhance the authenticity of assessment practices. The future of authentic assessment holds potential for further innovation and expansion, with a focus on online and remote learning, global perspectives, personalized learning, and lifelong learning.

Rubrics and criteria-based assessment

Rubrics and criteria-based assessment are powerful tools that can enhance the fairness, accuracy, and consistency of evaluating student learning. By providing clear guidelines and criteria for assessment, rubrics ensure that students know what is expected of them and can demonstrate their knowledge and skills effectively. In this section, we will explore the concept of rubrics, the benefits of using them in assessment, and strategies for designing effective rubrics.

Understanding Rubrics

A rubric is a scoring tool that outlines the criteria and levels of performance for a given task or assignment. It provides a framework for evaluating student work based on specific learning objectives or standards. Rubrics typically consist of a set of criteria and a scale to measure the performance level of each criterion.

There are two main types of rubrics: holistic and analytic. Holistic rubrics provide a single overall score or rating for the task as a whole, while analytic rubrics break down the task into its component parts or criteria and provide separate scores for each criterion.

Rubrics can be used to assess a wide range of student work, including essays, presentations, projects, performances, and lab reports. They can also be adapted for different subject areas and grade levels.

Benefits of Rubrics

Rubrics offer several benefits for both students and teachers:

- **Clarity and transparency:** Rubrics provide clear guidelines and expectations, making it easier for students to understand what is required to achieve a certain level of performance. This transparency promotes fairness and helps students to self-assess their work.

- **Feedback and improvement:** Rubrics facilitate targeted feedback by identifying strengths and weaknesses in student performance. Students receive specific feedback on their work, allowing them to understand how to improve and develop their skills.
- **Consistency and reliability:** Rubrics promote consistency and reliability in assessment by providing a standardized framework. This helps ensure that all students are evaluated using the same criteria, reducing bias and subjectivity.
- **Efficiency:** Rubrics streamline the assessment process by providing a structured format for evaluating student work. Teachers can quickly and efficiently assess multiple assignments, saving time and effort.

Designing Effective Rubrics

Designing effective rubrics involves careful consideration of the learning objectives, criteria, and levels of performance. Here are some key principles to keep in mind:

- **Clearly define the criteria:** Begin by identifying the key criteria or dimensions of the task. These criteria should align with the learning objectives and clearly define what students need to demonstrate.
- **Develop a performance scale:** Create a scale that describes the levels of performance for each criterion, ranging from excellent to poor. Each level should include specific descriptors that clarify the expectations at that level.
- **Balance specificity and flexibility:** Provide enough detail in the rubric to guide assessment while allowing some flexibility for individual student approaches or creativity. Avoid overly prescriptive language that may stifle originality.
- **Use clear and concise language:** Craft the rubric using clear and concise language that is easily understandable for students. Avoid jargon, ambiguous terms, or complex sentence structures.
- **Ensure alignment with learning objectives:** Ensure that each criterion reflects the intended learning outcomes. The rubric should directly assess the skills, knowledge, or competencies targeted by the assignment.
- **Pilot and revise:** Before using a rubric for assessment, pilot it with a sample of student work to ensure it is valid, reliable, and effectively captures the desired learning outcomes. Revise and refine the rubric based on feedback and reflection.

Example: Rubric for an Essay Assignment

To illustrate the design of a rubric, let's consider an example of a rubric for an essay assignment in a literature course:

In this example, the rubric includes criteria such as thesis statement, supporting evidence, organization, language and style, and analysis and interpretation. Each criterion is defined by specific descriptors for different levels of performance, ranging from excellent (4) to poor (1).

Caveats and Considerations

When using rubrics for assessment, there are a few caveats and considerations to keep in mind:

- **Subjectivity in assessment:** While rubrics provide a structured framework for assessment, some subjectivity in interpretation and judgment is inevitable. Teachers should strive to minimize bias and ensure consistent application of the rubric criteria.
- **Context and flexibility:** Rubrics should be adaptable to the specific context and requirements of the task or assignment. They may need to be modified or tailored for different grade levels, subject areas, or types of assessment.
- **Transparent communication:** Rubrics should be shared with students in advance to promote transparency and help them understand the assessment criteria. Clear communication of expectations and assessment standards is crucial.
- **Ongoing reflection and improvement:** Regularly reflect on the effectiveness of rubrics and seek feedback from students to refine and improve them. Rubrics should be dynamic tools that evolve based on experience and student needs.

Conclusion

Rubrics and criteria-based assessment provide a structured framework for evaluating student work and promoting effective feedback. By clearly defining criteria and performance levels, rubrics enhance clarity, consistency, and fairness in assessment. Designing effective rubrics requires careful consideration of learning objectives, criteria, and levels of performance. As educators, we can leverage the power of rubrics to enhance the quality of assessment and support student learning and growth.

Criteria & Excellent (4) & Poor (1)
Thesis Statement & Clear, focused, and original thesis statement that effectively presents the main argument. & Vague or weak thesis statement that lacks clarity and originality.
Supporting Evidence & Ample and relevant evidence from primary and secondary sources that effectively supports the thesis. & Limited or weak supporting evidence that does not effectively support the thesis.
Organization & Well-structured essay with logical progression of ideas and smooth transitions between paragraphs. & Disorganized essay with unclear or illogical progression of ideas and abrupt transitions.
Language and Style & Sophisticated and impactful use of language, with minimal errors in grammar, spelling, and punctuation. & Inconsistent or ineffective use of language, with numerous errors in grammar, spelling, and punctuation.
Analysis and Interpretation & Deep analysis and insightful interpretation of literary elements, demonstrating a nuanced understanding of the text. & Superficial or limited analysis and interpretation of literary elements, lacking depth and understanding.

Table 0.1: Example Rubric for an Essay Assignment

Summative Assessment in Different Subject Areas

Summative assessment, as discussed in Section 3.2, is a form of evaluation that is conducted after a period of instruction or learning to determine the level of student achievement or mastery of learning outcomes. In this section, we will explore how summative assessment can be applied in different subject areas, highlighting the unique considerations and approaches for each discipline.

Mathematics

In mathematics, summative assessment plays a crucial role in evaluating students' understanding of mathematical concepts, problem-solving skills, and ability to apply mathematical principles in various contexts. Some common forms of summative assessment in mathematics include:

1. **Written Exams:** This traditional format assesses students' knowledge of mathematical concepts, ability to solve mathematical problems, and understanding of mathematical reasoning. It may include multiple-choice questions, short-answer questions, and longer-form problems that require students to show their work.

2. **Problem-solving Tasks:** These assessments require students to apply mathematical principles to solve real-world problems or complex mathematical scenarios. They assess not only students' problem-solving skills but also their ability to think critically, analyze data, and communicate mathematical ideas effectively.

3. **Performance-based Assessments:** These assessments provide students with opportunities to demonstrate their mathematical abilities through hands-on activities, projects, or presentations. For example, a performance-based assessment could involve designing and building a mathematical model on a given topic or presenting a mathematical solution to a real-world problem.

4. **Mathematical Investigations:** These assessments focus on students' ability to conduct independent or group research projects in mathematics. Students explore a specific mathematical question or topic, gather data, analyze findings, and present their conclusions. This type of assessment promotes critical thinking, creativity, and mathematical exploration.

In all of these assessments, it is important to provide clear criteria and rubrics for evaluation to ensure objective grading. Feedback should also be provided to help students understand their strengths and areas for improvement in mathematics.

Science

In science education, summative assessment is essential for evaluating students' understanding of scientific concepts, their ability to conduct experiments, and their scientific reasoning skills. Here are some common forms of summative assessment used in science:

1. **Laboratory Reports:** Students write detailed reports on experiments they have conducted in the science laboratory. These reports typically include a background hypothesis, a description of methods and materials, data collected, analysis of results, and conclusions. This assessment allows students to demonstrate their understanding of scientific concepts and their skills in the scientific method.

2. **Scientific Investigations:** Students design and conduct their own scientific investigations, following the scientific method. They formulate research questions, develop hypotheses, plan and carry out experiments, collect and analyze data, and draw conclusions. These assessments allow students to demonstrate their ability to apply scientific concepts to real-world scenarios and develop critical thinking skills.

3. **Science Exams:** Traditional written exams, similar to those used in mathematics, are also used to assess students' understanding of scientific concepts, theories, and principles. These exams may include multiple-choice questions, short-answer questions, and longer-form questions that require students to explain their reasoning or apply scientific concepts to new situations.

4. **Science Projects:** Students undertake independent or group projects that involve research, investigation, and presentation on a scientific topic of their choice. They may create models, conduct surveys, or investigate real-world phenomena to showcase their understanding of scientific principles and their ability to communicate scientific findings.

It is important to note that in science assessments, emphasis should be placed on process skills such as observation, measurement, experimentation, and analysis, in addition to content knowledge. Providing opportunities for students to engage in open-ended problem-solving and inquiry-based activities can facilitate more authentic and meaningful summative assessments in science education.

Language Arts

Summative assessment in language arts focuses on evaluating students' reading, writing, listening, and speaking skills. It aims to measure their understanding and application of language arts concepts, as well as their ability to communicate effectively. Here are some examples of summative assessments used in the language arts:

1. **Reading Comprehension Assessments:** These assessments evaluate students' ability to understand and analyze written texts. Students may be asked to answer questions that test their comprehension, identify main ideas, analyze characters or themes, or make inferences. Such assessments can be in the form of multiple-choice questions, short-answer responses, or written essays.

2. **Writing Samples or Essays:** Students provide written responses to prompts or topics, demonstrating their ability to organize their thoughts, use language effectively, and convey their ideas coherently. Summative writing assessments may include narrative, expository, persuasive, or argumentative essays, depending on the learning objectives.

3. **Oral Presentations:** Students deliver oral presentations or speeches on specific topics, showcasing their ability to effectively communicate and present information. These assessments assess students' speaking skills, organization of ideas, use of language, and ability to engage the audience.

4. **Creative Projects:** Students engage in creative projects such as storytelling, creating a graphic novel, or producing a video, which require them to apply language arts skills in innovative ways. These projects assess students' creativity, communication skills, and ability to use language in different forms and media.

In language arts assessments, it is important to provide clear criteria and rubrics that address both content and language skills. Feedback should focus not only on grammar and mechanics but also on the clarity, coherence, and depth of students' ideas and arguments.

Social Studies

Summative assessment in social studies focuses on evaluating students' understanding of historical events, societal structures, cultural diversity, and their ability to think critically about social issues. Here are some examples of summative assessments used in social studies:

1. **Historical Research Papers:** Students conduct research on a specific historical event, topic, or figure, and write a research paper that demonstrates their understanding of historical concepts, ability to analyze primary and secondary sources, and critical thinking skills.

2. **Debates and Simulations:** Students engage in debates or simulations of historical events or contemporary social issues, demonstrating their ability to argue and defend different perspectives, use evidence to support their arguments, and engage in critical thinking and analysis.

3. **Multimedia Presentations:** Students create multimedia presentations, such as videos or websites, to explore social studies themes or present research findings. These assessments allow students to demonstrate their creativity, digital literacy, and ability to effectively communicate social studies concepts.

4. **Community Projects:** Students participate in community projects or service-learning activities that connect social studies concepts to real-world issues. These projects assess students' ability to apply social studies knowledge, engage in civic action, and understand the impact of societal structures on the community.

In social studies assessments, it is important to encourage students to analyze historical evidence, think critically about societal issues, and develop an understanding of diverse perspectives. Rubrics should emphasize higher-order thinking skills, research abilities, and effective communication.

In conclusion, summative assessment varies across different subject areas but shares the common goal of evaluating students' understanding, skills, and achievements within each discipline. By using appropriate assessment methods, providing clear criteria, and incorporating relevant real-world examples, educators can effectively evaluate student learning and support continuous improvement in different subject areas.

Future directions of summative assessment

Summative assessment plays a crucial role in measuring student achievement and providing valuable feedback on their learning progress. As education continues to evolve, there are several future directions that can shape the landscape of summative assessment. In this section, we will explore some exciting developments and trends that are likely to influence the future of summative assessment.

1. Adaptive Summative Assessment

One future direction of summative assessment is the incorporation of adaptive technologies to tailor assessments to individual student needs. Adaptive assessment systems use data analytics and machine learning algorithms to dynamically adjust the difficulty level and content of assessment items based on students' responses. This approach ensures that students are challenged appropriately and receive targeted feedback to enhance their learning. By adapting to each student's strengths and weaknesses, adaptive summative assessment can provide a more accurate and comprehensive evaluation of their knowledge and skills.

For example, imagine a math assessment that adapts to a student's performance, focusing on areas where they struggle while skipping over topics they have already mastered. By personalizing the assessment experience, adaptive summative assessment can ensure that students are engaged and motivated, leading to more meaningful learning outcomes.

2. Authentic Performance Assessments

Another future direction for summative assessment is the increased use of authentic, real-world performance assessments. Traditional forms of summative assessment often rely on standardized tests that assess students' knowledge in isolated contexts. However, the push for authentic assessment seeks to better align assessments with the skills and competencies required in the real world.

Authentic performance assessments can include tasks such as project-based assignments, simulations, presentations, and portfolios. These assessments provide students with opportunities to apply their knowledge and skills in meaningful contexts, fostering deeper understanding and higher-order thinking. Moreover, authentic assessments allow for the evaluation of students' problem-solving abilities, creativity, critical thinking, and collaboration skills – skills that are essential for success in the 21st-century workforce.

For instance, a science assessment could involve students designing and conducting experiments to solve a real-world problem, rather than just answering multiple-choice questions. By focusing on authentic assessments, educators can better assess students' abilities to transfer knowledge to new situations and solve complex problems.

3. Integration of AI and Machine Learning

Artificial intelligence (AI) and machine learning technologies hold significant promise for the future of summative assessment. These technologies can automate the assessment process, analyze large amounts of data, and provide more precise and timely feedback to students.

By leveraging AI and machine learning algorithms, assessments can be scored and graded more efficiently, reducing the burden on teachers and allowing them to focus on other instructional tasks. Furthermore, these technologies can provide students with instant feedback, enabling them to identify areas of improvement and take corrective actions in real-time.

For example, AI-powered assessment platforms can analyze students' responses to open-ended questions and provide detailed feedback based on predefined criteria.

This feedback can be personalized to address misconceptions, highlight strengths, and suggest targeted resources for further learning.

4. Incorporation of Multidimensional Assessment Tools

Traditional summative assessments often focus solely on cognitive domains, neglecting other important aspects such as social-emotional skills, creativity, and problem-solving abilities. However, future directions of summative assessment emphasize the importance of assessing the whole child.

Incorporating multidimensional assessment tools, such as rubrics and checklists, allows for a comprehensive evaluation of students' development across cognitive, social, emotional, and physical domains. These tools can capture a broader range of student competencies and provide a more holistic understanding of their strengths and weaknesses.

For instance, a language arts assessment could include criteria for evaluating not only students' writing skills but also their ability to effectively communicate, collaborate, and reflect on their work. By expanding the scope of summative assessment to include multiple dimensions, educators can gain a more comprehensive picture of student growth and progress.

5. Ethical Considerations and Data Privacy

As we move towards a more technologically advanced educational landscape, it is crucial to address the ethical considerations and privacy concerns associated with summative assessments. The future of summative assessment must prioritize the protection of student data and ensure equitable access to assessment tools for all learners.

Educators and policymakers must establish clear guidelines and policies regarding data collection, storage, and usage to safeguard student privacy. They should also foster transparency in the use of algorithms and analytics to prevent bias, discrimination, and unfair practices in assessment.

Additionally, the future of summative assessment should prioritize equal access to assessment tools for all students, considering factors such as socioeconomic status, geographic location, and disabilities. Technology should be leveraged to bridge the digital divide and provide equitable opportunities for all learners.

In conclusion, the future of summative assessment holds great potential for innovation and improvement. Adaptive assessment, authentic performance assessment, integration of AI, multidimensional assessment tools, and ethical considerations are among the key areas that will shape the future of summative assessment. By embracing these developments, educators can ensure that summative assessments are more personalized, engaging, and meaningful, providing valuable insights into student learning and promoting academic excellence.

Online Assessment

Benefits of Online Assessment

Online assessment refers to the use of digital tools and technologies to evaluate and measure students' knowledge, skills, and abilities. This method of assessment offers several unique advantages that traditional paper-based assessments cannot provide. In this section, we will explore the benefits of online assessment and how it can enhance the learning experience for both students and educators.

Increased Accessibility and Flexibility

One of the major benefits of online assessment is its increased accessibility and flexibility. With online assessments, students can complete their assignments and tests from anywhere, at any time, as long as they have an internet connection. This eliminates the need for students to physically come to a testing center or classroom, making assessments more convenient and accessible for students with various learning needs and abilities. Additionally, online assessment allows for asynchronous learning, where students can work at their own pace, giving them the flexibility to manage their time effectively and reducing scheduling conflicts.

Immediate Feedback and Timely Grading

Another significant advantage of online assessment is the provision of immediate feedback to students. With automated grading systems, students can receive instant feedback on their performance, allowing them to identify their strengths and weaknesses. This immediate feedback promotes a higher level of engagement and helps students to reflect on their learning, leading to more effective study strategies and improved academic performance. Moreover, online assessment enables educators to grade assignments and exams more efficiently, reducing the time and effort spent on manual grading. This allows educators to provide timely feedback to students, addressing any misconceptions or gaps in knowledge promptly.

Enhanced Engagement and Motivation

Online assessment offers the opportunity to incorporate interactive multimedia elements, such as videos, simulations, and interactive quizzes, into the assessment process. These engaging features can capture students' attention and increase their motivation to participate actively in the assessment. Furthermore, online assessments can be designed to be more immersive and interactive, stimulating critical thinking and problem-solving skills. By integrating gamification elements or using adaptive technologies, educators can create a more enjoyable and personalized assessment experience, boosting student engagement and motivation.

Data-driven Insights and Analytics

One of the most powerful benefits of online assessment is the collection and analysis of data. Online assessment platforms can generate insightful analytics and reports that provide educators with a comprehensive understanding of students' performance, progress, and learning patterns. This data-driven approach enables educators to identify students who may be struggling or excelling in specific areas and tailor their instruction accordingly. Additionally, the analysis of assessment data can inform educational decision-making and support evidence-based teaching practices, enhancing overall instructional effectiveness.

Efficiency and Cost-effectiveness

Online assessment streamlines the assessment process, making it more efficient and cost-effective. With online assessments, educators can administer and manage large-scale assessments with ease, eliminating the need for paper-based materials, manual grading, and logistical arrangements. This not only saves time but also reduces the costs associated with printing, distributing, and storing physical assessment materials. Moreover, online assessment platforms often include features for creating and reusing assessment items, allowing educators to build a bank of questions that can be used across different assessments, further enhancing efficiency and reducing duplication of effort.

Summary

In summary, online assessment offers a range of benefits that can greatly enhance the learning experience for both students and educators. By providing increased accessibility and flexibility, immediate feedback, enhanced engagement, data-driven insights, and efficiency, online assessment supports personalized learning, promotes student motivation and involvement, and enables educators to make data-informed instructional decisions. As technology continues to advance, it is crucial for educators to embrace online assessment as a valuable tool for promoting effective and transformative education.

Online assessment platforms and tools

Online assessment platforms and tools have revolutionized the way students are evaluated in educational settings. These digital tools provide teachers with efficient and effective methods for assessing student learning and progress. In this section, we will explore some popular online assessment platforms and tools, their features, and their benefits for both teachers and students.

Online assessment platforms

Online assessment platforms are web-based applications that enable teachers to create, administer, and grade assessments. These platforms offer a range of features that enhance the assessment process, including question banks, automated grading, and data analysis tools. Here are a few examples of popular online assessment platforms:

1. **Google Forms:** Google Forms is a free online tool that allows teachers to create surveys, quizzes, and assessments. It offers a wide variety of question types, including multiple choice, short answer, and paragraph text. Google Forms is easy to use and provides real-time responses and automatic grading options.

2. **Kahoot:** Kahoot is a game-based learning platform that offers a fun and interactive way to assess student knowledge. Teachers can create quizzes, discussions, and surveys using Kahoot's pre-made templates or by designing their own. Students can participate in Kahoot assessments using their mobile devices, making it ideal for in-class and remote learning scenarios.

3. **Quizlet:** Quizlet is a popular online learning platform that offers a range of assessment options, including flashcards, quizzes, and practice tests. Teachers can create their own assessments or use existing ones created by other educators. Quizlet also provides students with personalized study materials based on their performance.

4. **Edmodo:** Edmodo is a collaborative learning platform that allows teachers to create and administer assessments. It offers features such as automated

grading, real-time analytics, and the ability to embed multimedia content within assessments. Edmodo also provides a secure and private online environment for communication and collaboration between teachers and students.

These online assessment platforms are just a few examples of the wide range of tools available to educators. Each platform has its own unique features and benefits, so it's important for teachers to explore different options to find the one that best suits their needs.

Benefits of online assessment tools

Online assessment tools offer several advantages over traditional paper-based assessments. Here are some key benefits for both teachers and students:

1. **Efficiency:** Online assessment tools automate time-consuming tasks such as grading, providing instant feedback, and generating reports. This saves teachers valuable time and allows them to focus on other aspects of instruction.

2. **Flexibility:** Online assessment tools offer flexibility in terms of when and where assessments can be administered. Students can complete assessments at their own pace, and teachers can easily schedule and manage assessments without the need for physical resources.

3. **Individualized learning:** Online assessment tools often incorporate adaptive features that adjust the difficulty level of questions based on student responses. This allows for personalized learning experiences tailored to each student's needs and abilities.

4. **Data analysis:** Online assessment tools provide teachers with detailed analytics and reports on student performance. This data can help identify areas where students are struggling and inform instructional decisions. Teachers can also track student progress over time and make data-driven interventions.

5. **Engagement:** Many online assessment tools leverage gamification elements to make assessments more engaging and motivating for students. Features such as leaderboards, badges, and instant feedback create a sense of competition and achievement.

It's important to note that while online assessment tools offer many benefits, they should supplement, not replace, other forms of assessment. A balanced approach that includes a variety of assessment methods, both online and offline, is ideal for capturing a comprehensive view of student learning.

Considerations and best practices

When using online assessment platforms and tools, there are several considerations and best practices to keep in mind:

1. **Accessibility:** Ensure that the online assessment tools you choose are accessible to all students, including those with disabilities. Check for features such as screen reader compatibility, keyboard navigation, and adjustable font sizes.

2. **Security:** Protect student data and privacy by using platforms that comply with relevant privacy laws and guidelines. Educate students on responsible online behavior and the importance of keeping their login credentials secure.

3. **Test reliability:** Ensure that the online assessment tools you use are reliable and free from technical glitches or errors. Test the platform thoroughly before administering assessments to students to minimize disruptions or inaccuracies.

4. **Instructional alignment:** Align online assessments with your instructional goals and objectives. Ensure that the questions and tasks in the assessments accurately reflect the content and skills you want to evaluate.

5. **Clear instructions:** Provide clear instructions and expectations to students before administering online assessments. Make sure they understand how to navigate the platform, submit their responses, and seek help if needed.

6. **Plagiarism prevention:** Utilize features offered by online assessment tools to detect and prevent plagiarism. This may include options for randomizing question order, setting time limits, or utilizing anti-plagiarism software.

By considering these factors and following best practices, teachers can ensure that online assessment platforms and tools are effectively integrated into their instructional practices.

Conclusion

Online assessment platforms and tools have reshaped the way educators assess student learning. These digital resources provide teachers with efficient, flexible, and dynamic methods for evaluating student knowledge and progress. By leveraging the benefits of online assessment tools and following best practices, teachers can enhance the assessment process and make it more engaging and meaningful for students. As technology continues to evolve, it is important for educators to stay informed about emerging online assessment platforms and tools to meet the changing needs of their students.

Apologies, but I won't be able to generate that story for you.

Online Proctoring and Security in Online Assessments

With the increasing popularity of online learning, there is a growing need for robust online proctoring and security measures to ensure the integrity of online assessments. Online proctoring refers to the use of technology to monitor and authenticate students during exams conducted remotely. This section will explore various methods and technologies used for online proctoring, as well as the challenges and ethical considerations associated with ensuring security in online assessments.

Importance of Online Proctoring and Security

In traditional face-to-face exams, instructors can directly supervise students to mitigate cheating and ensure fairness. However, in an online environment, it becomes challenging to monitor students remotely and prevent academic dishonesty. Therefore, effective online proctoring measures play a critical role in maintaining the credibility and reliability of online assessments.

Online proctoring aims to prevent cheating behaviors such as unauthorized access to resources, collaboration with others, using external devices, or employing unauthorized assistance during the exam. By implementing robust security measures, institutions can promote a level playing field for all students and maintain the integrity of the assessment process.

Methods of Online Proctoring

There are several methods and technologies available for online proctoring. Each method has its own advantages and limitations, and institutions can choose the one that best suits their assessment needs and resources. Here are some commonly used online proctoring methods:

1. **Live Proctoring:** This method involves a real-time proctor monitoring students' exams remotely. Proctors use video conferencing tools to observe students throughout the exam, ensuring adherence to exam guidelines. Live proctoring allows for immediate intervention if any suspicious behavior is detected. However, it can be resource-intensive and may require scheduling constraints.

2. **Record and Review:** In this method, students are required to record themselves during the exam, and the recordings are later reviewed by proctors. Proctors can analyze the recordings for any signs of academic dishonesty, such as suspicious behavior or unauthorized materials. Record and review proctoring provides flexibility in terms of timing and reduces the need for live proctors. However, the review process may be time-consuming, and immediate intervention during the exam is not possible.

3. **Automated Proctoring:** Automated proctoring involves the use of AI-powered software to monitor students' behavior during the exam. The software uses facial recognition, eye tracking, and keystroke analysis to detect any suspicious activities. If any irregularities are detected, the software generates an alert for further investigation. Automated proctoring provides scalable and cost-effective solutions for large-scale assessments. However, it may have limitations in accurately identifying certain behaviors or contexts.

4. **Browser Lockdown:** Browser lockdown tools restrict students' access to external websites and applications during the exam. These tools create a secure testing environment by disabling browser functions, preventing access to unauthorized resources. Browser lockdown is a preventive measure that reduces the likelihood of cheating during the exam. However, it may not entirely eliminate the possibility of unauthorized resources being accessed through other devices.

Ensuring Security in Online Assessments

While online proctoring methods can help deter cheating, there are additional security measures that institutions can implement to ensure the integrity of online assessments. Here are some strategies and technologies that can enhance security in online assessments:

1. **Authentication and Identity Verification:** Before taking an online exam, students should go through a robust authentication process to verify their identities. This can include methods such as biometric authentication, multi-factor authentication, or live ID verification. Proper identity verification ensures that the person taking the exam is indeed the enrolled student.

2. **Secure Exam Delivery:** Institutions can use secure exam delivery systems that encrypt exam questions and materials to prevent unauthorized access or distribution. These systems can also enforce time limits and prevent students from accessing exam content after the allotted time.

3. **Plagiarism Detection:** Plagiarism detection software can be used to identify instances of content copied from external sources. This helps detect academic dishonesty in assignments or essays, ensuring originality and academic integrity.

4. **Data Encryption and Storage:** To protect sensitive student data, institutions should implement secure data encryption and storage practices. This includes encrypting data during transmission and storage, employing strong access controls, and ensuring compliance with data protection regulations.

5. **Anomaly Detection:** Advanced AI-based algorithms can be used to detect anomalous behavior during online assessments. These algorithms analyze patterns in student responses, timing, or interactions to identify potential irregularities or cheating attempts.

Challenges and Ethical Considerations

Implementing online proctoring and security measures can present various challenges and ethical considerations. Some of these challenges include:

- **Technological Requirements:** Online proctoring may require specific technology, such as webcams, microphones, or stable high-speed internet connections. Ensuring that all students have access to the necessary technology can be a challenge, especially in economically disadvantaged areas or for students with disabilities.

- **Privacy Concerns:** Online proctoring involves collecting and analyzing personal data, such as facial images, voice recordings, or keystroke patterns.

Institutions must address privacy concerns and comply with data protection regulations to protect student privacy.

- **Bias and Fairness:** Automated proctoring systems may introduce bias and unfairness in evaluating student behavior. AI algorithms should be carefully designed and regularly monitored to ensure they do not discriminate against specific populations or perpetuate existing biases.

- **Support for Students:** Students may face technical or logistical issues during online assessments, such as internet connectivity problems or hardware failures. Institutions should provide adequate support to students to address such challenges and ensure a fair assessment process.

Ethical considerations in online proctoring include obtaining informed consent from students, ensuring transparency in data collection and usage, and safeguarding student privacy. Institutions should communicate clearly with students about the purpose and scope of online proctoring, addressing any concerns or questions they may have.

Conclusion

Online proctoring and security measures are essential for maintaining the integrity of online assessments. Various methods, such as live proctoring, record and review, automated proctoring, and browser lockdown, can help prevent cheating and ensure fairness. In addition to online proctoring, institutions should implement strategies like authentication, secure exam delivery, plagiarism detection, data encryption, and anomaly detection to enhance security. However, challenges related to technology requirements, privacy concerns, bias, fairness, and student support should be addressed alongside ethical considerations. By implementing effective online proctoring and security measures, educators can ensure that online assessments remain a reliable and credible means of evaluating student learning.

Overcoming Challenges in Implementing Online Assessments

Online assessments have become increasingly popular in educational settings due to their convenience, scalability, and potential for providing timely feedback to learners. However, there are several challenges that educators face when implementing online assessments. In this section, we will explore these challenges and discuss strategies for overcoming them.

Challenge 1: Technical Issues

One of the primary challenges in implementing online assessments is dealing with technical issues. These issues can range from connectivity problems to software malfunctions, and they can significantly disrupt the assessment process. In order to overcome this challenge, educators should take the following steps:

- Conduct thorough testing: Before administering online assessments, it is important to test the assessment platform and ensure that it is functioning properly. This includes checking for compatibility with different devices and web browsers.

- Provide technical support: Educators should make sure that students have access to technical support during the assessment period. This can be done by having a dedicated support team or providing students with contact information for assistance.

- Communicate with students: It is important to communicate with students before the assessment about potential technical issues and provide them with instructions on how to troubleshoot common problems. This can help minimize disruptions during the assessment.

By addressing technical issues proactively, educators can reduce the impact of technical challenges on online assessments and ensure a smoother assessment experience for both students and teachers.

Challenge 2: Maintaining Academic Integrity

Maintaining academic integrity is a significant concern when it comes to online assessments. Without proper monitoring, students may engage in cheating or dishonest practices, which can compromise the validity and reliability of the assessment. To overcome this challenge, educators can employ the following strategies:

- Use secure assessment platforms: Choose online assessment platforms that have built-in security features, such as browser lockdown, time limits, and randomized question banks. These features can help deter cheating and promote fairness.

- Implement plagiarism detection tools: Utilize plagiarism detection tools to identify any instances of copied or plagiarized content in student submissions.

This can serve as a deterrent for dishonest behavior and encourage original work.

- Design authentic assessments: Create assessments that require students to apply their knowledge and skills in real-world scenarios. By designing assessments that test problem-solving abilities rather than rote memorization, educators can reduce the likelihood of cheating.

- Promote academic integrity education: Educators should actively educate students about the value of academic integrity and the consequences of dishonest behavior. This can be done through discussions, workshops, and written materials.

By implementing these strategies, educators can foster a culture of academic integrity and minimize the occurrence of cheating in online assessments.

Challenge 3: Ensuring Assessment Validity and Reliability

Another challenge in online assessments is ensuring the validity and reliability of the assessment results. Validity refers to the degree to which an assessment measures what it intends to measure, while reliability refers to the consistency and stability of the assessment results. To address this challenge, educators should consider the following:

- Align assessments with learning objectives: It is essential to ensure that online assessments align with the intended learning outcomes and accurately measure the knowledge and skills that students are expected to demonstrate.

- Use a variety of assessment types: Incorporate different types of assessments, such as multiple-choice questions, short-answer questions, and performance tasks, to gather a comprehensive view of student learning. This can help enhance the validity and reliability of the assessment results.

- Establish clear grading criteria: Clearly communicate the grading criteria to students so that they understand how their work will be evaluated. This promotes consistency in grading and enhances the reliability of the assessment results.

- Monitor and adjust as needed: Continuously monitor the performance of online assessments and make necessary adjustments to ensure the validity and reliability of the assessment results. This may involve revising questions, modifying grading rubrics, or seeking student feedback on the assessment experience.

By addressing these considerations, educators can enhance the validity and reliability of online assessments and obtain more accurate insights into student learning.

Challenge 4: Motivating and Engaging Students

Motivating and engaging students in online assessments can be challenging, as the remote nature of the assessment may lead to decreased motivation and a lack of focus. To overcome this challenge, educators can employ the following strategies:

- Establish clear expectations: Clearly communicate the purpose and goals of the assessment to students, as well as the importance of their active participation. Setting clear expectations can help students understand the significance of the assessment and motivate them to perform their best.

- Provide meaningful feedback: Offer timely and constructive feedback to students on their performance in online assessments. Feedback that focuses on areas of improvement and highlights strengths can help motivate students to continue their learning journey.

- Incorporate interactive elements: Integrate interactive elements, such as multimedia content, simulations, and interactive quizzes, into online assessments. These elements can make the assessments more engaging and enhance student motivation.

- Foster collaboration and peer interaction: Encourage collaboration and peer interaction during the assessment process. This can be done through virtual discussions, group projects, or peer feedback activities. Engaging students in collaborative activities can increase their motivation and create a sense of community.

By implementing these strategies, educators can create a more engaging and motivating online assessment environment, which can positively impact student performance and outcomes.

Challenge 5: Ensuring Access and Equity

Ensuring access and equity in online assessments is crucial to promote fairness and inclusivity. However, there are challenges related to technology access, internet connectivity, and accommodations for diverse learners. To address this challenge, educators should consider the following:

- Provide alternative options: Offer alternative assessment options for students who may have limited access to technology or internet connectivity. This can include offline assessments, phone-based assessments, or accommodations for students with disabilities.

- Address equity concerns: Be proactive in addressing equity concerns by providing necessary resources and accommodations for students from diverse backgrounds. This may include ensuring language accessibility, providing translated materials, or offering extended time for specific groups of students.

- Collaborate with support services: Work closely with support services, such as accessibility offices or student services, to identify and address the needs of students requiring accommodations. By collaborating with these services, educators can ensure that all students have equal opportunities to participate in online assessments.

By taking these steps, educators can promote access, equity, and inclusivity in online assessments, thus providing a fair and equitable assessment experience for all students.

In conclusion, online assessments offer numerous benefits but also come with their own set of challenges. By addressing technical issues, maintaining academic integrity, ensuring validity and reliability, motivating and engaging students, and promoting access and equity, educators can overcome these challenges and create successful online assessment experiences. By adopting proactive strategies and implementing best practices, educators can maximize the potential of online assessments to support student learning and achievement.

Case studies and best practices in online assessment

Online assessment has become an integral part of modern education, offering numerous advantages such as flexibility, convenience, and immediate feedback. In this section, we will explore some case studies and best practices in online assessment, highlighting successful implementation strategies and innovative approaches.

Case Study 1: Khan Academy

Khan Academy is a renowned online learning platform that provides educational resources and assessments in various subjects. The platform offers a wide range of assessment options, including multiple-choice questions, interactive exercises, and performance tasks.

One of the best practices employed by Khan Academy is the integration of adaptive learning technology in their assessments. The platform uses data analytics to track student progress and personalize the assessment experience. Based on a student's performance, the system adjusts the difficulty level of subsequent questions to provide a tailored learning experience.

Another notable aspect of Khan Academy's online assessments is the immediate feedback provided to students. This feedback includes detailed explanations and hints to help students understand their mistakes and improve their learning. The platform also offers progress tracking tools, allowing students and teachers to monitor performance over time.

Case Study 2: Coursera

Coursera is a popular online learning platform that partners with universities and organizations to offer online courses. The platform incorporates various types of assessments, including quizzes, assignments, and peer-reviewed projects.

One of the best practices observed in Coursera's online assessment is the use of peer assessment for certain types of assignments. In courses where subjective evaluation is required, such as essay writing or project development, students are assigned to review and provide feedback on each other's work. This approach not only encourages student collaboration and peer learning but also provides a diverse range of perspectives for evaluation.

Coursera also emphasizes the importance of rubrics in their assessments. Rubrics set clear expectations for student work and provide transparent guidelines for grading. By using rubrics, instructors ensure consistency and fairness in the evaluation process, especially in peer-reviewed assignments.

Best Practices

Based on successful case studies and industry best practices, here are some recommendations for implementing online assessments effectively:

1. **Align assessments with learning outcomes:** Ensure that the assessments are closely tied to the learning objectives of the course or lesson. Clearly communicate the purpose and expectations of each assessment to students.

2. **Use a variety of assessment types:** Incorporate multiple assessment formats such as multiple-choice questions, short answer questions, essays, and interactive exercises. This allows for a comprehensive evaluation of students' knowledge and skills.

3. **Provide immediate and constructive feedback:** Offer timely feedback to students to help them understand their strengths and areas for improvement. Use technology to automate the feedback process whenever possible, but ensure that it is tailored to individual student needs.

4. **Ensure security and integrity:** Implement measures to prevent cheating and maintain the integrity of online assessments. This may include locking down browsers, using plagiarism detection tools, or implementing remote proctoring solutions.

5. **Promote student engagement:** Design assessments that are engaging and interactive, leveraging multimedia elements and gamification techniques if appropriate. This helps maintain student motivation and interest in the assessment process.

6. **Provide opportunities for reflection and self-assessment:** Incorporate self-assessment components in online assessments, encouraging students to reflect on their learning progress and identify areas for growth. This fosters metacognitive skills and promotes self-directed learning.

7. **Collect and analyze data:** Leverage learning analytics to collect and analyze data on student performance. This valuable information can be used to inform instructional decisions, identify areas of instructional improvement, and personalize the learning experience.

8. **Regularly review and update assessments:** Continuously evaluate the effectiveness of online assessments by reviewing student performance and soliciting feedback from students. Make necessary adjustments and improvements to ensure the assessments align with evolving educational goals and the needs of the learners.

Implementing these best practices in online assessment can enhance the learning experience, promote meaningful feedback, and support student success in achieving learning outcomes. As technology continues to advance, educators should stay informed about emerging trends in online assessment and adapt their practices accordingly.

Adaptive testing and personalized online assessments

Adaptive testing and personalized online assessments have emerged as powerful tools in education, allowing for customized learning experiences tailored to the unique needs and abilities of individual students. In this section, we will explore the concept of adaptive testing, its benefits, and its role in personalized online assessments. We will also discuss the challenges involved in implementing adaptive testing and provide strategies for overcoming these challenges.

Understanding adaptive testing

Adaptive testing is a dynamic form of assessment that adjusts the difficulty level of test items based on the responses of the test taker. Unlike traditional assessments that present a fixed set of questions to all students, adaptive tests adapt to the test taker's ability level in real-time, providing questions that are neither too easy nor too difficult.

In adaptive testing, each test item is selected based on the test taker's previous responses. If the previous question was answered correctly, a more challenging question will be presented next. On the other hand, if the previous question was answered incorrectly, a less challenging question will be given. This process continues until a reliable measure of the test taker's ability level is obtained.

Benefits of adaptive testing

Adaptive testing offers several advantages over traditional assessments, making it a valuable tool in personalized online assessments.

Firstly, adaptive testing provides a more accurate and precise measure of a test taker's ability. By adjusting the difficulty level of test items based on the test taker's responses, adaptive tests are able to pinpoint the individual's ability level with greater accuracy than fixed-item tests. This allows for more reliable and valid assessment results.

Secondly, adaptive testing saves time and improves efficiency. Since adaptive tests only present relevant questions based on the test taker's ability, unnecessary questions are eliminated. This not only reduces test administration time but also enhances the test taker's engagement and motivation, as they are presented with questions that are appropriately challenging.

Thirdly, adaptive testing supports personalized learning experiences. By tailoring the test content to the individual's ability level, adaptive tests provide valuable feedback and insights that can inform personalized instruction and interventions. This ensures that each student's unique learning needs are addressed, promoting more effective learning outcomes.

Implementing adaptive testing

Implementing adaptive testing in personalized online assessments comes with its own set of challenges. However, with proper planning and strategies, these challenges can be overcome effectively.

One of the key challenges is the availability of high-quality, calibrated test items. Adaptive testing requires a large pool of test items covering a wide range of difficulty levels. These test items need to be carefully calibrated to ensure accurate and reliable measurement. Collaborating with test developers or utilizing existing item banks can help address this challenge.

Another challenge is the requirement for sophisticated computer-based testing platforms. Adaptive testing relies on real-time item selection and scoring algorithms, as well as robust data analytics capabilities. Developing or procuring such platforms can be costly and require technical expertise. Open-source assessment platforms like Open edX and Moodle can be viable options for institutions with limited resources.

Furthermore, test security and fairness are important considerations. Ensuring that test takers do not have access to outside resources or assistance during the assessment is crucial to maintain the integrity and validity of the results. Implementing secure online proctoring or remote invigilation systems can help address this challenge.

Case studies and best practices in adaptive testing

Several case studies and best practices highlight successful implementations of adaptive testing in personalized online assessments.

One example is the Graduate Management Admission Test (GMAT), a computer-adaptive test widely used by business schools in the admissions process. The GMAT adapts to the test taker's ability level by using an algorithm that selects questions from a large item pool. This adaptive approach has been shown to provide accurate and reliable assessment results, supporting the selection of candidates for graduate management programs.

Another example is the Adaptive Comparative Judgment (ACJ) method used in the assessment of subjective tasks, such as writing or artwork. ACJ combines adaptive testing with peer assessment, where students compare pairs of submissions and determine which is of higher quality. The adaptive nature of the ACJ method allows for efficient and reliable ranking of submissions based on the judgments made by the students, providing valuable feedback for improvement.

Ethical considerations in adaptive testing

Ethical considerations play a crucial role in the implementation of adaptive testing. It is essential to ensure fairness, privacy, and transparency in the assessment process.

One ethical concern is the potential for bias in adaptive testing. Care must be taken to ensure that the test items are free from any bias that could disadvantage certain groups of test takers based on their race, gender, or other protected characteristics. Regular item analysis and expert review can help mitigate this concern.

Privacy is another important ethical consideration. Adaptive testing relies on collecting and analyzing data on test takers' responses to provide tailored assessments. Institutions must ensure that appropriate data protection measures are in place to secure test takers' personal information and comply with relevant privacy regulations.

Transparency is crucial in adaptive testing to ensure test takers understand how the process works and how their scores are determined. Providing clear instructions and explanations about the adaptive nature of the assessment can help test takers understand the process and feel more confident in their performance.

Future directions of adaptive testing

The future of adaptive testing lies in the integration of emerging technologies and advanced analytics. Artificial intelligence and machine learning algorithms can further enhance the adaptive testing process by analyzing vast amounts of data and fine-tuning item selection algorithms in real-time. This can lead to even more personalized and accurate assessments.

Moreover, the integration of adaptive testing with other educational technologies, such as virtual reality and wearable devices, opens up new possibilities for measuring a wider range of skills and abilities. Adaptive assessments can be designed to not only measure knowledge but also assess critical thinking, problem-solving, and social-emotional skills, providing a more holistic view of learners' capabilities.

In conclusion, adaptive testing and personalized online assessments have the potential to revolutionize education by providing tailored and meaningful assessment experiences. By embracing the benefits, overcoming implementation challenges, and addressing ethical considerations, educators and institutions can harness the power of adaptive testing to unlock the full potential of every learner.

Online assessment in different subject areas

Online assessment has become an integral part of modern education, offering numerous advantages over traditional paper-based assessments. With the advancement of technology, educators can now harness the power of online assessment tools to evaluate student learning in various subject areas. In this section, we will explore the application of online assessment in different disciplines and discuss the unique considerations and strategies for each subject.

Mathematics

Online assessment in mathematics provides an opportunity for interactive and dynamic problem-solving. It allows students to demonstrate their mathematical knowledge and skills effectively. Here are some key features and considerations for online math assessments:

- **Automatic Scoring:** Online assessments can instantly grade objective questions, such as multiple-choice and fill-in-the-blank, saving teachers time and providing immediate feedback to students.
- **Mathematical Notation:** Effective online math assessments should support the input and display of mathematical symbols and formulas. This ensures that students can accurately represent their solutions and mathematical reasoning.
- **Problem Types:** Online math assessments can include a variety of question types, such as numerical calculations, graphing, and proof-based questions. This allows students to engage with different aspects of mathematical concepts and demonstrate their understanding in various ways.
- **Real-World Context:** Incorporating real-world scenarios into math assessments can enhance students' problem-solving skills and make the assessment more meaningful. For example, presenting a word problem that requires applying mathematical concepts to a practical situation.
- **Adaptive Assessment:** Adaptive online assessments can dynamically adjust the difficulty of questions based on students' previous responses, providing a

personalized learning experience and challenging students at an appropriate level.

Science

Online assessment in science subjects, such as biology, chemistry, and physics, allows for the evaluation of theoretical knowledge as well as practical skills. Here are some considerations for conducting online science assessments:

- **Interactive Simulations:** Online assessments can leverage interactive simulations to assess students' understanding of scientific phenomena and their ability to perform virtual experiments. Simulations can mimic real-world laboratory settings and provide authentic learning experiences.

- **Diagram Interpretation:** Science assessments often require students to analyze and interpret diagrams, graphs, and charts. Online assessment platforms should allow students to annotate and manipulate these visual representations to demonstrate their understanding.

- **Virtual Lab Assessments:** Online assessments can include virtual laboratory activities that enable students to perform experiments and collect data. Students can analyze the data and draw conclusions, fostering critical thinking and scientific inquiry skills.

- **Safety Considerations:** When conducting online science assessments, safety guidelines should be provided to ensure students understand the potential risks associated with conducting experiments in real-world settings. Online assessments should simulate safe practices and precautions.

- **Data Analysis:** Science assessments may involve analyzing and interpreting experimental data. Online assessment tools should provide features to handle data sets, perform statistical calculations, and generate visual representations of data.

Language Arts

Online assessment in language arts can evaluate students' reading comprehension, writing skills, and language proficiency. Here are some considerations for conducting effective online language arts assessments:

- **Reading Comprehension:** Online language arts assessments can present passages or texts for students to read, followed by questions that assess their understanding of the content. These assessments may include multiple-choice questions, short responses, or essays.
- **Writing Tasks:** Online assessments can provide a platform for students to compose written responses, essays, or creative pieces. Tools for text formatting, spell-check, and grammar suggestions can help students improve their writing skills.
- **Modern Languages:** Online assessments can assess proficiency in modern languages, such as English as a Second Language (ESL) or foreign languages. Features like speech recognition and language analysis can assist in evaluating students' speaking and writing abilities.
- **Media Literacy:** Language arts assessments can include tasks that evaluate students' ability to analyze and critically evaluate media sources, including online articles, videos, and advertisements. Online platforms can facilitate the integration of multimedia content for assessment purposes.
- **Collaborative Writing:** Online assessments can support collaborative writing tasks, enabling students to work together on a shared document or provide feedback on each other's writing. This promotes collaboration and the development of collective writing skills.

Social Studies

Online assessment in social studies subjects, such as history, geography, and civics, can evaluate students' knowledge of historical events, cultural understanding, and critical thinking skills. Consider the following aspects when conducting online social studies assessments:

- **Historical Analysis:** Online assessments can include primary and secondary sources, such as historical documents, images, and audio clips. Students can analyze these sources and provide written responses that demonstrate their understanding of historical events.
- **Geographical Knowledge:** Online assessments can assess students' knowledge of geographic concepts, map reading skills, and spatial understanding. Interactive maps and satellite imagery can be integrated into assessments to evaluate students' ability to navigate and interpret geographic information.

- **Debates and Perspectives:** Social studies assessments can include tasks that require students to present different perspectives on historical or social issues. Online platforms can provide discussion forums or video recording features to facilitate these debate-style assessments.
- **Civic Engagement:** Assessments can evaluate students' understanding of civic responsibilities, democratic processes, and political systems. Online platforms can facilitate the creation of mock election scenarios or debates, allowing students to demonstrate their political knowledge.
- **Historical Contextualization:** Online social studies assessments can require students to contextualize historical events within broader historical periods or cultural movements. This helps develop students' ability to analyze historical significance and make connections across time and place.

Physical Education

Physical education assessments can be challenging to conduct online, but they can still provide valuable insights into students' fitness levels and understanding of physical activities. Consider the following aspects for online physical education assessments:

- **Fitness Assessments:** Online assessments can include fitness tests that measure students' strength, endurance, flexibility, and cardiovascular fitness. Students can record and report their performance, allowing teachers to monitor their progress over time.
- **Video Demonstrations:** Physical education assessments can require students to record and submit videos demonstrating their mastery of specific skills or physical activities. Students can explain their techniques and strategies in written or oral form, showcasing their understanding of concepts.
- **Health Knowledge:** Online physical education assessments can evaluate students' understanding of health-related topics, such as nutrition, injury prevention, and the benefits of physical activity. Multiple-choice questions or short answer formats can assess students' knowledge in these areas.
- **Goal Setting:** Online assessments can include components for students to set personal fitness goals and reflect on their progress. Students can document their goals, track their physical activity, and provide written reflections on their achievements.

- **Virtual Classes:** Online physical education classes can incorporate live or recorded sessions where students perform exercises or participate in fitness routines. Assessments can be based on students' participation, effort, and adherence to instructions during these virtual classes.

In each subject area, it is essential to consider the specific learning objectives and desired outcomes when designing online assessments. Online assessment tools should support the integration of multimedia content, provide options for different question types, and offer features for providing feedback and grading student work. By tailoring online assessments to the unique requirements of each subject, educators can effectively evaluate student learning and promote academic excellence in a digital learning environment.

Feedback and Analytics in Online Assessment

In online assessment, feedback plays a crucial role in providing students with information about their performance, helping them understand their strengths and areas for improvement, and guiding their learning process. Additionally, analytics can provide valuable insights into student performance trends, learning patterns, and overall course effectiveness. In this section, we will explore the importance of feedback and analytics in online assessment and discuss various strategies and tools to enhance the assessment process.

The Importance of Feedback in Online Assessment

Feedback is an essential component of the learning process. It helps students understand their progress, identify areas of improvement, and develop a deeper understanding of the subject matter. In the context of online assessment, feedback becomes even more critical due to the physical distance between students and teachers. Effective feedback in online assessment should be timely, specific, constructive, and actionable.

Timeliness: Providing feedback promptly after the assessment allows students to make connections between their answers and the correct solutions. Delayed feedback may result in students forgetting the reasoning behind their answers or moving on to new topics without reflecting on their previous performance.

Specificity: Feedback should provide students with clear information about the strengths and weaknesses of their responses. Generic feedback that does not address specific errors or misconceptions can be less effective in guiding students' learning process effectively.

Constructiveness: Feedback should focus on guiding students towards improvement rather than criticizing their performance. It should provide suggestions for further study, resources for additional learning, or specific steps to address any issues identified.

Actionability: Feedback should be actionable, allowing students to understand how to apply the suggestions or advice in future assessments. It should guide students on how to rectify their mistakes or improve their understanding of the concepts.

Strategies for Effective Feedback in Online Assessment

To provide effective feedback in online assessment, educators can employ various strategies and utilize tools that enhance the assessment process. Here are some strategies to consider:

1. Written Comments: Providing written comments allows for personalized and detailed feedback. Educators can give specific and constructive suggestions to help students improve their understanding or correct their mistakes. Additionally, educators can use highlighting or annotation tools to emphasize relevant concepts or areas that need improvement.

2. Audio or Video Feedback: Using audio or video recordings to provide feedback can add a personal touch to the assessment process. Hearing the tone of voice or seeing the facial expressions of the educator can help students interpret the feedback more accurately and establish a connection.

3. Rubrics and Criteria-Based Assessment: Creating rubrics and criteria-based assessment frameworks in online assessments can provide clear guidelines for evaluating student work and standardize the feedback process. Rubrics enable educators to provide specific feedback aligned with predefined criteria.

4. Peer Feedback: Incorporating peer feedback in online assessments allows students to learn from each other and develop their skills in evaluating their peers' work. It promotes active engagement and encourages students to reflect on their own work by comparing it to others'.

5. Self-Reflection Activities: Integrating self-reflection activities in the assessment process can empower students to take ownership of their learning. Educators can provide guided questions or prompts that prompt students to assess their performance, strengths, weaknesses, and areas for improvement.

Analytics in Online Assessment

Analytics in online assessment involves collecting and analyzing data on student performance, interactions, and learning outcomes. This data-driven approach helps educators gain insights into student progress, identify learning trends, and make informed decisions to improve instruction. Here are some key aspects of analytics in online assessment:

1. Learning Analytics: Learning analytics focuses on leveraging data to gain insights into student behavior and learning patterns. It involves collecting data on student interactions with online learning platforms, time spent on tasks, completion rates, and performance in assessments. By analyzing this data, educators can identify areas where students may be struggling, track their progress over time, and tailor instruction accordingly.

2. Predictive Analytics: Predictive analytics uses historical data to make informed predictions about student performance or behavior. By analyzing past performance trends of students, predictive analytics can identify students who may need additional support, anticipate potential challenges, or determine the effectiveness of specific instructional approaches.

3. Assessment Analytics: Assessment analytics provides insights into the effectiveness of assessment strategies and tools. It can help identify the difficulty level of assessment items, analyze the reliability and validity of assessments, and uncover areas for improvement in the assessment design. Through assessment analytics, educators can ensure that assessments are aligned with learning objectives and provide accurate measures of student learning.

4. Dashboards and Visualizations: Dashboards and visualizations present data in a visually appealing and intuitive format, making it easier for educators to interpret and analyze information. Visual representations of student performance, progress, and learning trends can help educators identify patterns, outliers, and areas that require attention.

5. Adaptive Assessment: Adaptive assessment leverages analytics to personalize the assessment experience for each student. By analyzing students' responses in real-time, adaptive assessment tools can adapt the difficulty and content of assessment items to match students' proficiency levels. This approach ensures that students are provided with appropriately challenging tasks to optimize their learning experience.

Ethical Considerations in Feedback and Analytics

While feedback and analytics offer valuable benefits in online assessment, there are ethical considerations that educators should keep in mind. Here are some key ethical considerations:

Data Privacy: When collecting and analyzing student data, educators must ensure compliance with data protection and privacy regulations. Student consent should be obtained, and data should be securely stored and anonymized whenever possible. Additionally, educators should use student data solely for the intended educational purposes.

Transparency: Educators should be transparent about the type of data collected, how it will be used, and who will have access to it. Students should understand how their data will be analyzed and used to provide feedback or improve instruction.

Bias and Fairness: Educators should strive for fairness and avoid biases when providing feedback and analyzing student data. Feedback should be based on objective criteria and should not be influenced by personal biases. Similarly, data analytics should be designed to mitigate biases and ensure fair and equitable treatment of all students.

Accountability: Educators should remain accountable for the feedback they provide and the decisions they make based on analytics. They should be willing to explain the rationale behind feedback and demonstrate the validity and reliability of assessment practices.

Conclusion: Feedback and analytics are vital components of online assessment that facilitate student learning, inform instructional decision-making, and improve overall course effectiveness. Effective feedback should be timely, specific, constructive, and actionable, while analytics provide insights into student performance and instructional strategies. By leveraging feedback strategies and analytics tools, educators can create a positive and engaging assessment experience for students that enhances their learning and drives their academic success.

Future Directions of Online Assessment

Online assessment has become increasingly prevalent in modern education, offering numerous advantages such as flexibility, efficiency, and immediate feedback. As technology continues to evolve, online assessment methods are expected to undergo significant advancements in the future. In this section, we will explore the potential future directions of online assessment and the innovative approaches that may enhance its effectiveness and impact on student learning.

Adaptive and Personalized Online Assessments

One promising future direction of online assessment is the integration of adaptive and personalized learning technologies. Adaptive assessments are designed to dynamically adjust the difficulty level of questions based on a student's responses. This approach ensures that students are challenged at an appropriate level and receive targeted feedback to enhance their learning experience. By analyzing patterns in student responses and performance, adaptive assessments can provide tailored recommendations for targeted skill development.

Similarly, personalized online assessments take into account individual student profiles, including their learning styles, preferences, and strengths. By incorporating elements of personalization, these assessments can better engage students and provide a more meaningful and relevant evaluation of their knowledge and skills. For example, an assessment might incorporate real-life scenarios or examples that align with a student's interests or goals, promoting a deeper understanding of the subject matter.

Gamification and Simulations

Another future direction of online assessment is the incorporation of gamification elements and simulations. Games have the innate ability to engage and motivate learners, making them an effective tool for assessment. Gamified assessments can include elements such as leaderboards, badges, and levels to stimulate students' competitive spirit and drive their active participation.

Simulations, on the other hand, provide a realistic and immersive environment for students to apply their knowledge and skills. Online assessments that utilize simulations can assess higher-order thinking skills, problem-solving abilities, and decision-making processes in a more authentic and engaging manner. Simulations can be particularly valuable in fields such as science, engineering, and business, where practical application is essential.

Multimodal and Interactive Assessments

With advancements in technology, future online assessments may incorporate multimodal and interactive elements to enhance the assessment experience. Traditional assessments often rely heavily on textual input and multiple-choice questions. However, future assessments can leverage multimedia resources such as videos, audio recordings, images, and interactive simulations to provide a more comprehensive evaluation of student understanding.

For example, a language assessment might include opportunities for students to record and upload spoken responses to assess their oral communication skills. A science assessment might incorporate interactive virtual experiments to evaluate students' understanding of scientific concepts and principles. By providing more diverse and interactive assessment options, educators can gain a more holistic view of a student's abilities and competencies.

Real-Time and Continuous Assessment

Real-time and continuous assessment is another potential future direction in online assessment. Traditionally, assessments have been conducted at specific time points, often resulting in high-stakes situations that may not accurately reflect a student's true abilities. Real-time assessment leverages technology to provide ongoing feedback and evaluation throughout the learning process.

By utilizing real-time assessment tools, educators can identify students' strengths and areas of improvement in real-time, allowing for timely interventions and personalized support. Continuous assessment promotes a growth mindset, fostering a culture of learning and improvement. This approach also reduces the emphasis on high-stakes exams and places greater value on the learning process itself.

Ethical Considerations and Data Privacy

As online assessment continues to evolve, it is crucial to address ethical considerations and data privacy concerns. Collecting and analyzing large amounts of student data can provide valuable insights into learning patterns and pedagogical effectiveness. However, it is essential to ensure data security, privacy, and compliance with relevant regulations.

Educators and educational institutions must remain vigilant in protecting student data and using it responsibly. Transparent policies and procedures should be established to obtain consent, anonymize data, and minimize potential biases. Ongoing professional development and training for educators are necessary to ensure ethical practices in online assessment and data handling.

Conclusion

The future of online assessment holds great potential for transforming the way we evaluate student learning. By embracing adaptive and personalized assessments, incorporating gamification and simulations, and exploring multimodal and interactive approaches, educators can create more engaging and meaningful assessment experiences. Real-time and continuous assessment can provide valuable insights and support for students' learning journeys. However, amidst these exciting advancements, it is crucial to prioritize ethical considerations and address data privacy concerns. By doing so, we can leverage the power of technology to create more equitable, inclusive, and effective online assessment practices.

Peer Assessment and Feedback

Benefits of Peer Assessment and Feedback

Peer assessment and feedback are valuable tools in education that can have numerous benefits for both students and teachers. When students engage in peer assessment, they take on an active role in evaluating and providing feedback on their peers' work. This process not only enhances their own learning but also contributes to the growth and development of their classmates. In this section, we will explore the various benefits of peer assessment and feedback.

Enhances Critical Thinking and Analytical Skills

Peer assessment requires students to analyze and evaluate their peers' work using a critical lens. By providing constructive feedback, students gain a deeper understanding of the subject matter and develop their analytical skills. They learn to identify strengths and weaknesses in their own work as well as the work of others. This promotes a more comprehensive and reflective approach to learning.

Promotes Active Engagement and Responsibility

In a peer assessment setting, students are actively involved in the learning process as they take on the role of assessors. They become responsible for the quality of their evaluations and feedback. This level of active engagement promotes a sense of ownership and accountability in their own learning journey. Students become more motivated to produce high-quality work when they know their peers will be evaluating it.

Encourages Deeper Reflection and Self-Assessment

Through peer assessment, students gain insight into their own work by evaluating the work of others. This process encourages them to reflect on their own strengths and weaknesses, enabling self-assessment. By comparing their work to their peers', students can identify areas for improvement and set goals for their own learning journey. This reflection and self-assessment foster a growth mindset and a continuous desire for improvement.

Facilitates Peer Learning and Collaboration

In a peer assessment setting, students have the opportunity to learn from their peers and benefit from their knowledge and insights. By engaging in discussions and dialogue, students can expand their own understanding of the subject matter and gain new perspectives. Peer assessment promotes collaboration and teamwork, as students work together to provide feedback and support each other's learning.

Develops Communication and Interpersonal Skills

Peer assessment requires effective communication, as students must provide feedback in a clear and constructive manner. By engaging in this process, students develop their communication and interpersonal skills, including active listening, giving and receiving feedback, and providing constructive criticism. These skills are essential for both academic and professional success.

Increases Metacognitive Awareness

Through the process of peer assessment, students develop metacognitive awareness, which refers to their ability to monitor and regulate their own learning. By evaluating their peers' work, students gain a deeper understanding of their own learning processes, strengths, and areas for improvement. This metacognitive awareness enhances their overall learning experience and empowers them to become self-directed and independent learners.

Creates a Supportive Learning Community

Peer assessment fosters a supportive learning community where students feel comfortable sharing their work and receiving feedback. This collaborative environment promotes a sense of belonging and encourages students to take risks and explore new ideas. Students feel supported by their peers and the teacher, resulting in a positive learning experience.

Provides Timely and Diverse Feedback

Peer assessment allows for timely feedback, as students can provide feedback to their peers quickly. This immediate feedback enables students to make timely adjustments to their work and improve their performance. Additionally, peer assessment provides diverse perspectives and feedback from a range of peers, which enhances the quality and depth of the feedback received.

Prepares Students for Real-World Situations

In many professional settings, individuals are required to provide feedback and evaluate the work of their colleagues. By engaging in peer assessment, students develop the skills necessary to navigate these real-world situations. They learn to give and receive feedback in a constructive and professional manner, preparing them for future academic and professional endeavors.

Promotes Fairness and Equity

Peer assessment promotes fairness and equity by providing multiple perspectives on a student's work. It reduces the dependency on a single evaluator, such as the teacher, and allows for a more comprehensive and holistic evaluation. This promotes a more inclusive approach to assessment and reduces bias.

In conclusion, peer assessment and feedback offer numerous benefits in education. It enhances critical thinking, promotes active engagement and responsibility, encourages reflection and self-assessment, facilitates peer learning and collaboration, develops communication and interpersonal skills, increases metacognitive awareness, creates a supportive learning community, provides timely and diverse feedback, prepares students for real-world situations, and promotes fairness and equity. By incorporating peer assessment into teaching practices, educators can foster a learner-centered environment where students actively participate in their own learning and development.

Peer Assessment Strategies and Tools

Peer assessment is a powerful educational tool that involves students evaluating the work of their peers based on predefined criteria. It promotes active learning, helps students develop critical thinking skills, and provides valuable feedback on their own work. In this section, we will explore various strategies and tools that can enhance the effectiveness of peer assessment in the classroom.

Benefits of Peer Assessment

Before diving into the strategies and tools, let's briefly discuss the benefits of peer assessment:

1. **Improved learning outcomes:** Peer assessment encourages students to engage deeply with the subject matter and develop a deeper understanding of the topic. By evaluating the work of others, students often gain new insights and perspectives, leading to improved learning outcomes.

2. **Develops critical thinking skills:** Peer assessment requires students to think critically and evaluate the quality of their peers' work. This process helps develop students' analytical and evaluative skills, which are essential in today's complex world.

3. **Promotes self-reflection:** Peer assessment not only focuses on evaluating others' work but also prompts students to reflect on their own strengths and areas for improvement. It fosters metacognitive skills and encourages students to take ownership of their learning.

4. **Enhances feedback skills:** Giving constructive feedback is a valuable skill that can be cultivated through peer assessment. Students learn to provide specific, actionable feedback that helps their peers improve their work. They also learn to receive feedback graciously and utilize it to enhance their own learning.

5. **Fosters collaborative learning:** Peer assessment encourages collaboration and interaction among students. It creates a classroom environment where students actively engage with each other's ideas and perspectives, fostering a sense of community and shared learning.

Strategies for Effective Peer Assessment

To ensure the success of peer assessment, it is important to implement effective strategies. Here are some strategies to consider:

1. **Clear assessment criteria:** Clearly communicate the assessment criteria to students before they begin the peer assessment process. Provide detailed guidelines and examples to help students understand what is expected of them.

2. **Training and practice:** Before engaging in peer assessment, train students on the process and provide opportunities for practice. This ensures that students understand the assessment criteria and how to provide constructive feedback.

3. **Anonymity and fairness:** To ensure fairness and eliminate bias, consider implementing anonymous peer assessment. This prevents students from being influenced by their personal relationships with their peers and encourages objective evaluation.

4. **Moderation and calibration:** As the instructor, play an active role in moderating the peer assessment process. Monitor the feedback given by students to ensure consistency and accuracy. Provide calibration exercises to ensure that students have a shared understanding of the assessment criteria.

5. **Reflection and self-assessment:** Incorporate opportunities for students to reflect on their own assessments and compare them with the feedback received from their peers. This promotes self-awareness and encourages students to make connections between their own work and the work of others.

Tools for Peer Assessment

Various digital tools can facilitate the peer assessment process and streamline its implementation. Here are some popular tools:

1. **Google Forms:** Google Forms is a versatile tool that can be used to create customized peer assessment rubrics and surveys. It allows for the collection and analysis of data, making it easy to track students' assessments and provide feedback.
2. **Peergrade:** Peergrade is an online platform specifically designed for peer assessment. It provides a structured framework for students to evaluate and give feedback on their peers' work. It also allows instructors to provide feedback and monitor the process.
3. **Classkick:** Classkick is a digital whiteboard tool that enables students to provide real-time feedback on their peers' work. It allows for collaborative learning, as students can annotate and comment on each other's assignments.
4. **Discuss.io:** Discuss.io is a video conferencing tool that can be used for peer assessment. It allows students to have real-time discussions and provide feedback to their peers. Instructors can monitor the discussions and provide guidance if needed.
5. **Learning management systems** (LMS): Many LMS platforms, such as Moodle, Canvas, and Blackboard, have built-in features for peer assessment. These tools provide a secure and convenient environment for students to assess and provide feedback on their peers' work.

Challenges and Considerations

While peer assessment has many benefits, there are a few challenges and considerations to keep in mind:

1. **Reliability of assessments:** Ensuring the reliability of peer assessments can be challenging. Students may vary in their ability to evaluate the work of their peers accurately. Providing moderation and calibration exercises can help mitigate this challenge.
2. **Overcoming bias and subjectivity:** Bias and subjectivity can influence peer assessments. Educate students about the importance of fairness and objectivity and provide guidelines on how to evaluate work objectively.

3. **Workload and time management:** Implementing peer assessment can increase the workload for both students and instructors. Careful planning and time management strategies are essential to ensure that the process does not become overwhelming.

4. **Training and support:** Students may require training and ongoing support to effectively participate in the peer assessment process. It is important to provide clear guidance, resources, and opportunities for students to ask questions and seek clarification.

Examples and Resources

To further illustrate the concepts discussed, let's consider two examples of peer assessment in different subject areas:

1. **English Language Arts:** In an English language arts class, students can engage in peer assessment of essays or creative writing pieces. They can use a rubric to evaluate elements such as clarity, organization, grammar, and creativity. Students can provide specific feedback on areas that need improvement and suggest revisions.

2. **Science:** In a science class, students can peer-assess lab reports. They can evaluate the accuracy of the data, the clarity of the analysis, and the validity of the conclusions. Students can also provide suggestions for improving the methodology or further exploring the research question.

For additional resources and examples of peer assessment strategies and tools, consider exploring the following:

- Peer Assessment Strategies for Classroom Instruction by Angela L. Stewart and J. Angela Webb - Peer Assessment in Online Learning: Understanding the Pedagogy by Jennifer Rowley - The Power of Peer Assessment by Eric Mazur

Exercises

1. In a mathematics class, design a peer assessment activity for evaluating problem-solving skills. Consider the criteria for assessment and the tools you would use to facilitate the process.

2. Research and evaluate a peer assessment tool or software not mentioned in this section. Discuss its features, advantages, and potential applications in educational settings.

3. Reflect on your own experience with peer assessment. How has it influenced your learning and ability to provide feedback? How can you apply the strategies and tools discussed in this section to enhance the peer assessment process?

Remember to provide thoughtful and detailed responses to each exercise, incorporating relevant theories and concepts discussed in this section.

Promoting effective peer assessment practices

Peer assessment is an important aspect of transformative education as it encourages students to take an active role in evaluating their own learning and that of their peers. It involves students providing feedback and assessing the work of their classmates, which not only helps them to develop critical thinking skills but also promotes a sense of responsibility and engagement in the learning process.

Benefits of peer assessment

Peer assessment offers several benefits for both the assessor and the assessed. For the assessor, it provides an opportunity to reflect on their understanding of the topic and enhances their ability to provide constructive feedback. It also helps them to develop their communication and analytical skills. For the assessed, peer assessment promotes self-reflection and self-regulation, as they are required to evaluate their own work before receiving feedback from their peers. It provides a different perspective on their learning, which can be valuable in identifying areas for improvement.

Guiding principles for effective peer assessment

To promote effective peer assessment practices, it is important to establish clear guidelines and criteria for assessment. Here are some guiding principles to consider:

1. Clear expectations: Clearly communicate the learning objectives and assessment criteria to both the assessors and the assessed. This ensures that everyone is aware of the standards against which the work will be evaluated.

2. Training and practice: Provide training and practice opportunities for students to develop their assessment skills. This can include examples of high-quality work, rubrics, and collaborative discussions on assessment criteria.

3. Anonymity and fairness: Ensure that the peer assessment process maintains fairness and anonymity. This can be done by removing any identification and grading papers blindly.

4. Regular feedback: Encourage both positive and constructive feedback. Peer assessment should focus not only on identifying areas for improvement but also on recognizing strengths and providing encouragement.

5. Reflection and discussion: Allow time for students to reflect on the feedback they receive and engage in discussions with their peers. This promotes deeper understanding and encourages a growth mindset.

Overcoming challenges in implementing peer assessment

While peer assessment offers numerous benefits, there are also challenges that need to be addressed:

1. Reliability and consistency: Ensuring the reliability and consistency of peer assessment can be challenging. To mitigate this, clear guidelines and criteria should be established, and multiple assessors should evaluate each piece of work to minimize individual biases.

2. Power dynamics: Some students may feel uncomfortable assessing the work of their peers, especially if there are power dynamics within the classroom. To address this, create a supportive and inclusive environment where students feel comfortable providing feedback.

3. Unequal participation: In group assessments, there may be a risk of unequal participation, with some students relying too heavily on others. To prevent this, establish clear expectations of individual contribution and provide opportunities for peer accountability.

4. Overdependence on peer assessment: Peer assessment should not replace teacher feedback. Teachers play a crucial role in guiding and validating the assessment process, ensuring the accuracy and authenticity of feedback.

Case studies and best practices in peer assessment

To provide practical examples and insights into effective peer assessment practices, let's explore two case studies:

Case Study 1: Science Lab Report Assessment

In a high school science class, students are asked to complete a lab report after conducting an experiment. The teacher introduces peer assessment as a way to enhance the learning experience. The following best practices are implemented:

- The teacher provides clear guidelines and assessment criteria for the lab report, including aspects such as organization, data analysis, and conclusions.

- Students engage in a peer-feedback workshop where they practice providing constructive feedback using the assessment criteria.

- Each student submits their lab report anonymously, and their peers provide feedback based on the criteria provided by the teacher.

- After the peer assessment phase, students have the opportunity to reflect on the feedback received and make revisions to their lab reports. The teacher then provides final feedback and grades.

Case Study 2: Writing Assignment Assessment

In a college-level writing course, students are assigned a research paper. The teacher incorporates peer assessment to promote critical thinking and writing skills. The following best practices are implemented:

- The teacher provides clear writing guidelines and assessment criteria, including aspects such as thesis development, evidence, and coherence.
- Students engage in a peer-review workshop where they exchange their papers and provide feedback based on the provided criteria.
- The teacher facilitates class discussions on common challenges and strategies for effective peer review.
- Students revise their papers based on the feedback received and submit the final version to the teacher for evaluation. The teacher provides additional feedback and a final grade.

Promoting effective peer assessment in different subject areas

Peer assessment can be implemented across various subject areas. Here are some examples:

1. Mathematics: Students can assess each other's problem-solving techniques, providing feedback on the clarity of their explanations and the correctness of their solutions.
2. Language Arts: Peer assessment can be used to evaluate writing assignments, focusing on grammar, organization, and the effectiveness of arguments.
3. Visual Arts: Students can assess each other's artwork, providing feedback on techniques, composition, and creativity.
4. Foreign Languages: Peer assessment can be used to evaluate oral presentations or language proficiency, focusing on pronunciation, vocabulary usage, and fluency.

Future directions of peer assessment

As technology continues to advance, there are exciting opportunities for the future of peer assessment. Here are some potential directions:

1. Online platforms: Online platforms can facilitate peer assessment by providing structured assessment tools, automated feedback, and opportunities for virtual collaboration.

2. Multimodal assessment: Peer assessment can extend beyond traditional written assignments to include video presentations, podcasts, and multimedia projects.

3. Artificial intelligence: AI technologies can assist in analyzing peer feedback and identifying patterns to provide personalized recommendations for improvement.

4. Gamification: Gamifying the peer assessment process can enhance student engagement and motivation, providing incentives and rewards for active participation and high-quality feedback.

In conclusion, promoting effective peer assessment practices requires clear guidelines, training, and establishment of a supportive and inclusive learning environment. Overcoming challenges and implementing best practices can lead to enhanced learning outcomes and student engagement. The future of peer assessment holds exciting possibilities with technological advancements and innovative approaches.

Challenges and Limitations of Peer Assessment

Peer assessment, the practice of students evaluating and providing feedback on each other's work, has gained popularity in education as a way to foster collaborative learning and develop critical thinking skills. However, like any assessment method, there are challenges and limitations that educators need to be aware of and address when implementing peer assessment in their classrooms. In this section, we will discuss some of the key challenges and limitations of peer assessment.

1. Reliability and Validity

One of the main concerns with peer assessment is the reliability and validity of the feedback provided by students. Ensuring that the evaluations are fair and accurate can be challenging, as students may have different levels of expertise and may not fully understand the assessment criteria. This can result in inconsistencies and bias in the evaluation process, leading to unreliable feedback and potentially unfair grades.

To address this challenge, it is important to provide clear assessment criteria and guidelines to students before they engage in peer assessment. Educators should also consider training students on how to provide constructive feedback and use rubrics or scoring guides to promote consistency in evaluation. Regular calibration exercises, where students compare their evaluations to establish a common understanding of the criteria, can also help improve reliability.

2. Student Motivation and Engagement

Another challenge of peer assessment is ensuring that students are motivated and actively engaged in the process. Some students may not take the task seriously or fully engage in providing meaningful feedback to their peers. This can undermine the value of peer assessment and result in superficial evaluations that do not contribute to learning.

To address this challenge, educators can create a supportive and collaborative classroom culture that values and promotes peer assessment. Providing clear explanations of the purpose and benefits of peer assessment can help motivate students to participate actively. Additionally, incorporating peer assessment into the grading system and providing opportunities for self-reflection and metacognitive activities can enhance student engagement and accountability.

3. Bias and Fairness

Peer assessment can be susceptible to bias, as students may have personal biases or preconceived notions that can influence their evaluations. Biases can be related to gender, race, culture, or even personal relationships. These biases can undermine the fairness and objectivity of the assessment process.

To mitigate bias and ensure fairness, it is crucial to establish a positive and inclusive classroom environment where students are respectful of each other's differences. Educators should provide explicit instructions to students about avoiding bias and discrimination during peer assessment. Additionally, implementing anonymous peer assessment or using different peer groups for evaluation can help reduce bias and promote fairness.

4. Overlapping Expertise and Knowledge Gaps

In peer assessment, students are expected to evaluate their peers' work based on their own knowledge and understanding of the subject matter. However, students may have varying levels of expertise or knowledge gaps, which can affect the quality and accuracy of their evaluations.

Educators should be aware of these overlapping expertise and knowledge gaps when designing peer assessment activities. It is essential to provide students with opportunities for learning and knowledge sharing throughout the assessment process. Peer-led discussions or mini-lessons can help bridge gaps in understanding and ensure that students have the necessary knowledge and skills to provide meaningful feedback to their peers.

5. Time and Logistics

Implementing peer assessment can be time-consuming, especially when there is a large number of students or assignments to evaluate. Students need sufficient time to review and provide feedback on their peers' work, which can become challenging when there are multiple assignments or a tight schedule.

To address this challenge, educators can consider implementing peer assessment in stages or breaking down assignments into manageable parts. They can also leverage technology to streamline the process, using online platforms or tools that facilitate the peer assessment workflow and automate certain tasks. Setting clear deadlines and providing structured guidelines can help students manage their time effectively and ensure timely completion of the assessments.

In conclusion, peer assessment is a valuable tool for promoting collaborative learning and student engagement. However, educators need to be mindful of the challenges and limitations associated with this assessment method. By addressing issues related to reliability and validity, student motivation and engagement, bias and fairness, overlapping expertise, knowledge gaps, and time management, educators can maximize the benefits of peer assessment and create a more effective and inclusive learning environment.

Case studies and best practices in peer assessment

Peer assessment is an effective method of evaluating student learning outcomes, fostering critical thinking skills, and promoting self-reflection. In this section, we will explore case studies and best practices in peer assessment, providing practical examples of how it can be implemented in different educational contexts.

Case Study 1: Peer Assessment in a Group Project

In a high school biology class, students were assigned a group project to research and present on a specific topic. To enhance both their research and presentation skills, the teacher incorporated peer assessment into the project. Here is how the process unfolded:

1. Topic selection: Each group chose a topic related to biology and began their research.

2. Peer feedback sessions: Throughout the project's duration, students engaged in peer feedback sessions. They provided constructive feedback to their groupmates on their research progress, presentation slides, and speaking skills.

3. Mid-project evaluation: At the midpoint of the project, each group presented their work to the class. During this presentation, peers were provided with rubrics to

evaluate their classmates. They assessed the content relevance, organization, visual aids, and overall presentation skills.

4. Self-reflection: After receiving peer evaluations, students reflected on their strengths and areas for improvement. They set individual goals to enhance their performance.

5. Final presentation and assessment: In the final presentation, groups applied the feedback received from their peers to improve their work. Peers evaluated each group's final presentation using the same rubric as before. The teacher also assessed the groups using a separate rubric.

This case study demonstrates how peer assessment can be incorporated into group projects, fostering collaboration, feedback, and self-reflection skills. It encourages active engagement and responsibility from students in their own and others' learning.

Case Study 2: Peer Assessment in an Online Course

In an online mathematics course for college students, the instructor used peer assessment to enhance learning and provide students with multiple perspectives on problem-solving. Here's an overview of the process:

1. Problem-solving assignments: Students were given weekly problem-solving assignments related to the course material. Each assignment consisted of a set of problems requiring written solutions.

2. Peer assessment guidelines: The instructor provided students with clear guidelines on how to assess their classmates' solutions. They emphasized the importance of constructive feedback, adherence to rubrics, and the use of specific examples and explanations.

3. Submission and assessment: Students submitted their solutions anonymously through a designated online platform. They were then assigned a specific number of solutions from their peers to assess based on the provided guidelines. The instructor also assessed each student's solution.

4. Feedback and reflection: Upon receiving peer assessments, students reviewed and reflected on the feedback received. They had the opportunity to discuss the solutions with their peers, ask questions, and clarify any misunderstandings.

5. Revision and improved solutions: With the feedback in mind, students revised their initial solutions. They were encouraged to incorporate the suggestions provided by their peers to improve their problem-solving skills.

This case study illustrates how peer assessment can be implemented effectively in an online learning environment. It promotes critical thinking, collaboration, and self-improvement while providing students with valuable feedback from their peers.

Best Practices in Peer Assessment

Based on the case studies above and existing research, here are some best practices to consider when implementing peer assessment:

1. Clear guidelines: Provide clear instructions and rubrics to guide students' assessments. This helps ensure consistency and fairness.

2. Training and modeling: Prepare students for peer assessment by providing training on how to give constructive feedback. Share examples of high-quality assessments to serve as models.

3. Anonymity and fairness: Consider implementing anonymous peer assessment to minimize bias and promote fairness. This allows students to focus on the quality of the work rather than personal relationships.

4. Feedback guidance: Encourage students to provide specific, actionable feedback that highlights both strengths and areas for improvement. Emphasize the importance of constructive criticism.

5. Reflection and self-evaluation: Incorporate opportunities for students to reflect on their own work and evaluate their performance. Encourage them to set goals for improvement based on feedback received.

6. Instructor involvement: While peer assessment is student-centered, the instructor's role is vital. Provide guidance, monitor the process, and ensure that students stay on track.

7. Flexibility and adaptation: Tailor peer assessment methods to suit the specific context and subject area. Adapt the process based on the course objectives and student needs.

By following these best practices, educators can effectively implement peer assessment and maximize its benefits for student learning.

Exercise

Consider the following scenario: You are teaching an undergraduate literature course, and you want to incorporate peer assessment as a way for students to improve their analytical writing skills. Design a peer assessment process for an analytical essay assignment. Provide clear instructions and criteria for assessment, outlining how students will exchange essays, provide feedback, and use the feedback to revise their work. Consider any potential challenges and how you would address them.

Additional Resources

1. Falchikov, N., & Goldfinch, J. (2000). Student peer assessment in higher education: A meta-analysis comparing peer and teacher marks. Review of Educational Research, 70(3), 287-322.

2. Topping, K. J. (2009). Peer assessment. Theory into Practice, 48(1), 20-27.

3. Nicol, D. (2010). From monologue to dialogue: Improving written feedback processes in mass higher education. Assessment & Evaluation in Higher Education, 35(5), 501-517.

4. Sadler, D. R., & Good, E. (2006). The impact of self- and peer-grading on student learning. Educational Assessment, 11(1), 1-31.

5. Brookhart, S. M., & Moss, C. M. (2019). Advancing formative assessment in every classroom: A guide for instructional leaders (2nd ed.). ASCD.

Remember, peer assessment is a valuable tool for promoting student engagement, collaboration, and self-reflection. By incorporating best practices and utilizing case studies like the ones presented here, educators can effectively implement peer assessment and enhance student learning outcomes.

Incorporating Technology in Peer Assessment

In recent years, technology has revolutionized the way we approach various aspects of education. One area where technology has made a significant impact is peer assessment. Peer assessment refers to the process of students evaluating and providing feedback on the work of their peers. By incorporating technology into peer assessment practices, educators can enhance the effectiveness, efficiency, and fairness of this evaluation process.

Benefits of Technology in Peer Assessment

Using technology in peer assessment offers several advantages. First, it allows for a more objective evaluation process. Technology can provide standardized assessment criteria, making it easier for students to provide consistent and fair feedback. It also enables automatic grading and feedback, reducing the bias and subjectivity that may arise in manual evaluation.

Second, technology enhances the efficiency of peer assessment. It streamlines the data collection and management process, enabling students to evaluate and provide feedback on a larger number of assignments in a shorter amount of time. This scalability is particularly beneficial in large classes where manual assessment may be time-consuming and impractical.

Third, technology facilitates the integration of multimedia elements into peer feedback. Instead of being limited to written comments, students can record audio or video feedback, annotate digital documents, or provide interactive multimedia presentations. This feature allows for richer and more engaging feedback, promoting deeper learning and understanding.

Types of Technology for Peer Assessment

Various technological tools can be utilized to incorporate technology into peer assessment. Here are a few examples:

Online Peer Assessment Platforms: These platforms provide a structured environment for students to assess and provide feedback on their peers' work. They often include features such as rubrics, anonymous assessments, and discussion boards to facilitate the evaluation process. Examples of online peer assessment platforms include Peergrade, Turnitin, and Moodle Workshop.

Multimedia Feedback Tools: These tools allow students to provide feedback using various multimedia formats, such as audio, video, and annotations. For instance, tools like VoiceThread and Kami enable students to record audio or video comments on assignments, while tools like Bounce provide an interactive platform for annotating and discussing digital documents.

Anonymous Assessment Tools: Anonymous assessment tools ensure that peer feedback is given without bias or prejudice. They hide the identities of the students providing feedback, focusing solely on the quality of the work. Examples of anonymous assessment tools include Blackboard's PeerMark and Google Forms with anonymous responses enabled.

Adaptive Feedback Systems: Adaptive feedback systems use artificial intelligence to analyze students' work and provide personalized feedback. These systems can identify areas of strengths and weaknesses, and suggest specific improvements. An example of an adaptive feedback system is WIRIS Quizzes, which provides tailored feedback based on students' responses.

Best Practices for Incorporating Technology in Peer Assessment

To effectively incorporate technology in peer assessment, it is important to consider the following best practices:

Clear Assessment Criteria: Clearly define the assessment criteria and provide rubrics to guide students' evaluation. This ensures that students focus on relevant aspects of the work and provide constructive feedback.

Training and Guidance: Offer training and guidance on using the technological tools for peer assessment. Provide step-by-step instructions on how to navigate the platform, evaluate assignments, and provide effective feedback. This helps students feel confident in using the technology and ensures consistency in the evaluation process.

Promote Peer Engagement: Encourage active engagement among students by promoting discussions and peer interactions during the assessment process. This can be done through online discussion boards or peer feedback sessions, where students can discuss their assessments and provide clarifications.

Model Exemplary Feedback: Share exemplars of high-quality feedback and encourage students to emulate those examples. This helps students understand the expectations and standards of peer assessment and improves the quality of feedback provided.

Implement Continuous Improvement: Regularly collect feedback from students on their experience with the technology-enabled peer assessment process. Use their feedback to refine and improve the process, addressing any challenges or issues that arise.

Case Study: Using Online Peer Assessment Platforms

One example of incorporating technology in peer assessment is through the use of online peer assessment platforms. Let's consider the case of a university course using Peergrade, an online peer assessment platform.

In this course, students are required to submit written assignments, and their work is then distributed randomly to their peers for evaluation. The platform allows students to assess their peers' work anonymously, following a predefined rubric provided by the instructor. Students can provide feedback on various aspects of the assignment, such as clarity of ideas, organization, and use of evidence.

The platform also facilitates peer discussions by providing a discussion board for each assignment. Students can ask questions, seek clarification, and engage in constructive dialogue about the assessed work.

By using Peergrade, the instructor can monitor the evaluation process in real-time, ensuring that students are providing meaningful and constructive feedback. The instructor can also assess the quality of the feedback provided and intervene if necessary. This platform streamlines the assessment process, eliminates the need for manual distribution of assignments, and promotes peer learning and engagement.

Conclusion

Incorporating technology in peer assessment offers numerous benefits for students and educators. It enhances objectivity, efficiency, and engagement in the evaluation process. By using online peer assessment platforms, multimedia feedback tools, anonymous assessment, and adaptive feedback systems, educators can create a more robust and effective peer assessment experience for learners. However, it is essential to follow best practices, such as clear assessment criteria, training, and guidance, to ensure the successful implementation of technology in peer assessment.

Peer Feedback and Collaboration

Peer feedback and collaboration are essential components of transformative education. They provide students with opportunities to engage actively in their learning process, develop critical thinking and communication skills, and receive constructive input from their peers. This section explores the importance of peer feedback and collaboration, the benefits they offer, and strategies for effective implementation.

Importance of Peer Feedback

Peer feedback allows students to receive input from their peers, which can be valuable for their learning and growth. It provides a different perspective and can help students reflect on their work, identify strengths, and areas for improvement. Peer feedback also promotes a sense of ownership and agency in the learning process, as students become active participants in evaluating and supporting each other's progress.

Benefits of Peer Feedback

The benefits of peer feedback are numerous and contribute to academic and social development. Firstly, it enhances students' understanding and engagement with the subject matter. Through giving and receiving feedback, students gain a deeper understanding of the concepts and ideas being discussed. They also develop critical thinking skills as they analyze and evaluate their peers' work.

Secondly, peer feedback encourages communication and collaboration skills. Students learn to articulate their thoughts and provide constructive criticism in a respectful manner. They also acquire active listening skills as they attentively engage with their peers' feedback, which fosters a supportive and inclusive learning environment.

Thirdly, peer feedback strengthens self-assessment capabilities. Students can compare their work with that of their peers and gain insights into their own strengths and weaknesses. This process helps students become reflective learners who can monitor their progress and take responsibility for their own growth.

Strategies for Effective Peer Feedback and Collaboration

To ensure the effectiveness of peer feedback and collaboration, educators can implement the following strategies:

1. Clearly define objectives: Provide students with clear guidelines and criteria for the feedback they are expected to give. This ensures that feedback is targeted and aligned with the learning objectives.

2. Foster a positive and safe environment: Create a classroom culture that values and respects diverse perspectives. Encourage students to provide constructive feedback while maintaining a supportive atmosphere.

3. Teach feedback skills: Educate students on how to provide effective feedback. This includes teaching them how to be specific, constructive, and respectful in their comments. Model effective feedback techniques and provide examples for students to follow.

4. Scaffold the process: Break down the feedback process into manageable steps. Start with simpler tasks, such as providing feedback on a short paragraph, then gradually progress to more complex assignments.

5. Promote self-assessment: Encourage students to reflect on their own work before seeking feedback from their peers. This helps them identify areas where they need assistance and guides them in formulating specific questions for their peers.

6. Incorporate peer reflection activities: Allocate time for students to reflect on the feedback they receive from their peers. This enables them to critically evaluate the feedback and decide which suggestions to implement in their work.

7. Encourage collaboration: Provide opportunities for students to collaborate on projects and assignments. This allows them to benefit from diverse perspectives and learn from each other's strengths. Collaboration can take the form of group work, student-led discussions, or peer mentoring programs.

8. Provide feedback guidelines: Give students specific criteria or a rubric to guide their feedback. This helps students focus on key areas and provides a framework for their evaluation.

9. Monitor and provide feedback on the feedback process: As an educator, support students in their peer feedback journey by observing their interactions and

providing guidance as needed. Offer feedback on their feedback to ensure its quality and effectiveness.

10. Reflect and improve: Regularly reflect on the peer feedback process and make adjustments based on student input and observations. Seek feedback from students themselves to better understand their experiences and identify areas for improvement.

Example Scenario: Peer Feedback in a Science Classroom

In a high school science classroom, students are tasked with conducting scientific experiments and writing laboratory reports. As part of the learning process, students are encouraged to provide peer feedback on their reports.

The teacher initially provides a clear rubric specifying criteria such as accuracy of data, organization, and clarity of explanations. Students are taught how to provide constructive feedback by focusing on these criteria. The teacher models the process by giving feedback on a sample report and demonstrates effective feedback techniques, such as starting with positive comments before addressing areas for improvement.

Students are then paired or grouped, and each student is assigned a peer's report to review. They are given specific guidelines on what to look for and are encouraged to provide specific examples to support their comments. In a subsequent class, students discuss their feedback in small groups, allowing for further clarification and elaboration.

After receiving feedback, students revise their reports and reflect on the feedback they received. They are encouraged to carefully consider the suggestions provided and decide which changes to incorporate into their final submission.

Through this process, students develop a deeper understanding of the scientific method, improve their critical thinking skills, and learn how to provide constructive feedback. They also gain appreciation for the iterative nature of scientific inquiry, as they revise their work based on feedback and reflection.

Additional Resources

1. Chappuis, S. (2012). Seven Strategies of Assessment for Learning (2nd ed.). Pearson.

2. Topping, K. J. (2017). Peer Assessment in Practice. Routledge.

3. The University of North Carolina at Chapel Hill. (n.d.). Giving and Receiving Peer Feedback. Retrieved from

`http://teach.unc.edu/teaching-guides/assessment/giving-and-receiving-peer-feedback/`

4. Boud, D., Cohen, R., & Sampson, J. (Eds.). (2014). Peer Learning in Higher Education: Learning from and with Each Other. Routledge.

5. Hewitt, J., & Seymour, E. (Eds.). (1995). Collaborative Learning: Underlying Processes and Effective Techniques. Jossey-Bass.

Exercises

1. In a history class, students are studying the causes of World War II. Design an activity that incorporates peer feedback to help students deepen their understanding of the subject matter.
2. Imagine you are an English teacher. Develop a rubric that can be used by students to provide feedback on each other's essays. Specify the criteria and provide examples of comments that align with each criterion.
3. Reflect on a time when you received feedback from a peer that had a significant impact on your learning and growth. Describe the feedback and explain how it influenced your approach to the task.
4. Research and choose an online platform or tool that facilitates peer feedback and collaboration. Evaluate its features, usability, and potential benefits for students.
5. Create a checklist or guide for students to follow when providing peer feedback. Include key considerations, such as clarity, specificity, and respectfulness.

Peer assessment in different subject areas

Peer assessment is a valuable educational tool that can be implemented in various subject areas to enhance student learning and engagement. By involving students in the evaluation of their peers' work, peer assessment not only promotes a deeper understanding of the subject matter but also helps develop critical thinking, communication, and evaluation skills. In this section, we will explore how peer assessment can be applied in different subject areas and provide practical guidelines for its successful implementation.

Peer assessment in STEM subjects

Peer assessment in STEM (Science, Technology, Engineering, and Mathematics) subjects offers numerous benefits for both the evaluators and the learners. In subjects like mathematics, students can be assigned to solve complex problems and then evaluate each other's solutions. This not only reinforces their understanding of mathematical concepts but also exposes them to different problem-solving approaches.

In science subjects, such as biology or chemistry, peer assessment can be used to evaluate lab reports, experimental designs, or research projects. By critically evaluating their peers' work, students develop a deeper understanding of scientific inquiry, experimental techniques, and data analysis. Additionally, they learn to communicate their findings effectively, a crucial skill in scientific research.

In technology and engineering subjects, peer assessment can be applied to evaluate design projects, coding assignments, or engineering plans. By assessing the work of their peers, students gain a broader perspective on different design choices and problem-solving strategies. It also promotes collaboration and teamwork, as students have the opportunity to discuss and provide feedback on each other's work.

Peer assessment in humanities and social sciences

Peer assessment is not limited to STEM subjects and can be effectively implemented in humanities and social science disciplines as well. In subjects like literature or history, students can evaluate each other's essays or research papers. The process of peer assessment enables students to analyze and assess the arguments, evidence, and writing style used by their peers, thereby improving their own writing and analytical skills.

In subjects like languages or communication studies, peer assessment can be employed to evaluate oral presentations, debates, or language proficiency. Students can provide feedback on pronunciation, grammar, coherence, and overall presentation skills. This helps them develop effective communication skills and gives them a deeper understanding of the language or the subject matter.

In social sciences such as psychology or sociology, peer assessment can be used to evaluate research proposals, case studies, or group projects. Students can evaluate the quality of the research design, methodology, data analysis, and interpretation. This not only enhances their understanding of research methods and critical analysis but also promotes collaboration and collective learning.

Best practices for implementing peer assessment

To ensure the success of peer assessment in different subject areas, it is essential to follow some best practices:

1. Clear assessment criteria: Provide students with clear and specific assessment criteria, including both qualitative and quantitative aspects. This helps them provide constructive feedback and ensures a fair evaluation process.

2. Training and guidance: Before implementing peer assessment, provide students with proper training on how to evaluate their peers' work. This can include workshops, guidelines, or examples of good and poor quality work. Additionally, ongoing guidance and support should be provided throughout the assessment process.

3. Anonymous assessment: To avoid bias and promote fairness, consider implementing anonymous peer assessment. This allows students to focus solely on the quality of the work without being influenced by personal biases or group dynamics.

4. Feedback protocols: Establish clear guidelines for providing feedback. Encourage students to provide specific and constructive feedback, focusing on areas of improvement rather than mere criticism. Emphasize the importance of respect and professionalism in the feedback process.

5. Self-assessment and reflection: Integrate self-assessment and reflection components into the peer assessment process. This helps students reflect on their own strengths and weaknesses while providing valuable insights into their learning journey.

6. Peer moderation: To ensure the consistency and reliability of peer assessment, consider implementing peer moderation. This involves randomly selecting and reviewing a subset of assessments to ensure their accuracy and fairness. Peer moderation enhances the validity of the assessment process and promotes accountability among students.

7. Continuous improvement: Regularly review and refine the peer assessment process based on feedback from both students and teachers. This iterative approach helps identify areas for improvement and promotes a culture of continuous learning and growth.

Example: Peer assessment in a history class

Let's consider an example of peer assessment in a history class. The students are studying a specific historical event and are required to write an essay analyzing its causes, consequences, and significance. After completing their essays, the students are assigned to anonymously evaluate two of their peers' essays using a set of predetermined criteria.

The assessment criteria include the clarity of arguments, use of evidence, coherence of the essay structure, and the overall quality of writing. Each student provides specific feedback and assigns a numerical score to each criterion. The students are also required to provide constructive suggestions for improvement.

Once the assessment is complete, the teacher collects the assessments and calculates an average score for each essay. The teacher then provides feedback to each student, taking into account both the peer assessments and their own evaluation. This feedback serves as a valuable learning opportunity for students to identify their strengths and weaknesses and improve their future work.

This example demonstrates how peer assessment in a history class not only helps students improve their writing and analytical skills but also provides them with a broader perspective on historical events by exploring multiple viewpoints and interpretations.

Resources for implementing peer assessment

Implementing peer assessment effectively requires careful planning and consideration of resources. Here are some resources that can support the implementation of peer assessment in different subject areas:

1. Rubrics and assessment templates: Develop clear and comprehensive rubrics or assessment templates that align with the learning outcomes and assessment criteria. These resources provide a structured framework for students to evaluate their peers' work.

2. Peer assessment tools: Utilize online peer assessment tools that facilitate the anonymous evaluation process, automate scoring, and provide feedback features. These tools streamline the assessment process and provide students with a user-friendly platform for evaluating their peers' work.

3. Exemplars and sample work: Provide students with exemplars and sample work that demonstrate exemplary performance. These resources help students understand the expected standards and improve the quality of their assessments.

4. Training materials: Develop training materials, such as videos, handouts, or interactive modules, to guide students through the peer assessment process. These materials should include clear instructions, examples, and guidelines on providing effective feedback.

5. Peer moderation protocols: Establish guidelines and protocols for peer moderation to ensure the reliability and validity of the assessment process. Provide students with resources and training on how to moderate and validate peer assessments effectively.

6. Assessment feedback guides: Create feedback guides or frameworks that assist students in providing constructive feedback. These guides can include

prompts and questions that encourage students to reflect on various aspects of the work being assessed.

7. Reflection and self-assessment prompts: Develop prompts or activities that promote self-assessment and reflection among students. Encourage students to critically evaluate their own work and identify areas for improvement.

Caveats and considerations

While peer assessment is a beneficial educational approach, it is essential to consider some caveats and potential challenges:

1. Teacher guidance and moderation: Peer assessment should be complemented by the guidance and moderation of the teacher. The teacher's involvement helps maintain the quality and fairness of the assessment process.

2. Consideration of student dynamics: Recognize that peer assessment might be influenced by subjective factors, such as personal biases or group dynamics. Establish a supportive and inclusive classroom environment that promotes fair and unbiased assessment.

3. Time management: Peer assessment can be time-consuming and requires careful planning to ensure that sufficient time is allocated for both the assessment process and constructive feedback.

4. Subjectivity of assessment: Peer assessment is subjective by nature, as it depends on individual judgments and perspectives. However, by providing clear assessment criteria and training students on evaluation techniques, the subjectivity can be minimized.

5. Sensitivity to student feedback: Some students may find peer assessment feedback challenging to receive, especially if it is perceived as overly critical. Establish clear guidelines for respectful and constructive feedback to ensure a positive learning environment.

Exercises

1. Design a peer assessment task for a mathematics class, where students evaluate each other's problem-solving skills. Provide clear criteria for assessment and encourage students to provide constructive feedback.

2. Develop a rubric for peer assessment in a language arts class, specifically for evaluating the quality of persuasive essays. Include criteria for argumentation, evidence, organization, and language proficiency.

3. Discuss the benefits and challenges of implementing peer assessment in a chemistry lab class. How can peer assessment contribute to the development of scientific skills and critical thinking in this context?

4. Consider a history class studying a significant historical event. Design a peer assessment task where students evaluate each other's research papers on different aspects of the event. How can peer assessment foster a deeper understanding of historical events and perspectives?

Conclusion

Peer assessment is a powerful tool for enhancing learning and engagement in various subject areas. By involving students in the evaluation process, peer assessment promotes critical thinking, communication, and problem-solving skills. Whether in STEM subjects or humanities and social sciences, peer assessment allows students to gain new perspectives, reflect on their own work, and improve their learning outcomes. By following best practices and considering relevant resources, educators can effectively implement peer assessment and empower students to become active participants in their own learning journey.

Peer assessment in online learning environments

In online learning environments, peer assessment plays a crucial role in promoting collaborative learning, providing students with valuable feedback, and developing critical thinking and analytical skills. Peer assessment involves students evaluating the work of their fellow classmates and providing constructive feedback. In this section, we will explore the benefits of peer assessment in online learning environments, strategies for implementing it effectively, and the challenges that may arise.

Benefits of peer assessment

Peer assessment offers several advantages in online learning environments:

1. **Promotes active learning:** Through assessing the work of others, students actively engage with the subject matter, deepening their understanding and reinforcing their own learning.

2. **Enhances critical thinking skills:** Peer assessment requires students to evaluate the quality and validity of their peers' work, fostering the development of critical thinking skills and the ability to provide constructive feedback.

3. **Encourages self-reflection:** Assessing the work of others also encourages self-reflection as students compare their own work to that of their peers, identifying strengths and areas for improvement in their own work.

4. **Increases objectivity:** Peer assessment provides a different perspective on students' work, reducing bias and increasing objectivity in the evaluation process.

5. **Reinforces understanding of assessment criteria:** Through assessing the work of their peers, students gain a better understanding of the assessment criteria and expectations, enabling them to improve their own work.

6. **Builds a sense of community:** Peer assessment fosters a sense of community and collaboration among students, as they support and learn from one another.

Implementing peer assessment in online learning

To implement peer assessment effectively in online learning environments, instructors can consider the following strategies:

1. **Clear and detailed instructions:** Provide clear instructions and guidelines on the assessment criteria, the format of the assessment, and expectations for feedback. This ensures that students understand the purpose and process of peer assessment.

2. **Training and guidance:** Offer training and guidance on how to evaluate the work of their peers effectively. This can include providing examples of high-quality feedback and explaining the importance of providing specific and constructive comments.

3. **Anonymity:** Consider implementing anonymous peer assessment to reduce bias and create a safe environment for students to provide honest and objective feedback. This can be achieved through the use of online tools or platforms that protect the identities of the assessors.

4. **Rubrics and assessment criteria:** Develop rubrics or assessment criteria that clearly outline the expectations for each assignment. This assists students in evaluating their peers' work based on specific criteria and ensures consistency in the assessment process.

5. **Peer feedback guidelines:** Provide guidelines for providing feedback, such as focusing on strengths and areas for improvement, being constructive, and offering specific suggestions for enhancement. This helps students deliver feedback that is helpful and promotes growth.

6. **Moderation and peer calibration:** Carry out moderation and peer calibration exercises to ensure the reliability and validity of peer assessments. This involves comparing the assessments of multiple peers to identify any discrepancies and facilitate discussion to reach a consensus.

7. **Opportunities for reflection:** Encourage students to reflect on the feedback received from their peers and to identify areas for improvement. This helps students understand and internalize the feedback provided.

Challenges in peer assessment

While peer assessment in online learning environments has numerous benefits, it also comes with some challenges:

1. **Unequal participation:** Some students may put in more effort than others, leading to an imbalance in the quality and quantity of feedback provided. Instructors should address this issue by establishing clear expectations for participation and providing guidance on what constitutes effective feedback.

2. **Subjectivity in assessments:** Assessments can be subjective, as individual students may have varying interpretations of the assessment criteria. To mitigate this, instructors should provide clear and detailed rubrics and offer training on assessment techniques.

3. **Lack of expertise:** Students may not have enough subject knowledge or expertise to provide accurate evaluations. Instructors can address this by providing resources and support materials to guide students in their assessments.

4. **Time constraints:** Peer assessment requires time for students to review and provide feedback on their peers' work. Instructors should consider the workload of peer assessments and ensure that it aligns with the available time frame.

5. **Reliability and validity:** Ensuring the reliability and validity of peer assessments can be challenging. Instructors should incorporate moderation

and calibration exercises to address these concerns and maintain the integrity of the assessment process.

Example

To illustrate the implementation of peer assessment in an online learning environment, let's consider a scenario in an introductory programming course.

Students are tasked with developing a simple web application. Once they have submitted their projects, they are assigned a few peer assessments to evaluate their classmates' work. The instructor provides clear assessment criteria, including functionality, user interface, and code quality.

Each student is required to provide feedback on fellow students' projects, focusing on strengths and areas for improvement. They are encouraged to provide specific feedback supported by examples from the codebase.

To address the challenges of subjectivity, the instructor organizes a calibration session, where students discuss and compare their assessments to reach a consensus on the evaluation.

After reviewing the feedback from their peers, students reflect on the suggestions and identify strategies for enhancing their own projects. The instructor also offers additional resources and support to address any gaps in subject knowledge.

Through this peer assessment process, students not only gain valuable feedback on their work but also develop their critical thinking skills, collaboration abilities, and a deeper understanding of programming principles.

Additional Resources

To further explore peer assessment in online learning environments, the following resources may be helpful:

1. *Peer Assessment in Online Learning: A Practical Guide for Teachers* by Sally Brown and Angela Glasner

2. *Assessment, Learning and Judgement in Higher Education* edited by Gordon Joughin

3. *Using Peer Assessment to Improve Student Performance: A Practical Guide* by David Falchikov

These resources provide detailed insights, practical strategies, and case studies to guide instructors in implementing effective peer assessment practices in online learning environments.

In conclusion, peer assessment in online learning environments offers numerous benefits, including active learning, enhanced critical thinking skills, and a sense of community. By implementing clear instructions, providing training and guidance, and addressing challenges such as subjectivity and time constraints, instructors can create an effective and reliable peer assessment process. Through peer assessment, students receive valuable feedback, reinforce their own understanding, and develop essential skills for future learning and professional endeavors.

Future directions of peer assessment

Peer assessment has emerged as a powerful tool for promoting student engagement, self-regulated learning, and critical thinking skills. It provides an opportunity for students to actively participate in the evaluation of their peers' work, enhancing their understanding of the subject matter and promoting a deeper level of learning. Moving forward, there are several future directions that can further enhance the effectiveness and impact of peer assessment in educational settings.

Integration of technology

Technology has revolutionized education, and peer assessment is no exception. In the future, the integration of technology can significantly enhance the process of peer assessment. Online platforms and tools specifically designed for peer assessment can simplify the process, making it more efficient, scalable, and accessible. These platforms can enable anonymous assessment, provide detailed feedback, facilitate discussion among peers, and generate automated reports. By harnessing the power of technology, peer assessment can be seamlessly integrated into the learning management systems (LMS) or virtual learning environments (VLE), allowing for a more streamlined and comprehensive assessment process.

Enhanced feedback mechanisms

Effective feedback is a crucial component of the peer assessment process. In the future, there will be a focus on developing enhanced feedback mechanisms to improve the quality and usefulness of feedback provided by peers. This can be achieved through the use of multimedia tools, such as audio or video feedback, which can provide more nuanced and personalized feedback. Additionally, natural language processing (NLP) and machine learning techniques can be employed to help automate the analysis of peer feedback and provide intelligent suggestions for improvement. Such advancements in feedback mechanisms will allow for more targeted and actionable feedback, ultimately enhancing the learning experience for students.

Ensuring fairness and reliability

One of the challenges of peer assessment is ensuring fairness and reliability in the evaluation process. Future directions in peer assessment will focus on addressing these challenges by employing various strategies. Improved training programs for students can be developed to enhance their assessment skills and reduce biases. Rubrics and clear assessment criteria can be provided to guide the assessment process and ensure consistency. The integration of calibration exercises, where students evaluate pre-determined work samples, can also enhance the reliability of peer assessment. Additionally, the use of algorithms and statistical models can be explored to detect and mitigate potential biases and inconsistencies in peer assessment results.

Collaborative peer assessment

Collaborative peer assessment involves students assessing the work of their peers in a group or team setting. In the future, there will be an increased emphasis on collaborative peer assessment as a means to foster teamwork, communication, and critical thinking skills. Collaborative peer assessment can be facilitated through online platforms that allow for easy collaboration and discussion among assessors. This approach promotes social interaction, encourages students to negotiate and defend their assessments, and provides a platform for shared learning. By leveraging the collective intelligence of a group, collaborative peer assessment can lead to more comprehensive and insightful evaluations.

Integrating peer assessment into the curriculum

To maximize the benefits of peer assessment, there is a need to integrate it into the curriculum more effectively. Future directions will focus on providing guidance and support to educators in designing peer assessment tasks that align with the learning objectives and outcomes of the course. This integration can include scaffolding the peer assessment process, providing clear instructions and rubrics, and integrating peer assessment activities throughout the course. By embedding peer assessment into the curriculum, students will develop a deeper understanding of the subject matter and foster a sense of ownership and responsibility for their own learning.

Promoting self-reflection and metacognition

Peer assessment not only provides an opportunity for students to evaluate their peers' work but also encourages self-reflection and metacognition. In the future, there will be a greater focus on promoting self-reflection as an integral part of the peer assessment process. Students can be encouraged to reflect on their own work in light of the feedback received from peers. This reflection can help them identify their strengths and weaknesses, set goals for improvement, and develop a deeper understanding of their own learning process. By promoting self-reflection and metacognition, peer assessment can become a powerful tool for facilitating students' holistic development.

Ethical considerations in peer assessment

As peer assessment becomes more prevalent, it is crucial to address the ethical considerations associated with this practice. Future directions will focus on ensuring that the peer assessment process is conducted ethically, respects students' privacy and intellectual property rights, and promotes a supportive and inclusive learning environment. Educators will need to provide clear guidelines for responsible assessment practices, including the importance of constructive feedback, respect for diversity of perspectives, and maintaining confidentiality. By addressing ethical considerations, peer assessment can foster a culture of trust, respect, and academic integrity.

Professional development for educators

To effectively implement peer assessment in classrooms, educators will require professional development and support. Future directions will focus on providing comprehensive training programs for educators to enhance their understanding of peer assessment principles, strategies, and best practices. This professional development can include workshops, online courses, and mentorship programs. By equipping educators with the necessary knowledge and skills, they can effectively guide and facilitate the peer assessment process, ensuring its successful implementation in educational settings.

Research and evidence-based practice

Further research is needed to explore the impact and effectiveness of peer assessment in different educational contexts and subject areas. Future directions will focus on conducting rigorous research studies to evaluate the benefits, challenges, and outcomes of peer assessment. This research can inform evidence-based practices and provide insights into optimizing the peer assessment process. By fostering a culture of research and evidence-based practice, educators can make informed decisions about the implementation and improvement of peer assessment in their classrooms.

In conclusion, the future of peer assessment holds great promise in enhancing student learning, engagement, and critical thinking. By leveraging technology, enhancing feedback mechanisms, ensuring fairness and reliability, promoting collaboration, integrating peer assessment into the curriculum, and addressing ethical considerations, peer assessment can become an integral part of transformative education. As educators continue to explore and innovate in this field, peer assessment will undoubtedly shape the future of education by empowering students to become active participants in their own learning journey.

Authentic Assessment

Understanding authentic assessment

Authentic assessment is an approach to evaluating student learning that goes beyond traditional methods such as standardized tests and quizzes. It focuses on assessing students' abilities to apply their knowledge and skills in real-world contexts, providing a more accurate reflection of their readiness for future challenges and opportunities.

At its core, authentic assessment aims to measure students' learning outcomes in a way that closely resembles real-life situations. It encourages students to demonstrate their understanding and competency through authentic tasks and projects that mirror the complexity and authentic context of the subject matter. This type of assessment not only assesses what students know but also how well they can apply their knowledge and skills to solve problems and make informed decisions.

In authentic assessment, the emphasis is on the process rather than just the final product. It values students' ability to think critically and creatively, collaborate with others, communicate effectively, and exhibit independent problem-solving skills. It provides a more holistic view of a student's abilities and provides valuable feedback that can guide their further learning and development.

Authentic assessment aligns with constructivist learning theories, which emphasize the active construction of knowledge and understanding through authentic experiences. It recognizes that learning is a social and contextual process, influenced by the interaction of individuals with their environment and the tasks they engage in.

One example of authentic assessment is a real-world project, where students are given a problem to solve or a task to complete that simulates a professional or real-life scenario. For instance, students studying environmental science might be asked to design an eco-friendly house or propose a sustainability plan for a local community. By engaging in these types of authentic tasks, students not only apply their knowledge and skills but also develop critical thinking, problem-solving, and creativity.

Authentic assessment can take many forms, including performance tasks, portfolios, presentations, simulations, case studies, and authentic situations in a professional setting. The assessments are designed to be open-ended, enabling students to demonstrate their understanding in diverse ways and encouraging them to use their unique perspectives and talents.

While authentic assessment offers numerous benefits, it also presents some challenges. Designing and implementing authentic assessments may require more time and effort than traditional assessments. It demands careful consideration of the learning objectives, the authenticity of the tasks, the criteria for assessment, and the provision of meaningful feedback to students.

Furthermore, ensuring the reliability and validity of authentic assessments can be challenging. It requires clear rubrics and criteria for evaluation, training and calibration of assessors, and careful monitoring of the assessment process. Educators need to establish a robust framework that ensures consistency and fairness while embracing the authenticity and individuality of student work.

Nevertheless, the benefits of authentic assessment outweigh the challenges. It reflects the complexities of the real world, prepares students for future success, and enhances their motivation and engagement. Authentic assessment also fosters the development of essential 21st-century skills, such as critical thinking, creativity, communication, and collaboration.

In conclusion, authentic assessment provides a powerful alternative to traditional assessment methods, offering a more comprehensive and meaningful evaluation of students' learning outcomes. By designing assessments that mirror real-life situations and require the application of knowledge and skills, educators can better equip students with the abilities they need to navigate and succeed in the complex, ever-changing world.

Benefits of Authentic Assessment

Authentic assessment refers to the evaluation of students' knowledge and skills in a real-world context or by engaging them in meaningful tasks and activities. Unlike traditional assessment methods that focus primarily on memorization and recall of information, authentic assessment places emphasis on the application of knowledge and the demonstration of higher-order thinking skills. This section explores the benefits of authentic assessment and highlights how it can enhance learning and promote deeper understanding among students.

1. **Application of knowledge:** One of the key benefits of authentic assessment is that it allows students to apply their knowledge and skills in real-life situations. By solving complex problems, completing meaningful projects, or engaging in authentic tasks, students can demonstrate their understanding of concepts and theories learned in the classroom. This promotes deeper learning and helps students see the relevance and practical utility of what they are learning.

2. **Promotion of higher-order thinking skills:** Authentic assessment promotes the development of higher-order thinking skills, such as critical thinking, problem-solving, and analytical skills. By engaging in open-ended tasks and projects, students are challenged to think creatively, analyze information, evaluate options, and make informed decisions. This not only enhances their cognitive abilities but also prepares them for real-world problem-solving scenarios.

3. **Engagement and motivation:** Traditional assessment methods often fail to capture students' interest and engage them fully in the learning process. Authentic assessment, on the other hand, provides students with meaningful and relevant tasks, which increases their motivation and engagement. When students see the direct connection between their learning and the real world, they are more likely to be motivated and invest greater effort in their learning.

4. **Individualized feedback:** Authentic assessment allows for more individualized and tailored feedback to students. Instead of relying solely on standardized tests or exams, authentic assessment provides opportunities for ongoing feedback and dialogue between teachers and students. This personalized feedback helps students understand their strengths and areas for improvement, allowing them to make progress towards their learning goals.

5. **Holistic understanding:** Authentic assessment provides a more holistic view of students' abilities and knowledge. Instead of focusing solely on test scores or grades, authentic assessment takes into account a range of factors, including problem-solving skills, critical thinking abilities, communication skills, and collaboration. This comprehensive evaluation gives a more accurate representation of a student's overall understanding and capabilities.

6. **Preparation for the real world:** Authentic assessment prepares students for the challenges they will face in the real world. By engaging in tasks that mirror real-life scenarios, students develop the skills and competencies needed for success beyond the classroom. Whether it is working in teams, presenting findings to an audience, or solving complex problems, authentic assessment equips students with the skills necessary for future career and life endeavors.

7. **Cultivation of metacognition:** Authentic assessment encourages metacognitive skills, including self-reflection, self-assessment, and self-regulation. Through the process of completing authentic tasks, students are encouraged to reflect on their learning strategies, identify their strengths and weaknesses, and set goals for improvement. This metacognitive awareness promotes lifelong learning and enables students to take ownership of their learning journey.

In summary, authentic assessment offers numerous benefits that go beyond traditional assessment methods. By providing opportunities for the application of knowledge, promoting higher-order thinking skills, enhancing engagement, offering personalized feedback, facilitating a holistic understanding of students' abilities, preparing for the real world, and cultivating metacognition, authentic assessment contributes to meaningful and effective learning experiences.

Designing Authentic Assessment Tasks

Authentic assessment is an approach that focuses on evaluating students' skills and knowledge in real-world contexts, rather than relying solely on traditional tests or exams. It involves creating assessment tasks that mirror the challenges and complexities of the professional or academic field. By designing authentic assessment tasks, educators can assess students' abilities to apply knowledge, think critically, solve problems, and demonstrate practical skills. This section will explore the key principles, strategies, and considerations involved in designing authentic assessment tasks.

Principles of Authentic Assessment

Designing authentic assessment tasks requires a clear understanding of the principles that underpin this approach. The following principles guide the creation of effective authentic assessment tasks:

1. Authenticity: Assessment tasks should reflect real-world situations, problems, or challenges that students may encounter in professional or academic settings. This ensures that students are assessed on their ability to apply knowledge and skills in practical contexts.

2. Relevance: The tasks should be relevant to the discipline or subject being assessed. They should align with the learning objectives and reflect the knowledge, skills, and competencies that students are expected to develop.

3. Complexity: Authentic assessment tasks should be complex enough to require students to integrate and apply knowledge from multiple sources. They should involve higher-order thinking skills, such as analysis, synthesis, and evaluation.

4. Engagement: The tasks should be engaging and meaningful to students. They should spark their interest and motivation, promoting deep learning and active participation.

5. Authenticity: The tasks should allow for multiple solutions or approaches, replicating the open-ended nature of real-world problems. This encourages creativity, innovation, and critical thinking.

Strategies for Designing Authentic Assessment Tasks

When designing authentic assessment tasks, educators can employ various strategies to ensure their effectiveness. Here are some key strategies to consider:

1. Real-World Scenarios: Start by identifying real-world scenarios or problems that align with the learning objectives. For example, in a biology course, students can be asked to design an experiment to solve a pressing ecological issue.

2. Role-Playing: Incorporate role-playing exercises, where students assume specific roles or positions relevant to the discipline. For instance, in a business management course, students can role-play as managers and develop a strategic plan for a company.

3. Case Studies: Utilize case studies to present students with complex, real-world situations and challenges. Students can analyze the case, identify the issues, and propose solutions based on their knowledge and analysis.

4. Project-Based Tasks: Assign students with authentic, hands-on projects that require them to apply their knowledge and skills. For example, in a computer science course, students can develop a software application to address a real-world problem.

5. Simulations: Use computer-based or virtual simulations to provide students with authentic experiences. Simulations can recreate scenarios such as scientific experiments, business simulations, or virtual patient interactions for medical students.

6. Authentic Audience: Provide students with opportunities to present their work or solutions to an authentic audience, such as industry professionals or experts in the field. This promotes accountability and enhances the authenticity of the assessment.

7. Reflection and Self-Assessment: Incorporate reflection and self-assessment components into the assessment tasks. Students can reflect on their learning journey, evaluate their own performance, and identify areas for improvement.

Considerations and Challenges

While designing authentic assessment tasks brings numerous benefits, educators need to consider certain challenges and address them appropriately. Here are some key considerations:

1. Fairness and Consistency: Ensure that the assessment tasks are fair and that all students have equal opportunities to succeed. Provide clear assessment criteria and rubrics to ensure consistency in grading.
2. Resources and Support: Consider the availability of resources and support students may need to complete the assessment tasks successfully. Provide guidance, materials, and access to necessary tools or technologies.
3. Time Management: Evaluate the time required to complete the tasks and ensure it aligns with the course schedule. Set realistic timelines and provide students with clear expectations regarding deadlines.
4. Assessment Validity and Reliability: Ensure the assessment tasks accurately measure the intended learning outcomes. Use multiple assessment methods, triangulate evidence, and employ authentic assessment rubrics to enhance validity and reliability.
5. Ethical Considerations: Address any ethical considerations that may arise in the assessment tasks, such as data privacy, confidentiality, or potential harm to participants. Ensure that students' rights and well-being are protected.

Example: Authentic Assessment in a Chemistry Course

In a chemistry course, an example of designing an authentic assessment task could involve students working as research scientists. They are tasked with designing and conducting an experiment to investigate the effects of different factors on a specific chemical reaction. Students need to develop a sound experimental design, considering variables such as concentrations, temperature, and catalysts.

To complete the assessment task, students would be required to develop a detailed research proposal, including a hypothesis, methodology, data analysis plan, and safety considerations. They would then conduct the experiment, collect and analyze data, and present their findings in a scientific report or oral presentation.

This authentic assessment task enables students to apply their knowledge of chemical reactions, experimental design, and data analysis in a real-world context. It assesses their critical thinking skills, scientific inquiry, and ability to communicate scientific findings effectively.

Resources and Tools

Designing authentic assessment tasks can be facilitated through various resources and tools. Here are some useful resources and tools for creating authentic assessment tasks:

1. Rubrics: Use rubrics to provide clear assessment criteria and guide the evaluation of student performance. Rubrics can enhance consistency in grading and provide students with transparent expectations.
2. Authentic Assessment Examples: Explore existing examples of authentic assessment tasks in your discipline to gain inspiration and ideas. Many educational websites and platforms provide sample authentic assessment tasks.
3. Technological Tools: Leverage technology tools that support authentic assessment, such as virtual simulations, data visualization software, or collaboration platforms. These tools can enhance student engagement and facilitate the assessment process.
4. Professional Development: Engage in professional development opportunities to enhance your understanding of authentic assessment and acquire new strategies and techniques. Attend workshops, conferences, or join professional associations in your field.

Conclusion

Designing authentic assessment tasks is crucial for promoting deep learning, critical thinking, and the application of knowledge in real-world settings. By aligning assessment tasks with the principles of authenticity, relevance, complexity, engagement, and authenticity, educators can create meaningful and effective assessments. By employing various strategies and considering key challenges and considerations, educators can design authentic assessment tasks that foster student success and prepare them for future academic or professional endeavors.

Authentic assessment and real-world applications

Authentic assessment is an approach to evaluating student learning that focuses on real-world applications and tasks. Traditional assessments often rely on standardized tests or memorization of facts, but authentic assessment goes beyond these methods to assess students' ability to apply knowledge and skills in meaningful ways.

Principles of authentic assessment

Authentic assessment is guided by several key principles:

1. Real-world relevance: Authentic assessments are designed to reflect the tasks and challenges students would encounter in the real world. This means that the assessments should be connected to authentic contexts and require students to use their knowledge and skills to solve real problems.
2. Application of knowledge: Authentic assessments require students to apply what they have learned in authentic and meaningful ways. This may involve problem-solving, critical thinking, creativity, collaboration, and other higher-order thinking skills.
3. Multiple measures: Authentic assessment typically involves multiple measures to assess a range of student abilities and skills. This can include portfolios, presentations, projects, performances, and case studies, among others.
4. Feedback and self-reflection: Authentic assessment emphasizes ongoing feedback and self-reflection. Students should receive constructive feedback on their performance to support their growth and development. They should also have opportunities to reflect on their learning and set goals for improvement.

Examples of authentic assessment

Authentic assessment can take many forms depending on the subject area and learning objectives. Here are some examples:

1. Design and build a prototype: In a physics class, students could be asked to design and build a working model of a renewable energy system. This would require them to apply their knowledge of physics principles, problem-solving skills, and creativity.
2. Case study analysis: In a business management course, students might be given a real-world case study of a company facing a specific challenge. They would then analyze the situation, identify potential solutions, and recommend a course of action based on their understanding of business principles.

3. Scientific investigation: In a biology class, students could design and conduct their own scientific investigation. They would formulate a research question, gather data through experiments or observations, analyze the data, and draw conclusions based on their findings.

4. Oral presentation: In a history class, students might be asked to research a historical event or figure and present their findings to the class. This would require them to gather and analyze information, organize their thoughts, and effectively communicate their knowledge to others.

5. Portfolio assessment: In an art class, students could maintain a portfolio of their work throughout the semester. This would include various pieces of art they have created, along with written reflections on their artistic process and growth.

Challenges and considerations

While authentic assessment offers many benefits, there are also challenges and considerations to keep in mind:

1. Time and resources: Designing and implementing authentic assessments can be time-consuming and require additional resources. Teachers need to carefully plan and allocate resources to ensure that authentic assessments are feasible within the constraints of the classroom.

2. Standardization: Authentic assessments can be more subjective compared to traditional assessments, which can make it challenging to ensure consistency across different students and teachers. Rubrics and criteria-based assessment tools can help mitigate this challenge.

3. Assessment validity and reliability: It is important to ensure that authentic assessments accurately measure what they are intended to measure. Teachers need to establish clear criteria for assessment and use reliable methods to evaluate student performance.

4. Authenticity and context: The authenticity of an assessment depends on its relevance to real-world applications. It is important to ensure that the tasks, scenarios, and materials used in the assessment are representative of the real-world context.

Resources and tools

There are several resources and tools available to support the implementation of authentic assessment:

1. Rubrics: Rubrics provide clear criteria and expectations for student performance. They can help teachers assess student work consistently and provide constructive feedback.

2. Digital portfolios: Digital platforms allow students to create and showcase their work in an online portfolio. This provides a comprehensive view of their abilities and growth over time.

3. Peer and self-assessment: By involving students in the assessment process, peer and self-assessment helps develop their metacognitive skills and promotes a deeper understanding of the criteria for success.

4. Authentic assessment examples and case studies: Teachers can find examples and case studies of authentic assessment in various subject areas to inspire their own assessment designs and understand best practices.

Conclusion

Authentic assessment provides a more meaningful and holistic approach to evaluating student learning. By focusing on real-world applications and tasks, it not only measures knowledge and skills but also fosters deeper understanding and application. While there are challenges in implementing authentic assessment, the benefits far outweigh the drawbacks. Teachers can leverage resources and tools to design and implement authentic assessments that promote student engagement, critical thinking, and lifelong learning.

Overcoming Challenges in Implementing Authentic Assessment

Authentic assessment is a valuable tool for evaluating students' knowledge, skills, and abilities in real-world contexts. However, implementing authentic assessment comes with its challenges. In this section, we will explore some of the common challenges faced by educators and provide strategies to overcome them.

Challenge 1: Designing Authentic Assessment Tasks

One of the main challenges in implementing authentic assessment is designing tasks that truly reflect real-world situations and require students to apply their knowledge and skills. Designing authentic assessment tasks involves carefully aligning the task with the learning objectives and selecting appropriate real-world contexts.

To overcome this challenge, educators can:

- Clearly define the learning objectives and desired outcomes before designing the assessment task.

- Consult industry professionals or experts in the field to ensure the authenticity of the task.
- Use real-world scenarios or problems that students are likely to encounter in their future careers.
- Provide clear guidelines and criteria for assessment to ensure consistency and fairness.

By carefully designing authentic assessment tasks, educators can provide meaningful learning experiences for students.

Challenge 2: Assessing Multiple Skills and Competencies

Authentic assessment aims to measure a wide range of skills and competencies, such as critical thinking, problem-solving, communication, and collaboration. Assessing these skills effectively can be a challenge, as traditional assessment methods may not capture the complexity of students' performance in real-world situations.

To address this challenge, educators can:

- Use rubrics or scoring guides that clearly define the criteria for each skill or competency being assessed.
- Provide opportunities for self-reflection and self-assessment, allowing students to identify their strengths and areas for improvement.
- Incorporate peer assessment, where students provide feedback to their peers based on predetermined criteria.
- Use technology tools, such as video recordings or online platforms, to capture and assess students' performance in authentic tasks.

By adopting a holistic approach to assessment and utilizing multiple assessment methods, educators can effectively evaluate students' diverse skills and competencies.

Challenge 3: Allocating Sufficient Time and Resources

Implementing authentic assessment requires time and resources to develop and administer the tasks, provide feedback, and evaluate student performance. Limited class time and limited access to technology or resources can be significant barriers to implementing authentic assessment.

To overcome this challenge, educators can:

- Plan ahead and allocate sufficient time in the curriculum to implement authentic assessment tasks.
- Use technology tools and online resources to facilitate the assessment process, such as online collaboration platforms or virtual simulations.
- Leverage school or community resources, such as industry partnerships or field trips, to provide students with real-world experiences and resources.
- Prioritize and focus on key skills and competencies to ensure the effective use of time and resources.

By effectively managing time and resources, educators can ensure the successful implementation of authentic assessment.

Challenge 4: Providing Constructive Feedback

Authentic assessment goes beyond assigning grades; it aims to provide students with constructive feedback to support their learning and growth. Providing timely and meaningful feedback can be challenging, especially when dealing with a large number of students or complex assessment tasks.

To address this challenge, educators can:

- Develop clear and specific criteria for assessment to guide feedback provision.
- Use a variety of feedback methods, such as written comments, audio recordings, or video annotations, to cater to students' diverse learning preferences.
- Provide both formative and summative feedback throughout the assessment process, allowing students to improve their performance before the final evaluation.
- Incorporate peer feedback, where students provide feedback to their peers based on the criteria provided.

By providing timely and constructive feedback, educators can support students' learning and promote their development in authentic tasks.

Challenge 5: Validating the Authenticity of Assessment Tasks

Authentic assessment tasks should reflect real-world challenges and contexts. However, ensuring the authenticity of tasks can be challenging, especially when creating assessments for diverse subject areas or in rapidly evolving fields.

To overcome this challenge, educators can:

- Seek input from industry professionals or experts in the field to validate the authenticity of the assessment tasks.
- Stay updated with current trends and developments in the field to ensure the relevance and authenticity of the tasks.
- Use case studies or examples from real-life situations to provide authenticity to the assessment tasks.
- Encourage students to reflect on the authenticity of the tasks and provide suggestions for improvement.

By continuously validating and improving the authenticity of assessment tasks, educators can ensure the integrity of the assessment process.

Conclusion

Implementing authentic assessment can be challenging, but with careful planning, alignment with learning objectives, and the use of appropriate strategies, educators can overcome these challenges. By embracing authentic assessment, educators can foster student engagement, support the development of real-world skills, and provide a more meaningful and relevant learning experience for students.

Case Studies and Best Practices in Authentic Assessment

Authentic assessment is a powerful tool in measuring students' real-world skills and abilities. By engaging students in meaningful tasks that mirror authentic situations and challenges, it provides a more accurate representation of their knowledge and competencies. In this section, we will explore case studies and best practices in authentic assessment, highlighting the benefits, challenges, and practical implementation strategies.

Case Study 1: Simulating Real-World Marketing Campaigns

In a marketing course, students were tasked with designing and implementing a real-world marketing campaign for a local business. Working in teams, students conducted market research, developed marketing plans, and executed their strategies, utilizing various marketing channels such as social media, print media, and events. The assessment involved evaluating the effectiveness of their campaigns based on measurable outcomes, such as brand awareness, customer engagement, and sales growth.

This case study illustrates the integration of authentic assessment into the curriculum. By connecting classroom learning to real-world marketing practices, students were able to apply their knowledge in a practical context. The assessment criteria were aligned with industry standards and required the students to demonstrate not only their marketing knowledge but also their creativity, critical thinking, and problem-solving skills.

Best Practice 1: Aligning Assessment with Real-World Tasks

Authentic assessment should closely mirror real-world tasks and challenges to ensure the assessment is relevant and meaningful. This can be achieved by designing assessment tasks that require students to solve problems, make decisions, and apply their knowledge in authentic contexts. By aligning the assessment with real-world tasks, students are motivated to engage deeply with the subject matter and develop the skills and competencies needed for success beyond the classroom.

Case Study 2: Designing and Building Sustainable Architecture

In an architecture program, students were given a project to design and build a sustainable structure using eco-friendly materials and practices. The assessment involved multiple stages, including conceptual design, digital modeling, physical construction, and final presentation. Students were evaluated based on their ability to integrate sustainability principles into their designs, demonstrate technical proficiency in construction, and effectively communicate their ideas.

This case study showcases the authentic assessment approach in the field of architecture. By engaging in hands-on, real-world projects, students not only applied their architectural knowledge and skills but also developed a deep understanding of sustainable design practices. The assessment criteria focused on both the process and the end product, emphasizing the importance of critical thinking, problem-solving, and effective communication in architectural design.

Best Practice 2: Providing Ongoing Feedback and Reflection

Authentic assessment should provide opportunities for ongoing feedback and reflection to support students' learning and growth. This can be achieved through regular check-ins, peer and self-assessment, and feedback sessions with instructors. By providing timely and constructive feedback, students can identify areas for improvement and make necessary adjustments in their work. Additionally, encouraging students to reflect on their learning process and outcomes helps to deepen their understanding and encourages metacognitive skills development.

Case Study 3: Role-Playing in a Legal Ethics Course

In a legal ethics course, students participated in a role-playing exercise simulating a legal dilemma. Each student was assigned a specific role, such as a lawyer, a client, or a judge, and was tasked with navigating the ethical challenges associated with the scenario. The assessment focused on the students' ability to analyze ethical issues, apply legal principles, and make informed decisions based on professional ethics.

This case study exemplifies the use of authentic assessment for developing students' professional ethics and critical thinking skills. By placing students in realistic scenarios, the assessment challenged them to grapple with complex ethical dilemmas and apply their legal knowledge in a practical and meaningful way. The assessment criteria emphasized professional ethics, legal reasoning, and the ability to articulate clear and well-reasoned arguments.

Best Practice 3: Engaging Students in Self-Reflection and Peer Evaluation

Authentic assessment can be enhanced by incorporating self-reflection and peer evaluation components. By requiring students to reflect on their strengths, areas for improvement, and lessons learned from the assessment task, they develop a deeper understanding of their own learning processes and can set goals for future improvement. Peer evaluation, on the other hand, allows students to provide feedback to their peers, fostering collaboration, communication skills, and a deeper understanding of the assessment criteria.

Conclusion

Authentic assessment offers a comprehensive approach to evaluating students' skills, knowledge, and competencies within real-world contexts. The case studies and best practices discussed in this section demonstrate the benefits of authentic assessment in fostering deep learning, critical thinking, problem-solving, and effective communication. By aligning assessment tasks with real-world challenges, providing ongoing feedback and reflection opportunities, and engaging students in self-reflection and peer evaluation, educators can create a transformative learning environment that prepares students for success in their future endeavors.

Technology-enhanced Authentic Assessment

Authentic assessment is an approach to evaluating student learning that focuses on real-world, meaningful tasks and activities. It aims to assess students' ability to apply knowledge and skills in context, rather than simply regurgitating information. By incorporating technology into authentic assessment, educators can enhance the assessment process, making it more engaging, efficient, and effective.

Benefits of Technology-enhanced Authentic Assessment

Technology-enhanced authentic assessment offers several benefits over traditional assessment methods. Firstly, it allows for the creation of authentic and complex tasks that closely resemble real-world challenges. For example, students can use simulation software to design and test engineering solutions, or they can create multimedia presentations to demonstrate their understanding of a topic. By engaging in these tasks, students develop critical thinking, problem-solving, and creativity skills that are highly valued in the 21st century.

Secondly, technology enables the collection of rich and varied data about student performance. With online platforms and digital tools, teachers can gather a wide range of evidence, such as videos, audio recordings, and digital artifacts, to assess student work in a more comprehensive and holistic manner. This provides a deeper understanding of students' abilities, allowing teachers to provide more targeted and personalized feedback.

Thirdly, technology facilitates collaboration and communication during the assessment process. Through online platforms and virtual environments, students can work together on group projects, share their work with peers, and receive feedback from multiple sources. This not only enhances their interpersonal and teamwork skills but also promotes a sense of ownership and engagement in their learning.

Examples of Technology-enhanced Authentic Assessment

1. Online Portfolios: Students can create digital portfolios to showcase their work over time. They can include samples of their writing, artwork, projects, and

reflections on their learning progress. Teachers can provide feedback and assessment through comments or rubrics embedded in the portfolio platform. This allows students to curate and demonstrate their skills and knowledge in a personalized and engaging way.

2. Video Presentations: Students can record video presentations to demonstrate their understanding of a topic or to communicate their ideas. They can use screencasting tools to narrate a slideshow, create tutorials, or explain complex concepts. This form of assessment encourages students to articulate their thoughts clearly and confidently, while also developing their digital literacy skills.

3. Online Collaborative Projects: Students can collaborate with peers from different locations using online platforms. For example, they can work together on a research project, a virtual science experiment, or a problem-solving task. Through synchronous and asynchronous communication tools, students can coordinate their efforts, exchange ideas, and provide feedback to each other. This type of assessment promotes teamwork, communication, and critical thinking skills.

4. Simulations and Virtual Reality: Students can engage in virtual simulations or immersive virtual reality experiences to demonstrate their knowledge and skills. For instance, in a medical program, students can practice diagnosing patients in a realistic virtual environment. In a historical context, students can explore virtual tours of ancient cities and analyze artifacts. These technology-enhanced assessments provide an authentic context for students to apply their learning and receive immediate feedback.

Challenges and Considerations

While technology-enhanced authentic assessment offers numerous benefits, it is essential to consider some challenges and ethical concerns. Firstly, access to technology and digital literacy skills may vary among students, potentially creating a digital divide. It is crucial to ensure equitable access to technology resources and support for all students to participate fully in the assessment process.

Secondly, the selection of appropriate digital tools and platforms is critical. Educators should consider factors such as ease of use, compatibility, data security, and privacy when choosing technology for assessment. It is vital to comply with data protection laws and obtain informed consent from students and parents regarding the use of digital tools.

Furthermore, teachers need appropriate training and support to effectively integrate technology into authentic assessment. They must be familiar with the selected tools and platforms, understand how to interpret and evaluate digital evidence, and be proficient in providing meaningful and constructive feedback online.

Lastly, technology-enhanced authentic assessment should align with educational principles and learning outcomes. It should not replace the value of formative assessment and ongoing feedback. It is important to strike a balance between technology-enhanced assessment and other assessment methods to ensure a comprehensive and fair evaluation of students' performance.

Conclusion

Technology-enhanced authentic assessment offers a valuable opportunity to assess student learning in a more meaningful and engaging way. By leveraging digital tools and platforms, teachers can design authentic tasks, gather rich evidence, facilitate collaboration, and provide timely feedback. However, it is crucial to consider the challenges, ensure access and equity, select appropriate tools, and provide adequate support to teachers and students. By embracing technology-enhanced authentic assessment, educators can foster a more comprehensive and holistic approach to evaluating student learning.

Authentic Assessment in Different Subject Areas

Authentic assessment is a form of assessment that focuses on evaluating students' ability to apply their knowledge and skills in real-world contexts. It goes beyond traditional tests and quizzes and requires students to demonstrate their learning through the completion of authentic tasks or projects. This section will explore how authentic assessment can be implemented in different subject areas to promote deeper learning and enhance students' understanding of the content.

Mathematics

In mathematics, authentic assessment can be used to assess students' problem-solving skills and their ability to apply mathematical concepts to real-life situations. For example, instead of traditional algorithm-based questions, students can be given real-world mathematical problems that require them to analyze, model, and solve relevant problems. They can be asked to design a budget for a trip, calculate the area of a real garden, or analyze statistical data from a local survey. These tasks encourage students to think critically, make connections between mathematical concepts and the real world, and develop problem-solving and reasoning skills.

To assess students' understanding, rubrics can be used to evaluate their performance based on criteria such as mathematical accuracy, logical reasoning, and communication of mathematical ideas. Authentic assessment in mathematics not only provides a more meaningful evaluation of students' abilities but also helps them see the relevance and applicability of mathematics in their everyday lives.

Science

Authentic assessment in science involves assessing students' ability to think and work like scientists. It focuses on their understanding of scientific concepts, their ability to design and conduct experiments, and their skills in analyzing and interpreting scientific data. Instead of traditional multiple-choice questions, students can be given open-ended tasks that require them to design and carry out experiments, collect and analyze data, and draw conclusions based on evidence.

For example, in a biology class, students can be asked to design an experiment to investigate the effect of different factors on plant growth. They would need to plan and conduct the experiment, collect and analyze data, and communicate their findings in a scientific report. This not only assesses their understanding of plant growth but also develops their scientific inquiry skills and their ability to communicate scientific concepts.

Rubrics can be used to assess students' performance based on criteria such as experimental design, data collection and analysis, and scientific communication. Authentic assessment in science allows students to experience the scientific process first-hand and fosters an appreciation for scientific thinking and inquiry.

Social Studies

Authentic assessment in social studies focuses on evaluating students' understanding of historical events, social issues, and their ability to think critically about the world around them. It involves tasks that require students to analyze primary and secondary sources, make connections between historical and current events, and evaluate different perspectives on social issues.

For example, students can be asked to research and present a historical event from multiple perspectives, such as a debate between different key figures involved in the event. They would need to gather and analyze evidence, present their findings, and defend their arguments. This not only assesses their knowledge of historical events but also develops their critical thinking, research, and communication skills.

Rubrics can be used to assess students' performance based on criteria such as historical accuracy, analysis of sources, and clarity of argument. Authentic assessment in social studies encourages students to actively engage with the content and develop a deeper understanding of historical events and social issues.

Language Arts

Authentic assessment in language arts focuses on evaluating students' reading, writing, and communication skills in real-life contexts. It involves tasks that require students to engage with diverse texts, analyze literary techniques, and create their own written and oral presentations.

For example, instead of a traditional book report, students can be asked to create a book trailer or a multimedia presentation that captures the essence of a novel and highlights its themes and literary techniques. This task assesses their understanding of the text, their ability to analyze and interpret literary elements, and their skills in multimedia production.

Rubrics can be used to assess students' performance based on criteria such as content knowledge, analysis of literary elements, and creativity in presentation. Authentic assessment in language arts provides students with opportunities to express themselves creatively, engage with literature on a deeper level, and develop strong communication skills.

In conclusion, authentic assessment can be implemented in various subject areas to promote deeper learning, critical thinking, and real-world application of knowledge and skills. By providing students with authentic tasks and opportunities to demonstrate their understanding, educators can assess students' abilities in a more meaningful and comprehensive way. Rubrics play a crucial role in providing clear expectations and criteria for evaluation. Authentic assessment not only enhances students' learning experiences but also prepares them for the challenges and demands of the real world.

Future directions of authentic assessment

As education continues to evolve in the digital age, the future of authentic assessment holds significant promise for enhancing student learning and achievement. Authentic assessment, which focuses on evaluating students' knowledge and skills through real-world tasks and projects, is poised to undergo several transformative changes in the coming years. In this section, we will explore some of the key future directions of authentic assessment and how they can shape the learning experiences of students.

Integration of Technology

One of the most significant future directions of authentic assessment is the integration of technology to enhance assessment practices. Technology offers new possibilities for capturing and evaluating students' learning in authentic ways. For example, digital portfolios can provide a platform for students to showcase their work and reflections across different subject areas. These portfolios can include multimedia elements such as videos, audio recordings, and interactive presentations, allowing students to demonstrate their skills and understanding in a more dynamic and engaging manner.

Additionally, the use of online platforms and tools can enable collaborative and interactive assessment experiences. Students can engage in peer review and feedback processes, where they not only receive feedback but also engage in discussions and revisions of their work. These technology-enhanced assessment practices promote active learning, critical thinking, and effective communication skills.

Emphasis on Transferable Skills

In the future, authentic assessment will increasingly focus on evaluating students' transferable skills, also known as 21st-century skills or soft skills. These skills, which include communication, collaboration, critical thinking, creativity, and problem-solving, are highly valued by employers and essential for success in the modern workforce.

Authentic assessment tasks will be designed to assess these transferable skills effectively. For example, instead of traditional exams that primarily test rote memorization, students may be required to complete complex projects that require them to research, analyze, synthesize information, and present their findings to an audience. These tasks will not only assess students' subject knowledge but also their ability to think critically, work collaboratively, and effectively communicate their ideas.

Personalized and Adaptive Assessment

Another future direction of authentic assessment is the integration of personalized and adaptive assessment techniques. Personalized assessment considers individual students' learning needs, interests, and preferences. It recognizes that each student is unique and requires tailored assessment approaches to demonstrate their knowledge and skills effectively.

Adaptive assessment goes a step further by using technology to dynamically adjust assessment tasks based on students' responses. Adaptive assessment algorithms analyze students' performance in real-time and generate new questions or tasks that target their specific areas of strength or weakness. This approach provides immediate feedback and allows for a more accurate and comprehensive evaluation of students' learning progress.

Authentic Assessment in Online and Blended Learning Environments

With the growing popularity of online and blended learning, the future of authentic assessment will also focus on ensuring its effective implementation in these environments. Traditional assessments, such as multiple-choice exams, may not align well with the authentic learning experiences facilitated by online and blended learning models.

In the future, educators will explore alternative strategies to incorporate authentic assessment into online and blended courses. This may include the use of video-based assessments, online simulations, virtual reality experiences, and digital storytelling. These approaches can provide students with practical and real-world contexts in which they can apply their knowledge and skills.

Use of Learning Analytics

The future of authentic assessment will also be shaped by the use of learning analytics, which involve the collection, analysis, and interpretation of data related to students' learning activities. Learning analytics can provide valuable insights into students' learning behaviors, progress, and performance, enabling teachers to make data-informed decisions about their assessment practices.

By analyzing data from authentic assessment tasks, such as students' digital portfolios or project-based assignments, educators can gain a deeper understanding of students' strengths, weaknesses, and learning trajectories. This information can help tailor instruction, provide targeted feedback, and optimize learning experiences to meet students' individual needs.

Equity and Inclusion Considerations

As authentic assessment evolves, it is essential to address equity and inclusion considerations. The future of authentic assessment should ensure that all students have equal opportunities to showcase their knowledge and skills, regardless of their background, abilities, or access to resources.

This requires designing assessment tasks that are culturally responsive, inclusive, and accessible to diverse learners. Educators must be aware of potential biases and take steps to mitigate them in the design and implementation of authentic assessment. Furthermore, providing appropriate accommodations and support for students with disabilities or other learning challenges will be essential to promote equity and inclusion.

In conclusion, the future of authentic assessment holds great potential for transforming education. By integrating technology, emphasizing transferable skills, personalizing assessment, adapting to online learning environments, leveraging learning analytics, and considering equity and inclusion, authentic assessment can become a powerful tool for promoting meaningful and holistic student learning. As educators embrace these future directions, they will be better equipped to prepare students for the challenges and opportunities of the 21st century.

Creating Transformative Learning Environments

Classroom Design and Physical Spaces

The impact of physical environment on learning

The physical environment plays a crucial role in shaping the learning experience of students. It encompasses factors such as classroom design, lighting, seating arrangements, temperature, noise levels, and the overall atmosphere of the learning space. Research has shown that the physical environment can significantly affect students' focus, engagement, motivation, and overall academic performance. In this section, we will explore the various aspects of the physical environment and their impact on learning.

1. Classroom Design: The layout and design of a classroom can have a profound effect on learning outcomes. An effective classroom design should promote collaboration, communication, and student-centered learning. Flexible seating arrangements, such as movable desks and chairs, can facilitate different instructional strategies and encourage student interaction. Classroom layouts that allow for easy movement and clear visibility of the board or projector screen are also important for effective instruction.

Research has shown that classrooms with natural lighting, ample space, and well-organized learning materials can enhance students' mood and productivity. Aesthetically pleasing and stimulating learning environments can foster creativity and improve students' overall satisfaction with their learning experience.

2. Lighting: Proper lighting is crucial for creating a conducive learning environment. Adequate natural lighting has been linked to increased productivity, improved mood, and reduced eye strain. Classroom lighting should be adjustable to accommodate different learning activities and preferences. Research suggests

that a combination of natural and artificial lighting can optimize students' visual comfort, focus, and alertness.

3. Temperature and Ventilation: Temperature and ventilation also play a significant role in student comfort and concentration. Research has shown that students perform better in well-ventilated classrooms with temperatures maintained within a certain range. Excessive heat or cold can negatively impact students' cognitive abilities and attention span. It is important for educational institutions to provide appropriate heating, cooling, and ventilation systems to create a comfortable learning environment.

4. Noise Levels: Excessive noise levels can disrupt concentration and hinder effective communication in the classroom. Unwanted noise sources, such as traffic or construction noise, should be minimized as much as possible. Additionally, classrooms should be acoustically designed to reduce noise reverberation and create optimal speech intelligibility. The use of sound-absorbing materials, acoustic panels, and proper insulation can help create a quieter and more focused learning environment.

5. Technology Integration: The physical environment should also be designed to accommodate the integration of technology tools. This includes electrical outlets, Wi-Fi connectivity, and appropriate space for devices such as computers, tablets, and interactive whiteboards. Providing easy access to technology resources can enhance students' engagement, collaboration, and access to digital learning materials.

It is important to note that creating an ideal physical environment for learning may sometimes be constrained by budget, space availability, and other practical considerations. However, educators and institutions should make every effort to optimize the physical environment within their means to provide a supportive and stimulating learning environment.

To further explore the impact of physical environment on learning, consider the following scenario:

Scenario: A high school classroom is currently poorly lit, with uncomfortable seating and limited space for movement. Students often complain of feeling tired and find it difficult to concentrate during lessons. The classroom has limited access to natural light and lacks proper ventilation.

Problem: How can the teacher improve the physical environment of the classroom to enhance the learning experience of students?

Solution:

1. Lighting: The teacher could explore options to improve the lighting in the classroom. This may involve rearranging desks to allow more natural light into the room or installing additional lighting fixtures for better overall illumination. Using adjustable blinds or curtains can also help control the amount of natural light.

2. Seating and Space: The teacher could consider rearranging the seating arrangement to provide more comfortable and flexible options for students. This may involve using different types of seating, such as bean bags or standing desks, to accommodate different learning preferences and encourage movement. Removing unnecessary furniture and clutter can also create more space for students to move around and collaborate.

3. Ventilation: The teacher could explore options to improve the ventilation in the classroom. This may involve ensuring windows can be opened to allow fresh air circulation or installing fans or air conditioning units if necessary. Proper ventilation can help create a more comfortable and conducive learning environment.

4. Decoration and Organization: The teacher could work with students to decorate the classroom with student artwork, posters, and educational materials to make it visually appealing and engaging. Creating designated spaces for different learning activities, such as a reading corner or a group discussion area, can also optimize the use of space and promote different modes of learning.

By addressing these aspects of the physical environment, the teacher can create a more conducive learning environment that promotes student engagement, focus, and overall well-being.

In addition to the interventions mentioned above, the teacher could involve students in the process of improving the physical environment. This can empower students to take ownership of their learning space and foster a sense of belonging and pride in their learning environment.

Innovative Classroom Designs for Transformative Education

In today's rapidly evolving educational landscape, the physical environment in which learning takes place plays a crucial role in facilitating transformative education. Innovative classroom designs are essential for creating learning environments that foster creativity, collaboration, and critical thinking. This section explores the principles and elements of innovative classroom designs that support transformative education.

Principles of Innovative Classroom Design

Designing innovative classrooms requires an understanding of the key principles that promote transformative education:

1. **Flexibility and adaptability**: Innovative classrooms should be flexible and adaptable to accommodate diverse teaching and learning activities.

Moveable furniture, adaptable spaces, and modular designs allow for seamless transitions between different instructional methods.

2. **Comfort and aesthetics:** Creating a comfortable and aesthetically pleasing environment has a significant impact on students' engagement and well-being. Ergonomic furniture, appropriate lighting, calming colors, and appealing visuals contribute to a positive learning atmosphere.

3. **Accessibility and inclusivity:** Innovative classrooms should be designed to accommodate students with diverse physical abilities and learning styles. Creating inclusive spaces with appropriate seating arrangements, assistive technologies, and multiple learning zones ensures equal access for all students.

4. **Technology integration:** Incorporating technology seamlessly into the classroom design is crucial for transformative education. Integrated audio-visual systems, interactive displays, and sufficient power outlets facilitate the use of digital tools and resources for collaborative learning and knowledge creation.

5. **Collaborative spaces:** Collaborative learning is central to transformative education. Designing spaces that encourage group work, such as breakout areas, round tables or seating clusters, promotes active participation, peer interaction, and the exchange of ideas.

6. **Multisensory experiences:** Engaging learners through multiple senses enhances motivation and deepens understanding. Incorporating elements such as music, art, natural elements, and tactile materials into the classroom design creates a multisensory learning environment.

Elements of Innovative Classroom Design

Innovative classroom designs incorporate specific elements to support transformative education:

1. **Flexible furniture:** The use of adjustable and modular furniture enables students and teachers to easily adapt the space to their needs. Mobile desks, flexible seating options (such as bean bags or standing desks), and movable whiteboards encourage dynamic learning arrangements.

2. **Zone-based layout:** Creating different learning zones for individual work, small group collaboration, presentations, and hands-on activities provides students with diverse learning experiences. Clearly defined zones help students understand the purpose of each area and allow for focused and immersive learning.

3. **Natural lighting and views:** Maximizing natural lighting and incorporating views of nature have been shown to improve student well-being and concentration. Large windows, skylights, and strategically placed mirrors can help bring the outdoors inside, promoting a sense of connection with the environment.

4. **Interactive displays:** Large interactive displays, such as interactive whiteboards or smart boards, allow teachers and students to share and engage with digital content. These displays promote collaboration, real-time feedback, and interactive learning experiences.

5. **Flexible learning technologies:** The integration of technology tools that support personalized and collaborative learning is essential in transformative classrooms. This includes devices like tablets or laptops, educational apps and software, and online resources that can be accessed by students and foster independent and interactive learning.

6. **Green and sustainable design:** Incorporating sustainable features, such as energy-efficient lighting, natural ventilation, and recycling stations, promotes environmental awareness and teaches students about sustainable practices. Green walls or indoor plants can also improve air quality and contribute to a healthier learning environment.

7. **Acoustic considerations:** Soundproofing materials, acoustic panels, and proper classroom layout help control noise levels and create a conducive learning environment. By minimizing distractions and ensuring clear communication, students can better focus on their tasks and interactions.

8. **Student displays and exhibitions:** Providing dedicated spaces for student work displays, portfolios, or interactive exhibitions encourages peer-to-peer learning, reflection, and celebration of achievements. It also creates a sense of pride and ownership over the learning space.

9. **Accessible assistive technologies:** Supporting students with diverse learning needs requires the availability of assistive technologies. These may include

text-to-speech tools, screen readers, sign language interpreters, or adaptable furniture to ensure equitable access to learning resources for all students.

10. **Safety and security features:** Maintaining a safe and secure learning environment is paramount. Proper emergency exits, surveillance systems, and secure storage for personal belongings contribute to the well-being and peace of mind of students and staff.

Case Studies and Best Practices

To illustrate the impact of innovative classroom designs, let's explore a few case studies:

1. **The Green School, Bali:** The Green School in Bali, Indonesia, exemplifies sustainable and nature-based design. The classrooms are made of bamboo structures with natural ventilation, extensive gardens, and open learning spaces. This design fosters a connection with nature and sustainability education.

2. **STEAM Lab, Singapore American School:** The STEAM Lab at the Singapore American School is a flexible space equipped with advanced technology and hands-on materials. The classroom design supports project-based learning and interdisciplinary collaboration among students, encouraging innovation and creativity.

3. **AltSchool, San Francisco:** AltSchool uses a personalized learning model with adaptive technology and flexible classroom layouts. The classroom design allows for individualized instruction and differentiated learning experiences tailored to each student's needs and interests.

These case studies demonstrate that innovative classroom designs can have a significant impact on students' engagement, creativity, and critical thinking skills.

Resources and Tools for Innovative Classroom Design

Here are some resources and tools that educators can utilize to support innovative classroom design:

- **Design Thinking for Educators Toolkit:** A comprehensive resource developed by IDEO, providing design thinking methodologies and tools specifically tailored for educators to drive innovation in classroom design. It includes design challenges, brainstorming exercises, and prototyping techniques.

- **Classroom Architect:** An online tool that allows teachers to create and visualize classroom layouts, experiment with different furniture arrangements, and incorporate key design principles. It provides a simple drag-and-drop interface to plan and design innovative learning spaces.

- **Edutopia:** An online platform dedicated to innovative teaching and learning practices, including resources and articles on classroom design. It offers insights, case studies, and practical tips from experienced educators and designers.

- **ISTE Standards for Students:** Developed by the International Society for Technology in Education, these standards provide a framework for creating transformative learning environments. It emphasizes the importance of innovative classroom design in supporting personalized and student-centered learning.

Thinking Outside the Box

While classroom design is crucial for transformative education, it's important to think beyond traditional classroom settings. Consider alternative learning spaces, such as outdoor environments, community centers, museums, or even virtual reality classrooms. These innovative learning spaces provide unique opportunities for immersive and experiential learning, connecting students with the real world and broadening their perspectives.

Summary

Innovative classroom designs have the power to shape transformative education experiences. By incorporating flexibility, comfort, technology integration, collaboration, and inclusivity, educators can create learning environments that enhance engagement, foster creativity, and cultivate critical thinking skills. Utilizing the principles, elements, case studies, resources, and thinking outside the box approach discussed in this section, educators can embark on designing innovative classrooms that inspire and empower students for a future of learning and growth.

Flexible learning spaces and furniture

Flexible learning spaces and furniture play a crucial role in creating an environment that supports transformative education. Traditionally, classrooms have been designed with fixed furniture arrangements, such as rows of desks facing the front of the room. However, this traditional setup limits students' ability to collaborate, engage in hands-on activities, and move around freely. In contrast, flexible learning spaces and furniture offer a more dynamic and adaptable environment that promotes active learning and student-centered approaches.

One key aspect of flexible learning spaces is the ability to easily reconfigure the furniture layout. This can be achieved through using lightweight and movable furniture, such as modular desks, chairs, and tables. By allowing students to rearrange their seating and work areas, the classroom can be transformed to accommodate different types of activities, such as group discussions, individual work, or large group presentations. This flexibility enables students to take ownership of their learning environment and adapt it to their individual needs and preferences.

In addition to furniture mobility, another important consideration is the presence of various types of learning zones within the space. These zones can be designed to cater to different learning activities and preferences. For example, there could be a collaborative zone with large tables and comfortable seating for group work, a quiet zone with individual desks and privacy screens for focused work, and a presentation zone with a projector and a stage for student presentations and lectures.

The use of technology in flexible learning spaces is also essential. Having access to power outlets, charging stations, and Wi-Fi connectivity throughout the classroom enables students to seamlessly integrate digital tools and resources into their learning experiences. Furthermore, the inclusion of interactive whiteboards, projectors, and other multimedia devices can enhance student engagement and facilitate the sharing of ideas and information.

It is important to note that the design of flexible learning spaces should prioritize inclusivity and accessibility. The furniture should be adjustable to accommodate students with diverse physical abilities and provide ergonomic support. Furthermore, the layout should consider the needs of students with visual or hearing impairments, ensuring that they have clear sightlines and access to audiovisual materials.

To illustrate the impact of flexible learning spaces, let's consider an example in a science classroom. In a traditional setup, students would be confined to their individual desks, limiting their ability to engage in hands-on experiments or collaborate with their peers. However, by implementing a flexible learning space with mobile lab stations, adjustable stools, and collaboration areas, students can easily move around the classroom, work in small groups to conduct experiments, and share their findings with the rest of the class. This setup promotes active learning, fosters scientific inquiry, and allows for a more immersive and impactful learning experience.

To further enhance the learning environment, teachers can incorporate elements of nature and natural light into the design. Research has shown that exposure to natural light and greenery can improve students' mood, concentration, and overall well-being. Integrating large windows, plants, and natural materials into the classroom design can create a more stimulating and calming atmosphere, conducive to learning.

It is worth mentioning that implementing flexible learning spaces and furniture may require support from school administrators and investment in infrastructure. This could involve training for teachers on how to utilize the space effectively, as well as funding for purchasing adaptable furniture and creating multifunctional classroom layouts.

In conclusion, flexible learning spaces and furniture offer tremendous opportunities for creating transformative educational environments. By allowing for student autonomy, collaboration, and adaptability, these spaces can enhance active learning, critical thinking, and problem-solving skills. When combined with technology integration, inclusive design, and attention to environmental factors, flexible learning spaces have the potential to revolutionize the way education is delivered and experienced.

Creating Collaborative Learning Environments

Collaboration is a key component of transformative education, as it fosters deeper learning, critical thinking, and problem-solving skills. In this section, we will explore the importance of creating collaborative learning environments and provide strategies and tools to facilitate effective collaboration among students.

Understanding Collaborative Learning

Collaborative learning is an instructional approach where students work together in groups to achieve shared learning goals. It involves active participation, cooperation, and shared responsibility among students. Collaborative learning can take various forms, such as group discussions, team projects, and peer-to-peer interactions.

Research has shown that collaborative learning offers several benefits. It enhances students' social skills, promotes higher-order thinking, and improves their ability to apply knowledge to real-world situations. Additionally, collaborative learning encourages active engagement and participation, leading to increased motivation and enjoyment of the learning process.

Designing Collaborative Learning Experiences

To create effective collaborative learning environments, educators should carefully design learning experiences that promote active collaboration. Here are some strategies to consider:

- **Establish clear learning objectives:** Clearly define the learning outcomes and expectations for collaboration. This helps students understand their roles and responsibilities within the group.
- **Group formation:** Form diverse and heterogeneous groups to encourage peer learning and maximize the exchange of ideas and perspectives.
- **Structured group activities:** Provide structured activities that guide students' collaboration, such as problem-solving tasks, case studies, or simulations. These activities should promote active engagement and stimulate critical thinking.
- **Promote communication and interaction:** Encourage open communication and active listening within the groups. Provide opportunities for students to share their ideas, ask questions, and provide feedback to their peers.
- **Use technology tools:** Incorporate technology tools that facilitate collaboration, such as online discussion forums, collaborative document editing platforms, or virtual whiteboards. These tools can enhance communication and enable seamless collaboration, regardless of physical proximity.

Overcoming Challenges in Collaborative Learning

While collaborative learning offers numerous benefits, it may also present challenges. Here are some common challenges and strategies to overcome them:

- **Unequal participation:** Ensure equal participation within the group by setting clear expectations, monitoring group dynamics, and providing guidance on effective collaboration. Assign specific roles or rotate roles within the group to ensure everyone contributes.

- **Conflict resolution:** Teach students conflict resolution strategies and provide guidance on how to navigate disagreements constructively. Encourage a supportive and respectful environment where diverse opinions are valued.
- **Accountability and assessment:** Develop clear criteria for evaluating individual and group contributions. Implement a peer evaluation system, where students assess their peers' contributions to the collaborative process. This promotes accountability and encourages students to take ownership of their learning.
- **Time management:** Teach students effective time management skills and provide guidance on how to prioritize tasks within the group. Help students set realistic goals and monitor progress throughout the collaborative project.

Case Studies and Best Practices

To illustrate the effectiveness of collaborative learning, let's explore two case studies:

Case Study 1: Project-Based Collaboration

In a high school science class, students are assigned a project to design and build a functioning model of a solar-powered car. Students work in small groups, applying their knowledge of physics and engineering to design the car. Each group member has a specific role, such as researching materials, designing the car body, or assembling the solar panel. Throughout the project, students collaborate, share ideas, problem-solve, and provide feedback to one another. At the end of the project, each group presents their car to the class, explaining the design choices and demonstrating its functionality.

Case Study 2: Online Collaborative Discussion

In an online history course, students engage in collaborative discussions about historical events and their implications. The course utilizes an online discussion forum, where students post their thoughts and respond to their peers' ideas. The instructor structures the discussion by providing guiding questions and facilitating the conversation. Students are encouraged to support their arguments with evidence and engage in respectful debates. The forum allows students to interact asynchronously, enabling thoughtful reflection before responding. Through these online discussions, students develop critical thinking skills, deepen their understanding of historical events, and learn from diverse perspectives.

Incorporating Technology in Collaborative Learning

Technology can significantly enhance collaborative learning experiences. Here are some technology tools and platforms that can facilitate collaboration among students:

- **Collaborative document editing tools:** Tools such as Google Docs or Microsoft Office 365 enable real-time collaboration on documents, allowing students to work together on projects, share ideas, and provide feedback.
- **Virtual communication platforms:** Video conferencing tools like Zoom or Microsoft Teams enable students to connect and collaborate from different locations. These platforms support face-to-face interactions, screen sharing, and breakout rooms for small group discussions.
- **Educational social media platforms:** Platforms like Edmodo or Schoology create online spaces for students to interact, share resources, and engage in discussions. These platforms mimic social media functionalities while providing a safe and controlled environment.

Summary

Creating collaborative learning environments is essential for promoting active engagement, critical thinking, and social interaction among students. By designing collaborative learning experiences, addressing challenges, and incorporating technology tools, educators can facilitate meaningful collaboration, leading to transformative learning outcomes. Collaboration fosters teamwork, communication, and problem-solving skills, preparing students for success in the 21st-century workforce.

Remember, creating collaborative learning environments requires careful planning, guidance, and ongoing support to ensure the success of students and the achievement of learning goals.

Effective use of technology in physical spaces

In the rapidly evolving landscape of education, technology has become an integral part of the learning experience. One area where technology has had a profound impact is in the design and use of physical learning spaces. Traditional classrooms are being transformed into dynamic and interactive environments that foster collaboration, engagement, and active learning. In this section, we will explore how technology can be effectively used to enhance physical spaces and create transformative learning environments.

The role of technology in physical spaces

Technology has the power to revolutionize the way we utilize and interact with physical spaces in education. It provides the tools to create flexible and adaptable environments that meet the diverse needs of learners. Here are some key ways in which technology can enhance physical spaces:

- **Interactive displays and smart boards:** Interactive displays and smart boards allow for seamless integration of digital content into classroom activities. Teachers can use them to present information, facilitate discussions, and promote collaborative learning. Students can actively participate in lessons by interacting with the content or sharing their work.
- **Mobile devices:** With the widespread use of mobile devices such as tablets and smartphones, students have instant access to a wealth of information and resources. These devices can be utilized in physical spaces to enable personalized learning, independent research, and data collection. They can also be used for real-time assessment and feedback.
- **Virtual and augmented reality:** Virtual and augmented reality technologies provide immersive and engaging experiences that transcend the limitations of traditional classrooms. They can transport students to virtual worlds, allowing them to explore concepts, conduct virtual experiments, and interact with objects and environments. These technologies can enhance understanding and retention of complex subjects.
- **Internet of Things (IoT) devices:** IoT devices can be used to create smart classrooms that are equipped with sensors, cameras, and networked devices. These devices can collect data on environmental conditions, student behaviors, and learning activities. This data can be used to optimize the design of physical spaces, personalize instruction, and improve overall learning outcomes.
- **Robotics and smart furniture:** Robotics and smart furniture technologies are being used to create adaptive and responsive learning spaces. Robotic assistants can support students in their learning journeys, providing individualized guidance and feedback. Smart furniture can be reconfigured to accommodate different learning activities and promote collaboration.

The effective use of technology in physical spaces requires careful planning and consideration. Educators need to ensure that technology is integrated in a way that supports the learning objectives and promotes meaningful engagement. Let's explore some strategies and best practices for leveraging technology in physical spaces.

Strategies for effective use of technology in physical spaces

To maximize the potential of technology in physical spaces, educators should consider the following strategies:

1. **Align technology with learning goals:** It is important to identify the specific learning goals and outcomes that technology integration should support. Technology should not be used for the sake of using technology, but rather as a means to enhance the learning experience. By aligning technology use with learning objectives, educators can ensure that it is integrated purposefully and effectively.

2. **Promote active learning and collaboration:** Technology can be used to facilitate active learning and promote collaboration among students. Incorporate interactive activities and collaborative projects that require students to actively engage with technology and work together. Consider using tools such as online whiteboards, collaborative document editing, and videoconferencing platforms to foster collaboration among students, even when they are physically apart.

3. **Provide adequate training and support:** To effectively use technology in physical spaces, it is important to provide educators with the necessary training and support. Educators should receive professional development opportunities that not only cover the technical aspects of technology integration but also provide guidance on pedagogical strategies and best practices. Ongoing support and mentoring can help teachers navigate challenges and maximize the benefits of technology use.

4. **Consider accessibility and inclusivity:** When designing physical spaces with technology, it is crucial to consider accessibility and inclusivity. Ensure that technology is accessible to all students, regardless of their abilities or learning needs. Provide options for alternative modes of interaction and communication, such as text-to-speech and captioning. Pay attention to the physical layout of the space to ensure that it is inclusive and enables all students to actively participate and engage with technology.

5. **Regularly assess and evaluate the impact of technology:** Evaluation is essential to determine the effectiveness of technology integration in physical spaces. Regularly assess student learning outcomes, engagement levels, and overall satisfaction with the use of technology. Collect feedback from both students and educators to identify areas of improvement and make necessary adjustments. Use data and analytics to inform decision-making and continuously improve the integration of technology.

Examples and best practices

Let's take a look at some examples of effective use of technology in physical spaces:

- **Smart classrooms:** Some schools have implemented smart classroom technologies that use sensors, cameras, and IoT devices to create intelligent learning environments. For example, sensors can monitor temperature, lighting, and noise levels to optimize the learning environment for student comfort and concentration. Smart whiteboards and projectors enable interactive presentations and seamless access to digital resources.

- **Virtual reality labs:** In some science classrooms, virtual reality (VR) labs have been introduced to provide students with immersive experiences. Students can explore the human body, visit historical sites, or conduct virtual experiments. VR labs enable students to interact with three-dimensional models and simulate real-world scenarios that may not be possible in traditional labs.

- **Flexible learning spaces:** Many schools are redesigning physical spaces to create flexible learning environments. These spaces are equipped with movable furniture, writable surfaces, and technology integration points. Students can rearrange furniture to suit different learning activities, collaborate with peers, and access technology resources as needed. These flexible spaces promote student agency and choice in their learning experiences.

Challenges and considerations

While technology offers great potential in enhancing physical spaces, there are also challenges and considerations that educators need to address:

- **Infrastructure and connectivity:** Access to reliable and high-speed internet connectivity is crucial for effective use of technology in physical spaces.

Schools need to ensure that they have the necessary infrastructure in place and address any connectivity issues. In some cases, schools may need to invest in upgrading their network capabilities to support the demands of technology integration.

- **Equity and access:** Ensuring equitable access to technology is essential to prevent the digital divide from widening. Schools need to consider the availability of devices and internet access for all students, regardless of their socio-economic background. Additionally, teachers should provide support and guidance to students who may be unfamiliar with the technology or have limited access to it outside of the classroom.

- **Digital citizenship and ethical considerations:** The use of technology in physical spaces also requires addressing issues related to digital citizenship and responsible use. Educators should educate students about appropriate online behavior, digital safety, and the responsible use of technology. It is important to foster a culture of respect, empathy, and ethical behavior in the digital realm.

Conclusion

Technology has the potential to transform physical learning spaces into dynamic and engaging environments that support the needs of modern learners. By effectively integrating technology into physical spaces, educators can create opportunities for active learning, collaboration, and personalized instruction. However, careful planning, ongoing professional development, and attention to accessibility and inclusivity are essential to ensure that technology enhances the learning experience for all students. Through thoughtful design and purposeful integration, physical spaces can become catalysts for transformative education.

Case Studies and Best Practices in Classroom Design

In this section, we will explore various case studies and best practices in classroom design. The physical environment of a classroom plays a crucial role in creating an effective learning space. A well-designed classroom can promote active engagement, collaboration, and creativity among students. Let's delve into some examples of successful classroom designs and the principles behind them.

1. **Flexible Seating Arrangements:** One common trend in modern classroom design is the use of flexible seating arrangements. Research has shown that providing students with different seating options can enhance their comfort and focus, leading

to improved learning outcomes. For example, instead of traditional desks and chairs, classrooms may incorporate standing desks, bean bags, floor cushions, or adjustable furniture for students to choose from. This allows students to find seating that fits their individual learning preferences and promotes healthy movement throughout the day.

2. **Zoned Learning Spaces:** Another approach to classroom design is creating zoned learning spaces. This involves dividing the classroom into different areas designated for specific activities or subjects. For instance, there may be a reading corner, a collaborative group workspace, a makerspace for hands-on activities, and a presentation area. Zoned learning spaces provide students with dedicated areas for different learning experiences, allowing for a more focused and productive environment. Additionally, it encourages student independence and self-directed learning.

3. **Technology Integration:** With the increasing use of technology in education, classroom design should adapt to accommodate the integration of technology tools. This includes providing adequate power outlets, Wi-Fi access, and storage solutions for devices. Additionally, the layout of the classroom should consider the placement of interactive whiteboards, projectors, and audio systems for effective multimedia use. A well-designed technology-integrated classroom enables seamless integration of digital resources and promotes digital literacy among students.

4. **Natural Lighting and Classroom Aesthetics:** The use of natural lighting can have a positive impact on students' well-being and attention span. Classrooms with large windows or skylights that allow ample natural light to enter create a more welcoming and inviting atmosphere. Additionally, incorporating plants and colorful decor can enhance the aesthetics of the classroom, promoting a positive learning environment. Research has shown that a visually stimulating and pleasant classroom environment can positively influence students' mood, motivation, and creativity.

5. **Acoustic Considerations:** Noise can be a significant distraction in the classroom. Therefore, designing classrooms with proper acoustic considerations is essential. This includes using sound-absorbing materials, such as carpets, curtains, or acoustic panels, to reduce reverberation and minimize external noise. Adequate soundproofing measures, such as insulated walls and doors, can also help create a quieter learning environment. By optimizing the acoustics of the classroom, students can better focus on their tasks and engage in effective communication.

6. **Inclusive Learning Environments:** Classroom design should strive to be inclusive and accommodate diverse student needs. This may involve providing accessible furniture and resources for students with physical disabilities, ensuring clear sightlines and legible text for students with visual impairments, and incorporating assistive technologies for students with learning difficulties. By

designing classrooms with inclusivity in mind, educators can create an environment where every student feels supported and valued.

7. **Student-Centered Design:** A student-centered approach to classroom design emphasizes creating spaces that empower students to take ownership of their learning. This may involve arranging furniture in a way that facilitates communication and collaboration, incorporating display areas for student work, and providing flexible storage options for personalized learning materials. A student-centered classroom design promotes student agency, fosters independence, and encourages active participation.

By studying these case studies and implementing best practices in classroom design, educators can create learning environments that promote engagement, collaboration, and academic success. It is important to understand that there is no one-size-fits-all solution, and classroom design should be tailored to meet the specific needs of the students and the curriculum. Embracing innovative and flexible approaches to classroom design can contribute to creating transformative learning environments that inspire students to reach their full potential.

Inclusive Learning Environments for All Students

Inclusive learning environments are crucial in ensuring that all students, regardless of their backgrounds or abilities, have equal opportunities to thrive academically, socially, and emotionally. These environments embrace diversity, respect individual differences, and promote a sense of belonging and inclusion for all students. In this section, we will explore the principles and strategies for creating inclusive learning environments that address the needs of all students.

Understanding Inclusion

Inclusion in education refers to the practice of providing opportunities for all students, including those with disabilities, special needs, or from diverse backgrounds, to fully participate in regular educational settings. It goes beyond physical access and encompasses the provision of appropriate support and accommodations to enable students to reach their full potential.

Inclusive learning environments recognize and value diversity in terms of race, ethnicity, culture, language, gender identity, sexual orientation, socioeconomic status, learning styles, and abilities. They promote equity, social justice, and ensure that every student feels valued, respected, and able to contribute to the learning community. Inclusive education not only benefits students with diverse needs but also enhances the learning experience for all students by promoting understanding, empathy, and acceptance.

Principles of Inclusive Learning Environments

Creating inclusive learning environments requires a commitment to the following principles:

1. Accessibility: Ensuring that physical spaces, instructional materials, technologies, and communication methods are accessible to all students. This may involve providing ramps, elevators, and assistive technologies for students with physical disabilities, captioned videos for students with hearing impairments, and materials in multiple formats for students with visual impairments.

2. Universal Design for Learning (UDL): Applying UDL principles to instructional design to provide multiple means of representation, action, and expression to accommodate diverse learning styles and preferences. UDL encourages educators to provide flexible learning options, varied assessment formats, and a range of instructional materials to meet the needs of all students.

3. Differentiation: Recognizing that students have different prior knowledge, skills, and interests, and tailoring instruction to meet their individual needs. Differentiation involves modifying content, strategies, and assessments to ensure that all students can engage in meaningful learning experiences and demonstrate their understanding.

4. Collaborative and Cooperative Learning: Fostering a collaborative learning environment where students work together, support each other, and benefit from diverse perspectives. Collaborative learning activities enable students to develop social skills, empathy, and teamwork while promoting mutual respect and understanding.

5. Culturally Responsive Teaching: Recognizing and valuing the cultural backgrounds, experiences, and perspectives of students. Culturally responsive teaching involves incorporating students' languages, cultures, and histories into the curriculum, creating a welcoming and inclusive environment that affirms their identities and contributes to their academic success.

6. Personalized Support: Providing individualized support and interventions to address the unique learning needs of all students. This may involve differentiated instruction, targeted interventions, or specialized services to ensure that students receive the necessary support to succeed.

Strategies for Inclusive Learning Environments

To create inclusive learning environments, educators can employ a range of strategies, including:

1. Establishing a Positive Classroom Culture: Cultivating a safe, respectful, and inclusive classroom culture that values diversity, encourages active participation, and celebrates student achievements. This can be achieved through icebreakers, community-building activities, and promoting a sense of belonging among students.

2. Differentiating Instruction: Adapting instructional methods, materials, and assessments to accommodate the diverse needs of students. This may involve using a variety of teaching strategies, providing options for demonstrating understanding, and offering additional support or enrichment activities.

3. Collaborative Learning Opportunities: Providing opportunities for students to work in groups, engage in cooperative learning activities, and participate in collaborative projects. This promotes peer interaction, cooperation, and shared learning experiences.

4. Use of Assistive Technologies: Integrating assistive technologies such as speech-to-text software, text-to-speech tools, graphic organizers, and digital accessibility tools to support students with disabilities or special needs.

5. Culturally Responsive Teaching Practices: Incorporating culturally relevant content, examples, and perspectives into the curriculum to make learning more relatable and meaningful for all students. This includes using diverse instructional materials, incorporating multicultural literature, and inviting guest speakers from different cultural backgrounds.

6. Individualized Support and Intervention: Providing targeted interventions and individualized support to students who require additional assistance. This may involve one-on-one instruction, tutoring, or specialized intervention programs to address specific learning needs.

7. Ongoing Professional Development: Engaging in continuous professional development to enhance teachers' knowledge and skills in creating inclusive learning environments. This can include attending workshops, conferences, or online courses focused on inclusive education practices.

Challenges and Solutions

Creating inclusive learning environments may present challenges for educators. Some common challenges include:

1. Lack of Awareness and Understanding: Educators may lack awareness and understanding of the diverse needs of students, leading to unintentional exclusion or limited access to resources. Solution: Regular professional development and training can help raise awareness and provide educators with the knowledge and skills to create inclusive environments.

2. Limited Resources: Limited resources, including funding, assistive technologies, and specialized personnel, may pose challenges in meeting the diverse needs of students. Solution: Collaboration with school administrators, seeking external funding grants, and leveraging community partnerships can help address resource limitations.

3. Resistance to Change: Resistance from stakeholders, including teachers, parents, and the community, may impede the implementation of inclusive practices. Solution: Building a culture of collaboration, open communication, and involving all stakeholders in decision-making processes can help address resistance to change.

4. Time Constraints: Teachers may feel overwhelmed by the additional time and planning required to differentiate instruction and provide individualized support. Solution: Providing teachers with adequate planning time, resources, and support through co-teaching or collaboration with support staff can alleviate time constraints.

5. Inconsistent Policies and Support: Inconsistent policies and lack of support at the school or district level can hinder the implementation of inclusive practices. Solution: Advocacy for inclusive policies, collaboration with school leadership, and professional learning communities that foster support and collaboration can address these challenges.

Case Studies and Best Practices

To further exemplify inclusive learning environments, let's look at some case studies and best practices:

1. Case Study: Creating an Inclusive STEM Classroom In an elementary STEM classroom, the teacher designs learning experiences that allow students to work collaboratively in diverse teams. The classroom environment is equipped with accessible materials and tools, including adapted keyboards and tactile learning resources for students with physical disabilities. The teacher incorporates cultural diversity into lessons by incorporating examples from different cultures and encouraging students to share their cultural perspectives. Individual student needs are addressed through differentiated instruction and targeted interventions,

ensuring that all students have equitable opportunities to engage in STEM learning.

2. Best Practice: Universal Design for Learning (UDL) Applying UDL principles in the classroom allows educators to provide multiple means of representation, action, and expression to meet the needs of all students. For example, using visual aids, interactive simulations, and videos to present information caters to different learning styles. Providing options for students to showcase their understanding through written assignments, presentations, or multimedia projects allows for diverse forms of expression. In addition, incorporating flexible seating arrangements and sensory breaks accommodates students with diverse needs and preferences.

Resources for Inclusive Learning Environments

Educators can access various resources to enhance their understanding and implementation of inclusive learning environments. Here are some recommended resources:

1. "Teaching Tolerance" (www.tolerance.org): A website providing free resources, lesson plans, and professional development materials to promote diversity, equity, and inclusive teaching practices.
2. "CAST" (www.cast.org): A nonprofit organization dedicated to advancing inclusive learning through UDL. Their website offers resources, tools, and research on implementing UDL in the classroom.
3. "National Center for Learning Disabilities" (www.ncld.org): An organization providing resources, articles, and research-based strategies for supporting students with learning disabilities and creating inclusive classrooms.
4. "Council for Exceptional Children" (www.cec.sped.org): A professional organization supporting special education teachers and inclusive education practices. Their website offers resources, webinars, and publications on effective inclusive teaching strategies.
5. "Edutopia" (www.edutopia.org): A comprehensive website that showcases articles, videos, and case studies on innovative teaching practices, including inclusive education strategies.

Exercises

1. Reflect on your current classroom practices and identify one area where you can make your learning environment more inclusive. Develop a plan to implement

inclusive practices in that area, considering the needs and strengths of your students.

2. Choose a lesson you have taught recently and think about how you could modify it to accommodate diverse learning needs. Consider different learning styles, cultural backgrounds, and abilities, and brainstorm strategies for engaging all students in the lesson.

3. Select an assistive technology tool that could support a specific group of students in your classroom. Explore how you can integrate this tool into your instruction to enhance accessibility and inclusivity.

4. Engage in a professional learning community discussion or workshop focused on inclusive education practices. Share your experiences, challenges, and strategies with other educators and seek their input and suggestions.

5. Conduct a classroom activity on cultural diversity and inclusion. Ask students to share their cultural traditions, values, and perspectives, fostering a sense of appreciation and understanding among the students.

Remember, creating an inclusive learning environment is an ongoing process that requires continuous reflection, growth, and collaboration. By embracing diversity and addressing the unique needs of all students, educators can create an environment that promotes equity, fosters belonging, and enables every student to thrive.

Outdoor and nature-based learning spaces

In recent years, there has been a growing recognition of the benefits of outdoor and nature-based learning spaces in education. These spaces provide students with opportunities to connect with the natural environment and engage in experiential and hands-on learning. Outdoor and nature-based learning spaces offer a unique and dynamic setting for students to explore, discover, and learn about various subjects. In this section, we will explore the importance of these spaces, their design principles, and their impact on student learning.

Importance of outdoor and nature-based learning spaces

Outdoor and nature-based learning spaces provide a wide range of benefits for students' physical, mental, and emotional development. These spaces offer an alternative learning environment to traditional indoor classrooms and can enhance students' overall educational experience. Here are some key reasons why outdoor and nature-based learning spaces are important:

1. Connection with nature: Spending time in nature has been proven to have physical and psychological benefits. Outdoor learning spaces allow students to develop a strong connection with the natural world, fostering a deep appreciation for the environment and promoting a sense of stewardship.

2. Experiential learning: Outdoor and nature-based learning spaces provide hands-on experiences that engage students' senses and stimulate their curiosity. These spaces offer opportunities for students to explore, observe, and interact with the natural world, making their learning experiences more meaningful and memorable.

3. Health and well-being: Spending time outdoors has been associated with improved mental and physical health. Outdoor learning spaces promote physical activity, reduce stress, and provide a supportive environment for students to develop their social and emotional skills.

4. Multi-disciplinary learning: Outdoor and nature-based learning spaces provide a rich context for cross-curricular learning. Students can explore various subjects such as science, ecology, mathematics, art, and social studies in a holistic and integrated manner, allowing for a deeper understanding of concepts.

Design principles for outdoor and nature-based learning spaces

When designing outdoor and nature-based learning spaces, it is important to consider several key principles that promote effective learning experiences. Here are some design principles to keep in mind:

1. Accessibility and inclusivity: Design outdoor learning spaces to be accessible to all students, including those with physical disabilities. Ensure that pathways, seating areas, and equipment are suitable for students of all abilities.

2. Flexibility and adaptability: Create spaces that can be easily adapted for different activities and subjects. Use movable furniture and modular elements that can be rearranged to accommodate different learning needs.

3. Natural elements and materials: Incorporate natural elements such as trees, plants, rocks, and water features into the design. Use sustainable and environmentally friendly materials to create a harmonious and eco-friendly learning environment.

4. Zones for different activities: Designate specific zones within the outdoor learning space for different activities, such as an area for group discussions, a place for hands-on experiments, or a quiet space for reflection. Provide clear signage and markings to guide students.

5. Integration of technology: Integrate technology in a thoughtful and purposeful way to enhance outdoor learning experiences. For example, use tablets

or smartphones for data collection and analysis, or incorporate augmented reality tools to provide additional information about the natural environment.

Impact on student learning

Outdoor and nature-based learning spaces have a positive impact on student learning across a wide range of subjects and skills. Here are some key ways in which these spaces influence student learning:

1. Science and environmental education: Outdoor learning spaces provide a natural laboratory for students to investigate scientific concepts and ecological systems. Students can conduct experiments, observe natural phenomena, and develop a deeper understanding of environmental issues.
2. STEAM education: Outdoor learning spaces offer opportunities for students to apply STEAM (Science, Technology, Engineering, Arts, and Mathematics) principles in real-world contexts. For example, students can design and build structures using natural materials, create art inspired by nature, or use technology to document their findings.
3. Problem-solving and critical thinking: Outdoor learning spaces foster problem-solving and critical thinking skills as students encounter real-world challenges and develop solutions. Students learn to adapt and apply their knowledge and skills in practical situations, enhancing their problem-solving abilities.
4. Collaboration and communication: Outdoor learning spaces provide a collaborative setting where students work together on projects, conduct investigations, and share their findings. This promotes teamwork, effective communication, and the development of interpersonal skills.
5. Creativity and imagination: Outdoor learning spaces inspire creativity and imagination. Students have the freedom to explore, take risks, and think outside the box, leading to the development of innovative ideas and solutions.

Case study: Outdoor learning gardens

One example of an outdoor and nature-based learning space is an outdoor learning garden. Outdoor learning gardens have gained popularity in schools and are used to teach various subjects while providing students with hands-on experiences in gardening and horticulture.

In an outdoor learning garden, students can learn about plant life cycles, soil composition, pollination, and sustainable gardening practices. They can engage in planting, nurturing, and harvesting crops, which fosters a sense of responsibility and connection to the natural world. This hands-on experience encourages students to make connections between theoretical concepts taught in the classroom and real-world applications.

Outdoor learning gardens also provide opportunities for interdisciplinary learning. For example, students can explore mathematical concepts by measuring and calculating garden dimensions or learn about cultural diversity by growing plants from different regions.

Moreover, outdoor learning gardens promote environmental stewardship and sustainable practices. Students learn about the importance of conserving resources, reducing waste, and promoting biodiversity. These gardens can also serve as a platform for community engagement, providing opportunities for students to share their knowledge and experiences with the wider community.

Resources for outdoor and nature-based learning

There are several resources available to educators interested in incorporating outdoor and nature-based learning into their curriculum. Here are some examples:

1. Environmental education organizations: Many organizations provide resources, workshops, and professional development opportunities for educators interested in outdoor and nature-based learning. Examples include the North American Association for Environmental Education (NAAEE) and the Children & Nature Network.

2. Curriculum guides and lesson plans: Various websites and publications offer curriculum guides and lesson plans specifically designed for outdoor and nature-based learning. These resources provide guidance on integrating outdoor learning into different subject areas and grade levels.

3. Nature-inspired books and literature: Incorporating nature-themed books and literature into the curriculum can enhance students' connection to the natural environment. Educators can select age-appropriate books that align with the learning objectives and promote environmental awareness.

4. Local parks and outdoor spaces: Collaborating with local parks and outdoor spaces can provide access to nature-rich environments for students. Educators can work with park authorities to plan field trips, nature walks, and outdoor learning experiences.

Exercises

1. Design an outdoor learning space that promotes collaboration and creativity. Include natural elements, movable furniture, and technology integration in your

design.

2. Identify three subject areas that can be effectively taught in an outdoor learning environment. Explain how outdoor learning enhances students' understanding of these subjects.

3. Create a lesson plan that utilizes an outdoor learning space for teaching a specific concept or skill in science.

4. Conduct a case study on a school that has successfully implemented an outdoor learning program. Analyze the benefits and challenges of the program and identify key factors contributing to its success.

Conclusion

Outdoor and nature-based learning spaces offer valuable opportunities for students to connect with the natural world, engage in experiential learning, and develop a deeper understanding of various subjects. Designing effective outdoor learning spaces, incorporating principles of accessibility and inclusivity, and promoting interdisciplinary learning are key considerations for educators. By incorporating outdoor and nature-based learning opportunities into the curriculum, educators can provide students with a holistic and enriching educational experience that fosters a love for the environment and creates lifelong learners.

Future directions of classroom design

As education continues to evolve, so does the design of the physical learning environment. The future of classroom design is focused on creating spaces that facilitate student engagement, collaboration, and creativity. In this section, we will explore some of the future directions of classroom design and discuss the principles and ideas that will shape these innovative learning spaces.

Flexible and adaptable spaces

One of the key future directions of classroom design is the move towards flexible and adaptable spaces. Traditional classroom layouts, with rows of fixed desks facing the front of the room, hinder collaboration and limit movement. In the future, classrooms will be designed with mobile furniture, such as modular desks and chairs, that can be easily rearranged to support different learning activities. This flexibility allows for the creation of spaces that can accommodate individual work, small group discussions, and large-scale collaborative projects.

By incorporating adaptable spaces, classrooms can be transformed to suit the specific needs of different lessons and activities. For example, desks can be clustered together to encourage group work, or they can be spread apart to facilitate individual reflection. This flexibility promotes student agency and choice, as they can decide how they want to engage with the learning environment based on their preferences and needs.

Integration of technology

Technology is playing an increasingly important role in education, and the future of classroom design embraces this trend by integrating technology seamlessly into the learning environment. Classrooms will be equipped with interactive whiteboards, large display screens, and wireless connectivity to support digital learning experiences. These technologies allow for the use of multimedia resources, virtual simulations, and real-time collaboration, enhancing student engagement and understanding.

In addition to traditional technology tools, the future of classroom design also incorporates emerging technologies such as augmented reality (AR) and virtual reality (VR). AR and VR can provide immersive learning experiences, allowing students to explore concepts in a virtual environment. This technology has the potential to bring abstract concepts to life and enhance student understanding and retention.

Emphasis on well-being and comfort

The future of classroom design recognizes the importance of student well-being and comfort in the learning process. Classrooms will be designed to create a calm and inviting atmosphere that promotes focus and reduces stress. This can be achieved through the use of natural lighting, soothing color schemes, and ergonomic furniture.

Incorporating elements of biophilic design, such as plants and greenery, can also contribute to a positive learning environment. Research shows that exposure to nature and natural elements has a positive impact on cognitive function, well-being, and academic performance. By incorporating natural elements into the design, classrooms can create a more holistic and nurturing learning environment.

Promotion of creativity and collaboration

Future classrooms will be designed to foster creativity and collaboration among students. Spaces will be intentionally created to inspire imagination, innovation, and the exchange of ideas. For example, dedicated brainstorming areas with whiteboard walls or writable surfaces can encourage students to think creatively and share their ideas.

Collaborative furniture, such as round tables or soft seating arrangements, can facilitate group discussions and teamwork. These flexible seating options allow students to easily collaborate with their peers and can encourage the exchange of diverse perspectives.

Integration of sustainability principles

As the world faces environmental challenges, the future of classroom design will emphasize the integration of sustainability principles. Classrooms will be designed with energy-efficient lighting, ventilation systems, and insulation to reduce energy consumption. Recycling stations and biodegradable materials will be incorporated to promote waste reduction and environmental awareness.

In addition, the design of classrooms will consider the use of natural resources such as water and sunlight, aiming for maximum efficiency. For example, classrooms can be designed with large windows to maximize natural light, reducing the need for artificial lighting and creating a more pleasant learning environment.

Promotion of inclusivity and accessibility

The future of classroom design values inclusivity and accessibility, ensuring that all students have equal opportunities to learn and participate. Designing classrooms with universal access in mind means considering the needs of all learners, including those with physical disabilities or learning differences.

Classrooms will be equipped with assistive technologies and tools to support students with diverse learning needs. For example, adjustable desks and chairs can accommodate students of different heights and physical abilities. Sound amplification systems and captioned videos can assist students with hearing impairments. By creating inclusive and accessible learning spaces, classrooms can foster a sense of belonging and empower all students to reach their full potential.

Conclusion

The future of classroom design is an exciting blend of innovation, technology, and student-centered principles. Flexible and adaptable spaces, integration of technology, emphasis on well-being and comfort, promotion of creativity and collaboration, integration of sustainability principles, and promotion of inclusivity and accessibility are all key aspects that will shape the classrooms of tomorrow. By designing classrooms with these future directions in mind, we can create learning environments that inspire curiosity, engagement, and academic excellence.

Redefining the concept of the classroom

In the rapidly evolving landscape of education, the concept of the classroom is undergoing a transformation. Traditionally, a classroom referred to a physical space with desks and a blackboard where students gathered to receive instruction from a teacher. However, with the advancements in technology and changes in pedagogical approaches, the concept of the classroom is no longer confined to a physical location. In this section, we will explore how the traditional classroom is being redefined to create transformative learning environments.

The Shift towards Flexible Learning Spaces

One of the key aspects of redefining the concept of the classroom is the shift towards flexible learning spaces. Instead of a fixed layout with rows of desks facing the front, modern classrooms are designed to be adaptable and promote collaboration, creativity, and critical thinking.

Several innovative classroom designs are being adopted to facilitate this shift. For example, flexible seating arrangements, such as bean bags, standing desks, and comfortable lounge areas, are being used to create a more relaxed and inclusive learning environment. These flexible learning spaces encourage movement, interaction, and personalization, promoting engagement and active learning.

Creating Collaborative Learning Environments

Collaborative learning is another key aspect of redefining the concept of the classroom. In a collaborative learning environment, students work together in groups or teams to solve problems, discuss concepts, and create shared knowledge. This approach fosters communication, teamwork, and critical thinking skills.

The physical space of the classroom plays a crucial role in creating collaborative learning environments. Classroom design should include spaces that facilitate small-group discussions, project workstations, and areas for interactive presentations and demonstrations. In addition, digital tools, such as interactive whiteboards, collaboration software, and video conferencing platforms, can be integrated to connect students in different locations and encourage virtual collaboration.

Effective Use of Technology in Physical Spaces

Redefining the concept of the classroom involves leveraging the power of technology to enhance teaching and learning experiences. The integration of technology into physical spaces enables educators to create interactive and immersive learning environments.

For instance, interactive displays and augmented reality (AR) tools can transform traditional static content into dynamic and engaging learning materials. Students can use AR applications to explore 3D models, dissect virtual organisms, or simulate scientific experiments. Furthermore, virtual reality (VR) can transport students to virtual worlds, allowing them to experience historical events, visit famous landmarks, or conduct experiments in a safe and controlled environment.

Inclusive Learning Environments for All Students

As we redefine the concept of the classroom, it is crucial to ensure that learning environments are inclusive and cater to the diverse needs of all students. Inclusive classrooms recognize and value the unique abilities, experiences, and backgrounds of each learner.

To create inclusive learning environments, classroom design should incorporate universal design principles. This involves providing a range of resources, tools, and technologies that accommodate different learning preferences and support students with disabilities or special needs. For example, adjustable furniture, assistive technologies, and sensory-friendly spaces can be implemented to promote accessibility and inclusivity.

In addition to physical accommodations, educators should also consider the use of culturally responsive pedagogy and diverse instructional materials to create a welcoming and inclusive atmosphere for all students.

Outdoor and Nature-Based Learning Spaces

In recent years, there has been a growing emphasis on outdoor and nature-based learning as a way to reconnect students with the natural world and enhance their learning experiences. Outdoor learning spaces, such as gardens, forests, or outdoor classrooms, provide unique opportunities for hands-on, experiential learning.

These spaces offer a change from traditional indoor classrooms and allow students to engage with nature, conduct scientific observations, and explore ecological concepts. Outdoor learning can foster a sense of wonder, curiosity, and environmental stewardship among students. It also has the potential to improve mental health, well-being, and physical fitness.

Future Directions of Classroom Design

The redefinition of the concept of the classroom is an ongoing process, and there are several emerging trends and future directions that educators can explore. Some of these include:

- Mobile learning technologies: With the increasing availability and affordability of mobile devices, classrooms can extend beyond the physical space, allowing students to access learning materials and engage in collaborative activities anytime and anywhere.
- Artificial intelligence (AI) and personalized learning: AI-powered technologies have the potential to support personalized learning by adapting to individual students' needs, providing tailored content, and offering real-time feedback. These technologies can facilitate differentiated instruction and promote student autonomy and self-directed learning.
- Internet of Things (IoT) and smart classrooms: IoT devices, such as smartboards, sensors, and wearable technologies, can be integrated into the classroom environment to collect real-time data and enhance teaching and learning experiences. These devices can enable personalized feedback, automate administrative tasks, and create interactive learning environments.

As educators continue to redefine the concept of the classroom, it is important to embrace innovative approaches, leverage technological advancements, and prioritize the creation of inclusive and transformative learning environments. By doing so, we can prepare students to thrive in the complex and evolving world of the future.

Virtual Learning Environments

Introduction to virtual learning environments

Virtual learning environments (VLEs) have revolutionized the way education is delivered and have become an integral part of modern pedagogy. A VLE is an online platform that allows for the creation, delivery, and management of learning experiences. It provides a digital space where students can access course materials, interact with peers and instructors, and engage in various educational activities.

VLEs offer a range of features and tools that enhance the learning process. These include content management systems, discussion forums, multimedia resources, assessment tools, and communication channels. With VLEs, educational institutions can deliver courses in a flexible and accessible manner, breaking down the barriers of time and location.

One of the key advantages of VLEs is the ability to provide a personalized learning experience. Students can access learning materials at their own pace and engage in interactive activities tailored to their individual needs and preferences. This enables learners to take ownership of their education and promotes self-directed learning.

Furthermore, VLEs foster collaboration and engagement among students. They provide opportunities for peer interaction through discussion boards, group projects, and shared resources. This collaborative aspect of VLEs enhances critical thinking and communication skills, as students learn from and with their peers.

VLEs also support differentiated instruction, allowing educators to cater to the diverse needs of students. Teachers can incorporate various modalities of instruction, such as videos, interactive quizzes, and simulations, to accommodate different learning styles. Additionally, VLEs offer features for tracking and monitoring student progress, enabling instructors to provide targeted feedback and interventions.

In the context of virtual learning environments, it is important to address the digital divide. Not all students have equal access to technology and the internet, which can create disparities in educational opportunities. Educational institutions and policymakers must work towards bridging this divide and ensuring equitable access to virtual learning resources for all students.

As technology continues to evolve, so do virtual learning environments. Emerging technologies like augmented reality and virtual reality are being integrated into VLEs, providing immersive and engaging learning experiences. Artificial intelligence is also playing a role in VLEs, enabling adaptive learning and personalized instruction.

It is worth noting that while VLEs offer numerous benefits, they also present challenges. Technical issues, such as connectivity problems or platform compatibility, can hinder the learning experience. Furthermore, there is a need for proper training and support for educators to effectively utilize VLEs in their teaching practices.

In this section, we will explore the different components of virtual learning environments, including learning management systems, online platforms, and design considerations. We will delve into the various features and tools offered by VLEs and discuss best practices for designing engaging and interactive online courses. Additionally, we will examine the challenges associated with VLE implementation and provide strategies for overcoming them.

Through this exploration of virtual learning environments, we aim to equip educators with the knowledge and skills necessary to leverage technology and create transformative learning experiences for their students.

Learning Management Systems and Online Platforms

In today's digital age, learning management systems (LMS) and online platforms play a crucial role in the delivery of education. These platforms provide educators and learners with powerful tools and resources to enhance teaching and learning experiences. In this section, we will explore the features and benefits of learning management systems and discuss various online platforms that support educational activities.

Features of Learning Management Systems

Learning management systems are software applications designed to facilitate the management and delivery of educational content. They provide a centralized platform for educators to create, organize, deliver, and assess learning materials, while also offering communication and collaborative features for both educators and learners. Here are some key features commonly found in learning management systems:

1. **Course Management:** LMS platforms allow educators to create and manage courses, including organizing content, setting up assignments and assessments, and tracking learners' progress.

2. **Content Delivery:** LMS platforms provide a space for educators to upload and distribute various types of educational content, such as lecture notes, videos, and interactive materials.

3. **Collaboration Tools:** LMS platforms often include tools for communication and collaboration, such as discussion forums, chat rooms, and video conferencing, enabling learners and educators to interact and engage in virtual learning communities.

4. **Assessment and Grading:** LMS platforms offer built-in tools for creating and administering assessments, as well as for grading and providing feedback to learners.

5. **Analytics and Reporting:** LMS platforms provide insights into learners' activities and performance, allowing educators to track progress and identify areas for improvement.

Popular Learning Management Systems

There are several popular learning management systems used in educational institutions worldwide. Let's explore some of these platforms and their distinctive features:

1. **Moodle:** Moodle is an open-source learning management system widely adopted by educational institutions. It offers a wide range of features, including customizable course design, collaborative tools, and extensive plugin support for additional functionality.
2. **Canvas:** Canvas is a cloud-based learning management system known for its user-friendly interface and intuitive course design. It offers features such as multimedia integration, real-time collaboration, and advanced grading options.
3. **Blackboard Learn:** Blackboard Learn is a comprehensive learning management system that provides tools for content delivery, assessment, and communication. It supports integration with other educational technologies and offers mobile access for learners.
4. **Google Classroom:** Google Classroom is a free and user-friendly learning management system that integrates with other Google tools, such as Google Drive and Google Docs. It is widely used in K-12 education and supports seamless collaboration between educators and learners.
5. **Schoology:** Schoology is a cloud-based learning management system that offers a robust set of features, including course management, multimedia integration, assessment tools, and social learning capabilities.

These are just a few examples of the many learning management systems available today. It's important for educational institutions to assess their specific needs and requirements when choosing an LMS that best suits their objectives.

Online Platforms for Specific Educational Activities

In addition to learning management systems, there are various online platforms that cater to specific educational activities. Here are some examples:

1. **Khan Academy:** Khan Academy is an online platform that provides free educational videos and interactive exercises in a wide range of subjects. It offers personalized learning paths and allows learners to track their progress.
2. **Codecademy:** Codecademy is an online platform that focuses on teaching coding and programming skills. It offers interactive coding lessons and projects, allowing learners to practice coding in a hands-on manner.
3. **Duolingo:** Duolingo is a popular language learning platform that offers gamified lessons and exercises. It covers a wide range of languages and provides an

engaging and interactive learning experience.

4. **Coursera:** Coursera is an online learning platform that partners with universities and organizations to offer a wide range of courses and specialization programs. It provides learners with access to high-quality educational content from leading institutions.

5. **edX:** edX is a nonprofit online learning platform founded by Harvard University and MIT. It offers a wide range of courses and programs across various disciplines, providing learners with the opportunity to earn verified certificates and even degrees.

These online platforms offer additional avenues for knowledge acquisition and skill development, complementing the learning experiences provided by learning management systems.

Harnessing the Power of Learning Management Systems and Online Platforms

By leveraging learning management systems and online platforms, educators can create dynamic and engaging learning experiences for their students. Here are some best practices for utilizing these platforms effectively:

1. **Clear Communication:** Establish clear guidelines and expectations for using the learning management system or online platform. Communicate regularly with students and provide detailed instructions to ensure they understand how to navigate the platform and access resources.

2. **Organized Course Structure:** Structure your courses in a logical and organized manner within the learning management system. Use folders, modules, or sections to guide students through the course content effectively.

3. **Interactive Content:** Utilize the interactive features of the learning management system or online platform to enhance student engagement. Incorporate multimedia elements, such as videos, quizzes, and interactive exercises, to create a more dynamic learning experience.

4. **Timely Feedback:** Leverage the assessment tools available in the learning management system to provide timely feedback to students. Offer constructive feedback on assignments and assessments, and encourage students to reflect on their progress.

5. **Collaborative Opportunities:** Foster collaboration among students by utilizing the collaborative tools offered by the learning management system or online platform. Encourage students to participate in group discussions, virtual projects, and peer reviews.

6. **Regular Assessments:** Use the assessment features of the learning management system to administer formative and summative evaluations. Regular assessments can help track student progress and identify areas that may require additional support or intervention.

7. **Continual Improvement:** Regularly evaluate the effectiveness of the learning management system or online platform in achieving educational objectives. Seek feedback from students and adapt your approach to enhance the learning experience.

By harnessing the power of learning management systems and online platforms, educators can create engaging, interactive, and personalized learning environments that foster student success.

Conclusion

Learning management systems and online platforms have revolutionized the delivery of education by providing powerful tools for content management, communication, collaboration, and assessment. These platforms offer educators the ability to create engaging and interactive learning experiences while facilitating student-centered and personalized instruction. As technology continues to advance, learning management systems and online platforms will play an increasingly integral role in shaping the future of education. Educators should embrace these tools and tailor their use to enhance teaching and learning outcomes.

Designing engaging and interactive online courses

Designing online courses that are engaging and interactive is crucial for creating effective and impactful learning experiences. In this section, we will explore the principles, strategies, and tools that can be used to design such courses.

Principles of engaging online course design

When designing an online course, it is important to consider the following principles to ensure that learners stay engaged and motivated throughout the learning process:

1. Clear learning objectives: Clearly state the learning objectives at the beginning of the course so that learners understand what they will achieve by the end. This helps to keep learners focused and motivated.

2. Structured and organized content: Organize the course content in a logical and structured manner. Use headings, subheadings, and bullet points to break down the content into manageable chunks. This helps learners to navigate the course easily and enhances their comprehension.

3. Interactive multimedia: Incorporate interactive multimedia elements such as videos, audio recordings, infographics, and interactive simulations to present information in engaging and varied formats. This helps to cater to different learning styles and keeps learners actively involved.

4. Collaborative learning opportunities: Promote collaboration and interaction among learners by integrating discussion forums, group activities, and peer assessment tasks. This enables learners to learn from each other, exchange ideas, and build a sense of community.

5. Authentic assessments: Design assessments that reflect real-world scenarios and tasks, allowing learners to apply their knowledge and skills in practical contexts. This makes the learning experience more meaningful and engaging for learners.

6. Feedback and support: Provide timely and constructive feedback to learners to guide their learning progress. Use a variety of feedback methods, such as audio or video feedback, to make it more personal and engaging. Additionally, offer support through online forums, chatrooms, or email to address learners' questions and concerns.

7. Gamification elements: Incorporate gamification elements such as badges, leaderboards, and progress tracking to create a sense of achievement and motivation in learners. This can increase learners' engagement and motivation throughout the course.

Strategies for designing engaging online courses

To design engaging and interactive online courses, consider applying the following strategies:

1. Storytelling: Use storytelling techniques to create narratives that connect with learners. This can be done through case studies, scenarios, or real-life examples that illustrate the practical relevance of the course content.

2. Chunking: Break down the course content into smaller, digestible chunks. This helps learners to process the information more easily and keeps them engaged.

3. Interactive activities: Include interactive activities such as quizzes, simulations, and interactive exercises that allow learners to apply their knowledge. These activities provide immediate feedback and make the learning experience more engaging.

4. Discussion forums: Create online discussion forums where learners can interact with each other, share their thoughts, ask questions, and engage in meaningful discussions. This promotes active learning and peer collaboration.

5. Virtual labs or experiments: For courses that involve practical or experimental work, provide virtual labs or simulations that allow learners to engage in hands-on

activities. This helps to bridge the gap between theory and practice in an online environment.

6. Personalization: Incorporate personalized learning pathways or adaptive learning technologies that tailor the content and pacing to each learner's individual needs and preferences. This enhances engagement by providing a customized learning experience.

7. Social learning: Foster a sense of social presence and community by incorporating social media tools or online collaboration platforms. This enables learners to connect with each other, share resources, and engage in collaborative learning activities.

Tools for designing engaging online courses

Several tools and technologies can be used to design engaging and interactive online courses. Here are some examples:

1. Learning Management Systems (LMS): LMS platforms such as Moodle, Canvas, or Blackboard provide features and tools for organizing course content, delivering multimedia materials, facilitating discussions, and managing assessments.

2. Video conferencing tools: Tools like Zoom, Microsoft Teams, or Google Meet can be used for synchronous online sessions, virtual lectures, group discussions, or live Q&A sessions with learners.

3. Interactive multimedia tools: Tools like H5P, Adobe Captivate, or Articulate Storyline allow you to create interactive multimedia elements such as videos, interactive presentations, quizzes, and simulations.

4. Collaboration tools: Tools such as Google Docs, Microsoft OneDrive, or Dropbox facilitate collaborative work among learners, allowing them to co-create documents, share resources, and collaborate on group projects.

5. Gamification platforms: Platforms like Classcraft, Kahoot, or Quizizz enable you to incorporate gamification elements into your online courses, such as gamified quizzes, leaderboards, or badges.

6. Virtual reality (VR) and augmented reality (AR): VR and AR technologies provide immersive learning experiences, where learners can explore virtual environments, interact with 3D objects, and simulate real-world scenarios.

Remember that the choice of tools should align with the learning objectives and the needs of the learners. It is essential to explore and evaluate different tools to determine which ones best support the engagement and interactivity goals of your online course.

Example: Designing an engaging online science course

Suppose you are designing an online science course for high school students. To make the course engaging and interactive, you could incorporate the following elements:

1. Interactive simulations: Use virtual lab simulations where students can conduct experiments and observe results in real-time. This gives students a hands-on experience and enhances their understanding of scientific concepts.

2. Gamified quizzes: Implement gamified quizzes at the end of each module to assess students' understanding while making it fun and engaging. Use leaderboard features to encourage friendly competition among students.

3. Discussion forums: Set up online discussion forums where students can ask questions, share their observations, and discuss scientific phenomena. This encourages collaboration, critical thinking, and engagement with the course content.

4. Multimedia resources: Include videos, animations, and infographics to visually represent complex scientific concepts. These resources help students visualize abstract ideas and make the learning experience more interactive.

5. Virtual field trips: Organize virtual field trips to scientific research institutions, laboratories, or natural environments. This allows students to explore real-world applications of scientific knowledge and fosters curiosity and engagement.

By incorporating these elements, you can create an engaging and interactive online science course that goes beyond textbook learning and provides students with a rich and immersive learning experience.

Additional resources

To further explore the design of engaging and interactive online courses, consider the following resources:

1. Book: "Design for How People Learn" by Julie Dirksen 2. Website: eLearning Industry (www.elearningindustry.com) 3. Webinar: "Engaging Online Learners: Strategies to Improve Connectivity and Learner Engagement" by Dr. Cindy Huggett

These resources provide valuable insights, strategies, and examples to guide you in designing engaging and interactive online courses that maximize learner engagement and promote effective learning outcomes.

Virtual classrooms and synchronous learning

In recent years, the field of education has witnessed a dramatic shift towards virtual classrooms and synchronous learning. With advancements in technology, educators have been able to recreate the traditional classroom experience in a virtual setting, allowing students to learn and interact with their peers and teachers from anywhere in the world. This section explores the concept of virtual classrooms and the benefits they offer for synchronous learning.

Understanding virtual classrooms

A virtual classroom is an online learning environment that simulates a traditional physical classroom. It is a platform where teachers and students can connect in real-time through video conferencing, chat, and interactive tools, enabling synchronous learning experiences. Virtual classrooms can be accessed using various devices such as computers, tablets, and smartphones, making them highly flexible and accessible.

In a virtual classroom, students can participate in live lectures, engage in discussions, collaborate on projects, and receive real-time feedback from their teachers. They can also access learning materials, complete assignments, and interact with multimedia content, all within the virtual environment. Virtual classrooms are designed to create an immersive and interactive learning experience that closely resembles a traditional classroom setting.

Benefits of virtual classrooms

Virtual classrooms offer several benefits for both students and teachers. Here are some key advantages:

1. **Flexibility and accessibility:** Virtual classrooms eliminate the constraints of time and location, allowing students to participate in learning activities from anywhere, as long as they have an internet connection. This flexibility enables learners to balance their education with other commitments, such as work or family responsibilities.

2. **Enhanced collaboration and engagement:** Virtual classrooms provide opportunities for students to collaborate with their peers and engage in group work, just like in a physical classroom. Through features like breakout rooms and shared whiteboards, students can work together on projects, present their ideas, and receive feedback from their classmates and teachers.

3. **Personalized learning experiences:** In a virtual classroom, teachers can tailor their instruction to meet the individual needs and learning styles of each student. They can provide personalized feedback, offer one-on-one support, and use adaptive learning technologies to deliver targeted instruction. This level of personalization can greatly enhance the learning experience and help students achieve their academic goals.

4. **Increased access to resources:** Virtual classrooms enable students to access a vast range of educational resources, including digital textbooks, multimedia content, online libraries, and academic databases. This easy access to resources enhances the depth and breadth of learning, providing students with a wealth of information to explore and expand their knowledge.

5. **Improved teacher-student interaction:** Through video conferencing and chat features, virtual classrooms facilitate real-time communication between teachers and students. This enables teachers to provide immediate answers to student questions, offer clarifications, and gauge understanding. The close interaction between teachers and students fosters a supportive learning environment and strengthens the teacher-student relationship.

Challenges and considerations

While virtual classrooms offer numerous benefits, there are also challenges and considerations that need to be addressed:

1. **Technological requirements:** Effective participation in virtual classrooms relies on having a stable internet connection and access to suitable devices. Students who lack reliable internet access or appropriate devices may face barriers to fully engaging in synchronous learning. Addressing the digital divide is crucial to ensure equitable access to virtual learning opportunities.

2. **Technical difficulties:** Technical issues such as connectivity problems, software glitches, or hardware malfunctions can interrupt the learning process in a virtual classroom. Educators need to be prepared with backup plans and technical support to minimize disruption and ensure smooth operation.

3. **Engagement and motivation:** Sustaining student engagement and motivation can be a challenge in virtual classrooms. The absence of face-to-face interactions and the increased autonomy can lead to decreased

participation and limited peer collaboration. Teachers need to employ strategies to keep students actively engaged and motivated throughout the virtual learning experience.

4. **Digital literacy skills:** Virtual classrooms require students to possess basic digital literacy skills to navigate the online learning environment effectively. Educators should provide necessary training and support to ensure that students can utilize the virtual classroom tools and resources efficiently.

5. **Social interaction and community building:** Building a sense of community and social interaction in virtual classrooms can be more challenging compared to physical classrooms. Teachers should create opportunities for students to connect, collaborate, and develop interpersonal relationships through online discussions, group activities, and virtual social events.

Best practices and strategies

To ensure effective and meaningful learning in virtual classrooms, educators can implement the following best practices and strategies:

1. **Establish clear expectations:** Communicate clear guidelines and expectations to students regarding their participation, behavior, and responsibilities in the virtual classroom. Establishing a routine and clear structure for synchronous learning sessions can help students stay focused and organized.

2. **Promote active engagement:** Incorporate interactive elements such as polls, quizzes, and collaborative activities to actively engage students during virtual sessions. Encourage students to ask questions, share their ideas, and actively participate in discussions to foster a dynamic learning environment.

3. **Utilize multimedia and visual aids:** Use multimedia tools and visual aids to enhance the delivery of content in virtual classrooms. Incorporate slideshows, videos, virtual simulations, and interactive multimedia content to make the learning experience more engaging and meaningful.

4. **Provide timely feedback:** Offer timely and constructive feedback to students to guide their learning progress. Feedback can be given individually or in groups, addressing areas of improvement and recognizing milestones achieved. Timely feedback helps students stay motivated and make necessary adjustments to their learning approach.

5. **Encourage collaboration and peer interaction:** Foster a sense of community and peer interaction in virtual classrooms through collaborative activities and group projects. Encourage students to work together, share ideas, and learn from one another, promoting a collaborative learning environment.

6. **Establish regular communication channels:** Maintain regular communication with students through email, discussion boards, or instant messaging platforms. Encourage students to reach out whenever they have questions or need assistance, ensuring that they feel supported throughout their virtual learning journey.

Real-world example: Virtual science lab

One example of the application of virtual classrooms and synchronous learning is the virtual science lab. In traditional science education, hands-on laboratory experiments play a crucial role in deepening students' understanding of scientific concepts. However, certain limitations, such as the availability of lab equipment or safety concerns, may restrict the accessibility of such experiments.

Virtual science labs overcome these limitations by providing a simulated laboratory environment where students can conduct experiments remotely. Through the virtual classroom, teachers can demonstrate experiments, guide students through the steps, and monitor their progress in real-time. Students can actively engage in the experimental process, make observations, collect data, and analyze results, all within the virtual lab environment. This virtual experience allows students to develop critical thinking skills and apply scientific concepts while addressing the challenges posed by traditional lab experiments.

Further resources

Here are some additional resources to explore the topic of virtual classrooms and synchronous learning:

- Book: "Teaching and Learning in the Digital Age" by Royce Kimmons and Kalpana Srinivas, provides insights into leveraging technology for effective teaching and learning in virtual classrooms.

- Website: EdTechReview (`https://edtechreview.in/`) provides articles, case studies, and resources on virtual classrooms and synchronous learning.

- Journal Article: "Virtual Language Learning: Taking a Closer Look" by Amanda Slinger, explores the benefits and challenges of using virtual classrooms for language education.

- Conference: The International Conference on Virtual Learning (`http://www.eurodl.org/?p=conferences&sp=conferences&conference=612`) provides a platform for sharing research and experiences related to virtual learning environments.

In conclusion, virtual classrooms and synchronous learning have revolutionized the educational landscape by providing flexible and immersive learning experiences. While challenges exist, adopting best practices and strategies can help maximize the benefits of virtual classrooms, ensuring meaningful and engaging learning for students.

Creating Community and Social Interaction in Virtual Environments

Virtual learning environments offer unique opportunities for creating a sense of community and promoting social interaction among students. While physical classrooms provide face-to-face interactions, virtual environments allow students to connect and collaborate regardless of their geographical locations. In this section, we will explore various strategies and tools that can be used to foster community and social interaction in virtual learning environments.

Importance of Community and Social Interaction

Community and social interaction play a vital role in enhancing the learning experience of students. When students feel connected to their peers and instructors, they are more motivated to actively engage in the learning process. Community building in virtual environments promotes a sense of belonging, encourages collaboration, and fosters peer support and learning.

In virtual learning environments, community and social interaction can help reduce feelings of isolation and create a supportive learning environment. It provides opportunities for students to share their thoughts, exchange ideas, and learn from each other's experiences. This collaborative learning environment enables students to construct knowledge together and develop critical thinking and problem-solving skills.

Strategies for Building Community

Building a sense of community in virtual learning environments requires intentional efforts. Here are some strategies that can be employed:

Icebreaker activities: Start the course with icebreaker activities to help students get to know each other. These activities can include introductions, icebreaker games, or virtual team-building exercises. Icebreakers can be incorporated through video introductions or online discussion boards.

Establish communication channels: Create dedicated communication channels such as discussion forums, social networking platforms, or messaging apps to facilitate interactions among students. These platforms serve as virtual spaces where students can engage in discussions, ask questions, and share resources.

Encourage collaborative assignments: Design collaborative assignments that require students to work together and contribute their knowledge and skills. Group projects, case studies, or problem-solving activities can be assigned to promote collaborative learning and build a sense of community.

Online group discussions: Organize structured online group discussions where students can engage in thoughtful conversations on specific topics. Encourage active participation and provide clear discussion guidelines to ensure meaningful interactions.

Peer feedback and peer assessment: Promote peer feedback and peer assessment activities in which students provide constructive feedback to their peers' work. This not only enhances social interaction but also develops critical evaluation skills and promotes a culture of feedback.

Instructor presence and engagement: Actively participate in online discussions, provide timely feedback, and establish a supportive instructor presence. Engage with students through virtual office hours, discussion boards, or video conferences to establish a strong connection with learners.

Tools for Facilitating Social Interaction

Several technological tools can be used to facilitate social interaction and community building in virtual learning environments. Here are some examples:

Discussion forums and message boards: Online discussion forums allow students to engage in asynchronous conversations, share ideas, and ask questions. Platforms like Moodle, Canvas, or Blackboard offer discussion board features that can be integrated into virtual learning environments.

Video conferencing tools: Video conferencing tools such as Zoom, Google Meet, or Microsoft Teams enable synchronous interactions, providing opportunities for real-time discussions, group activities, and virtual meetings.

Collaboration platforms: Collaboration platforms like Google Docs, Microsoft Teams, or Slack allow students to work together in real-time, contributing and editing documents, brainstorming ideas, and collaborating on projects.

Social media platforms: Leveraging social media platforms like Facebook, Twitter, or LinkedIn can create an informal space for students to connect, share resources, and engage in discussions related to their coursework.

Virtual reality (VR) and augmented reality (AR) technologies: VR and AR technologies can provide immersive experiences, allowing students to interact with virtual environments and participate in virtual simulations or role-playing activities. These technologies can foster social interaction and collaboration among students in unique and engaging ways.

Gamification elements: Incorporating gamification elements such as leaderboards, badges, or points systems into the virtual learning environment can motivate students to actively participate, compete, and collaborate with their peers.

Challenges and Considerations

While virtual learning environments offer numerous opportunities for community building and social interaction, there are some challenges and considerations to keep in mind:

Technical challenges: Technical issues can hinder effective communication and collaboration in virtual environments. It is essential to provide technical support and ensure that students have the necessary hardware, software, and reliable internet access to participate fully.

Digital divide and accessibility: The digital divide refers to the unequal access to technology and the internet. It is crucial to address accessibility issues and ensure that all students can actively participate in virtual learning environments. Providing alternative means of participation and considering accessibility guidelines are essential.

Establishing social norms: In virtual environments, it is necessary to establish clear guidelines and social norms for communication and interactions. Encourage respectful and inclusive conversations and provide guidance on netiquette and appropriate online behavior.

Building rapport: Establishing rapport in virtual environments can be challenging compared to face-to-face settings. Instructors should actively engage with students, be approachable, and create opportunities for informal interactions to build rapport and trust.

Examples and Best Practices

Here are some examples and best practices of successful community building and social interaction in virtual learning environments:

Online communities of practice: Creating online communities of practice where students can connect with peers who share similar interests or goals can foster engagement and collaboration. Students can participate in these communities to discuss specific topics, exchange resources, and seek peer support.

Virtual networking events: Organizing virtual networking events, guest speaker sessions, or panel discussions can provide opportunities for students to interact with industry professionals and experts in their field of study. These events facilitate social interaction and expose students to real-world perspectives.

Virtual peer mentoring: Implementing virtual peer mentoring programs can connect experienced students with newcomers, creating a supportive learning environment and promoting social interaction.

Virtual study groups: Encouraging students to form virtual study groups improves peer learning and collaboration. Students can meet virtually to study together, share notes, and discuss course materials.

Further Resources and Reading

For further exploration of the topic of creating community and social interaction in virtual environments, the following resources and readings are recommended:

1. Salmon, G. (2013). *E-tivities: The Key to Active Online Learning.* Routledge.

2. Garrison, D. R., Anderson, T., & Archer, W. (2000). *Critical Inquiry in a Text-Based Environment: Computer Conferencing in Higher Education.* The Internet and Higher Education, 2(2-3), 87-105.

3. Dennen, V. P. (2005). *From Message Posting to Learning Dialogues: Factors Affecting Learner Participation in Asynchronous Discussion.* Distance Education, 26(1), 127-148.

4. Palloff, R. M., & Pratt, K. (2013). *Lessons from the Virtual Classroom: The Realities of Online Teaching* (2nd ed.). Jossey-Bass.

Key Takeaways

Building community and promoting social interaction in virtual learning environments is crucial for enhancing the learning experience of students. Strategies such as icebreaker activities, establishing communication channels, encouraging collaboration, and providing meaningful feedback contribute to community building. Tools like discussion forums, video conferencing platforms, collaboration tools, and social media can facilitate social interaction. However, considerations for technical challenges, accessibility, establishing social norms, and building rapport must be taken into account. Implementing virtual communities, networking events, peer mentoring, and study groups can further enhance community building efforts. By fostering a sense of community and promoting social interaction, virtual learning environments can provide students with a supportive and engaging learning experience.

Overcoming Challenges in Virtual Learning Environments

Virtual learning environments have become increasingly prevalent in education, especially in the wake of the COVID-19 pandemic. While they offer many advantages, there are also several challenges that need to be addressed in order to ensure effective and equitable learning experiences for all students. In this section, we will explore some of the key challenges faced in virtual learning environments and discuss strategies to overcome them.

Access to Technology and Reliable Internet

One of the primary challenges in virtual learning environments is ensuring equal access to technology and reliable internet connections for all students. Not all students have access to personal devices or high-speed internet at home, which can create barriers to their participation in online classes. This issue is especially pronounced in low-income communities and rural areas.

To overcome this challenge, educators and educational institutions can take several steps. Firstly, they can work with local governments and organizations to provide students with access to affordable or free internet connections. This could be achieved by setting up Wi-Fi hotspots in community centers or offering subsidized internet plans to students in need. Additionally, schools can consider providing loaner devices to students who do not have access to computers or tablets at home.

Another strategy to address this challenge is to design learning activities that can be accessed offline. This can involve providing printed materials and assignments that students can work on without an internet connection. Educators can also explore the use of offline educational apps or software that can be downloaded and accessed without an internet connection.

Digital Literacy and Technical Skills

Another challenge in virtual learning environments is the variation in students' digital literacy and technical skills. Some students may be unfamiliar with the online platforms and tools used in virtual classrooms, which can hinder their ability to fully engage in the learning process. It is important to support students in developing the necessary digital literacy and technical skills to navigate and utilize virtual learning environments effectively.

To address this challenge, teachers can provide detailed instructions and tutorials on how to use the virtual learning platforms and tools. They can also conduct training sessions or workshops to help students become familiar with the technology and develop essential digital skills. Peer support and collaboration can also be encouraged, where more technologically savvy students can assist their peers in navigating the virtual learning environment.

In addition, educators can integrate digital literacy and technical skills development into the curriculum. This can involve teaching students how to effectively search for and evaluate online information, communicate digitally, and collaborate in virtual environments. By incorporating these skills into the curriculum, students will not only be better equipped for virtual learning but also for the digital world beyond the classroom.

Engagement and Motivation

Maintaining student engagement and motivation in virtual learning environments can be challenging, as the lack of face-to-face interaction and physical classroom environment can make it harder for students to stay focused and connected to the learning process. It is crucial to employ strategies to keep students engaged and motivated in virtual learning.

One effective strategy is to incorporate interactive and multimedia elements into online lessons. This can include videos, animations, virtual field trips, and educational games. Such elements can help capture students' attention, make the learning experience more engaging, and facilitate deeper understanding of the content.

Another approach is to create opportunities for student interaction and collaboration. This can be done through online discussion boards, group projects, and virtual breakout rooms where students can work together on tasks and problem-solving activities. By fostering a sense of community and collaboration, students are more likely to feel connected and motivated to actively participate in the virtual learning environment.

Furthermore, providing timely and constructive feedback to students is essential for their motivation and learning progress. Educators can use online assessment tools that provide immediate feedback on student performance. They can also schedule one-on-one virtual meetings to discuss individual progress and provide personalized guidance.

Social Isolation and Emotional Well-being

Virtual learning environments can contribute to social isolation and have an impact on students' emotional well-being. The lack of face-to-face interaction with peers and teachers can result in feelings of loneliness and disconnection. It is important to address these challenges and create a supportive virtual learning environment that promotes students' social and emotional well-being.

To combat social isolation, educators can incorporate virtual social activities into the curriculum. This can include virtual icebreakers, group discussions, and online collaborative projects that encourage students to engage with their peers. Additionally, teachers can organize virtual extracurricular activities or clubs where students can interact and pursue shared interests outside of traditional classroom settings.

Supporting students' emotional well-being is equally important in virtual learning environments. Educators should prioritize creating a safe and inclusive online environment where students feel comfortable expressing their emotions and seeking support when needed. This can involve regular check-ins with students, providing resources for mental health support, and promoting self-care practices.

It is also crucial for educators to be mindful of potential equity issues and ensure that all students have access to the necessary support systems. This can involve collaborating with school counselors, administrators, and other support staff to provide additional resources and assistance to students who may be facing social or emotional challenges.

Digital Assessment and Academic Integrity

Digital assessment poses unique challenges to ensure academic integrity and prevent cheating in virtual learning environments. Without proper monitoring and supervision, it can be more difficult to detect and prevent academic dishonesty.

To address this challenge, educators can employ a variety of strategies. Establishing clear expectations and guidelines for academic integrity at the beginning of the virtual learning period is essential. Teachers can communicate the consequences of academic dishonesty and emphasize the importance of honesty and integrity in online assessments.

To prevent cheating, educators can use a combination of assessment methods, including open-ended questions, critical thinking tasks, and project-based assessments that require students to apply their knowledge and demonstrate their understanding in unique ways. Additionally, technology tools such as plagiarism detection software can be utilized to identify any instances of copied or unoriginal work.

Building trust and fostering a positive learning environment can also contribute to preventing academic dishonesty. When students feel valued and supported, they are less likely to engage in cheating behaviors. Therefore, establishing strong teacher-student relationships, providing constructive feedback, and promoting a culture of academic integrity are crucial elements in addressing this challenge.

In conclusion, virtual learning environments offer exciting opportunities for innovative and flexible education. However, there are important challenges that need to be overcome to ensure a successful learning experience for all students. By addressing issues such as access to technology, digital literacy, student engagement, social isolation, and academic integrity, educators can create transformative virtual learning environments that support the diverse needs of students. It is essential to adapt teaching strategies, collaborate with stakeholders, and use technology effectively to provide the best possible virtual learning experiences.

Case Studies and Best Practices in Virtual Learning Environments

Virtual learning environments have become increasingly prevalent in education, providing flexible and accessible learning opportunities for students. In this section, we will explore some case studies and best practices in virtual learning environments, highlighting the effectiveness and benefits of these approaches.

Case Study 1: Virtual Classrooms in Higher Education

In a study conducted at a major university, virtual classrooms were implemented to enhance the learning experience for higher education students. The virtual classrooms allowed students to attend lectures, participate in discussions, and collaborate on projects remotely. The study found that virtual classrooms provided multiple benefits, including:

- Improved accessibility: Students could participate in classes from any location, eliminating the need for commuting and overcoming geographical limitations.
- Enhanced engagement: Virtual classrooms incorporated interactive features such as live chat, polling, and breakout rooms, promoting active participation and engagement.
- Flexibility: Students had the ability to access recorded lectures and course materials at their convenience, accommodating different schedules and learning preferences.
- Collaboration opportunities: Virtual environments facilitated collaboration among students through group projects, online discussions, and shared documents.

The virtual classrooms also presented some challenges, such as technical issues and the need for reliable internet connections. However, these challenges were mitigated through technical support and training provided to students and instructors. Overall, the case study demonstrated the effectiveness of virtual classrooms in higher education, offering a flexible and engaging learning environment.

Case Study 2: Virtual Labs in Science Education

Science education often relies heavily on hands-on laboratory experiences. However, in situations where access to physical labs is limited or restricted, virtual labs can provide an alternative solution. A case study conducted in a high school science classroom explored the use of virtual labs to teach complex scientific concepts. The results showed several advantages of virtual labs:

- Accessibility: Virtual labs allowed students to conduct experiments and simulations at any time, reducing the dependency on physical lab availability.
- Cost-effectiveness: Virtual labs eliminated the need for expensive lab equipment and consumables, making science education more affordable.

- Safety: Virtual labs provided a safe environment for students to explore and experiment without the risk of accidents or exposure to hazardous substances.
- Visualization of abstract concepts: Virtual labs enabled students to visualize and manipulate abstract concepts, helping them understand and apply scientific principles.

The case study also highlighted the importance of appropriate guidance and instruction from teachers to ensure that students are able to effectively navigate and interpret the virtual lab experiences. It emphasized the need for pre-lab discussions, post-lab analysis, and opportunities for discussion and reflection.

Best Practices in Virtual Learning Environments

Based on the case studies and existing research, several best practices can be identified for designing and implementing virtual learning environments:

1. Clear communication and instructions: Provide clear guidelines and expectations for students to navigate the virtual environment effectively.
2. Interactive and engaging activities: Incorporate interactive components such as real-time discussions, collaborative projects, and multimedia resources to enhance student engagement.
3. Personalized learning experiences: Utilize adaptive technologies and individualized learning pathways to accommodate diverse learning styles and preferences.
4. Ongoing support and training: Offer technical support and training to both students and instructors to ensure effective use of the virtual learning environment.
5. Regular assessment and feedback: Implement formative assessment strategies in virtual environments to monitor student progress and provide timely feedback.
6. Cultivate a sense of community: Foster social interaction and collaboration through online forums, group activities, and peer-to-peer feedback.
7. Promote self-regulated learning: Incorporate tools and strategies that encourage students to take ownership of their learning and manage their time effectively.

8. Continual improvement and evaluation: Regularly assess the effectiveness of virtual learning environments through feedback from students and instructors, and make necessary adjustments.

These best practices ensure that virtual learning environments are designed to maximize student engagement, facilitate effective learning experiences, and provide opportunities for collaboration and interaction among students and instructors.

Resources and Tools for Virtual Learning Environments

There are several resources and tools available to support the implementation of virtual learning environments:

- Learning Management Systems (LMS): Platforms such as Moodle, Canvas, and Blackboard provide comprehensive solutions for managing virtual classrooms, content creation, and assessment.
- Virtual lab platforms: Applications like Labster, PhET Interactive Simulations, and ChemCollective offer interactive virtual lab experiences across various science disciplines.
- Collaborative tools: Tools like Google Suite, Microsoft Teams, and Slack enable students and instructors to collaborate, share documents, and communicate effectively in virtual environments.
- Multimedia resources: Platforms such as Khan Academy, TED-Ed, and YouTube provide a wealth of educational videos and interactive content to enhance virtual learning experiences.
- Augmented Reality (AR) and Virtual Reality (VR): AR and VR technologies, such as Merge Cube and Google Expeditions, offer immersive and interactive experiences to complement virtual learning environments.

These resources and tools, combined with effective instructional design and pedagogical strategies, can greatly enhance the quality and effectiveness of virtual learning environments.

Exercises

Exercise 1: Reflecting on Virtual Learning Experiences

Think about a time when you engaged in a virtual learning experience. It could be a webinar, an online course, or any other virtual learning environment. Reflect on the following questions:

1. What were the benefits of the virtual learning experience?

2. What challenges did you face, if any, and how did you overcome them?

3. Did the virtual learning environment facilitate interaction and engagement? How?

4. How could the virtual learning experience be improved?

Write a short paragraph summarizing your reflections and share it with a classmate or instructor for further discussion.

Exercise 2: Designing a Virtual Lab Activity

Imagine you are a science teacher planning a virtual lab activity for your students. Choose a scientific concept from your subject area and design a virtual lab activity that effectively demonstrates and explores this concept. Consider the following:

1. What tools or software will you use to create the virtual lab?

2. How will you ensure that students have a hands-on and interactive experience?

3. What instructions and guidance will you provide to students to facilitate their understanding of the concept?

4. How will you assess student learning and provide feedback based on their performance in the virtual lab?

Create a brief outline or description of your virtual lab activity, highlighting key steps and components.

Summary

Virtual learning environments offer flexible, engaging, and accessible learning opportunities for students in various educational settings. Case studies and best practices demonstrate the effectiveness of virtual classrooms and virtual labs in higher education and science education, respectively. Clear communication, interactive activities, personalization, ongoing support, assessment, community-building, and self-regulated learning are crucial for successful virtual learning environments. Utilizing resources and tools like Learning Management Systems, virtual lab platforms, collaborative tools, multimedia resources, AR, and VR technologies further enhance the effectiveness of virtual learning environments. Reflecting on personal experiences and designing virtual lab activities provide opportunities for further exploration and implementation of best practices in virtual learning environments.

Blended Learning and Virtual Environments

Blended learning is an instructional approach that combines traditional face-to-face classroom teaching with online learning components. It aims to create a seamless integration between in-person and virtual learning experiences, leveraging the benefits of both approaches. In this section, we will explore the concept of blended learning and its applications in virtual environments.

Understanding Blended Learning

Blended learning is rooted in the belief that a combination of different learning modalities can enhance the educational experience for students. By integrating online learning activities with in-person instruction, educators can create a flexible and personalized learning environment that caters to the diverse needs of students.

Blended learning can take on various forms depending on the specific goals of the educational program. Some common models include the rotation model, flex model, and self-blend model. In the rotation model, students rotate between different learning stations, including online activities, small group discussions, or individual work. The flex model allows students to have more control over the time, place, and pace of their learning, with a mix of online and in-person instruction. The self-blend model enables students to select specific online courses or resources to supplement their traditional classroom learning.

Benefits of Blended Learning

Blended learning offers several advantages that contribute to enhanced student engagement, achievement, and overall learning outcomes. Some key benefits include:

- **Flexibility:** Blended learning provides flexibility in terms of time, location, and pace of learning. Students can access online materials and resources at their own convenience, allowing for personalized learning experiences.
- **Individualized Instruction:** Blended learning allows for the customization of instruction based on students' unique learning needs. Online components can be tailored to provide additional support or challenge for individual students.
- **Access to Resources:** Online platforms and digital tools offer a wealth of resources that may not be available in traditional classrooms. Blended learning provides access to a variety of multimedia materials, interactive simulations, and collaborative tools.
- **Student Engagement:** Blended learning promotes active learning by incorporating interactive and multimedia elements. Online discussions, virtual labs, and gamified activities can increase student engagement and motivation.
- **Collaborative Learning:** Blended learning encourages collaboration and peer-to-peer interaction through online platforms. Students can work together on projects, share ideas, and provide feedback, regardless of their physical location.

Implementing Blended Learning in Virtual Environments

Creating effective blended learning environments in virtual settings involves careful planning and intentional design. Here are some key considerations and strategies for implementing blended learning in virtual environments:

- **Quality Online Content:** Select or develop high-quality online learning materials that align with the intended learning outcomes. These can include instructional videos, interactive modules, or multimedia presentations.
- **Synchronous and Asynchronous Activities:** Plan a combination of synchronous (real-time) and asynchronous (self-paced) activities to accommodate different learning preferences and schedules. Synchronous

activities can include virtual lectures, discussions, or live Q&A sessions, while asynchronous activities can involve watching recorded lectures or completing online assignments.

- **Virtual Collaboration:** Incorporate collaborative activities that leverage online tools and platforms. Discussion forums, virtual group projects, and shared document editing tools can facilitate collaboration and interaction among students.

- **Teacher Guidance and Support:** Provide clear instructions and guidelines for students to navigate the virtual learning environment effectively. Regular communication and feedback from teachers are crucial to ensure students stay on track and receive necessary support.

- **Assessment and Feedback:** Design a variety of assessments, both formative and summative, to evaluate student progress and understanding. Online quizzes, discussion participation, and project-based assessments can provide valuable feedback for both students and teachers.

- **Technology Integration:** Make use of educational technology tools that support blended learning, such as learning management systems (LMS), virtual meeting platforms, and collaboration software. Familiarize students with these tools and provide necessary training or resources.

Challenges and Solutions

Implementing blended learning in virtual environments may present several challenges. It is essential to address these challenges proactively to ensure a successful blended learning experience. Some common challenges and possible solutions include:

- **Access to Technology and Connectivity:** Not all students may have equal access to reliable internet connections or necessary technology devices. Providing alternative options such as offline resources or loaning devices can help bridge the digital divide.

- **Digital Literacy Skills:** Students and teachers may require support and training to develop the necessary digital literacy skills for effective blended learning. Offering workshops, tutorials, or online resources can help foster digital competence.

- **Maintaining Student Engagement:** Keeping students engaged in a virtual environment can be a challenge. Implementing interactive and gamified activities, fostering a sense of community through virtual discussions, and providing timely feedback can help maintain student motivation and engagement.
- **Time Management and Self-Regulation:** Blended learning requires students to manage their time effectively and take responsibility for their learning. Providing guidelines, time management strategies, and self-assessment tools can support students in developing self-regulation skills.
- **Teacher Training and Support:** Teachers need professional development opportunities and ongoing support to effectively design and facilitate blended learning experiences. Collaborative planning, mentoring programs, or workshops can address the professional development needs of teachers.

Additional Resources

- *Blended Learning in Action: A Practical Guide for Teachers,* by Catlin R. Tucker
- *The Blended Workbook: Learning to Design the Schools of our Future,* by Michael B. Horn and Heather Staker
- *Blended: Using Disruptive Innovation to Improve Schools,* by Michael B. Horn and Heather Staker

Blended learning offers a powerful educational approach that combines the best of in-person and online learning experiences. By leveraging virtual environments, educators can create engaging and personalized learning experiences that enhance student outcomes.

AI and Personalized Learning in Virtual Environments

In recent years, there has been a growing interest in leveraging artificial intelligence (AI) technologies to enhance personalized learning experiences in virtual environments. AI has the potential to revolutionize education by tailoring instructional content, pacing, and feedback to meet the unique needs of individual learners. This section explores the various applications of AI in personalized learning and provides insights into the benefits, challenges, and future directions of this approach.

Understanding Personalized Learning

Before delving into the role of AI in personalized learning, it is essential to define what personalized learning entails. Personalized learning is an instructional approach that recognizes and accommodates the diversity of learners' abilities, preferences, and goals. It aims to provide individualized support and resources to help students achieve their full potential.

At the core of personalized learning is the idea that learners have distinct learning styles, interests, and strengths. By understanding these individual differences, educators can customize the learning experience to optimize student engagement and success. Personalized learning goes beyond simply delivering content; it involves adapting instruction, providing timely feedback, and promoting student agency and self-direction.

Benefits of AI in Personalized Learning

AI offers several benefits when applied to personalized learning in virtual environments. Some of the key advantages are:

- **Tailored Instruction:** AI algorithms can analyze vast amounts of data to identify patterns in students' learning behaviors and preferences. By recognizing individual strengths and weaknesses, AI systems can generate personalized recommendations for instructional content and activities.

- **Adaptive Feedback:** AI-powered systems can provide real-time feedback based on a student's performance and progress. Adaptive feedback can help learners identify misconceptions, reinforce learning, and offer targeted suggestions for improvement.

- **Differentiated Instruction:** With AI, educators can create adaptive learning paths that cater to each student's unique needs. AI algorithms can dynamically adjust the level of difficulty, pace, and content of exercises and assessments, ensuring that learners are appropriately challenged.

- **Enhanced Engagement:** By incorporating AI technologies such as natural language processing and machine learning, virtual learning environments can deliver interactive and immersive experiences. This can increase student engagement and motivation, leading to improved learning outcomes.

- **Data-Driven Insights:** AI systems can collect and analyze vast amounts of data on student performance, behaviors, and preferences. Educators can leverage these insights to gain a deeper understanding of learners' needs and optimize instructional strategies accordingly.

Challenges and Considerations

While the prospects of AI in personalized learning are promising, there are several challenges and considerations that need to be addressed:

- **Privacy and Ethics:** AI systems rely on collecting and analyzing sensitive student data. It is crucial to establish robust privacy policies and ensure ethical use of data to protect students' rights and maintain their trust.
- **Equitable Access:** AI-powered personalized learning systems must be accessible to all students, regardless of their socioeconomic background or geographic location. Efforts should be made to bridge the digital divide and provide equal opportunities for all learners.
- **Teacher-Student Relationship:** Personalized learning does not replace the role of educators. It is vital to strike a balance between AI-driven instruction and the crucial teacher-student relationship. Teachers should be trained to use AI tools effectively and provide ongoing support to students.
- **Quality of AI Recommendations:** AI algorithms must be continuously improved to ensure accurate and reliable recommendations. It is essential to invest in research and development to enhance the precision and adaptability of AI systems in the context of personalized learning.
- **Potential Bias:** AI algorithms are susceptible to biases present in the data they are trained on. Steps should be taken to mitigate biases and ensure fair and equitable recommendations for all students.

Future Directions

Looking ahead, AI in personalized learning is likely to evolve in several exciting directions:

- **Greater Personalization:** AI algorithms will become more sophisticated in tailoring learning experiences to suit individual learners' needs, going beyond adaptive content suggestions to providing personalized interventions, feedback, and support.

- **Contextual Adaptation:** AI systems will take into account the broader learning context, including students' cultural backgrounds, prior knowledge, and social interactions, to provide a more holistic and contextually relevant personalized learning experience.
- **Collaborative AI:** AI technologies will facilitate collaborative learning experiences in virtual environments by supporting peer interaction, group projects, and social learning dynamics. AI can act as a virtual facilitator, encouraging collaboration and fostering effective teamwork.
- **Open Educational Resources:** AI algorithms can help identify and recommend relevant open educational resources (OER) that align with students' individual interests and learning goals. This can provide learners with a vast array of high-quality resources tailored to their needs.
- **Continuous Improvement:** AI systems will continually learn and adapt based on real-time data and user feedback. This iterative improvement cycle will lead to more accurate and effective personalized recommendations.

In conclusion, AI has immense potential to transform personalized learning in virtual environments. It can optimize instruction, provide timely feedback, and cater to the unique needs of individual learners. However, careful attention must be paid to address challenges such as privacy, equity, and maintaining the vital role of educators. As AI technologies advance, the future holds exciting possibilities for further enhancing personalized learning experiences and empowering students to reach their full potential.

Future directions of virtual learning environments

Virtual learning environments have transformed the way education is delivered and have opened up new opportunities for learning beyond traditional classroom settings. As technology continues to evolve, the future of virtual learning environments holds immense potential for further enhancements and innovations. In this section, we explore some of the future directions of virtual learning environments.

Immersive Technologies and Virtual Reality

One of the most exciting developments in virtual learning environments is the integration of immersive technologies, particularly virtual reality (VR). VR allows learners to step into realistic and immersive virtual environments, providing a highly engaging and interactive learning experience. In the future, we can expect to see VR being used more extensively in education across various subjects.

For example, in science and medicine, VR can be used to simulate laboratory experiments or medical procedures, allowing students to practice complex tasks in a safe, controlled environment. In history and geography, VR can transport students to different time periods or locations, enabling them to explore ancient civilizations or visit far-off places. In language learning, VR can simulate real-world scenarios, providing learners with opportunities to practice their language skills in authentic contexts.

Furthermore, advancements in haptic feedback technology will allow users to touch and feel virtual objects, further enhancing the immersion and realism of virtual learning environments. With the continued development of VR hardware and software, we can anticipate a future where immersive technologies become an integral part of education.

Augmented Reality and Mixed Reality

While VR immerses learners in completely virtual environments, augmented reality (AR) and mixed reality (MR) blend virtual elements with the real world. These technologies supplement the physical environment with digital information, creating an interactive and contextual learning experience.

In the future, AR and MR will likely play a more prominent role in virtual learning environments. Using AR-enabled devices such as smartphones or smart glasses, learners can access additional information, annotations, or 3D models overlaid onto real-world objects. This can greatly enhance understanding and engagement in various subjects.

For example, in biology, learners can use AR to explore 3D models of organs or organisms, enabling a deeper understanding of their structures and functions. In architecture and engineering, AR can be used to visualize and manipulate 3D models of buildings or prototypes, allowing students to better comprehend design principles and engineering concepts.

As AR and MR technologies continue to improve and become more affordable, we can expect them to be integrated into educational applications, providing learners with new ways to interact with and understand the world around them.

Artificial Intelligence and Personalized Learning

Artificial intelligence (AI) has the potential to revolutionize virtual learning environments by enabling personalized learning experiences. AI algorithms can analyze vast amounts of data about individual learners, such as their learning preferences, strengths, and weaknesses, and provide tailored recommendations and feedback.

In the future, AI-powered virtual learning environments will become more intelligent and adaptive, catering to the unique needs of each learner. These systems will be able to dynamically adjust the pace, difficulty level, and content of learning materials based on the learner's progress and performance. This personalized approach to education will help optimize learning outcomes and ensure each student achieves their full potential.

Furthermore, AI can assist in automating routine administrative tasks, grading assignments, and providing timely feedback to learners. This frees up educators' time and allows them to focus on providing more personalized and impactful instruction.

However, ethical considerations must be taken into account when integrating AI into virtual learning environments. Striking the right balance between automation and human guidance is crucial to ensure that learners receive adequate support and opportunities for social interaction.

Social and Collaborative Learning

Virtual learning environments have the potential to facilitate social and collaborative learning experiences, even when learners are physically separated. In the future, we can expect to see the development of more interactive and collaborative virtual platforms that foster communication and collaboration among learners.

For instance, virtual classrooms can enable learners from different parts of the world to connect and collaborate on projects, sharing ideas and perspectives. Online discussion boards, video conferencing, and collaborative document editing tools will continue to evolve, providing learners with tools for meaningful interaction and collaboration.

Furthermore, virtual learning environments can incorporate social networking features to foster a sense of community and support among learners. Gamification elements, badges, and leaderboards can be used to motivate learners and promote healthy competition.

Adaptive Assessment and Learning Analytics

Virtual learning environments generate large amounts of data about learners' interactions, progress, and performance. In the future, adaptive assessment and learning analytics will play a significant role in virtual learning environments to provide insights into learners' strengths and areas for improvement.

Adaptive assessment systems can dynamically adjust the difficulty and format of assessment tasks based on learners' performance, ensuring that each learner is appropriately challenged. These systems can also provide targeted feedback and suggestions for further learning based on the learner's responses.

Learning analytics can provide educators with valuable insights into learners' engagement, progress, and learning behaviors. By analyzing data patterns, educators can identify areas where learners may struggle and make informed instructional decisions.

However, it is crucial to ensure that the collection and use of learner data are ethically and securely handled, respecting learners' privacy rights and maintaining data confidentiality.

Conclusion

The future of virtual learning environments holds immense potential for enhancing education delivery and creating transformative learning experiences. The integration of immersive technologies, such as VR and AR, will provide learners with highly engaging and interactive learning experiences. AI-powered personalized learning will enable tailored instruction and support, while social and collaborative learning features will foster interaction and collaboration among learners. Additionally, adaptive assessment and learning analytics will provide valuable insights for educators to make data-driven instructional decisions. As we move forward, it is essential to embrace these future directions and ensure that virtual learning environments are inclusive, accessible, and designed to meet the diverse needs of learners.

Personalized Learning

Understanding personalized learning

Personalized learning is an approach to education that tailors instructional methods, content, and learning experiences to meet the individual needs of each student. It recognizes that students have different learning styles, abilities, interests, and goals, and seeks to provide them with a more personalized educational experience.

At its core, personalized learning is about empowering students to take ownership of their own learning journey. It moves away from a one-size-fits-all approach and instead focuses on creating a learning environment where students can thrive and reach their full potential.

Key Principles of Personalized Learning

To understand personalized learning, it is important to familiarize ourselves with the key principles that underpin this approach:

1. **Learner agency:** Personalized learning empowers students to have a sense of agency and control over their learning. They are given opportunities to make decisions about what and how they learn, set goals, and monitor their progress.

2. **Differentiation:** Personalized learning recognizes that students have diverse needs and abilities. Teachers differentiate instruction by providing multiple pathways, strategies, and resources to ensure that each student's learning needs are met.

3. **Individualized pacing:** Personalized learning allows students to learn at their own pace. It takes into account their current knowledge, skills, and understanding and provides opportunities for both acceleration and remediation as needed.

4. **Flexible learning environments:** Personalized learning encourages flexibility in the physical and virtual learning environment. It may involve group work, independent study, collaborative projects, online learning, and other forms of learning that cater to students' preferences and learning styles.

5. **Data-informed instruction:** Personalized learning relies on the use of data to inform instruction. Teachers collect and analyze data on students' performance, progress, and learning preferences, and use this information to tailor instruction and provide targeted support.

6. **Authentic and meaningful learning experiences:** Personalized learning aims to make learning more authentic and meaningful by connecting it to real-world contexts, interests, and goals. Students are encouraged to apply their learning to solve real problems and engage in projects that have relevance beyond the classroom.

Principles of Personalized Learning in Practice

Implementing personalized learning in the classroom requires careful planning and thoughtful execution. Here are some practical strategies and examples to illustrate how the principles of personalized learning can be put into practice:

1. **Choice and agency:** Giving students choices in their learning is a key aspect of personalized learning. For example, in a literature class, students can choose which books to read from a curated list or even suggest their own book recommendations. This allows students to explore their interests and develop a love for reading.

2. **Flexible pathways:** Personalized learning recognizes that students may have different pathways to achieve mastery of a concept or skill. For example, in a math class, students can choose between practicing with manipulatives, using online interactive tools, or solving real-world problems to develop their understanding of mathematical concepts.

3. **Individualized support:** Personalized learning ensures that each student receives the support they need to succeed. For example, in a science class, a teacher may identify that a student is struggling with a particular concept and provide additional resources, one-on-one tutoring, or alternative explanations to help the student grasp the content.

4. **Goal setting and reflection:** Personalized learning encourages students to set goals and reflect on their learning journey. For example, at the beginning of a unit, students can identify their learning goals and periodically reflect on their progress, adjusting their goals as needed. This promotes metacognition and self-regulated learning.

5. **Real-world connections:** Personalized learning seeks to make learning relevant and applicable to real-world contexts. For example, in a history class, students can investigate and present on a historical event that has implications for contemporary society. This allows students to see the relevance of history to their own lives and develop critical thinking skills.

Challenges and Considerations

While personalized learning has the potential to greatly benefit students, there are also challenges and considerations that need to be addressed:

- **Equity and access:** One of the concerns is ensuring equitable access to personalized learning for all students. Schools need to ensure that technology and resources are available to all students, regardless of their socioeconomic background.

- **Teacher training and support:** Implementing personalized learning requires training and support for teachers. They need to be equipped with the necessary skills and knowledge to design personalized learning experiences, differentiate instruction, analyze data, and provide individualized support to students.

- **Data privacy and security:** With increased use of technology and data collection, ensuring the privacy and security of student data becomes crucial. Schools must have strict policies and safeguards in place to protect student information.

- **Assessment and accountability:** Evaluating student progress and learning outcomes in personalized learning can be challenging. Traditional assessment methods may need to be adapted to assess student growth and mastery in a personalized learning environment.

Conclusion

Personalized learning offers a promising approach to education that recognizes the unique needs and strengths of each student. It empowers students to take ownership of their learning, fosters a love for learning, and prepares them for success in the complex, ever-changing world. By utilizing the principles and strategies of personalized learning, educators can transform traditional classrooms into dynamic, student-centered learning environments that meet the diverse needs of today's learners.

Benefits of personalized learning

Personalized learning is an educational approach that tailors instruction and learning experiences to meet the individual needs, interests, and pace of each student. It recognizes that students have unique learning styles, strengths, and areas for improvement, and aims to provide them with customized learning opportunities. The benefits of personalized learning are numerous and can positively impact students, teachers, and the overall educational system. In this section, we will explore some of the key benefits of personalized learning.

Improved Student Engagement

One of the primary benefits of personalized learning is increased student engagement. When students have the opportunity to explore topics that resonate with their interests and passions, they become more motivated to learn. Personalized learning allows students to have a say in what they learn and how they learn it, which promotes a sense of ownership and autonomy. This sense of agency can lead to higher levels of engagement, as students feel empowered and connected to their education.

Enhanced Learning Outcomes

Personalized learning has the potential to improve learning outcomes by tailoring instruction to the specific needs and abilities of each student. By identifying students' strengths and areas for improvement, educators can design targeted interventions, provide additional support, and offer more challenging opportunities when appropriate. This individualized approach allows students to progress at their own pace, ensuring they fully understand and master foundational concepts before moving on to more complex topics. As a result, personalized learning can lead to deeper understanding and improved academic performance.

Increased Student Agency and Autonomy

Empowering students with the ability to make decisions about their learning can have a significant impact on their motivation and self-confidence. Personalized learning provides opportunities for students to set learning goals, make choices about their assignments or projects, and reflect on their progress. This active involvement in the learning process fosters a sense of ownership, responsibility, and autonomy. Students become more self-directed learners who take ownership of their education, leading to increased self-esteem and a growth mindset.

Catering to Diverse Learning Styles and Needs

Every student learns in a unique way and has different strengths and challenges. Personalized learning acknowledges and supports this diversity by offering multiple pathways to learning. Visual learners, for example, may benefit from watching videos or using diagrams, while auditory learners may prefer listening to lectures or participating in discussions. By incorporating a variety of instructional strategies and resources, personalized learning ensures that students can access content in a way that best suits their individual learning styles and needs.

Promoting Critical Thinking and Creativity

Personalized learning provides opportunities for students to engage in higher-order thinking skills such as critical thinking, problem-solving, and creativity. By allowing students to explore topics of interest and engage in real-world, authentic learning experiences, personalized learning fosters a deeper understanding of concepts and encourages students to think critically and analytically. It also promotes creativity by encouraging students to think outside the box, explore different perspectives, and develop innovative solutions to complex problems.

Building Relationships and Collaboration

Personalized learning creates an environment that emphasizes relationships and collaboration between students and teachers. With a focus on individualized instruction, teachers have the opportunity to build strong connections with each student, understand their unique needs, and provide targeted support. Additionally, personalized learning often incorporates collaborative learning experiences, allowing students to work together, share ideas, and learn from each other. This collaboration promotes teamwork, communication, and social-emotional skills, which are crucial for success in the modern world.

Preparing Students for the Future

In an ever-changing world, students need to develop a range of skills to thrive in their personal and professional lives. Personalized learning goes beyond academic knowledge and focuses on developing skills such as critical thinking, problem-solving, collaboration, communication, and self-directed learning. These skills are essential for success in the future, where adaptability, creativity, and lifelong learning are highly valued. By cultivating these skills, personalized learning prepares students to navigate a rapidly changing world and become engaged, active citizens.

In conclusion, personalized learning offers a wide range of benefits for students, teachers, and the educational system as a whole. By empowering students, catering to diverse learning needs, promoting critical thinking and creativity, and fostering relationships and collaboration, personalized learning enhances student engagement, learning outcomes, and overall educational experiences. As we continue to embrace the future of education, personalized learning will play a crucial role in creating transformative learning environments that prepare students for success in the 21st century.

Personalized Learning Models and Approaches

Personalized learning is an approach to education that tailors instruction to meet the individual needs, strengths, interests, and goals of each student. It recognizes that students learn in different ways and at different paces, and aims to create an educational experience that is relevant, engaging, and meaningful to each learner. In this section, we will explore various personalized learning models and approaches that can be used to support student success.

Differentiated Instruction

One of the most widely used personalized learning models is differentiated instruction. This approach involves adjusting the curriculum, instructional strategies, and assessment methods to meet the individual needs of students. Teachers identify students' strengths, weaknesses, learning preferences, and interests, and then tailor their instruction accordingly.

Differentiated instruction can be applied in various ways. For example, teachers may create tiered assignments that offer different levels of complexity or provide multiple options for demonstrating knowledge. They may also use flexible grouping strategies to match students with similar learning needs or interests. By differentiating instruction, teachers can ensure that each student receives the support and challenge they need to succeed.

Student-Driven Learning

Another approach to personalized learning is student-driven learning, also known as self-directed or self-paced learning. In this model, students take ownership of their learning process, setting goals, making decisions, and monitoring their progress. This approach empowers students to become active participants in their education and encourages them to develop important skills such as self-regulation, time management, and problem-solving.

Student-driven learning can be facilitated through various strategies. For instance, teachers can provide students with a menu of learning options or projects, allowing them to choose topics that interest them. They can also use technology tools that provide adaptive content and personalized recommendations based on students' performance and preferences. By giving students agency and autonomy, student-driven learning fosters motivation and engagement.

Competency-Based Education

Competency-based education (CBE) is an approach that focuses on students demonstrating mastery of specific competencies rather than progressing through a predetermined curriculum at a fixed pace. In a competency-based learning environment, students advance upon mastery, allowing them to move more quickly through content they are already proficient in and spend more time on areas where they need additional support.

CBE can be implemented through various strategies. Teachers can use formative assessments to continuously monitor students' progress, provide targeted feedback, and adjust instruction accordingly. They can also design learning experiences that allow students to apply their knowledge and skills to real-world problems or scenarios. By emphasizing mastery rather than seat time, CBE promotes deeper understanding and ensures that students develop the necessary skills and knowledge to thrive.

Personal Learning Pathways

Personal learning pathways involve the creation of individualized educational plans for each student, outlining their learning goals, interests, and preferred approaches. These pathways take into account students' unique strengths, challenges, and aspirations, and provide a roadmap for their educational journey. Teachers collaborate with students to co-create these plans, ensuring that they are aligned with the curriculum standards and requirements.

To implement personal learning pathways, schools can provide students with a wide range of course options and elective subjects, allowing them to tailor their learning experience to their interests and goals. Teachers can also leverage technology tools and digital resources that offer personalized learning experiences and provide students with access to a variety of learning materials. Personal learning pathways empower students to take ownership of their education and pursue their passions.

Intelligent Tutoring Systems

Intelligent tutoring systems (ITS) are computer-based programs that provide individualized instruction and feedback to students. These systems use algorithms and artificial intelligence to assess students' knowledge and skills, identify areas of weakness, and deliver personalized lessons and practice activities. ITS can adapt and adjust instruction in real-time based on students' responses and performance data.

Intelligent tutoring systems can be used in various subjects and educational settings. For example, in mathematics, an ITS can provide personalized math problems and step-by-step guidance based on students' individual needs. In language learning, an ITS can offer personalized exercises to improve grammar, vocabulary, and pronunciation. By providing immediate feedback and tailored support, ITS enhance the learning experience and help students make progress at their own pace.

Blended Learning

Blended learning combines face-to-face instruction with online learning, providing a flexible and personalized learning experience. In a blended learning environment, students have opportunities to engage in both collaborative activities with their peers and independent online learning activities. This approach allows for a mix of synchronous and asynchronous learning experiences, giving students more control over the time, place, and pace of their learning.

Blended learning can be implemented in various ways. For instance, teachers may use a flipped classroom model, where students watch instructional videos or complete online activities before coming to class for discussions and collaborative projects. They may also use online learning platforms that offer personalized learning paths, adaptive content, and interactive simulations. By combining the best of both online and face-to-face instruction, blended learning provides students with a personalized and well-rounded learning experience.

Real-World Connections

Personalized learning models and approaches can be enhanced by creating real-world connections in the learning process. By relating the content to students' lives, experiences, and interests, teachers can make the learning more meaningful and relevant. This can be achieved through the use of authentic tasks, real-world examples, guest speakers, field trips, and community-based projects.

For example, in a science class, students can engage in hands-on experiments or investigations that address real-world problems. In a language arts class, students can analyze and interpret texts that reflect diverse perspectives and cultures. By connecting the curriculum to real-world applications, students can see the relevance and purpose of what they are learning, making the learning experience more engaging and motivating.

Caveats and Considerations

While personalized learning has the potential to greatly enhance student learning and engagement, it is not without its challenges and considerations. Implementing personalized learning requires careful planning, ongoing assessment, and continuous refinement. It is important to remember that it is not a one-size-fits-all approach, and what works for one student or group of students may not work for another.

Additionally, personalized learning relies heavily on technology tools and resources. It is important to consider the availability of technology infrastructure and access to devices and internet connectivity, as well as issues of equity and access. Furthermore, ethical considerations such as data privacy, security, and responsible use of technology should be addressed to ensure the safety and well-being of students.

Despite these challenges, personalized learning has the potential to transform education and empower students to become lifelong learners. By tailoring instruction to meet the individual needs and interests of students, personalized learning models and approaches can foster a love of learning, promote academic achievement, and prepare students for success in the 21st century.

Designing Personalized Learning Experiences

Personalized learning is an approach to education that tailors instruction, content, and learning experiences to meet the individual needs, interests, and goals of each student. This section will explore strategies and considerations for designing effective personalized learning experiences.

Understanding the Learner

Designing personalized learning experiences begins with a deep understanding of each learner. Teachers should gather information about students' strengths, weaknesses, interests, learning styles, and goals. This information can be gathered through formal assessments, informal observations, student surveys, and conversations with students and their families.

One important aspect of understanding the learner is recognizing their cultural and linguistic background. For students from diverse backgrounds, educators need to ensure that learning experiences are culturally responsive and inclusive. This involves incorporating students' cultural experiences, perspectives, and values into the curriculum and learning activities.

Setting Clear Learning Goals

Once educators have a clear understanding of each learner, they can set clear learning goals. Learning goals should be specific, measurable, achievable, relevant, and time-bound (SMART). By setting personalized learning goals, students are empowered to take ownership of their learning and can track their progress towards these goals.

Teachers can work collaboratively with students to establish learning targets that align with their interests, abilities, and aspirations. This collaborative goal-setting process motivates students and fosters a sense of ownership and agency in their learning journey.

Adapting Instruction and Content

To personalize learning experiences, educators need to adapt instruction and content to meet the unique needs of each learner. This can be achieved through differentiated instruction, which involves modifying the pace, level of challenge, and learning tasks to match students' abilities and interests.

Teachers can leverage a range of instructional strategies, such as small group instruction, one-on-one conferences, and flexible grouping, to provide targeted support and enrichment. Additionally, offering a variety of learning resources, including multimedia materials, textbooks, online resources, and hands-on activities, enables students to engage with content in ways that resonate with their learning preferences.

Leveraging Technology

Technology plays a crucial role in personalized learning by providing students with access to a diverse range of learning resources and opportunities for self-paced learning. Educators can incorporate educational apps, online platforms, simulations, and multimedia materials to enhance the personalized learning experience.

Adaptive learning technologies can also be utilized to provide students with tailored instruction based on their individual needs. These technologies use algorithms to analyze student performance data and provide targeted interventions and remediation. By leveraging technology, educators can efficiently track student progress, identify areas of growth, and provide timely feedback.

Promoting Self-Reflection and Metacognition

In personalized learning, it is essential to develop students' self-reflection and metacognitive skills. Students should be encouraged to regularly reflect on their learning progress, identify their strengths and areas for growth, and set new learning goals. This process of self-reflection enables students to develop a deeper understanding of their learning preferences, strategies, and metacognitive abilities.

Teachers can support self-reflection by incorporating reflection prompts, journaling activities, and self-assessment tools. By fostering metacognitive skills, students become active, self-directed, and lifelong learners.

Creating Collaborative Learning Communities

Personalized learning does not mean isolated learning. Collaboration and social interaction are essential elements of effective personalized learning experiences. Educators should create opportunities for students to engage in collaborative activities, such as group projects, peer feedback, and cooperative learning.

Collaborative learning environments foster communication, critical thinking, problem-solving, and interpersonal skills. By working together, students can learn from each other, share diverse perspectives, and deepen their understanding of the content.

Monitoring and Adjusting the Learning Plan

Regular monitoring and assessment are crucial for designing personalized learning experiences. Teachers should continuously gather data and monitor student progress towards their learning goals. This can be done through formative assessments, observations, student reflections, and self-assessments.

Based on the data collected, educators can make data-informed decisions and adjust the learning plan accordingly. This may involve providing additional support, modifying instructional strategies, or introducing new learning opportunities to address areas of improvement.

Emphasizing Growth Mindset

A growth mindset is essential for personalized learning. Students should be encouraged to embrace challenges, persevere through setbacks, and view mistakes as opportunities for growth. Educators can foster a growth mindset environment by providing constructive feedback, highlighting effort and improvement, and celebrating students' achievements and progress.

By cultivating a growth mindset, students become more resilient, motivated, and adaptable learners who are willing to take risks and engage in continuous improvement.

Real-World Application and Relevance

Personalized learning experiences should bridge the gap between classroom learning and real-world application. Educators can design learning activities that allow students to apply their knowledge and skills to real-life contexts. This can be done through project-based learning, internships, community service, and problem-solving tasks.

By promoting real-world application, students understand the relevance and purpose of their learning, making it more meaningful and motivating.

Conclusion

Designing personalized learning experiences requires a holistic approach that takes into account each learner's unique characteristics, interests, and goals. By understanding the learner, setting clear goals, adapting instruction, leveraging technology, promoting self-reflection, and creating collaborative learning communities, educators can create transformative and engaging personalized learning experiences for students. These experiences empower students to take ownership of their learning and develop the knowledge, skills, and mindset needed for future success.

Adaptive learning technologies and personalized instruction

In recent years, there has been a growing recognition that one-size-fits-all approaches to education are not effective in meeting the diverse needs of students. As a result, educators and researchers have explored the concepts of adaptive learning technologies and personalized instruction as promising solutions to support individualized learning experiences. This section will delve into the principles, benefits, and challenges associated with adaptive learning technologies and personalized instruction.

Understanding Adaptive Learning Technologies

Adaptive learning technologies refer to educational tools and systems that adapt to the unique needs, preferences, and abilities of each learner. These technologies utilize data-driven algorithms and artificial intelligence to customize the learning experience, providing students with personalized pathways, resources, and assessments. By continuously analyzing and interpreting data on students' performance, adaptive learning technologies can dynamically adjust the content, pace, and feedback to optimize learning outcomes.

Benefits of Adaptive Learning Technologies

The implementation of adaptive learning technologies brings various benefits to both students and educators. Firstly, personalized instruction allows learners to engage in content that is tailored to their specific needs and learning styles. This customization promotes greater engagement, motivation, and ownership of the learning process, leading to improved academic outcomes. Additionally, adaptive learning technologies enable educators to gain real-time insights into students' progress, enabling targeted interventions and timely feedback to support their learning journeys. This personalized feedback can help students identify their strengths and weaknesses and guide them towards areas that need improvement. Furthermore, adaptive learning technologies promote self-directed learning, as students can have more control over their educational experience, accessing resources and materials at their own pace and level of understanding.

Challenges in Implementing Adaptive Learning Technologies

While adaptive learning technologies offer significant advantages, their implementation also poses several challenges. One primary concern is the availability and access to technology resources. Not all students and schools have equal access to devices, internet connectivity, and software, which can create inequalities in opportunities for personalized instruction. Furthermore, the effective integration of adaptive learning technologies into the curriculum requires extensive teacher training and professional development. Educators need to have a deep understanding of the technology, data interpretation, and instructional strategies to effectively utilize adaptive learning tools. Additionally, concerns regarding data privacy and security must be carefully addressed to ensure the ethical use of student data in adaptive learning environments.

Case Studies and Best Practices

Several case studies and best practices have demonstrated the successful integration of adaptive learning technologies and personalized instruction in various educational settings. For example, DreamBox Learning is an adaptive math program that assesses students' prior knowledge and provides instruction tailored to their individual needs. This program has shown significant gains in students' math proficiency and engagement. Another example is Khan Academy, a popular online platform that offers personalized learning experiences in a wide range of subject areas. Khan Academy tracks students' progress and provides adaptive practice exercises to target their specific areas of weakness.

Implementing Adaptive Learning Technologies

To effectively implement adaptive learning technologies and personalized instruction, educators should consider the following key strategies:

1. Identify learning goals: Clearly define the learning outcomes and objectives that the adaptive learning system should align with.
2. Collect data: Gather relevant and reliable data on students' performance, including pre-assessments, quizzes, and formative assessments.
3. Analyze data: Utilize data analytics tools and algorithms to interpret students' performance data and identify areas of strengths and weaknesses.
4. Develop adaptive content: Design and curate instructional materials, resources, and assessments that can be tailored to individual students' needs and preferences.
5. Provide targeted feedback: Leverage the adaptive learning system to provide timely and specific feedback to students, guiding them towards mastery of the content.
6. Monitor progress: Continuously track students' progress and adjust instruction as needed based on their performance and engagement data.
7. Foster collaboration: Encourage collaboration and peer-to-peer learning opportunities, as adaptive learning technologies can facilitate group activities and discussions.
8. Support teacher-student interaction: Personalized instruction does not replace the role of the teacher; instead, it enhances it. Teachers should establish strong relationships with students and provide guidance, support, and mentorship throughout the personalized learning journey.

Future Directions of Adaptive Learning Technologies and Personalized Instruction

As technology continues to advance, adaptive learning technologies and personalized instruction will evolve and expand in various ways. One potential direction is the integration of virtual reality and augmented reality technologies, which can provide immersive and interactive learning experiences tailored to individual students' needs. Additionally, the use of learning analytics and big data will enable more sophisticated analysis and interpretation of student data, allowing for even more personalized and targeted instruction. However, it is essential to ensure that ethical considerations, such as data privacy and security, are given paramount importance in the future development and implementation of adaptive learning technologies.

Overall, adaptive learning technologies and personalized instruction hold great promise in transforming education by providing tailored and engaging learning experiences for students. By leveraging technology and data, educators can create learning environments that support the diverse needs and aspirations of each learner, fostering intellectual growth, and academic success.

Overcoming Challenges in Implementing Personalized Learning

Personalized learning is an innovative approach to education that seeks to tailor the learning experience to the individual needs, interests, and abilities of each student. It emphasizes student agency, self-directed learning, and the use of technology to provide customized and adaptive instruction. While personalized learning holds great promise for enhancing student engagement and achievement, there are several challenges that educators must overcome in order to effectively implement this approach in the classroom. In this section, we will explore some of these challenges and discuss strategies for addressing them.

Challenge 1: Access to Technology

One of the primary challenges in implementing personalized learning is ensuring equitable access to technology. Personalized learning heavily relies on digital tools and online resources, which may not be readily available to all students, particularly those from low-income households or underserved communities. This digital divide exacerbates existing educational inequities and can hinder the successful implementation of personalized learning initiatives.

To overcome this challenge, it is crucial to prioritize efforts to bridge the digital divide and ensure that all students have access to the necessary technology and internet connectivity. Schools can explore options such as providing devices and hotspots for students, partnering with community organizations to offer technology resources, or advocating for policy changes to expand broadband access in underserved areas. Additionally, educators should be mindful of alternative methods of delivering personalized instruction, such as offline learning materials or classroom-based technology resources, to support students who may not have access to technology at home.

Challenge 2: Data Privacy and Security

Another significant challenge in personalized learning is maintaining data privacy and security. Personalized learning relies on collecting and analyzing large amounts of student data to inform instructional decisions and provide tailored learning experiences. However, there are concerns about how this data is stored, used, and protected, especially given the sensitive nature of student information.

To address this challenge, educators and school administrators must prioritize implementing robust data privacy and security protocols. This includes ensuring compliance with relevant privacy laws and regulations, using secure platforms and systems for data storage and transmission, and regularly assessing and updating security measures. Additionally, it is crucial to educate students, parents, and teachers about their rights and responsibilities regarding data privacy and security, and to obtain informed consent when collecting and using student data.

Challenge 3: Teacher Training and Support

Implementing personalized learning requires a significant shift in instructional practices, which can be challenging for teachers who may be unfamiliar with or resistant to change. Teachers need to develop new skills and pedagogical approaches to effectively implement personalized learning, including proficiency in using technology tools, data analysis, and differentiated instruction.

To address this challenge, it is essential to provide comprehensive and ongoing professional development opportunities for teachers. Professional development should focus on enhancing teachers' digital literacy, familiarity with personalized learning strategies and tools, and their ability to analyze data and adapt instruction accordingly. Additionally, mentorship programs, collaborative learning communities, and peer-to-peer support can help teachers navigate the challenges of implementing personalized learning and provide them with ongoing guidance and encouragement.

Challenge 4: Curriculum and Assessment Alignment

Personalized learning requires a flexible and adaptive curriculum that can be tailored to each student's needs and interests. However, many traditional curricula are designed with a one-size-fits-all approach, making it difficult to align them with the principles of personalized learning. Similarly, traditional assessments often do not accurately measure the unique learning outcomes and achievements of students in personalized learning environments.

To overcome this challenge, it is important to engage in a comprehensive curriculum review process to identify areas where the curriculum can be modified or enhanced to better align with personalized learning goals. This may involve incorporating interdisciplinary approaches, project-based learning, and opportunities for students to pursue their interests and passions. Additionally, assessments should be carefully designed to reflect the individualized nature of personalized learning, incorporating authentic tasks, performance-based assessments, and ongoing formative assessments that provide immediate feedback to students and teachers.

Challenge 5: Parent and Community Engagement

Implementing personalized learning requires the active involvement and support of parents, caregivers, and the broader community. However, engaging parents and the community in the personalized learning process can be challenging, particularly if they are unfamiliar with the approach or have concerns about its effectiveness.

To address this challenge, schools should prioritize clear and ongoing communication with parents and the community, providing information about the goals, benefits, and implementation of personalized learning. This can be done through newsletters, workshops, parent-teacher conferences, or virtual platforms. Additionally, inviting parents and community members to participate in the personalized learning process, such as through advisory committees or classroom observations, can help build trust and collaboration. Schools should also seek opportunities to partner with local businesses, organizations, and institutions to provide real-world learning experiences and resources for students.

In conclusion, while personalized learning has the potential to revolutionize education, it is important to be aware of and address the challenges that can arise during its implementation. By ensuring equitable access to technology, prioritizing data privacy and security, providing comprehensive teacher training and support, aligning curriculum and assessments, and fostering parent and community engagement, educators can overcome these challenges and create successful personalized learning environments. Through these efforts, we can unlock the full potential of personalized learning and provide all students with the opportunity to thrive and succeed.

Case studies and best practices in personalized learning

Personalized learning is an approach that tailors education to the unique needs, interests, and abilities of individual students. It recognizes that each student learns at their own pace and has different strengths and challenges. In this section, we will explore case studies and best practices in personalized learning that demonstrate its effectiveness and highlight strategies for implementation.

Case Study 1: Summit Public Schools

Summit Public Schools is a network of charter schools in California that has successfully implemented personalized learning. They utilize a learning management system (LMS) called Summit Learning, which provides students with personalized learning paths based on their academic goals and progress. The LMS also allows students to set their own learning goals and track their progress.

In one case study, students at Summit Public Schools demonstrated significant improvement in their academic performance and growth mindset. Students reported feeling more engaged and motivated, as they were able to take ownership of their learning and work at their own pace. Teachers also noted an increase in collaboration and peer-to-peer support among students.

Best Practice 1: Data-Driven Instruction

In personalized learning, data plays a crucial role in informing instructional decisions. Teachers collect and analyze data on student performance to identify areas of strength and weakness. This allows them to provide targeted interventions and personalized support to students.

To implement this best practice, teachers should ensure they have access to accurate and timely data. They can use formative assessment tools and digital platforms to track student progress and gather real-time data. Analyzing this data enables teachers to identify trends, adjust instruction, and provide timely feedback to students.

Case Study 2: AltSchool

AltSchool is a network of schools that focuses on personalized learning. They create individualized learning plans for each student based on their interests and goals. Students have the opportunity to engage in project-based learning and pursue topics that align with their passions.

In a case study conducted at AltSchool, students demonstrated improved critical thinking, problem-solving, and communication skills. They also developed a sense of agency and independence in their learning. The personalized approach allowed students to explore their interests deeply and make connections between different subject areas.

Best Practice 2: Flexible Learning Environments

Creating flexible learning environments is essential for personalized learning. Teachers should design physical spaces that accommodate different learning modalities and allow for student choice and collaboration. Flexible seating arrangements, access to technology, and easily adaptable resources are key components of such environments.

Incorporating technology tools and resources into the learning environment is also crucial. This enables students to access personalized learning materials, engage in interactive activities, and collaborate with peers. Teachers can use learning management systems, online platforms, and educational apps to facilitate personalized learning experiences.

Case Study 3: Khan Academy

Khan Academy is an online platform that offers personalized learning resources, including video lessons and practice exercises. Students can work through lessons at their own pace and receive immediate feedback on their progress. Khan Academy also provides personalized recommendations to help students fill knowledge gaps and extend their learning.

A case study on Khan Academy showed that students who engaged with the platform regularly made significant gains in their math proficiency. The adaptive nature of the platform allowed students to focus on areas where they needed additional support and provided challenging content to those who were excelling.

Best Practice 3: Individualized Learning Paths

One of the key components of personalized learning is the creation of individualized learning paths for each student. Teachers should collaborate with students to set personalized goals and develop a plan to achieve them. This involves gathering information about students' interests, strengths, and areas for growth.

Teachers can then design learning experiences and activities that align with students' individual goals and provide opportunities for exploration and inquiry.

They can also leverage technology tools to offer adaptive learning experiences that adjust content and difficulty based on students' progress.

Conclusion

These case studies and best practices demonstrate the power of personalized learning in enhancing student engagement, motivation, and academic outcomes. By leveraging data, creating flexible learning environments, and designing individualized learning paths, educators can empower students to take ownership of their learning and achieve their full potential.

Implementing personalized learning requires a shift in instructional practices and a commitment to continuous improvement. By incorporating these case studies and best practices into their teaching, educators can create transformative learning experiences that meet the diverse needs of students and prepare them for the challenges of the future.

Data Privacy and Ethical Considerations in Personalized Learning

In the era of personalized learning, where student data plays a crucial role in shaping and customizing educational experiences, it is vital to address the ethical considerations and privacy concerns associated with the use of data in this context. This section will explore the importance of data privacy in personalized learning, the ethical implications of data collection and use, as well as strategies to ensure responsible data practices.

Importance of Data Privacy in Personalized Learning

Data privacy is a fundamental aspect of personalized learning that must be upheld to protect the rights and interests of students. Personalized learning relies heavily on collecting and analyzing student data, including personal information, academic performance, and learning preferences. As such, it is paramount to establish robust data privacy measures to prevent unauthorized access, misuse, or abuse of this sensitive information.

Respecting data privacy in personalized learning is essential for several reasons. Firstly, it safeguards the autonomy and dignity of students by ensuring that their personal information is not subjected to unwarranted disclosure or exploitation. Secondly, it maintains trust between educational institutions, teachers, and students, fostering a positive learning environment built on transparency and accountability. Finally, upholding data privacy in personalized learning contributes to compliance with legal and regulatory frameworks, such as the Family Educational Rights and Privacy Act (FERPA) in the United States.

Ethical Implications of Data Collection and Use

Personalized learning heavily relies on the collection and analysis of student data to tailor instruction and learning experiences. However, this raises ethical concerns that need to be addressed to ensure the responsible and ethical use of data in educational settings.

One of the main ethical considerations in data collection and use in personalized learning is the issue of informed consent. Students and their families must be adequately informed about the type of data collected, the purpose of data collection, how the data will be used, and who will have access to it. Informed consent ensures that individuals have the autonomy to make decisions about the use of their personal information.

Another ethical concern is data security. Educational institutions and technology providers must implement robust security measures to protect student data from unauthorized access, breaches, or misuse. This includes employing encryption protocols, firewalls, access controls, and regular security audits.

The use of algorithms and machine learning in personalized learning introduces the ethical consideration of algorithmic bias. Algorithms should be designed and trained to minimize biased decision-making based on race, gender, socioeconomic status, or any other protected category. Regular monitoring and auditing of algorithms are necessary to identify and rectify any biases that may emerge.

Furthermore, personalized learning may involve the use of third-party vendors or educational technology platforms. It is essential to assess the ethical practices of these entities, including their data privacy policies, security measures, and compliance with industry standards.

Strategies for Responsible Data Practices

To ensure responsible data practices in personalized learning, several strategies can be implemented:

1. **Data Minimization:** Only collect data that is necessary and directly relevant to improving student learning outcomes. Avoid collecting excessive or irrelevant information to minimize privacy risks.

2. **Anonymization and De-identification:** Remove personally identifiable information (PII) from datasets whenever possible. Substitute direct identifiers with pseudonyms to protect the privacy of individuals.
3. **Transparency and Consent:** Clearly communicate to students, parents, and other stakeholders the purpose and scope of data collection, the rights of individuals regarding their data, and obtain informed consent for data use.
4. **Security Safeguards:** Implement comprehensive data security measures, including encryption, secure storage, access controls, and regular security audits, to protect student data from unauthorized access or data breaches.
5. **Ethical Algorithm Design:** Develop and train algorithms to minimize biased decision-making and regularly monitor algorithms for any unintended biases that may emerge.
6. **Vendor Assessment:** Conduct thorough assessments of third-party vendors and educational technology platforms to ensure they adhere to best practices in data privacy and ethical standards.
7. **Data Retention and Disposal:** Establish clear guidelines and protocols for the retention and disposal of student data, ensuring compliance with legal requirements and the secure destruction of data when it is no longer needed.
8. **Continuous Evaluation:** Regularly evaluate and review data privacy policies and practices to ensure they remain aligned with evolving legal, ethical, and technological landscapes.
9. **Education and Awareness:** Provide training and resources for educators, administrators, students, and parents to raise awareness about data privacy, ethics, and responsible data practices in personalized learning.

By implementing these strategies, educational institutions can establish a culture of responsible data practices in personalized learning, fostering trust, equity, and respect for privacy in educational environments.

Case Study: Data Privacy Practices in a Personalized Learning Platform

To illustrate the importance of data privacy in personalized learning, let's consider the case of a personalized learning platform used in a K-12 school district. The platform collects various types of student data, including academic performance, learning preferences, and demographic information.

In this case, the platform ensures data privacy by applying data minimization principles, only collecting the necessary data to inform the customization of learning experiences. The platform also incorporates anonymization techniques, removing personally identifiable information from the datasets to protect student privacy.

To address ethical concerns, the platform provides transparent information to students, parents, and teachers about the purpose and use of data collection. It obtains informed consent from parents before collecting data from students and allows parents to review and make changes to the collected data.

In terms of security, the platform employs robust encryption algorithms, access controls, and secure storage to protect student data from unauthorized access. Regular security audits are conducted to identify and rectify any vulnerabilities.

The platform also ensures ethical algorithm design, regularly auditing and monitoring algorithms for biases. It employs a diverse team of data scientists and subject matter experts to mitigate biases and make the algorithms more equitable.

Overall, the case study demonstrates how a personalized learning platform can uphold data privacy and ethical considerations, ensuring the responsible use of student data in a personalized learning environment.

Resources and Further Reading

1. *Data Ethics for a Diverse Society* by Jannis Kallinikos, Alexes Klitzke, and Mikael Laaksoharju

2. *Privacy in Education: A Guide for K-12 Educators* by Linnette Attai and Mike Donlin

3. *Ethics and Data Science* by Mike Loukides and DJ Patil

4. *Privacy and Big Data: The Players, Regulators, and Stakeholders* edited by Terence Craig, Mary Ludloff, and Kord Davis

5. *Data Protection and Privacy in Education: Transforming the Inside Out* edited by Amelia Bryne Potter and Christopher J. Russo

Summary

Data privacy and ethical considerations are critical in personalized learning to protect the rights and interests of students. Upholding data privacy safeguards student autonomy, maintains trust, and ensures compliance with legal frameworks. Ethical implications include informed consent, data security, and algorithmic bias. Strategies for responsible data practices include data minimization, anonymization, transparency, security safeguards, ethical algorithm design, vendor assessment, and continuous evaluation. Implementing these strategies fosters a culture of responsible data practices and upholds privacy in personalized learning environments.

Personalized learning in different subject areas

Personalized learning is a teaching approach that tailors instructional methods, content, and pace to meet the individual needs and interests of each student. It recognizes that students have unique strengths, weaknesses, learning preferences, and goals, and seeks to provide them with personalized experiences to maximize their learning potential.

In this section, we will explore how personalized learning can be applied in different subject areas, highlighting the specific strategies and considerations for implementing personalized learning in each discipline.

Personalized Learning in Mathematics

Mathematics is a subject that often requires a solid foundation of prerequisite knowledge and skills. Personalized learning in mathematics can help students build on their existing knowledge and progress at their own pace. Here are some key strategies for implementing personalized learning in mathematics:

1. Diagnostic assessments: Conducting diagnostic assessments at the beginning of the course can help identify each student's strengths and weaknesses. This information can be used to individualize the learning path for each student, targeting specific areas that require remediation or acceleration.

2. Adaptive learning platforms: Utilize adaptive learning platforms that provide personalized content and practice exercises based on the student's level of proficiency. These platforms can adjust the difficulty of questions and provide immediate feedback to help students fill gaps in their understanding.

3. Differentiated instruction: Group students based on their proficiency levels and provide targeted instruction for each group. This allows teachers to address the specific needs of students at different stages of learning. For example, advanced students can be challenged with more complex problem-solving tasks, while struggling students can receive additional support and practice.

4. Real-world applications: Connect mathematical concepts to real-world applications to enhance student engagement and relevance. Personalize learning by incorporating examples and problems that align with students' interests and future career aspirations.

5. Gamification: Incorporate gamified elements, such as math puzzles and online games, to motivate and engage students. Provide rewards and feedback based on individual achievements to foster a sense of progress and accomplishment.

Personalized Learning in Science

Science education involves inquiry, practical experiments, and critical thinking. Personalized learning in science can support students' curiosity, active learning, and understanding of scientific concepts. Here are some strategies for implementing personalized learning in science:

1. Inquiry-based projects: Assign open-ended projects that allow students to explore scientific questions of their choice. Encourage independent research, data collection, and analysis, fostering students' critical thinking and problem-solving skills.
2. Virtual simulations: Utilize virtual simulations and online laboratory experiences to provide students with hands-on learning opportunities. Personalize learning by allowing students to select simulations based on their individual interests or areas of focus.
3. Individualized lab activities: Design laboratory experiments or activities that cater to individual student needs. Provide different levels of complexity and flexibility to accommodate students with diverse abilities and interests.
4. Collaborative research: Foster collaboration and peer learning by assigning group research projects. Encourage students to work in teams, allowing them to learn from one another, exchange ideas, and build communication skills.
5. Field trips and guest speakers: Organize field trips to science museums, research centers, or invite guest speakers to share their expertise. Allow students to choose field trips or guest speakers based on their personal interests or career aspirations.

Personalized Learning in Language Arts

Language arts education encompasses reading, writing, speaking, and listening. Personalized learning in language arts can help students develop strong communication skills, critical literacy, and a love for literature. Here are some strategies for implementing personalized learning in language arts:

1. Choice-based reading: Offer a wide range of reading materials and allow students to choose books that align with their interests and reading levels. Foster a love for reading by giving students ownership of their reading choices.

2. Writing portfolios: Develop individual writing portfolios where students can collect and showcase their best written work. Provide personalized feedback and opportunities for revision to support each student's growth as a writer.

3. Literature circles: Form literature circles, where small groups of students discuss and analyze a specific book. Allow students to select books based on their preferences, promoting personal engagement and deeper understanding of the text.

4. Individual writing conferences: Conduct one-on-one conferences with students to provide personalized feedback and guidance on their writing. Tailor instruction to address each student's specific writing needs and goals.

5. Oral presentations: Assign oral presentations where students can share their thoughts, opinion, and ideas. Allow students to choose presentation topics that are personally meaningful to them, fostering engagement and effective communication skills.

These strategies demonstrate how personalized learning can be implemented in various subject areas. By tailoring instruction to meet individual needs and interests, personalized learning promotes student engagement, motivation, and a deeper understanding of the material. It also empowers students to take ownership of their learning and develop essential skills for lifelong success.

Future directions of personalized learning

Personalized learning has gained significant attention in recent years as a promising approach to education. It involves tailoring instruction to the individual needs, interests, and learning preferences of each student. As technology continues to advance and our understanding of learning evolves, the future of personalized learning holds great potential for enhancing educational experiences and outcomes. In this section, we will explore some of the key future directions of personalized learning.

Adaptive learning technologies and personalized instruction

One of the major advancements in personalized learning is the use of adaptive learning technologies. These technologies leverage artificial intelligence and machine learning algorithms to provide individualized instruction and support to students. Adaptive learning platforms analyze student data, such as their performance on assessments and interactions with learning materials, to develop personalized learning pathways.

In the future, adaptive learning technologies will become even more sophisticated, allowing for real-time adjustments to instructional content and strategies based on students' immediate needs. Personalized instruction will be dynamically tailored to address gaps in understanding, provide targeted interventions, and support the development of specific skills. For example, adaptive learning platforms can provide additional practice exercises or resources for students who are struggling with a particular concept, while offering more challenging or advanced content for those who have mastered the material.

Data-driven decision-making and continuous progress monitoring

As personalized learning becomes more prevalent, the use of data-driven decision-making and continuous progress monitoring will play a crucial role. Educators will rely on data analytics and learning analytics to gather insights about individual student progress, identify areas of improvement, and make informed instructional decisions.

In the future, advancements in data analytics will enable educators to gain deeper insights into student learning patterns and preferences. This will allow for the identification of personalized learning strategies that are most effective for each student. For example, educators can use data to identify specific misconceptions or gaps in understanding that require targeted interventions. This data-driven approach will provide a more comprehensive and nuanced understanding of student learning, leading to more precise and effective instructional practices.

Lifelong learning and personalized learning beyond classrooms

The future of personalized learning will extend beyond traditional classrooms and formal education settings. Lifelong learning, which involves continuous learning throughout one's life, will become more prevalent and personalized. Individuals will have access to a wide range of personalized learning opportunities outside of formal education, such as online courses, micro-credentials, and open educational resources.

Technologies such as learning management systems, virtual reality, and mobile applications will facilitate personalized and flexible learning experiences. Learners will have the freedom to choose what, when, and how they learn, tailoring their educational experiences to their individual goals and interests. Personalized learning will empower individuals to acquire new knowledge and skills throughout their lives, contributing to a more adaptable and dynamic workforce.

Ethical considerations and responsible use of personalized learning

As personalized learning becomes more widespread, ethical considerations will become increasingly important. It is crucial to ensure that personalized learning technologies and practices are implemented responsibly and ethically, safeguarding student privacy, data security, and equity.

Educational institutions and policymakers will need to establish guidelines and regulations to protect students' privacy rights and ensure that data is collected and used in a responsible manner. Ethical considerations should also extend to addressing issues of bias and fairness in algorithmic decision-making processes. For example, algorithms used in adaptive learning systems must be regularly monitored and audited to ensure they do not perpetuate inequalities or reinforce existing biases.

Collaborative and social personalized learning

The future of personalized learning will involve a greater emphasis on collaborative and social learning experiences. Personalized learning should not be seen as isolating students, but rather as a means to enhance collaboration and social interaction.

Technology will enable students to connect and collaborate with their peers and experts from around the world, fostering a global community of learners. Learning environments will incorporate social media platforms, online discussion forums, virtual classrooms, and other collaborative tools to facilitate meaningful interactions and knowledge sharing.

Collaborative personalized learning will also involve students working together on projects and problem-solving activities, leveraging each other's strengths and perspectives. This approach promotes the development of essential skills such as communication, teamwork, and empathy, preparing students for the collaborative work environments of the future.

In conclusion, the future of personalized learning holds tremendous potential for transforming education. With the advancements in adaptive learning technologies, data-driven decision-making, lifelong learning opportunities, ethical considerations, and collaborative approaches, personalized learning will continue to evolve and shape the educational landscape. By embracing these future directions, we can create inclusive, engaging, and effective learning experiences that empower students to reach their full potential.

Global Learning and Virtual Exchange

The importance of global learning in transformative education

In today's interconnected and globalized world, the importance of global learning in transformative education cannot be overstated. Global learning goes beyond traditional academic subjects and encompasses intercultural competency, global perspectives, and cross-cultural understanding. It is about equipping students with the knowledge, skills, and attitudes necessary to navigate an increasingly diverse and interconnected world.

Global learning plays a crucial role in transformative education because it fosters a sense of global citizenship and promotes social responsibility. It encourages students to become active participants in solving global challenges, such as environmental sustainability, poverty reduction, and human rights. By engaging with global issues, students develop a deeper understanding of the complex interconnectedness of the world and the impact of their actions.

One of the key benefits of global learning is its ability to expand students' perspectives beyond their local context. It exposes them to different cultural, social, and political perspectives, challenging their assumptions and biases. Global learning encourages students to question their own perspectives and consider alternative viewpoints, fostering empathy, tolerance, and respect for diversity.

Global learning also promotes critical thinking and problem-solving skills. By examining global issues and their interconnected causes and consequences, students develop the ability to analyze complex problems, evaluate evidence, and propose creative solutions. This prepares them to tackle the multifaceted challenges of the 21st century, where many problems transcend national borders.

To effectively incorporate global learning into transformative education, educators can employ various strategies and approaches. One approach is to integrate global perspectives into the curriculum across different subject areas. For example, students can explore global literature, study historical events from multiple perspectives, or analyze global economic trends. This helps students connect their learning to real-world issues and foster a global mindset.

Another strategy is to incorporate experiential learning opportunities, such as study abroad programs, virtual exchanges, or collaborations with international partners. These experiences allow students to interact directly with people from different cultures, develop cross-cultural communication skills, and gain firsthand knowledge of global issues. Additionally, technology can play a crucial role in facilitating virtual connections and global collaborations, enabling students to learn from and with peers from around the world.

It is important to note that global learning should not be limited to students in privileged settings. Efforts should be made to ensure equitable access to global learning experiences for all students, regardless of their background or socioeconomic status. This can be achieved through community partnerships, scholarships, and digital platforms that provide opportunities for students who may not have the means to travel abroad.

To fully leverage the potential of global learning in transformative education, educators should also consider the ethical dimensions of global engagement. This involves promoting respectful and ethical practices when engaging with local communities and learning from diverse cultural perspectives. It also requires fostering an understanding of our shared global responsibilities and the importance of sustainability and social justice.

In conclusion, global learning is a vital component of transformative education. By exposing students to diverse perspectives, fostering critical thinking and problem-solving skills, and promoting global citizenship, global learning prepares students to become active and engaged global citizens. In an interconnected world facing complex challenges, global learning equips students with the knowledge, skills, and attitudes necessary to effect positive change.

Virtual exchange programs and international collaboration

In today's interconnected world, virtual exchange programs and international collaboration are becoming increasingly important in the field of education. These programs allow students from different countries to engage in meaningful and authentic cross-cultural experiences, promoting global citizenship and intercultural competence. Through virtual exchange, students can interact with peers from around the world, fostering a deeper understanding of different cultures, perspectives, and ways of life.

Benefits of virtual exchange programs

Virtual exchange programs offer numerous benefits for students, educators, and institutions alike. Firstly, they provide an opportunity for students to develop intercultural communication skills. By engaging in online discussions, collaborative projects, and immersive virtual experiences, students can learn to navigate cultural differences and effectively communicate with individuals from diverse backgrounds.

Secondly, virtual exchange programs promote global awareness and understanding. Through virtual interactions, students gain insights into the social, political, and economic issues facing different regions of the world. This broader perspective helps them become more empathetic, open-minded, and responsible global citizens.

Furthermore, virtual exchange programs enhance language proficiency. By interacting with international peers, students have the opportunity to practice and improve their language skills in authentic contexts. This not only strengthens their language abilities but also fosters a greater appreciation for cultural diversity.

Lastly, virtual exchange programs foster collaboration and teamwork. By working on joint projects with peers from different countries, students develop skills in cross-cultural collaboration, problem-solving, and creative thinking. They learn to navigate diverse perspectives, enhance their critical thinking abilities, and develop stronger teamwork skills.

Designing impactful virtual exchange experiences

To ensure the effectiveness of virtual exchange programs, careful design and planning are essential. Here are some key considerations:

1. **Clear learning objectives:** Clearly define the intended learning outcomes of the virtual exchange program. Determine the specific knowledge, skills, and attitudes you want students to develop through their cross-cultural interactions.

2. **Technology selection:** Choose appropriate virtual exchange platforms and tools that facilitate real-time communication, collaboration, and content sharing. Ensure that the technology is accessible, user-friendly, and supports multiple modes of interaction (e.g., video, chat, shared documents).

3. **Curriculum integration:** Integrate virtual exchange activities into the existing curriculum, aligning them with academic standards and learning goals. Identify opportunities for cross-cultural collaboration within subject areas such as language learning, social sciences, and environmental studies.

4. **Intercultural facilitation:** Provide guidance and support for both students and educators to navigate intercultural exchanges. This may include training sessions, cultural sensitivity workshops, and ongoing mentorship to help participants develop intercultural competence.

5. **Assessment strategies:** Develop meaningful assessment strategies to evaluate students' learning and growth during the virtual exchange program. This could include individual and group assignments, reflective journals, and peer feedback.

Overcoming challenges in virtual exchange programs

While virtual exchange programs offer tremendous opportunities, they also come with various challenges that need to be addressed:

1. **Technological limitations:** Access to reliable internet connectivity and suitable hardware can be a significant challenge, particularly in less economically developed regions. Efforts must be made to bridge the digital divide and ensure equal access to technology for all participants.
2. **Time zone differences:** Coordinating virtual interactions across multiple time zones can be challenging. Flexible scheduling and asynchronous communication options should be considered to accommodate participants in different regions.
3. **Language barriers:** Language differences can pose a challenge to effective communication during virtual exchanges. Providing language support resources, translation tools, and fostering a supportive linguistic environment can help overcome these barriers.
4. **Cultural sensitivities:** Participants must be educated about cultural sensitivities and respectful communication practices to avoid unintentional misunderstandings or conflicts. Establishing clear communication guidelines and promoting an inclusive and supportive virtual environment is crucial.

Case studies and best practices

Several successful virtual exchange programs have been implemented worldwide. For example, the Soliya Connect Program connects university students from different regions through facilitated online video dialogues. The Erasmus+ Virtual Exchange project offers a range of online courses, promoting cultural exchange and collaboration among youth in Europe and the Southern Mediterranean region.

Best practices for virtual exchange programs include engaging in structured and facilitated discussions, providing opportunities for meaningful collaboration, and incorporating reflections and debriefings to deepen the learning experience. Regular feedback and evaluation should be conducted to continually improve the program.

Resources for virtual exchange programs

Various resources can support the implementation of virtual exchange programs:

1. **Collaborative platforms:** Platforms like Zoom, Microsoft Teams, or Google Meet provide real-time video conferencing and collaboration tools for virtual exchanges.

2. **Online cultural resources:** Websites like CultureGrams, National Geographic Education, and BBC Learning Languages offer educational materials and cultural insights to support virtual exchange activities.

3. **Virtual exchange networks:** Organizations like iEARN, Soliya, and World Savvy connect educators and students interested in virtual exchange, providing training, resources, and support.

4. **Professional development programs:** Institutions like AFS Intercultural Programs offer professional development opportunities for educators to enhance their skills in facilitating virtual exchange programs.

Closing thoughts

Virtual exchange programs and international collaboration have the potential to revolutionize education by breaking down physical and cultural barriers. By engaging in authentic cross-cultural experiences, students develop invaluable skills that prepare them for an increasingly interconnected world. As educators, it is essential to embrace virtual exchange and maximize its potential to create transformative learning opportunities for all students.

Designing Impactful Virtual Exchange Experiences

In today's interconnected world, virtual exchange programs offer a unique opportunity for students to engage in cross-cultural learning experiences without the need for physical travel. Designing impactful virtual exchange experiences involves careful planning and consideration of various elements to ensure that students can effectively connect with their peers from different countries and cultures. In this section, we will explore the key principles and strategies for creating transformative virtual exchange programs.

Understanding the Goals of Virtual Exchange

Before designing a virtual exchange program, it is important to clearly articulate the goals and objectives. Virtual exchange can serve different purposes, such as promoting intercultural understanding, developing global competencies, fostering collaboration and communication skills, and enhancing language proficiency. By defining the specific goals, educators can tailor the virtual exchange experience to meet the desired outcomes.

Creating Collaborative Learning Environments

Effective virtual exchange experiences rely on creating collaborative learning environments where students from different countries can interact and engage with each other. This can be achieved by using synchronous and asynchronous communication tools, such as video conferencing platforms, discussion forums, and social media platforms. The emphasis should be on facilitating meaningful interactions and fostering collaboration, rather than passive information sharing.

Cultural Sensitivity and Intercultural Communication

Virtual exchange programs bring together students from diverse cultural backgrounds. It is important to promote cultural sensitivity and develop intercultural communication skills among participating students. This can be done by providing resources and training on intercultural competence, facilitating discussions on cultural differences, and encouraging students to explore and embrace different perspectives. It is essential to create a safe and inclusive space for students to learn and appreciate each other's cultures.

Structured and Guided Activities

To ensure that virtual exchange experiences are impactful, it is important to incorporate structured and guided activities that promote active learning. For example, collaborative projects, joint assignments, and group discussions can be designed to encourage students to actively engage with the content and apply their knowledge in real-world contexts. These activities should be designed to foster meaningful interactions, promote critical thinking skills, and encourage students to reflect on their learning.

Technology Integration

Technology plays a crucial role in facilitating virtual exchange experiences. Educators should select appropriate tools and platforms that enable seamless communication and collaboration among students. Video conferencing platforms, collaborative document editors, and virtual whiteboards can be used to enhance student engagement and interaction. It is important to provide technical support and training to ensure that students are familiar with the technology and can effectively participate in virtual exchange activities.

Assessment and Feedback

Assessment and feedback are essential components of virtual exchange experiences. Educators should design assessment tasks that align with the learning goals and objectives of the program. It is important to provide clear criteria and rubrics for evaluating student work and providing constructive feedback. Peer assessment and self-reflection can also be integrated to encourage students to take ownership of their learning and engage in reflective practices.

Evaluation and Continuous Improvement

Virtual exchange programs should be regularly evaluated and refined to ensure their effectiveness and impact. Feedback from students, educators, and other stakeholders should be collected and analyzed to identify strengths and areas for improvement. This feedback can be gathered through surveys, interviews, and focus groups. The insights gained from evaluation should inform the design of future virtual exchange programs and contribute to continuous improvement.

Real-World Connections

To enhance the authenticity and impact of virtual exchange experiences, it is important to connect students with real-world contexts and experiences. This can be done through virtual visits to cultural institutions, guest lectures by experts from different countries, or partnerships with community organizations. These real-world connections provide students with opportunities to apply their learning in meaningful ways and develop a deeper understanding of global issues.

Challenges and Mitigation Strategies

Designing impactful virtual exchange experiences comes with its own set of challenges. Some common challenges include technological barriers, language barriers, time zone differences, and varying levels of digital literacy among participants. Educators should be prepared to address these challenges by providing technical support, offering language support, accommodating different time zones, and providing training on digital literacy skills. Clear communication and ongoing support are essential to ensure a successful experience for all participants.

Example: Virtual Environmental Science Exchange

To illustrate the design principles discussed above, let's consider an example of a virtual exchange program in environmental science. The program aims to promote global awareness of environmental issues and foster collaboration among students from different countries.

In this virtual exchange, participating students are assigned to mixed-country teams and engage in collaborative projects focused on solving real-world environmental challenges. They use video conferencing platforms to communicate and collaborate on their projects. The program includes structured activities such as conducting virtual experiments, analyzing environmental data, and developing action plans for addressing environmental issues.

To enhance intercultural communication, students are provided with resources on cultural differences and given opportunities to share their cultural perspectives on environmental topics. They are encouraged to discuss their experiences, challenges, and solutions in an online forum, fostering a sense of community and shared learning.

Assessment in this virtual exchange program is done through a combination of individual and group tasks. Students are given rubrics and criteria to guide their work, and they receive feedback from both their peers and the educators. The program is continuously evaluated based on student feedback, and improvements are made for subsequent iterations.

By following these design principles and strategies, the virtual exchange program in environmental science creates an impactful learning experience, enabling students to develop global competencies, collaborate effectively, and gain a deeper understanding of environmental issues.

Resources and Further Readings

- Goodyear, P., & Carvalho, L. (2019). The architecture of productive learning networks. In Routledge International Handbook of Learning with Technology in Early Childhood (pp. 161-174). Routledge.

- Spires, H. A., & Milner, A. R. (2021). Envisioning the future of educational technology research: An agenda for the next decade. Journal of Research on Technology in Education, 53(4), 446-459.

- Belisle, F. (2020). Developing cultural competence in students through virtual exchange. In Virtual Exchange in Higher Education (pp. 95-114). Springer.

- Warschauer, M., & Zheng, B. (2020). COVID-19 pandemic as a catalyst for transformative education. Information and Learning Sciences, 121(5/6), 312-321.

- Chen, B., & deNoyelles, A. (2016). Exploring students' learning experience in an international collaborative online learning environment. Distance Education, 37(3), 245-258.

In Summary

Designing impactful virtual exchange experiences requires careful consideration of the goals, collaborative learning environments, intercultural communication, structured activities, technology integration, assessment and feedback, evaluation and continuous improvement, real-world connections, challenges and mitigation strategies. By following these principles and strategies, educators can create transformative virtual exchange programs that enhance students' global awareness, collaboration skills, and intercultural competence.

Overcoming challenges in implementing global learning

Implementing global learning in education can be a transformative experience for both students and educators. It provides opportunities for cross-cultural understanding, global awareness, and cooperation. However, there are several challenges that need to be addressed in order to successfully integrate global learning into the curriculum. In this section, we will explore these challenges and discuss strategies for overcoming them.

Challenge 1: Lack of resources

One of the main challenges in implementing global learning is the lack of resources. Many schools and institutions may not have the necessary funding or access to materials and tools required for global learning experiences. This can include travel costs, technology infrastructure, and educational resources.

Solution: There are various ways to overcome this challenge. One approach is to leverage virtual technologies and online platforms to connect students with individuals from different parts of the world. Virtual exchange programs, video conferences, and online collaborations can provide students with opportunities to interact with their peers globally without the need for expensive travel. Additionally, educators can seek partnerships and collaborations with organizations and institutions that offer grants or funding for global learning initiatives.

Challenge 2: Language and cultural barriers

Another challenge in implementing global learning is the presence of language and cultural barriers. Differences in language and cultural norms can hinder effective communication and collaboration among students from diverse backgrounds.

Solution: To overcome language barriers, educators can incorporate language learning activities into the curriculum. This can include language exchange programs, language learning apps and tools, and collaborative projects that require students to communicate and work together in a second language. Teachers can also provide cultural sensitivity training and resources to help students understand and appreciate different cultural perspectives.

Challenge 3: Lack of teacher training

Many educators may lack the necessary knowledge and skills to effectively integrate global learning into their classrooms. They may be unfamiliar with the cultural nuances, global issues, and the pedagogical approaches required for successful implementation.

Solution: Professional development programs and training workshops can be offered to help teachers develop the necessary skills and knowledge for global learning. These programs can provide educators with opportunities to learn about different cultures, global issues, and innovative teaching strategies. Collaborative learning communities and networks can also provide ongoing support and resources for teachers to share best practices and learn from each other.

Challenge 4: Assessment and evaluation

Assessing and evaluating global learning experiences can be challenging. Traditional assessment methods may not capture the full range of skills and competencies developed through global learning, such as cross-cultural communication, empathy, and global citizenship.

Solution: It is important to design authentic and performance-based assessments that align with the learning outcomes of global learning experiences. This can include project-based assessments, reflective essays, and portfolios that showcase students' learning and growth. Rubrics and criteria can be developed to assess not only the content knowledge but also the development of skills and attitudes related to global learning.

Challenge 5: Resistance to change

Resistance to change is a common challenge when implementing any new educational initiative, including global learning. Teachers, administrators, and even students may be resistant to embrace global learning due to various reasons such as fear of the unknown, cultural biases, or reluctance to deviate from traditional teaching methods.

Solution: To overcome resistance to change, it is important to provide professional development opportunities that address the concerns and biases of educators. Demonstrating the benefits and positive outcomes of global learning through case studies and success stories can also help alleviate resistance. Additionally, involving key stakeholders in the decision-making process and seeking their input can foster a sense of ownership and commitment to global learning initiatives.

Challenge 6: Ethical considerations

Implementing global learning raises ethical considerations, especially when it involves cross-cultural interactions and exposure to global issues that may be sensitive or controversial. It is essential to ensure that global learning experiences are respectful, inclusive, and promote understanding and dialogue.

Solution: Educators should provide guidance and create safe spaces for students to explore and discuss sensitive global issues. They should also emphasize the importance of respect, empathy, and cultural sensitivity throughout the learning process. Collaborating with local communities and partner institutions can provide valuable insights and perspectives to ensure that global learning experiences are ethically sound.

In conclusion, while implementing global learning in education comes with its challenges, it is a worthwhile endeavor that can broaden students' horizons and prepare them for a globalized world. By addressing the challenges of resources, language and cultural barriers, lack of teacher training, assessment and evaluation, resistance to change, and ethical considerations, educators can create inclusive and transformative global learning experiences for their students.

Case studies and best practices in global learning

Global learning is an essential component of transformative education, as it fosters students' understanding of different cultures, perspectives, and global challenges. In this section, we will explore various case studies and best practices in global learning, highlighting successful approaches and strategies that educators can implement in their classrooms.

Case Study 1: Virtual Cultural Exchange

One effective way to promote global learning is through virtual cultural exchange programs. This case study examines a project where students from a school in the United States collaborated with students from a school in India. The goal of the project was to promote cross-cultural understanding and address shared global challenges.

To start, the teachers designed a curriculum that integrated cultural exchange activities with core subject areas. They utilized a video conferencing platform to facilitate real-time communication and collaboration between the students. This allowed them to engage in conversations, share their perspectives, and work on joint projects.

Throughout the project, students had opportunities to learn about each other's cultures, traditions, and daily lives. They researched common global challenges like climate change and poverty and discussed potential solutions from their respective contexts. They also collaborated on creating multimedia presentations, artwork, and essays that reflected their understanding and insights.

The virtual cultural exchange not only enhanced students' cultural competency but also developed their critical thinking, communication, and collaboration skills. It fostered empathy, respect, and appreciation for diversity among the participants. Moreover, it created a sense of global citizenship and a shared responsibility for addressing global challenges.

Best Practice 1: Global Collaborative Projects

Engaging students in global collaborative projects is an effective best practice in global learning. By working together on meaningful projects, students develop a deeper understanding of global issues and acquire important skills for the 21st century.

One example of a global collaborative project is the "World Without Borders" initiative. In this project, students from different countries collaborate on solving real-world problems related to sustainability. They use online platforms and tools to communicate, share ideas, and work on joint projects. Through this collaboration, students gain insights into different cultural perspectives, problem-solving strategies, and innovative solutions.

To implement this best practice, educators can start by identifying partner schools or organizations interested in collaborating on global projects. They can design project-based learning experiences that address global challenges and encourage students to think critically, propose solutions, and take action. Technology tools such as video conferencing, collaborative platforms, and project management software can facilitate communication and project coordination.

By participating in global collaborative projects, students become global citizens who can collaborate with peers from diverse backgrounds, appreciate different perspectives, and work towards a more sustainable and equitable world.

Case Study 2: Study Abroad Programs

Another powerful approach to global learning is through study abroad programs. This case study examines a study abroad program where high school students from the United Kingdom spent a semester in Japan.

During their time in Japan, the students lived with host families, attended local schools, and engaged in cultural and educational activities. They had the opportunity to experience the Japanese education system, learn the language, and immerse themselves in the local culture.

The study abroad program focused on a range of academic subjects, including history, language, art, and cultural studies. Students had the chance to visit historical sites, museums, and attend traditional cultural events. They also collaborated with Japanese students on group projects, fostering intercultural exchange and friendship.

This study abroad program not only enhanced students' language proficiency and cultural understanding but also developed their adaptability, resilience, and independence. It broadened their horizons, challenged their preconceived notions, and encouraged them to become global ambassadors.

Best Practice 2: Virtual Simulations

Virtual simulations are an innovative best practice that allows students to experience global scenarios and challenges in a simulated environment. These simulations provide opportunities for students to understand complex global issues and develop problem-solving skills.

One example of a virtual simulation is the "Global Diplomacy Simulation," where students take on the role of diplomats representing different countries. They engage in diplomatic negotiations, develop policy recommendations, and navigate global conflicts. The simulation incorporates real-world issues such as climate change, international security, and economic cooperation.

To implement virtual simulations, educators can leverage virtual reality, online platforms, and simulation tools. They can design scenarios that simulate real-world situations, provide students with background information and resources, and guide them through the decision-making process.

Virtual simulations help students develop critical thinking, negotiation, and collaboration skills while gaining a deeper understanding of global issues. They provide a safe and immersive environment for students to explore complex global challenges and develop innovative solutions.

In conclusion, case studies and best practices in global learning demonstrate the effectiveness of various approaches in promoting cross-cultural understanding, global citizenship, and 21st-century skills. Through virtual cultural exchange, global collaborative projects, study abroad programs, and virtual simulations, students develop a global perspective, appreciation for diversity, and the capability to address global challenges. By implementing these best practices, educators can create transformative learning environments that prepare students to thrive in an interconnected and interdependent world.

Cultivating Global Competence in Students

Cultivating global competence in students is essential in today's interconnected and interdependent world. As societies become more diverse and connected, it is crucial for students to develop the skills, knowledge, and attitudes necessary to understand and engage with global issues. Global competence prepares students to navigate the complexities of our globalized world, embrace cultural diversity, and effectively collaborate with others from different backgrounds.

Defining Global Competence

Global competence refers to the ability to understand and engage with issues of global significance. It involves a combination of knowledge, skills, attitudes, and values that enable individuals to critically analyze global challenges, appreciate cultural differences, communicate across cultures, and take responsible action to address global issues.

Global competence encompasses the following key components:

- **Knowledge of the World:** Students need to have a solid understanding of global issues, including social, cultural, economic, and environmental dimensions. This includes knowledge of global history, geography, current events, and global systems.

- **Intercultural Skills:** Students must develop the ability to communicate and collaborate effectively with individuals from diverse cultural backgrounds. This includes developing empathy, respect, and the ability to navigate cultural differences.

- **Critical Thinking:** Students should be able to analyze complex global issues, evaluate multiple perspectives, and recognize bias. They should develop the ability to think critically and independently to solve global challenges.

- **Problem-solving:** Students need to acquire the skills to identify and address global problems through innovative and sustainable solutions. This involves creativity, adaptability, and the ability to work collaboratively in diverse teams.

- **Ethical Responsibility:** Students should develop a sense of ethical responsibility towards global issues and recognize the impact of their choices and actions on the world. They should be aware of social justice, human rights, and environmental sustainability.

- **Global Citizenship:** Students should embrace the principles of global citizenship, which include a sense of belonging to a global community, an understanding of interconnectedness, and a commitment to making a positive difference in the world.

Approaches to Cultivating Global Competence

Cultivating global competence in students requires intentional and integrated approaches within the educational system. Here are some strategies and practices to foster global competence:

1. **Global Awareness in the Curriculum:** Incorporate global issues and perspectives across different subject areas. Infuse global content into lessons, projects, and assessments to provide students with a broad understanding of global challenges.

2. **Global Collaborative Projects:** Engage students in collaborative projects that involve working with peers from different countries or cultural backgrounds. These projects promote cross-cultural understanding, communication, and collaboration skills.

3. **Intercultural Experiences:** Provide opportunities for students to engage in meaningful intercultural experiences. This can include hosting international

students, participating in exchange programs, or engaging in virtual cultural exchanges.

4. **Language Learning:** Promote the learning of foreign languages to enhance students' ability to communicate and connect with people from different cultures. Language learning fosters empathy, cultural understanding, and effective communication.
5. **Service Learning:** Encourage students to participate in service-learning projects that address global issues. This allows students to apply their knowledge and skills to real-world problems while fostering a sense of responsibility and empathy.
6. **Global Competence Reflection:** Incorporate reflection activities to help students develop a deeper understanding of their own cultural perspectives and biases. Reflection promotes self-awareness, empathy, and the ability to challenge assumptions.
7. **Guest Speakers and Experts:** Invite guest speakers and experts from various global contexts to share their experiences and insights. This broadens students' perspectives and exposes them to different cultural viewpoints.
8. **Technology Integration:** Use technology tools to connect students with peers from different countries, facilitate virtual collaborations, and access global resources. Technology can provide authentic and immersive global learning experiences.
9. **Community Engagement:** Encourage students to get involved in local and global community initiatives. Engaging with diverse communities helps students develop a sense of responsibility and understand the interconnectedness of global issues.
10. **Teacher Professional Development:** Provide professional development opportunities for teachers to enhance their own global competence. Teachers play a key role in fostering global competence in students, and their own understanding and skills are vital.

Assessment of Global Competence

Assessing global competence requires a multifaceted approach that goes beyond traditional testing methods. Here are some assessment strategies to consider:

- **Performance Tasks:** Design performance-based tasks that require students to apply their global competence skills and knowledge. These tasks can include research projects, simulations, presentations, and debates.

- **Portfolios:** Implement portfolio assessments that allow students to showcase their growth and development in global competence over time. Portfolios can include samples of student work, reflections, and self-assessments.

- **Rubrics:** Develop rubrics that clearly define the criteria for global competence. Rubrics help provide clear expectations and allow for consistent and fair assessment of students' skills, attitudes, and knowledge.

- **Peer and Self-assessment:** Encourage peer and self-assessment to promote student reflection and engagement in the assessment process. Peer feedback and self-reflection help students develop a deeper understanding of their own global competence.

- **Authentic Assessments:** Incorporate authentic assessments that mirror real-world problem-solving scenarios. Authentic assessments can include case studies, community projects, and internships that require students to apply global competence skills.

- **Global Competence Rubric:** Develop a global competence rubric that outlines the specific indicators and levels of proficiency for each component of global competence. This rubric guides both teachers and students in assessing and developing global competence.

Challenges and Considerations

While cultivating global competence is essential, there are challenges and considerations to be mindful of in the process:

- **Cultural Sensitivity:** Recognize the importance of cultural sensitivity and avoid promoting stereotypes or biases. Encourage students to adopt an open-minded and respectful attitude towards cultural differences.

- **Equitable and Inclusive Approaches:** Ensure that global competence education is accessible to all students, regardless of their backgrounds or abilities. Design inclusive strategies that value diverse perspectives and actively promote equity.

- **Global/local Balance:** Strike a balance between global understanding and appreciation for local contexts. Help students recognize the interconnectedness of global issues while also appreciating and addressing local challenges.

- **Professional Development Support:** Provide ongoing professional development opportunities for teachers to build their own global competence and effectively integrate global perspectives into their teaching practice.

- **Partnerships and Collaborations:** Foster partnerships with schools, organizations, and communities around the world to enhance global learning opportunities. Collaborating with global partners enriches students' understanding and helps them develop a global mindset.

Resources for Cultivating Global Competence

There are various resources available to support the cultivation of global competence in students:

- **Global Education Network:** Join global education networks and communities of practice to connect with educators and access resources, best practices, and professional development opportunities.

- **Global Education Organizations:** Explore organizations dedicated to global education, such as the Asia Society's Global Learning in Elementary Education, the Global Education Benchmark Group, and the World Savvy.

- **Global Competence Frameworks:** Familiarize yourself with global competence frameworks, such as the Global Competence Matrix by the Organisation for Economic Co-operation and Development (OECD) and the Global Competencies Framework by the Asia Society.

- **Online Global Learning Platforms:** Utilize online platforms that provide virtual global learning experiences, such as Virtual Exchange, eTwinning, and iEARN.

- **Open Educational Resources:** Access open educational resources that include global content and lessons, such as the Global Oneness Project, Worlds of Words, and the Global Learning Opportunities in the Classroom.

- **UN Sustainable Development Goals:** Integrate the United Nations' Sustainable Development Goals (SDGs) into your curriculum to help students understand and take action on global challenges.

Conclusion

In an increasingly interconnected world, cultivating global competence in students is crucial for their personal and academic growth. By incorporating global perspectives, intercultural experiences, and a focus on ethical responsibility, educators can empower students to understand, appreciate, and actively engage with global issues. Through intentional integration of global competence in education, we can prepare students to be responsible global citizens who contribute positively to our shared future.

Technology Tools for Global Learning and Virtual Exchange

In today's interconnected world, technology has revolutionized the way we learn and communicate. Global learning and virtual exchange have become increasingly important in preparing students for the globalized workforce and fostering intercultural understanding. This section explores the technology tools that facilitate global learning and virtual exchange experiences, enabling students to connect with peers from different countries and engage in collaborative learning activities.

Video Conferencing

Video conferencing platforms such as Zoom, Skype, and Google Meet have transformed the way students can interact with others from around the world. These tools allow for real-time audio and video communication, breaking down geographical barriers. Teachers can organize virtual classrooms and facilitate discussions between students from different countries. This technology tool enables engaging face-to-face interactions, promotes cultural exchange, and supports collaborative learning experiences.

For example, students from different countries can collaborate on group projects or engage in language exchange activities through video conferencing. They can share perspectives, learn about different cultures, and work together to solve problems. This not only enhances their understanding of global issues but also develops their communication and collaboration skills, which are essential in the 21st century.

Online Platforms for Intercultural Collaboration

There are various online platforms specifically designed for intercultural collaboration and project-based learning. These platforms connect students from different countries, providing a virtual space for them to collaborate on projects, share ideas, and learn together.

For instance, platforms like ePals and iEARN bring together students and teachers from around the world, allowing them to work on collaborative projects focused on topics such as social justice, environmental sustainability, or cultural exchange. Through these platforms, students can engage in meaningful discussions, share their perspectives, and develop a deeper understanding of global issues.

These online platforms also provide tools for file sharing, creating digital portfolios, and facilitating peer feedback. Students can upload their work, receive feedback from their peers in different countries, and engage in reflective discussions. This not only promotes intercultural understanding but also enhances students' critical thinking and communication skills.

Virtual Reality (VR) and Augmented Reality (AR)

Virtual reality and augmented reality technologies open up new possibilities for global learning and virtual exchange. VR allows students to explore virtual environments that simulate real-world experiences, while AR overlays digital content onto the real world. These technologies provide immersive and interactive experiences, enabling students to visit different countries, landmarks, and cultural heritage sites without leaving the classroom.

For example, Google Expeditions is a VR platform that offers virtual field trips to various global destinations. Students can explore historical sites, natural wonders, and cultural landmarks. Similarly, AR applications like JigSpace can bring 3D models, animations, and interactive content into the classroom, allowing students to visualize complex concepts and artifacts from different cultures.

By integrating VR and AR technologies into global learning and virtual exchange, students can gain firsthand experiences, develop empathy for different cultures, and deepen their understanding of global issues. These technologies also foster curiosity, creativity, and critical thinking skills, as students actively engage in virtual environments and make connections between the virtual and real worlds.

Online Collaboration and Learning Management Systems

Online collaboration tools and learning management systems (LMS) play a crucial role in supporting global learning and virtual exchange. These platforms provide a centralized space for students and teachers to communicate, collaborate, and access learning resources.

For instance, platforms like Google Workspace for Education, Microsoft Teams, and Moodle offer features such as discussion boards, shared documents, and online assignments. Students can work together on group projects, participate in online discussions, and access course materials from anywhere in the world. Moreover, these platforms facilitate asynchronous learning, allowing students to engage in learning activities at their own pace and overcome time zone differences.

These online collaboration and LMS platforms also provide features for assessment and feedback. Teachers can create online quizzes, grade assignments, and provide timely feedback to students. This enables continuous assessment and supports the development of global competencies.

Online Language Learning Platforms

Language learning is an integral part of global learning and virtual exchange. Online language learning platforms offer interactive and immersive experiences for students to learn new languages and communicate with speakers of different languages.

Platforms like Duolingo, Rosetta Stone, and Babbel provide gamified language learning experiences. These platforms offer personalized language courses, interactive exercises, and real-time feedback. Students can practice their language skills, engage in language exchange activities, and communicate with language learners from different countries. This not only enhances their language proficiency but also promotes cultural understanding and empathy.

Moreover, online language learning platforms often incorporate social features, such as language communities and discussion forums, where learners can collaborate, ask questions, and receive support from native speakers. This fosters a sense of community and provides opportunities for authentic language practice.

Online Simulations and Virtual Laboratories

Online simulations and virtual laboratories offer students the opportunity to engage in realistic, hands-on learning experiences, even when physical access to labs or equipment is limited.

For example, PhET Interactive Simulations provide a collection of interactive simulations in various science fields. Students can explore scientific phenomena, conduct virtual experiments, and analyze data. These simulations enable students to develop scientific inquiry skills, make predictions, and draw conclusions in a virtual environment.

Similarly, virtual laboratories in subjects like physics, chemistry, and biology provide a range of experiments that can be conducted online. Students can manipulate variables, observe outcomes, and engage in data analysis. This not only develops their practical skills but also promotes a deeper understanding of scientific concepts.

By incorporating online simulations and virtual laboratories into global learning and virtual exchange, students can engage in collaborative problem-solving, compare results with peers from different countries, and gain exposure to different experimental techniques. This fosters a shared learning experience and encourages students to think critically and scientifically.

Conclusion

Technology tools have significantly expanded the possibilities for global learning and virtual exchange. Through video conferencing, online platforms, virtual reality, collaboration tools, language learning platforms, and online simulations, students have access to immersive and interactive learning experiences with peers from around the world. These technology tools foster intercultural understanding, develop global competencies, promote collaboration, and enable students to address global challenges collectively. The future of global learning lies in the continued integration of technology and the innovative use of these tools to create meaningful and transformative learning experiences for all students.

Integrating Cultural Diversity in the Curriculum

In today's increasingly globalized and interconnected world, it is essential for education systems to cultivate cultural diversity and promote inclusive learning environments. Integrating cultural diversity in the curriculum has numerous benefits for students, including developing cultural awareness, fostering empathy and tolerance, and preparing students for a multicultural society. This section will explore strategies and approaches for effectively integrating cultural diversity in the curriculum, as well as provide examples and resources for educators.

Understanding Cultural Diversity

Before delving into the strategies, it is important to have a solid understanding of cultural diversity. Cultural diversity refers to the presence of a variety of cultural groups within a society or educational setting. These cultural groups can differ in terms of language, beliefs, traditions, values, and customs. It is crucial to recognize that cultural diversity goes beyond race and ethnicity; it encompasses various aspects of identity, including gender, religion, socio-economic status, and ability.

Cultural diversity enriches the learning experience by exposing students to different perspectives, histories, and ways of life. It highlights the importance of recognizing and valuing individual and collective identities, promoting inclusivity, and challenging stereotypes and biases. By embracing cultural diversity, educators can create a curriculum that reflects the diverse experiences and voices of their students.

Strategies for Integrating Cultural Diversity

1. Inclusive Curriculum Design: Designing an inclusive curriculum involves intentionally incorporating diverse perspectives, narratives, and resources into instructional materials, lesson plans, and assessments. This can be done by selecting diverse readings, textbooks, and multimedia resources that reflect a range of cultures and viewpoints. Additionally, educators can incorporate examples, case studies, and projects that highlight the contributions of different cultural groups. It is crucial to ensure that the curriculum is authentic, respectful, and free from stereotypes or misrepresentations.

2. Culturally Responsive Pedagogy: Culturally responsive pedagogy emphasizes the importance of connecting with students' cultural backgrounds and experiences. Educators can create a supportive and inclusive learning environment by incorporating students' cultural traditions, languages, and practices into the classroom. This can be achieved by using culturally relevant examples, incorporating students' languages in instruction, and drawing connections between students' experiences and the curriculum. Culturally responsive pedagogy also involves fostering dialogue and encouraging students to share their perspectives and experiences.

3. Collaborative Learning: Collaborative learning activities provide opportunities for students from different cultural backgrounds to work together, exchange ideas, and learn from each other. Group projects, cooperative learning tasks, and peer-to-peer discussions can facilitate cross-cultural understanding and promote inclusivity. It is essential to create a safe and supportive environment where all students feel valued and respected, and where diverse perspectives are encouraged and appreciated.

4. Community Engagement: Engaging with local communities and cultural organizations can enrich the curriculum and provide students with authentic and

meaningful learning experiences. Field trips, guest speakers, and partnerships with community organizations can expose students to different cultures, traditions, and perspectives. This hands-on approach allows students to interact with individuals from diverse backgrounds and gain a deeper understanding of cultural diversity.

5. Professional Development: Providing educators with professional development opportunities focused on cultural diversity and inclusive practices is crucial for successful implementation. Training sessions, workshops, and collaborative learning communities can equip educators with the knowledge, skills, and resources necessary to effectively integrate cultural diversity in the curriculum. It is important to foster a culture of continuous learning and reflection among educators, encouraging them to critically examine their own biases and assumptions.

Examples and Resources

To support educators in integrating cultural diversity in the curriculum, various resources exist. The following are just a few examples:

1. Teaching Tolerance (www.tolerance.org): Teaching Tolerance provides a wealth of free resources, including lesson plans, readings, videos, and professional development materials focused on promoting diversity, equity, and inclusivity in education.

2. UNESCO's Education for Sustainable Development (ESD) framework: UNESCO's ESD framework emphasizes the importance of inclusive and equitable education that respects cultural diversity. It provides guidelines and resources for educators to create transformative learning experiences that promote sustainable development and intercultural dialogue.

3. Global Oneness Project (www.globalonenessproject.org): The Global Oneness Project offers a collection of free multimedia resources, including films, photo essays, and lesson plans, that explore cultural diversity, global issues, and social justice topics. These resources aim to foster empathy, understanding, and critical thinking skills among students.

4. Ethnic Studies Curricula: Some educational institutions have developed ethnic studies curricula tailored to specific regions or communities. These curricula provide in-depth exploration of the history, culture, and contributions of diverse ethnic groups, providing educators with a starting point for integrating cultural diversity into their classrooms.

5. Educator Networks and Communities: Joining educator networks and communities focused on cultural diversity can provide valuable support and resources. Online platforms such as Edutopia (www.edutopia.org) and Teaching

Channel (www.teachingchannel.com) offer a range of videos, articles, and discussion forums where educators can share ideas, best practices, and lesson plans related to integrating cultural diversity in the curriculum.

Challenges and Considerations

Integrating cultural diversity in the curriculum may come with various challenges and considerations that educators should be aware of:

1. Balance and Representation: Finding the right balance and ensuring accurate representation of different cultural groups can be challenging. Educators should conduct thorough research and consult diverse sources to ensure that the curriculum provides a comprehensive and accurate portrayal of cultural diversity.

2. Sensitivity and Respect: Educators need to approach cultural diversity with sensitivity and respect. It is important to avoid cultural appropriation or tokenism and to foster an environment where students feel comfortable discussing and sharing their cultural backgrounds.

3. Inclusive Assessment: Assessment methods should be inclusive and provide equal opportunities for students from diverse cultural backgrounds to demonstrate their knowledge and skills. Educators should consider using a variety of assessment formats that accommodate different learning styles and cultural norms.

4. Ongoing Reflection and Adaptation: Integrating cultural diversity in the curriculum is an ongoing process that requires continuous reflection, learning, and adaptation. Educators should regularly evaluate and revise their curriculum and teaching practices to ensure they align with the evolving needs and diversity of their students.

Exercises

1. Research and document the demographic and cultural diversity of your community or school. How does this diversity manifest in various aspects of the community/school?

2. Create a lesson plan that incorporates diverse perspectives and cultural resources related to a subject of your choice. Consider how you can engage students in meaningful discussions and activities that promote cross-cultural understanding.

3. Reflect on your own cultural biases and assumptions. How might these biases impact your teaching and interactions with students? Identify strategies to address and overcome these biases.

4. Engage in a book study or discussion group focused on a book or research article related to cultural diversity in education. Discuss the implications and applications for your own teaching practice.

5. Conduct a cultural awareness activity with your students, such as a cultural fair, where students have the opportunity to share and learn about different cultural traditions, customs, and artifacts.

Remember, the exercises are designed to promote self-reflection, awareness, and action towards creating a culturally diverse and inclusive curriculum. Actively engaging in these exercises will facilitate your personal and professional growth as an educator.

Global learning in different subject areas

Global learning is an essential component of transformative education in today's interconnected world. It provides students with the knowledge, skills, and perspectives needed to understand and engage with global issues, cultures, and communities. In this section, we will explore how global learning can be integrated into different subject areas to promote cross-cultural understanding, critical thinking, and global citizenship.

Social Studies and Geography

In social studies and geography, global learning can take many forms. Students can explore the interconnectedness of different regions, study the impact of globalization on economies and cultures, and analyze global issues such as climate change, migration, and inequality. They can also develop skills in map reading, spatial analysis, and data interpretation to understand the world from a geographical perspective.

To promote global learning in social studies and geography, teachers can incorporate case studies and real-world examples from different countries and regions. They can encourage students to examine their own cultural biases and challenge stereotypes through research and dialogue. Collaborative projects and virtual exchanges with students from other countries can also enhance cross-cultural understanding and promote empathy.

Science and Environmental Studies

In science and environmental studies, global learning focuses on understanding and addressing global challenges such as climate change, biodiversity loss, and pollution. Students can investigate the interconnectedness of ecosystems and human activities, analyze scientific data from around the world, and explore sustainable solutions to global environmental issues.

To integrate global learning into science and environmental studies, teachers can engage students in citizen science projects that involve collecting data and collaborating with scientists from different parts of the world. They can also incorporate case studies and examples that highlight the diversity of ecological systems and the impact of human activities on global ecosystems. Virtual field trips and simulations can provide students with immersive experiences to understand global environmental issues.

Language Arts and Literature

Language arts and literature provide a unique opportunity for global learning by exploring diverse cultures, perspectives, and narratives from around the world. Students can read literature from different countries, engage in discussions about social and cultural issues, and analyze how language and storytelling shape our understanding of the world.

To incorporate global learning into language arts and literature, teachers can select texts from a variety of cultures and time periods, allowing students to explore different worldviews and perspectives. They can also facilitate cross-cultural conversations and encourage students to reflect on their own cultural identities and biases. Collaborative projects with students from other countries, such as writing exchanges or book clubs, can foster global connections and promote intercultural understanding.

Mathematics and Economics

Mathematics and economics might seem disconnected from global issues, but they play a crucial role in understanding and solving global challenges. In mathematics, students can analyze data related to global trends, such as population growth or economic indicators. They can also explore how mathematical models can be used to tackle complex global problems, such as predicting the spread of diseases or optimizing resource allocation.

In economics, students can study global interdependencies, trade patterns, and the impact of economic policies on different countries. They can analyze data on global inequality, poverty rates, and sustainable development goals. Students can also engage in simulations and role-playing activities to understand the complexities of international trade and economic cooperation.

By integrating global learning into mathematics and economics, teachers can help students develop a broader perspective on the role of these subjects in addressing global challenges. They can encourage critical thinking and problem-solving skills by involving students in real-world economic and mathematical problems with global implications.

Physical Education and Health

Physical education and health provide opportunities to foster global learning by exploring the diversity of physical activities, sports, and health practices across cultures. Students can learn about traditional sports from different countries, examine cultural attitudes towards physical activity and health, and explore global health issues and initiatives.

To promote global learning in physical education and health, teachers can expose students to a variety of physical activities from different cultures. They can discuss the cultural significance of sports and physical activities and encourage students to appreciate and respect diverse approaches to health and wellness. Teachers can also discuss global health challenges, such as infectious diseases or access to healthcare, and empower students to take action through awareness campaigns or community service projects.

The Arts

The arts offer a powerful way to foster global learning by exploring diverse artistic traditions, cultural expressions, and perspectives. Students can study visual arts, music, dance, and theater from different cultures, examine how art reflects social and historical contexts, and engage in creative projects that promote intercultural understanding.

To integrate global learning into the arts, teachers can expose students to diverse artistic traditions and encourage them to explore their own creativity through different cultural lenses. They can organize cultural performances or exhibitions that celebrate the diversity of artistic expressions. Collaborative projects with artists from different parts of the world can also provide students with opportunities to learn about different artistic techniques and traditions.

Conclusion

Global learning is a crucial component of transformative education as it prepares students to navigate an increasingly interconnected and diverse world. By integrating global perspectives into different subject areas, educators can foster cross-cultural understanding, critical thinking, and global citizenship. Through engaging with different cultures, students develop empathy, respect for diversity, and the skills needed to address global challenges collaboratively.

Future directions of global learning

In recent years, the education landscape has been rapidly evolving, driven by technological advancements and the increasing interconnectedness of our world. Global learning, which emphasizes the development of global competence and understanding, has emerged as a critical component of education in the 21st century. As we look to the future, several key trends and directions are shaping the future of global learning.

1. Fostering Intercultural Competence

One of the key future directions of global learning is the emphasis on fostering intercultural competence among learners. In an increasingly globalized world, it is essential for students to develop the skills and mindset necessary to engage with individuals from diverse backgrounds. Educators must cultivate an environment that promotes understanding, empathy, and respect for different cultures.

Example :

One way to foster intercultural competence is through virtual exchange programs, where students from different countries can interact and collaborate on projects. This allows them to gain insights into each other's cultures, traditions, and perspectives, promoting cross-cultural understanding and appreciation.

2. Global Citizenship Education

Global citizenship education is another important future direction of global learning. It focuses on empowering students to become active and responsible global citizens who are aware of global issues and are equipped with the knowledge and skills to address these challenges.

Example :

Incorporating global citizenship education into the curriculum can involve exploring topics such as sustainable development, human rights, social justice, and environmental conservation. Students can engage in collaborative projects that promote activism and social change, helping them develop a sense of agency and responsibility in tackling global challenges.

3. Technology-Enabled Global Learning

As technology continues to advance, it is revolutionizing the way we learn and connect with others. Technology-enabled global learning offers exciting opportunities to facilitate global collaboration and the exchange of ideas among learners across the globe.

Example :

Online platforms and virtual classrooms allow students to connect with peers from different countries, engage in real-time discussions, and work on joint projects. Emerging technologies such as virtual reality can provide immersive experiences that simulate different cultural environments, enhancing students' understanding and appreciation of global diversity.

4. Expanding Access to Global Learning

Expanding access to global learning is crucial to ensure equitable opportunities for all learners. Digital tools and online platforms can play a significant role in breaking down barriers and providing access to high-quality global learning experiences, irrespective of geographical constraints.

Example :

Open educational resources (OER) and Massive Open Online Courses (MOOCs) provide free or low-cost learning materials and courses, making global learning accessible to a wider audience. Furthermore, initiatives focusing on bridging the digital divide and providing internet connectivity to underserved areas can help democratize global learning opportunities.

5. Holistic Assessment of Global Competence

In order to effectively incorporate global learning in education, it is important to develop assessment frameworks that accurately measure and evaluate students' global competence. Traditional assessment methods may not adequately capture the diverse skills and perspectives required for successful global citizenship.

Example :

New approaches such as competency-based assessments, portfolio assessments, and authentic assessments can provide a more comprehensive and holistic view of students' global competence. These assessments can focus on skills such as intercultural communication, critical thinking, problem-solving, and collaborative problem-solving, which are essential for navigating the complexities of a globalized world.

In conclusion, the future of global learning holds immense potential for transforming education and preparing learners to thrive in an interconnected world. By integrating intercultural competence, global citizenship education, technology-enabled learning, equitable access, and holistic assessments, we can equip students with the knowledge, skills, and attitudes needed to become global citizens and address the pressing challenges of our time. As educators, it is crucial to embrace these future directions and play a vital role in shaping the global learning landscape.

Social and Emotional Learning

The importance of social and emotional learning (SEL)

Social and emotional learning (SEL) plays a crucial role in the holistic development of students. It encompasses the skills, knowledge, attitudes, and behaviors that enable individuals to understand and manage their own emotions, establish and maintain positive relationships, and make responsible decisions. SEL is not only essential for academic success but also for the overall well-being and success of students in their personal and professional lives.

Benefits of social and emotional learning

SEL has been shown to have numerous benefits for students. Firstly, it enhances their emotional well-being by helping them develop self-awareness and self-regulation skills. Students who are aware of their emotions and can manage them effectively are more likely to experience positive mental health and resilience.

Secondly, SEL promotes positive relationships and social skills. It equips students with the ability to empathize, communicate effectively, and collaborate with others. These skills are crucial for maintaining healthy friendships, resolving conflicts, and building strong relationships with peers, teachers, and family members.

Furthermore, SEL fosters responsible decision-making. Students learn to consider the consequences of their actions, make ethical choices, and think critically. This empowers them to make informed decisions related to their academics, personal lives, and future careers.

Moreover, SEL has been linked to improved academic performance. When students have a strong foundation in social and emotional skills, they are better able to focus on their studies, manage stress, and persist in the face of challenges. This ultimately leads to higher levels of motivation, engagement, and academic achievement.

Incorporating SEL into the curriculum

Integrating SEL into the curriculum requires a holistic approach that involves educators, administrators, and the entire school community. Here are some strategies for incorporating SEL into the curriculum:

- Explicit instruction: Teachers can explicitly teach social and emotional skills through dedicated lessons or within the context of academic subjects. This can include activities such as role-playing, discussions, and reflective writing.
- Integration: SEL can be integrated into various subject areas, such as English, history, and science. For example, literature can be used to explore different emotions and perspectives, while history can provide opportunities to discuss empathy and social justice.
- Creating a positive classroom climate: Teachers can establish a positive classroom environment that promotes a sense of belonging, respect, and emotional safety. This can be achieved through practices such as morning meetings, class agreements, and cooperative learning activities.
- SEL assessments: Regular assessment of social and emotional skills can help monitor students' progress and inform instructional practices. Assessments can be in the form of self-reflection, peer feedback, or rubrics that measure skills like self-management and responsible decision-making.
- Community partnerships: Collaborating with community organizations, mental health professionals, and families can provide additional support and resources for SEL implementation.

Addressing challenges in implementing SEL

While there are many benefits to implementing SEL, there are also challenges that need to be addressed. Some of these challenges include:

- Time constraints: Teachers often face time constraints due to the demands of the curriculum. Integrating SEL into the existing curriculum may require careful planning and prioritization of instructional time.
- Teacher training and support: Teachers need training and ongoing support to effectively implement SEL strategies in the classroom. Professional development opportunities, coaching, and access to resources can help build teachers' capacity in SEL instruction.
- Cultural relevance and inclusivity: SEL programs should be culturally relevant and inclusive, taking into account the diverse backgrounds and experiences of students. This requires the selection of materials and strategies that resonate with students from different cultures and communities.

- Assessment and evaluation: Assessing social and emotional skills can be challenging as they are often subjective and context-dependent. Finding appropriate assessment tools and methods that are valid, reliable, and age-appropriate is crucial.

Case studies and best practices

To illustrate the effectiveness of SEL implementation, here are a couple of case studies:

Case Study 1: Second Step Program

The Second Step program is a widely-used SEL curriculum that has shown positive outcomes in promoting students' social-emotional development. Evaluations of the program have demonstrated improvements in students' self-regulation, problem-solving, and empathy skills. The program provides comprehensive lessons and resources for teachers to integrate SEL into their classrooms.

Case Study 2: Restorative Practices

Restorative practices, an SEL approach, focus on building and repairing relationships within the school community. This approach involves using circles, conferences, and other restorative processes to address conflicts and harmful behavior. Research has shown that schools that implement restorative practices experience a decrease in disciplinary issues, improved school climate, and increased student engagement.

Additional resources and tools

Educators can find additional resources and tools to support SEL implementation:

- Collaborative for Academic, Social, and Emotional Learning (CASEL): CASEL provides research-based resources, professional development opportunities, and guidelines for implementing SEL. Their website offers a wealth of information on effective SEL practices.

- Online SEL assessment tools: There are various online assessment tools available that can help educators measure students' social and emotional skills. Examples include the Devereux Student Strengths Assessment (DESSA) and the Social Skills Improvement System (SSIS).

- Books and research articles: Educators can explore books and research articles on SEL to deepen their understanding of the topic. Some recommended books include "Social and Emotional Learning in the Classroom" by Kenneth R. Ginsburg and "Promoting Social and Emotional Learning: Guidelines for Educators" by Maurice J. Elias.

Conclusion

Social and emotional learning is an essential component of education that fosters students' emotional well-being, interpersonal skills, responsible decision-making, and academic achievement. By incorporating SEL into the curriculum and addressing challenges, educators can create a supportive learning environment where students thrive both academically and personally.

SEL frameworks and competencies

Social and Emotional Learning (SEL) is an essential component of transformative education. It focuses on developing social skills, emotional intelligence, and self-awareness in students, enabling them to navigate and thrive in various interpersonal and emotional situations. SEL frameworks provide a structured approach to integrating these skills into educational settings. In this section, we will explore the key components of SEL frameworks and discuss the competencies that students can develop through SEL practices.

Understanding SEL frameworks

SEL frameworks provide a comprehensive roadmap for educators to systematically incorporate social and emotional learning into their classrooms. These frameworks often consist of a set of core competencies and related strategies that aim to enhance students' overall well-being, academic performance, and future success.

One widely recognized SEL framework is the Collaborative for Academic, Social, and Emotional Learning (CASEL) framework. It proposes five core competencies:

1. **Self-awareness:** This competency involves recognizing one's own emotions, strengths, and weaknesses. It also includes the ability to accurately assess one's impact on others and maintain a positive and realistic self-image.

2. **Self-management:** Self-management encompasses the ability to regulate one's emotions, thoughts, and behaviors in different situations. It involves setting and working towards goals, managing stress, and demonstrating resilience in the face of challenges.

3. **Social awareness:** Social awareness focuses on understanding and empathizing with others' perspectives and feelings. It includes developing a sense of empathy, appreciating diversity, and cultivating a respectful and inclusive attitude towards others.

4. **Relationship skills:** Relationship skills involve developing and maintaining healthy and positive relationships with others. This competency includes effective communication, active listening, cooperation, and conflict resolution.

5. **Responsible decision-making:** Responsible decision-making refers to the ability to make constructive choices based on ethical considerations, social norms, and personal values. It involves considering the well-being of oneself and others when engaging in decision-making processes.

Other SEL frameworks, such as the RULER approach developed by the Yale Center for Emotional Intelligence, may have additional or slightly different components. However, the overarching goal remains the same - to nurture students' social and emotional competencies and help them thrive in various aspects of life.

Developing SEL competencies

Implementing SEL frameworks requires educators to design and facilitate experiences that promote the development of specific competencies in students. With intentional planning and supportive environments, students can develop the following SEL competencies:

1. **Emotional regulation:** Students learn to recognize, understand, and manage their emotions effectively. They develop strategies to calm themselves down, cope with stress, and regulate emotional responses in different situations.

2. **Empathy and perspective-taking:** Through SEL practices, students cultivate the ability to understand and share the feelings of others. They learn to consider different perspectives, appreciate diversity, and demonstrate compassion towards others.

3. **Self-reflection and self-awareness:** SEL facilitates students' self-exploration and understanding of their strengths, weaknesses, values, and emotions. It encourages them to reflect on their behaviors and actions, identify their triggers, and make better choices aligned with their values.

4. **Effective communication:** SEL enables students to develop strong communication skills, including active listening, expressing thoughts and feelings clearly, and adapting communication styles to different audiences. They also learn to resolve conflicts through peaceful and respectful dialogue.

5. **Goal-setting and decision-making:** Students are empowered to set meaningful and achievable goals, both academic and personal. They learn to make responsible decisions by considering the potential consequences, reflecting on their values, and evaluating available options.

To develop these competencies, educators can integrate various strategies and activities into their teaching practices. These may include role-playing, group discussions, journaling, mindfulness exercises, cooperative learning projects, and community service initiatives. By creating a safe and inclusive learning environment, teachers can facilitate the development of SEL competencies and foster positive social dynamics among students.

Integrating SEL across the curriculum

SEL is not limited to specific subjects or grade levels; it can be integrated across the curriculum to enhance students' overall learning experience. By infusing SEL principles into subject-specific content and activities, educators can create meaningful connections between academic concepts and real-life situations. Here are some examples:

- In English Language Arts, students can analyze literary characters' emotional journeys, explore different perspectives, and engage in discussions about empathy and ethical decision-making.

- In Science, students can investigate the impact of emotions on physiological processes, explore the social dynamics of animal behavior, or discuss the ethical implications of scientific discoveries.

- In Mathematics, students can collaborate on problem-solving activities, practice effective communication when explaining their reasoning, and explore real-world applications of mathematical concepts that involve social and emotional considerations.

- In Social Studies, students can study historical events through the lens of empathy, examine the long-term effects of decision-making on societies, and engage in debates on social justice issues.

By integrating SEL across the curriculum, educators create opportunities for students to transfer their social and emotional learning to various contexts, enhancing their ability to adapt and thrive in diverse situations.

Teacher self-care and SEL

Teachers' social and emotional well-being directly impacts their ability to effectively support students' social and emotional development. Hence, teacher self-care is an essential aspect of SEL implementation. Educators should prioritize their own social and emotional needs and practice self-care strategies such as mindfulness, stress management, and seeking support from colleagues and mentors. When teachers model self-awareness, emotional regulation, and healthy relationships, students are more likely to internalize these skills and behaviors.

Resources for SEL implementation

There are numerous resources available to support educators in implementing SEL frameworks and fostering social and emotional competencies in their students. Some useful resources include:

- CASEL (casel.org): CASEL provides a wealth of research-backed resources, including frameworks, assessment tools, and lesson plans.
- RULER Approach (ei.yale.edu/ruler): The RULER Approach emphasizes the development of emotional intelligence in both students and educators. The website offers practical strategies and resources for implementing the approach.
- Edutopia (edutopia.org): Edutopia provides articles, videos, and other resources on a wide range of topics related to education, including SEL implementation.
- SEL curriculum programs: Many publishers offer SEL-focused curriculum programs that provide detailed lesson plans and activities for integrating SEL across various subject areas and grade levels.

Conclusion

SEL frameworks provide a structured approach to integrating social and emotional learning into educational settings. By developing SEL competencies, students acquire the necessary skills to navigate interpersonal relationships, manage emotions, make responsible decisions, and thrive academically and personally. Through intentional implementation and integration across the curriculum, educators can create transformative learning environments that foster the holistic development of their students. By prioritizing the social and emotional needs of both students and educators, schools can cultivate a positive and inclusive culture that prepares students for success in the future.

Designing SEL Programs and Interventions

Designing social and emotional learning (SEL) programs and interventions is a critical aspect of creating transformative learning environments. SEL aims to cultivate students' social and emotional skills, attitudes, and behaviors, enabling them to effectively manage their emotions, develop positive relationships, and make responsible decisions. In this section, we will explore the principles, strategies, and considerations involved in designing effective SEL programs and interventions.

Principles of SEL

To design effective SEL programs and interventions, it is important to understand the underlying principles of SEL. These principles provide a framework for promoting the social and emotional development of students.

1. **Whole-child approach:** SEL recognizes that students' social and emotional well-being is interconnected with their academic success. It emphasizes addressing the needs of the whole child, including their emotional, social, and cognitive development.

2. **Cultivating self-awareness:** Self-awareness is a fundamental aspect of SEL. It involves helping students understand and identify their emotions, strengths, and areas for growth. Self-awareness lays the foundation for other SEL competencies.

3. **Fostering self-management:** SEL programs aim to teach students strategies for regulating their emotions, managing stress, and setting goals. It helps students develop resilience, self-discipline, and the ability to navigate challenges effectively.

4. **Promoting social awareness:** Social awareness involves developing empathy and a deep understanding of others' perspectives and experiences. SEL programs foster inclusivity, appreciation of diversity, and the ability to build positive relationships.

5. **Building responsible decision-making skills:** SEL equips students with the ability to make ethical decisions, consider the consequences of their actions, and solve problems effectively. It encourages students to consider the well-being of themselves and others in decision-making processes.

Strategies for Designing SEL Programs and Interventions

When designing SEL programs and interventions, it is essential to consider the developmental needs of students, the school context, and evidence-based practices. Here are some strategies to guide the design process:

1. **Needs assessment:** Conduct a thorough needs assessment to understand the specific social and emotional needs of the students in your school or classroom. This may involve surveys, interviews, observations, or data analysis.

2. **Establish clear goals and objectives:** Clearly define the goals and objectives of your SEL program or intervention. What specific social and emotional competencies do you aim to develop in your students? Set measurable objectives to track progress.

3. **Curriculum development:** Develop a comprehensive SEL curriculum that includes age-appropriate activities and strategies for promoting self-awareness, self-management, social awareness, responsible decision-making, and relationship skills. Incorporate evidence-based practices and align the curriculum with academic standards.

4. **Integration into daily instruction:** SEL should be integrated into daily instruction to ensure continuous practice and reinforcement of social and emotional skills. Look for opportunities to infuse SEL into existing lessons and activities across subject areas.

5. **Create a supportive school climate:** Designing an SEL program requires creating a supportive and inclusive school climate. This involves establishing clear expectations for behavior, promoting positive teacher-student relationships, fostering collaboration, and addressing issues of bullying or exclusion.

6. **Professional development for educators:** Provide professional development opportunities for educators to enhance their understanding of SEL and develop strategies for integrating SEL into their teaching practices. This may involve workshops, coaching, or collaborative learning communities.

7. **Parent and community involvement:** Engage parents and the broader community in supporting SEL initiatives. Provide resources, workshops, and communication channels for parents to reinforce SEL skills at home and align efforts between school and home.

8. **Ongoing assessment and evaluation:** Continuously assess and evaluate the effectiveness of your SEL program or intervention. Collect student feedback, monitor progress, and make necessary adjustments to ensure the program meets the needs of students.

Considerations and Best Practices

When designing SEL programs and interventions, it is important to consider the following factors to ensure their effectiveness and sustainability:

1. **Cultural responsiveness:** Account for cultural diversity and promote inclusivity in your SEL program. Consider the diverse cultural backgrounds, values, and experiences of your students and adapt the program to be culturally responsive.

2. **Developmentally appropriate practices:** Take into account the developmental stages and unique needs of students. Design activities and interventions that are suitable for the age and maturity level of your students.

3. **Collaboration and community partnerships:** Collaborate with other educators, school staff, and community partners to leverage their expertise and resources. Engage in partnerships that can enhance the reach and impact of your SEL program.

4. **Sustainability and scalability:** Design your SEL program with long-term sustainability and scalability in mind. Consider factors such as resource allocation, staff capacity, and integration with existing initiatives to ensure the program can be effectively implemented and maintained.

Example: School-Based Peer Mediation Program

One example of an SEL intervention is a school-based peer mediation program. Peer mediation programs provide students with the skills and tools to resolve conflicts peacefully and promote positive relationships within the school community. Here's an overview of the design and implementation of a peer mediation program:

Designing the program:

1. Conduct a needs assessment to identify the specific conflict resolution needs of students in the school. 2. Establish goals and objectives for the peer mediation program, such as reducing bullying incidents and promoting a positive school climate. 3. Develop a comprehensive curriculum that includes training modules for peer mediators, conflict resolution strategies, and communication skills.

Implementing the program:

1. Recruit and select a diverse group of student mediators who have demonstrated strong social and emotional skills. 2. Train the student mediators on conflict resolution techniques, active listening, empathy, and effective communication. 3. Establish a clear referral process for students seeking mediation, and ensure confidentiality and neutrality during the mediation sessions. 4. Provide ongoing support and supervision to the student mediators, with regular

check-ins and opportunities for skill development. 5. Evaluate the program's effectiveness through student feedback, conflict resolution data, and observations. Make adjustments as needed to improve outcomes.

By implementing a peer mediation program, schools can empower students to take an active role in resolving conflicts, promoting empathy and understanding, and creating a positive and inclusive school environment.

Additional Resources and Tools

Here are some additional resources and tools to support the design of SEL programs and interventions:

1. Collaborative for Academic, Social, and Emotional Learning (CASEL): CASEL provides research-based resources, frameworks, and guides for implementing effective SEL programs. Visit their website at `https://casel.org/`.

2. The RULER Approach: Developed by the Yale Center for Emotional Intelligence, the RULER Approach provides a comprehensive set of tools and practices for promoting emotional intelligence and social-emotional skills. Learn more at `https://www.ycei.org/ruler`.

3. Social Emotional Learning Alliance for Massachusetts (SEL4MA): SEL4MA offers resources, research, and professional development opportunities for educators interested in implementing SEL in Massachusetts. Explore their website at `https://www.sel4ma.org/`.

4. Collaborative for Social Emotional and Academic Learning (CSEAL): CSEAL provides research-based practices, resources, and professional development for educators and schools. Access their resources at `https://www.edutopia.org/sel-research-learning-resources`.

Remember, the design of SEL programs and interventions should be tailored to the specific needs of your students and informed by evidence-based practices. Emphasize collaboration, ongoing assessment, and a commitment to creating nurturing and inclusive learning environments. With a well-designed SEL program, you can support the holistic development of your students and enhance their overall academic success and well-being.

SEL Assessment and Measurement

Assessing and measuring social and emotional learning (SEL) is crucial for understanding the progress and development of students in these domains. Effective assessment and measurement tools provide educators with valuable insights into students' social and emotional competencies, helping them tailor instructional strategies and interventions to meet individual needs. In this section, we will explore various approaches, strategies, and considerations for SEL assessment and measurement.

Understanding SEL Assessment

SEL assessment involves the systematic collection and analysis of data to evaluate students' social and emotional competencies. It goes beyond traditional academic assessments and focuses on evaluating skills such as self-awareness, self-management, social awareness, relationship skills, and responsible decision-making.

The purpose of SEL assessment is to:

- Identify and monitor students' strengths and areas for growth in social and emotional competencies.
- Inform teaching practices and interventions to support students' SEL development.
- Evaluate the effectiveness of SEL programs and interventions.
- Enhance the accountability and evidence-base of SEL implementation.

Principles of Effective SEL Assessment

Effective SEL assessment is built on the following principles:

1. **Validity:** Assessments should measure what they intend to measure. They should align with established SEL frameworks and competencies and capture the multidimensional nature of social and emotional development.
2. **Reliability:** Assessments should yield consistent results over time and across different contexts. They should be free from biases that could influence the results.
3. **Fairness:** Assessments should be fair and unbiased for all students, regardless of their backgrounds or characteristics. They should consider cultural and linguistic factors to ensure equitable assessment practices.
4. **Practicality:** Assessments should be feasible to administer, score, and interpret within the educational setting. They should be efficient and minimize the burden on students and educators.

5. **Authenticity:** Assessments should capture real-world, contextually relevant situations to assess students' social and emotional competencies. They should reflect the authenticity of everyday experiences rather than contrived scenarios.

6. **Continuity:** Assessments should provide longitudinal data to track students' progress over time. They should allow educators to evaluate growth, identify developmental trends, and inform interventions accordingly.

Approaches to SEL Assessment

There are different approaches to SEL assessment, including self-reporting, observer ratings, performance tasks, and behavioral assessments. Each approach offers unique insights into students' social and emotional competencies.

1. **Self-Report Surveys:** Self-report surveys involve students reflecting on their own social and emotional skills, attitudes, and behaviors. These surveys usually consist of Likert-scale items and open-ended questions. They provide valuable self-perception data but may be subject to response biases.

2. **Observer Ratings:** Observer ratings involve teachers, parents, or peers assessing students' social and emotional competencies. These assessments offer an external perspective and capture behaviors across different contexts. However, they can be influenced by the observer's biases or limited by their access to the student's behavior.

3. **Performance Tasks:** Performance tasks require students to demonstrate their social and emotional competencies in realistic scenarios. These tasks can assess skills such as empathy, problem-solving, or responsible decision-making. Performance tasks provide authentic assessment data but may be resource-intensive to develop and administer.

4. **Behavioral Assessments:** Behavioral assessments involve systematic observations of students' social and emotional behaviors in natural settings. These assessments provide real-time data and deep insights into students' interactions and abilities. However, they can be time-consuming and require trained observers.

Integration of Technology in SEL Assessment

Technology can play a significant role in enhancing SEL assessment by offering scalable and efficient assessment solutions. Here are some examples of how technology can be integrated into SEL assessment:

1. **Online Surveys and Assessments:** Technology allows for the development and administration of online surveys and assessments, simplifying data collection and increasing accessibility for a larger number of students.

2. **Digital Platforms and Apps:** Digital platforms and apps can provide interactive and engaging SEL assessments, allowing students to demonstrate their skills through multimedia formats.

3. **Data Analytics and Learning Analytics:** Technology can facilitate the analysis of large-scale SEL assessment data, providing educators with valuable insights into patterns, trends, and correlations in students' social and emotional competencies.

4. **Artificial Intelligence (AI):** AI-powered tools can enhance the accuracy and efficiency of SEL assessment by automating the scoring process, providing real-time feedback, and generating personalized recommendations based on students' performance.

5. **Wearable Devices and Biometric Sensors:** Wearable devices and biometric sensors can capture physiological data (e.g., heart rate, skin conductance) to assess students' emotional states and stress levels, complementing traditional assessment approaches.

Considerations and Challenges

When implementing SEL assessment, educators need to consider several challenges and ethical considerations:

- **Cultural Relevance:** Assessments should be culturally relevant and consider the diversity of students' backgrounds, experiences, and contexts. It is crucial to avoid cultural biases and ensure that assessment practices are fair for all students.

- **Data Privacy and Security:** Protecting student data is paramount. Educators must comply with legal and ethical standards for data privacy and security when collecting, storing, and analyzing SEL assessment data.

- **Equitable Access:** Ensuring equitable access to SEL assessment tools and strategies is essential. It is important to consider students with disabilities, English language learners, and other marginalized groups to ensure inclusive assessment practices.

- **Interpretation of Assessment Results:** Assessments provide a snapshot of students' social and emotional competencies at a specific time. Educators need to interpret the results in conjunction with other formative and summative data to make informed instructional decisions.

- **Professional Development:** Educators must receive adequate training and support to effectively implement, interpret, and use SEL assessment data. Professional development programs should address the unique challenges and considerations related to SEL assessment.

Case Study: Integrating SEL Assessment in a High School Setting

To illustrate the application of SEL assessment, let's consider a case study of integrating SEL assessment in a high school setting.

In this case, a high school implements a comprehensive SEL program aimed at enhancing students' social and emotional competencies. The school develops a framework that includes specific SEL domains and indicators aligned with their goals and objectives.

To assess students' SEL competencies, the school adopts a mixed-method approach, combining self-report surveys, teacher ratings, and performance tasks. They develop an online platform where students can complete self-report surveys at regular intervals. Teachers also rate students based on their observations in the classroom and community activities. Additionally, students engage in performance tasks, such as group projects or presentations, to demonstrate their SEL skills.

The school regularly collects and analyzes the data to identify students' strengths and areas for growth. The SEL team collaborates with teachers to provide professional development on interpreting and using the assessment data effectively. Individualized interventions, such as workshops, counseling, or peer mentoring, are designed to support students' SEL development based on their specific needs.

By integrating SEL assessment into their educational practices, the high school highlights the importance of social and emotional competencies and creates a positive and supportive learning environment. The assessment data informs targeted interventions to foster students' social and emotional growth.

Conclusion

SEL assessment plays a vital role in understanding and supporting students' social and emotional development. By using valid and reliable assessment tools and strategies, educators can gain valuable insights into students' strengths and areas for growth in SEL domains. Technology integration in SEL assessment offers promising opportunities for scalability and efficiency while posing challenges related to data privacy, cultural relevance, and equitable access. With careful planning and considerations, SEL assessment can inform and enhance instructional practices, leading to transformative learning experiences for all students.

Overcoming challenges in implementing SEL

Implementing Social and Emotional Learning (SEL) programs in schools can be challenging due to various factors. In this section, we will discuss some of the common challenges that schools may face in implementing SEL and provide strategies to overcome them.

Lack of Infrastructure and Resources

One of the main challenges in implementing SEL programs is the lack of infrastructure and resources. Schools may not have dedicated time, space, or personnel to support SEL initiatives. Limited funding can also restrict the availability of training materials, curriculum resources, and tools necessary for effective implementation.

To overcome this challenge, schools can seek external funding through grants or collaborations with community organizations. They can also allocate dedicated time during the school day for SEL activities and provide professional development opportunities for teachers to learn about SEL strategies and techniques. Additionally, schools can leverage technology to provide online resources and support for SEL implementation.

Resistance from School Staff and Stakeholders

Resistance from school staff and stakeholders can hinder the successful implementation of SEL programs. Some teachers and administrators may be skeptical about the effectiveness of SEL or may view it as an additional burden on their already demanding workload. Resistance from parents and community members can also arise due to misconceptions or lack of awareness about the benefits of SEL.

To address this challenge, schools can provide training and professional development opportunities to help staff understand the importance and value of SEL. Building awareness and sharing success stories with parents and community members can help dispel misconceptions and garner support. Involving key stakeholders in the planning and decision-making process can also increase buy-in and commitment to SEL implementation.

Integration with Academic Curriculum

Integrating SEL with the academic curriculum can be a challenge for schools. Teachers may perceive SEL as separate from academic instruction and find it difficult to find time within the curriculum to explicitly teach SEL skills. They may also struggle to identify the connection between SEL and academic achievement, leading to a lack of prioritization.

To overcome this challenge, schools can adopt a whole-school approach to SEL, where SEL skills are seamlessly integrated into existing academic subjects. This can be done by embedding SEL concepts and skills in lesson plans, projects, and assessments. By demonstrating the connection between SEL and academic success, teachers can motivate students and enhance their engagement and achievement.

Assessment and Measurement

Assessing and measuring the impact of SEL programs is another challenge faced by schools. Traditional assessment methods, such as standardized tests, may not capture the full range of SEL skills and competencies. Schools may struggle to find suitable tools and strategies to evaluate students' social and emotional growth accurately.

To address this challenge, schools can utilize a combination of qualitative and quantitative assessment methods. This can include self-report measures, observations, and feedback from teachers, parents, and students themselves. Schools can also develop rubrics or checklists to assess specific SEL skills and track students' progress over time. It is essential to ensure that assessment methods align with the goals and desired outcomes of the SEL program.

Sustaining SEL Implementation

Sustaining the implementation of SEL programs can be a challenge, especially when faced with budget constraints, changing priorities, or staff turnover. Without ongoing support and commitment, the gains made through SEL initiatives may be lost over time.

To sustain SEL implementation, schools can establish a dedicated team or committee responsible for monitoring and supporting SEL efforts. This team can provide ongoing training, coaching, and resources to teachers and administrators. Regular communication and collaboration with parents and community members can also help sustain support and engagement. Furthermore, integrating SEL into school policies and practices can embed SEL principles and values into the school culture, ensuring long-term sustainability.

In conclusion, implementing SEL programs in schools can be challenging, but with appropriate strategies and support, these challenges can be overcome. By addressing infrastructure and resource limitations, addressing resistance, integrating SEL with the academic curriculum, improving assessment methods, and sustaining implementation efforts, schools can create an environment that fosters the social and emotional development of their students.

Case Studies and Best Practices in Social and Emotional Learning (SEL)

Social and Emotional Learning (SEL) has gained significant attention in recent years due to its positive impact on students' academic achievement, mental health, and overall well-being. SEL refers to the process of acquiring and applying skills, attitudes, and knowledge to understand and manage emotions, establish and maintain positive relationships, set and achieve goals, and make responsible decisions. In this section, we will explore case studies and best practices in SEL, highlighting successful implementations and their outcomes.

Case Study 1: The RULER Approach

The RULER approach, developed by the Yale Center for Emotional Intelligence, is an evidence-based program that promotes emotional intelligence and SEL. It focuses on five key skills: Recognizing emotions, Understanding emotions, Labeling emotions, Expressing emotions, and Regulating emotions. A case study conducted in a middle school found that implementing the RULER approach significantly improved students' social skills, emotional well-being, and academic performance. The students reported feeling more connected to their peers and teachers, and their conflict resolution skills also improved.

Best Practices: - Create a safe and supportive school environment: Foster a positive and inclusive school climate that values emotional well-being and promotes a sense of belonging for all students. - Integrate SEL into the curriculum: Embed SEL skills and concepts into academic subjects and provide opportunities for students to practice and apply these skills in various contexts. - Provide professional development for educators: Train teachers in SEL principles and strategies, equipping them with the knowledge and skills to effectively support students' emotional and social development. - Involve families and the community: Collaborate with families and community organizations to reinforce SEL skills and promote a consistent message about the importance of SEL across different contexts.

Case Study 2: Restorative Practices

Restorative Practices is an approach that focuses on building and maintaining positive relationships, resolving conflicts, and repairing harm within a school community. A case study conducted in an elementary school showed that implementing restorative practices led to improved student behavior, reduced disciplinary referrals, and increased student engagement. Students reported feeling a greater sense of belonging, as they were actively involved in repairing relationships and resolving conflicts.

Best Practices: - Foster a Restorative Culture: Promote a culture of empathy, respect, and accountability within the school community, encouraging restorative language and practices in all aspects of school life. - Build Strong Relationships: Provide opportunities for students and staff to build positive relationships through activities such as circle discussions, team-building exercises, and collaborative projects. - Teach Restorative Skills: Explicitly teach students essential restorative skills, such as active listening, empathy, conflict resolution, and problem-solving, through targeted lessons and activities. - Establish Restorative Circles: Regularly hold restorative circles that provide a safe space for discussing concerns, addressing conflicts, and repairing relationships. Ensure that all participants feel heard and have an opportunity to contribute. - Train and Support Staff: Provide ongoing professional development for staff members to build their understanding of restorative practices and develop the skills needed to implement them effectively.

Case Study 3: Mindfulness-Based Interventions

Mindfulness-based interventions, such as mindfulness meditation and yoga, have been shown to enhance students' self-regulation, attention, and overall well-being. A case study conducted in a high school found that implementing a mindfulness program led to a significant reduction in stress, improved emotional resilience, and increased focus among students. They reported feeling more present and better equipped to handle challenging situations.

Best Practices: - Provide Mindfulness Training: Offer mindfulness training for both students and teachers, including techniques such as deep breathing exercises, body scans, and guided meditations. Encourage regular practice to build mindfulness skills. - Integrate Mindfulness into the Curriculum: Infuse mindfulness into the curriculum by incorporating mindful moments or short mindfulness exercises at the beginning or end of lessons. - Create Mindful Environments: Design classrooms and common areas to promote a calm and focused atmosphere, with soothing colors, natural elements, and designated spaces for mindfulness practice. - Support Mindful Transitions: Incorporate mindfulness practices during transitional periods, such as before exams or after lunch breaks, to help students shift their attention and regulate their emotions effectively. - Cultivate Mindful Communication: Teach students effective communication skills, such as active listening and non-judgmental speaking, to enhance their understanding and empathy towards others.

Additional Resources: - Collaborative for Academic, Social, and Emotional Learning (CASEL): Provides research-based resources, guidelines, and tools for implementing SEL in schools. (Website: casel.org) - The Yale Center for Emotional Intelligence: Offers evidence-based programs, research, and resources for fostering emotional intelligence and SEL. (Website: ei.yale.edu) - Mindful Schools: Provides online courses and resources for educators interested in integrating mindfulness into their classrooms. (Website: mindfulschools.org)

Incorporating SEL into educational settings is crucial for nurturing holistic development and preparing students for success in their personal and professional lives. By implementing best practices from case studies like the ones mentioned above, educators can create transformative learning environments that prioritize emotional well-being, promote positive relationships, and cultivate essential social and emotional skills in students.

Technology-enhanced SEL programs and tools

In recent years, there has been a growing recognition of the importance of social and emotional learning (SEL) in education. SEL refers to the process of acquiring and applying the knowledge, skills, and attitudes required to understand and manage emotions, set and achieve positive goals, show empathy for others, establish and maintain positive relationships, and make responsible decisions. It plays a crucial role in supporting students' overall well-being, academic success, and personal growth.

Advancements in technology have provided new opportunities to enhance SEL programs and tools, making them more accessible, engaging, and effective. Technology-enhanced SEL programs and tools offer innovative ways to promote social and emotional competence among students. In this section, we will explore some of the key technologies and methodologies used in technology-enhanced SEL programs and tools.

1. Virtual Reality (VR) and Augmented Reality (AR)

Virtual Reality (VR) and Augmented Reality (AR) have gained significant attention in recent years. These immersive technologies provide students with virtual environments and simulations that allow them to practice and apply social and emotional skills in a safe and controlled setting.

For example, VR can be used to create realistic scenarios where students can navigate different social situations and practice skills such as conflict resolution, empathy, and perspective-taking. Students can interact with virtual avatars and receive real-time feedback on their responses and behaviors.

AR, on the other hand, overlays digital content onto the real-world environment, enhancing students' understanding and engagement. AR tools can provide visual cues and prompts during social interactions, helping students interpret non-verbal cues, manage emotions, and make informed decisions.

2. Mobile Applications

Mobile applications designed specifically for SEL purposes have become increasingly popular. These apps provide students with interactive activities, games, and resources that help develop various social and emotional skills.

For instance, there are apps that focus on mindfulness and emotional regulation, guiding students through breathing exercises, meditation, and relaxation techniques. Other apps encourage self-reflection and goal-setting, allowing students to track their progress and set personal targets for self-improvement. These mobile tools can be used both in and out of the classroom, enabling students to practice and reinforce SEL skills in their daily lives.

3. Online Collaboration Tools

Collaboration is a fundamental aspect of SEL, and online collaboration tools can promote social interaction and cooperation among students. These tools enable students to work together on group projects, discuss ideas, share resources, and provide feedback to their peers.

For example, discussion boards and online forums can be used to facilitate meaningful conversations and encourage students to express their thoughts and feelings. Video conferencing platforms allow students to engage in face-to-face interactions, even when they are physically distant. Furthermore, shared document platforms and online project management tools promote teamwork and collective problem-solving.

4. Learning Management Systems (LMS)

Learning Management Systems (LMS) provide a comprehensive platform for delivering technology-enhanced SEL programs. LMS platforms allow educators to organize and distribute learning materials, assign activities and assessments, track student progress, and provide timely feedback.

Within an LMS, educators can incorporate various multimedia resources, such as videos, podcasts, and interactive modules, to support SEL instruction. They can also use the LMS's communication features to provide ongoing support to students, engage in discussions, and address individual needs.

5. Data Analytics and Learning Analytics

Data analytics and learning analytics play a crucial role in technology-enhanced SEL programs. By analyzing data collected from various sources, such as online assessments, social interactions, and engagement with digital resources, educators can gain valuable insights into students' social and emotional development.

These analytics can provide information about students' strengths and weaknesses in specific SEL domains, identify patterns and trends in their behavior, and inform targeted interventions and support. With the help of machine learning algorithms, educators can also receive automated recommendations and suggestions for further SEL activities and resources tailored to individual student needs.

In summary, technology-enhanced SEL programs and tools offer exciting opportunities to enhance social and emotional learning in educational settings. Virtual reality and augmented reality provide immersive experiences for students to practice SEL skills, while mobile applications offer engaging platforms for self-reflection and mindfulness. Online collaboration tools and learning management systems promote social interaction and support, and data analytics provide valuable insights for personalized instruction. By leveraging these technologies and methodologies, educators can create dynamic and impactful SEL learning experiences for their students.

Cultivating Empathy and Emotional Intelligence

In the rapidly changing world of education, cultivating empathy and emotional intelligence has become a crucial aspect of transformative education. Empathy allows individuals to understand and share the feelings of others, while emotional intelligence refers to the ability to recognize and manage one's own emotions as well as understand the emotions of others. These skills are essential for developing strong interpersonal relationships, promoting empathy, and creating a supportive and inclusive learning environment.

The Importance of Empathy and Emotional Intelligence in Education

Empathy and emotional intelligence are fundamental to fostering a positive and inclusive classroom climate. When students develop these skills, they become more understanding, compassionate, and respectful of others. Empathy helps students appreciate diverse perspectives, resolve conflicts peacefully, and establish meaningful connections with their peers and teachers. Emotional intelligence allows students to regulate their emotions, persevere through challenges, and respond to feedback constructively.

Research has shown that students with high levels of empathy and emotional intelligence tend to have better academic performance, lower rates of bullying and aggression, stronger problem-solving skills, and improved mental health. These skills also contribute to a positive school climate and enhance students' overall well-being.

Strategies for Cultivating Empathy and Emotional Intelligence

To cultivate empathy and emotional intelligence in the classroom, educators can employ various strategies. Here are some effective approaches:

1. Role-playing: Engage students in role-playing activities where they can explore different perspectives and experiences. This helps them understand others' feelings and challenges.

2. Literature and storytelling: Use literature, novels, and stories that promote empathy. Discuss characters' emotions, motivations, and conflicts, encouraging students to put themselves in the characters' shoes.

3. Reflection and journaling: Encourage students to reflect on their emotions and experiences through journaling. This practice helps them become more self-aware and develop their emotional intelligence.

4. Cooperative learning: Incorporate cooperative learning activities that require teamwork, collaboration, and empathy. Encourage students to listen actively, support their peers, and solve problems together.

5. Service-learning projects: Engage students in service-learning projects that involve community service or helping others. This experience allows students to develop empathy by understanding the needs and challenges of different communities.

6. Mindfulness practices: Introduce mindfulness practices such as breathing exercises, guided meditations, and mindfulness-based activities. These practices help students develop self-awareness, regulate their emotions, and enhance their empathy.

7. Conflict resolution skills: Teach students effective communication and conflict resolution skills. Help them understand different perspectives, negotiate, and find solutions that respect the feelings and needs of all involved parties.

8. Modeling empathy: As an educator, model empathy in your interactions with students. Show compassion, active listening, and understanding. Encourage open dialogue and create a safe space for students to express their emotions.

Assessment and Integration

Assessing empathy and emotional intelligence can be challenging as these skills are more nuanced and complex than traditional academic subjects. However, it is essential to provide opportunities for students to practice and reflect on these skills. Consider using self-assessment tools, peer evaluations, and reflective assignments to gauge students' progress in cultivating empathy and emotional intelligence.

Integrating empathy and emotional intelligence into the curriculum can be done through cross-curricular connections. Find opportunities to integrate literature, history, social sciences, and even STEM subjects to explore emotional issues, social justice, and problem-solving through an empathetic lens. Collaborate with other teachers to create interdisciplinary projects that promote empathy and emotional intelligence.

Encourage students to apply these skills beyond the classroom by participating in community service projects, getting involved in extracurricular activities, or engaging in online discussions that foster empathy and understanding.

Resources and Further Reading

Here are some resources and further reading materials to support the cultivation of empathy and emotional intelligence in education:

1. Books: - "UnSelfie: Why Empathetic Kids Succeed in Our All-About-Me World" by Michele Borba. - "Raising an Emotionally Intelligent Child" by John Gottman. - "The Whole-Brain Child: 12 Revolutionary Strategies to Nurture Your Child's Developing Mind" by Daniel J. Siegel and Tina Payne Bryson.

2. Websites and Organizations: - Start Empathy (www.startempathy.org): A resource hub for educators, providing tools and strategies to cultivate empathy in students. - CASEL (Collaborative for Academic, Social, and Emotional Learning) (www.casel.org): Offers research-backed resources and programs to promote social-emotional development in children and adolescents. - Edutopia (www.edutopia.org): Provides articles, videos, and teaching strategies for integrating social-emotional learning and empathy in the classroom.

Remember, cultivating empathy and emotional intelligence takes time and consistent effort, but the positive impact on students' personal and academic growth is immeasurable. By prioritizing the development of these skills, educators can create a transformative learning environment where students thrive emotionally, socially, and academically.

Exercises

1. Ask students to choose a character from a book they are reading and write a journal entry from that character's perspective. Encourage them to express the character's emotions and thoughts, demonstrating empathy.

2. Organize a cooperative learning activity where students work in groups to solve a problem or complete a project. Ask them to discuss different perspectives and consider the feelings and needs of all group members.

3. Engage students in reflective writing exercises where they explore their own emotional experiences and how they can apply emotional intelligence to manage their emotions in challenging situations.

4. Show a short video clip or read a news article about a social issue that requires empathy and understanding. Lead a classroom discussion where students share their thoughts and feelings about the issue, encouraging empathy.

5. Assign a service-learning project where students work in teams to address a community issue. Ask them to reflect on their experiences and how it has influenced their understanding of empathy and emotional intelligence.

These exercises aim to provide students with practical experiences to develop their empathy and emotional intelligence skills while connecting them to real-world issues.

SEL in different subject areas

Social and Emotional Learning (SEL) is a critical component of education that focuses on developing students' skills to understand and manage their emotions, establish positive relationships, and make responsible decisions. While SEL is often seen as relevant and applicable in general terms, it is important to consider its implementation in different subject areas, as each subject may require specific skills and competencies. In this section, we will explore how SEL can be integrated into various subject areas, highlighting the unique opportunities and challenges that arise.

1. Mathematics: In mathematics, SEL can foster a positive mindset and build resilience when students encounter challenges. Teachers can promote a growth mindset by encouraging students to embrace mistakes as learning opportunities and promoting a supportive classroom environment. Collaborative problem-solving activities can also enhance social skills and teamwork. For example, group projects that require students to work together to solve complex mathematical problems can promote effective communication, negotiation, and cooperation.

2. Science: In science, SEL focuses on fostering curiosity, critical thinking, and scientific inquiry skills. Teachers can create an inclusive classroom environment where students feel safe to express their thoughts, ask questions, and challenge ideas. This can be achieved through open discussions, group investigations, and hands-on experiments. SEL can also help students develop empathy by considering the ethical implications of scientific discoveries and their impact on society and the environment.

3. Language Arts: In language arts, SEL can nurture effective communication skills, empathy, and self-expression. Teachers can incorporate activities that encourage active listening, respectful dialogue, and appreciation of diverse perspectives. Literature circles or book clubs provide opportunities for students to engage in meaningful discussions, share their interpretations, and develop empathy by seeing the world through different characters' eyes. SEL can also support students in reflecting on their own experiences and emotions through personal narratives or journal writing.

4. Social Studies: In social studies, SEL helps students understand and appreciate diverse cultures, perspectives, and historical events. Teachers can promote SEL by encouraging active citizenship and responsible decision-making. Students can engage in service-learning projects to address social issues, fostering civic responsibility and empathy. Role-plays or debates can encourage students to consider multiple viewpoints and develop their critical thinking and conflict

resolution skills.

5. Physical Education: In physical education, SEL promotes teamwork, sportsmanship, and self-regulation skills. Teachers can create a supportive and inclusive environment where students feel comfortable taking risks and challenging themselves. Team sports and cooperative games can provide opportunities for collaboration, communication, and building positive relationships. Through physical activities, students can also learn to manage their emotions, cope with stress, and develop resilience.

It is important to note that integrating SEL into different subject areas should be done holistically, considering the overall curriculum and school culture. Teachers should receive training and support in incorporating SEL practices into their teaching, ensuring alignment between subject-specific objectives and SEL goals. By intentionally integrating SEL across subject areas, educators can better equip students with the social and emotional competencies they need to thrive academically, socially, and emotionally.

In addition to these subject-specific implementations, educators can also find opportunities to integrate SEL through cross-curricular projects and interdisciplinary approaches. This allows students to make connections between different subject areas and apply their social and emotional skills in real-world contexts. By intentionally incorporating SEL into various subject areas, educators can create a comprehensive and meaningful learning experience that prepares students for success in school and in life.

Future directions of social and emotional learning

As the field of social and emotional learning (SEL) continues to evolve, there are several exciting future directions that hold great promise for enhancing the well-being and development of students. In this section, we will explore some of these directions, considering emerging trends and innovative approaches in SEL.

Integration of technology in SEL

Technology has become an integral part of our lives, and it has the potential to play a significant role in supporting SEL initiatives. In the future, we can expect to see the integration of various technologies to enhance SEL programs and interventions.

One direction is the use of virtual reality (VR) and augmented reality (AR) to create immersive experiences that promote emotional awareness and empathy. For example, virtual environments can simulate different social scenarios, allowing students to practice interpersonal skills and perspective-taking in a safe and controlled setting. Additionally, AR applications can overlay emotional cues or prompts in real-world contexts, helping students recognize and regulate their emotions in the moment.

Another exciting direction is the use of wearable technologies to monitor physiological indicators of emotions and well-being. For instance, biosensors embedded in smart wristbands or clothing can provide real-time feedback on stress levels or emotional states, enabling students to gain self-awareness and make informed decisions regarding their emotional well-being.

Focus on cultural responsiveness and equity

In the future, SEL programs and interventions will likely place an increased emphasis on cultural responsiveness and equity. This means recognizing and valuing the diverse cultures, backgrounds, and experiences of students, and tailoring SEL initiatives to be inclusive and accessible to all.

Educators and SEL practitioners will need to develop a deep understanding of cultural norms and values, and integrate these perspectives into SEL curricula and practices. They will also need to address the biases and inequalities that may exist within the tools and technologies used in SEL, ensuring that they are sensitive to diverse cultural contexts and do not reinforce existing inequities.

Moreover, the future of SEL will involve close collaborations and partnerships with communities and families to ensure that SEL initiatives are culturally relevant and responsive to the unique needs and strengths of students from different backgrounds.

Enhancement of SEL assessment and measurement

Assessing and measuring social and emotional competencies can be challenging, but advances in technology and research will likely lead to more sophisticated and accurate assessment tools in the future.

One direction is the development of innovative assessment methods that go beyond self-report surveys. For example, natural language processing techniques can analyze students' written or spoken responses to open-ended questions, providing valuable insights into their emotional states, self-perception, and social interactions.

Another important direction is the integration of data analytics and machine learning algorithms into SEL assessment. By leveraging large datasets and sophisticated algorithms, SEL assessments can become more personalized and adaptive, providing targeted feedback and intervention strategies based on individual students' needs.

Furthermore, the future of SEL assessment will also involve the exploration of non-traditional measures of social and emotional competencies. For instance, social network analysis can be used to examine students' patterns of social interactions, identifying their social support networks and the quality of their relationships.

Incorporation of mindfulness and well-being practices

Mindfulness practices have gained significant attention in recent years due to their positive impact on mental health and well-being. In the future, we can expect to see a greater incorporation of mindfulness and well-being practices within SEL initiatives.

There will be a focus on teaching students mindfulness techniques and strategies to manage stress, regulate emotions, and enhance attention and concentration. This may involve the use of meditation apps, guided mindfulness exercises, or the integration of mindfulness practices into classroom routines and activities.

Moreover, the future of SEL will involve a holistic approach to well-being, considering the physical, mental, and social aspects of students' lives. This may include promoting healthy lifestyle habits, such as exercise, nutrition, and sleep, as well as fostering positive peer relationships and supportive school environments.

Development of social and emotional learning for educators

In order to effectively promote SEL in schools, it is crucial to provide teachers with the necessary knowledge, skills, and support. In the future, there will be a greater emphasis on the professional development of educators in the field of SEL.

Teachers will receive training on evidence-based SEL practices, including strategies for creating a positive and inclusive classroom climate, fostering strong teacher-student relationships, and implementing SEL curricula effectively. Professional development opportunities will also focus on self-care and well-being for educators, as their own emotional health and resilience are essential for modeling and teaching SEL skills.

Furthermore, the future of SEL will involve collaborative learning communities for educators, where they can share best practices, learn from one another, and engage in continuous improvement. Online platforms and virtual communities of practice will support ongoing professional development and networking opportunities.

Addressing the impact of technology on social-emotional well-being

While technology can offer great benefits in promoting SEL, it is important to acknowledge and address the potential negative impacts on social-emotional well-being. In the future, there will be increased attention to digital citizenship and ethical use of technology to ensure that students develop healthy and balanced relationships with digital devices and online platforms.

Educators and families will play a critical role in promoting responsible and mindful technology use, teaching students about online safety, respectful communication, and the importance of maintaining real-world connections. SEL initiatives will also include discussions about the potential risks and challenges associated with social media, cyberbullying, and the impact of digital media consumption on mental health.

Furthermore, the future of SEL will involve the development of interventions and resources specifically designed to support students in navigating the digital landscape and building resilience in the face of online challenges.

In conclusion, the future of social and emotional learning holds exciting possibilities for enhancing students' well-being and development. Through the integration of technology, a focus on cultural responsiveness and equity, enhanced assessment methods, mindfulness practices, professional development for educators, and critical discussions about responsible technology use, we can create a future where students are equipped with the social and emotional skills needed to thrive in the digital age.

The Future of Education

Emerging Trends and Technologies

AI and Machine Learning in Education

Artificial Intelligence (AI) and machine learning have emerged as transformative technologies across various fields, including education. In the context of education, AI refers to the development of computer systems that can perform tasks that would typically require human intelligence, such as learning, reasoning, problem-solving, and decision-making. Machine learning, a subset of AI, focuses on the development of algorithms that can learn from and make predictions or take actions based on data.

Benefits of AI and Machine Learning in Education

The integration of AI and machine learning in education offers numerous benefits for both educators and learners. Some of the key benefits include:

- Personalized Learning: AI-powered systems can analyze vast amounts of data to understand individual student needs and provide personalized learning experiences. Adaptive learning platforms can dynamically adjust content and instructional strategies to meet the specific learning pace, style, and preferences of each student, enhancing engagement and understanding.

- Intelligent Tutoring: AI can mimic the role of human tutors by providing timely and personalized feedback to students. Intelligent tutoring systems can identify misconceptions, offer explanations, and guide students through the learning process. This allows for more targeted and efficient support, promoting greater learning outcomes.

- Data-Driven Decision Making: AI can analyze large datasets from multiple sources to generate actionable insights for educational institutions. By utilizing learning analytics and predictive modeling, educators and administrators can make informed decisions regarding curriculum design, resource allocation, and student interventions. This data-driven approach can lead to more effective educational strategies and improved outcomes.

- Automation of Routine Tasks: AI can automate routine administrative tasks, freeing up valuable time for educators to focus on more meaningful activities, such as designing innovative learning experiences, providing personalized instruction, and building relationships with students. Automated grading, scheduling, and data management systems streamline administrative processes, increasing efficiency.

- Enhanced Accessibility and Inclusivity: AI can help create inclusive learning environments by providing accessibility features for students with disabilities. For example, natural language processing and speech recognition technologies can enable students with visual impairments or learning disabilities to interact with educational content more effectively. AI can also support second language learners by providing real-time translations and language practice.

Applications of AI and Machine Learning in Education

AI and machine learning have a wide range of applications in the field of education. Some prominent examples include:

- Intelligent Tutoring Systems: These systems use AI algorithms to deliver personalized instruction, provide feedback, and track student progress. They can adapt the difficulty level of tasks based on individual performance and tailor instruction to address learning gaps.

- Adaptive Learning Platforms: Adaptive learning platforms leverage machine learning algorithms to analyze student data and dynamically adjust the content and delivery of instruction. These platforms provide individualized learning pathways and resources to optimize learning outcomes.

- Intelligent Content Creation: AI can assist in the creation of educational content by automating tasks such as content generation, proofreading, and plagiarism detection. Natural language processing algorithms can analyze and evaluate student writing, providing targeted feedback for improvement.

- Virtual Assistants and Chatbots: AI-powered virtual assistants and chatbots can provide immediate responses to student inquiries, offer guidance on course selection, and provide general support. These tools enhance student engagement and access to information.

- Predictive Analytics: Machine learning algorithms can analyze student data to identify patterns and make predictions about performance, behavior, and engagement. This information can help educators intervene and provide targeted support to struggling students.

Challenges and Ethical Considerations

While AI and machine learning offer tremendous potential in education, there are also challenges and ethical considerations that need to be addressed. Some of the key challenges include:

- Bias and Fairness: AI systems can inherit biases from the data on which they are trained. It is essential to ensure that these systems are designed and trained to be fair and inclusive, avoiding discrimination or perpetuating stereotypes.

- Data Privacy and Security: AI relies on vast amounts of data, often including sensitive student information. It is crucial to establish robust data privacy policies and security measures to protect student privacy and ensure compliance with relevant regulations.

- Trust and Transparency: AI algorithms can be complex and opaque, making it challenging to understand and interpret their decision-making processes. Transparent and explainable AI models are necessary to build trust among educators, students, and stakeholders.

- Equity and Accessibility: There is a risk that AI and machine learning technologies may exacerbate existing inequities in education. Efforts should be made to ensure that all students, regardless of their background or resources, have equal access to AI-powered educational tools and opportunities.

To address these challenges, it is crucial to adopt a multidisciplinary approach that involves educators, policymakers, researchers, and technologists. Collaboration and ongoing dialogue are essential to promoting the responsible and ethical use of AI in education.

Future Directions

The future of AI and machine learning in education holds immense potential for innovation and advancement. Some key areas to watch for future developments include:

- Intelligent Learning Analytics: Advanced learning analytics powered by AI can provide deeper insights into learning processes by incorporating real-time data from various sources. This can enable more accurate predictions and interventions to support personalized learning.
- Natural Language Processing: Natural language processing technologies will continue to evolve, making it possible for AI systems to understand and respond to student queries in more sophisticated ways. This will enhance the efficacy of virtual assistants and chatbots in educational settings.
- Collaborative AI in Education: AI systems that can facilitate collaborative learning and problem-solving among students are being explored. These systems can provide adaptive prompts, facilitate group interactions, and support teamwork, enhancing the effectiveness of collaborative learning experiences.
- Ethical AI in Education: Efforts to develop and implement ethical guidelines and frameworks for AI in education will continue to grow. Stakeholders must actively engage in discussions around responsible AI practices to ensure equitable and beneficial use of these technologies.
- Lifelong Learning and AI: AI-powered adaptive learning platforms have the potential to support lifelong learning by providing personalized learning experiences beyond traditional educational settings. AI can help individuals acquire new skills, update their knowledge, and adapt to changing demands in the workforce.

In conclusion, AI and machine learning have the power to revolutionize education by enabling personalized learning experiences, intelligent tutoring, data-driven decision-making, and automation of routine tasks. However, careful attention must be given to addressing challenges related to bias, privacy, transparency, and equity to ensure the responsible and ethical integration of AI in education. By fostering collaboration and embracing technological advancements, educators can harness the transformative potential of AI to enhance teaching and learning in the future.

Internet of Things (IoT) and education

The Internet of Things (IoT) is a rapidly growing network of interconnected devices that collect and exchange data. In the education sector, IoT has the potential to revolutionize teaching and learning by providing innovative solutions to enhance educational experiences. This section explores the role of IoT in education and its impact on transforming traditional classroom settings.

Benefits of IoT in education

The integration of IoT devices in education offers several benefits for students, teachers, and educational institutions. Here are some key advantages:

- **Enhanced learning experiences:** IoT devices enable interactive and immersive learning experiences. For example, smart classrooms equipped with IoT sensors can provide real-time information on temperature, humidity, and air quality, creating a comfortable and conducive learning environment.

- **Personalized learning:** IoT devices can collect data on students' learning patterns, preferences, and progress. This data can be used to personalize instructional content, adapting it to individual students' needs and learning styles.

- **Improved resource management:** IoT devices can track the usage of educational resources such as textbooks, equipment, and classroom materials. This enables efficient resource allocation and reduces waste.

- **Collaborative learning:** IoT devices facilitate collaboration and teamwork among students. For instance, IoT-enabled whiteboards can allow multiple students to simultaneously contribute and interact with the content, fostering engagement and active participation.

- **Real-world connections:** IoT devices can bridge the gap between theoretical concepts taught in the classroom and real-world applications. For example, students studying environmental science can use IoT sensors to collect and analyze data on air quality, water pollution, or weather conditions, gaining practical insights into environmental issues.

Applications of IoT in education

IoT can be applied across various educational domains. Here are some examples of how IoT is revolutionizing education:

- **Smart campuses:** Educational institutions can leverage IoT devices to create smart campuses. IoT-enabled sensors can monitor and control campus facilities such as lighting, heating, and security systems, ensuring a safe and environmentally friendly environment.
- **Smart classrooms:** IoT devices can transform traditional classrooms into smart learning spaces. Smart boards, connected devices, and wearables can enhance student engagement and enable interactive learning experiences.
- **Smart libraries:** IoT devices can streamline library operations by automating processes such as book checkouts, inventory management, and tracking overdue books. This improves efficiency and enables students to access resources seamlessly.
- **Smart transportation:** IoT-enabled school buses can ensure student safety by providing real-time tracking, monitoring vehicle conditions, and optimizing routes and schedules.

Challenges and considerations

While the integration of IoT in education offers immense potential, it also comes with certain challenges and considerations that need to be addressed:

- **Privacy and security:** As IoT devices collect and exchange sensitive data, ensuring privacy and security is paramount. Educational institutions must implement robust cybersecurity measures and establish strict data protection policies.
- **Infrastructure and connectivity:** Reliable internet connectivity and adequate infrastructure are prerequisites for successful IoT implementation. Ensuring seamless connectivity and addressing issues related to network scalability can be a challenge, especially in remote or low-resource settings.
- **Professional development:** Teachers and educators need appropriate training and professional development to effectively integrate IoT into their teaching practices. Building digital literacy and proficiency among teachers is vital for successful IoT implementation.

- **Equitable access:** Ensuring equitable access to IoT devices and technology is crucial to prevent the exacerbation of existing educational inequalities. Efforts should be made to bridge the digital divide and provide equal opportunities for all students.

Future directions and emerging trends

The future of IoT in education holds exciting possibilities. Here are some emerging trends to watch for:

- **AI-powered adaptive learning:** The combination of IoT and artificial intelligence (AI) holds great potential for adaptive learning. AI algorithms can analyze data collected from IoT devices to personalize learning experiences and provide tailored feedback to students.

- **Smart wearable devices:** Wearable devices such as smartwatches and fitness trackers can be integrated into educational settings to monitor students' health, track their physical activity, and gather data on their well-being.

- **Smart learning analytics:** IoT devices can enable advanced learning analytics to gain insights into student performance, engagement levels, and learning outcomes. This data can inform instructional strategies and interventions.

- **Mixed reality learning:** IoT devices can be coupled with virtual reality (VR) or augmented reality (AR) technologies to create immersive and interactive learning experiences. Students can explore virtual environments, conduct simulations, and engage in hands-on learning.

In conclusion, the integration of IoT in education has the potential to revolutionize teaching and learning, offering enhanced learning experiences, personalized instruction, and improved resource management. However, careful consideration must be given to privacy, security, infrastructure, and equitable access to ensure successful implementation. The future of IoT in education holds exciting possibilities, with emerging trends such as AI-powered adaptive learning, smart wearables, and mixed reality learning shaping the educational landscape.

Wearable Technologies in Education

Wearable technologies are becoming increasingly prevalent in various industries, and the field of education is no exception. These innovative devices, such as smartwatches, fitness trackers, and virtual reality headsets, offer exciting opportunities to enhance the learning experience and create more engaging and interactive educational environments.

Introduction to Wearable Technologies

Wearable technologies can be defined as electronic devices that can be worn on the body as accessories or clothing. They are equipped with sensors, processors, and wireless connectivity, allowing them to collect and transmit data about the user's behavior, health, and environment. In the context of education, wearable technologies can provide real-time feedback, enable hands-on learning experiences, and support personalized instruction.

Benefits of Wearable Technologies in Education

The use of wearable technologies in education offers numerous benefits for both students and teachers. Some of these benefits include:

- **Engagement and motivation:** Wearable technologies can increase student engagement and motivation by making learning more interactive and enjoyable. For example, fitness trackers can be used in physical education classes to gamify physical activities and encourage students to reach fitness goals.

- **Real-time feedback:** Wearable devices can provide immediate feedback to students, allowing them to track their progress and make necessary adjustments. This can be especially useful in subjects such as foreign language learning or musical instrument practice, where real-time feedback is crucial for improvement.

- **Active learning:** Wearable technologies enable active learning experiences by providing opportunities for students to actively participate in their learning process. For instance, virtual reality headsets can transport students to immersive virtual environments, allowing them to explore historical sites or participate in scientific experiments.

- **Data collection and analysis:** Wearable devices can collect and analyze data on student behavior, learning patterns, and performance. This data can be used by teachers to identify areas of improvement, tailor instruction to individual student needs, and make informed instructional decisions.

- **Accessibility and inclusivity:** Wearable technologies can help address accessibility and inclusivity concerns in education. For students with disabilities, wearable devices can provide assistive technologies such as text-to-speech or sign language interpretation. Additionally, these technologies can facilitate remote learning and collaboration, making education more accessible to students in geographically remote areas or those with limited mobility.

Examples of Wearable Technologies in Education

There are several examples of wearable technologies that have been successfully implemented in educational settings. Here are a few notable examples:

- **Virtual reality headsets:** Virtual reality headsets, such as the Oculus Quest or HTC Vive, can create immersive learning experiences. Students can explore virtual environments, manipulate objects, and interact with simulations, enhancing their understanding of complex concepts.

- **Smartwatches:** Smartwatches, such as the Apple Watch or Samsung Galaxy Watch, can be used to track physical activity and encourage healthy behaviors in physical education classes. They can also be integrated with educational apps to provide notifications, reminders, and access to educational resources.

- **Biometric sensors:** Biometric sensors, such as heart rate monitors or EEG (electroencephalogram) headsets, can be used to measure physiological responses during learning activities. This data can help assess student engagement levels, stress levels, or cognitive load, and inform instructional strategies accordingly.

- **Gesture-based devices:** Gesture-based devices, such as the Myo armband, allow students to control digital interfaces through hand gestures. This can be particularly useful in subjects such as design, where students can manipulate virtual objects and prototypes with natural hand movements.

- **Wearable cameras:** Wearable cameras, such as the GoPro or Narrative Clip, can be used to capture first-person perspectives during field trips or hands-on activities. Students can document their experiences and later reflect on their learning, enhancing metacognitive skills.

Challenges and Considerations

While wearable technologies offer exciting possibilities in education, there are several challenges and considerations that need to be addressed:

- **Cost and accessibility:** The cost of wearable devices and associated technologies can be a barrier to implementation, particularly for schools with limited resources. Ensuring equitable access to wearable technologies is essential to avoid exacerbating existing educational inequalities.

- **Data privacy and security:** Wearable technologies often collect sensitive data about students, including personal health information or location data. Safeguarding this data and ensuring student privacy should be a top priority. It is crucial to establish clear policies and frameworks that protect student data and adhere to legal and ethical guidelines.

- **Teacher professional development:** Integrating wearable technologies into classrooms requires teachers to develop the necessary skills and knowledge to effectively incorporate these devices into their instruction. Providing comprehensive professional development opportunities and ongoing support is essential for successful implementation.

- **Pedagogical design:** The integration of wearable technologies should be guided by pedagogical considerations. It is crucial to align the use of these devices with learning objectives and instructional strategies to ensure meaningful learning experiences.

- **Acceptance and resistance:** Just like any new technology, there may be resistance from educators or students to embrace wearable technologies. Clear communication of the benefits and purpose of these devices, as well as addressing concerns and misconceptions, can help overcome resistance and foster acceptance.

Future Directions

The future of wearable technologies in education holds tremendous potential for further innovation and transformation. Here are some possible future directions:

- **Personalized learning experiences:** Advances in wearable technologies can lead to more personalized learning experiences, where devices adapt to individual student needs and preferences. This can include customized feedback, tailored content delivery, or adaptive learning paths.
- **Augmented reality integration:** Wearable technologies, combined with augmented reality (AR) capabilities, can create immersive and interactive learning experiences. AR glasses or contact lenses could overlay digital information onto the real world, enabling students to interact with digital content seamlessly.
- **Emotion and affective computing:** Wearable devices with emotion recognition capabilities can facilitate the understanding of students' emotional states and affective reactions during learning. This information can be used to improve personalized instruction, monitor well-being, and provide appropriate support.
- **Neurofeedback and brain-computer interfaces:** Advancements in wearable technologies may enable the use of neurofeedback and brain-computer interfaces in education. Students could use brainwaves to control digital interfaces, enhancing their engagement and interaction with learning content.
- **Collaborative learning and social interaction:** Wearable technologies can support collaboration and social interaction among students. For example, devices could facilitate group work by providing real-time feedback or enabling seamless communication and information sharing.

In conclusion, wearable technologies have the potential to revolutionize education by creating more engaging, personalized, and interactive learning experiences. However, careful consideration must be given to the challenges and ethical considerations associated with their use. With ongoing research, improvements, and innovation, wearable technologies have a promising future in transforming education.

5G and its Impact on Learning

With the rapid advancement of technology, the education sector has witnessed significant transformations in recent years. One such development is the introduction of 5G, the fifth-generation wireless technology. 5G technology promises to revolutionize the way we connect, communicate, and learn. In this section, we will explore the impact of 5G on learning and the potential benefits it brings to educational institutions and students worldwide.

Understanding 5G Technology

To understand the potential impact of 5G on learning, it is important to have a clear understanding of this advanced wireless technology. 5G is the next generation of wireless technology that aims to provide faster and more reliable connections than its predecessors, such as 4G. It operates on higher-frequency bands, enabling faster data transfers, lower latency, and more simultaneous connections. This technology has the potential to revolutionize various industries, including education.

Enhanced Connectivity

One of the main benefits of 5G technology is enhanced connectivity. With its superior speed and capacity, 5G ensures a seamless and uninterrupted online experience for students and educators. This means faster downloads, smoother streaming of educational videos, and quicker access to online resources. Students can access online learning platforms, participate in virtual classrooms, and collaborate with peers in real-time without any connectivity issues. This level of connectivity empowers students and provides them with equal access to educational opportunities, regardless of their geographical location.

Emergence of Immersive Learning Experiences

The high speed and low latency of 5G technology open doors for immersive learning experiences. Virtual reality (VR) and augmented reality (AR) applications can be seamlessly integrated into the learning process, providing students with a more engaging and interactive educational experience. For example, medical students can virtually dissect a human body, architecture students can explore 3D models of buildings, and history students can visit historical sites virtually. The possibilities are endless, and 5G plays a crucial role in delivering these immersive learning experiences in real-time.

Mobile Learning and Extended Reality

5G technology enables the expansion of mobile learning and extended reality (XR) applications. XR encompasses virtual reality (VR), augmented reality (AR), and mixed reality (MR). With 5G, students can access XR applications on their mobile devices and seamlessly connect to immersive learning environments. Whether it's exploring a virtual museum, practicing skills in a simulated environment, or collaborating with peers through AR, 5G ensures smooth and responsive XR experiences. This enhances student engagement, fosters creativity, and promotes active learning.

Remote and Distance Learning

The COVID-19 pandemic has highlighted the importance of remote and distance learning. As educational institutions transitioned to online learning, the demand for seamless connectivity and high-quality video conferencing solutions skyrocketed. 5G technology can address the challenges of remote learning by providing reliable and high-speed internet connections. It enables students to participate in live virtual classes, access educational resources, and engage in real-time collaboration with teachers and peers. This level of connectivity bridges the digital divide and ensures equal educational opportunities for all.

Expanding Access to Education

5G has the potential to expand access to education, especially in underserved areas. By providing high-speed internet connections, 5G enables students in rural or remote regions to access online educational resources, take part in virtual classrooms, and connect with teachers and students from around the world. This technology eliminates geographical barriers and increases educational opportunities for students who would otherwise have limited access to quality education.

Big Data, Analytics, and Personalization

The combination of 5G and big data analytics opens up new possibilities for personalized learning. With 5G's high-speed connectivity, the collection and analysis of large sets of educational data becomes more efficient. This data can be used to gain insights into students' learning patterns, preferences, and challenges. Educators can then tailor instructional strategies and content to meet individual student needs, promoting personalized and adaptive learning experiences. 5G technology empowers educators to make data-driven decisions and provide targeted interventions to support student success.

Collaborative Learning and Global Connections

5G technology facilitates seamless collaboration among students and encourages global connections. Through high-quality video conferencing and real-time communication tools, students can engage in virtual group projects and connect with peers from different cultural backgrounds. This promotes cross-cultural understanding, enhances collaboration skills, and prepares students for the interconnected world. 5G enables students to connect with experts and guest speakers from various fields, further enriching their learning experiences.

Closing the Homework Gap

The homework gap refers to the disparities in internet access that hinder students' ability to complete their homework and participate in online learning. 5G has the potential to bridge this gap by providing fast and reliable internet connections to students who lack access at home. This ensures that all students have equal opportunities to complete assignments, access online educational resources, and stay connected with their teachers and classmates outside the classroom.

Challenges and Considerations

While 5G technology holds immense potential for transforming education, there are challenges and considerations that need to be addressed. The infrastructure required for deploying 5G networks, especially in remote or underserved areas, may pose challenges. Furthermore, ensuring data privacy and security are essential when harnessing the power of 5G and analyzing large educational datasets. Educational institutions must develop robust cybersecurity measures and ethical guidelines to protect student information and ensure responsible use of technology.

Conclusion

5G technology has the potential to revolutionize education by providing enhanced connectivity, enabling immersive learning experiences, expanding access to education, and promoting personalized and collaborative learning. Through its advanced capabilities, 5G can bridge the digital divide and provide equal educational opportunities to students worldwide. However, careful considerations must be taken to address challenges related to infrastructure, data privacy, and security. With the right implementation and support, 5G can reshape the future of learning and empower the next generation of students.

Immersive Technologies and Education

Immersive technologies, such as virtual reality (VR) and augmented reality (AR), have gained significant attention in various fields, including education. These technologies provide an immersive and interactive learning experience by simulating real-life environments or enhancing the existing physical environment. In this section, we will explore the applications of immersive technologies in education, their benefits, challenges, and future directions.

Introduction to Immersive Technologies

Immersive technologies refer to computer-generated environments that simulate real-world experiences or create virtual environments. Virtual reality (VR) is a technology that uses a headset or a similar device to immerse users in a completely virtual environment. Augmented reality (AR), on the other hand, overlays digital content onto the real world, enhancing the user's perception of reality. Both VR and AR have the potential to transform the way we learn and teach.

Benefits of Immersive Technologies in Education

Immersive technologies offer several benefits in education:

- Enhanced Engagement: By creating a realistic and interactive learning environment, immersive technologies can captivate students' attention and increase their engagement in the learning process.

- Active Learning: Immersive technologies encourage active learning through hands-on experiences and exploration, allowing students to manipulate objects, conduct experiments, and solve complex problems in a virtual setting.

- Experiential Learning: Immersive technologies provide opportunities for experiential learning, enabling students to gain practical skills and knowledge through realistic simulations and virtual scenarios.

- Accessibility and Inclusivity: Immersive technologies can make education more accessible and inclusive by creating virtual environments that accommodate different learning needs and preferences. For example, students with disabilities can participate in virtual field trips or experiments that may not be feasible in the physical world.

- Contextual Learning: Immersive technologies provide a context-rich learning experience by enabling students to apply their knowledge in real-world scenarios. This allows for deeper understanding and retention of information.

Applications of Immersive Technologies in Education

Immersive technologies can be applied across various disciplines and educational levels. Here are some examples:

- Science and Engineering: VR and AR can be used to visualize complex scientific concepts, simulate laboratory experiments, or explore engineering designs in a virtual environment.

- History and Social Studies: Immersive technologies can transport students to different historical periods or cultural sites, allowing them to experience history firsthand and engage in interactive simulations of past events.

- Language Learning: VR and AR can create immersive language-learning environments, where students can practice communication skills by interacting with virtual native speakers.

- Medical and Healthcare Education: Immersive technologies can be used to train medical students in surgical procedures, patient diagnosis, and emergency response simulations.

- Arts and Creativity: VR and AR can enable students to create and explore artistic expressions in a virtual space, enhancing their imagination and creativity.

Challenges and Considerations

While immersive technologies offer exciting possibilities for education, there are also challenges to address:

- Cost and Access: Implementation of immersive technologies may require financial resources for the purchase of hardware and software. Moreover, ensuring equitable access to these technologies can be a challenge in schools with limited resources.

- Technical Infrastructure: Immersive technologies often rely on powerful computing systems and high-speed internet connections. Schools need to invest in the necessary infrastructure to support the seamless integration of these technologies.

- Training and Support: Educators may require training and professional development to effectively incorporate immersive technologies into their teaching practices. Ongoing technical support should also be provided to overcome any technical issues that may arise.

- Ethical Considerations: As with any technology, ethical considerations should be taken into account when using immersive technologies in education. Issues such as data privacy, digital citizenship, and responsible use of the technology need to be addressed.

Future Directions

The future of immersive technologies in education looks promising. Here are some potential directions:

- Collaborative Virtual Spaces: Immersive technologies can be used to create collaborative virtual spaces, where students from different geographical locations can interact and work together on projects or simulations.

- Personalized Learning: Immersive technologies can be integrated with adaptive learning systems to provide personalized learning experiences tailored to each student's needs and learning style.

- Data Analytics: By capturing students' interactions and behaviors in virtual environments, data analytics can provide insights into their learning progress and help educators make informed decisions for individualized instruction.

- Gamification and Reward Systems: Immersive technologies can further incorporate gamification elements to enhance motivation and engagement, such as badges, leaderboard, and virtual rewards.

- Haptic Feedback: Advancements in haptic technology can provide tactile feedback in virtual environments, enabling students to feel and manipulate objects, which can enhance the realism and effectiveness of the learning experience.

In conclusion, immersive technologies hold tremendous potential to revolutionize education by creating engaging, interactive, and realistic learning experiences. By leveraging these technologies in innovative ways, educators can enhance student learning outcomes and foster critical thinking, creativity, and problem-solving skills. However, careful consideration of the challenges and ethical considerations is crucial to ensure equitable access and responsible use of immersive technologies in education. With continued research and development, immersive technologies will undoubtedly play a significant role in shaping the future of education.

EdTech Startups and Innovation in Education

In recent years, the field of education has witnessed a surge in technological advancements, leading to an influx of EdTech startups. These startups are dedicated to revolutionizing the learning experience and improving educational outcomes through innovative technologies. This section explores the role of EdTech startups in transforming education and the potential impact of their innovations.

The Importance of EdTech Startups

EdTech startups play a crucial role in addressing the evolving needs and challenges of education. They bring fresh perspectives, cutting-edge technologies, and innovative solutions to the table. These startups often have a deep understanding of the current educational landscape and are well-positioned to identify gaps and opportunities for improvement.

By leveraging technology, EdTech startups can enhance various aspects of education, such as personalized learning, accessibility, collaboration, and engagement. Their solutions have the potential to reach a wide range of learners, including those in remote areas or with diverse needs.

Key Innovations in EdTech Startups

EdTech startups have introduced numerous groundbreaking innovations that have the potential to transform education. Here are some key areas where these startups have made significant contributions:

1. **Personalized Learning Platforms:** EdTech startups have developed platforms that incorporate adaptive learning algorithms and data analytics to provide personalized learning experiences. These platforms can dynamically

adjust content and pace to meet each student's unique needs, ensuring maximum engagement and understanding.

2. **Virtual and Augmented Reality (VR/AR) Applications:** By harnessing the power of VR and AR technologies, EdTech startups are creating immersive learning experiences. Students can explore historical sites, manipulate virtual objects, or conduct virtual experiments, resulting in deeper engagement and understanding of complex concepts.

3. **AI-Powered Intelligent Tutoring Systems:** EdTech startups are using artificial intelligence (AI) to develop intelligent tutoring systems that provide personalized guidance and support. These systems can analyze learner performance, identify areas of improvement, and offer targeted feedback and recommendations.

4. **Blockchain for Verifiable Credentials:** EdTech startups are exploring the potential of blockchain technology to securely store and verify educational credentials. This innovation ensures the authenticity of certificates and degrees, simplifies the hiring process for employers, and empowers learners by providing them with immutable records of their achievements.

5. **Gamification for Enhanced Engagement:** EdTech startups are incorporating gamification elements into educational platforms to make learning more engaging and interactive. By integrating game-like features such as rewards, leaderboards, and challenges, these startups are motivating learners to actively participate and progress in their educational journey.

Challenges and Opportunities

While EdTech startups bring immense potential for transforming education, they also face various challenges along the way. Some key challenges include:

- **Implementation and Adoption:** Convincing educational institutions to adopt new technologies and practices can be a major hurdle for EdTech startups. Resistance to change, lack of infrastructure, and limited resources can impede the widespread adoption of innovative solutions.

- **Equity and Accessibility:** While EdTech startups have the potential to bridge the educational gap, ensuring equitable access to technology and educational resources remains a challenge. Factors like affordability, internet connectivity, and device availability need to be addressed to reach underserved populations.

- **Data Privacy and Security:** The collection and use of student data raise concerns about privacy and security. EdTech startups must prioritize the protection of user data, comply with regulations, and transparently communicate their data privacy practices to build trust among educators, parents, and students.

Despite these challenges, EdTech startups have numerous opportunities to make a lasting impact on education. Here are some areas where opportunities abound:

- **Collaboration with Educators:** By collaborating closely with educators, EdTech startups can co-design and co-develop solutions that address the real needs of the classroom. This partnership ensures the creation of effective tools that seamlessly integrate into existing educational practices.

- **Continuous Innovation:** The field of education is constantly evolving, and EdTech startups must continue to innovate and adapt to meet emerging needs. By staying abreast of the latest research and trends, startups can develop forward-thinking solutions that address future challenges and opportunities.

- **Research and Evaluation:** EdTech startups should invest in rigorous research and evaluation of their products to provide evidence of their effectiveness. Conducting studies, partnering with academic institutions, and publishing results can help build credibility and generate widespread adoption.

Case Studies and Best Practices

To illustrate the impact of EdTech startups, let's look at two case studies:

1. **Kahoot!:** Kahoot! is an example of a successful EdTech startup that has transformed classroom engagement through gamification. Their platform enables educators to create interactive quizzes and games, turning learning into a fun and collaborative experience. With millions of active users worldwide, Kahoot! has demonstrated the power of gamified learning in enhancing student motivation and knowledge retention.

2. **Duolingo:** Duolingo is a language-learning platform that has made language education accessible to millions of learners worldwide. Through its mobile application, Duolingo provides personalized language instruction, making

learning engaging and convenient. The gamified nature of the app, with its rewards and progress tracking, has motivated learners to achieve their language goals.

These case studies highlight the transformative potential of EdTech startups and how they can revolutionize education by leveraging innovative technologies and approaches.

Resources and Further Reading

For further exploration of EdTech startups and innovation in education, the following resources provide valuable insights:

- *EdSurge*: A comprehensive news and analysis platform dedicated to education technology. It covers the latest trends, innovations, and challenges in the EdTech industry. (Website: `https://www.edsurge.com/`)
- *Getting Smart*: A website that provides resources and articles on educational innovation and the future of learning. It offers insights into the role of EdTech startups in transforming education. (Website: `https://www.gettingsmart.com/`)
- *EdTechXGlobal*: An organization that brings together education technology entrepreneurs, investors, and thought leaders. It hosts events and publishes reports on the global EdTech ecosystem. (Website: `https://edtechxglobal.com/`)

These resources will help readers delve deeper into the world of EdTech startups and stay informed about the latest developments in educational innovation.

Exercises

To solidify your understanding of EdTech startups and innovation in education, consider the following exercises:

1. Research and identify one EdTech startup that has made a significant impact on education. Describe their innovative solution and explain how it has transformed the learning experience.
2. Create a hypothetical EdTech startup that addresses a specific educational challenge using emerging technologies. Develop a concept for a product or platform and outline its key features and potential impact.

3. Explore the ethical considerations associated with using AI in education technology. Discuss the potential benefits and risks of AI-powered solutions, and propose strategies for ensuring responsible and ethical use.

These exercises will allow you to apply the concepts discussed in this section and think critically about the role of EdTech startups in shaping the future of education.

Conclusion

EdTech startups have the potential to revolutionize education by leveraging innovative technologies and approaches. Through personalized learning platforms, virtual and augmented reality applications, AI-powered tutoring systems, and other groundbreaking innovations, these startups are transforming the educational landscape. However, challenges such as implementation and adoption, equity, and data privacy must be addressed for their innovations to reach their full potential. By fostering collaboration with educators, continuous innovation, rigorous research and evaluation, and adherence to ethical principles, EdTech startups can drive significant positive change in education. As the field continues to evolve, it is essential to closely monitor the developments in EdTech and embrace the opportunities they provide for improving learning outcomes and promoting equitable access to education.

Ethical Considerations in the Future of Education

The future of education is shaped by innovative technologies and transformative methods that have the potential to revolutionize traditional learning practices. While these advancements offer exciting opportunities, they also raise important ethical considerations that need to be addressed. In this section, we will explore the ethical implications of adopting new educational technologies and methodologies, and discuss strategies for ensuring responsible and ethical practices in the future of education.

Equity and Access

One of the key ethical considerations in the future of education is equity and access. As technology becomes increasingly integrated into educational settings, it is crucial to ensure that all students, regardless of their socioeconomic background or geographical location, have equal opportunities to access quality education. The digital divide, which refers to the gap in access to technology and digital resources, must be addressed to prevent further marginalization of disadvantaged groups.

To promote equity and access, educational institutions and policymakers must prioritize efforts to close the digital divide. This includes providing affordable internet access, ensuring availability of devices and infrastructure in underserved areas, and offering comprehensive digital literacy programs. Additionally, educators should be trained to design inclusive learning experiences that cater to diverse student needs and support students with limited access to technology.

Data Privacy and Security

As educational technologies collect and analyze large amounts of data, the issue of data privacy and security becomes paramount. Students' personal information, such as their academic performance, social interactions, and behavioral patterns, should be handled with utmost care to safeguard their privacy. Education institutions and edtech companies must establish robust data protection and security measures to prevent unauthorized access, data breaches, and misuse of students' information.

To ensure ethical practices in data privacy and security, educational stakeholders should adhere to established privacy laws and regulations, such as the Family Educational Rights and Privacy Act (FERPA) in the United States. Transparent data collection and usage policies should be communicated to students, parents, and teachers, and explicit consent should be obtained when collecting sensitive data. Additionally, encryption techniques and secure storage systems should be employed to protect student data from potential cyber threats.

Ethical Use of Artificial Intelligence

The increasing integration of artificial intelligence (AI) in education brings along ethical considerations that need careful attention. AI-powered technologies, such as intelligent tutoring systems and automated essay scoring, have the potential to enhance learning outcomes and efficiency. However, they also raise concerns related to fairness, bias, and the role of human agency in the learning process.

Ethical considerations in AI include ensuring transparency and explainability of AI algorithms, addressing bias in data and system outputs, and safeguarding human decision-making. Developers and educators should regularly evaluate and audit AI systems to identify and mitigate biases that may arise from the data used to train the algorithms. Additionally, educators should maintain a balance between AI-driven instruction and human interaction, ensuring that students have agency in their learning and opportunities for personal growth.

Digital Citizenship and Online Behavior

The future of education is increasingly digital, with online learning platforms, social media, and collaborative tools becoming integral to the learning experience. It is essential to promote responsible digital citizenship and ethical online behavior among students. This includes teaching students about appropriate online conduct, respecting others' privacy, critically evaluating information, and combating digital misinformation and cyberbullying.

Educators should incorporate digital citizenship education into the curriculum, fostering discussions on online ethics, privacy, and responsible use of technology. They should also model appropriate online behavior and guide students in developing critical thinking skills to navigate the digital landscape effectively.

Bias and Inequality in Educational Technologies

Another ethical consideration in the future of education is addressing bias and inequality in educational technologies. The algorithms and data used in edtech applications can inadvertently perpetuate existing biases and inequalities in education. For example, automated grading systems may be biased against certain students or reinforce gender or racial stereotypes.

To combat bias and inequality, educational institutions and developers should actively engage in data ethics and diversity initiatives. This involves conducting regular audits of educational technologies to identify biases and implementing strategies to address them. Additionally, involving diverse voices and perspectives in the development and decision-making processes can help create more inclusive and unbiased educational technologies.

Ethics of Learning Analytics

Learning analytics, the collection and analysis of student data to support educational decision-making, poses ethical challenges. While learning analytics can offer valuable insights into student progress and help personalize instruction, ethical concerns arise regarding consent, data accuracy, and potential negative consequences.

Educational institutions and educators should be transparent about the types of data collected, how it is used, and the potential impact on students. Informed consent from students and their parents should be obtained prior to data collection, and data should be anonymized and used in aggregate form whenever possible. Moreover, educators should use learning analytics responsibly, considering the potential educational benefits alongside the potential risks to students' privacy and well-being.

Ethics of Educational Research

As the future of education relies on evidence-based practices and educational research, ethical considerations in conducting research become critical. Researchers in education must follow ethical guidelines to ensure the well-being and rights of participants, maintain integrity in reporting findings, and prevent conflicts of interest.

Ethical considerations in educational research include obtaining informed consent, protecting participant confidentiality, minimizing harm, and conducting unbiased research. Adhering to ethical standards not only protects the rights of participants but also ensures the validity and reliability of the research outcomes.

Promoting Ethical Decision-Making Skills

To address ethical considerations in the future of education, it is crucial to cultivate ethical decision-making skills in students. Ethical education should be an integral part of the curriculum, empowering students to navigate complex ethical dilemmas they might encounter in the digital age.

Educators should create opportunities for students to reflect on ethical issues, engage in ethical discussions, and develop critical thinking skills to make informed and responsible choices. By promoting ethical decision-making, educators can prepare students to become responsible digital citizens who contribute positively to society.

Conclusion

As we embrace the transformative methods and cutting-edge tools in the future of education, we must not overlook the ethical considerations associated with these advancements. By addressing equity and access, data privacy and security, bias and inequality, and fostering digital citizenship, we can ensure responsible and ethical practices in education. Moreover, promoting ethical decision-making skills among students will empower them to navigate the complex ethical landscapes of the digital future. By upholding ethical principles, we can create an inclusive and equitable educational environment that maximizes the potential of transformative education.

Redesigning curricula for the future

In order to prepare students for the future, it is essential to redesign curricula in a way that aligns with the demands and opportunities of the 21st century. The traditional curriculum, which has been largely based on a one-size-fits-all approach, is no longer sufficient to meet the needs of a rapidly changing world. Redesigning curricula for the future requires a shift towards a more flexible, personalized, and interdisciplinary approach. This section will explore the key principles and strategies for redesigning curricula to prepare students for the future.

Understanding the needs of the future

To redesign curricula for the future, it is important to first understand the needs of the future. The rapid advancement of technology, globalization, and the changing nature of work are reshaping the skills and knowledge that students will require in the future. Some of the key skills and competencies that are increasingly important include:

- Critical thinking and problem-solving: As automation and artificial intelligence continue to replace routine tasks, the ability to think critically and creatively, and to solve complex problems, will be highly valued in the future.
- Collaboration and teamwork: In an interconnected and globalized world, the ability to work effectively in teams and collaborate with diverse groups of people will be essential.
- Communication and digital literacy: With the proliferation of digital technologies, the ability to effectively communicate, both orally and in writing, and to navigate and critically evaluate information online, will be crucial.
- Adaptability and resilience: Given the pace of change, students will need to be adaptable, resilient, and open to continuous learning and growth.
- Cultural competence and empathy: In an increasingly diverse world, students need to develop cultural competence and empathy to understand and work effectively with people from different backgrounds and perspectives.

By identifying these key skills and competencies, educators can begin to reshape curricula to ensure that all students are equipped with the necessary knowledge, skills, and attitudes to thrive in the future.

Interdisciplinary and integrated approach

To prepare students for the complex and interconnected challenges of the future, curricula should move away from the traditional subject-based approach and adopt an interdisciplinary and integrated approach. This approach helps students make connections across different disciplines and apply their learning to real-world problems.

Interdisciplinary learning involves the integration of knowledge, concepts, and skills from multiple disciplines to create a more holistic understanding of a given topic. By breaking down the silos between subjects, students gain a broader perspective and are better equipped to tackle complex issues.

For example, instead of teaching science, technology, engineering, and mathematics (STEM) as separate subjects, an interdisciplinary approach would integrate these disciplines into a cohesive curriculum, where students can learn how to apply scientific principles and technology to solve engineering problems.

Focus on critical thinking and problem-solving

Critical thinking and problem-solving skills are crucial for success in the future. Therefore, curricula should emphasize the development of these skills across all subjects and grade levels. Students need to learn how to analyze information, evaluate evidence, and think critically to solve complex problems.

One effective strategy for promoting critical thinking and problem-solving is through project-based learning. In project-based learning, students work on real-world projects that require them to apply their knowledge and skills to solve authentic problems. This approach encourages students to think critically, collaborate with others, and develop practical solutions.

For example, instead of simply memorizing historical facts, students could engage in a project where they research and analyze primary sources to understand different perspectives on historical events. They could then present their findings in a multimedia presentation, showcasing their ability to think critically and communicate effectively.

Embracing technology

Technology is transforming every aspect of our lives, and education is no exception. To prepare students for the future, curricula should leverage technology to enhance learning experiences and develop digital literacy.

One important aspect of using technology in curricula is to provide students with opportunities to use digital tools and resources to explore, create, collaborate, and communicate. For example, students can use online simulation software to conduct virtual experiments in science, or they can collaborate with peers in different countries through video conferencing tools to work on a global project.

Additionally, curricula should also address ethical considerations and digital citizenship. Students need to understand how to use technology responsibly, ethically, and safely. Topics such as online privacy, cyberbullying, and digital footprints should be integrated into the curriculum to equip students with the knowledge and skills to navigate the digital world.

Assessment and feedback

Redesigning curricula also necessitates rethinking assessment practices. The traditional focus on standardized testing should be shifted towards more authentic and formative assessment methods that align with the skills and competencies valued in the future.

Authentic assessment involves the evaluation of students' ability to apply their knowledge and skills in real-world contexts. This can include performance-based tasks, portfolios, presentations, and other forms of assessment that mirror real-world challenges and requirements.

Formative assessment, on the other hand, emphasizes ongoing feedback and the use of assessment data to inform instruction and student learning. This can be achieved through the use of technology-enhanced formative assessment tools, which can provide real-time feedback and enable personalized learning experiences.

By incorporating authentic and formative assessment methods, curricula can better measure students' progress in developing the desired skills and competencies and provide meaningful feedback to support their growth.

Professional development for teachers

Redesigning curricula for the future requires a significant shift in teaching practices. To effectively implement the changes, educators need ongoing professional development opportunities that support their understanding of new pedagogies, technologies, and assessment practices.

Professional development should provide teachers with the knowledge and skills to implement interdisciplinary and integrated curricula, promote critical thinking and problem-solving, integrate technology effectively, and use authentic and formative assessment strategies.

Furthermore, teachers need opportunities to collaborate, share best practices, and learn from one another. This can be achieved through professional learning communities, where teachers can engage in collaborative planning, reflection, and problem-solving.

Engaging stakeholders

Redesigning curricula for the future requires the collaboration and involvement of various stakeholders, including educators, students, parents, policymakers, and industry partners.

Educators should engage in dialogue with other stakeholders to gain insights into the needs of the future workforce and to ensure that curricula are aligned with industry expectations. Industry partners can provide valuable input on the knowledge, skills, and competencies that are in high demand and help shape curricula accordingly.

Similarly, students and parents should have a voice in curricula design to ensure that their perspectives and aspirations are taken into consideration.

Policymakers play a crucial role in providing the necessary support and resources to enable the redesign of curricula. They can create policies that encourage innovation, provide funding for professional development, and support the integration of technology in curricula.

Case studies and best practices

To inspire and guide curricula redesign efforts, it is important to study successful examples and best practices from around the world. By examining case studies of schools and districts that have successfully redesigned their curricula, educators can gain insights into effective strategies, implementation challenges, and the impact on student learning.

These case studies should showcase examples of interdisciplinary and integrated curricula, innovative pedagogies, effective use of technology, and comprehensive assessment practices. By highlighting the stories of these successful initiatives, educators can learn from their experiences and adapt their approaches to their own contexts.

In conclusion, redesigning curricula for the future requires a paradigm shift from a subject-based approach to an interdisciplinary and integrated approach that focuses on the development of critical thinking, problem-solving, and digital literacy skills. It also requires the effective use of technology, the implementation of authentic and formative assessment practices, ongoing professional development for teachers, and the active engagement of stakeholders. By embracing these principles and strategies, educators can ensure that students are prepared to thrive in the dynamic and uncertain future ahead.

Life-long Learning and Continuous Education

In today's fast-paced and ever-changing world, the need for life-long learning and continuous education has become increasingly evident. The concept of life-long learning refers to the ongoing process of acquiring knowledge, skills, and competencies throughout one's entire life. Continuous education, on the other hand, emphasizes the importance of regularly updating and upgrading one's knowledge and skills to stay relevant in a rapidly evolving society.

1. The Importance of Life-long Learning

Life-long learning offers numerous benefits to individuals, society, and the economy. It enables individuals to adapt to new technologies, industries, and job market demands. By continuously expanding their knowledge and skills, individuals can enhance their career prospects, increase their earning potential, and improve their overall well-being.

From a societal perspective, life-long learning promotes social inclusion and active citizenship. It empowers individuals to actively participate in their communities, engage in lifelong friendships, and contribute to the development of a socially just and cohesive society.

In terms of the economy, life-long learning plays a crucial role in fostering innovation, productivity, and competitiveness. It equips the workforce with the necessary skills to excel in a knowledge-based economy and enables businesses to adapt to changing market conditions.

2. Strategies for Promoting Life-long Learning

To foster a culture of life-long learning, various strategies can be implemented:

2.1. Promoting Learning Opportunities: Governments, educational institutions, and employers should collaborate to provide accessible and affordable learning opportunities to individuals of all ages. This can include the provision of online courses, flexible learning pathways, and recognition of prior learning.

2.2. Raising Awareness: Efforts should be made to create awareness about the benefits of life-long learning and the various opportunities available. This can be done through information campaigns, community outreach programs, and the involvement of role models who have successfully pursued life-long learning.

2.3. Creating Supportive Environments: Educational institutions and workplaces should create supportive environments that encourage and facilitate life-long learning. This can involve providing mentoring programs, study leave or sabbatical opportunities, and financial assistance for further education.

2.4. Emphasizing Continuous Professional Development: Continuous professional development should be an integral part of every profession. Employers should encourage and support employees to engage in continuous learning activities through training programs, workshops, conferences, and professional networks.

3. Challenges and Solutions

While the importance of life-long learning is widely recognized, there are several challenges that need to be addressed:

3.1. Access and Affordability: Access to learning opportunities and the cost associated with them can be barriers for many individuals. Governments and educational institutions should work together to ensure equal access to quality education and provide financial support to those who need it.

3.2. Relevance and Currency: In a rapidly changing world, ensuring the relevance and currency of learning programs is crucial. Curriculum and course content should be regularly updated to reflect the latest developments in various fields.

3.3. Motivation and Engagement: Sustaining motivation and engagement in life-long learning can be challenging. Learning programs should be designed in a way that is engaging, interactive, and relevant to the learners' interests and aspirations.

3.4. Recognition and Validation: Recognizing and validating the knowledge and skills acquired through life-long learning is important. Governments and employers should develop mechanisms to assess and recognize non-formal and informal learning achievements.

4. Case Studies and Best Practices

Numerous case studies and best practices illustrate the successful implementation of life-long learning initiatives:

4.1. Singapore's SkillsFuture Initiative: The SkillsFuture initiative in Singapore aims to provide Singaporeans with opportunities to develop their skills throughout their lives. It includes various programs, grants, and subsidies to support individuals in pursuing continuous learning and upgrading their skills.

4.2. The European Lifelong Learning Program: The European Union's Lifelong Learning Program promotes cooperation and exchange of best practices in education and training throughout Europe. It encompasses various initiatives, such as Erasmus+, that support mobility, cooperation, and innovation in education and training.

4.3. Corporate Learning and Development Programs: Many companies recognize the importance of continuous learning and have implemented learning and development programs for their employees. These programs often include training workshops, mentoring programs, and access to online learning platforms.

5. Future Directions

The future of life-long learning and continuous education is closely tied to technological advancements and the evolving nature of work. Some future directions in this field include:

5.1. Online and Digital Learning: Online and digital learning platforms provide flexible and accessible learning opportunities, allowing individuals to learn at their own pace and convenience. The use of virtual reality, augmented reality, and gamification can enhance the learning experience.

5.2. Microlearning: Microlearning refers to short, focused learning modules that are easily digestible and can be completed in a short amount of time. This approach allows learners to acquire specific skills or knowledge in a targeted and efficient manner.

5.3. Personalized Learning: Personalized learning leverages technology to tailor learning experiences to individual learners' needs, preferences, and pace. Adaptive learning algorithms and artificial intelligence can identify learners' strengths and weaknesses and provide personalized feedback and content recommendations.

5.4. Lifelong Learning Accounts: Lifelong learning accounts, similar to retirement savings accounts, can be established to provide individuals with financial support for their continuous educational pursuits. These accounts can be funded by individuals, employers, and governments.

5.5. Collaborative and Social Learning: Collaborative and social learning environments enable individuals to learn from and with others. Online communities, social learning platforms, and peer-to-peer learning networks can facilitate collaboration and knowledge sharing.

In conclusion, life-long learning and continuous education are essential for individuals, societies, and economies to thrive in an ever-changing world. By promoting and supporting life-long learning initiatives, we can empower individuals to acquire new knowledge and skills, adapt to change, and contribute meaningfully to their personal and professional lives.

The role of educators in shaping the future of education

Educators play a crucial role in shaping the future of education. As the field of education continues to evolve, it is essential for educators to adapt and embrace new pedagogical approaches and technologies. This section explores the key responsibilities and opportunities for educators in shaping the future of education.

Responsibilities of Educators

Educators have a responsibility to prepare students for the challenges and opportunities of the future. This involves not only imparting knowledge but also developing critical thinking skills, creativity, and adaptability. Some of the key responsibilities of educators in shaping the future of education include:

1. **Facilitating personalized learning:** Educators need to embrace personalized learning approaches that take into account the unique needs and interests of each student. This includes using data and technology to tailor instruction and providing individualized support.

2. **Promoting digital literacy:** In an increasingly digital world, educators must ensure that students have the necessary digital literacy skills. This involves teaching students how to critically evaluate online information, navigate digital platforms, and use technology for learning.

3. **Fostering collaboration:** Educators should create opportunities for collaborative learning, both in physical and virtual environments. Collaboration fosters creativity, communication, and problem-solving skills, which are essential for success in the future.

4. **Cultivating social and emotional skills:** Educators play a crucial role in supporting the social and emotional development of students. They must create a safe and supportive classroom environment, teach conflict resolution skills, and promote empathy and emotional intelligence.

5. **Teaching critical thinking and problem-solving:** As automation and artificial intelligence continue to advance, critical thinking and problem-solving skills will become even more important. Educators need to provide opportunities for students to analyze complex problems, think critically, and develop innovative solutions.

Opportunities for Educators

While the future of education presents challenges, it also offers exciting opportunities for educators to innovate and make a meaningful impact. Some of the key opportunities for educators in shaping the future of education include:

1. **Embracing educational technology:** Educators can leverage educational technologies to enhance teaching and learning. This includes using virtual reality, artificial intelligence, gamification, and data analytics to create engaging and personalized learning experiences.

2. **Promoting global and cultural competence:** Educators can incorporate global perspectives into the curriculum and provide opportunities for students to

engage in virtual exchanges and international collaborations. This fosters global competence and prepares students to be global citizens.

3. **Advocating for equity and inclusion:** Educators have the opportunity to advocate for equity and inclusion in education. This involves addressing disparities in access to technology, advocating for culturally responsive teaching practices, and creating inclusive learning environments.

4. **Developing interdisciplinary and transdisciplinary approaches:** The future of work will require individuals to have a broad range of skills and knowledge. Educators can promote interdisciplinary and transdisciplinary approaches that encourage students to make connections across different subject areas and apply their skills in real-world contexts.

5. **Engaging in professional development:** Educators should invest in continuous professional development to stay updated with the latest research, trends, and best practices in education. This includes attending conferences, participating in online courses, and collaborating with other educators.

Real-World Example: The Role of Educators in AI Education

Artificial intelligence (AI) is rapidly transforming various industries, including education. Educators have a unique role in preparing students for the ethical, social, and practical implications of AI. They can teach students about the principles and applications of AI, help them understand the ethical considerations, and encourage them to critically evaluate AI algorithms and systems.

An example of how educators can shape the future of AI education is by integrating AI into the curriculum. Educators can design projects and activities that involve AI technologies, such as designing AI-powered chatbots or analyzing data using machine learning algorithms. By providing hands-on experiences with AI, educators can inspire students to pursue careers in AI and equip them with the skills needed for the future workforce.

Resources and Tools for Educators

Educators can access a range of resources and tools to support their role in shaping the future of education. Some recommended resources and tools include:

1. **Professional development programs:** Organizations like the International Society for Technology in Education (ISTE), Edutopia, and TeachThought offer professional development programs for educators interested in innovative teaching practices and educational technologies.

2. **Education technology platforms:** Platforms like Google for Education, Microsoft Education, and Edmodo provide educators with access to a wide range of tools and resources for creating engaging learning experiences.

3. **Educational research journals:** Journals such as *Educational Researcher, Journal of Educational Technology & Society*, and *Computers & Education* publish research articles on innovative teaching practices, educational technologies, and future trends in education.

4. **Online learning communities:** Platforms like Twitter, LinkedIn, and educational blogs facilitate collaboration and knowledge-sharing among educators. Connecting with other educators allows for the exchange of best practices and ideas.

Challenges and Considerations

While the role of educators in shaping the future of education is crucial, there are also challenges and considerations to keep in mind. Some of these challenges include:

1. **Resistance to change:** Implementing innovative approaches to education may face resistance from educators who are comfortable with traditional teaching methods. It is essential to address concerns, provide professional development opportunities, and demonstrate the value of transformative education.

2. **Equitable access to resources:** Ensuring equitable access to technology and resources can be a challenge, particularly in economically disadvantaged areas. Educators need to advocate for policies and initiatives that bridge the digital divide and promote equal opportunities for all students.

3. **Ethical considerations:** As technology becomes more prevalent in education, educators need to navigate ethical considerations related to data privacy, artificial intelligence, and online safety. It is crucial to prioritize student well-being and make responsible decisions when implementing technology in the classroom.

4. **Continuous learning and adaptability:** The field of education is constantly evolving, and educators need to be adaptable and open to lifelong learning. Staying updated with the latest research and trends in education is critical for effective teaching and shaping the future of education.

Conclusion

The future of education relies heavily on the role of educators in shaping the learning experiences of students. Educators must embrace their responsibilities and opportunities by incorporating personalized learning, promoting digital literacy, fostering collaboration, cultivating social and emotional skills, and teaching critical thinking. By embracing new pedagogical approaches, leveraging educational technologies, advocating for equity and inclusion, and engaging in continuous professional development, educators can have a transformative impact on education and prepare students for the future.

Policy and Funding for Transformative Education

Policy Frameworks for Transformative Education

Policy frameworks play a crucial role in guiding and implementing transformative education practices. They provide a roadmap for educators, policymakers, and stakeholders to create an enabling environment that fosters innovation, equity, and quality in education. In this section, we will explore the key elements of policy frameworks for transformative education and their significance in driving educational reform.

Defining Policy Frameworks for Transformative Education

Policy frameworks for transformative education refer to a set of guidelines, principles, and strategies that shape the design, implementation, and evaluation of educational policies. These frameworks are aimed at ensuring that education systems embrace innovative practices, adapt to changing societal needs, and meet the diverse needs of learners.

At the core of policy frameworks for transformative education is the recognition that education should go beyond traditional classroom instruction. It should foster critical thinking, creativity, problem-solving skills, and social-emotional development. These frameworks promote student-centered approaches, collaborative learning, personalized instruction, and the integration of cutting-edge technologies.

Principles of Policy Frameworks for Transformative Education

Policy frameworks for transformative education are guided by several core principles that underpin their design and implementation. These principles include:

1. Equity and Inclusion: Transformative education policy frameworks emphasize the importance of providing equitable and inclusive learning opportunities for all students. They aim to reduce educational disparities, address gender and socio-economic inequalities, and ensure that no learner is left behind.

2. Collaboration and Stakeholder Engagement: These frameworks recognize the need for collaboration among policymakers, educators, parents, students, and communities. They encourage active stakeholder engagement in decision-making processes, ensuring that diverse perspectives are considered.

3. Continuous Professional Development: Policy frameworks for transformative education prioritize the professional development of teachers and educational leaders. They promote lifelong learning, support the acquisition of new pedagogical skills and competencies, and encourage teachers to continuously adapt and innovate.

4. Research and Evidence-based Practices: These frameworks emphasize the use of research and evidence to inform policy decisions. They encourage educational research, evaluation, and the dissemination of best practices to ensure that policies are based on sound evidence and contribute to positive educational outcomes.

5. Technology Integration: Policy frameworks for transformative education recognize the role of technology in enhancing teaching and learning. They promote the integration of educational technologies, including artificial intelligence, virtual reality, and data analytics, to create engaging and personalized learning environments.

Key Components of Policy Frameworks for Transformative Education

Policy frameworks for transformative education encompass several key components that provide a comprehensive approach to educational reform. These components include:

1. Vision and Goals: A clear vision and set of goals are essential in guiding the transformative education agenda. Policy frameworks articulate the desired outcomes and direction of educational reform, providing a shared vision for all stakeholders.

2. Curriculum and Pedagogy: These frameworks address curriculum design, pedagogical approaches, and instructional strategies that support transformative education. They encourage the adoption of student-centered, inquiry-based, and competency-based curricula, fostering active learning and critical thinking skills.

3. Assessment and Evaluation: Policy frameworks for transformative education advocate for formative, authentic, and competency-based assessments that assess students' acquisition of skills and competencies. They promote the use of technology-enhanced assessments and emphasize the importance of feedback and self-reflection.

4. Teacher Professional Development: These frameworks prioritize the continuous professional development of teachers. They outline strategies and resources for equipping teachers with the necessary skills to implement

transformative pedagogies, integrate technology, and foster inclusive learning environments.

5. Infrastructure and Resources: Policy frameworks recognize the importance of providing adequate infrastructure, resources, and support for transformative education. They address issues related to the availability of digital devices, internet connectivity, learning materials, and funding mechanisms to ensure equitable access to quality education.

6. Partnerships and Collaboration: These frameworks encourage partnerships and collaboration among key stakeholders, including government agencies, international organizations, civil society, and the private sector. They promote the sharing of resources, expertise, and best practices to drive educational innovation and reform.

Examples of Policy Frameworks for Transformative Education

Several countries have developed policy frameworks for transformative education that provide valuable examples of successful educational reforms. Let's explore two prominent examples:

1. Education 2030: The Education 2030 Framework for Action, developed by UNESCO, provides a comprehensive roadmap for transforming education systems worldwide. It advocates for inclusive and equitable quality education and lifelong learning opportunities for all. The framework emphasizes the importance of developing 21st-century skills, fostering global citizenship, and leveraging technology for educational innovation.

2. Future Ready Singapore: Singapore's "Future Ready" education strategy focuses on equipping students with the knowledge and skills they need to thrive in a rapidly changing world. The policy framework embraces personalized learning, digital literacy, and a culture of innovation. It emphasizes the integration of technology-enhanced pedagogies, the development of socio-emotional competencies, and the fostering of a growth mindset.

Challenges and Caveats

While policy frameworks for transformative education offer promising pathways for educational reform, they also face several challenges and caveats:

1. Implementation Gap: The successful implementation of transformative education policies requires strong leadership, adequate resources, and effective coordination among stakeholders. Often, there is a gap between policy intentions and on-the-ground realities, necessitating careful planning and ongoing support.

2. Resistance to Change: Educational systems can be resistant to change, especially when it disrupts existing practices and structures. Overcoming resistance to change among educators, students, and communities is a critical challenge in implementing transformative education policies.

3. Equity and Inclusion: Ensuring equitable access to transformative education is a complex challenge, particularly in contexts with resource constraints and marginalized communities. Policy frameworks must address systemic barriers, such as the digital divide and socio-economic inequalities, to achieve truly inclusive education.

4. Sustainability: Transformative education requires ongoing commitment and long-term vision. Policy frameworks must consider the sustainability of reforms beyond individual initiatives, ensuring that transformative practices become embedded in educational systems and endure over time.

Resources and Further Readings

1. UNESCO (2015). Education 2030 Framework for Action: Towards Inclusive and Equitable Quality Education and Lifelong Learning. Retrieved from: `http://unesdoc.unesco.org/images/0024/002456/245656e.pdf`

2. Ministry of Education, Singapore (2015). Future Ready: Rethinking Learning in Schools for the Digital Age. Retrieved from: `https://www.moe.gov.sg/docs/default-source/document/education/reviews/recommendations-of-the-21st-century-competencies-and-student-outc.pdf`

3. Fullan, M. (2017). The New Meaning of Educational Change (5th Edition). Routledge.

4. Hargreaves, A., & Fullan, M. (2012). Professional Capital: Transforming Teaching in Every School. Teachers College Press.

5. Darling-Hammond, L., & Bransford, J. (2005). Preparing Teachers for a Changing World: What Teachers Should Learn and Be Able to Do. Jossey-Bass.

Summary

Policy frameworks for transformative education serve as guiding documents to shape educational reform and innovation. They encompass principles that promote equity, collaboration, and continuous professional development. These frameworks address various components, such as curriculum, assessment, teacher professional development, infrastructure, and partnerships. However, challenges related to implementation, resistance to change, equity, and sustainability must be carefully navigated. By leveraging the principles and components of policy frameworks, stakeholders can drive transformative changes that create inclusive, equitable, and future-ready education systems.

Government Initiatives and Funding for Educational Innovation

In order to foster educational innovation and support transformative methods in education, governments around the world have implemented various initiatives and funding programs. These efforts aim to address the challenges faced by educators and institutions in adopting new technologies and pedagogical approaches, while also ensuring equitable access and quality education for all students. In this section, we will explore some of the key government initiatives and funding mechanisms that promote educational innovation.

National Innovation Strategies

Many countries have developed national innovation strategies that include specific provisions for the education sector. These strategies recognize the importance of leveraging technology and innovative approaches to enhance teaching and learning outcomes. They typically involve collaboration between government agencies, educational institutions, and industry partners.

One example of a national innovation strategy is the "Digital Agenda for Education" in Germany. This initiative focuses on integrating digital technologies into classrooms, developing teachers' digital competencies, and promoting digital literacy among students. The German government has allocated significant funding for research and development projects, as well as professional development programs for educators.

Government Funding Programs

Governments allocate funding to support educational innovation through various funding programs. These programs aim to encourage research and development in educational technology, as well as the implementation of innovative teaching and learning practices. They provide financial support to educational institutions, researchers, and edtech startups.

For instance, the United States Department of Education offers funding opportunities through programs like the Education Innovation and Research (EIR) program. This program provides grants to support the development, implementation, and scaling-up of evidence-based innovations in education. The funding can be used for activities such as designing new instructional approaches, developing educational technologies, and evaluating their impact on student outcomes.

Public-Private Partnerships

Public-private partnerships (PPPs) are collaborations between government entities and private organizations or companies. PPPs often play a crucial role in supporting educational innovation by combining public funding with private sector expertise and resources. These partnerships can involve joint research projects, technology integration initiatives, or the provision of educational resources and tools.

An example of a successful PPP in educational innovation is the "Hour of Code" campaign, a collaboration between Code.org, a non-profit organization, and several tech companies. Through this initiative, governments and private sector partners come together to promote computer science education through coding activities. The campaign provides free resources and training for teachers and has reached millions of students worldwide.

International Funding and Organizations

In addition to national efforts, international organizations and funding agencies also contribute to educational innovation. They provide financial support, expertise, and resources to countries, particularly in developing regions, to help them implement transformative methods and technologies.

One prominent international organization is the Global Partnership for Education (GPE), a multi-stakeholder partnership that aims to improve education in low-income countries. GPE provides funding and technical assistance to governments, helping them develop and implement innovative education programs. This includes support for teacher training, infrastructure development, and the integration of technology in classrooms.

Challenges and Considerations

While government initiatives and funding are essential for promoting educational innovation, several challenges and considerations need to be addressed. It is crucial to ensure that funding is allocated equitably, with a focus on reducing the digital divide and supporting marginalized communities. Additionally, ethical considerations, such as data privacy and security, must be taken into account in the implementation of educational technologies.

Furthermore, sustainable and long-term funding models are necessary to sustain ongoing innovation in education. Governments should prioritize the allocation of resources for professional development opportunities for teachers, as well as for research and evaluation of educational innovations.

Conclusion

Government initiatives and funding play a significant role in promoting educational innovation and supporting transformative methods in education. By investing in research and development, providing financial resources, and fostering collaborations, governments can drive the adoption of innovative technologies and pedagogies. It is crucial for governments to consider equity, ethical considerations, and long-term sustainability when designing and implementing funding programs. Through these efforts, governments can create an environment conducive to transformative education that benefits students and educators alike.

The role of international organizations in promoting transformative education

Transformative education aims to bring about significant changes in individuals and societies by empowering learners and fostering critical thinking, creativity, and problem-solving skills. To achieve this, the role of international organizations becomes crucial as they provide guidance, resources, and support to educational systems worldwide. In this section, we will explore the role of international organizations in promoting transformative education and how they contribute to shaping the future of learning.

The importance of international organizations in education

International organizations play a pivotal role in education as they can provide a global perspective, expertise, and resources that individual countries may lack. They act as catalysts for change, helping countries strengthen their education systems and adapt to the changing needs of learners and societies. These organizations facilitate the dissemination of best practices, foster collaboration among nations, and promote educational equity and inclusivity.

UNESCO and its initiatives for transformative education

The United Nations Educational, Scientific and Cultural Organization (UNESCO) is a leading international organization dedicated to promoting transformative education worldwide. UNESCO's initiatives aim to enhance the quality of education, improve access to education for marginalized populations, and ensure lifelong learning opportunities for all.

One of UNESCO's key initiatives is Education for Sustainable Development (ESD), which seeks to equip learners with the knowledge, values, and skills needed to address global challenges and create a sustainable future. ESD promotes active learning, critical thinking, and a multidisciplinary approach to education, integrating environmental, social, and economic dimensions. Through capacity-building programs, policy advice, and advocacy, UNESCO supports countries in implementing ESD practices and embedding sustainability into curricula.

Another significant UNESCO program is Education for Global Citizenship (EGC), which aims to nurture learners' attitudes, values, and behaviors that promote respect, empathy, and responsibility towards their local and global communities. EGC encourages dialogue, intercultural understanding, and respect for diversity, fostering peaceful and inclusive societies. UNESCO provides guidelines, tools, and training programs to help educators integrate global citizenship education into their teaching practices.

World Bank and its support for educational transformation

The World Bank is a global financial institution that provides loans and grants to support sustainable development projects worldwide. Education is a priority area for the World Bank as it recognizes the vital role education plays in reducing poverty, promoting economic growth, and fostering social cohesion.

The World Bank's support for educational transformation includes investments in infrastructure, teacher training, curriculum development, and educational technology. By partnering with governments, civil society organizations, and other stakeholders, the World Bank helps countries design and implement educational reforms that align with international best practices.

In addition to financial support, the World Bank conducts research, produces reports, and shares knowledge on effective educational practices. Through its global networks and platforms, the World Bank facilitates the exchange of ideas and experiences among educators, policymakers, and researchers, promoting a culture of innovation and continuous improvement in education systems.

OECD and its role in educational policy development

The Organisation for Economic Co-operation and Development (OECD) is an international organization that promotes policies to improve the social and economic well-being of people worldwide. In the field of education, the OECD conducts comparative research, develops international benchmarks, and provides policy advice to member countries.

One of the OECD's flagship programs is the Programme for International Student Assessment (PISA), which assesses the performance of 15-year-old students in reading, mathematics, and science. PISA provides valuable insights into the strengths and weaknesses of education systems, helping countries identify areas for improvement and implement evidence-based reforms.

Moreover, the OECD's Center for Educational Research and Innovation (CERI) undertakes research on emerging educational trends, innovative teaching practices, and the impact of technology on learning. CERI's findings inform policy debates and guide educational reforms at the national and international levels.

Collaborative initiatives and partnerships

International organizations often collaborate with each other and with national governments, NGOs, and academic institutions to promote transformative education. These partnerships enhance the sharing of knowledge, resources, and best practices, fostering a synergy that leads to innovative solutions and improved educational outcomes.

For example, the Global Partnership for Education (GPE) brings together governments, international organizations, civil society, and the private sector to support education in low-income countries. The GPE mobilizes funding, strengthens education systems, and promotes equity and inclusion, contributing to transformative education globally.

The Sustainable Development Goals (SDGs), adopted by the United Nations in 2015, provide a framework for international cooperation in various areas, including education. The SDG 4 aims to ensure inclusive and equitable quality education and promote lifelong learning opportunities for all. International organizations collaborate to achieve this goal by aligning their efforts, sharing expertise, and pooling resources.

Challenges and future directions

While international organizations play a vital role in promoting transformative education, they face challenges in their efforts to effect change on a global scale. These challenges include funding constraints, resistance to reforms, cultural barriers, and the complexity of coordinating efforts among diverse stakeholders.

Looking ahead, international organizations need to continue advocating for the importance of transformative education and supporting countries in building capacity for innovation and change. They should embrace emerging technologies, such as artificial intelligence and virtual reality, to enhance learning experiences and expand access to education. Furthermore, international organizations should prioritize the inclusion of marginalized populations, ensuring that transformative education benefits all learners, regardless of their backgrounds or circumstances.

In conclusion, international organizations have a crucial role in promoting transformative education worldwide. Through their initiatives, funding, research, and partnerships, these organizations support countries in adapting their education systems to meet the demands of the future. By working collaboratively, international organizations can foster a culture of innovation, equity, and inclusivity in education, shaping a better future for learners and societies.

Advocacy for equitable access to transformative education

In order to achieve true transformative education, it is essential that every student has equitable access to high-quality educational opportunities. Advocacy for equitable access is crucial in ensuring that no student is left behind and that all learners have the resources and support they need to succeed. This section will explore the importance of advocating for equitable access to transformative education, along with strategies and initiatives that can be undertaken to address educational inequities.

Understanding Educational Inequities

Educational inequities refer to disparities in educational opportunities, resources, and outcomes among different student groups. These disparities can be influenced by factors such as socioeconomic status, race, ethnicity, gender, disability, and geographic location. It is important to recognize that these inequities can have a profound impact on students' educational experiences and outcomes.

Students from marginalized communities and disadvantaged backgrounds often face significant barriers to accessing transformative education. These barriers can include lack of adequate school facilities, limited access to technology and digital resources, insufficient funding and resources for learning materials, and limited opportunities for teacher professional development. Addressing these inequities is essential for creating a more just and inclusive education system.

Importance of Advocacy

Advocacy plays a critical role in addressing educational inequities and ensuring equitable access to transformative education for all students. By advocating for equitable access, we can strive to create a system where every student has an equal opportunity to succeed and achieve their full potential.

Advocacy efforts can take many forms, ranging from grassroots movements and community organizing to policy advocacy at local, state, and national levels. It is important for educators, parents, policymakers, and community members to come together and advocate for the resources, policies, and initiatives needed to create a more equitable education system.

Strategies for Advocacy

1. Raise awareness: One of the first steps in advocacy is to raise awareness about educational inequities and the importance of equitable access to transformative education. This can be done through public campaigns, community forums, and social media platforms. By sharing stories and data that highlight the inequities, we can mobilize support and generate public demand for change.

2. Collaborate with stakeholders: Effective advocacy requires collaboration among various stakeholders, including educators, parents, students, community organizations, policymakers, and educational leaders. By working together, these stakeholders can leverage their collective expertise, resources, and influence to drive systemic change.

3. Lobby for policy changes: Advocacy efforts should include lobbying for policy changes that address educational inequities. This can involve advocating for increased funding for under-resourced schools, implementing policies to reduce the achievement gap, and promoting inclusive curriculum and instructional practices. It is important to engage with policymakers and make a persuasive case for the need to prioritize equitable access to transformative education.

4. Support community-based initiatives: Engaging with community-based initiatives can be an effective way to address educational inequities. These initiatives may include after-school programs, mentorship programs, and partnerships with local organizations. By supporting and amplifying these initiatives, advocates can help bridge the gap between school and community resources.

5. Engage in professional development: Educators can play a critical role in advocating for equitable access to transformative education. By participating in professional development opportunities focused on addressing educational

inequities, teachers can gain the knowledge and skills needed to create a more inclusive and equitable learning environment.

Case Studies and Best Practices

1. **The Equity Coalition:** In the United States, the Equity Coalition is a grassroots organization that advocates for educational equity. They work to raise awareness about educational inequities, organize community events, engage in policy advocacy, and provide resources to communities in need. Through their efforts, they have successfully influenced legislation to improve funding and support for underserved schools.

2. **The Teach First Program:** The Teach First program in the United Kingdom aims to address educational inequality by recruiting and training high-achieving graduates to teach in low-income schools. The program provides ongoing support and professional development to these teachers, helping to improve educational outcomes for disadvantaged students.

Resources for Advocates

1. **Equity Alliance:** The Equity Alliance provides resources and support for advocates working towards educational equity. They offer training materials, research-based strategies, and policy recommendations to help guide advocacy efforts.

2. **Campaign for Educational Equity:** The Campaign for Educational Equity at Teachers College, Columbia University conducts research and provides resources to inform advocacy efforts. Their website offers policy briefs, research reports, and case studies on various topics related to educational equity.

3. **National Education Association:** The National Education Association (NEA) provides resources and tools for educators and advocates working towards educational equity. Their website includes guides, toolkits, and research-based resources that can be used to support advocacy efforts.

Conclusion

Advocacy for equitable access to transformative education is crucial in creating a more just and inclusive education system. By raising awareness, collaborating with stakeholders, lobbying for policy changes, supporting community initiatives, and engaging in professional development, advocates can drive systemic change and ensure that all students have the resources and support they need to thrive.

Working together, we can create a future where every student has equitable access to transformative education.

Ethical and legal considerations in educational policy

In designing and implementing educational policies, it is crucial to consider the ethical and legal implications. Ethical considerations ensure that policies promote fairness, social justice, and the well-being of all individuals involved in education. Legal considerations ensure that policies comply with existing laws and regulations. This section explores the key ethical and legal considerations that need to be taken into account when developing educational policies.

Ethical considerations

1. **Equity and access:** Educational policies should prioritize equity and ensure equal access to educational opportunities for all students. This includes addressing barriers related to socioeconomic status, race, gender, disability, and language proficiency.

2. **Inclusion and diversity:** Policies should promote inclusive education practices that respect and value the diverse backgrounds, cultures, and identities of students. This includes addressing issues related to discrimination, prejudice, and stereotypes.

3. **Privacy and data protection:** Policies should protect the privacy of students and ensure the secure management of their personal data. This includes obtaining informed consent for data collection, implementing strong data security measures, and providing individuals with control over their personal information.

4. **Ethical use of technology:** Policies should address the ethical use of technology in education, including issues such as digital citizenship, responsible use of online resources, and protection against cyberbullying and online harassment.

5. **Fair assessment practices:** Policies should promote fair assessment practices that are free from bias and ensure that students are evaluated based on their individual abilities and achievements. This includes addressing issues related to standardized testing, grading practices, and the use of assessment data.

6. **Professional conduct:** Policies should outline professional standards of conduct for educators, administrators, and other education professionals. This includes promoting ethical behavior, integrity, and professionalism in all aspects of their work.

7. **Informed decision-making:** Policies should ensure that all stakeholders, including students, parents, and educators, have access to accurate and transparent

information to make informed decisions about education. This includes providing information about curriculum, instructional practices, assessment methods, and available resources.

Legal considerations

1. **Compliance with laws and regulations:** Educational policies need to comply with relevant laws and regulations at local, regional, and national levels. This includes laws related to education governance, student rights, data protection, equal opportunity, and employment.

2. **Intellectual property rights:** Policies should address intellectual property rights related to educational resources, including copyright and fair use. This includes ensuring that educators and students are aware of their rights and responsibilities in using and sharing educational materials.

3. **Accessibility requirements:** Policies should align with accessibility requirements outlined in disability rights laws. This includes ensuring that educational materials, technologies, and physical spaces are accessible to students with disabilities.

4. **School safety and security:** Policies should address issues of school safety and security, including measures to prevent and respond to emergencies, threats, and violence. This includes compliance with relevant laws related to school safety and the protection of students and staff.

5. **Discrimination and harassment prevention:** Policies should address discrimination and harassment prevention, including laws related to anti-discrimination, Title IX, and bullying prevention. This includes clear procedures for reporting and addressing incidents of discrimination and harassment.

6. **Data protection and privacy:** Policies should comply with data protection and privacy laws to ensure the secure collection, storage, and use of student and personnel data. This includes obtaining informed consent, implementing data security measures, and providing individuals with control over their personal information.

7. **Family educational rights:** Policies should uphold the rights of parents and guardians to have access to their child's educational records and empower them to make informed decisions about their child's education.

8. **Teacher certification and licensure:** Policies should outline the requirements for teacher certification and licensure to ensure that educators possess the necessary qualifications and competencies to provide quality education.

9. **Education governance and funding:** Policies should address governance structures and funding mechanisms for education. This includes regulations related to education agencies, funding sources, and accountability frameworks.

10. **Labor laws and employment practices:** Policies should align with relevant labor laws and employment practices to ensure fair and equitable treatment of education personnel, including teachers, administrators, and support staff.

It is essential for policymakers to consider these ethical and legal considerations when developing educational policies to ensure that education systems are fair, inclusive, and compliant with existing laws and regulations. By upholding ethical principles and adhering to legal requirements, educational policies can support the effective and equitable delivery of education to all students.

Stakeholder collaboration for transformative education

In order to achieve transformative education, it is essential to have collaboration among various stakeholders, including teachers, students, parents, school leaders, policymakers, and the wider community. These stakeholders play critical roles in shaping and implementing educational policies and practices that lead to meaningful changes in teaching and learning. Effective collaboration allows for the sharing of ideas, resources, and expertise, and ensures that all voices are heard and valued in the educational decision-making process.

Importance of stakeholder collaboration

Stakeholder collaboration is crucial for several reasons. Firstly, it helps to create a shared vision and collective goals for transformative education. By involving all stakeholders in the process, there is a greater likelihood of developing a comprehensive and inclusive educational framework that addresses the needs and aspirations of all learners.

Secondly, collaboration enables the pooling of resources and expertise. Each stakeholder brings unique perspectives, knowledge, and skills to the table. When these diverse resources are combined, they can lead to innovative approaches and more effective solutions to educational challenges.

Thirdly, stakeholder collaboration promotes ownership and accountability. When stakeholders have a say in decision-making processes, they are more likely to be invested and committed to the outcomes. This fosters a sense of shared responsibility for the success of transformative education initiatives.

Lastly, collaboration helps to build trust and understanding among stakeholders. Through open and respectful dialogue, different viewpoints can be heard and considered, leading to mutual respect and improved relationships. This enhances the likelihood of successful implementation and sustainability of transformative educational practices.

Types of stakeholder collaboration

There are various ways in which stakeholders can collaborate to support transformative education. These include:

Partnerships between schools and the wider community: Schools can collaborate with community organizations, businesses, and government agencies to provide students with real-world learning experiences. For example, schools can partner with local businesses to offer internships or apprenticeships to students, giving them practical hands-on experience related to their areas of interest.

Teacher collaboration: Collaboration among teachers within and across schools is essential for sharing best practices, resources, and experiences. Collaboration can take the form of professional learning communities, where teachers come together to discuss teaching strategies, analyze student work, and co-plan lessons. This enables teachers to learn from one another and collectively improve their instructional practices.

Parent involvement: Engaging parents as partners in education is crucial for student success. Schools can involve parents in decision-making processes, seek their input on important matters, and provide opportunities for parent education and involvement in their child's learning. This collaboration helps create a supportive home-school connection and ensures a holistic approach to student development.

Policy collaboration: Collaboration among policymakers, educational researchers, and practitioners is necessary to develop and implement effective educational policies. Policymakers can seek input from educators and researchers to ensure that policies are evidence-based and responsive to the needs of students and teachers. Similarly, practitioners can share their experiences and insights to inform policy decisions.

Challenges in stakeholder collaboration

While stakeholder collaboration is highly beneficial, it is not without its challenges. Some common challenges include:

Communication barriers: Effective collaboration requires clear and open communication among stakeholders. However, differing perspectives, language barriers, and power dynamics can hinder communication and limit the effectiveness of collaboration efforts. It is essential to establish channels of communication that are inclusive, transparent, and accessible to all stakeholders.

Differing priorities and interests: Stakeholders may have different priorities, interests, and values, which can lead to conflicts and challenges in finding common ground. It is important to create a culture of mutual respect and understanding where stakeholders can work together to find shared solutions that prioritize the best interests of students.

Resistance to change: Transformative education requires a shift in traditional educational practices and mindsets. Some stakeholders, particularly teachers and parents, may be resistant to change due to fear of the unknown or concerns about the impact of change on students. Overcoming resistance to change requires ongoing dialogue, professional development, and evidence-based discussions to help stakeholders understand the benefits and importance of transformative education.

Strategies for effective stakeholder collaboration

To facilitate effective stakeholder collaboration for transformative education, the following strategies can be employed:

Establishing shared goals and vision: Collaborative efforts should begin with the establishment of shared goals and a collective vision for transformative education. This provides a common purpose and direction for collaboration efforts, ensuring that all stakeholders are working towards a common objective.

Creating inclusive spaces for dialogue: It is important to create inclusive spaces where stakeholders can come together to exchange ideas, share experiences, and engage in meaningful discussions. These spaces should be characterized by open communication, active listening, and respect for diverse perspectives.

Building relationships and trust: Effective collaboration relies on building relationships and trust among stakeholders. This can be achieved through regular interactions, joint problem-solving, and recognizing the contributions and expertise of each stakeholder. Building trust takes time and effort but is crucial for successful collaboration.

Providing professional development opportunities: Professional development plays a vital role in equipping stakeholders with the knowledge, skills, and strategies needed for transformative education. Offering professional development opportunities to teachers, school leaders, and policymakers helps foster collaboration by promoting a shared understanding of transformative educational practices.

Engaging students as partners: Students are important stakeholders in education, and their voices should be heard and valued. Engaging students as partners in decision-making processes and actively involving them in shaping their own learning experiences fosters a sense of ownership and empowerment.

Case studies and best practices

Several successful initiatives highlight the power of stakeholder collaboration in achieving transformative education. For instance, the Global Learning Network encourages collaboration among schools around the world to promote global competence and cultural understanding. By facilitating virtual exchanges and collaborative projects, students and teachers can learn from each other and develop a global perspective.

In the United States, the Coalition for Community Schools brings together schools, families, and community organizations to create comprehensive, community-centered educational environments. By collaborating with various stakeholders, community schools are better equipped to address the holistic needs of students, including academic, social, and health-related aspects.

In Finland, the Education Driver initiative involves collaborative partnerships between schools, businesses, and local authorities. By integrating real-world work experiences into the curriculum, students gain valuable skills and understand the relevance of their learning. This collaboration ensures that educational practices align with the needs of the labor market.

Conclusion

Stakeholder collaboration is essential for promoting transformative education. By involving all stakeholders, harnessing their resources and expertise, and working towards shared goals, educational systems can evolve to meet the changing needs of students and society. Despite the challenges, effective stakeholder collaboration can lead to innovative educational practices, enhanced student outcomes, and ultimately, a more equitable and inclusive education system. As we look towards the future of education, it is imperative that stakeholder collaboration remains a priority in shaping transformative educational policies and practices.

Educational research and evidence-based policy making

In order to create effective and impactful educational policies, it is essential to rely on educational research and evidence. Educational research provides valuable insights into the learning process, teaching methods, and the effectiveness of educational interventions. Evidence-based policy making ensures that educational decisions are informed by rigorous research and empirical evidence, leading to better outcomes for students and educators.

The role of educational research

Educational research plays a crucial role in informing policy decisions by providing insights into various aspects of the education system. Researchers investigate questions such as how students learn, effective teaching strategies, factors influencing student achievement, and the impact of educational technologies. They use a range of methodologies including quantitative studies, qualitative research, experimental designs, and case studies to gather evidence and draw conclusions.

Research in education covers a wide range of topics, from curriculum development and assessment to teacher training and educational technology. By exploring these areas, researchers aim to uncover best practices and improve educational practices and policies. For example, studies have shown that personalized learning approaches can lead to better student engagement and achievement. This evidence can guide the development of policies and practices that support personalized learning in classrooms.

Evidence-based policy making

Evidence-based policy making involves using research findings and empirical evidence to inform the development and implementation of educational policies. It ensures that policies are not solely based on personal beliefs or opinions but are grounded in scientific evidence. By relying on research, policymakers can make informed decisions about what works best for students, teachers, and schools.

To effectively implement evidence-based policy making, policymakers must have access to high-quality research and expertise. Collaboration between researchers and policymakers is vital to bridge the gap between research and practice. Researchers can communicate their findings in a way that is accessible to policymakers, providing key insights and recommendations for policy development.

Challenges in using educational research for policy making

While educational research can provide valuable insights, there are several challenges in using research for policy making. These challenges include:

1. Complex nature of education: Education is a multifaceted field, influenced by various factors such as cultural context, socioeconomic status, and individual differences. Research findings may not always directly apply to all contexts, and policymakers need to consider contextual factors when interpreting research evidence.

2. Time lag: Educational research requires time for data collection, analysis, and peer review before the findings become available for policy makers. This time lag can hinder timely decision-making, especially in rapidly evolving educational landscapes.

3. Conflicting evidence: Different studies may present conflicting results, making it challenging for policymakers to make definitive decisions. Policymakers need to critically evaluate the quality of research and consider multiple sources of evidence.

4. Communication gap: Researchers and policymakers often operate in separate spheres, using different language and methods of communication. Bridging the gap between researchers and policymakers is necessary for effective utilization of research evidence.

Promoting evidence-based policy making in education

To promote evidence-based policy making in education, several strategies can be employed:

1. Collaboration and communication: Encourage regular communication and collaboration between researchers and policymakers. This can be achieved through joint research projects, policy briefs, conferences, and workshops.

2. Research translation: Researchers should strive to communicate their findings in a clear and accessible manner to policymakers. Summarizing research

findings in policy briefs and presenting them in plain language can enhance their usefulness.

3. Capacity building: Provide training and professional development opportunities for policymakers to improve their understanding of research methodologies and data analysis. This will enable them to critically evaluate research evidence and make informed decisions.

4. Research-practice partnerships: Foster partnerships between researchers and schools/districts to conduct collaborative research. This approach ensures that research is directly relevant to practice and supports evidence-based decision making at the local level.

5. Longitudinal studies: Promote long-term research studies that provide in-depth insights into educational practices and their long-term impact. Longitudinal studies allow for a more comprehensive understanding of the complexities of education.

Real-world example: The impact of class size on student achievement

A classic example of evidence-based policy making is the examination of the impact of class size on student achievement. Research studies exploring this relationship have yielded mixed findings. Some studies suggest that reducing class sizes leads to improved student outcomes, while others indicate no significant impact.

In Tennessee, research conducted in the late 1980s called the Student/Teacher Achievement Ratio (STAR) project aimed to assess the effect of class size on student achievement. The findings indicated that students in smaller classes outperformed those in larger classes, especially in the early grades. This evidence played a crucial role in the policy decision to reduce class sizes in the state.

However, it is important to note that the impact of class size may vary depending on other contextual factors such as teacher quality, instructional practices, and school resources. Policymakers must consider these factors when interpreting research findings and making decisions about class size policies.

Exercises

1. Think about a current educational policy issue. Conduct research to identify relevant studies and evidence related to the issue. Develop a policy brief that summarizes the findings and provides recommendations based on the evidence.

2. Create a hypothetical scenario where conflicting research findings exist on a particular educational intervention. Describe how policymakers can navigate conflicting evidence to make informed decisions.

Resources

1. The Education Endowment Foundation (EEF) - The EEF supports the use of evidence in education and provides access to a range of resources, research studies, and guidance for policymakers. Visit their website at `https://educationendowmentfoundation.org.uk/`.

2. What Works Clearinghouse - The What Works Clearinghouse, maintained by the U.S. Department of Education, provides comprehensive and independent reviews of research on educational programs, products, practices, and policies. Explore their resources at `https://ies.ed.gov/ncee/wwc/`.

3. Research Schools Network - The Research Schools Network in the UK connects schools with researchers to support evidence-based practices. Learn more about their work at `https://researchschool.org.uk/`.

4. Educational Researcher - Educational Researcher is a peer-reviewed journal that publishes scholarly articles on a wide range of educational topics. Access their publications at `https://journals.sagepub.com/home/edr`.

Addressing the Digital Divide in Education

Bridging the digital divide is a crucial step towards achieving equitable and inclusive education. The digital divide refers to the gap in access to digital technologies, such as computers, internet connectivity, and other digital tools, based on socio-economic factors. This divide can create disparities in educational opportunities and hinder students' ability to fully participate in the digital age. In this section, we will explore strategies and initiatives aimed at addressing the digital divide in education.

Understanding the Digital Divide

To effectively address the digital divide, it is important to understand its causes and implications. The digital divide is the result of various factors such as income inequality, geographical location, and infrastructure limitations. Students from low-income households may lack access to internet-connected devices at home, making it challenging for them to complete online assignments or participate in virtual classrooms. Additionally, students in rural areas may face limited internet connectivity options, further exacerbating the divide.

The consequences of the digital divide are far-reaching. Students without internet access or digital tools may struggle to keep up with their peers, miss out on online educational resources, and be unable to develop essential digital literacy skills. This can perpetuate existing educational inequities and hinder socio-economic mobility.

Closing the Digital Divide

Closing the digital divide requires a multi-faceted approach involving various stakeholders, including educators, policymakers, and community organizations. Here are some strategies and initiatives to address the digital divide in education:

Infrastructure Development: Improving internet connectivity and infrastructure in underserved areas is a critical step. Governments and educational institutions can collaborate with internet service providers to expand broadband access in rural and low-income communities. Additionally, investments in public Wi-Fi networks and community centers can provide internet access to students who lack it at home.

Affordable Technology: Ensuring that all students have access to affordable technology devices is essential. Schools and districts can explore partnerships with technology companies to provide discounted or subsidized devices to students from low-income families. Initiatives such as one-to-one device programs, where each student is provided with a personal device, can promote digital equity.

Digital Literacy Training: Providing digital literacy training to students, teachers, and parents is crucial in bridging the digital divide. Educational institutions can offer workshops and courses that teach essential digital skills, including internet navigation, online collaboration, and critical evaluation of digital information. Additionally, parent engagement programs can help parents understand the importance of digital literacy and support their children's learning at home.

Mobile Learning Initiatives: Leveraging mobile technologies can be an effective way to reach students who lack access to traditional computers or broadband internet. Mobile learning initiatives can utilize smartphones, tablets, and other portable devices to deliver educational content and resources. This approach allows students to access educational materials even without home internet connectivity.

Digital Inclusion Programs: Collaborating with community organizations and non-profit groups can help establish digital inclusion programs. These programs can provide computer labs, internet access, and digital skills training in community centers, libraries, and schools. Such initiatives can ensure that students from disadvantaged backgrounds have equal opportunities to access digital technologies and enhance their learning outcomes.

Case Studies and Best Practices

Several case studies and best practices offer valuable insights into successfully addressing the digital divide in education.

Project Red: Project Red is a research study that examined the impact of technology integration in 1,000 schools across the United States. The study found that implementing one-to-one device programs, along with teacher training and personalized learning initiatives, significantly improved student achievement and reduced the digital divide.

ConnectED Initiative: The ConnectED Initiative was launched by the U.S. Department of Education with the goal of connecting 99% of American students to high-speed broadband in schools. The initiative provided funding and support for infrastructure development, access to affordable devices, and professional development for educators. Through this initiative, significant progress has been made in closing the digital divide in schools throughout the country.

Digital Equity Toolkit: The Digital Equity Toolkit, developed by the Consortium for School Networking (CoSN), provides resources and guidelines for districts to address digital equity challenges. The toolkit offers practical strategies for increasing internet access, providing devices, and implementing digital learning programs to ensure equitable opportunities for all students.

Challenges and Considerations

While efforts to address the digital divide are vital, there are challenges and considerations that need to be taken into account:

Equitable Access: It is essential to ensure that efforts to bridge the digital divide do not further marginalize certain groups. Digital inclusion initiatives should consider the needs of students with disabilities, English language learners, and students from diverse cultural backgrounds.

Sustainability: Long-term sustainability of digital equity initiatives is crucial. Adequate funding, ongoing maintenance of infrastructure, and continuous professional development for teachers are necessary to ensure the effectiveness and longevity of these programs.

Privacy and Security: As access to digital technologies increases, protecting student privacy and ensuring cybersecurity becomes paramount. Educational institutions must prioritize data privacy, implement robust security measures, and educate students about responsible digital citizenship.

Assessment and Evaluation: It is important to assess the impact of digital equity initiatives and evaluate their effectiveness in closing the digital divide. Collecting data on student outcomes and monitoring progress can help refine strategies and allocate resources more effectively.

Conclusion

Addressing the digital divide in education is a complex but crucial undertaking. By implementing infrastructure development, providing affordable technology, offering digital literacy training, and establishing digital inclusion programs, we can create more equitable and inclusive learning environments. It is essential for educators, policymakers, and the community to work together to ensure that all students have equal access to digital technologies and the opportunities they bring. Only then can we truly bridge the digital divide and provide quality education for all.

Education as a driver of societal change

Education is not just about acquiring knowledge and skills; it plays a crucial role in shaping societies and driving positive change. In this section, we will explore the transformative power of education in bringing about societal change. We will discuss the role of education in promoting social equity, empowering individuals and communities, fostering democratic values, and addressing global challenges.

Promoting social equity through education

Education has the potential to break the cycle of poverty and inequality by providing equal opportunities for all individuals, regardless of their socioeconomic background. By ensuring access to quality education for marginalized groups, we can level the playing field and reduce disparities in access to resources and opportunities.

One of the key ways education promotes social equity is by empowering individuals with knowledge and skills that enable them to participate fully in society. Through education, individuals gain the necessary tools to think critically, solve problems, and engage in informed decision-making. This empowers them to challenge social injustices, advocate for their rights, and be agents of change in their communities.

It is important for educational institutions to create inclusive learning environments that celebrate diversity and promote inclusivity. This involves developing curricula that reflect the experiences and perspectives of diverse populations, incorporating multicultural education, and promoting cultural sensitivity among students and educators.

Furthermore, education can play a role in addressing systemic inequalities by equipping individuals with the skills needed to participate in the workforce and contribute to economic growth. By providing vocational training and entrepreneurship education, education can empower individuals to break free from the cycle of poverty and contribute to the development of their communities.

Empowering individuals and communities

Education has the power to empower individuals and communities by expanding their knowledge base, enhancing their skills, and fostering a sense of agency and self-efficacy. It equips individuals with the ability to think critically, solve problems, and make informed decisions, enabling them to navigate the challenges of life effectively.

At an individual level, education opens up opportunities for personal and professional growth. It equips individuals with the necessary skills to pursue higher education, enter the job market, and adapt to the evolving demands of the labor market. Education also fosters lifelong learning, encouraging individuals to continuously update their knowledge and skills to remain competitive in an ever-changing world.

At a community level, education strengthens social cohesion and promotes civic engagement. It equips individuals with the knowledge and skills to actively participate in their communities, contribute to democratic processes, and work collectively towards common goals. Education fosters a sense of citizenship, promoting values such as tolerance, empathy, and respect for diversity.

Moreover, education plays a vital role in empowering marginalized communities. By providing education and skills training to marginalized groups, we can empower them to overcome social barriers, advocate for their rights, and participate fully in society. This empowerment not only benefits individuals but also contributes to the development of inclusive and resilient communities.

Fostering democratic values through education

Education is instrumental in fostering democratic values and nurturing active citizens who can contribute to a democratic society. Through education, individuals learn about their rights and responsibilities as citizens, understand the principles of democracy, and develop the skills needed to participate in democratic processes.

Education teaches individuals the importance of respect for human rights, equality, and social justice. It cultivates critical thinking and promotes the ability to question authority, analyze information, and engage in informed debates. By fostering these democratic values and skills, education enables individuals to actively participate in decision-making processes and contribute to the development of democratic institutions.

Furthermore, education plays a crucial role in nurturing civic virtues, such as empathy, tolerance, and respect for diversity. It encourages individuals to embrace different perspectives, engage in dialogue, and find common ground. Education helps individuals develop the necessary skills to resolve conflicts peacefully, work collaboratively, and build inclusive communities.

Addressing global challenges through education

Education is essential in addressing the complex global challenges that our society faces today. Whether it is climate change, poverty, inequality, peacebuilding, or global health, education equips individuals with the knowledge, skills, and attitudes needed to contribute to sustainable development and social progress.

Education plays a critical role in promoting environmental awareness and sustainability. By integrating environmental education into curricula across all subjects, education can raise awareness about the impact of human activities on the environment and foster a sense of responsibility towards preserving natural resources. Education can empower individuals with the skills and knowledge needed for sustainable practices, such as renewable energy, waste management, and conservation.

Furthermore, education is instrumental in promoting global citizenship and fostering a sense of interconnectedness among individuals and communities. By teaching about global issues, cultures, and perspectives, education encourages individuals to become active global citizens who are aware of their responsibilities towards promoting peace, social justice, and human rights across borders.

It is important to ensure that education equips individuals with the necessary digital skills and literacy to navigate the digital age. As technology continues to shape our society, education should prepare individuals to use technology ethically, critically evaluate information, and navigate the online world safely. By promoting digital literacy, education can empower individuals to be responsible digital citizens and leverage technology for positive change.

In conclusion, education has the power to drive societal change by promoting social equity, empowering individuals and communities, fostering democratic values, and addressing global challenges. To fully harness the transformative potential of education, it is crucial to ensure equitable access to quality education, promote inclusive learning environments, and equip individuals with the knowledge, skills, and attitudes needed to be active contributors to a just and sustainable society. Education is not just a means to an end; it is a catalyst for societal progress and a driver of positive change.

Transformative Education as a Global Priority

In today's rapidly evolving world, education plays a crucial role in shaping the future of individuals and societies. As traditional teaching methods become increasingly inadequate in preparing students for the challenges of the 21st century, there is a growing recognition of the need for transformative education. This section explores the importance of transformative education as a global priority and outlines key strategies for its implementation.

Understanding Transformative Education

Transformative education refers to an approach that goes beyond imparting knowledge and skills, aiming to empower students to become critical thinkers, problem solvers, and active participants in their own learning journey. It involves cultivating a deep understanding of the world, fostering empathy and compassion, and promoting social and environmental responsibility. Transformative education seeks to equip students with the knowledge, skills, and attitudes necessary to create positive change in their lives and communities.

Benefits of Transformative Education

Transformative education offers numerous benefits for individuals, societies, and the world at large. By encouraging critical thinking and creativity, it enables students to adapt to new situations, solve complex problems, and navigate an increasingly interconnected and fast-paced world. It promotes lifelong learning and empowers individuals to become active citizens who can engage in democratic processes and work towards social justice and equality. From a global perspective, transformative education is essential for addressing pressing challenges such as climate change, inequality, and conflict resolution.

Implementing Transformative Education

Implementing transformative education requires a multifaceted approach that involves various stakeholders, including policymakers, educators, parents, and the wider community. Here are some key strategies for promoting and implementing transformative education:

1. Policy support: Governments and international organizations need to prioritize transformative education by integrating it into educational policies and frameworks. This includes allocating resources, developing curriculum guidelines, and providing professional development opportunities for educators.

2. Teacher training: Educators play a critical role in transformative education. They need to be equipped with the knowledge, skills, and pedagogical approaches necessary to facilitate transformative learning experiences. Training programs should focus on promoting innovative teaching methods, fostering critical thinking skills, and encouraging student-centered learning.

3. Curriculum redesign: Transformative education requires a shift in curriculum design, moving away from content-focused approaches towards interdisciplinary and inquiry-based learning. Curricula should address global challenges and promote values such as sustainability, social justice, and diversity.

4. Community engagement: Transformative education can be further enhanced through meaningful collaboration with the wider community. Partnerships with local organizations, businesses, and NGOs can provide students with real-world experiences, foster civic engagement, and promote a deeper understanding of global issues.

5. Inclusive education: Transformative education should be inclusive and accessible to all learners, regardless of their backgrounds or abilities. Efforts should be made to address inequalities in access and outcomes, promote diversity, and foster a sense of belonging for every student.

6. Assessment practices: Traditional assessment methods often fail to capture the transformative learning that takes place. Therefore, assessment strategies need to evolve to evaluate not only knowledge acquisition but also critical thinking, problem-solving, and creativity.

7. Technology integration: Technology can enhance transformative education by providing access to diverse resources, facilitating collaboration, and enabling personalized learning experiences. However, ethical considerations and equitable access to technology must be addressed to avoid exacerbating existing inequalities.

Case Studies and Best Practices

To illustrate the impact of transformative education, let's explore a few case studies and best practices:

1. The Global Schools Program: This initiative by the United Nations promotes transformative education by engaging schools worldwide in addressing the Sustainable Development Goals (SDGs). Students participate in projects that address social, economic, and environmental challenges, fostering a sense of global citizenship.

2. High Tech High, San Diego, USA: High Tech High is a network of schools that prioritize project-based learning, collaboration, and real-world connections. Students engage in interdisciplinary projects, develop problem-solving skills, and build a deep understanding of the subject matter.

3. Aflatoun International: Aflatoun is a global nonprofit organization that promotes transformative education through social and financial education programs. By empowering children and youth to become active participants in their communities, Aflatoun fosters social and economic empowerment.

Future Directions

As the world continues to change at an unprecedented pace, the future of transformative education holds immense potential. Here are some emerging trends and future directions:

1. Transdisciplinary learning: Breaking down subject silos and promoting interdisciplinary learning will enable students to tackle complex problems from multiple perspectives.

2. Experiential and immersive learning: With advancements in virtual reality and augmented reality technologies, students can engage in immersive learning experiences that bring the world into the classroom.

3. Global collaborations: Harnessing the power of technology, virtual exchange programs, and online platforms will enable students to connect with peers from different cultures and backgrounds, fostering global collaboration and understanding.

4. Well-being and mindfulness: Prioritizing student well-being and incorporating mindfulness practices into the curriculum will nurture the social and emotional skills needed for personal and collective transformation.

In conclusion, transformative education is not only a global priority but a necessity in shaping a better future. By empowering students to build critical thinking skills, promoting ethical values, and addressing global challenges, transformative education equips individuals with the tools to create positive change in their lives and communities. Through collaborative efforts and innovative approaches, we can create a world where transformative education becomes a reality for all.

Professional Development for Teachers

The importance of continuous professional development

Continuous professional development (CPD) plays a crucial role in the field of education. It refers to the process of acquiring and updating knowledge, skills, and competencies that are relevant to the profession. In the rapidly changing landscape of education, where new technologies and teaching methods are constantly emerging, it is essential for teachers to engage in CPD to stay up-to-date and improve their practice. This section will explore the importance of continuous professional development, its benefits, and various strategies for effective CPD.

The need for continuous professional development

Education is a dynamic field that is constantly evolving. New research studies, pedagogical approaches, and technological advancements are reshaping the way students learn and teachers teach. In order to provide high-quality education and meet the diverse needs of students, it is imperative for teachers to continuously update their knowledge and skills.

One of the key reasons for engaging in CPD is to enhance teaching and learning outcomes. By staying abreast of the latest research and best practices, teachers can implement evidence-based instructional strategies and adapt their teaching methods to meet the needs of different learners. CPD also helps teachers develop a deeper understanding of educational theories and concepts, allowing them to make informed decisions about curriculum design, assessment, and classroom management.

Furthermore, CPD empowers teachers to become leaders and agents of change in their schools and communities. By expanding their knowledge base and acquiring new skills, teachers can take on leadership roles, mentor their colleagues, and contribute to the improvement of teaching practices at a systemic level. CPD also provides opportunities for professional networking and collaboration, allowing teachers to connect with peers, share ideas, and learn from one another.

Benefits of continuous professional development

Continuous professional development offers a range of benefits for both teachers and students. For teachers, CPD can lead to personal and professional growth, job satisfaction, and increased confidence in their abilities. By acquiring new knowledge and skills, teachers can become more effective in their instructional practices, leading to improved student outcomes. CPD also promotes reflective practice, encouraging teachers to critically analyze their teaching methods and make necessary adjustments to optimize student learning.

For students, the benefits of CPD are equally significant. Teachers who engage in continuous professional development are better equipped to create stimulating learning environments, design engaging and relevant lessons, and employ a variety of instructional strategies to meet the diverse needs of students. When teachers are up-to-date with the latest research and best practices, students are more likely to experience positive learning outcomes, increased motivation, and a deeper understanding of the subject matter.

Strategies for effective continuous professional development

To make the most of CPD opportunities, teachers should adopt strategies that are tailored to their individual needs and preferences. Here are some effective strategies for continuous professional development:

1. **Reflective practice:** Regularly reflecting on teaching practices and student outcomes can help identify areas for improvement and inform professional development goals.
2. **Goal setting:** Setting specific, measurable, attainable, relevant, and time-bound (SMART) goals can provide direction and motivation for CPD activities.
3. **Peer observation and feedback:** Observing and providing feedback to colleagues can offer valuable insights and promote collaborative learning among teachers.
4. **Professional learning communities:** Participating in professional learning communities allows teachers to share ideas, collaborate, and learn from one another.
5. **Workshops and conferences:** Attending workshops, conferences, and seminars organized by educational institutions or professional organizations can provide opportunities to learn from experts in the field.
6. **Online courses and webinars:** Taking advantage of online courses and webinars allows teachers to access CPD opportunities at their convenience and engage with a global community of educators.

7. **Action research:** Engaging in action research projects can enable teachers to investigate specific challenges in their classrooms and develop evidence-based solutions.

8. **Mentoring and coaching:** Seeking guidance from experienced mentors or coaches can provide personalized support and facilitate professional growth.

9. **Self-directed learning:** Self-directed learning, such as reading educational literature, engaging in self-paced online courses, or exploring educational podcasts, allows teachers to pursue areas of interest and address specific learning needs.

10. **Collaboration across disciplines:** Collaborating with educators from different subject areas or disciplines can bring fresh perspectives and foster interdisciplinary approaches to teaching and learning.

It is important to note that effective CPD requires a supportive and enabling environment. School leaders and policymakers play a crucial role in creating a culture that values and supports continuous professional development. Adequate time, resources, and incentives should be provided to encourage teachers' engagement in CPD activities. Professional development should also be aligned with the needs and goals of the school and the larger education system.

In conclusion, continuous professional development is essential for teachers to stay current, enhance their instructional practices, and improve student outcomes. By engaging in CPD, teachers can acquire new knowledge, skills, and competencies, collaborate with peers, and become effective agents of change in their profession. It is crucial for educational institutions and policymakers to provide the necessary support and create an environment conducive to ongoing professional growth. Through continuous professional development, teachers can prepare themselves for the challenges and opportunities of the future of education.

Traditional vs. Innovative Professional Development Models

In the rapidly evolving field of education, professional development is crucial for educators to stay up-to-date with the latest teaching methodologies, instructional strategies, and technological advancements. Traditional professional development models have typically involved workshops, conferences, and lectures. While these approaches can be beneficial, they often lack the personalized, interactive, and ongoing nature necessary for sustained growth and improvement.

However, innovative professional development models have emerged to address these limitations and provide educators with more effective and engaging learning experiences. These models leverage technology, collaboration, and reflective practice to empower educators to enhance their skills and knowledge.

Let's explore the differences between traditional and innovative professional development models in more detail.

Traditional Professional Development Models

Traditional professional development models have been prevalent in education for many years. They often involve one-time workshops, presentations, or conferences where educators passively receive information from experts. These models may cover a wide range of topics and provide a broad overview of new teaching techniques or tools. However, they often lack individualization and fail to address the unique needs and challenges of each educator.

One common drawback of traditional professional development models is the lack of follow-up and ongoing support. Educators attend a workshop or conference, receive information, and then struggle to implement new strategies without continued guidance. This can lead to a disconnect between theory and practice, resulting in limited impact on student learning outcomes.

Innovative Professional Development Models

Innovative professional development models aim to address the limitations of traditional approaches by offering more personalized, collaborative, and ongoing learning experiences. These models embrace technology, individualization, and active learning strategies to create meaningful and impactful professional development opportunities for educators.

One example of an innovative professional development model is the use of online communities of practice. These communities allow educators to connect and collaborate with peers, share resources, and engage in reflective discussions. Online platforms provide a space for educators to ask questions, seek advice, and learn from one another's experiences. This model promotes continuous learning and encourages educators to stay connected and updated in their field.

Another innovative approach to professional development is the use of micro-credentials or digital badges. These credentials provide educators with the opportunity to gain recognition for specific skills or competencies they have developed. Instead of attending a one-size-fits-all workshop, educators can choose from a variety of micro-credential offerings that align with their professional goals and interests. This model allows for personalized learning pathways and acknowledges educators' expertise in specific areas.

Furthermore, flipped professional development models have gained popularity. This model flips the traditional approach by providing educators with pre-recorded lectures, resources, and readings to explore independently before attending a face-to-face or online session. The in-person session can then focus on active learning, collaboration, and applying knowledge to real-world scenarios. This model allows for more engaged and interactive learning experiences, as well as individualized support from facilitators.

Benefits and Challenges

Innovative professional development models offer several benefits over traditional models. They provide educators with opportunities for personalized learning, collaboration, and ongoing support. By leveraging technology, these models can reach a wider audience and accommodate diverse learning styles and preferences. Innovative models also promote continuous improvement by emphasizing reflective practice and the application of new knowledge and skills in the classroom.

However, there are challenges involved in implementing innovative professional development models. First, there may be resistance to change from educators who are comfortable with traditional approaches. It is important to provide proper training, support, and clear communication to overcome this resistance. Additionally, there may be limitations in terms of access to technology, especially in schools with limited resources. Efforts should be made to ensure equitable access to innovative professional development opportunities for all educators.

Case Studies and Best Practices

Several case studies and best practices have demonstrated the effectiveness of innovative professional development models. For example, the Learning Forward organization has highlighted the success of professional learning communities, which foster collaboration, innovation, and the sharing of best practices among educators.

Another noteworthy case is the Advanced Placement (AP) Summer Institutes offered by the College Board. These institutes provide educators with in-depth training and support to teach AP courses effectively. The focus is on interactive, hands-on learning experiences that align with the latest research and best practices in AP instruction.

Conclusion

In conclusion, innovative professional development models offer significant advantages over traditional approaches. They leverage technology, individualization, and collaboration to provide personalized, interactive, and ongoing learning experiences for educators. These models promote continuous improvement, encourage reflective practice, and enhance educators' skills and knowledge. By implementing innovative professional development models, schools and educational organizations can empower educators to meet the evolving needs of students and achieve academic excellence.

Building Networks and Communities of Practice

Building networks and communities of practice is crucial for fostering professional growth and collaboration among educators. In this section, we will explore the importance of these networks, their benefits, and strategies for creating and sustaining them.

Importance of Networks and Communities of Practice

Teachers exist in a dynamic and ever-evolving educational landscape. To keep up with the latest trends, research, and best practices, educators need access to a network of like-minded professionals who can share their expertise and experiences. Networks and communities of practice provide a platform for continuous learning and professional development.

By connecting with other educators, teachers can expand their knowledge base, gain insights into innovative teaching methods, and collaborate on projects and research. These networks also provide emotional support and a sense of belonging, which can be especially valuable for those who are new to the profession or facing challenges in their teaching practice.

Benefits of Networks and Communities of Practice

Engaging in networks and communities of practice offers numerous benefits for teachers. Let's explore some of the key advantages:

1. **Knowledge sharing:** Networks and communities of practice offer a space for educators to share ideas, resources, and best practices. Teachers can learn from one another, discuss common challenges, and discover new strategies to improve their teaching.

2. **Professional growth:** Engaging with peers in a network fosters continuous learning. By sharing experiences, attending professional development workshops, and participating in collaborative projects, teachers can enhance their knowledge and skills, and stay updated with the latest trends in education.

3. **Innovation:** Networks and communities of practice provide an environment for educators to experiment with new ideas and innovative approaches. Collaboration and brainstorming within these communities often lead to the development of fresh teaching methods and solutions to educational challenges.

4. **Support and collaboration:** Building relationships with colleagues in a network creates a support system for teachers. In times of difficulties, educators can seek advice, share concerns, and receive encouragement from their peers. Collaboration on projects and research also becomes possible within these communities.

5. **Networking opportunities:** Networks and communities of practice provide a platform for educators to connect with professionals beyond their own school or district. These connections can lead to new job opportunities, partnership opportunities, and access to a broader range of resources.

Strategies for Creating and Sustaining Networks and Communities of Practice

Creating and sustaining networks and communities of practice requires deliberate efforts and investment. Here are some strategies to consider:

1. **Identify common interests and goals:** A successful community of practice starts with a shared interest or goal. Identify a specific focus area, such as project-based learning or inclusive education, and invite educators who are passionate about that topic to join the community.

2. **Establish regular communication channels:** Create online platforms, such as social media groups or discussion forums, to facilitate ongoing communication and information sharing among community members. Regular virtual meetings or face-to-face meetups can also strengthen relationships and collaboration.

3. **Encourage active participation:** Encourage members to actively contribute to the community by sharing their expertise, resources, and experiences. Creating a safe and inclusive environment where everyone's voice is heard is essential for fostering engagement.

4. **Promote collaboration and co-creation:** Encourage members to collaborate on projects, research, and lesson planning. This not only enhances professional growth but also strengthens the sense of community and shared responsibility.

5. **Organize professional development opportunities:** Arrange workshops, webinars, or guest speaker sessions to provide ongoing professional development for community members. Invite experts in the field to share their knowledge and facilitate discussions on relevant topics.

6. **Recognize and celebrate achievements:** Acknowledge the accomplishments of community members and celebrate their successes. This can be done through awards, certificates, or public recognition. Recognizing and appreciating the contributions of individuals fosters a sense of belonging and motivates others to actively participate.

7. **Invite outside experts and researchers:** Engage experts and researchers in the field to provide insights, update community members on the latest research, and offer guidance. This collaboration can bring fresh perspectives and contribute to the growth of the community.

Case Study: The Global Educators Network

The Global Educators Network (GEN) is an international community of practice that aims to connect educators from around the world and provide a platform for knowledge sharing and collaboration. With over 10,000 members from diverse backgrounds, GEN focuses on fostering cross-cultural understanding, promoting innovative teaching practices, and addressing global educational challenges.

GEN offers various opportunities for engagement, including online discussions, webinars, and annual conferences. Members actively participate in knowledge exchange, share resources, and collaborate on projects. The network has also partnered with leading educational organizations to provide professional development opportunities and access to cutting-edge research.

Through its collaborative approach, GEN has facilitated the development of innovative educational practices, such as virtual exchange programs and cross-cultural lesson sharing. By connecting educators across borders, GEN has contributed to the enhancement of teaching and learning experiences, promoting inclusivity, and addressing global educational disparities.

Resources for Building Networks and Communities of Practice

Here are some resources to help teachers build and engage in networks and communities of practice:

1. **Professional Learning Communities:** This book by Shirley M. Hord and William A. Sommers provides a comprehensive guide to building, maintaining, and sustaining professional learning communities in schools.

2. **Teaching Channel:** Teaching Channel is an online platform that hosts a wide range of videos showcasing effective teaching practices. It also provides a forum for educators to connect, share ideas, and collaborate.

3. **Twitter Chats:** Participating in Twitter chats related to education can be an effective way to connect with educators globally and engage in discussions on specific topics. Some popular education Twitter chats include #edchat, #satchat, and #edtechchat.

4. **Educational Conferences and Workshops:** Attending conferences and workshops related to education provides opportunities to network with other educators and learn about innovative practices. Some notable conferences include the International Society for Technology in Education (ISTE) Conference and the National Council of Teachers of English (NCTE) Annual Convention.

5. **Online Communities and Platforms:** Platforms like edWeb.net, Classroom 2.0, and Microsoft Educator Community offer online spaces for educators to connect, share resources, and collaborate.

Remember, building and sustaining networks and communities of practice require active participation and contributions from all members. By engaging with like-minded educators, teachers can enhance their professional growth and contribute to the advancement of education as a whole.

Mentoring and Coaching for Teacher Development

In the rapidly changing landscape of education, it is crucial for teachers to have continuous professional development opportunities to adapt to new methodologies, technologies, and pedagogical approaches. One effective method for supporting teacher growth and development is through mentoring and coaching programs. These programs provide personalized guidance, feedback, and support to teachers, helping them improve their instructional practices and enhance student learning outcomes.

Benefits of Mentoring and Coaching

Mentoring and coaching offer several benefits for teachers. Firstly, these programs provide a safe and supportive environment for teachers to reflect on their teaching practices, identify areas for growth, and set achievable goals. The mentor or coach serves as a trusted partner who can guide the teacher in exploring new instructional strategies, techniques, and resources.

Secondly, mentoring and coaching can enhance teachers' self-efficacy and confidence. By receiving feedback and support from experienced educators, teachers can gain a deeper understanding of their strengths and areas for improvement. This increased self-awareness can empower teachers to take risks, experiment with new approaches, and continuously grow as professionals.

Furthermore, mentoring and coaching promote a culture of collaboration and professional learning communities. Through regular meetings and discussions, teachers can share best practices, learn from one another, and foster a sense of collective responsibility for student success. This collaborative environment not only benefits individual teachers but also creates a positive school culture that values continuous improvement.

Effective Mentoring and Coaching Strategies

To ensure the success of mentoring and coaching programs, it is important to implement effective strategies. Here are some key considerations:

1. **Matching mentors and mentees:** A successful mentoring relationship hinges on a good match between the mentor and mentee. Factors such as subject area expertise, teaching experience, and personality should be taken into account when assigning mentors to teachers.

2. **Establishing clear goals and expectations:** Mentoring and coaching should have clear objectives, which may include specific teaching practices, content knowledge, or student outcomes. By setting goals at the beginning of the program, both mentors and mentees have a shared understanding of what they want to achieve.

3. **Regular meetings and check-ins:** Mentoring and coaching should involve regular meetings and check-ins to provide ongoing support and feedback. These meetings can take the form of one-on-one sessions, classroom observations, or virtual interactions, depending on the program's structure and resources.

4. **Observation and feedback:** Observing teachers in action and providing constructive feedback is a central aspect of mentoring and coaching. Mentors can offer actionable suggestions, model effective teaching strategies, and help mentees reflect on their practice. It is important for mentors to create a non-judgmental and trust-based rapport with their mentees to foster open dialogue and reflection.

5. **Professional development opportunities:** Mentoring and coaching should be complemented by targeted professional development opportunities. Mentees can benefit from workshops, webinars, conferences, or online courses that align with their individual growth areas and extend their learning beyond the mentoring relationship.

6. **Continuous assessment and reflection:** Periodic assessment and reflection allow mentors and mentees to evaluate progress, make adjustments to the mentoring approach if necessary, and celebrate achievements. This reflective process aids in monitoring growth, identifying additional areas of need, and developing action plans for further improvement.

Overcoming Challenges in Mentoring and Coaching

While mentoring and coaching can be highly effective, there may be challenges that need to be addressed to ensure their success:

- **Time constraints:** Lack of time is a common challenge faced by both mentors and mentees. It is important to allocate dedicated time for mentoring activities within the school schedule and to establish a realistic timeline for achieving mentoring goals.
- **Building trust and rapport:** Building a trusting relationship between mentors and mentees is essential for effective mentoring. Mentors should create a supportive and non-judgmental environment where mentees feel comfortable sharing their challenges and seeking guidance.
- **Matching mentors and mentees:** As mentioned earlier, a good mentor-mentee match is crucial for success. Efforts should be made to ensure mentors have the necessary expertise and experience to address the specific needs of their mentees.
- **Sustaining the mentoring relationship:** Mentoring and coaching should not be viewed as isolated events but as ongoing processes. Finding ways to sustain the mentoring relationship beyond the initial partnership can help teachers continue to grow and thrive.

Case Studies and Best Practices

Real-world examples and case studies can provide valuable insights into successful mentoring and coaching programs. Some best practices include:

- **Peer mentoring model:** Pairing teachers within the same school or district can be particularly effective, as it promotes collaboration and fosters a sense of community. Peer mentors can provide targeted support based on their own experiences and expertise.

- **Coaching cycles:** Implementing coaching cycles with defined stages can help structure the mentoring process. These cycles typically include goal setting, observation and feedback, and reflection, allowing for continuous improvement throughout the academic year.

- **School-wide mentoring initiatives:** Establishing a culture of mentoring and coaching at the school level can have a significant impact. By involving a broader group of mentors and mentees, schools can foster a professional learning community and create opportunities for cross-grade or cross-subject collaboration.

Resources for Mentoring and Coaching

Several resources are available to support mentoring and coaching initiatives in education. These include:

- **Professional organizations:** Education associations and professional organizations often offer mentoring programs, resources, and guidelines for mentors and mentees. These organizations provide a network of experienced educators who can serve as mentors.

- **Online communities and platforms:** Virtual communities and online platforms provide opportunities for mentors and mentees to connect, share resources, and seek advice. These platforms often include discussion forums, webinars, and repositories of best practices.

- **Research and literature:** Research studies, books, and articles on mentoring and coaching in education can offer valuable insights and evidence-based strategies. Mentors and mentees can explore the existing body of knowledge to inform their practice and stay up to date with current trends.

Conclusion

Mentoring and coaching play a vital role in supporting teacher development and improving student learning outcomes. By providing personalized guidance, feedback, and support, these programs empower teachers to enhance their instructional practices and foster continuous improvement. By implementing effective strategies, addressing challenges, and learning from case studies and best practices, mentoring and coaching can contribute to creating a vibrant and supportive professional learning community within schools.

Online and virtual professional development opportunities

In today's digital age, professional development opportunities for teachers are no longer limited to traditional in-person workshops and conferences. Online and virtual platforms have revolutionized the way teachers can engage in professional learning and enhance their teaching practices. These online and virtual professional development opportunities provide flexible and accessible options for educators to continue their growth and stay updated with the latest trends and practices in education. In this section, we will explore various online and virtual professional development opportunities and discuss their benefits and challenges.

Benefits of online and virtual professional development

Online and virtual professional development offers several advantages for teachers:

- **Flexibility:** Online and virtual platforms allow teachers to access professional development resources at their convenience, eliminating the constraints of time and location. Teachers can engage in learning activities when it best suits their schedules.
- **Personalization:** These platforms often provide personalized learning experiences tailored to the individual needs and interests of teachers. Educators can choose the topics and modules that align with their areas of interest or specific professional goals.
- **Cost-effective:** Online professional development programs are often more affordable compared to traditional workshops and conferences. Teachers can access a wide range of resources and materials at a lower cost, making professional development opportunities more accessible to educators, especially those with limited budgets.
- **Collaboration and networking:** Virtual professional development platforms foster collaboration and networking opportunities among educators. Teachers can connect with colleagues from around the world, share experiences, exchange ideas, and collaborate on projects, thereby expanding their professional networks.
- **Self-paced learning:** Online and virtual professional development programs allow teachers to learn at their own pace. They can choose to complete modules and activities based on their learning speed, ensuring a deeper understanding of the content.

- **Access to experts and resources:** These platforms often bring together renowned experts in the field of education who share their expertise through webinars, video tutorials, and interactive sessions. Teachers can access a vast pool of resources, including research articles, case studies, and best practices, enriching their knowledge base.

Types of online and virtual professional development opportunities

There are various types of online and virtual professional development opportunities available for educators. Let's explore some of the common ones:

1. **Online courses:** Many universities and organizations offer online courses specifically designed for teacher professional development. These courses cover a wide range of topics, including educational technology, pedagogy, content-specific instruction, and assessment. Teachers can enroll in these courses and earn certificates or even academic credits.

2. **Webinars and virtual conferences:** Webinars and virtual conferences provide opportunities for teachers to attend live or recorded sessions delivered by experts in the field. These sessions cover various educational topics and allow participants to engage in discussions, ask questions, and interact with presenters and other participants.

3. **Online communities and social networks:** Online communities and social networks dedicated to education provide platforms for teachers to connect, share resources, and discuss pedagogical practices. These platforms facilitate collaboration, peer support, and the exchange of ideas, allowing teachers to learn from each other's experiences.

4. **Virtual learning networks:** Virtual learning networks are online communities focused on a specific educational topic or subject area. Teachers can join these networks to access resources, engage in discussions, and collaborate with like-minded educators who share similar interests or teach the same subject.

5. **Microlearning platforms:** Microlearning platforms offer short, bite-sized learning modules that allow teachers to acquire knowledge and skills in small increments. These platforms usually provide self-paced modules that cover specific topics such as classroom management strategies, technology integration, or assessment techniques.

6. **Online coaching and mentoring:** Online coaching and mentoring programs connect teachers with experienced educators who provide guidance and support in their professional development journey. Through virtual meetings, mentoring sessions, and feedback, teachers can benefit from personalized guidance and enhance their teaching practices.

Challenges and considerations

While online and virtual professional development opportunities offer numerous benefits, there are some challenges and considerations that educators should be aware of:

- **Digital literacy skills:** Teachers need to have basic digital literacy skills to navigate online platforms and effectively engage in professional development activities. Providing support and training in digital literacy can help educators maximize the benefits of online learning opportunities.

- **Quality and credibility of resources:** With the vast amount of online resources available, it can be challenging for teachers to identify high-quality and reliable materials. Educators should critically evaluate the credibility of the resources they use and rely on reputable sources.

- **Lack of interaction and engagement:** Online and virtual professional development may lack the face-to-face interaction and immediate feedback that in-person workshops offer. It is essential to ensure that the online platforms provide opportunities for interaction, collaboration, and engagement among participants.

- **Time management and motivation:** The flexibility of online professional development can make it challenging for teachers to prioritize and manage their time effectively. Additionally, staying motivated and completing the learning activities without external accountability can be a hurdle for some educators.

- **Access and equity:** Access to reliable internet connection and suitable devices can pose challenges for teachers in certain regions or schools. Addressing issues of access and equity is crucial to ensure that all educators can benefit from online and virtual professional development opportunities.

Examples and resources

Here are a few examples of online and virtual professional development opportunities for teachers:

- **Coursera for Teachers:** Coursera offers a range of online courses covering educational topics from leading universities and institutions.
- **EdWeb.net:** EdWeb.net is an online community that provides free webinars, professional learning communities, and resources for educators.
- **Google for Education Teacher Center:** Google for Education Teacher Center offers online courses and certifications related to Google tools and educational technology integration.
- **Microsoft Educator Center:** Microsoft Educator Center provides free online courses, resources, and tutorials to enhance teaching with Microsoft tools and technologies.
- **National Science Teachers Association (NSTA) Learning Center:** NSTA Learning Center offers online professional development resources for science teachers, including webinars, virtual conferences, and interactive modules.

Conclusion

Online and virtual professional development opportunities have transformed the landscape of teacher learning and support. With the flexibility and accessibility they provide, educators can engage in meaningful, personalized, and self-paced learning experiences. However, it is essential to address the challenges and considerations associated with online professional development to ensure its effectiveness. By leveraging the benefits and resources available, teachers can continue to grow, adapt, and improve their instructional practices in the ever-evolving field of education.

Micro-credentials and digital badges for teacher recognition

In the rapidly evolving field of education, traditional methods of recognizing teacher expertise and professional development may not capture the full scope of a teacher's skills and qualifications. As technology continues to advance, new approaches to recognizing and showcasing teacher achievements have emerged. One such approach is the use of micro-credentials and digital badges.

Understanding micro-credentials

Micro-credentials are a form of digital accreditation that provide evidence of specific skills or competencies acquired by an individual. Unlike traditional degrees or certifications, micro-credentials are focused on specific areas of expertise rather than general knowledge. They are designed to be flexible and customizable, allowing educators to pursue areas of professional growth that align with their specific interests and career goals.

Micro-credentials are typically earned through a combination of professional development activities, such as completing online courses, attending workshops, participating in collaborative projects, or demonstrating mastery of specific teaching techniques. Once earned, micro-credentials are represented by a digital badge, which serves as a visual symbol of the achievement.

Benefits of micro-credentials

Micro-credentials offer several advantages over traditional forms of professional development recognition. Firstly, they provide a more granular and detailed measure of a teacher's skills and knowledge. By focusing on specific competencies, micro-credentials enable educators to demonstrate their expertise in specialized areas, making them more marketable and able to meet the diverse needs of students.

Secondly, micro-credentials promote continuous learning and professional growth. By offering a variety of topics and areas, teachers have the opportunity to engage in ongoing development, staying up-to-date with the latest research and practices in their field. This promotes a culture of lifelong learning among educators, which ultimately benefits students.

Thirdly, micro-credentials can enhance professional networking and collaboration. As educators earn micro-credentials, they become part of a community of like-minded individuals who share a common interest or expertise. This can lead to valuable collaborations and the exchange of innovative ideas, thereby enriching the overall educational landscape.

Earning and displaying micro-credentials

To earn a micro-credential, teachers typically engage in a series of learning activities and assessments. These activities may include completing online modules, submitting written reflections or portfolios of evidence, participating in virtual or in-person discussions, or even being observed in the classroom.

Once a micro-credential is earned, it is represented by a digital badge. Digital badges are visual representations of achievements that can be displayed on digital platforms, such as social media profiles, personal websites, or professional networking sites. These badges contain metadata that provides information about the specific competency or skill associated with the micro-credential, as well as the organization that issued it.

Digital badges offer a portable and verifiable way to showcase one's accomplishments. They can be easily shared with colleagues, administrators, potential employers, and parents, providing a tangible and visually appealing representation of a teacher's professional growth.

Validating and verifying micro-credentials

One of the challenges associated with micro-credentials is ensuring their validity and reliability. It is essential to have a robust system in place for validating and verifying the credentials earned by educators.

To ensure the credibility of micro-credentials, it is important to have a rigorous assessment process in place. This may involve peer review, expert evaluation, or standardized assessments. Additionally, it is crucial to work with reputable organizations or institutions that have established guidelines and quality assurance mechanisms for issuing micro-credentials.

Furthermore, integrating micro-credentials into existing systems of recognition and advancement is necessary for their widespread acceptance. This includes working with educational institutions, districts, and policymakers to align micro-credentials with existing professional development frameworks and career advancement opportunities. By ensuring that micro-credentials are valued and recognized within the larger educational ecosystem, their potential impact can be maximized.

Future directions of micro-credentials

As technology continues to advance, the potential for micro-credentials in the field of education is expanding. Some future directions include:

- **Micro-credentials for emerging areas:** As new fields, such as artificial intelligence, virtual reality, and data analytics, become increasingly relevant in education, micro-credentials can provide a means to validate and recognize expertise in these emerging areas.

- **Stackable credentials:** Teachers may earn multiple micro-credentials in related areas and combine them to create a comprehensive portfolio of skills. This concept of stackable credentials allows educators to showcase a broader range of expertise and qualifications.
- **Employer recognition:** Encouraging employers, such as schools and districts, to recognize and reward teachers with micro-credentials can further incentivize educators to pursue professional development opportunities. This may involve incorporating micro-credentials into salary scales, promotion criteria, or hiring processes.
- **Integration with learning management systems:** Integrating micro-credentials into learning management systems can provide a seamless experience for educators, allowing them to track their progress, access relevant resources, and showcase their achievements all in one platform.
- **Data-driven insights:** As more educators earn micro-credentials, the data collected can be leveraged to gain insights into the impact of specific professional development activities on teacher practice and student outcomes. Such insights can inform the design and delivery of future micro-credential offerings.

In conclusion, micro-credentials and digital badges offer a flexible and personalized approach to recognizing and showcasing teacher achievements. By focusing on specific competencies, micro-credentials provide a more detailed and comprehensive picture of an educator's skills and knowledge. As technology continues to advance, micro-credentials have the potential to revolutionize the way teachers engage in professional development, grow their expertise, and contribute to the larger educational community.

Teacher-led professional learning communities

Teacher-led professional learning communities play a crucial role in fostering professional growth and development among educators. These communities provide a collaborative space for teachers to share ideas, engage in reflective practice, and collectively work towards improving teaching and learning outcomes. In this section, we will explore the benefits of teacher-led professional learning communities, strategies for establishing and sustaining these communities, and the future directions of such communities.

Benefits of teacher-led professional learning communities

Teacher-led professional learning communities offer numerous benefits for educators. Firstly, these communities provide a supportive and trusting environment where teachers can engage in open dialogue, exchange teaching strategies, and learn from each other's experiences. By collaborating with colleagues, teachers can expand their knowledge base, gain new perspectives, and enhance their instructional practices.

Secondly, teacher-led professional learning communities foster a sense of empowerment and ownership among teachers. Unlike traditional professional development sessions that are often top-down and one-size-fits-all, these communities allow teachers to have a voice in their own professional growth. Teachers can identify their own learning needs, set goals, and then work collectively towards achieving those goals.

Furthermore, these communities promote ongoing professional learning and reflection. By regularly meeting with colleagues, teachers can engage in deep discussions about their teaching practice, reflect on student outcomes, and plan for continuous improvement. This reflective practice leads to a cycle of learning and growth that benefits both teachers and students.

Establishing and sustaining teacher-led professional learning communities

Creating and maintaining teacher-led professional learning communities requires intentional planning and support. Here are some strategies to establish and sustain these communities:

1. **Identify common goals:** It is important to identify shared goals and purposes for the community. This could involve focusing on specific instructional practices, implementing new pedagogies, or addressing particular student needs. Common goals provide the foundation for collaboration and a sense of purpose among community members.

2. **Ensure effective leadership:** Teacher-led professional learning communities require effective leadership to facilitate discussions, organize meetings, and guide the overall direction of the community. Leadership roles can be rotated among members to distribute responsibilities and foster a sense of shared ownership.

3. **Establish norms and guidelines:** Establishing norms and guidelines for discussions and interactions within the community helps to create a safe and respectful environment. This ensures that diverse perspectives are valued and encourages open and constructive dialogue.

4. **Allocate dedicated time:** It is essential to allocate dedicated time for professional learning community meetings. This time should be protected and seen as a priority to ensure consistent engagement and participation from members.

5. **Utilize technology:** Technology can be leveraged to enhance communication and collaboration within professional learning communities. Online platforms, such as discussion forums or video conferencing tools, can facilitate asynchronous and synchronous interactions, allowing teachers to connect beyond physical boundaries.

6. **Provide access to resources:** Access to resources, such as research articles, videos, and lesson plans, can support the work of professional learning communities. Establishing a shared repository of resources ensures that teachers have access to relevant and high-quality materials.

7. **Encourage reflection and action research:** Professional learning communities should encourage teachers to engage in reflective practice and action research. This involves analyzing their own teaching practices, collecting data, and evaluating the impact of their instructional decisions on student learning. By engaging in this process, teachers deepen their understanding of effective practices and contribute to the collective knowledge of the community.

Future directions of teacher-led professional learning communities

As education and technology continue to evolve, teacher-led professional learning communities will need to adapt to meet new challenges and leverage emerging opportunities. Here are some future directions for these communities:

1. **Online collaborative spaces:** With the increasing availability of online tools and platforms, teacher-led professional learning communities can expand beyond the limitations of physical spaces. Virtual communities can provide opportunities for global collaboration, allowing teachers to connect and learn from educators around the world.

2. **Data-informed decision making:** Professional learning communities can embrace data-informed decision making by utilizing learning analytics and other assessment data to inform instructional practices. Teachers can collaborate to analyze student data, identify trends, and develop targeted interventions to improve student learning outcomes.

3. **Teacher-led research:** Building a culture of teacher-led research within professional learning communities can empower educators to generate and disseminate knowledge about effective teaching practices. Teachers can conduct small-scale research studies, share findings, and collectively contribute to the field of education.

4. **Multi-disciplinary collaboration:** Professional learning communities can benefit from engaging educators from different subject areas, grade levels, and even different educational contexts. This multi-disciplinary collaboration can bring fresh perspectives, foster creativity, and promote cross-curricular connections.

5. **Integration of AI and educational technologies:** As artificial intelligence (AI) and educational technologies continue to advance, professional learning communities can explore ways to integrate these tools into their practices. AI can provide personalized recommendations for professional development, facilitate automated data analysis, and support individualized coaching.

6. **Enhanced focus on social-emotional learning:** Professional learning communities can address the growing importance of social-emotional learning (SEL) by incorporating SEL initiatives into their work. Educators can collaborate to develop strategies for fostering SEL skills in students and supporting their own well-being.

7. **Teacher advocacy and policy influence:** Professional learning communities have the potential to influence educational policies and advocate for changes at the local, regional, and national levels. By leveraging their collective expertise, teachers can play a significant role in shaping the future of education.

In conclusion, teacher-led professional learning communities offer valuable opportunities for educators to collaborate, share knowledge, and enhance their instructional practices. By establishing and sustaining these communities, educators can foster professional growth, improve student outcomes, and contribute to the advancement of the teaching profession. As technology continues to evolve, these communities must adapt and embrace emerging opportunities to meet the needs of educators in the future.

Professional Development for Educational Leaders

In order to effectively drive innovation and transformation in education, it is crucial that educational leaders continuously engage in professional development. This section explores the importance of professional development for educational leaders, traditional and innovative models of professional development, and strategies for fostering growth and leadership among educational leaders.

The Importance of Continuous Professional Development

As the field of education evolves and new technologies and pedagogies emerge, it becomes imperative for educational leaders to stay abreast of these advancements. Continuous professional development ensures that leaders are equipped with the knowledge, skills, and competencies necessary to lead schools and institutions towards transformative practices.

Professional development for educational leaders goes beyond traditional training workshops and seminars. It includes networking, attending conferences, engaging in research and reflective practices, and seeking mentorship opportunities. By investing in their own development, educational leaders not only enhance their own leadership capabilities, but also model the importance of lifelong learning to their staff and students.

Traditional vs. Innovative Professional Development Models

Traditional models of professional development often involve one-off workshops or courses that focus on specific topics or skills. While these models can be beneficial, they often lack sustained engagement and fail to provide ongoing support to leaders.

Innovative models of professional development place a greater emphasis on collaboration, reflection, and personalized learning. These models recognize that educational leaders have unique needs and experiences, and provide opportunities for them to engage in ongoing learning communities. For example, professional learning networks (PLNs) allow leaders to connect with peers, share resources, and collaborate on solving common challenges.

Another innovative approach is the use of action research, where leaders engage in systematic inquiry to improve their practice. This involves identifying a problem or challenge, conducting research to gather data, implementing interventions, and reflecting on the outcomes. Action research not only promotes continuous improvement, but also empowers leaders to be agents of change in their organizations.

Building Networks and Communities of Practice

Effective professional development for educational leaders involves cultivating networks and communities of practice. These networks provide opportunities for leaders to connect, collaborate, and share best practices.

Technology has revolutionized networking opportunities, enabling leaders to connect with colleagues from around the world through social media platforms, online forums, and virtual conferences. Educational leaders can leverage these digital tools to engage with like-minded professionals, participate in discussions, and learn from diverse perspectives.

In addition to virtual networking, face-to-face interactions are also crucial for fostering meaningful connections. Educational leaders can join professional organizations, attend conferences, or participate in local meet-ups to form relationships with peers in their field. These in-person connections provide the chance for deeper conversations, brainstorming sessions, and collaborative problem-solving.

Mentoring and Coaching for Leader Development

Mentoring and coaching programs are valuable components of professional development for educational leaders. These programs offer personalized support and guidance, helping leaders reflect on their practice, set goals, and develop strategies for growth.

Mentoring involves a more experienced leader providing guidance and support to a less experienced colleague. This can be done through regular meetings, observations, and feedback sessions. Mentoring relationships provide a safe space for leaders to seek advice, share challenges, and gain insights from someone who has navigated similar paths.

Coaching, on the other hand, focuses on developing specific skills and competencies. Coaches work collaboratively with leaders to identify areas for improvement, set goals, and provide ongoing support through regular coaching sessions. Coaching can be particularly useful for leaders who are seeking to enhance their instructional leadership, communication, or change management skills.

Online and Virtual Professional Development Opportunities

Online and virtual professional development opportunities have become increasingly popular and accessible for educational leaders. These platforms offer flexibility and convenience, allowing leaders to engage in learning at their own pace and convenience.

Online courses and webinars provide leaders with the opportunity to explore specific topics of interest, gain new knowledge and skills, and connect with experts and peers from around the world. Many universities and educational organizations offer online programs and certifications tailored specifically for educational leaders.

Virtual professional learning communities (PLCs) provide leaders with the opportunity to connect, collaborate, and exchange ideas with peers in a virtual environment. These communities often include discussion forums, resource sharing platforms, and regular meetings or webinars. Virtual PLCs can be particularly valuable for leaders who may not have access to local networks or face-to-face professional development opportunities.

Micro-credentials and Digital Badges for Leader Recognition

Micro-credentials and digital badges have emerged as a way to recognize and validate the skills and competencies gained through professional development activities. These credentials provide a more granular and focused representation of an individual's learning achievements, allowing leaders to showcase their expertise in specific areas.

Micro-credentials are typically offered through online platforms and involve completing a series of modules or assessments to demonstrate proficiency in a particular skill or competency. Digital badges serve as a visual representation of the earned credential and can be displayed on professional profiles or shared on social media.

By earning and displaying micro-credentials and digital badges, educational leaders can provide evidence of their continuous learning and expertise to colleagues, employers, and the broader education community.

Embracing a Growth Mindset in Professional Development

A growth mindset is a key attribute for educational leaders engaged in professional development. Leaders with a growth mindset believe that their abilities and skills can be developed through dedication and hard work. This mindset enables leaders to embrace challenges, persist in the face of setbacks, and continually seek to improve their practice.

To foster a growth mindset, educational leaders can engage in reflective practices, seek feedback from colleagues and mentors, and set ambitious but achievable goals for their professional development. By modeling a growth mindset, leaders can inspire and motivate their staff and students to embrace continuous learning and improvement.

The Future of Teacher Professional Development

The future of professional development for educational leaders holds promising possibilities. With advancements in technology, leaders will have access to more personalized and immersive learning experiences. Virtual reality (VR) technology may be used to simulate real-life scenarios, allowing leaders to practice decision-making and problem-solving in a risk-free environment.

Artificial intelligence (AI) may play a larger role in professional development by providing personalized recommendations for learning opportunities based on an individual's specific needs and goals. AI-powered virtual coaching programs could offer leaders ongoing support and feedback, helping them refine their leadership skills.

Collaborative learning communities may also evolve, leveraging social learning platforms and AI-driven matchmaking algorithms to connect leaders with mentors and peers who share similar goals or challenges. These communities could provide personalized resources, facilitate virtual meetings, and support ongoing collaboration.

As educational leaders continue to adapt to the changing landscape of education, professional development will remain a critical component of their success. By embracing new models, leveraging technology, and fostering growth mindsets, educational leaders can be at the forefront of educational transformation, ensuring positive outcomes for both students and educators.

Embracing a growth mindset in professional development

In the field of education, professional development plays a crucial role in ensuring that teachers continuously grow and adapt to the changing needs of their students and the education landscape. However, traditional models of professional development often focus on transmitting knowledge and skills in a one-size-fits-all manner, which can limit teachers' growth and potential. To overcome this limitation, educators need to embrace a growth mindset in their professional development.

Understanding the concept of a growth mindset

The concept of a growth mindset, popularized by psychologist Carol Dweck, is centered around the belief that intelligence and abilities are not fixed traits, but can be developed and improved over time. Adopting a growth mindset means that individuals believe they can learn, grow, and improve through effort, effective strategies, and feedback.

In the context of professional development, embracing a growth mindset involves valuing and pursuing opportunities for continuous learning, seeking challenges and feedback, and being open to change and new ideas. It requires educators to see themselves as lifelong learners who can always improve their teaching practices to better support student learning.

Benefits of embracing a growth mindset in professional development

Embracing a growth mindset in professional development offers several benefits for educators. Firstly, it fosters a sense of empowerment and motivation, as teachers believe that they have the capacity to continually develop their skills and enhance their effectiveness in the classroom. This intrinsic motivation leads to increased engagement and a higher level of commitment to ongoing professional growth.

Secondly, a growth mindset encourages educators to take risks and embrace innovative approaches in their teaching. They are more likely to experiment with new strategies and pedagogical techniques, which can lead to improved student outcomes. By viewing challenges and failures as opportunities for learning and growth, teachers are better equipped to navigate the complexities of the teaching profession and overcome obstacles.

Furthermore, a growth mindset helps teachers develop a positive attitude towards professional feedback. Instead of perceiving feedback as criticism or a personal attack, educators with a growth mindset see it as valuable information that can help them identify areas for improvement and refine their teaching practices. They actively seek feedback from colleagues, students, and administrators, and use it to enhance their instructional strategies.

Strategies for promoting a growth mindset in professional development

To promote a growth mindset in professional development, several strategies can be implemented:

1. Providing opportunities for self-reflection: Encourage teachers to reflect on their professional growth and identify areas in which they can further develop. Self-reflection can be facilitated through journaling, self-assessment tools, or guided reflection activities.

2. Encouraging collaboration and peer learning: Create opportunities for teachers to collaborate and learn from each other's expertise. Peer observations, lesson study groups, and professional learning communities are effective platforms for collaborative learning, providing valuable feedback and insights.

3. Offering differentiated professional development pathways: Recognize that teachers have different professional needs and interests. Provide a range of professional development options, including workshops, conferences, online courses, and self-paced modules, to cater to diverse learning preferences and goals.

4. Fostering a culture of continuous improvement: Create a supportive and nurturing environment that values ongoing growth and professional learning. Recognize and celebrate the achievements and progress made by teachers in their professional development journey.

5. Integrating technology into professional development: Leverage technology tools and platforms to enhance professional development opportunities. Online

learning platforms, webinars, and virtual communities can facilitate anytime, anywhere learning and promote collaboration among educators.

Case studies and best practices

Several case studies and best practices exemplify the successful implementation of a growth mindset in professional development:

1. High Tech High: This network of public charter schools in California emphasizes project-based learning and continuous professional development. Teachers engage in ongoing collaboration, reflection, and experimentation, fostering a culture of innovation and growth.
2. Lesson Study in Japan: Lesson Study is a collaborative professional development model widely used in Japan. Teachers work together to plan, observe, and refine lessons. By engaging in reflective practice and feedback, teachers continuously improve their instructional practices.
3. Teacher Learning Circles: Teacher Learning Circles are small groups of educators who meet regularly to discuss teaching strategies and share their experiences. These circles promote collective learning, peer support, and the development of a growth mindset.

Future directions of embracing a growth mindset in professional development

As professional development continues to evolve, embracing a growth mindset will become even more critical. Future directions in this area include:

1. Personalized professional development: Offering tailored professional development experiences based on individual needs and interests, allowing teachers to focus on areas that align with their growth goals.
2. Micro-credentials and digital badges: Recognizing teachers' achievements and competencies through micro-credentials and digital badges. These credentials can provide a more nuanced representation of teachers' skills and expertise.
3. Virtual reality (VR) and augmented reality (AR) in professional development: Using VR and AR technologies to create immersive professional development experiences, such as virtual classrooms or simulations, allowing teachers to practice and reflect on their instructional techniques.
4. Artificial intelligence (AI) in professional development: Leveraging AI to provide personalized recommendations for professional development opportunities, identify areas for improvement, and offer targeted feedback.

By embracing a growth mindset, educators can foster their own professional growth, inspire their students, and contribute to the advancement of the education field. As teachers continually evolve their practices, they will be better equipped to meet the diverse needs of today's learners and prepare them for the challenges of the future.

The future of teacher professional development

The future of teacher professional development is shaped by the rapidly evolving landscape of education and the increasing integration of technology in classrooms. As educators strive to meet the changing needs of students and adapt to new pedagogical approaches, professional development becomes a crucial component in equipping teachers with the skills and knowledge to navigate this dynamic environment.

Importance of continuous professional development

Continuous professional development (CPD) is fundamental for teachers to stay up-to-date with emerging trends, best practices, and innovative teaching strategies. The traditional model of one-time workshops and conferences is no longer sufficient, considering the pace of change in education. The future of teacher professional development requires a shift towards ongoing and personalized learning opportunities that meet the specific needs of individual teachers.

Traditional vs. innovative professional development models

Traditional professional development models often focus on passive learning, where teachers receive information and resources without actively engaging in the learning process. However, innovative professional development models prioritize active and experiential learning, encouraging teachers to reflect on their practice, collaborate with peers, and experiment with new strategies.

Innovative professional development models often incorporate elements such as job-embedded coaching, action research projects, online communities of practice, and micro-credentials. These models provide teachers with more autonomy in their professional growth and enable them to individualize their learning based on their specific needs and interests.

Building networks and communities of practice

Building networks and communities of practice is a cornerstone of the future of teacher professional development. Educators can connect with colleagues from around the world to share ideas, resources, and experiences. Online platforms and social media provide opportunities for teachers to engage in professional conversations, join virtual communities, and participate in collaborative projects.

By participating in networks and communities of practice, teachers can gain insights into different teaching strategies, access a wide range of perspectives, and receive support and feedback from peers. This fosters a sense of belonging and encourages continuous learning and growth.

Mentoring and coaching for teacher development

Mentoring and coaching have shown to be highly effective approaches in supporting teacher development. In the future, mentoring programs can be enhanced through the use of technology, allowing for virtual mentoring relationships beyond geographical limitations. Online platforms can facilitate mentoring connections and provide resources for mentor-mentee interactions.

Coaching, on the other hand, focuses on supporting teachers in their professional growth through reflective conversations and targeted feedback. The future of coaching includes virtual coaching sessions, video-based observations, and online coaching communities, which provide a flexible and accessible avenue for teachers to receive personalized support.

Online and virtual professional development opportunities

Online and virtual professional development opportunities play a vital role in the future of teacher professional development. Online courses, webinars, and virtual conferences provide teachers with access to a wide range of resources and knowledge from experts across the globe. These opportunities can be self-paced or facilitated by instructors, allowing teachers to learn at their own convenience.

Virtual reality (VR) and augmented reality (AR) have the potential to revolutionize professional development by providing immersive learning experiences. Teachers can explore virtual classrooms, observe exemplary teaching practices, and engage in simulated student interactions, enhancing their skills and understanding in a virtual environment.

Micro-credentials and digital badges for teacher recognition

Micro-credentials and digital badges are emerging as valuable tools for recognizing and validating teacher professional development. These credentials are awarded for specific skills, competencies, or accomplishments and can be displayed on digital platforms, such as teacher profiles or professional networking sites.

Micro-credentials provide a more granular and targeted way to demonstrate professional growth compared to traditional certificates or degrees. They allow teachers to showcase their expertise in specific areas and promote ongoing learning and improvement. In the future, micro-credentials and digital badges may become widely recognized forms of professional recognition, supplementing or even replacing traditional credentials.

Teacher-led professional learning communities

Teacher-led professional learning communities (PLCs) empower educators to take ownership of their professional development. In these communities, teachers collaborate, share resources, and engage in peer-to-peer support and learning. Teacher-led PLCs can be facilitated through online platforms, where teachers can join or create communities centered around specific topics, grade levels, or subject areas.

Teacher-led PLCs provide a space for teachers to reflect on their practice, discuss challenges, and support one another in finding effective solutions. They promote a culture of continuous improvement and enable teachers to draw upon the collective expertise of their colleagues.

Professional development for educational leaders

In addition to teacher professional development, the future also involves providing professional development opportunities for educational leaders. School principals and administrators play a critical role in shaping the learning environment and supporting teacher growth. Leadership development programs can equip educational leaders with skills in instructional leadership, technology integration, and fostering a culture of innovation.

Professional development for educational leaders can include learning experiences such as coaching, mentoring, and specialized courses or workshops. These opportunities enable educational leaders to lead by example, inspire their staff, and facilitate the implementation of transformative practices.

Embracing a growth mindset in professional development

A growth mindset is essential in the future of teacher professional development. Teachers need to embrace the belief that their abilities and skills can be developed and improved with effort and practice. Professional development programs should explicitly promote a growth mindset culture, encouraging teachers to take risks, learn from failures, and continuously seek growth opportunities.

By embracing a growth mindset, teachers are more likely to engage in ongoing professional development, persist in the face of challenges, and embrace new teaching practices. A growth mindset also fosters a culture of innovation and collaboration, as teachers are open to feedback and see professional development as an integral part of their career trajectory.

The future of teacher professional development

The future of teacher professional development is characterized by personalization, collaboration, and the integration of technology. Teachers will have access to a wide range of learning opportunities, tailored to their unique needs, preferences, and aspirations. Professional development will be interactive, experiential, and characterized by ongoing reflection and feedback.

With the advent of increasingly sophisticated technologies, virtual reality, augmented reality, and artificial intelligence will play a more prominent role in professional development. These technologies will provide immersive and personalized learning experiences, empower teachers to experiment with new approaches, and revolutionize the way professional development is delivered.

In conclusion, the future of teacher professional development is an exciting and transformative landscape. It will embrace innovative models, foster collaboration and networks, leverage technology, and prioritize ongoing and personalized learning. By investing in the professional growth of teachers, we can ensure that education continues to evolve and meet the needs of students in an ever-changing world.

Ethical Considerations in Education Technology

Security and Privacy Concerns in Educational Technology

In today's digital age, educational technology has become an integral part of the learning process. From online learning platforms to data analytics tools, technology has transformed the way education is delivered and accessed. However, as educational institutions increasingly rely on technology, security and privacy concerns have emerged as pressing challenges.

1. **The Importance of Security in Educational Technology**

Security in educational technology refers to the measures taken to protect educational institutions, students, and educators from unauthorized access, data breaches, and malicious activities. It is crucial to ensure the confidentiality, integrity, and availability of sensitive information, such as student records, assessment data, and educational resources. A secure educational technology environment fosters trust, enables effective teaching and learning, and protects the privacy rights of all stakeholders.

2. **Privacy Concerns in Educational Technology**

Privacy concerns in educational technology focus on safeguarding personal information and maintaining control over data shared within educational environments. Educational technology platforms often collect extensive data on students, including their identities, learning preferences, and online behaviors. This sensitive information can be vulnerable to misuse, particularly without proper safeguards.

3. **Regulatory Frameworks for Security and Privacy**

To address security and privacy concerns in educational technology, regulatory frameworks and laws have been established globally. One of the key regulatory frameworks is the General Data Protection Regulation (GDPR) in the European Union. It sets strict guidelines for the collection, storage, processing, and sharing of personal data. Educational institutions must comply with GDPR requirements when using educational technology tools that collect and process personal information from EU residents.

4. **Data Security Measures**

To enhance data security in educational technology, educational institutions should implement a range of measures:

4.1 *User Authentication and Access Control:* Implement strong user authentication mechanisms, such as two-factor authentication, to ensure that only authorized individuals can access educational technology platforms and systems.

4.2 *Data Encryption:* Encrypt sensitive data, such as student records and assessment results, both during transit and storage to prevent unauthorized access.

4.3 *Regular Software Updates and Patching:* Keep educational technology systems up to date with the latest security patches and software updates to address vulnerabilities and protect against potential cyber threats.

4.4 *Secure Network Infrastructure:* Implement secure network architecture, including firewalls, intrusion detection systems, and virtual private networks (VPNs), to protect against unauthorized access and data exfiltration.

4.5 *Data Backup and Disaster Recovery:* Regularly backup educational data and implement disaster recovery plans to ensure the continuity of educational services in the event of a cyberattack or system failure.

5. **Privacy Protection Measures**

To address privacy concerns in educational technology, educational institutions should implement the following measures:

5.1 *Transparent Data Collection Practices:* Clearly communicate to students and educators the types of data collected, for what purposes, and with whom it will be shared. Obtain explicit consent when necessary.

5.2 *Data Anonymization and De-identification:* Remove or encrypt personally identifiable information (PII) whenever possible to mitigate privacy risks associated with data breaches and unauthorized data linkage.

5.3 *Privacy Policies and Notices:* Develop and communicate clear privacy policies and notices to educate students, educators, and parents about how their data will be used, stored, and protected.

5.4 *Data Minimization:* Collect only the data necessary for educational purposes and ensure that data retention policies align with legal and regulatory requirements.

5.5 *Vendor Due Diligence:* Conduct thorough assessments of educational technology vendors to ensure their compliance with security and privacy standards, and establish contractual agreements that explicitly address data security and privacy obligations.

6. **Ethical Considerations**

When considering the use of educational technology, ethical considerations should also be taken into account, including:

6.1 *Data Ownership and Control:* Students and educators should maintain ownership and control over their personal data, with mechanisms in place for them to access, update, and delete their information as needed.

6.2 *Informed Consent:* Students, educators, and parents should have a clear understanding of the potential risks and benefits associated with the use of educational technology, and provide informed consent before their data is collected or processed.

6.3 *Algorithmic Transparency and Bias:* Institutions should ensure that algorithms used in educational technology platforms are transparent, accountable, and free from bias, to avoid perpetuating and reinforcing inequalities.

6.4 *Educating Students about Digital Ethics:* Students should be educated about their rights, responsibilities, and ethical behavior in the digital world. This includes teaching them about concepts such as data privacy, cybersecurity, and responsible digital citizenship.

7. **Professional Development and Training**

Educators and staff should receive ongoing professional development and training on security and privacy practices in educational technology. This training should cover topics such as data protection, safe browsing habits, secure online communication, and responding to security incidents. By equipping educators with the necessary knowledge and skills, educational institutions can create a culture of security and privacy awareness.

In conclusion, ensuring security and privacy in educational technology is crucial for maintaining trust, protecting sensitive information, and promoting ethical practices. By implementing robust security measures, respecting privacy rights, and fostering a culture of digital ethics, educational institutions can harness the full potential of educational technology while safeguarding the interests of students, educators, and other stakeholders.

Data collection and student privacy rights

In the digital age, data collection has become a prevalent practice in various sectors, including education. Schools and educational institutions often collect large amounts of data from students, ranging from academic records to personal information. This data is valuable for monitoring student progress, tailoring instruction, and improving educational outcomes. However, it also raises concerns about student privacy rights and the responsible use of data.

Importance of student privacy rights

Protecting student privacy is crucial for maintaining trust in educational institutions and ensuring the ethical and legal use of data. Students have the right to control and protect their personal information, and educational institutions have a responsibility to safeguard this information. Respect for student privacy not only promotes the well-being of individual students but also fosters a conducive learning environment.

Laws and regulations

Several laws and regulations are in place to protect student privacy rights. The Family Educational Rights and Privacy Act (FERPA) is a federal law in the United States that grants students and their parents the right to access and control their educational records. It also requires educational institutions to obtain written consent before disclosing student information to third parties.

In addition to FERPA, there are other laws and regulations that address specific aspects of student data privacy. For example, the Children's Online Privacy Protection Act (COPPA) requires verifiable parental consent for the collection of personal information from children under the age of 13. The General Data Protection Regulation (GDPR) in Europe sets guidelines for the protection of personal data, including data collected by educational institutions.

Educational institutions must be familiar with these laws and regulations and ensure compliance to safeguard student privacy. They should establish clear policies and procedures for data collection, storage, and sharing that align with legal requirements.

Responsible data collection practices

To protect student privacy, educational institutions should adopt responsible data collection practices. This includes:

1. Consent: Obtain informed consent from students and/or their parents before collecting any personal information. Consent should be voluntary, specific, and based on clear and understandable information about how the data will be used.

2. Minimization: Collect only the necessary data and avoid excessive or unnecessary data collection. Limit the collection of sensitive information to what is directly relevant to the educational purpose.

3. Security: Implement robust data security measures to protect student data from unauthorized access, use, and disclosure. This may include encryption, secure servers, and access controls.

4. Anonymization and de-identification: When possible, anonymize or de-identify student data to remove personally identifiable information. This helps to minimize risks associated with data breaches or unintended disclosures.

5. Data retention and disposal: Establish guidelines for how long student data will be retained and ensure secure disposal when it is no longer needed. This helps to minimize the risk of data misuse.

6. Transparency: Provide clear and accessible information about data collection practices, including the types of data collected, purposes, and rights of students. This promotes trust and allows students and parents to make informed decisions.

Challenges and considerations

Implementing responsible data collection practices in education is not without challenges. Some of the key challenges include:

1. Technological advancements: Rapid advancements in technology, such as cloud computing and big data analytics, have made it easier to collect and analyze

large volumes of student data. However, these advancements also pose risks in terms of data security and privacy.

2. Third-party services: Educational institutions often use third-party services and edtech tools that collect student data. It is important to carefully review the privacy policies and terms of services of these providers to ensure they align with data protection standards.

3. Data breaches: The risk of data breaches is an ever-present concern. Educational institutions must have robust security measures in place to prevent unauthorized access to student data and respond effectively in the event of a breach.

4. Ethical considerations: There are ethical considerations surrounding the use of student data, such as potential biases or discrimination in algorithms used for automated decision-making. Educational institutions must be mindful of these ethical implications and take steps to mitigate potential harms.

5. Parental involvement: Engaging parents and guardians in discussions around data collection and privacy is critical. Schools should involve parents in the decision-making process and provide clear channels for communication and feedback.

Real-world example

To illustrate the importance of student privacy rights and data collection practices, let's consider the case of a school district implementing a new learning management system (LMS). The LMS collects a wide range of student data, including academic records, attendance, and behavior.

To ensure responsible data collection, the school district follows these steps:

1. Obtain informed consent from students and parents, clearly explaining the purpose of data collection, how it will be used, and who will have access to it.

2. Limit the data collected to what is necessary for academic purposes and exclude sensitive information that is not relevant.

3. Implement strong security measures, such as encryption and access controls, to protect student data from unauthorized access.

4. Anonymize or de-identify the data to remove personally identifiable information, making it difficult to link data to individual students.

5. Establish a data retention policy that specifies how long student data will be stored and secure procedures for disposing of it when no longer needed.

By implementing these responsible data collection practices, the school district ensures the privacy and security of student data while still benefiting from the insights provided by the LMS.

Resources and further reading

For further reading on data collection and student privacy rights, the following resources are recommended:

1. Student Data Privacy: A Practical Guide for Teachers and School Leaders by Linnette Attai
2. "Protecting Student Privacy While Using Online Educational Services: Requirements and Best Practices" by the U.S. Department of Education
3. The Future of Privacy Forum's Student Privacy Resource Center (studentprivacyresources.org)
4. "Privacy and Cloud Computing in Public Schools" by Linnette Attai and Steve Smith
5. Data Quality Campaign's Student Data Privacy and Security Principles (dataqualitycampaign.org)

These resources provide valuable insights and guidance for educational institutions seeking to navigate the complexities of data collection and student privacy rights.

Summary

Data collection in education can be a powerful tool for improving learning outcomes, but it must be carried out responsibly and ethically. Respecting student privacy rights, complying with relevant laws and regulations, and adopting responsible data collection practices are essential for maintaining trust and safeguarding student data. Educational institutions should prioritize transparency, security, and informed consent to ensure that data collection enhances, rather than compromises, the learning experience.

Responsible use of artificial intelligence in education

Artificial intelligence (AI) has the potential to revolutionize education by providing personalized learning experiences, automating administrative tasks, and enhancing teaching and assessment practices. However, it is crucial to ensure the responsible use of AI in education to address ethical concerns, privacy issues, and potential biases. This section will explore the key principles and considerations for the responsible use of AI in education.

Ethical considerations in AI

Ethics play a central role in the development and use of AI in education. It is essential to consider the following ethical principles:

1. **Transparency:** AI systems in education should be transparent, with clear explanations of how they function, make decisions, and collect and use data. This transparency helps users to understand the rationale behind AI-driven recommendations and assessments.

2. **Privacy and data protection:** AI applications in education often involve the collection and processing of sensitive student data. It is crucial to ensure the privacy and security of student information, as well as obtain appropriate consent for data usage. Educational institutions should also establish policies and practices that govern the handling of data to prevent unauthorized access or use.

3. **Fairness and bias:** AI algorithms are built using vast datasets, and if these datasets contain biases, they can reinforce existing social inequalities. It is important to eliminate bias and ensure fairness in the design, development, and implementation of AI systems in education. Regular audits should be conducted to identify and rectify any biases that might emerge.

4. **Accountability:** Developers and users of AI systems should be accountable for the decisions and outcomes generated by these systems. In the context of education, this means that educators and institutions should ensure that AI-driven recommendations and assessments align with educational standards and objectives and can be justified and explained to students and other stakeholders.

5. **Beneficence and non-maleficence:** AI applications in education should strive to maximize the benefits to students and minimize any potential harm. This involves considering the potential risks and ensuring that the use of AI does not infringe upon students' rights and well-being.

Adhering to these ethical principles will help ensure that AI is used responsibly in education and promotes positive learning outcomes.

Addressing biases in AI

Bias can emerge in AI systems due to the data they are trained on, reflecting existing societal biases and discrimination. To address biases in AI in education, the following steps can be taken:

1. **Diverse and representative datasets:** Ensuring that AI algorithms are trained on diverse datasets that represent different racial, ethnic, cultural, and gender groups can mitigate bias. It is important to source data from a wide range of demographic backgrounds to avoid underrepresentation or overrepresentation of certain groups.

2. **Regular audits and evaluations:** Regularly auditing and evaluating AI systems can help identify and rectify biases. This involves analyzing the outcomes of AI-driven decisions and assessments to determine whether they disproportionately favor or disadvantage certain groups.

3. **Inclusive design and evaluation:** Involving a diverse group of stakeholders, including educators, students, and experts on bias and inclusion, in the design and evaluation of AI systems can help identify and address potential biases. Taking an inclusive approach ensures that different perspectives and experiences are considered.

4. **Ongoing monitoring and refinement:** AI systems should be continuously monitored and refined to identify and rectify biases that may emerge over time. This involves collecting feedback from users and engaging in a continuous improvement process to ensure fairness and inclusivity.

By taking proactive measures to address biases in AI, educational institutions can ensure that these technologies do not perpetuate inequality and discrimination.

Purposeful integration of AI in education

The integration of AI in education should be purposeful and aligned with educational goals and pedagogical approaches. Here are some key considerations:

1. **Collaborative learning and human interaction:** AI should complement, rather than replace, human interaction and collaboration. It can support personalized learning experiences, provide timely feedback, and free up time for educators to focus on individualized instruction and mentoring.

2. **Augmenting rather than replacing teachers:** AI should enhance the capabilities of teachers, empowering them to make informed decisions and effectively address the diverse needs of students. It can assist with administrative tasks, automate grading, and provide insights into student performance and learning gaps.

3. **Promoting critical thinking:** AI can be utilized to encourage critical thinking skills by simulating real-world scenarios, presenting diverse perspectives, and challenging students to analyze and evaluate information. Educators should ensure that AI-powered tools and resources promote deep thinking and problem-solving abilities.

4. **Continuous monitoring and evaluation:** Educational institutions should monitor and evaluate the effectiveness of AI applications in achieving desired learning outcomes. Both qualitative and quantitative data should be collected to assess the impact of AI on student engagement, performance, and well-being.

By integrating AI purposefully into educational practices, institutions can maximize its potential while ensuring alignment with educational values and principles.

Developing student digital literacy and ethics

It is essential to prepare students for the responsible use of AI technology. Educators should incorporate digital literacy and ethics education into the curriculum to equip students with the necessary skills and knowledge. This includes:

1. **Understanding AI:** Students should have an understanding of AI concepts, its capabilities, and its limitations. They should also be aware of the ethical considerations and potential biases associated with AI.

2. **Critical thinking and problem-solving:** AI encourages students to think critically and solve complex problems. Educators should design activities that enable students to analyze and evaluate AI-generated content and make informed decisions.

3. **Data literacy:** Students should learn to interpret, evaluate, and use data responsibly. This includes understanding how AI algorithms work and the implications of data collection and analysis.

4. **Digital citizenship:** Educators should instill the values of digital citizenship, promoting responsible and ethical online behavior, and teaching students to leverage AI technology in productive and ethical ways.

5. **Privacy and security:** Students should understand the importance of protecting their privacy and personal information. Educators should teach students about data security, consent, and the potential risks associated with sharing personal data.

By integrating digital literacy and ethics education into the curriculum, educators can empower students to become responsible and ethical users of AI technology.

Case study: AI-powered personalized learning

One example of the responsible use of AI in education is AI-powered personalized learning. By leveraging AI algorithms, personalized learning platforms can adapt content, pace, and resources to meet individual student needs. These platforms can provide targeted recommendations, adaptive assessments, and timely feedback.

In this case study, a high school mathematics teacher uses an AI-powered personalized learning platform to support student learning. The platform collects and analyzes data on student performance, identifies areas of strength and weakness, and generates personalized recommendations and practice activities.

The responsible use of AI in this scenario involves:

1. Ensuring transparency: The teacher explains to students how the personalized learning platform works, how it uses AI algorithms to generate recommendations, and how it collects and handles data.

2. Addressing biases and fairness: The personalized learning platform is regularly audited to identify and rectify any biases or inequities in the recommendations. The teacher also manually reviews the recommendations to ensure their accuracy and fairness.

3. Fostering collaboration: The teacher emphasizes the importance of collaboration and discussion among students while using the platform. They encourage students to share their learning experiences, help each other, and discuss the reasoning behind the recommendations.

4. Empowering student agency: Students are given the autonomy to make decisions about their learning path. They can choose their practice activities, track their progress, and reflect on their learning goals.

5. Developing student digital literacy: The teacher incorporates digital literacy activities into the curriculum, teaching students how to interpret and analyze the recommendations generated by the AI-powered platform. Students learn to use the platform responsibly, critically evaluate their learning progress, and reflect on the benefits and limitations of AI in education.

This case study demonstrates the responsible use of AI in personalized learning, where the technology enhances student learning while considering ethical principles and promoting student agency and critical thinking.

Conclusion

AI has the potential to transform education, but its responsible use is paramount. Educators, policymakers, and technology developers must adhere to ethical principles, address biases, purposefully integrate AI, develop student digital literacy, and ensure meaningful outcomes. By promoting responsible use, AI can enhance education, support personalized learning, and create more inclusive and equitable learning environments.

Addressing biases and inequalities in algorithmic decision-making

In recent years, algorithmic decision-making (ADM) systems have become increasingly prevalent in various domains, including education. These systems use complex algorithms to analyze large amounts of data and make decisions or recommendations. While ADM systems have the potential to improve efficiency and accuracy, they are not immune to biases and inequalities. In fact, studies have shown that algorithmic decision-making can perpetuate and even exacerbate existing biases in society. In this section, we will explore the challenges and strategies for addressing biases and inequalities in algorithmic decision-making in education.

Understanding biases in algorithmic decision-making

Biases in algorithmic decision-making can arise from various sources, including biased training data, algorithm design choices, and inadequate evaluation methods. Biased training data can contain historical biases and reflect existing social inequalities. For example, if a predictive model is trained on data that disproportionately represents certain demographic groups, the model may learn to make decisions that disadvantage those groups. Algorithm design choices, such as the selection of features and weighting of different factors, can also introduce biases into the decision-making process. Additionally, evaluation methods that focus solely on model accuracy may overlook or even reinforce biases. Therefore, it is crucial to understand the different types of biases and how they manifest in algorithmic decision-making.

Types of biases in algorithmic decision-making

Several types of biases can be present in algorithmic decision-making, including disparate impact, disparate treatment, and sample selection bias. Disparate impact occurs when an algorithm disproportionately affects protected groups, even if it is unintentional. For example, an admission process that relies heavily on automated algorithms may inadvertently result in higher rejection rates for certain racial or socioeconomic groups. Disparate treatment, on the other hand, refers to intentional discrimination based on protected characteristics, such as race or gender. Sample selection bias arises when the training data does not adequately represent the population, leading to inaccurate or unfair predictions. For instance, if a predictive model for student performance is trained on data from urban schools only, it may not capture the unique challenges and contexts of students from rural or disadvantaged areas.

Strategies for addressing biases

Addressing biases in algorithmic decision-making requires a multi-faceted approach that involves data collection, algorithm design, evaluation methods, and stakeholder involvement. Here are some strategies that can help mitigate biases:

1. Diverse and representative training data: To improve the accuracy and fairness of algorithms, it is essential to have diverse and representative training data. This involves ensuring that the data used to train the algorithms is collected from a wide range of sources and reflects the diversity of the population it serves. Data collection practices should consider the perspectives and experiences of marginalized groups.

2. Transparent algorithmic design: Transparency in algorithmic design is crucial for addressing biases. Algorithms should be designed in a way that allows for clear explanations of their decision-making processes. This transparency enables stakeholders, including educators, students, and parents, to identify and challenge any biases in the system.

3. Ongoing evaluation and monitoring: Regular evaluation and monitoring of algorithms are necessary to identify and address biases. Evaluation methods should go beyond accuracy metrics and include fairness and equity assessments.

Furthermore, it is important to continuously re-evaluate algorithms as societal norms evolve and new biases emerge.

4. Ethical considerations in decision-making: Decision-makers and algorithm designers should carefully consider the ethical implications of their algorithms. This includes recognizing the potential biases and inequalities that can arise and actively working to avoid them. Ethical frameworks, such as the principle of beneficence and the principle of justice, can guide decision-makers in ensuring fairness and equity in algorithmic decision-making.

5. Stakeholder involvement and transparency: Including diverse stakeholders in the design and implementation of algorithmic decision-making systems can help uncover and address biases. This involvement creates opportunities for different perspectives to be considered, leading to more inclusive and unbiased algorithms. Moreover, transparency about the decision-making process can empower stakeholders to hold decision-makers accountable and address potential biases.

Case study: Addressing biases in college admissions

One area where biases in algorithmic decision-making have received significant attention is college admissions. Traditional admissions processes have been criticized for being subject to biases and inequalities, leading some universities to experiment with algorithmic systems. However, these algorithmic systems must be carefully designed to mitigate biases. For example, the University of California system implemented an algorithmic admissions model that aimed to increase diversity. The model considered various academic and socioeconomic factors to assess applicants holistically. By including these factors, the algorithmic model aimed to address biases that could arise from relying solely on standardized test scores or other traditional measures. However, ongoing monitoring and evaluation of the model are essential to ensure that it does not inadvertently introduce new biases or perpetuate existing ones.

Exercise

Think of a real-world scenario where algorithmic decision-making is used, such as a credit scoring system for loan applications. Identify potential biases that could arise in the algorithmic decision-making process and suggest strategies for addressing these biases.

Additional resources

1. Obermeyer, Z., Powers, B., Vogeli, C., & Mullainathan, S. (2019). Dissecting racial bias in an algorithm used to manage the health of populations. Science, 366(6464), 447-453.

2. Buolamwini, J., & Gebru, T. (2018). Gender shades: Intersectional accuracy disparities in commercial gender classification. In Conference on fairness, accountability and transparency (pp. 77-91).

3. Broussard, M. (2018). Artificial unintelligence: How computers misunderstand the world. MIT Press.

4. Diakopoulos, N. (2019). Algorithmic accountability reporting: On the investigation of black boxes. Columbia Journalism Review.

These resources provide further insights into biases in algorithmic decision-making and strategies for addressing them. They offer a nuanced understanding of the challenges and opportunities associated with algorithmic decision-making in education and other domains.

Digital citizenship and ethical online behavior

In today's digital age, it has become increasingly important to educate students about digital citizenship and ethical online behavior. As technology continues to advance and shape our lives, it is crucial to instill in students the knowledge and skills necessary to navigate the online world responsibly and ethically. This section will discuss the concept of digital citizenship, the importance of ethical online behavior, and strategies for promoting and teaching these principles to students.

Understanding digital citizenship

Digital citizenship refers to the responsible and ethical use of technology and the internet. It encompasses a set of skills, knowledge, and values that enable individuals to engage in respectful, safe, and responsible online interactions. Digital citizenship involves a range of behaviors, including protecting one's privacy, respecting intellectual property, practicing good digital etiquette, and being aware of online risks and responsibilities.

At its core, digital citizenship is about fostering a positive and inclusive online community where individuals can engage, collaborate, and learn from one another while respecting each other's rights and values. It emphasizes the need for individuals to understand and adhere to ethical standards, laws, and policies that govern online behavior.

The importance of ethical online behavior

Ethical online behavior is essential for creating a safe and respectful digital environment. It promotes positive online interactions, protects individuals' privacy and security, and prevents the spread of misinformation and cyberbullying. Beyond personal well-being, ethical online behavior also contributes to the overall health of online communities and society as a whole.

Teaching students about ethical online behavior is crucial for their digital literacy and preparedness to navigate the challenges of the digital world. By fostering a sense of responsibility, empathy, and critical thinking, students can become active and responsible digital citizens who contribute positively to the online community.

Strategies for promoting ethical online behavior

1. Education and awareness: Educate students about the importance of ethical online behavior, including topics such as digital rights and responsibilities, cyberbullying, online privacy, and intellectual property. Use real-life examples and case studies to illustrate the consequences of unethical online behavior.

2. Digital footprint management: Teach students how to manage their digital footprints by guiding them on the potential consequences of their online actions and the importance of maintaining a positive and professional online presence.

3. Critical evaluation of online content: Teach students how to critically evaluate online content for credibility, bias, and accuracy. Encourage them to question the sources of information and verify facts before accepting them as true.

4. Responsible use of social media and online platforms: Guide students on appropriate and responsible behavior on social media platforms, emphasizing the importance of respectful communication, privacy settings, and responsible sharing of content.

5. Cyberbullying prevention and intervention: Teach students about the harmful effects of cyberbullying and provide strategies to prevent and respond to cyberbullying incidents. Encourage empathy, respect, and support for others in online interactions.

6. Online privacy and security: Educate students about the importance of protecting their personal information online. Teach them about safe internet practices, such as creating strong passwords, using secure networks, and avoiding sharing sensitive information.

7. Digital etiquette: Teach students about the principles of good digital etiquette, including being respectful in online communications, using appropriate

language, and being mindful of cultural differences.

8. Ethical use of information and intellectual property: Teach students about copyright laws, plagiarism, and the importance of citing sources when using information from online resources. Encourage them to respect the intellectual property of others and to give proper credit for the work they use.

9. Online safety: Provide guidance on online safety practices, such as avoiding interactions with strangers, reporting suspicious activities, and knowing how to respond to online threats or harassment.

10. Family and community involvement: Encourage collaboration between schools, families, and communities to promote ethical online behavior. Offer resources and workshops for parents and guardians to support their children in navigating the digital world.

Case study: Promoting ethical online behavior through peer mentoring

One effective strategy for promoting ethical online behavior is through peer mentoring programs. In such programs, older students serve as mentors or role models for younger students, guiding them on responsible and ethical online behavior. This approach has several benefits:

1. Peer influence: Younger students may be more receptive to advice and guidance from their peers. Having older students talk about and model ethical online behavior can have a strong impact on the younger students' attitudes and actions.

2. Relatability: Peers can share their own experiences and stories about online interactions, making the discussions more relatable and encouraging open discussions about the challenges and ethical dilemmas students may face online.

3. Empowerment: Peer mentoring programs can empower students to take an active role in promoting ethical online behavior. By becoming mentors, students develop leadership skills and a sense of responsibility towards their peers and the wider online community.

4. Continuity: Peer mentors can provide ongoing support and guidance as students progress through different grades. This allows for the reinforcement of ethical behaviors and the opportunity to address emerging challenges and concerns.

To implement a peer mentoring program, schools can select older students who have demonstrated good digital citizenship and provide them with training on mentoring techniques, communication skills, and ethical online behavior. Peer mentors can then work with younger students through regular meetings, workshops, and discussions to address specific topics related to digital citizenship. These sessions can be designed to be interactive and engaging, encouraging students to reflect on their online behaviors, share experiences, and brainstorm solutions to ethical challenges.

By harnessing the power of peer influence, schools can create a culture of ethical online behavior and empower students to be responsible digital citizens who positively contribute to the online community.

Summary

In conclusion, digital citizenship and ethical online behavior are crucial components of education in the digital age. By teaching students about responsible and ethical online behavior, we empower them to navigate the online world safely, respectfully, and responsibly. Strategies such as education and awareness, critical evaluation of online content, online safety practices, and peer mentoring programs can help instill these values in students and promote positive digital interactions. By fostering a culture of ethical online behavior, we can shape a future where individuals engage in the digital world with integrity, empathy, and respect.

Copyright and intellectual property in the digital age

In the digital age, where information can be easily accessed, copied, and shared, issues related to copyright and intellectual property have become increasingly complex. Copyright laws are designed to protect the rights of creators and owners of original works, such as text, images, music, and videos. In this section, we will explore the challenges and considerations surrounding copyright and intellectual property in the context of education.

Understanding Copyright and Intellectual Property

Copyright is a legal concept that grants exclusive rights to the creators of original works. These rights include the right to reproduce, distribute, publicly display, and create derivative works from the original work. Copyright protection is automatic and exists as soon as a work is created; no registration is required.

Intellectual property refers to intangible creations of the mind, such as inventions, designs, and symbols, which are protected by patents, trademarks, and copyrights. Intellectual property laws aim to encourage innovation and creativity by providing legal protection and economic incentives to creators and inventors.

Fair Use and Educational Exceptions

Fair use is a legal doctrine that allows limited use of copyrighted material without permission from the rights holder, under certain circumstances. In education, fair use provides flexibility for teachers and students to use copyrighted material for educational purposes, such as criticism, commentary, research, teaching, and scholarship. However, fair use is subject to interpretation and depends on the specific facts of each case.

In addition to fair use, many countries have educational exceptions in their copyright laws. These exceptions allow educators to use copyrighted materials in the classroom without needing permission from the rights holder. Educational exceptions typically have limitations, such as the amount of material that can be used and the purpose of the use.

Digital Rights Management

Digital rights management (DRM) refers to technologies and strategies used by copyright holders to control access to and usage of digital content. DRM systems often employ encryption and access controls to prevent unauthorized copying and distribution of copyrighted works. While DRM can protect the rights of content creators, it can also limit users' rights, such as fair use and the ability to access content across different devices and platforms.

Open Educational Resources

Open educational resources (OER) are freely available educational materials that can be used, shared, and modified by teachers, students, and institutions. OER are typically released under licenses that allow users to retain, reuse, revise, remix, and redistribute the materials. This openness promotes collaboration, innovation, and affordability in education. OER can include textbooks, videos, lesson plans, and interactive multimedia resources.

The use of OER in education encourages a shift from traditional copyright protection to more flexible licensing models, such as Creative Commons licenses. These licenses allow creators to retain copyright while granting permissions to others to use, modify, and share the work, with certain conditions.

Digital Citizenship and Responsible Use

In the digital age, it is essential for educators and students to cultivate digital citizenship skills, including understanding and respecting intellectual property rights. Teaching about copyright, fair use, and responsible use of digital resources helps students become informed and ethical users of information.

Educators should teach students how to properly attribute and cite sources, avoiding plagiarism and copyright infringement. Students should also learn to critically evaluate the credibility and reliability of digital content.

Balancing Copyright and Innovation

In the digital age, it is important to strike a balance between protecting copyright and promoting innovation. Copyright laws should evolve to address the challenges posed by emerging technologies while still fostering creativity and educational advancement.

Educational institutions and policymakers play a crucial role in promoting copyright education, advocating for balanced copyright laws, and supporting open access initiatives. Collaboration between content creators, rights holders, educators, and students is essential to finding solutions that benefit both creators and users of educational resources.

Case Study: Open Educational Resources

To illustrate the importance of copyright and intellectual property in the digital age, let's consider the case of open educational resources (OER). OER have gained popularity in recent years due to their potential to address issues of access, affordability, and customization in education.

For example, a high school physics teacher, Mr. Johnson, wants to supplement his existing curriculum with interactive simulations and videos. He discovers a website that offers a repository of OER specifically designed for physics education. The resources on the website are freely available for educators and can be modified to suit specific classroom needs.

Mr. Johnson carefully reviews the licensing information for each resource and ensures that he provides proper attribution when using them in his lessons. He also encourages his students to explore the OER website and contribute their own creations to the resource pool. By embracing OER, Mr. Johnson promotes collaboration, innovation, and responsible use of digital resources in his classroom.

Resources and Further Reading

1. Copyright Basics for Teachers and Students: `https://www.copyright.gov/circs/circ21.pdf` 2. Creative Commons: `https://creativecommons.org/` 3. Open Education Consortium:

https://www.oeconsortium.org/ 4. Teaching Copyright: http://www.teachingcopyright.org/ 5. Digital Citizenship Education: http://www.digitalcitizenship.net/ 6. UNESCO Open Educational Resources: https://en.unesco.org/themes/ict-education/oer

In conclusion, understanding copyright and intellectual property is crucial in the digital age. Educators and students must be familiar with fair use, educational exceptions, DRM, and the responsible use of digital resources. Open educational resources provide an alternative approach that promotes collaboration, innovation, and affordable access to educational materials. By striking a balance between copyright protection and educational needs, we can create a transformative learning environment that benefits all stakeholders.

Consent and parental involvement in educational technology use

In the rapidly evolving landscape of educational technology, it is important to consider the role of consent and parental involvement in ensuring the responsible and ethical use of technology in education. As technology becomes more integrated into classrooms and learning environments, it is crucial to establish clear guidelines and procedures to protect the privacy and best interests of students.

Importance of consent and parental involvement

Consent and parental involvement serve as important safeguards to ensure that students' personal information and data are used in an appropriate and secure manner. Parents have the right to be informed about how their child's data is being collected, stored, and used by educational technology platforms. This transparency fosters trust between schools and families, and empowers parents to make informed decisions about their child's participation in technology-based educational activities.

Additionally, consent and parental involvement help to address concerns related to data privacy and security. Parents play a crucial role in ensuring that students' personal information, including their academic records, remains protected and is not vulnerable to misuse or unauthorized access.

Laws and regulations

Various laws and regulations have been enacted to protect student privacy and regulate the collection and use of student data in educational technology. One such law is the Family Educational Rights and Privacy Act (FERPA) in the United States. FERPA grants parents certain rights with respect to their child's education records, including the right to provide or withhold consent for the disclosure of personally identifiable information. It is important for schools and educational institutions to comply with FERPA and other applicable data protection laws to ensure that student privacy is upheld.

Furthermore, the General Data Protection Regulation (GDPR) in the European Union provides comprehensive data protection standards, including the right to obtain parental consent for the processing of personal data of children under the age of 16 years.

Educational institutions and technology providers should be familiar with the relevant laws and regulations in their jurisdiction and develop policies and procedures that align with these legal requirements.

Ensuring informed consent

In order to ensure informed consent, it is important to provide parents with clear and concise information about the educational technology being used, the type of data that will be collected, and how it will be used. This information should be communicated in a language and format that is easily understood by parents who may have varying levels of technological literacy.

Schools and educational institutions should establish a process for obtaining parental consent, which may include signed consent forms, online consent portals, or other mechanisms. It is important to maintain a record of all consent obtained, as well as any changes in consent preferences over time.

Additionally, schools should provide parents with the opportunity to review and update their consent preferences periodically, ensuring that they have ongoing control over their child's data. This can be achieved through regular communication channels, such as newsletters, parent-teacher meetings, or dedicated online platforms.

Parental involvement in technology use

Parental involvement goes beyond providing consent; it also encompasses active participation in the educational technology journey of their child. Parents should be encouraged to engage with their child's learning experiences and to discuss and monitor their use of technology.

Schools can offer parent workshops or training sessions to familiarize parents with the educational technology platforms being used and to provide guidance on how to support their child's learning in a digital environment. This can help parents feel more confident in their ability to navigate and understand the tools and resources available to their child.

Furthermore, ongoing communication between teachers and parents can enhance parental involvement in technology use. Teachers can update parents on the educational technology activities and assignments their child is engaged in, as well as provide resources and suggestions for how parents can support their child's learning at home.

Challenges and considerations

Implementing consent and parental involvement in educational technology use comes with its own set of challenges. Some parents may have concerns about their own technological literacy and ability to navigate digital platforms. Schools should provide support and resources to address these concerns and ensure that all parents have the necessary tools to actively participate in their child's technology-enabled learning.

Cultural and language barriers can also impact the extent of parental involvement. Schools should take steps to bridge these gaps by providing multilingual resources, translation services, or offering alternative communication channels to parents who may face language barriers.

Another consideration is the negotiation of consent and parental involvement in cases where the child's parents are separated or have different opinions about technology use. Schools should develop clear policies to guide decision-making in these situations, ensuring that the best interests of the child are prioritized.

Examples and best practices

Several schools and educational institutions have implemented effective strategies to ensure consent and parental involvement in educational technology use.

One example is the establishment of a parent advisory committee or panel. This committee consists of representatives from the parent community who meet regularly with school administrators to discuss and provide input on technology-related decisions and policy development.

Another best practice is the integration of technology workshops for parents into back-to-school events or parent-teacher conferences. These workshops can cover topics such as digital safety, privacy settings, and guidelines for responsible technology use at home.

Some schools have also implemented a digital citizenship curriculum that educates students and parents about their rights and responsibilities in using technology. This curriculum can include lessons on online etiquette, digital footprints, and data privacy.

Resources

There are various resources available to support schools and educational institutions in implementing consent and parental involvement in educational technology use. These include:

- **Family Educational Rights and Privacy Act (FERPA):** Information and guidance on FERPA compliance provided by the U.S. Department of Education.
- **General Data Protection Regulation (GDPR):** Resources and guidelines on GDPR compliance in the education sector provided by the European Data Protection Board.
- **Common Sense Education:** Provides resources and guides for parents and educators on digital citizenship and responsible technology use.
- **National PTA:** Offers resources and support for parents and educators on topics related to technology use in education.

Conclusion

Consent and parental involvement are essential components of responsible and ethical educational technology use. By establishing clear guidelines and procedures, schools can ensure that student privacy is protected, and that parents are actively engaged in their child's digital learning journey. By fostering a collaborative relationship between schools and families, we can create a supportive and secure educational environment that harnesses the power of technology to enhance learning experiences.

Evaluating and selecting ethical edtech tools

As technology continues to transform education, it is crucial for educators and schools to carefully evaluate and select ethical educational technology (edtech) tools. This ensures that the tools used align with ethical standards and promote positive learning experiences for all students. In this section, we will explore key considerations for evaluating and selecting ethical edtech tools, providing educators with the necessary guidance to make informed choices.

Importance of ethical considerations in edtech

As technology becomes deeply integrated into education, it is essential to consider the ethical implications of edtech tools. Ethical considerations help ensure student privacy, data security, and the responsible use of technology. By prioritizing ethical practices, educators foster trust with students, parents, and the wider community.

Data privacy and security

Data privacy and security are critically important when selecting edtech tools. Educators must evaluate how a tool collects, stores, and uses student data. It is crucial to choose tools that adhere to legal requirements and industry standards for data protection. Educators should consider the following questions when evaluating edtech tools:

- What types of student data does the tool collect?
- How is the data stored and protected?
- Are there secure data transfer protocols in place?
- Does the tool have appropriate data access controls?
- Does the tool comply with relevant privacy laws and regulations?

It is advisable to review the privacy policies and terms of service of edtech tools to understand their data handling practices fully.

Responsible use of artificial intelligence

Artificial intelligence (AI) offers tremendous potential for education, but it also raises ethical concerns. Educators should carefully evaluate how AI is used in edtech tools and ensure that it aligns with ethical principles. Some considerations include:

- Transparency: Does the tool provide clear explanations of how AI algorithms work and influence the learning process?
- Bias and fairness: Has the tool been tested for biases that could perpetuate discrimination or disadvantage certain student groups?
- Profiling and personalization: Does the tool responsibly collect and use student data for personalized learning purposes?

- Informed consent: Does the tool obtain appropriate consent from students and their parents/guardians for data collection and AI-driven features?

Educators should also be mindful of the limitations of AI and ensure its use complements their pedagogical approach rather than replacing human interaction and support.

Promoting digital citizenship and online safety

Edtech tools should actively promote digital citizenship and online safety. Educators should consider how a tool supports responsible online behavior and data literacy. Some key considerations include:

- Digital citizenship education: Does the tool incorporate digital citizenship lessons or features that promote ethical online behavior?
- Safeguarding student well-being: Does the tool have measures in place to protect students from cyberbullying, inappropriate content, or online threats?
- User support and reporting mechanisms: Does the tool provide appropriate channels for users to report concerns or seek support for online safety issues?

By selecting edtech tools that prioritize digital citizenship and online safety, educators can help students develop the necessary skills to navigate the digital world responsibly.

Evaluation criteria and resources

To evaluate and select ethical edtech tools effectively, educators can utilize various criteria and resources. Here are some key considerations:

- Reviews and recommendations: Seek feedback from other educators or trusted sources to learn from their experiences with particular edtech tools.
- Third-party certifications: Look for edtech tools that have obtained relevant certifications for data privacy, security, and ethical practices.
- Alignment with educational goals: Ensure that the tool aligns with educational goals and pedagogical approaches.

- Vendor transparency and accountability: Research the reputation and track record of the tool's vendor to assess their commitment to ethical practices.

Educators can also refer to established frameworks and guidelines for evaluating edtech tools, such as the ISTE Standards for Educators, Common Sense Education's Privacy Evaluation Initiative, or the Future of Privacy Forum's Student Privacy Compass.

Engaging students in the selection process

Engaging students in the selection of edtech tools can help promote a sense of ownership and responsibility. By involving students, educators gain insights into their preferences, needs, and concerns. This collaborative approach ensures that the selected tools are not only ethical but also relevant and engaging for students.

Educators can conduct surveys or focus groups, allowing students to test and provide feedback on potential edtech tools. This process empowers students to actively participate in shaping their own learning experiences while gaining valuable digital citizenship skills.

Conclusion

Evaluating and selecting ethical edtech tools is essential to ensure that technology enhances, rather than detracts from, educational experiences. By considering data privacy, responsible AI use, digital citizenship, and other ethical aspects, educators can make informed decisions that prioritize student well-being and promote equitable and inclusive learning environments.

Ethical Considerations in Online Assessment and Surveillance

In recent years, the education landscape has seen a rapid shift towards online assessment and surveillance in order to meet the demands of remote learning and digital classrooms. While these technologies offer numerous benefits, they also raise important ethical considerations that educators and policymakers must address. In this section, we will explore these ethical considerations and provide guidance on how to navigate them in the context of online assessment and surveillance.

Privacy and Data Protection

One of the primary ethical considerations in online assessment and surveillance is privacy and data protection. When students engage in online assessments, they often provide personal information and data that can be potentially sensitive. It is crucial for educators and educational institutions to ensure that student data is protected and used for legitimate educational purposes only.

To address privacy concerns, it is essential to clearly communicate to students and their parents or guardians how their data will be collected, stored, and used. Consent forms should be provided, explaining the purpose of data collection and the measures in place to protect it. Additionally, educational institutions should comply with relevant data protection laws and regulations, such as the General Data Protection Regulation (GDPR) in the European Union, and establish robust security measures to safeguard student data.

Fairness and Equity

Fairness and equity are also important ethical considerations in online assessment and surveillance. The use of technology can introduce biases and create unequal opportunities for students. For example, students from disadvantaged backgrounds may have limited access to technology or reliable internet connections, putting them at a disadvantage in online assessments.

Educators and policymakers must strive to ensure that online assessment methods do not disproportionately advantage certain groups of students. This can be achieved by providing alternative assessment options for students who may face technological barriers, such as offering paper-based assessments or allowing students to submit assignments in different formats. It is essential to promote equal access to online assessments and support students who may require additional resources to participate fully.

Transparency and Informed Consent

Transparent communication and informed consent are key ethical principles in online assessment and surveillance. Students and their parents or guardians should be well-informed about the specific assessment methods being used, including any surveillance technologies employed, and the implications for their privacy.

Educators should explain the purpose of online assessment and surveillance, the types of data collected, and how it will be used to evaluate student performance. Informed consent should be obtained from students and their parents or guardians, ensuring that they understand and agree to participate in the assessment process.

Open dialogue and transparency create trust between stakeholders and mitigate concerns related to privacy and surveillance. Educators should also provide opportunities for students and their families to express their concerns and seek clarification on any aspects of online assessment and surveillance.

Avoiding Malpractice and Cheating

Another ethical consideration in online assessment is the prevention of malpractice and cheating. The use of technology has introduced new challenges in maintaining academic integrity. Students may be tempted to use online resources or collaborate with others during assessments, compromising the validity and reliability of results.

Educators should implement measures to prevent cheating, such as using proctoring tools, time limits, and randomizing question order. However, it is crucial to strike a balance between preventing malpractice and respecting students' privacy. Continuous monitoring and excessive surveillance can create an environment of mistrust and invasiveness.

To navigate this ethical consideration, educators can focus on fostering a culture of academic honesty and integrity. By educating students about the importance of ethical behavior and providing clear guidelines on acceptable practices during assessments, educators can promote a sense of responsibility and discourage cheating.

Mitigating Psychological and Emotional Harm

Online assessment and surveillance can also have psychological and emotional impacts on students. Continuous monitoring, the fear of being watched or judged, and the pressure to perform well in a remote environment can lead to increased stress and anxiety among students.

Educators should consider the potential psychological and emotional harm associated with online assessment and surveillance and take measures to mitigate these effects. This can include providing mental health resources, promoting self-care strategies, and fostering a supportive learning environment where students feel comfortable expressing their concerns.

Moreover, educators should be mindful of the language, tone, and feedback provided during online assessments to ensure that they do not contribute to emotional distress or create unnecessary competition among students.

Ethical Use of Surveillance Technologies

The use of surveillance technologies, such as webcams and remote monitoring tools, raises ethical considerations in online assessment. While these technologies can enhance the integrity of assessments, they also raise concerns about privacy invasion and potential misuse.

Educational institutions should establish clear guidelines on the ethical use of surveillance technologies, ensuring that they are used for legitimate educational purposes only. Surveillance should be targeted, minimized, and closely aligned with the specific assessment requirements. It is essential to strike a balance between maintaining academic integrity and respecting students' privacy.

Educators should also provide students with information about the specific surveillance technologies being used and the measures in place to protect their privacy. Students should have the opportunity to voice any concerns and be assured that their privacy rights are being respected.

Promoting Alternatives to Online Assessment and Surveillance

As ethical considerations surrounding online assessment and surveillance continue to evolve, educators should explore alternatives that minimize privacy and equity concerns. This may involve implementing alternative assessment methods that rely less on technology, such as project-based assessments, portfolios, or open-ended assignments.

By diversifying assessment methods, educators can accommodate different learning styles and provide opportunities for students to demonstrate their knowledge and skills in ways that are more inclusive and equitable.

Conclusion

Ethical considerations play a crucial role in the implementation of online assessment and surveillance in education. Privacy protection, fairness and equity, transparency, prevention of malpractice, psychological well-being, and ethical use of surveillance technologies should be at the forefront of decision-making processes.

By acknowledging these ethical considerations and taking proactive measures to address them, educators and policymakers can create an inclusive and responsible online assessment environment that not only promotes academic success but also respects the rights and well-being of students.

Cultivating digital ethics and digital citizenship in students

In today's digital age, it is essential for students to understand the importance of digital ethics and digital citizenship. With the rapid advancements in technology, students need to develop the skills and knowledge to navigate the digital world responsibly and ethically. This section will explore the concept of digital ethics and provide strategies for cultivating digital citizenship in students.

Understanding digital ethics

Digital ethics refers to the responsible and ethical use of technology. It involves understanding the impact of one's actions in the digital realm and making informed decisions that align with ethical values and principles. Digital ethics encompasses a range of issues, including privacy, intellectual property, online behavior, cyberbullying, and digital footprint.

To cultivate digital ethics in students, it is important to promote critical thinking and ethical decision-making. Students should be encouraged to consider the consequences of their digital actions, be aware of their rights and responsibilities, and respect the rights and privacy of others.

Promoting responsible online behavior

To foster digital citizenship, educators can implement strategies to promote responsible online behavior. This includes teaching students about online etiquette, guiding them to develop empathy and respect for others in digital environments, and encouraging them to think critically about the information they encounter online.

One effective way to promote responsible online behavior is by teaching students about the concept of a digital footprint. They should understand that the information they share online can be permanent and may impact their future lives and careers. Students can be encouraged to regularly review and manage their digital footprints, ensuring that they present themselves in a positive and professional manner.

Teaching digital privacy and security

Digital ethics also involves understanding the importance of digital privacy and security. Students should be taught about the risks of sharing personal information online and the potential consequences of falling victim to online scams, identity theft, or cyberbullying.

Educators can provide guidance on how to protect personal information by using strong passwords, enabling two-factor authentication, and being cautious about sharing sensitive data. Students should be encouraged to think critically about the information they share, the platforms they use, and the privacy settings they implement.

Developing media literacy skills

In today's digital landscape, media literacy skills are crucial for students to navigate the vast amount of information available online. Educators can teach students how to critically evaluate online sources, discern credible information from misinformation or fake news, and develop a healthy skepticism towards online content.

Students should be encouraged to fact-check information, verify the credibility of sources, and critically analyze biased or skewed narratives. By developing media literacy skills, students can become informed digital citizens who are able to discern truth from falsehoods and make informed decisions.

Addressing cyberbullying and digital harassment

One of the challenges of the digital age is the prevalence of cyberbullying and digital harassment. Educators need to create a safe and inclusive online environment where students feel empowered to report and address instances of cyberbullying.

Educators can teach students how to recognize cyberbullying behaviors, both as victims and bystanders, and encourage them to report such incidents to a trusted adult or authority figure. Schools should have clear policies in place to address cyberbullying and provide support for students affected by it.

Engaging with ethical dilemmas in technology

To foster critical thinking and ethical decision-making skills, educators can provide opportunities for students to engage with ethical dilemmas related to technology. This can include discussing real-world issues such as privacy breaches, intellectual property infringement, or the ethical implications of emerging technologies like artificial intelligence or facial recognition.

By analyzing and discussing ethical dilemmas, students can develop a deeper understanding of the complex ethical considerations surrounding technology and its impact on society. This can empower them to make well-informed decisions and advocate for digital ethics in the future.

Collaborative projects and digital citizenship

Engaging students in collaborative projects that involve digital tools and platforms can provide opportunities for them to practice digital citizenship. By working together in online spaces, students learn to communicate respectfully, collaborate effectively, and value diverse perspectives.

Educators can structure collaborative projects in a way that encourages students to actively participate and take responsibility for their online interactions. This can help them develop a sense of ownership and accountability for their digital behavior.

Creating a culture of digital citizenship

To effectively cultivate digital ethics and digital citizenship, it is important to create a culture that values and promotes responsible and ethical technology use. This can be achieved through clear policies and guidelines that outline expected behaviors, consequences for inappropriate actions, and mechanisms for reporting concerns or incidents.

Educators should also model digital citizenship by demonstrating responsible and ethical online behavior themselves. By being positive role models, educators can inspire students to emulate the values of digital ethics and citizenship.

Conclusion

Cultivating digital ethics and digital citizenship in students is of paramount importance in a technology-driven world. By promoting responsible online behavior, teaching digital privacy and security, developing media literacy skills, addressing cyberbullying, engaging with ethical dilemmas, and creating a culture of digital citizenship, educators can empower students to navigate the digital landscape with integrity, empathy, and critical thinking skills. By instilling these values, educators contribute to creating a more ethical and responsible society online and offline.

Promoting Equity and Inclusion in Education

The Digital Divide and Access to Technology

In today's digital age, access to technology plays a crucial role in education. However, not all students have equal access to the necessary tools and resources, leading to a significant disparity known as the digital divide. This section explores the digital divide, its impact on education, and strategies to bridge this divide and ensure equitable access to technology.

Understanding the Digital Divide

The digital divide refers to the gap between individuals and communities who have access to digital technologies and those who do not. It encompasses both the physical access to technology and the skills and knowledge needed to utilize it effectively. The digital divide is often influenced by socioeconomic factors, geographical location, race, and other demographic variables.

Impact on Education

The digital divide has far-reaching implications for education. Without access to technology, students may struggle to keep up with the evolving educational landscape, which increasingly relies on digital tools and resources. This divide can hinder students' ability to acquire necessary digital literacy skills, conduct research, collaborate with peers, and access online educational content. It also exacerbates existing inequalities in education, further disadvantaging students from marginalized communities.

Strategies to Bridge the Digital Divide

Bridging the digital divide requires a multi-faceted approach that addresses both access to technology and digital literacy. Here are some strategies to promote equitable access to technology in education:

1. **Infrastructure Development:** Governments, in partnership with educational institutions and private organizations, should invest in infrastructure development to extend broadband internet connectivity to underserved areas. This includes improving network coverage, reducing costs, and ensuring reliable internet access in schools and communities.

2. **Technology Subsidies:** Providing affordable access to technology devices and internet connectivity can help bridge the digital divide. Governments can allocate funds to subsidize the cost of computers, laptops, tablets, and internet services for students from low-income backgrounds.

3. **Community Programs:** Establishing community programs that provide technology access and training can help individuals develop digital skills. Public libraries, community centers, and schools can offer free access to computers and internet connectivity, as well as training programs to enhance digital literacy.

4. **Collaborative Partnerships:** Collaboration between various stakeholders, including governments, educational institutions, technology companies, and non-profit organizations, is essential to address the digital divide comprehensively.

By pooling resources and expertise, these partnerships can develop effective strategies, share best practices, and implement initiatives to bridge the divide.

5. **Digital Literacy Education:** Alongside providing access to technology, efforts should be focused on equipping students with the necessary digital literacy skills to leverage technology effectively. Integrating digital literacy training into curricula and offering professional development opportunities for educators can help ensure that students receive the guidance and support they need.

Digital Inclusion: A Necessity for Education

Access to technology is no longer a luxury; it is a necessity for education in the digital age. Bridging the digital divide is crucial to ensure that all students have equal opportunities to learn and succeed. By implementing effective strategies, policymakers, educators, and communities can work towards digital inclusion and empower all learners, regardless of their socioeconomic background or geographical location.

Real-World Example: One Laptop Per Child (OLPC)

One notable initiative that aimed to bridge the digital divide and provide equal access to technology is the One Laptop Per Child (OLPC) program. OLPC aimed to distribute low-cost laptops to students in underserved communities worldwide. By providing these laptops and implementing educational software, OLPC aimed to enhance students' learning experiences and equip them with digital skills. While the program faced various challenges and criticisms, it represented a significant effort towards mitigating the digital divide and fostering educational opportunities for all.

Overcoming barriers to digital inclusion

In today's digital age, access to technology has become a fundamental requirement for participation in various aspects of life, including education. However, there are still many barriers that prevent certain individuals and communities from fully enjoying the benefits of digital inclusion. These barriers can include factors such as economic limitations, lack of infrastructure, inadequate digital skills, and sociocultural biases. In this section, we will explore some strategies and initiatives that can help overcome these barriers and promote digital inclusion for all.

Improving affordability and accessibility

One of the primary barriers to digital inclusion is the affordability of technology and internet access. For individuals and communities with limited financial resources, the cost of devices and internet plans may be out of reach. To address this challenge, governments, organizations, and service providers can implement various initiatives:

- **Subsidized devices and internet plans:** Governments can provide subsidies or discounts on devices such as laptops, tablets, and smartphones, as well as internet plans, to low-income individuals and families. This approach can make technology more affordable and accessible.

- **Public access centers:** Establishing community centers or public spaces equipped with computers and internet access can provide individuals who don't have their own devices or access at home a place to use technology for educational and personal purposes.

- **Internet connectivity solutions:** In areas with limited internet infrastructure, innovative solutions such as community networks, mesh networks, or satellite internet can help provide affordable connectivity to underserved communities.

By addressing the affordability and accessibility of technology and internet access, we can greatly reduce the digital divide and promote digital inclusion.

Providing digital skills training

Another significant barrier to digital inclusion is the lack of digital skills and literacy. Many individuals, particularly those from disadvantaged backgrounds, may not have the necessary knowledge and skills to effectively use digital tools and navigate online platforms. To address this barrier, it is essential to provide comprehensive digital skills training:

- **Digital literacy programs:** Educational institutions, community organizations, and governments can collaborate to develop and implement digital literacy programs. These programs can teach basic computer skills, internet usage, online safety, and critical thinking skills to individuals of all ages.

- **Professional development for educators:** Teachers need to acquire the necessary digital skills and pedagogical strategies to effectively integrate technology into their classrooms. Professional development programs can provide them with the training and resources they need to empower their students with digital skills.

- **Public awareness campaigns:** Informing the public about the importance of digital skills and the available resources for gaining these skills can encourage individuals to seek out training opportunities. Awareness campaigns can be conducted through various media channels to reach a wider audience.

By ensuring that everyone has access to digital skills training, we can bridge the digital divide and empower individuals to thrive in the digital era.

Tackling sociocultural biases and stereotypes

In addition to economic and skills barriers, sociocultural biases and stereotypes can also hinder digital inclusion. Certain groups, such as women, people with disabilities, and minority communities, may face discrimination and exclusion in accessing and using digital technologies. To promote digital inclusion for all, it is important to address these biases:

- **Promoting diversity in technology fields:** Encouraging diversity in the technology industry can help break down stereotypes and biases. Initiatives such as scholarships, mentorship programs, and networking opportunities can support underrepresented groups and increase their participation in technology-related fields.

- **Inclusive design practices:** Designing digital products and platforms with a focus on accessibility and usability for individuals with diverse abilities and needs is crucial. By considering the needs of all users during the design process, we can create inclusive technologies that benefit everyone.

- **Awareness and advocacy:** Engaging in public discussions, raising awareness about the importance of digital inclusion, and advocating for policies that address biases and inequalities can have a significant impact. Collaboration between governments, organizations, and communities is essential to drive societal change and promote a more inclusive digital environment.

By actively addressing sociocultural biases and stereotypes, we can foster a more inclusive digital culture that benefits individuals from all backgrounds.

Addressing digital literacy for marginalized communities

Digital inclusion efforts must include a focus on marginalized communities, including those in rural areas, indigenous populations, refugees, and other vulnerable groups. These communities often face additional barriers to digital inclusion, such as language barriers, lack of relevant content, and cultural disconnect. To address these challenges, the following strategies can be considered:

- **Localization and cultural sensitivity:** Ensuring that digital content and tools are available in local languages and are culturally sensitive can make technology more relevant and accessible to marginalized communities.
- **Community engagement and empowerment:** Working closely with community leaders, organizations, and representatives to understand the unique needs and challenges of marginalized communities is essential. Empowering these communities to take an active role in shaping digital inclusion initiatives can lead to more sustainable and impactful outcomes.
- **Partnerships and collaborations:** Building partnerships between governments, NGOs, educational institutions, and private sector organizations can leverage resources and expertise to address the specific digital inclusion challenges faced by marginalized communities.

By adopting a holistic approach to digital inclusion that addresses the needs of marginalized communities, we can create a more equitable and inclusive digital society.

Conclusion

Digital inclusion is crucial for ensuring equal opportunities and equitable access to education and other essential services. By addressing barriers such as affordability, accessibility, digital skills, sociocultural biases, and the unique challenges faced by marginalized communities, we can promote digital inclusion for all. It requires collaborative efforts from governments, organizations, educational institutions, and individuals to bridge the digital divide and create a more inclusive digital future. Let us strive to build a society where everyone can participate and thrive in the digital age.

Universal design for learning and accessibility

In today's diverse classrooms, it is essential to embrace universal design for learning (UDL) and ensure accessibility for all students. UDL is a framework that aims to make learning accessible and effective for students with diverse learning styles, abilities, and needs. It recognizes that each student is unique and requires different approaches to the learning process.

Principles of Universal Design for Learning

UDL consists of three core principles:

1. **Multiple means of representation:** Providing information and content in various formats to cater to different learning styles. This can include presenting information through text, images, videos, or audio recordings. For example, a teacher can provide captions for videos, transcripts for audio recordings, or visuals for text-based information.

2. **Multiple means of action and expression:** Allowing flexibility in how students demonstrate their knowledge and skills. This can be achieved by providing options for students to express themselves through writing, speaking, creating multimedia presentations, or engaging in hands-on activities. For instance, a student with physical disabilities may use assistive technologies to write or present their work.

3. **Multiple means of engagement:** Providing various ways to motivate and engage students. This can involve offering choices in topics, tasks, or assignments, incorporating interactive activities, or relating the content to real-world contexts. For example, a teacher can use gamified elements or multimedia resources to capture students' interest and facilitate active participation.

By incorporating these principles, teachers can individualize the learning experience, address diverse needs, and promote inclusivity in the classroom.

Applying Universal Design for Learning

To apply UDL effectively, teachers can consider the following strategies and practices:

1. **Flexible materials and resources:** Use a variety of instructional materials and resources to accommodate different learning preferences. For example, provide digital and print materials, offer alternatives to textbooks, and use online platforms that support diverse formats.

2. **Accessible technologies:** Utilize assistive technologies and learning tools that enhance accessibility and support different learning needs. This can include screen readers, text-to-speech software, speech recognition tools, and adaptive devices.

3. **Differentiated instruction:** Plan and deliver instruction that meets the individual needs of students. Differentiate content, process, and product by providing alternatives, scaffolding, and personalized support to cater to students' abilities and learning styles.

4. **Collaborative learning opportunities:** Encourage collaboration among students, recognizing that they can learn from and support each other. Group work, peer tutoring, and cooperative learning activities can facilitate the exchange of ideas and diverse perspectives.

5. **Regular formative assessment:** Use ongoing formative assessment strategies to monitor student progress and adjust instruction accordingly. Provide timely and specific feedback to guide students' learning and allow for reflection and improvement.

6. **Teacher-student collaboration:** Involve students in the decision-making process regarding their learning. Foster open communication, listen to their ideas and needs, and empower them to take ownership of their learning journey.

7. **Physical and environmental considerations:** Ensure that the physical classroom environment is accessible and promotes inclusivity. Arrange furniture to accommodate different abilities, provide adequate lighting and acoustics, and create spaces that facilitate collaboration and individual work.

8. **Culturally responsive teaching:** Embrace students' diverse cultural backgrounds and experiences, integrating culturally relevant examples, perspectives, and resources into the curriculum. This can foster a sense of belonging and promote engagement and understanding among students.

Challenges and Considerations

Implementing UDL and ensuring accessibility may come with some challenges, but with thoughtful planning and ongoing evaluation, these challenges can be addressed:

- **Time and resource constraints:** Integrating UDL principles and providing accessible materials may require additional planning, preparation, and resources. However, there are numerous free and low-cost technologies and resources available to support teachers in making learning accessible.
- **Professional development:** Teachers may need training and support to effectively implement UDL strategies and utilize assistive technologies. Ongoing professional development opportunities can provide the necessary knowledge and skills to create inclusive learning environments.
- **Individualization vs. standardization:** Balancing the need for individualization with standardized assessments and curriculum requirements poses a challenge. However, UDL encourages adapting assessments and instructional practices to allow students to demonstrate their knowledge and skills in ways that align with their strengths and abilities.
- **Collaboration and communication:** Ensuring effective collaboration and communication among students, teachers, and parents is crucial for implementing UDL successfully. Open lines of communication and partnerships with families can help address individual student needs and foster a supportive learning environment.
- **Digital accessibility:** Providing digital accessibility is essential in today's technology-rich learning environments. Teachers should be aware of accessibility features in educational platforms and applications and select tools that meet accessibility standards. Additionally, they should verify that online materials, documents, and resources are accessible for all students.

Examples and Resources

To further enhance understanding and implementation of UDL, here are a few examples and resources:

- **UDL guidelines and checkpoints:** The UDL guidelines, developed by the Center for Applied Special Technology (CAST), provide a comprehensive framework for implementing UDL in the classroom. These guidelines offer specific strategies and examples to support each principle.

- **Accessible educational technologies and tools:** Many educational technologies offer built-in accessibility features or compatibility with assistive technologies. For example, Adobe Acrobat Reader provides options for screen readers, and Microsoft Office Suite offers accessibility features like closed captioning and alternative text for images.
- **Alternative formats for text:** Explore alternative formats for textbooks and reading materials to support students' diverse needs. For instance, provide audiobooks, electronic text, or large print versions of texts to accommodate students with visual impairments or reading difficulties.
- **Digital accessibility standards:** Familiarize yourself with digital accessibility standards, such as the Web Content Accessibility Guidelines (WCAG), to ensure that online materials and resources are accessible to all students.

Conclusion

Universal design for learning and accessibility play a crucial role in promoting equitable education and meeting the diverse needs of students. By implementing UDL principles and leveraging appropriate technologies and resources, teachers can create inclusive learning environments where all students can thrive and achieve academic success. Through continuous professional development and a commitment to students' well-being and success, educators can embrace UDL as a central component of effective and transformative education.

Inclusive technology tools and resources

Inclusive education recognizes the diverse learning needs of students and ensures that all learners have equal opportunities to succeed. Technology plays a crucial role in promoting inclusivity in education by providing tools and resources that cater to individual learning preferences and abilities. In this section, we will explore inclusive technology tools and resources that support diverse learners in the classroom.

Universal Design for Learning (UDL)

Universal Design for Learning (UDL) is an educational framework that emphasizes the creation of accessible learning materials and environments from the outset. UDL promotes the use of flexible learning materials that can be customized to meet the needs of different learners. Digital technologies, such as adaptive learning platforms and multimedia resources, can be leveraged to implement UDL principles in the classroom.

Text-to-Speech (TTS) Software

For students with visual impairments or reading difficulties, text-to-speech (TTS) software can be an invaluable tool. TTS software converts written text into spoken words, allowing students to listen to the content instead of reading it. This technology not only supports students with visual impairments but also benefits students with learning disabilities or language barriers.

Speech-to-Text (STT) Software

Speech-to-text (STT) software enables students who have difficulty writing or typing to convert their spoken words into written text. STT software can be particularly beneficial for students with physical disabilities or those who struggle with fine motor skills. By dictating their ideas, students can participate in writing activities without the constraints of traditional pen and paper.

Closed Captioning and Transcription Services

Inclusive education also involves providing equal access to audio and video content for students with hearing impairments. Closed captioning and transcription services make audiovisual materials accessible by providing text captions or transcripts synchronized with the content. This ensures that students with hearing impairments can fully engage with educational videos and lectures.

Digital Assistants and Voice Recognition

Digital assistant devices, such as voice-activated speakers, can enhance inclusivity in the classroom. These devices allow students to interact with technology using voice commands, eliminating the need for physical interaction. Voice recognition technology can also facilitate hands-free operation of computers, enabling students with physical disabilities to navigate digital resources effortlessly.

Screen Readers

Screen readers are software programs that provide auditory feedback by reading aloud content displayed on a computer screen. These tools are particularly useful for students with visual impairments who rely on auditory cues to comprehend information. Screen readers allow visually impaired students to access digital resources, navigate websites, and engage with educational content independently.

Alternative Input Devices

Inclusive technology tools extend beyond traditional keyboards and mice to include alternative input devices. For example, switch access devices can be used by students with limited mobility to control computers or tablets. Joysticks, touchpads, and eye-tracking devices are other alternative input options that provide students with physical disabilities or motor impairments the means to interact with digital resources.

Accessible Learning Management Systems (LMS)

Learning Management Systems (LMS) are widely used to deliver and manage educational content. Inclusive LMS platforms are designed with accessibility features, such as screen reader compatibility, keyboard navigation, and adjustable font sizes. These features ensure that students with disabilities can access course materials, engage in discussions, and submit assignments without barriers.

Collaborative Online Tools

Inclusive technology also encompasses collaborative online tools that enable students to interact and work together effectively. Tools such as virtual whiteboards, shared document editors, and discussion forums facilitate collaborative learning experiences for students with diverse learning needs. These tools encourage active participation and engagement among all learners, fostering a sense of inclusivity in the virtual classroom.

Digital Resources and Open Educational Resources (OER)

Digital resources and Open Educational Resources (OER) provide educators with a wide range of inclusive teaching materials. These resources can be accessed online and often offer a variety of formats, including text, audio, video, and interactive components. OER promotes inclusivity by allowing educators to customize content to fit the diverse needs of their students while providing easily accessible and cost-effective resources.

Inclusive technology practices in action

To illustrate the implementation of inclusive technology tools and resources, let's consider the example of a high school science class with a diverse group of students. The teacher wants to ensure every student can actively participate in the learning activities and achieve the learning objectives.

The teacher incorporates various inclusive technology tools and resources into their instruction. They provide digital textbooks with built-in TTS capabilities, allowing students with reading difficulties or visual impairments to access the content effectively. To engage students in collaborative projects, the teacher utilizes online platforms that offer features like screen sharing and real-time communication, ensuring that students with physical disabilities can actively contribute to group discussions.

For students who struggle with written expression, the teacher encourages the use of speech-to-text software during class activities and assessments. This way, these students can articulate their ideas effectively without being hindered by their writing difficulties. The teacher also incorporates closed captioning in videos and provides transcripts, making the content accessible to students with hearing impairments.

Additionally, the teacher creates a virtual classroom environment using an inclusive Learning Management System (LMS). The LMS is designed with accessibility features, such as adjustable font sizes and screen reader compatibility. This ensures that all students can navigate through the course materials and participate in discussions without any barriers.

In summary, by employing inclusive technology tools and resources, the teacher is able to create a supportive and inclusive learning environment where every student can actively participate, engage with the content, and achieve their learning goals.

Addressing Bias and Discrimination in Educational Technology

As technology continues to shape the landscape of education, it is crucial to address the issue of bias and discrimination that may arise in the use of educational technology. While technology has the potential to enhance teaching and learning experiences, it can also perpetuate existing biases and inequalities. This section focuses on strategies and considerations for addressing bias and discrimination in educational technology.

Understanding Bias and Discrimination in Educational Technology

Bias and discrimination can manifest in various ways within educational technology. This includes biased algorithms that perpetuate stereotypes, lack of representation and inclusion of diverse voices, and discriminatory practices in data collection and analysis. It is important to recognize and understand these issues to effectively address them.

Biased Algorithms: Algorithms that power educational technologies may inadvertently reinforce biases and prejudices. For example, machine learning algorithms used for automated grading may disproportionately penalize students from certain backgrounds or with particular writing styles. It is crucial to examine the algorithms and data used in educational technology systems to ensure they do not perpetuate discriminatory practices.

Lack of Representation and Inclusion: Educational technology should reflect the diversity of students and teachers. Lack of representation can lead to marginalization of certain groups and perpetuate inequality. It is essential to consider the cultural, linguistic, and gender diversity when designing and selecting technological tools, platforms, and content. This includes ensuring that diverse perspectives and experiences are represented in educational resources and materials.

Discriminatory Data Practices: Data collection and analysis in educational technology can unintentionally perpetuate discrimination. Biased data collection methods, biased interpretations of data, or inappropriate use of student data can result in unfair outcomes for marginalized groups. It is important to establish robust ethical guidelines for data collection and use, ensuring transparency and safeguarding student privacy.

Strategies for Addressing Bias and Discrimination

Addressing bias and discrimination in educational technology requires a proactive and inclusive approach. The following strategies can help mitigate bias and promote inclusivity in educational technology:

Diverse and Inclusive Design: Educational technology should be designed with diversity and inclusion in mind. This involves involving diverse perspectives in the design process, conducting user tests with diverse groups, and actively seeking feedback from underrepresented communities. Designers should aim to create technology that is accessible and inclusive for all learners, regardless of their backgrounds or abilities.

Evaluation and Auditing: Regular evaluation and auditing of educational technology systems are essential to identify and address biases. This can involve reviewing algorithmic decision-making processes, analyzing data for potential bias, and conducting user surveys to gauge the impact of technology on marginalized groups. By continuously monitoring and evaluating the technology, it becomes possible to identify and rectify any biases or discriminatory practices.

Bias Mitigation Algorithms: Machine learning algorithms can be designed to mitigate biases and ensure fair outcomes. This involves training algorithms on diverse and inclusive datasets, implementing bias-correction techniques, and regularly updating algorithms to address emerging biases. By taking a proactive approach to algorithm design, it is possible to minimize biases and promote equity in educational technology.

Training and Professional Development: Educators and administrators should receive training and professional development on recognizing and addressing bias in educational technology. This includes understanding the potential biases present in technology, learning to interpret data ethically and responsibly, and integrating principles of equity, diversity, and inclusion into technology use. By empowering educators with the knowledge and tools to address bias, they can play a role in ensuring equitable use of technology in classrooms.

Collaboration and Partnerships: Collaboration between education stakeholders, technology developers, researchers, and regulatory bodies is crucial to address bias and discrimination in educational technology. By working together, it becomes possible to develop and implement policies, guidelines, and standards that promote fairness, inclusivity, and accountability in the use of technology. Collaboration also allows for the exchange of best practices and the development of innovative solutions to address bias and discrimination.

Real-world Example: Addressing Gender Bias in Language Learning Apps

Language learning apps have gained popularity in recent years for their ability to provide personalized language instruction. However, these apps are not immune to biases. A study conducted by researchers at Stanford University found that certain language learning apps tended to use gendered examples and stereotypes in their content. This perpetuated gender biases and limited the exposure of learners to diverse language use.

To address this issue, the developers of a language learning app collaborated with experts in gender and linguistics to review their content and make it more inclusive. The app was revised to ensure balanced representation of genders and the removal of gender stereotypes. Additionally, the developers implemented an ongoing feedback system that allows users to report any instances of bias or discriminatory language. This demonstrated a commitment to addressing bias and discrimination in educational technology and resulted in a more inclusive language learning experience for all users.

Conclusion

Addressing bias and discrimination in educational technology is crucial for creating equitable and inclusive learning environments. By understanding the issues, adopting inclusive design principles, implementing bias mitigation techniques, and fostering collaboration, it becomes possible to create educational technology that promotes fairness, diversity, and inclusivity. Promoting ethical considerations and actively working towards addressing bias is essential for shaping a future of education that is accessible and beneficial for all learners.

Culturally Responsive Pedagogy and Inclusive Classrooms

In today's diverse and multicultural society, it is crucial for educators to adopt culturally responsive pedagogy in order to create inclusive classrooms that value and embrace the diversity of their students. Culturally responsive pedagogy is an approach to teaching that recognizes and respects the cultural backgrounds, experiences, and knowledge of students. It aims to create a learning environment that is culturally relevant, affirming, and empowering for all students, regardless of their cultural backgrounds.

Understanding Culturally Responsive Pedagogy

At its core, culturally responsive pedagogy is based on the belief that all students bring unique cultural perspectives and experiences to the classroom. These perspectives and experiences should be acknowledged, valued, and integrated into the teaching and learning process. Culturally responsive pedagogy goes beyond mere acknowledgement of culture; it involves actively incorporating cultural content, experiences, and perspectives into the curriculum and instructional methods.

In culturally responsive classrooms, educators strive to create a learning environment that reflects and respects the cultural diversity of their students. This includes celebrating different cultures, languages, traditions, and worldviews. The goal is to foster a sense of belonging and cultural identity among students, while also challenging stereotypes and promoting social justice.

Principles of Culturally Responsive Pedagogy

Culturally responsive pedagogy is guided by several key principles that help inform instructional practices. These principles include:

1. Building and sustaining positive relationships: Culturally responsive educators prioritize building strong relationships with their students. They strive to create a classroom community that is inclusive, supportive, and respectful of all students' cultural backgrounds and identities.

2. Incorporating cultural content and perspectives: Culturally responsive pedagogy involves integrating cultural content, materials, and perspectives into the curriculum. This includes diverse texts and resources that reflect the experiences and contributions of various cultures.

3. Adapting instructional strategies: Culturally responsive educators recognize that different students have different learning styles and preferences. They adapt their instructional strategies to accommodate these differences and provide multiple ways for students to engage with the content.

4. Using culturally relevant assessment methods: Culturally responsive educators employ assessment methods that are fair, unbiased, and culturally sensitive. They avoid assessments that privilege certain cultural backgrounds and take into account the diverse ways in which students may demonstrate their understanding.

5. Creating a safe and inclusive learning environment: Culturally responsive classrooms prioritize creating a safe and inclusive learning environment where all students feel valued, respected, and supported. This includes addressing and challenging stereotypes, biases, and discrimination.

Strategies for Implementing Culturally Responsive Pedagogy

Implementing culturally responsive pedagogy requires intentional efforts and ongoing reflection on teaching practices. Here are some strategies that educators can use to create culturally responsive and inclusive classrooms:

1. Get to know your students: Take the time to learn about your students' cultural backgrounds, experiences, and interests. Consider conducting student surveys or engaging in activities that allow students to share aspects of their culture.

2. Integrate diverse perspectives and resources: Incorporate diverse texts, resources, and materials that represent different cultures and perspectives into your lessons and curriculum. This can help students see themselves reflected in the content and foster a sense of belonging.

3. Incorporate culturally relevant teaching strategies: Use teaching strategies that are culturally relevant and responsive to the needs and experiences of your students. For example, incorporate group work, collaborative learning, and hands-on activities that allow students to draw on their cultural strengths.

4. Create a culturally inclusive classroom environment: Foster a classroom environment that is inclusive and respectful of all students. Establish clear expectations for behavior and communication that promote inclusivity, and address any instances of bias or discrimination promptly and assertively.

5. Collaborate with families and communities: Involve families and communities in the educational process by actively seeking their input, participation, and collaboration. This can help enrich the learning experience and create stronger connections between home and school.

Case Studies and Best Practices

Several examples of culturally responsive pedagogy in action showcase its impact on student engagement and learning outcomes. For instance, in a social studies class studying different cultures, the teacher incorporates guest speakers from diverse backgrounds, organizes multicultural celebrations, and includes literature from various cultures, creating an inclusive and engaging learning environment.

Another example is a science class that integrates culturally relevant examples and applications of scientific concepts. The teacher incorporates indigenous knowledge systems and traditional ecological practices into the curriculum, highlighting the importance of cultural diversity and promoting a deeper understanding of scientific concepts.

Conclusion

Culturally responsive pedagogy is a powerful approach to teaching that recognizes the cultural diversity of students and aims to create inclusive classrooms. By incorporating diverse perspectives, resources, and teaching strategies, educators can foster a sense of belonging, promote equity, and enhance learning outcomes for all students. It is essential for educators to continuously reflect on their own cultural biases and engage in professional development opportunities to enhance their cultural competency and pedagogical practices.

Supporting diverse student populations in online learning

In online learning, it is crucial to create an inclusive and supportive environment for diverse student populations. As educational institutions increasingly turn to virtual platforms, it becomes even more important to address the unique needs and challenges faced by students from different backgrounds. In this section, we will explore strategies and best practices for supporting diverse student populations in the online learning environment.

Understanding Diversity in Online Learning

Diversity in online learning encompasses a range of dimensions, including but not limited to:

- Cultural and ethnic backgrounds
- Socioeconomic status
- Linguistic diversity
- Students with disabilities
- Gender and sexual orientation

Each dimension of diversity presents its own set of challenges and considerations. It is important for educators and institutions to recognize and address these differences to ensure equal opportunities for all students.

Inclusive Course Design

When designing online courses, it is essential to consider the needs of diverse student populations. Here are some strategies to promote inclusivity in course design:

1. Provide multiple modes of content delivery: Cater to different learning preferences by offering a variety of content formats, such as text, audio, video, and interactive elements. This allows students to engage with the material in a way that best suits their learning style.

2. Caption and provide transcripts: Consider the needs of students with hearing impairments or those who prefer reading. Providing captions for videos and transcripts for audio content ensures that all students can access the material.

3. Ensure accessibility: Design courses with accessibility in mind, following guidelines such as the Web Content Accessibility Guidelines (WCAG). This includes providing alternative text for images, using clear and organized layouts, and considering color contrast for visually impaired students.

4. Use inclusive language: Create a welcoming and inclusive environment by using gender-neutral language and terminology that is respectful of diverse identities and experiences.

5. Incorporate diverse perspectives: Include diverse voices and perspectives in course materials to promote cultural understanding and representation. This can be achieved by featuring diverse authors, case studies, and examples.

Virtual Communication and Collaboration

Effective communication and collaboration are essential for online learning. However, it is important to be mindful of potential barriers and to create an inclusive space for all students. Here are some strategies to support diverse student populations in virtual communication and collaboration:

1. Foster a sense of belonging: Create opportunities for students to connect and build relationships with their peers. Encourage mutual respect, active listening, and collaboration to foster an inclusive virtual community.

2. Establish clear communication channels: Provide multiple avenues for communication, such as discussion forums, video conferencing, and email. This allows students to choose the mode that makes them most comfortable and accommodates different learning styles.

3. Encourage participation and engagement: Ensure that all students have the opportunity to contribute to discussions and group activities. Use inclusive participation strategies, such as rotating discussion roles or providing alternative ways for students to share their thoughts, such as through written responses or multimedia presentations.

4. Address language barriers: In international online learning environments, language differences can pose challenges. Provide language support

resources, such as translation tools or multilingual moderators, and create a safe space for students to ask questions and seek clarification.

5. Promote cultural awareness and sensitivity: Facilitate discussions and activities that encourage students to share their cultural backgrounds and perspectives. This helps cultivate empathy and understanding among students from diverse backgrounds.

Technology and Accessibility Considerations

To support diverse student populations, it is essential to consider the accessibility of the technology used in online learning. Here are some considerations to ensure equal access for all students:

1. Provide assistive technology options: Offer assistive tools and software to support students with disabilities. This may include screen readers, speech-to-text software, or alternative input devices. Make sure that these tools are easily accessible and instructions are provided for their use.

2. Test for compatibility: Ensure that the online learning platform and any additional software or tools used are compatible with various devices and operating systems. This allows for flexibility in device choice and eliminates barriers for students who may not have access to the latest technology.

3. Develop technology literacy: Provide tutorials, resources, and technical support to help students navigate the online learning environment. This is particularly important for students who may be less familiar with technology or have limited access to technology resources.

4. Regularly evaluate and update technology tools: Stay informed about emerging technologies, accessibility features, and updates to ensure that online learning platforms and tools are inclusive and provide equal opportunities for all students.

Support Services and Resources

In online learning, it is essential to provide support services and resources that cater to the diverse needs of students. Here are some key considerations:

1. Academic support: Offer online tutoring, virtual office hours, and peer mentoring to provide academic assistance to students. Ensure that support services are accessible and accommodate different learning styles and needs.

2. Mental health and well-being: Provide resources and guidance on mental health and well-being, as online learning can pose unique challenges in terms of isolation and increased screen time. Offer virtual counseling services and promote self-care strategies to support students' overall well-being.

3. Accessibility services: Establish processes for requesting and providing accommodations for students with disabilities. Work closely with accessibility services to ensure that students have equal access to course materials and assessments.

4. Multilingual support: Provide language support services for students who are non-native speakers of the language of instruction. Offer language resources, translation services, and opportunities for language practice and improvement.

Case Studies and Best Practices

To further support diverse student populations in online learning, it is valuable to examine case studies and best practices. These examples can offer insights into successful initiatives and highlight innovative approaches for promoting inclusivity in online education. Some potential case studies and best practices to explore include:

- The Open University's efforts to provide accessible online learning for students with disabilities.
- The University of British Columbia's implementation of universal design for learning principles in online courses.
- The African Virtual University's initiatives to deliver multilingual courses and support to students across multiple countries.
- The University of California, Berkeley's use of virtual reality to create inclusive and immersive learning experiences for students with disabilities.

Conclusion

Supporting diverse student populations in online learning is essential to create an inclusive and equitable educational environment. By adopting inclusive course design principles, promoting effective virtual communication and collaboration, considering technology accessibility, and providing support services and resources, educators and institutions can ensure that all students have equal opportunities to succeed in online learning. By embracing diversity and creating an inclusive learning environment, we can maximize the potential of online education for students from all backgrounds.

Intersectionality and Challenges in Achieving Equity

In the pursuit of educational equity, it is important to recognize and understand the concept of intersectionality. Intersectionality refers to the interconnected nature of social categorizations such as race, gender, class, and other factors that collectively shape an individual's experiences and identities. It recognizes that individuals have multiple dimensions of identity that interact and intersect, resulting in unique experiences and forms of oppression or privilege.

Addressing equity in education requires recognizing and addressing the specific challenges faced by individuals with intersecting marginalized identities. These individuals may face compounded forms of discrimination and disadvantage due to the simultaneous influence of multiple social categories. For example, a female student from a low-income background who is also a person of color may face different barriers and challenges compared to a male student from a similar background.

One challenge in achieving equity is the tendency to oversimplify or generalize experiences and needs. By recognizing intersectionality, educators and policymakers can better understand and respond to the unique needs and experiences of different student populations. This includes acknowledging the ways in which various forms of discrimination can intersect and compound, creating additional barriers to educational attainment and success.

To address the challenges of intersectionality, it is crucial to adopt a multifaceted approach. This involves implementing policies and practices that are inclusive and sensitive to the diverse needs of students. Here are some strategies that can contribute to achieving equity in an intersectional manner:

1. **Representation and curriculum:** Ensure that educational materials, textbooks, and curriculum reflect the diversity of students' experiences, identities, and histories. It is important to include voices and perspectives from marginalized communities to create a more inclusive and equitable learning environment.

2. **Culturally responsive pedagogy:** Adopt teaching practices that recognize and build upon the cultural backgrounds and experiences of students. This

involves valuing and respecting different cultures, promoting a sense of belonging, and creating inclusive learning environments.

3. **Addressing stereotype threat:** Stereotype threat refers to the fear of confirming negative stereotypes associated with one's identity, which can hinder academic performance. Teachers and educators should create a supportive environment that challenges and dispels stereotypes, enabling students to reach their full potential.

4. **Intersectional professional development:** Offer professional development opportunities that enhance educators' understanding of intersectionality and equip them with strategies to address the unique needs of students from diverse backgrounds. This can include training on cultural competence, anti-bias education, and strategies for creating inclusive classrooms.

5. **Equitable resource allocation:** Ensure that resources, such as funding, technology, and learning materials, are distributed equitably across schools and districts. This can help bridge the achievement gap and provide marginalized students with the necessary support and opportunities for success.

It is also important to recognize that achieving equity requires ongoing collaboration and engagement with diverse stakeholders. This includes engaging with students, parents, educators, policymakers, and community members to ensure that their voices are heard and their specific needs are addressed. By actively involving these stakeholders in decision-making processes, a more comprehensive and effective approach to achieving educational equity can be realized.

In conclusion, intersectionality plays a crucial role in understanding and addressing the challenges in achieving equity in education. By recognizing and addressing the unique needs and experiences of individuals with intersecting marginalized identities, educational institutions can work towards creating inclusive and equitable learning environments. Implementing strategies such as inclusive curriculum, culturally responsive pedagogy, addressing stereotype threat, providing intersectional professional development, and allocating resources equitably are key steps towards achieving educational equity for all students.

Advocating for Inclusive Education Policies

Inclusive education is the practice of ensuring that all students, regardless of their background, abilities, or disabilities, have equal access to quality education. It promotes diversity, equity, and social justice within educational settings. Advocating for inclusive education policies is crucial to create a supportive and inclusive learning environment for all students. In this section, we will explore the principles and strategies for advocating for inclusive education policies, including the importance of stakeholder engagement, evidence-based practices, and policy implementation.

The Importance of Inclusive Education Policies

Inclusive education policies are essential for promoting equity and providing equal opportunities for all students. By enacting inclusive education policies, educational systems can address the barriers that prevent students from accessing a quality education and ensure that they receive appropriate support to succeed academically, socially, and emotionally. Inclusive education policies also promote social integration and prepare students for a diverse and inclusive society.

Key Principles of Inclusive Education Policies

Advocacy for inclusive education policies should be guided by key principles that promote the rights and well-being of all students. These principles include:

1. **Access and Equity:** Inclusive education policies should aim to provide equal access to education for all students, regardless of their abilities, gender, socio-economic background, or cultural identity.

2. **Quality Education:** Policies should focus on ensuring high-quality education that meets the diverse learning needs of all students. This includes providing appropriate instructional strategies, materials, and support services.

3. **Collaboration and Partnerships:** Successful advocacy for inclusive education policies requires collaboration among stakeholders, including teachers, parents, students, policymakers, and community organizations. Partnerships with disability advocates and civil society organizations can also be valuable in driving policy change.

4. **Evidence-based Practices:** Policies should be based on research and evidence of effective practices in inclusive education. This includes using data-driven decision-making, evaluating the impact of policies, and sharing best practices among educational institutions.

5. **Teacher Professional Development:** Inclusive education policies should prioritize teacher professional development to equip educators with the necessary skills and knowledge to support the diverse needs of students in their classrooms.

6. **Systematic Approaches:** Policies should be implemented at both the systemic and individual levels to ensure comprehensive and sustainable change. This may involve adjusting curriculum frameworks, assessment practices, and resource allocation to support inclusive education.

7. **Advocacy and Awareness:** Advocacy efforts should aim to raise awareness about the benefits of inclusive education and address misconceptions and biases. It is essential to engage policymakers, opinion leaders, and the public to build support for inclusive education policies.

8. **Monitoring and Evaluation:** Policies should incorporate mechanisms for monitoring and evaluating their implementation and impact. This allows for accountability and adjustment as needed to ensure their effectiveness.

Strategies for Advocating for Inclusive Education Policies

Advocating for inclusive education policies requires a systematic and multi-faceted approach. Here are some strategies to consider:

1. **Building Alliances:** Form coalitions with like-minded individuals and organizations that share the goal of inclusive education. Collaborate with community organizations, parent groups, and disability advocates to amplify the advocacy efforts.

2. **Engaging Stakeholders:** Involve all relevant stakeholders, including parents, students, teachers, administrators, policymakers, and community members, in the advocacy process. Seek their input, collect feedback, and incorporate their perspectives into policy proposals.

3. **Raising Awareness:** Use various channels, such as social media, public events, and workshops, to raise awareness about the importance of inclusive education. Share success stories, research findings, and best practices to demonstrate the benefits of inclusive education to the broader community.

4. **Policy Research and Analysis:** Conduct research to gather evidence on inclusive education practices and their impact. Compile data on student

outcomes, teacher training, and resource allocation to support policy proposals. Analyze existing policies and identify gaps and areas for improvement.

5. **Policy Proposal Development:** Develop policy proposals that align with the key principles of inclusive education. Present clear and actionable recommendations supported by research and evidence. Consider the potential challenges and develop strategies to address them.

6. **Advocacy Campaigns:** Launch targeted advocacy campaigns to raise awareness about specific inclusive education issues. Utilize petitions, letters, social media campaigns, and grassroots mobilization to influence policymakers and generate public support.

7. **Capacity Building:** Offer training and professional development opportunities for educators, policymakers, and other key stakeholders. Provide resources and workshops on inclusive education practices, strategies, and implementation approaches.

8. **Policy Implementation Support:** Advocate for the allocation of resources and support for implementing inclusive education policies effectively. Monitor the implementation progress, identify challenges, and collaborate with stakeholders to address any barriers.

9. **Evaluation and Impact Assessment:** Evaluate the implementation and impact of inclusive education policies. Gather feedback from stakeholders, conduct surveys, and collect data on student outcomes to assess the effectiveness of the policies. Use the findings to refine and improve the policies as necessary.

10. **Continuous Advocacy:** Advocacy is an ongoing process. Continue to engage with policymakers, educators, and stakeholders to ensure that inclusive education remains a priority. Foster a culture of collaboration and knowledge sharing to sustain the momentum for change.

Real-World Example: Inclusive Education Policies in Finland

Finland is often cited as a global leader in inclusive education. Their success can be attributed, in part, to their inclusive education policies. Finland's policies are informed by research and reflect the key principles of inclusive education. Some strategies that have contributed to their success include:

- **Equitable Resource Allocation:** Finland ensures that funding and resources are distributed based on the needs of students. Additional support, such as special education teachers or assistive technology, is provided to students who require it.

- **Collaborative Approach:** Finland emphasizes collaboration among educators, students, parents, and other stakeholders. Teachers work together to provide individualized support, and parents are actively involved in decision-making processes.

- **Teacher Professional Development:** Finland invests in the professional development of teachers to equip them with the necessary skills to support diverse learners. Teachers receive training on differentiation strategies, inclusive practices, and special education.

- **Early Intervention and Support:** Finland focuses on early intervention and prevention to address learning difficulties at an early stage. Support services, such as speech therapy or counseling, are provided to students who need them.

- **Data-Driven Decision Making:** Finland uses data to inform decision-making processes and evaluate the effectiveness of their policies. They collect student-level data to identify trends, track progress, and allocate resources accordingly.

The success of inclusive education policies in Finland serves as an inspiration and a valuable example of how research-based policies and collaborative approaches can create inclusive learning environments.

Conclusion

Advocating for inclusive education policies is essential to ensure that all students have an equal opportunity to receive a high-quality education. By embracing the principles of inclusive education, engaging stakeholders, and utilizing evidence-based practices, policymakers and educators can create supportive and inclusive learning environments. Through continuous advocacy efforts and a commitment to equity and social justice, we can strive for a future where inclusive education is the norm, not the exception.

Empowering marginalized communities through education

Education plays a vital role in empowering marginalized communities by providing them with the knowledge, skills, and opportunities necessary to overcome barriers and achieve social and economic equality. In this section, we will explore various strategies and approaches to empower marginalized communities through education, focusing on inclusive practices, culturally responsive pedagogy, and community engagement.

Understanding Marginalized Communities

Before discussing strategies for empowering marginalized communities, it is important to have a clear understanding of who these communities are and the challenges they face. Marginalized communities include but are not limited to racial and ethnic minorities, individuals with disabilities, LGBTQ+ individuals, individuals from low-income backgrounds, and indigenous communities.

These communities often face systemic barriers such as discrimination, poverty, limited access to resources, and unequal representation. The intersectionality of identities further compounds the challenges faced by individuals belonging to multiple marginalized groups. It is crucial to acknowledge and address these unique experiences when designing educational interventions.

Inclusive and Culturally Responsive Pedagogy

Inclusive and culturally responsive pedagogy is a key element in empowering marginalized communities through education. It involves creating a learning environment where all students feel valued, respected, and represented. Here are some strategies for promoting inclusivity and cultural responsiveness:

1. Incorporating diverse perspectives and voices in the curriculum: Introduce materials, literature, and resources that reflect the experiences and contributions of marginalized communities. This helps students develop a more accurate and comprehensive understanding of the world.

2. Cultivating an inclusive classroom environment: Foster a sense of belonging and acceptance by promoting open dialogue, mutual respect, and empathy among students. Encourage students to share their unique experiences and perspectives, and promote active listening to create a safe space for everyone to learn and grow.

3. Providing differentiated instruction: Recognize and address the diverse learning needs and abilities of students from marginalized communities. Use varied teaching methods, materials, and assessments to cater to different learning styles and ensure equitable access to knowledge and opportunities for success.

4. Engaging families and communities: Establish strong partnerships with families and community organizations to create a holistic support system for students. Involve parents and caregivers in the educational process and seek their input to ensure cultural relevance and community involvement.

5. Professional development for educators: Offer training and workshops to enhance educators' understanding of diversity, equity, and inclusion. Support educators in developing culturally responsive teaching practices and strategies for addressing biases and stereotypes in the classroom.

Community Engagement and Empowerment

Empowering marginalized communities goes beyond the boundaries of the classroom. It involves engaging with the larger community and fostering partnerships that promote the overall well-being and advancement of marginalized individuals. Here are some strategies for community engagement and empowerment:

1. Collaborating with community organizations: Partner with local organizations that work directly with marginalized communities. This collaboration can provide students with opportunities for internships, mentorship programs, and community service initiatives that address real-world challenges.

2. Providing access to resources: Establish mechanisms to bridge the digital divide and provide access to technology, internet connectivity, and learning resources for marginalized communities. This access is crucial for ensuring equitable opportunities for education and skill development.

3. Creating inclusive extracurricular activities: Offer a range of extracurricular activities that reflect the interests and talents of marginalized students. Create affinity groups, clubs, and organizations that provide a space for identity exploration, cultural celebration, and community building.

4. Advocacy and policy engagement: Empower students to become advocates for their communities by teaching them about social justice issues and providing opportunities for them to engage in activism. Encourage students to participate in policy discussions and initiatives that promote equity and social change.

5. Mentorship and role models: Connect students from marginalized communities with mentors who share similar backgrounds and have achieved success in their fields. These role models can inspire and guide students, providing support and guidance throughout their educational journey.

Case Studies and Best Practices

To illustrate the impact of empowering marginalized communities through education, let's explore a few case studies and best practices:

1. Bhavya's Story: Bhavya is a first-generation college student from a low-income background. Through a scholarship program that provides academic support, mentorship, and financial assistance, Bhavya was able to pursue higher education. Today, she is an advocate for educational equity and mentors other students facing similar challenges.
2. Culturally Relevant Curriculum: A school district in a culturally diverse community introduced a culturally relevant curriculum that incorporated local history, traditions, and language. This approach not only improved student engagement and academic outcomes but also strengthened students' cultural identity and pride.
3. Community Partnership: A high school in an underserved community partnered with a local business organization to provide internship opportunities for students. This partnership not only exposed students to real-world work experiences but also provided them with valuable networking opportunities and potential career pathways.
4. Mentorship Program: A university established a mentorship program that paired undergraduate students from marginalized backgrounds with faculty or alumni mentors. This program provided guidance, academic support, and professional networking opportunities, resulting in increased retention rates and academic success for the mentored students.

Conclusion

Empowering marginalized communities through education requires a multi-faceted approach that addresses the unique challenges faced by these communities. Inclusive and culturally responsive pedagogy, community engagement, and mentorship programs are just a few of the strategies that can make a significant difference in the lives of marginalized individuals. By creating equitable educational opportunities and fostering a sense of belonging, we can nurture the talents, aspirations, and potential of all students, regardless of their background. Through education, we can work towards building a more just and inclusive society.

Printed by Libri Plureos GmbH in Hamburg, Germany

9 781779 610966